Lecture Notes in Computer Science 13192

More information about this subseries at https://link.springer.com/bookseries/7409

Malte Smits (Ed.)

Information for a Better World: Shaping the Global Future

17th International Conference, iConference 2022
Virtual Event, February 28 – March 4, 2022
Proceedings, Part I

 Springer

Editor
Malte Smits 🆔
Humboldt-Universität zu Berlin
Berlin, Germany

ISSN 0302-9743   ISSN 1611-3349 (electronic)
Lecture Notes in Computer Science
ISBN 978-3-030-96956-1   ISBN 978-3-030-96957-8 (eBook)
https://doi.org/10.1007/978-3-030-96957-8

LNCS Sublibrary: SL3 – Information Systems and Applications, incl. Internet/Web, and HCI

This Springer imprint is published by the registered company Springer Nature Switzerland AG
The registered company address is: Gewerbestrasse 11, 6330 Cham, Switzerland

Preface

This year's iConference looked at building post-COVID realities in a world that has adapted to home offices and connecting in digital spaces and that gave us many reasons to reflect on our approach to research, information technology, and communication. In these challenging and difficult times researchers from all over the world came together and worked on current issues, trying to understand more of what we need when it comes to social justice, sustainability, government, and the workplace. What can we improve together? How does a better world look to us?

iConference 2022 was hosted by the iSchools at Kyushu University, University College Dublin, and the University of Texas at Austin under the motto "Information for a Better World: Shaping the Global Future", encouraging a positive and enthusiastic view on the coming years – shared and discussed by attendants in a plethora of presentations, interactive events, and colloquiums. It was the seventeenth event in the iConference series and the third to be held virtually, taking place online between February 28 and March 4, 2022.

The conference chairs accepted a total of 32 full research papers and 29 short research papers along with 35 posters. The submissions were reviewed, scored, and reworked with the help of 255 active peer reviewers in a double-blind review process. Participants also hosted 10 workshops to share information and discuss various topics. Similarly, the Doctoral Colloqium, the Early Career Colloquium, and the Student Symposium held a total of 73 presentations and meetings.

For the fifth time the full and short research papers are published in Springer's Lecture Notes in Computer Science (LNCS). The proceedings are sorted into the following seven categories: Library and Information Science, Information Governance and Ethics, Data Science, Human-Computer Interaction and Technology, Information Behaviour and Retrieval, Health Informatics, and Communities and Media.

We would like to thank all the reviewers for their invaluable effort, expertise, and work. A big thank you also goes to the other chairs for their hard work and prowess. Without them this conference would not have been possible. Our gratitude goes out to everyone who worked on this conference and those who joined and participated in any way, shape, or form.

With a bright and hopeful vision, the iConference again brought researchers together and created and empowered connections between scholars and scientists to grow something that is way bigger than the sum of its parts. Together we explored "Information for a Better World: Shaping the Global Future".

January 2022

Malte Smits
Kristin Eschenfelder
Lihong "Nick" Zhou
Makoto Kato
Henriette Roued-Cunliffe
Michael Twidale

Organization

iConference 2022 was organized by the iSchools at Kyushu University, Japan; University College Dublin, Ireland; and the University of Texas at Austin, USA.

Conference Chairs

Amber Cushing	University College Dublin, Ireland
Kenneth R. Fleischmann	University of Texas at Austin, USA
Emi Ishita	Kyushu University, Japan
Eric Meyer	University of Texas at Austin, USA
Kalpana Shankar	University College Dublin, Ireland
Yoichi Tomiura	Kyushu University, Japan

Full Research Paper Chairs

Kristin Eschenfelder	University of Wisconsin-Madison, USA
Lihong "Nick" Zhou	University of Wuhan, China

Short Research Paper Chairs

Makoto Kato	University of Tsukuba, Japan
Henriette Roued-Cunliffe	University of Copenhagen, Denmark
Michael Twidale	University of Illinois Urbana-Champaign, USA

Poster Chairs

Preben Hansen	Stockholm University, Sweden
Pengyi Zhang	Peking University, China

Interactive Events Chairs

Gillian Oliver	Monash University, Australia
Virginia Ortíz-Repiso	Universidad Carlos Ill de Madrid, Spain

Doctoral Colloquium Chairs

Ben Cowan	University College Dublin, Ireland
Mohammad Jarrahi	University of North Carolina at Chapel Hill, USA
Atsuyuki Moroshima	University of Tsukuba, Japan

Student Symposium Chairs

Koraljika Golub	Linnaeus University, Sweden
Colin Rhinesmith	Simmons University, USA
Di Wang	Wuhan University, China

Early Career Colloquium Chairs

Doug Oard	University of Maryland, USA
Natalie Pang	University of Singapore, Singapore
António Lucas Soares	University of Porto, Portugal

Social Activity Chairs

Shaobo Liang	Wuhan University, China
Ulrike Liebner	Humboldt-Universität zu Berlin, Germany

Proceedings Chair

Malte Smits	Humboldt-Universität zu Berlin, Germany

Conference Coordinators

Executive Director

Michael Seadle	iSchools Organization

Director of Communications

Clark Heideger	iSchools Organization

Business Manager

Slava Sterzer	iSchools Organization

Program Manager

Katharina Toeppe	iSchools Organization

Social Media

Cynthia Ding	iSchools Organization

Additional Reviewers

Jacob Abbott
Waseem Afzal
Noa Aharony
Jae-wook Ahn
Isola Ajiferuke
Bader Albahlal
Nicole D. Alemanne
Daniel Gelaw Alemneh
Hamed Alhoori
Reham Alhuraiti
Anas Hamad Alsuhaibani
Xiaomi An
Misita Anwar
Muhmammad Naveed Anwar
Catherine Arnott-Smith
Leif Azzopardi
Cristina Robles Bahm
Alex Ball
Zoe Bartliff
Andrew Berry
Nanyi Bi
Toine Bogers
Maria Bonn
Sarah Bratt
Jo Ann M. Brooks
Sarah A. Buchanan
John Budd
Julia Bullard
Yao Cai
Biddy Casselden
Tamy Chambers
Wayland Chang
Tiffany Chao
Hsin-liang Chen
Jiangping Chen
Chola Chhetri
Rachel Ivy Clarke
Anthony Joseph Corso
Andrew Cox
Sally Jo Cunningham
Amber L. Cushing
Rebecca Davis
Shengli Deng

Bridget Disney
Brian Dobreski
Philip Doty
Kedma Duarte
Ricardo Eito-Brun
Avsalom Elmalech
Heidi Enwald
Kristin Eschenfelder
Bruce Ferwerda
Rachel Fleming-May
Fred Fonseca
Henry Alexis Gabb
Maria Gäde
Chunmei Gan
Victor Garcia-Font
John Gathegi
Tali Gazit
Yegin Genc
Susan Elizabeth German
Dion Goh
Patrick Thomas Golden
Melissa Gross
Michael Gryk
Kailash Gupta
Ayse Gursoy
Lala Hajibayova
Carina Hallqvist
Jenna Hartel
Bruce Hartpence
Daqing He
Jiangen He
Viviane Hessami
Alison Hicks
Kelly M. Hoffman
Chris Holstrom
Liang Hong
Kun Huang
Ching Yin Huang
Shuiqing Huang
Isto Huvila
Aylin Imeri (Ilhan)
Sharon Ince
Charles Inskip

Yvette Iribe Ramirez
Vanessa Irvin
Wei Jeng
Tingting Jiang
Michael Jones
Heidi Julien
Nicolas Jullien
Jaap Kamps
Unmil Karadkar
Páraic Kerrigan
Heikki Keskustalo
Jigya Khabar
Yeolib Kim
Vanessa Kitzie
Bart Knijnenburg
Kyungwon Koh
Kolina Koltai
Adam Kriesberg
Keeheon Lee
Jian-Sin Lee
Kijung Lee
Lo Lee
Myeong Lee
Noah Lenstra
Shijuan Li
Guangjian Li
Kai Li
Meng-Hao Li
Ying Li
Louise Limberg
Jenny Lindberg
Henry Linger
Zack Lischer-Katz
Ping Liu
Xiaobin Lu
Kun Lu
Ana Lucic
Christopher Lueg
Haakon Lund
Haiqun Ma
Jinxuan Ma
Lai Ma
Craig MacDonald
Jin Mao
Kate Marek

Matthew S. Mayernik
Philipp Mayr-Schlegel
Claire McGuinness
Pamela Ann McKinney
David McMenemy
Shuyuan Ho Metcalfe
Shawne Miksa
A. J. Million
J. Elizabeth Mills
Stasa Milojevic
Chao Min
Lorri Mon
Camilla Moring
Valerie Nesset
Chaoqun Ni
David M. Nichols
Jan Nolin
Rebecca Noone
Casey O'Donnell
Sanghee Oh
Benedict Salazar Olgado
Peter Organisciak
Felipe Ortega
Abraham Oshni Alvandi
Kathleen Padova
Min Sook Park
Sohyun Park
Hyoungjoo Park
Bo Pei
Diane Pennington
Vivien Petras
Bobby Phuritsabam
Mary Pietrowicz
Ola Pilerot
Alex Poole
Jennifer Proctor
Jian Qin
Marie L. Radford
Arcot Rajasekar
Susan Rathbun-Grubb
Ming Ren
Gabby Resch
Angela U. Rieks
Milly Romeijn-Stout
Philip Romero-Masters

Howard Rosenbaum
Ariel Rosenfeld
Vassilis Routsis
Ehsan Sabaghian
Ashley Sands
Madelyn Rose Sanfilippo
Sally Sanger
Anindita Sarker
Steve Sawyer
Laura Sbaffi
Kirsten Schlebbe
Rainforest Scully-Blaker
Michael Seadle
Ryan Shaw
Stephen C. Slota
Mads Solberg
Shijie Song
Clay Spinuzzi
Beth St. Jean
Gretchen Renee Stahlman
Hrvoje Stancic
Caroline Stratton
Besiki Stvilia
Shigeo Sugimoto
Tanja Svarre
Sue Yeon Syn
Anna Maria Tammaro
Yi Tang
Andrea Karoline Thomer
Chunhua Tsai
Tien-I Tsai
Yuen-Hsien Tseng
Pertti Vakkari
Frans van der Sluis
Nitin Verma
Travis Wagner
Jieyu Wang
Lin Wang
Xiangnyu Wang

Xiaoguang Wang
Yanyan Wang
Yi-Yu Wang
Xiaofei Wei
Martin Weiss
Brian Wentz
Rachel Williams
R. Jason Winning
Dietmar Wolfram
Adam Worrall
Steven John Wright
I-Chin Wu
Qiuhui Xiao
Juan Xie
Iris Xie
Lifang Xu
Shenmeng Xu
Xiao Xue
Hui Yan
Erjia Yan
Gal Yavetz
Ayoung Yoon
Sarah Young
Bei Yu
Chuanming Yu
Liangzhi Yu
Xianjin Zha
Chengzhi Zhang
Chenwei Zhang
Jinchao Zhang
Mei Zhang
Xiaojuan Zhang
Xinyu Zhang
Yan Zhang
Ziming Zhang
Yiming Zhao
Yuxiang (Chris) Zhao
Qinghua Zhu
Zhiya Zuo

Contents – Part I

Information Governance and Ethics

Data Science

Human-Computer Interaction and Technology

Contents – Part II

Communities and Media

Health Informatics

Library and Information Science

Bibliometric Analysis and Data Visualization of Archival Science Journal Literature (1971–2020)

Yu-Ting Huang[1] (ID) and Chiao-Min Lin[2](✉) (ID)

[1] Graduate Institute of Library, Information and Archival Studies, National Chengchi University, No. 64, Sec. 2, Zhinan Rd., Wenshan District, Taipei City 11605, Taiwan
[2] Graduate Institute of Library, Information and Archival Studies, National Chengchi University, No. 64, Sec. 2, Zhinan Rd., Wenshan, Taipei 11605, Taiwan
cmlin@nccu.edu.tw

Abstract. Literature publications in archival science have been critical to the recognition of archival science as an independent discipline. The public access to archives has been popularized with the rise of information freedom since 1970, and the research of international archival study has increased year by year. In recent years, data visualization of literature has become the trend of bibliometric analysis. However, there is still a lack of data visualization analysis about international archival science research results.

Therefore, this study used a Scopus database for international journal papers retrieval and employed a bibliometric method to analyze the achievements of international journal articles. The publication quantity, research topics, authors, and journal characteristics were conducted and analyzed. The visualization tools were also taken to present literature keyword distribution and the relationship of subject concepts. The analysis of archival science research literature in international journals could show the whole picture of research trends and changes of archival science in the past 50 years (1971–2020).

Keywords: Archival studies · Bibliometric analysis · Data visualization

1 Introduction

1.1 Purpose

Bibliometric method, as the methodology to understand the knowledge structure of specific discipline and professional connotation through statistics and comparison analysis of types or year of research literature in specific coverage, aims to present the subject concern trend and change of the discipline and to generate more knowledge contexts from existing literature to form the core structure for professional development [1].

Archival study, as the discipline stressing on the combination of professional research with the development of practical technologies, precedes archival research literature analysis to provide the development potential issues for archival endeavor and reference

M. Smits (Ed.): iConference 2022, LNCS 13192, pp. 3–11, 2022.
https://doi.org/10.1007/978-3-030-96957-8_1

for evaluating existing management technologies as well as understands the development trend and characteristics of archival study and subjects requiring reinforcement [1, 2]. Freedom of Information Act was successively announced in various countries in the 1970s and policies to promote freedom of governmental information were promoted; besides, the development of information technology drove the emergence of preserving archives and applying information with new technologies to enhance the development of professional research and practical technology and further generate a large amount of research literature. The combination of the bibliometric method with visualization analysis and data mining emerged internationally in past years to attempt to analyze research literature in specific professional fields and dig out richer research results from diverse perspectives.

Research on the discussion of archival literature with the combination of bibliometric and visualization analyses is comparatively scarce. This study analyzed development trends and characteristics of the papers of archival science research in 1971–2020 with bibliometric analysis and VOSviewer visualization tool. The questions discussed include the situation of the growth in the number of archival journal papers in English, the interdisciplinary distribution of research papers in English, the distribution of research author, article journal, and papers publishing institution, as well as the correlation between core subject and the lexical concept of archival research.

1.2   Literature Review

Regarding research with the combination of bibliometric and visualization analyses, Lewis, Alpib, and Kristine (2017) applied Science of Science (Sci2) visualization tool to produce the visualization network of author citation and organization citation of journals in libraries, analyze the citation of the relevant holdings, and dig out the potential cooperative research opportunities for the reference of the journals holdings development strategies [3]. Wang (2018) collected literature in digital humanities through WOS database for the bibliometric analysis and applied visualization tools of VOSviewer and CiteSpace to produce and compare the author, category, reference, and keyword in relevant research to explain the development trend and limitations of research on digital humanities [4].

Mokhtari, Roumiyani, and Saberi (2019) used VOSviewer for calculating the network relationship of keyword co-occurrence and co-citation of literature in Journal of Artificial Societies and Social Simulation (JASSS) in 2000–2018 to present the growth size of the journal and the partnership with other academic publications [5]. Sun and Yuan (2020) collected research literature in English with the topic of library and information science for bibliometric analysis and cluster analysis of literature subject through databases of Web of Science and Essential Science Indicators (ESI) and generated the social network of co-authors and cooperative institutions with VOSviewer [6]. The previously mentioned research results revealed that network relationship was the frequently used visualization method. The network relationship of archival research topic is therefore presented with visualized image.

2 Methods

2.1 Data Sources

The bibliographic access in this study focuses on English journal papers, and the bibliographic data set was collected with Scopus. Scopus established by Elsevier is the bibliographic database with the comparatively complete collection of papers with interdisciplinary peer review and provides the functions of detailed bibliography output and brief bibliographic analysis. To take care of literature subject accuracy and rate of quantity recovery, keywords and the year of data limited in 1971–2020 are utilized for the retrieval, and the type of literature and language is limited to journal papers and English, respectively, for the retrieval. Total 7,389 pieces of papers are inquired, and the briefly retrieval result matches the retrieval concept.

2.2 Analysis Methods

The bibliometric analysis items contain the growth of papers, disciplinary subject distribution, high-productivity author, high article journal, and papers source institution in past years, and the statistical diagram is applied to present the analysis result. For papers subject analysis, VOSviewer, developed by Centre for Science and Technology Studies, Leiden University, is used for calculating keyword co-occurrence word frequency of all literature and drawing the keyword subject network to show the correlations between core research topic and subject term in archival research.

3 Results

3.1 Publication Quantity

No more than 10 papers on archival science written in English were produced annually in 1970–1977, while the growth trend appeared annually more than 100 English papers after 2000 and achieved annually more than 600 in 2020 (see Fig. 1).

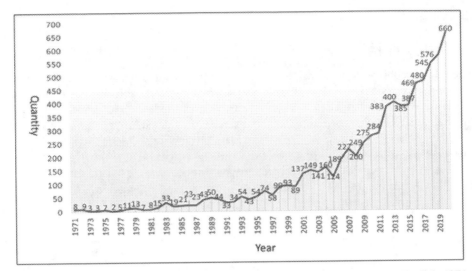

Fig. 1. The change of publication quantity about archival science journal papers in English, 1971–2020. (Data adapted from the Scopus database.)

3.2 Subject Area

The discipline distribution in Scopus database shows that English archival journal papers covers several disciplines, which are ranked as social science (26.0%), arts and humanities (15.7%), computer science (11.0%), medicine (6.9%), engineering (6.0%), earth and planetary sciences (6.0%), environmental science (4.2%), agricultural and biological science (3.8%), business, management and accounting (3.2%), physics and astronomy

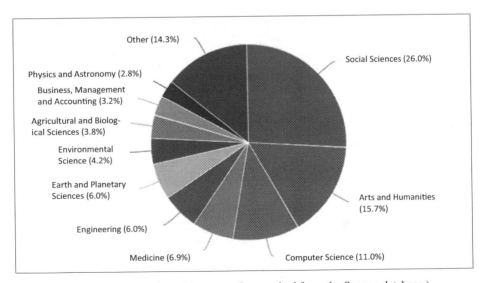

Fig. 2. Documents by subject area. (Image cited from the Scopus database.)

(2.8%), and others (14.3%). Summing up research on various disciplines related to archival research, it is in common that archives are used as the review materials for the development of the professional field as well as the archival data management and application in various fields (see Fig. 2).

3.3 Authors

Authors, according to the literature output, are ranked Kitagawa (15), Caswell (14), Evans (12), Kimura (12), Ngoepe (11), Shepherd (11), Leinonen (10), McKemmish (10), Netshakhuma (10), Yakel (10), and Yusof (10) (see Fig. 3). The literature output does not concentrate on a specific author.

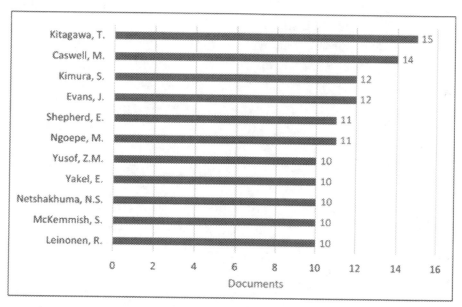

Fig. 3. Order of high-productivity authors (Data adapted from the Scopus database.)

3.4 High-Article Journal

Journals with more than 100 archival research literatures contain Archival Science (241), Journal of Archival Organization (147), and Records Management Journal (102); journals with top 10 quantity of papers are shown in Table 1. The professional fields in journals cover archival study and practice, astronomy, digital image, and engineering and information; it also presents that archival data could support research on other disciplines (Table 1).

Most journal papers related to archival research published before 1980 appeared on Proceedings of SPIE The International Society for Optical Engineering; after 1995, the quantity of literature in Archival Science and Journal of Archival Organization continuously grew; and, after 2000, the quantity of literature published on Journal of Digital Imaging and American Archivist increased largely. It reveals that the quantity of papers in professional journals discussing archival study and archival technology is largely increasing in past years, while the quantity of research papers of journals with applied archival data in other disciplines is not stable (see Fig. 4).

Table 1. Journals with top 10 quantity of papers

Sequence	Jounal name	Quantity	Proportion (%)
1	Archival Science	241	3.2%
2	Journal of Archival Organization	147	1.9%
3	Records Management Journal	102	1.3%
4	Archives and Manuscripts	86	1.2%
5	Astronomy and Astrophysics	81	1.0%
6	Archives and Records	69	0.9%
7	Journal of Digital Imaging	62	0.8%
8	Proceedings of SPIE the International Society for Optical Engineering	61	0.8%
9	Slavic and East European Information Resources	57	0.7%
10	American Archivist	47	0.6%

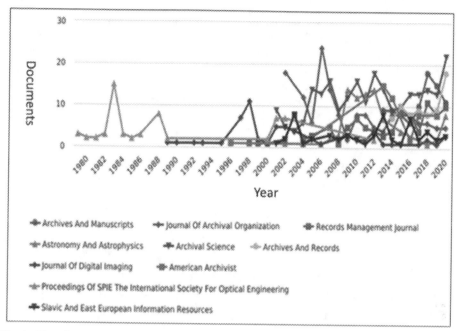

Fig. 4. Year distribution of high-article journal in 1971–2020 (Image cited from Scopus database.)

3.5 Institution of Papers

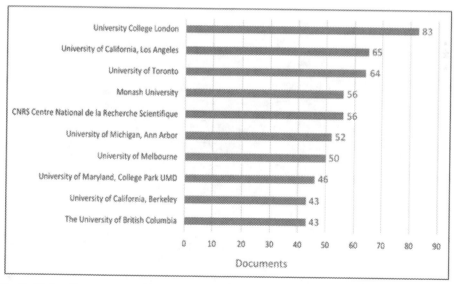

Fig. 5. Order of papers source institutions in 1971–2020 (Data adapted from the Scopus database.)

Among top 10 papers source institutions, University College London (83) shows the highest productivity, followed by University of California, Los Angeles (65) and University of Toronto (64) (see Fig. 5). 9 out of top 10 institutions are English-speaking countries and 5 of them are in the USA, revealing that the USA is the major country for the development of English archival research literature and languages used for literature would affect the visibility of literature publication of research institutions.

3.6 Topics Analysis

The co-occurrence word frequency is used for keyword selection, and a total of 61 terms appear more than 30 times. After filtering 3 keywords not related to the edge topic of archival study (archival tissue, archival tag, and archival tags), the co-occurrence subject network output with keyword as the topic contains 58 keywords, and 8 topics are clustered (see Fig. 6).The clusters including (1) Cluster 1—archival value and function, (2) Cluster 2—theory of records and archives management, (3) Cluster 3—application of archival history, (4) Cluster 4—digital archive, (5) Cluster 5—operation and management issues of digital archives(organization), (6) Cluster 6—archival description, (7) Cluster 7—manuscript and special archives management, and (8) Cluster 8—practice of archival institution. Cluster 4 "digital archive" appears the most links, i.e. the broadest topics being applied, and is currently the main trend of archival research. Cluster 1 "archival value and function" shows the most word frequency co-occurrence, revealing that it is the subject the most commonly appears and is the core concept of archival research.

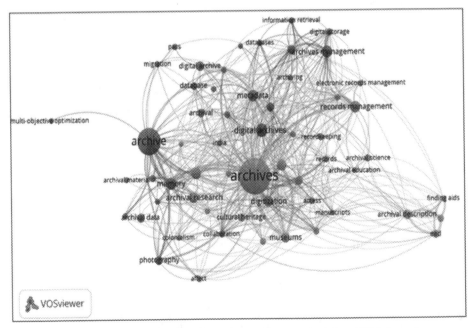

Fig. 6. Papers subject correlation network (Image cited from VOSviewer.)

4   Conclusion

English archival science journal papers appeared no more than10 articles annually in the 1970s but reached more than 600 articles annually in 2020. It reveals the continuous concern about archival research and the development potential to constantly generate research issues. Discipline distribution and high-article journal analysis results show that the application of archival research covers various professional fields, including social science, computer science, and medicine, etc. Most of those fields mainly use archives for reviewing discipline development history or the research on archival data management in the field, which shows the characteristic of archival research being able to combine with practical work in different fields. High-productivity author analysis reveals that archival journal papers does not concentrate on specific authors, but the papers source institution analysis reveals that the language used for literature obviously affects the visibility of literature published in research institutions and might affect the visibility of the international publication; especially, the USA presents the advantage of journal papers output and the publication.

Being affected by information environment, archival science research topic is developing towards archival digitization and electronic archive management. The most broadly discussed topics are "archival value and function" and "digital archives", revealing that not only is the digital application of archival data continuously discussed, but the value and function of archives are also given new meanings in the digital era, to present the archival value and the dynamic development of archival research. Such a result also proves the factors in the increasing quantity of archival science research literature. The correlations among archival research literatures could be deeply discussed with data mining of literature content in the future.

References

1. Lin, C.: Review and outlook of domestic research on archival management. In: Conference Papers of Library and Information Science Research Review and Foresight Edited by Taiwan Association of Library and Information Science Education (2020)
2. Stephenson, M.S.: Deciding not to build the wall: research and the archival profession. Archivaria **32**, 145–151 (1991)
3. Lewis, D., Alpib, M., Kristine, M.: Bibliometric network analysis and visualization for serials librarians: an introduction to Sci2. Serials Rev. **43**(3/4), 239–245 (2017)
4. Wang, Q.: Distribution features and intellectual structures of digital humanities: a bibliometric analysis. J. Documentation **74**(1), 223–246 (2018)
5. Mokhtari, H., Roumiyani, A., Saberi, M.K.: Bibliometric analysis and visualization of the journal of artificial societies and social simulation (JASSS) between 2000 and 2018. Webology **16**(1), 166–183 (2019)
6. Sun, J., Yuan, B.-Z.: Bibliometric mapping of top papers in library and information science based on the essential science indicators database. Malays. J. Libr. Inf. Sci. **25**(2), 61–76 (2020)

Analysis of the Dynamics Among State Libraries, Local Libraries, and Citizens in the United States

Motoko Yamagishi[1]($\boxtimes$), Masanori Koizumi[2] (iD), and Michael M. Widdersheim[3] (iD)

[1] Graduate School of Comprehensive Human Sciences, University of Tsukuba, 1-2 Kasuga, Tsukuba 305-8550, Ibaraki, Japan
s1711578@klis.tsukuba.ac.jp
[2] Faculty of Library, Information and Media Science, University of Tsukuba, 1-2 Kasuga, Tsukuba 305-8550, Ibaraki, Japan
[3] School of Library and Information Management, Emporia State University, 1 Kellogg Circle, Emporia, KS 66801, USA

Abstract. This study explores the policy dimensions of public libraries in the United States from 2000 to 2021. A longitudinal document analysis was conducted using strategic plans, grant evaluation reports, Web pages, and other materials produced by the New York State Library. The purpose of this study was to describe the interrelationships that exist between local, state, and federal policies in response to emerging societal problems. Findings indicate a changing focus in key strategies. In response to evolving social issues, library policy transitioned away from an emphasis on electronic collections and toward an emphasis on the use of library spaces for community services and programs targeting specific populations. The policies encourage investment in collections and services that influence citizens' lives. Other salient emerging goals include broadening partnerships with public and private agencies, securing alternative funding streams, and meeting minimum public library standards. At the same time, it was found that dynamic relationships exist between local, state, and federal policies. While state policies undoubtedly affect local library operations, the reverse is also true, and state policymakers look to innovative local library systems when developing future strategies. The findings of this study are significant because they build on previous literature in the cultural policy field by further elaborating public library policy dynamics from an understudied context.

Keywords: Democracy · Library policies · Policy analysis · Public libraries · United States · New York

1 Research Background

The climate for public libraries in the 21st century has changed dramatically due to emerging information technologies and changing immigrant populations. These changes have resulted in social problems, such as informational and social divides, which have accumulated throughout the past but are now manifesting. The Black Lives Matter movement and protests for Trump's border wall are two high-profile examples of recent cases in the United States that are just the tip of the iceberg. They speak to a larger, global phenomenon of deeply divided societies.

Amidst these challenges, national governments have sought stronger democracies, and public libraries have an essential role to play in this initiative. For over a century, public libraries have had core democratic functions, such as lending books and assisting literacy for reading, in order to secure the right to know and correct inequality among citizens. Previous literature, including Jaeger et al., analyzed historical transitions of U.S. public libraries from the perspective of political discourse in order to describe four eras of U.S. public libraries [1]. At a time when society requires stronger democratic institutions to overcome divisions, public libraries have become increasingly important. For instance, Kranich [2] mentions that if libraries are to remain a cornerstone of democracy, they must recognize that they are moving from an informed, monitorial citizen model of service to an engaged, strong democracy model. But how have public libraries come to embrace this new role?

In the United States, library buildings have historically been built by active citizens or philanthropists like Andrew Carnegie. Currently, however, American society cannot cope with social problems using the power of civil society alone since the societal changes are too drastic. In order to solve social problems, government policies have become critical. This applies to public library policies. As one salient example of how this has worked, national governments in Scandinavia, together with regional and local governmental bodies, have been constructing new public library buildings since the beginning of the 21st century (e.g. and DOKK1 in Aarhus, Denmark, in 2015 [3] and Helsinki Central Library Oodi in 2018 in Finland [4]). In these turbulent times, governments have exhibited strong leadership with ambitious policies.

Against this backdrop, Widdersheim et al. conducted an international comparative analysis of the policies and cultural characteristics of public libraries in the United States, Norway, and Japan. In this research, public library policies in the United States have been shown to consist of several layers that include national, state, and local governments [5]. In the United States, new public libraries have also been reinvented for the 21st century, e.g. New York Public Library. It remains to be seen, however, how exactly these layers of policies have functioned in the U.S. While U.S. federal laws do not define specific services, and libraries are regulated by the states, the strategic plans of states can tell us much about how public policies function nationwide.

2   Previous Research

There are research gaps in what characteristics library policy has and how it has changed in its details. These gaps exist especially in the interrelationships and interactions between the different layers of policies, especially in the U.S. A number of articles in a recent volume focus on cultural policies related to public libraries. For example, in 2020, Rydbeck and Johnston describe statistics and legislation from several European nations [6]; Henningsen and Larsen analyze Norwegian policy documents related to digitalization [7]; Blomgren analyzes policy documents in Sweden related to digitalization

[8]. Stokstad presents findings from a document analysis and interviews related to the implementation of two national policies in Norway [9]; Tóth analyzes how Visegrád countries responded to and implemented the European Commission's recommendations on digitization and digital preservation [10]; and Vårheim, Skare, and Stokstad describe a Norwegian library agency within the context of Norwegian cultural policy [11]. Each of these articles focuses on cultural policy in Europe. It remains to be seen how these analyzes compare to cultural policy in the United States. Following Widdersheim, Koizumi, and Larsen, in 2021, there could be further analysis of the relationships between the national, regional, and local policy levels [5]. In addition to recent articles, Political Dynamics of the Cultural Sector is an ongoing project at Oslo Metropolitan University that seeks to understand in part policymaking processes in the cultural sector [12]. The results of this project have yet to be published.

3 Research Purpose

The purpose of this study is to clarify the relationships between the policies of American state libraries and local public libraries, and the actual management strategies of public libraries. Specifically, drawing from the macrological analysis by Widdersheim et al. in 2021 [5], the purpose of this study is to elucidate the policies of American public libraries on a micrological scale using the case of New York State from 2000 to 2021. In doing so, this study will also clarify the transitions of public library policies in the American government.

    This research fills the gap from previous research by providing an overview of traits about the details of library policies and their transitions over time. This study focuses on the mechanisms of policies, policy strategies, and the actual services of public libraries.

4 Research Methods - Document Analysis

Source materials analyzed for this study include public library policies and annual reports of New York State Library. These policy documents describe how to provide services and spaces for the New York State Library and other local public libraries in New York State. Annual Reports and other reports give us examples of actual services that have been provided using the funds. In this study, strategic plans and policies were analyzed in order to clarify the wide-ranging roles of libraries in current society. The temporal boundaries of this study range from the years 2000 to 2021. These materials were analyzed by careful reading and by extracting essential key words related to policy transitions. New York State Library was selected to represent state library policy across the U.S. more generally.

    The materials analyzed from the New York State Library were Library Services and Technology Act Five-year Strategic Plans, consisting of 85 total pages and 1 Web page; Library Services and Technology Act Five-Year Evaluation Reports, which were 4 in total with 196 pages total; New York State Library Development Strategic Plans, consisting of 7 reports with 26 total pages and 4 Web pages; New York State Public Library Minimum Standards which were 2 documents and a 4-page comparison table; a 2020 Vision and Plan for Library Service in New York state document that was 22 pages long, 1 report on LSTA grant utilization from 1998 to 2013 which was 1 Web page; LSTA Service Improvement Projects that were 5 reports with 38 total pages and 3 Web pages; and 2 LSTA Service Improvement Project reports which were 38 pages total and 3 Web pages which together describe the main targets of the grant. For the Library Services and Technology Act Five-Year Strategic Plans and the Library Services and Technology Act Five-Year Evaluation Reports, the goals and strategies were extracted and analyzed. There were 371 pages total and 9 Web pages. For the New York State Library Strategic Plans, which were published online by the Division of Library Development for the years 2000 to 2021, research consisted of careful reading, memos, and some coding applied to the materials in order to document the dynamic transitions of the New York State Library's policies.

5   Research Results

5.1   Shifting Goals of Library Policies in New York State

Seven of New York State Library's recent strategic plans from 1999 to 2022 set goals that all public libraries should pursue in order to cope with social problems. Through the analysis, six elements were identified: 1) collections and civil life, 2) electronic resources, 3) policies and funding, 4) services and programs, 5) spaces and buildings, and 6) staff.

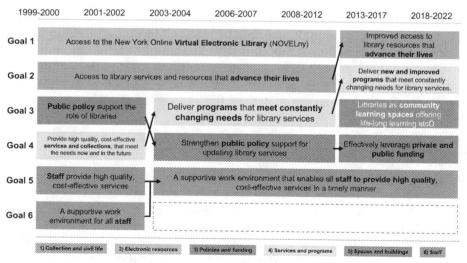

Fig. 1. Transition of goals and their elements in New York library strategic plans.

The transitions of these six goals are shown in Fig. 1. In the figure, the same goals over the years can be tracked because they are distinguished by color. As can be seen, the goals as described in the two documents from 1999 to 2002 were almost the same, each with 6 goals. Then, since 2003, there were 5 goals due to the integration of goals

5 and 6 in 2003. There were no major changes from 2003 to 2012, except that since 2013 the description of Goal 1, or the New York Online Virtual Electronic Library, disappeared, and a new community learning space was described instead. The remaining goals shifted accordingly. From 2013, Goal 4 shifted from "strengthen public policy support for updating library services" to "effectively leverage private and public funding." With no increase in support forecasted from the state, it was necessary to advocate that public libraries seek out private funding. These shifting goals of New York State's public library policies were spurred by societal changes, and the goals of the state library were then realized through more specific strategies of local public libraries. These transitions are explained in more detail below.

5.2   Shifting Key Strategies of Library Policies in New York State

In the section of key strategies in the New York State Library documents, the strategies describe detailed tactics for how public libraries in the state can realize the goals described in state library policy (see Fig. 2).

As an especially distinctive strategy, the policy in 1999–2000 emphasized compliance with minimum standards for public libraries, described in more detail below. As a second goal, just as the Internet became widespread, it was important to build a wide range of basic digital infrastructure, as seen by the goal to "support obtaining money to use for technology." LSTA began funding digitization projects in 1998 for libraries in New York State. The Brooklyn Public Library received $81,225 in 1998, $69,500 in 1999, and $69,500 in 2000 to gradually digitize materials and redesign websites. This broad funding strategy coincided with the large-scale spread of the Internet. By 2013, LSTA's Digitization Projects had a total of $1,552,907 in grants.

Related to community engagement, strategies in 2001–2002 instructed libraries to provide basic computer skills. Similarly, as seen in English literacy and information literacy skill acquisition services, as well as access to medical and consumer health information, services that supported individuals' lifestyles were emphasized over traditional lending services. There was an emphasis on services such as NOVELny that were created in order to provide citizens access to 21st century information through the library system. Strategies related to NOVELny were completed by 2012, and from 2013 onward they disappeared. The Mohawk Valley Library Association is an example of a library that provided health information. The Mohawk Valley Library Association received a $29,760 grant to help the community learn about consumer health resources on the Internet and to hold farm safety day camps for children.

In 2003–2004, in addition to the approach from the previous years that emphasized targeted citizen services, library services for addressing language barriers for adults and young people were described. Furthermore, in collaboration with the Office of Elementary, Middle, Secondary and Continuing Education and the Department of Labor, library services were introduced that enhanced access to labor development and economic revitalization. In addition, in order to improve library services, one of the public policies was to develop advocacy tools in coordination with the community. Community-conscious strategies continue to be seen from this year forward. As an example, the Nassau Library System, with a $33,460 grant, enhanced library services to the Latin community by introducing collections and training staff for Spanish-speaking adults. Similarly, the Queens

Borough Public Library, with a $36,875 grant, provided State Correctional Facilities with a library outreach service for prisoners reading languages other than English and Spanish.

The contents of the 2006–2007 year do not differ significantly from the previous year.

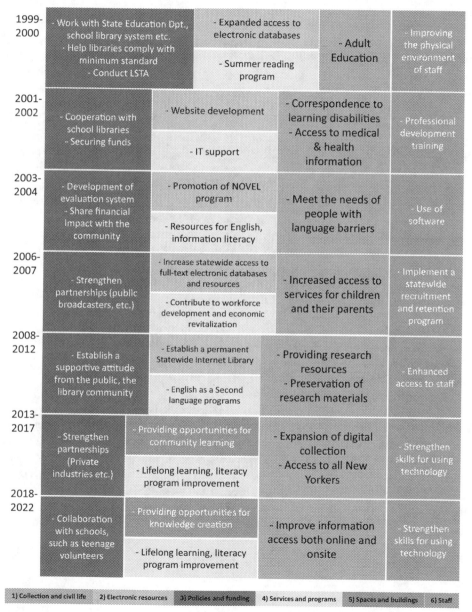

	1) Collection and civil life	2) Electronic resources	3) Policies and funding	4) Services and programs	5) Spaces and buildings	6) Staff
1999-2000	- Work with State Education Dpt., school library system etc. - Help libraries comply with minimum standard - Conduct LSTA	- Expanded access to electronic databases - Summer reading program		- Adult Education	- Improving the physical environment of staff	
2001-2002	- Cooperation with school libraries - Securing funds	- Website development - IT support		- Correspondence to learning disabilities - Access to medical & health information	- Professional development training	
2003-2004	- Development of evaluation system - Share financial impact with the community	- Promotion of NOVEL program - Resources for English, information literacy		- Meet the needs of people with language barriers	- Use of software	
2006-2007	- Strengthen partnerships (public broadcasters, etc.)	- Increase statewide access to full-text electronic databases and resources - Contribute to workforce development and economic revitalization		- Increased access to services for children and their parents	- Implement a statewide recruitment and retention program	
2008-2012	- Establish a supportive attitude from the public, the library community	- Establish a permanent Statewide Internet Library - English as a Second language programs		- Providing research resources - Preservation of research materials	- Enhanced access to staff	
2013-2017	- Strengthen partnerships (Private industries etc.)	- Providing opportunities for community learning - Lifelong learning, literacy program improvement		- Expansion of digital collection - Access to all New Yorkers	- Strengthen skills for using technology	
2018-2022	- Collaboration with schools, such as teenage volunteers	- Providing opportunities for knowledge creation - Lifelong learning, literacy program improvement		- Improve information access both online and onsite	- Strengthen skills for using technology	

Fig. 2. Transition of key strategies and characteristic items in each year.

However, partnerships with public broadcasters and literacy providers were added, and users with special needs and toddlers and parents were emphasized. Other factors that were emphasized in the strategies in previous years were continued. Erie 2-Chautauqua-Cattaraugus BOCES (LEA) has undertaken a joint project with several organizations, including Buffalo City SLS, with a $30,000 grant. The project provided librarians and teachers with literacy training as a workshop to facilitate communication between the library and the school.

From 2008–2012, more detailed descriptions of services were added. For example, as an expansion of services from previous years, services for toddlers and those with learning disabilities were added. Moreover, collaboration with school libraries was emphasized. Since then, strategies that emphasize early childhood education were emphasized. In addition, digital technologies that preserve research materials in multiple formats are described. It can be said from this period that digitization initiatives expanded. This can be said to indicate that the digitization of materials expanded with the times. As an example, the Long Island Library Resources Council gave lectures and workshops for librarians from 2008 to 2010 with a $21,250 grant to promote digitization of Long Island regional materials. Similarly, from 2010 to 2012, with a $21,215 grant, it continued to carry out projects to digitize historical, cultural, governmental and industrial material.

The years 2013–2017 emphasized a wide range of community learning and intellectual creation opportunities to support the lives of citizens. This included programs to enhance literacy, labor development, public participation, and financial awareness. As in the previous years, it was shown that with regard to electronic resources, public access to the digital collection of cultural facilities through the library was expanded, and collections of electronic resources were also expanded. In addition, libraries were encouraged to utilize not only public funds but also private funds such as private companies and non-profit sectors for improving services. It can be seen that partnerships with the private sector became more important as public funds were reduced. As an example of a service opportunity for intellectual creation, the New York Public Library hosted a Summer Program called "Living Cities" with a $35,400 state grant. This was a workshop for young people to improve cross-cultural skills, information literacy, and knowledge of global sustainability issues.

In 2018–2022, although there was no significant change from the previous year, each strategy was described more concretely. For example, strengthening partnerships included more diverse institutions such as state museums, state archives, and the Office of Educational Television and Public Broadcasting. In collaboration with schools, it was important to expand activities led by teens, such as volunteer services. In particular, since 2018, the state library website provided information on opioids, providing guidance to prevent opioid overdose in public places, making it a social issue.

Throughout all of the policies, there has always been an emphasis on building the capacity of library staff. Because the content of policy descriptions about library staff has continually increased, the wide range of competencies of library staff has changed in line with the times.

5.3 Changes in Minimum Standards in New York State

The minimum standards for public libraries consisted of 11 sections until 2020, but from 2021 the sections increased to 14. The added content includes "provides programming" (Sect. 9), "Provides library staff with annual technology training, appropriate to their position" (Sect. 13), "Establishes and maintains partnerships with other educational, cultural or community organizations which enable the library" (Sect. 14), and every item contains the phrase "to address community needs." These added Sects. (9, 13, 14) reflect strategy element number 1, "Collection and civil lives," shown in red in Fig. 1 and 2. Furthermore, Sect. 9 of the minimum standards reflects element 4, "Services and programs," shown in light blue in Fig. 1 and 2, and Sect. 13 reflects element 6, "Staff," shown in orange. With changes in goals 3 and 4 in the State library policies in Fig. 1, Sect. 14 was added to the minimum standards, reflecting element 3, "Policies and funding," shown in dark blue in Fig. 1 and 2.

Other sections in the standards that were changed include "periodically evaluates the effectiveness of the library's programs, services and collections" (Sect. 6), and "programs" has been added alongside services and collection, thus supporting programs. In addition, the technology-related sections "power and data infrastructure" (Sect. 8) and "Internet connectivity to address community needs and facilitate access to information" (Sect. 10) were added. This indicates that it is necessary for libraries to provide a minimum level of network infrastructure, thus guaranteeing access to online information. In the other sections, the word "community" was frequently used, and the word "meet" was used until 2020, but this was changed to "address" in 2021.

The New York State Library 2020 Vision has 60 strategic recommendations for all library types, including 16 items for public libraries. It shows what libraries should do in the absence of increased state funding. One distinctive recommendation is "All public libraries proactively create and collect local content and serve as a catalyst for civic engagement to promote civil discourse and confront society's most difficult problems" (24). It aims to position libraries as places for citizen participation and as places for discussion, which is related to element 6, "spaces and buildings," shown in green in Fig. 1 and 2.

6 Discussion and Conclusion

The significant increase in the number of pages and detailed descriptions in the key strategies over time suggests that the goals and strategies of the state library have become more critical in response to social problems.

As described above, the state library has flexibly and dynamically invested in funding to public libraries every year in order to cope with emerging social problems. Based on that investment, local public libraries have created new services. At the same time, the power of state library policies has increasingly strengthened since it is difficult for local libraries alone to react in community-responsive ways. State library policies reference Federal level laws, such as LSTA, and include ideal partnerships with local public libraries for funding.

While state strategic plans influenced local library services to an extent, the reverse was also true: New York State Library observed and reacted to advanced public libraries like the New York Public Library by incorporating those libraries' new services and roles into future strategies. In addition to this, the New York State Library responded to federal laws related to libraries. This is to say that there exists an interrelationship among local public libraries, the state library, and the federal government. In other words, there is a dynamic relationship in public library political discourse.

Future research will conduct a further analysis of the dynamic mechanisms among policies, strategies, and citizens through several cases in the United States.

Acknowledgement. This work was supported by JSPS KAKENHI Grant Number 20H04479.

References

1. Jaeger, P.T., Gorham, U., Sarin, L.C., Bertot, J.C.: Libraries, policy, and politics in a democracy: four historical epochs. Libr. Q. Inform. Commun. Policy **83**, 166–181 (2013)
2. Kranich, C.N.: Libraries and strong democracy: moving from an informed to a participatory 21st century citizenry. Indiana Libr. **32**, 13–20 (2009)
3. Østergård, M.: 6. Dokk1 – Re-inventing Space Praxis: a Mash-up Library, a Democratic Space, a City Lounge or a Space for Diversity? In: Koen, D., Lesneski, T.E. (eds.) Library Design for the 21st Century: Collaborative Strategies to Ensure Success, pp. 91–103. De Gruyter Saur, Berlin, Boston (2018)
4. Haavisto, T.: 14. A Dream Come True of Citizens – the New Helsinki Central Library. In: Koen, D., Lesneski, T.E. (eds.) Library Design for the 21st Century: Collaborative Strategies to Ensure Success, pp. 203–213. De Gruyter Saur, Berlin, Boston (2018)
5. Widdersheim, M.M., Koizumi, M., Larsen, H.: Cultural policy, the public sphere, and public libraries: a comparison of Norwegian, American, and Japanese models. Int. J. Cult. Policy **27**, 358–376 (2021)
6. Rydbeck, K., Johnston, J.: LAM institutions: a cross-country comparison of legislation and statistics on services and use. In: Audunson, R., et al. (eds.) Libraries, Archives and Museums as Democratic Spaces in a Digital Age, pp. 25–52. De Gruyter Saur, GmbH, Germany (2020)
7. Henningsen, E., Larsen, H.: The digitalization imperative: Sacralization of technology in LAM policies. In: Audunson, R., et al. (eds.) Libraries, Archives and Museums as Democratic Spaces in a Digital Age, pp. 53–72. De Gruyter Saur, GmbH, Germany (2020)
8. Blomgren, R.: The institutions go digital. In: Audunson, R., et al. (eds.) Libraries, Archives and Museums as Democratic Spaces in a Digital Age, pp. 73–90. De Gruyter Saur, GmbH, Germany (2020)
9. Stokstad, S.: Norwegian national policies for digitalization in the LAM sector - Imperative and implementation. In: Audunson, R., et al. (eds.) Libraries, Archives and Museums as Democratic Spaces in a Digital Age, pp. 91–109. De Gruyter Saur, GmbH, Germany (2020)
10. Tóth, M.: Organization and funding of digitization in the Visegrád countries. In: Audunson, R., et al. (eds.) Libraries, Archives and Museums as Democratic Spaces in a Digital Age, pp. 111–131. DE GRUYTER SAUR, GmbH, Germany (2020)
11. Vårheim, A., Skare, R., Stokstad, S.: Institutional convergence and divergence in Norwegian cultural policy: Central government LAM organization 1999–2019. In: Audunson, R., et al. (eds.) Libraries, Archives and Museums as Democratic Spaces in a Digital Age, pp. 133–162. De Gruyter Saur, GmbH, Germany (2020)
12. Henningsen, E.: Political Dynamics of the Cultural Sector (POLYCUL). https://www.oslomet.no/en/research/research-projects/political-dynamics-of-the-cultural-sector-polycul. Accessed 08 Sept 2021

Controversial 'Black Legend' Concept as Misinformation or Disinformation Related to History: Where Do We Go from Here in 21st Century Information Field?

Josep Cobarsí-Morales(✉) ⓘ

Computer Science, Universitat Oberta de Catalunya, Multimedia and Telecommunication Studies, Rambla de Poblenou 156, 08018 Barcelona, Spain
jcobarsi@uoc.edu

Abstract. The controversial concept of 'Black Legend' ('Leyenda Negra') as a distortion of the history of a nation or other relevant historical actor has been in place since early 20th century (mostly referred to Spain and Hispanic world so far, but potentially in a more general way) [2, 3]. The present paper reviews multidisciplinary the scientifical studies in 21st century related to this concept, so to gather its state of the art, limitations and potential for the information field. From the review, four main suggestions for future research are proposed: 1) Refine the concept with the help of knowledge management theory and stakeholder theory, to enhance its general application in an interdisciplinary environment, 2) Reconsider the term itself, 3) Clearly establish the gaps between present popular culture or established knowledge, and scientific updated knowledge about history, taking into account multidisciplinary methods and sources (including primary documental sources when suitable), 4) Measure and discuss the gaps with the help of automated extraction and analysis of terms applied to selected corpus of digital content, such as Wikipedia, popular literature, scientific literature or multimedia/audiovisual production.

Keywords: 'Black Legend' · Misinformation · Disinformation · Popular culture · Memory · Scientific knowledge · Digital content

1 Introduction

The term 'Black Legend' may sound weird, outdated or even shocking, for many readers, especially if they are not familiarized with Spanish language and culture. On the other hand, it may have more positive connotations for some specific readers, such as video gamers [59] or fans of nautical topics [60]. Anyway, this paper is not about controversial terminology, nor about videogames or about nautical topics. It's devoted to the study of misinformation or disinformation related to historical events (either real misinformation/disinformation or just perceived as such).

The term 'Black Legend' ('Leyenda Negra' in the original Spanish language) was first popularized at early 20th century by Julián Juderías [1] referred specifically to

Spanish history, although it was used at late 19th by other authors, either referred to Spain as a country (Emilia Pardo Bazán and Vicente Blasco Ibáñez) or to Napoleón as an historical figure (Arhur Lévy).

We may take as initial concept from an historian, the one stated by Powell, referred specifically to Spain [2]:

"The basic premise ... is that Spaniards have shown themselves, historically, to be uniquely cruel, bigoted, tyrannical, obscurantists, lazy, fanatical, greedy, and treacherous; that is, that they differ so much from other peoples in these traits that Spaniards and Spanish history must be viewed and understood in terms not ordinarily used in describing and interpreting other people."

In a more general formulation, referred to any country, Manuel Fernández Alvarez defined it as intentional distortion oriented to disinformation for political reasons [3]:

"... the careful distortion of the history of a nation, perpetrated by its enemies, in order to better fight it. And a distortion as monstrous as possible, with the goal of achieving a specific aim: the moral disqualification of the nation, whose supremacy must be fought in every way possible."

In this sense, according to Elvira Roca Barea [4] the formation of a 'Black Legend' referred to the most prominent nation of a multicultural empire is a universal phenomenon. She addresses specifically the cases of Rome, Russia, United States and Spain.

The concept itself, and specifically when referred to Spain, is controversial. Some authors dispute this very notion: García Cárcel and Mateo Bretos state is rather a Spaniard self-perception about how their history is presented abroad [5], Keen defends the historical descriptions about Spanish empire are fair in broad terms [6]. Also, it must be taken into account that 'Black Legend' is not the only possible distortion of history, but there are also others such as: 'Golden Legend', nationalisms, etc.

Taking all of this into account we aim at this paper to answer two questions:

1) How scientifical studies in the 21st century refer to the concept of 'Black Legend' as a real or just perceived case of misinformation/disinformation? Which are the most significant trends about it?
2) Which potentiality may have this concept for information studies, in present and near future?

Then the remaining of this paper is as follows:

In Sect. 2, we formalize objectives and methodology. In Sect. 3, we present the preliminary results of the review about this topic. Finally, in Sect. 4, we articulate a discussion about the interest of this topic for the information field and some gaps which deserve further research, including reformulation of the concept and reconsideration of the term itself, and conclusions are set up.

2   Objectives and Methodology

The objectives of this paper are stated as follows:

1) Knowing the present concept of 'Black Legend' in the scientific literature and the most significand trends about related research.
2) Gathering the potential interest and significance of this concept for information studies, as well as present limitations, in the era of digital information and data

In order to achieve it, a search of the term 'Black Legend' and its equivalent in Spanish language 'Leyenda Negra' was conducted through Web of Science scientific database (title, keywords and abstract), in the period from the beginning of 2000 to the end of 2020. Content of titles, keywords and abstract was analyzed, so to gather: focus on historical or cultural facts, methodology and sources, intellectual position about the concept. For a few specific papers, also full text was consulted. Tentatively, registers were retrieved to supposedly similar or related terms, such as 'hispanophobia' or 'dark legend', with very few significant additional results that are not included in this review.

3   Results of the Review

Out of 78 registers retrieved 76 were relevant to the topic, and 51 referred to Spanish 'Black Legend' in broad sense: Spain as a country, Imperial Spain, Spanish Monarchy, Hispanic culture, Hispanic world, or similar. The other 25 registers referred to a wide range of persons, countries or institutions (one or two references each one), such as: Imperial Portugal [7, 8], city of Tijuana, Jean Calvin, Boris Yeltsin, a few large companies from Mexico, Borgia family, Teutonic Order, etc. So, it's confirmed that 'Black Legend' is mostly Spanish related in scientific literature nowadays, although it has some use in a more general sense referred to other countries, geographical zones or relevant historical persons or organizations.

Regarding Spanish 'Black Legend', 34 studies take it into account as an historic concept related to the analysis of the past, with no focus on its possible projection to present time. This stem of literature is shown in the three following tables.

Table 1 shows the 13 studies about non-Hispanic actors and/or related cultural production (mostly from Western Europe).

Some of them are based on very specific plays or authors related to the topic: Reginald Scot [10], Inca Garcilaso de la Vega [11], Leonardo Sciascia [13], British soldiers in the Napoleonic war [14], Titus Andronicus [15], operas [7, 21]. In fact [11] refers not properly said to Inca Garcilaso who was a prominent Hispanic author in 16th century, but to the use of his writings against Imperial Spain by French and English, and later on by Irish against Imperial Britain as a hinted way to oppose colonialism.

Other papers have a broader focus. In this sense, it's relevant the study of Sell Maestro [9] about the cooperation of England and Nederland to set up most of the basis of 'Black Legend' discourse in 16th century. Villagrana [12] deals with the derogatory racialization of Spaniards as a relevant element of the 'Black Legend', in some way related to [15] and [18]. Murry [19] explains the use of Spanish writings to set up through the time a negative perception by English public opinion of the evangelization in New World by Spaniards. Flannery [16] states a curious point: the impact of 'Black Legend' based perceptions as a bias for the underestimation of the military capability of Spain as an enemy in a campaign of Seven Years War. And Iserov explains the evolution of North American attitude about its Hispanic neighbors before and after achieving them the independence [21].

All in all, these contributions show significant facets of the formation and evolution of the so called 'Black Legend' discourse in Western culture related to a wide range of cultural production.

Table 1. Past focused studies about only non-Hispanic actors and/or related cultural production

First author (year)	Content
Sell Maestro (2020) [9]	'Black Legend' in Nederland and England in the Sixteenth Century
Méndez (2020) [10]	Hispanophobic discourse in The Discoverie of Witchcraft by Reginald Scot (1584)
Orr (2020) [11]	French, English and Irish plays on 18th century based on Inca Garcilaso de la Vega
Villagrana (2020) [12]	Racialization of Spaniards by late 16th century English polemic
Pioli (2019) [13]	Spanish image in Leonardo Sciascia (1912–1989)
Daly (2018) [14]	Perceptions about Spain and France of British soldiers fighting Napoleonics in Iberic Peninsula, through their letters (1808–1814)
Ndiaye (2016) [15]	Spanish dimension of Gothic with Titus Andronicus
Flannery (2016) [16]	Seven Years War in Philippines (1756–1763)
Nunez Ronchi (2014) [17]	First American-themed operas (the Purcells, Vivaldi, Rameau, Graun), early 18th century
Gonzalez (2014) [18]	Use made in the early modern era of medieval narratives about the fall of Jerusalem
Murry (2013) [19]	Changing English perceptions of Spanish evangelization in the Americas in early modern era
Iserov (2011) [20]	Evolution of the North American attitude towards its Southern neighbours in early 19th century
Andrews (2007) [21]	Study of Meyerbeer's last grand opera, L'Africaine (1865)

Table 2 shows the 18 studies found about only Hispanic actors and/or related cultural production (in broad sense: that is including Spain itself in Imperial and post-Imperial era, and Hispanic countries before and after achieving their independence).

The most important stem of this literature shows how Spanish cultural and/or political agents react more or less consciously (and sometimes through overreaction or clumsy reaction) about it, in broad terms not quite successfully [23–26, 30, 32, 34–36, 38, 39].

On the other hand, a few contributions focus on the assumption in Latin American countries of the 'Black Legend' discourse as an element for the formation of their national identity [26, 28], but also show sometimes more critical visions about it in these countries [29, 33].

Finally, specific contributions focus on singular biographies which could be considered as counterexamples [31] or offer a critical point of view and new knowledge about this topic related to specific cases [37].

Table 2. Past focused studies about only Hispanic actors and/or related cultural production

First author (year)	Content
Gomez Cabia (2020) [22]	Spanish literature of the Baroque
Calderon Argelich (2020) [23]	1867–1868 controversy about Philip II
Rodriguez-Milan (2020) [24]	Late 17th century Spanish novatores
Dominguez (2019) [25]	Spanish apologists during Illustration
Martin-Marquez (2019) [26]	Reformulation of Black Legend by Cuban prisoners in 19th century
Sanchez Jimenez (2018) [27]	National stereotypes in Cervantes''Persiles'
Castilla Urbano (2018) [28]	Use of Las Casas' Brevísima Relación in 19th century to support independence from Spain
Ruiz Velasco Barba (2018) [29]	Evolution of Mexican nationalism (19th century)
Guibovich Perez (2017) [30]	Late Inquisition in Peru (early 19th century)
Del Real (2017) [31]	Plays of Cabeza de Vaca and Sor Juana Inés de la Cruz as counterexamples of 'Black Legend'
Mateos (2017) [32]	Benito Perez Galdos's Fortunata y Jacinta (1887) in terms of the Spanish politics at that time
Reyna Berrotaran (2015) [33]	Pablo Cabrera (1857–1936), rebuider of Argentinian colonial history against 'Black Legend'
Jimenez (2013) [34]	Quevedo, Lope de Vega and Spain's image in early 17th century
Yurchik (2011) [35]	Spanish enlightened reaction towards the negative stereotypes about Spain typical for French literature of the 18th century
Guastu (2009) [36]	Cultural and editorial production developed by some Spanish Jesuits, in order to refute the'Black Legend' (18th century)
Carrasco (2007) [37]	Analysis the 'myth' of Pablo Olavide as martyr of the Spanish Inquisition (18th century)
Glesener (2005) [38]	Spaniards' vision of the Flemish through letters of soldiers and officials (late 16th century and early 17th century)
Stone (2002) [39]	Study of Lope de Vega English characters (1598–1612)

Table 3 shows the 3 studies retrieved about both Hispanic and non-Hispanic actors and/or related cultural production. These are quite interesting approaches, but unfortunately the use of such a plural range of sources is not usual.

Table 3. Past focused studies about Hispanic and non-Hispanic actors and/or related cultural production

First author (year)	Content
Munoz Areyzaga (2020) [40]	Review of scientific texts about the pre-Columbian past, produced between the 17th and 18th centuries
Bigelow (2016) [41]	Mining in colonial Latin America
Lopez Palmero (2016) [42]	Destruction of Hugonot French settlements in Florida (1565)

On the other hand, Table 4 shows 16 papers related in some way to present time (21st century in wide terms).

A few papers explore the presence of 'Black Legend' discourse in 21th century cultural products, either films [45, 57], TV Series [44] or novels [53, 58].

A significant stem of literature traces the long-term influence of the assumption of these ideas (or the opposition to them) in the intellectual and political discussion, including present time [43, 47, 48, 56]. In this sense, a couple of papers are devoted specifically to the distortion due the 'Black Legend' over the history of science and the attempts to counter it [50, 56]. Other specific example concerns history of music [49].

A couple of interesting examples are devoted to fact checking: about the manipulation of Las Casas Brevísima relación translations for disinformation purposes [55], and the study about Spanish genetic trace found not significant, which contradicts popular traditional believes in Nederland [46].

Finally, a couple of relevant papers show a more critical view about Spain and this concept: an explanation of the use of the supposed 'Black Legend' as an element of Spanish nationalist discourse with no historical factual base [51]; a description of the Spanish contribution to the racist categorization and practices [54].

As a summary of the review, the most relevant points about (Spanish) 'Black Legend' are as follows:

Out of 51 papers, 35 are historical studies strictly focused in the past, while other 16 study it with a significant relation with present time. So, the number of papers devoted to the projection of this concept to present time culture, although being a minority, is enough significant.

Regarding the conceptual basis, most of the papers are aligned in broad terms with the concepts of 'Black Legend' stated by [2] or [3], with some significant exceptions. For instance, papers [23, 51] and [54] deny it as a valid historical concept or describe its undue appropriation by conservative actors, and in this sense are aligned to [5] and [6]. On the other hand, the authors of 21st century fictions such as mentioned in [44, 45, 53, 57, 58] don't match exactly with the definitions of [2] or [3]. They use it as a catchy element of popular culture for their own fun fiction and business purposes, rather than

Table 4. Studies related to present time

First author (year)	Content
Favio Osorio (2020) [43]	Analysis of Carlos Rangel's book: from the good savage to the good revolutionary
Lim (2019) [44]	Analysis of TV Serie Aguila Roja
Leetoy & Linan (2018) [45]	Contemporary cultural appropriations of the 'Black Legend', in fictional content such as The Pirates of the Caribbean
Larmuseau et al. (2018) [46]	Genetic trace of Spaniards in Nederlands: popular believes vs scientific evidence
Bauer (2018) [47]	Reflection on Edmundo O'Gorman's The invention of America
Maestro Cano (2018) [48]	Analysis of Weber's thinking
Martin Saez (2018) [49]	Myths about Farinelli (18th century) and its trace in present musicology
Slater & Lopez-Terrada (2017) [50]	Responses to the 'Black Legend' in history of science
Park (2017) [51]	So called 'Black Legend' explained as a nationalist discourse, not as an historical fact
Pimentel & Pardo-Tomas (2017) [52]	History of early modern Spanish science in late 20th century
Dhondt (2017) [53]	Analysis of the historical novel Triptico de la infamia (2015) by the Colombian author Pablo Montoya
Soto (2017) [54]	The Spanish role in the construction of racial categories and racially determined practices
Valdeon (2017) [55]	Manipulation of Las Casas Brevísima relación translations
Fernandez Sebastian (2015) [56]	Long lasting vision of Iberian and since early decades of 19th century of the history of their own countries
Burcar (2015) [57]	Discoursive analysis of Disney's Little Mermaid, Pocahontas and Aladdin
Bazzano (2016) [58]	Use of 'Black Legend' related elements by Sardinian novelists

consciously for political reasons. They may contribute to misinformation, but are not intentionally disinformation-oriented actors.

Paradoxically, a significant contribution to the diffusion and popularity of 'Black Legend' related misinformation and disinformation impacts has been due across time to pro-Hispanic actors who have overreacted to it and/or have reacted not wisely. This idea is present for instance in [35] and [50].

As a multidisciplinary topic of interest, papers concerned about it belong mostly to Arts & Humanities subjects, and other few of them relate to Communication. A very exceptional one, from the disciplinary point of view, is the one about Genetics [46]. Also, a very specific one is the devoted to mining in colonial Latin America, which uses etymology of terms to trace indigenous contribution to colonial mining and metallurgy [41].

Regarding the methodology, content analysis and discourse analysis are the most usual, including translations' analytics, with the mentioned exceptions regarding genetic fact-checking [46].

Acknowledging the relevance of the so called 'Black Legend' as a bias in past and present historical knowledge about Hispanic world (or eventually, the generalization of the term to be applied to the study of historical perception of other nations and actors), doesn't imply this is the only bias possible. Also, Golden Legend, nationalism and other bias influence across the time and contribute to misinformation and disinformation [29, 56].

Although the term as such, according to this review, refers mostly to Hispanic world, the presence of the term referred to other nations and actors is significant and deserves further search.

4   Discussion and Conclusions

The concept of 'Black Legend' as a distortion of the image of a nation or other historical actors, suggests after reviewed in 21st century scientific literature, a few lines of research, mostly related to the following two points:

First, refine the concept, so to enhance its general application in an interdisciplinary environment. For this purpose, it would be helpful to distinguish between scientifical knowledge vs popular culture or established knowledge, and to clarify the potential role of different actors: ones who consciously devote themselves to disinformation, others who use or propagate unconsciously for entertaining or other purposes, others who overreact, etc. Knowledge management theory and stakeholder theory could be useful about it.

In this sense, we propose as a first approach an alternative and more general formulation of the concept, broadly inspired by [3] and taking into account the convenience to reconsider the original term:

"'Black Legend' or 'Dark Legend': Is the careful distortion of the history of a nation (or other relevant historical actor, including persons or organizations) perpetrated by its enemies, in order to better fight it. It's aimed to disqualify or erode its memory and/or its present reputation through intentional disinformation, which is conducted by culturally relevant stakeholders during a certain period of time. Typically, this distortion pollutes in the long term the knowledge base and memory related to this nation (or other relevant historical actor), either popular culture or established knowledge or both, so that later on other stakeholders contribute unconsciously and unintentionally to prolong in time this distortion through misinformation."

Secondly, many images and stereotypes regarding Spanish 'Black Legend' are deeply embedded in Western popular culture and established knowledge. Many of them may become obsolete and wrong according to the evolution of scientifical knowledge, while others could be confirmed. In this sense, in order to establish an improved base of knowledge about this historical case (or about other similar cases), a better multidisciplinary connection is needed, with a more significant presence of genetics, archaeology, economics history, engineering, etc. so to clearly establish the gaps between present scientific knowledge and information available to general public. And is not to forget the knowledge and access to primary historical sources previous to digital era [61]. Also, automatic extraction and analysis of terms applied to digital content (such as Wikipedia, digital corpus of popular or scientific literature, multimedia and audiovisual production, etc.) could help to measure and discuss distortions in knowledge and memory, as a first step to eventually mitigate them. Off course this proposal has its limitations, knowledge and memory about historical facts are prone to competing interpretations and debates. Anyway, those interpretations and debates could benefit from new approaches oriented to improve updated knowledge about those historical facts.

In this sense, from our review we suggest at least three stems of relevant distortion or gaps which deserve further attention about this specific case: 1) the manipulation and weaponization of the translations of Hispanic authors contemporary to Hispanic colonial period, such as reported in [28]; 2) the undervaluation or silence about Hispanic contributions (including indigenous contributions) to global science and technology, such as studied in [41]; 3) the derogatory racialization as an issue, as pointed by [12]. Anyway, sceptical visions about this concept, such as those in [51] and [54] should be taken into account as well.

Let's remark finally, this review has been mostly devoted to Spain and Hispanic world, as a prominent historical case studied by literature, but the concept and the research suggested may be applied more generally to any nation or any relevant historical actor being object of controversial points of view and potential target of misinformation and disinformation.

References

1. Juderías, J.: La leyenda negra. Estudios del concepto de España en el extranjero. Araluce, Barcelona (1917)
2. Powell, P.W.: Tree of hate: propaganda and prejudices affecting United States relations with Hispanic world. University of New Mexico Press, Alburquerque (1971)
3. Fernández Alvarez, M.: Sombras y luces de la España imperial. Espasa Calpe, Madrid (2005)
4. Roca Barea, E.: Imperiofobia y leyenda negra: Roma, Rusia. Estados Unidos y el Imperio español. Siruela, Madrid (2018)

5. García Cárcel, G., Mateo Bretos, L.: Leyenda negra. Compañía Europea de Comunicación e Informació, Madrid (1991)
6. Keen, B.: The Black Legend revisited: assumptions and realities. Hisp. Am. Hist. Rev. **49**(4), 703–719 (1969)
7. Xavier, A.B.: Parecem indianos na cor e na feição: a "lenda negra" e a indianização dos portugueses. Etnográfica **18**(1), 111–133 (2014)
8. Halikowski-Smith, S.: 'Insolence and pride': problems with the representation of the South-East Asian Portuguese communities in Alexander Hamilton's 'A New Account of the East Indies' (1727). J. Roy. Asiatic Soc. **19**, 213–234 (2009)
9. Sell Maestro, A.: The black legend in the Low Countries and England in the Sixteenth Century: a comparative study of its origins and main topics. Tiempos Modernos-Revista Electrónica de Historia Moderna **10**(40), 40–57 (2020)
10. Méndez, A.: Espana a traves de los ojos de un demonologo ingles: leyenda negra, brujeria y supersticion en THE Discoverie of Witchcraft (1584) de Reginald Scot. Bull. Span. Stud. **97**(5), 701–727 (2020)
11. Orr, B.: Indigenous critique and the eighteenth-century English stage. Postcolonial Stud. **23**(3), 284–299 (2020)
12. Villagrana, J.J.: The apocalyptic spanish race. J. Early Modern Cult. Stud. **20**(1), 1–28 (2020)
13. Pioli, M.: L'immaginario spagnolo di leonardo sciascia: genealogie mediterranee. Ital. Stud. **74**(4), 427–441 (2019)
14. Daly, G.: British soldiers and the legend of Napoleon. Hist. J. **61**(1), 131–153 (2018)
15. Ndiaye, N.: Aaron's roots: spaniards, englishmen, and blackamoors in titus andronicus. Early Theatre **19**(2), 59–80 (2016)
16. Flannery, K.P.: Battlefield diplomacy and empire-building in the indo-pacific world during the seven years' war. Itinerario-International J. Hist. Eur. Expansion Global Interact. **40**(3), 467–488 (2016)
17. Nunez Ronchi, A.: American Indians on the European Lyric stage: from the purcell brothers (1695) to Carl Heinrich Graun (1755). Revista de Indias **74**(261), 483–505 (2014)
18. Gonzalez, C.: Vespasiano in America: conquistadors, gold, anti-Semitism, and the Spanish Black Legend. J. Mediev. Iber. Stud. **6**(2), 237–250 (2014)
19. Murry, G.: Tears of the Indians or superficial conversion? Jose de Acosta, the Black Legenf, and the Spanish evangelization of the New World. Catholic Hist. Rev. **99**(1), 29–51 (2013)
20. Iserov, A.A.: United States and the Fight for Independence of Latin America. Elektronnyi nauchno-obrazovatel'nyi zhurnal Istoriya **6**, 21–22 (2011)
21. Andrews, J.: Meyerbeer's L''Africaine': French grand opera and the Iberian exotic (Giacomo Meyerbeer). Modern Laguage Rev. **102**, 108+ (2007)
22. Gomez Cabia, F.: Mowing the shadows in silence. Literature as an aberrated form of philosophical thought in Spain of the Baroque. STOA **11**(22), 141–170 (2020)
23. Calderon Argelich, A.: Shades of Philip II: the Black Legend and the uses of history in the crisis of moderantism (1867–1868). Cuadernos de Historia Contemporanea **42**, 173–195 (2020)
24. Rodriguez-Milan, R.: Noah's grandson and St. James: rewriting the past in eighteenth-century Spain. Eur. Legacy-Towards New Paradigms **25**(7–8), 733–742 (2020)
25. Dominguez, J.P.: España contra las luces: antiilustrados, apologistas y el triunfo de la leyenda negra (1759–1808). Bull. Span. Stud. **96**(2), 219–240 (2019)
26. Martin-Marquez, S.: Transported Identities: global trafficking and late-imperial subjectivity in cuban narratives on African penal colonies. J. Lat. Am. Stud. **51**(1), 1–30 (2019)
27. Sanchez Jimenez, A.: Cervantes and the Northern peoples: an imagologic approach. Atalanta-Revista de las Letras Barrocas **6**(1), 129–147 (2018)

28. Castilla Urbano, F.: Bartolome de las Casas and the independence of Spanish America: the edition of his writings by Juan Antonio Llorente. Revista de Hispanismo Filosófico **23**, 39–61 (2018)
29. Ruiz Velasco Barba, R.: En torno a discursos y representacions del nacionalismo católico en México. Revista de historia americana y argentina **53**(1), 203–233 (2018)
30. Guibovich Perez, P.M.: The last years of the Inquisition in the Viceroyalty of Peru (1813–1820). Ayer **108**, 49–78 (2017)
31. Del Real, A.: The conquered conqueror Alvar Nunez Cabeza de Vaca and the conquered conqueror Sor Juana Ines de la Cruz. Analysis of two divergent identities from two brief Works. Ars Humanitas **11**(2), 232–244 (2017)
32. Mateos, A.: Fortunata, L'Africaine: slavery and semitism in Spain's modern empire. Rev. Estud. Hisp. **51**(2), 441–465 (2017)
33. Reyna Berrotaran, D.: Doctor Honoris Causa Monsenor Pablo Cabrera: historiographical lines a tribute. Coordenadas-Revista de historia local y regional **2**(2), 81–100 (2015)
34. Jimenez, A.: Quevedo and Lope (poetry and theatre) in 1609: patriotism and building of a nation State in La Espana defendida and La Jerusalen conquistada. Perinola-Revista de Investigacion Quevediana **17**, 27+ (2013)
35. Yurchik, E.E.: La leyenda negra en la literatura de la Ilustracion espanyola. Elektronnyi nauchno-obrazovatel'nyi zhurnal Istoriya **8**, 17–18 (2011)
36. Guasti, N.: Sketches of the Italian exili of the Spaish Jesuites. Hispania Sacra **61**(123), 257–278 (2009)
37. Carrasco, R.: A myth in movement: Pablo de Olavide and Gospel in Triumph. Rev. Chil. Lit. **71**, 19–42 (2007)
38. Glesener, T.: Flanders and the Flemish in the Spanish imaginary lore of the XVIth century. Revue du Nord **87**(360–361), 337+ (2005)
39. Stone, R.S.: With art everything is overcome: Images of English in Lope de Vega. Bull. Comediantes **54**(2), 249–269 (2002)
40. Munoz Areyzaga, E.: The construction of the pre Columbian past as an identity element of the mexican territory, through a dialogical dynamic between Nueva Espana and the West, in the 17th and 18th centuries. Revista Hmanidades **10**(2) https://doi.org/10.15517/h.v10i2.41195 (2020)
41. Bigelow, A.: Incorporating indigenous knowledge into extractive economies: the science of colonial silver. Extractive Ind. Soc. Int. J. **3**(1), 117–123 (2016)
42. Lopez Palmero, M.: The discursive dimensions of the Spanish attack on the French colony of Florida (1565). Magallanica-Revista de Historia Moderna **2**(4), 136–151 (2016)
43. Favio Osorio, L.: Latin American myths: Validity of the work Del buen salvaje al buen revolucionario. Telos-Revista interdisciplinària en ciencias sociales **22**(2), 310–324 (2020)
44. Lim, J.: Aguila Roja: the demythification of black legend and the will to overcome. Cross-Cultural Stud. **54**, 333–370 (2019)
45. Leetoy, S., Linan, M.: Barbarossa - Bar(bar)ossa - Barbossa: the permanence of the black legend as a discourse of otherness. Chasqui-Revista Latinoamericana de Comunicación **137**, 223–243 (2018)
46. Larmuseau, M.H.D., Calafell, F., Princen, S.A., Decorte, R., Soen, V.: The black legend on the Spanish presence in the low countries: Verifying shared beliefs on genetic ancestry. Am. J. Phys. Anthropol. **166**(1), 219–227 (2018)
47. Bauer, R.: The white legend edmundo O'Gorman, hemispheric studies, and the paradigm of new world exceptionalism. English Language Notes **56**(2), 51–54 (2018)
48. Maestro Cano, I.C.: The weber thesis on capitalism in the 500th anniversary of the protestant reformation. ILU-Revista de Ciencias de las Religiones **23**, 149–173 (2018)
49. Martin Saez, D.: The legend of Farinelli in Spain: historiograhy. Mithology and Politics. Revista de Musicologia **41**(1), 41–77 (2018)

50. Slater, J., Lopez-Terrada, M.: Being beyond: the Black Legend and how we got over it. Hist. Sci. **55**(2), 148–166 (2017)
51. Park, P.K.: The black legend as a nationalist discourse. Korean J. Hispanic Stud. **10**(1), 55–81 (2017)
52. Pimentel, J., Pardo-Tomas, J.: And yet, we were modern. The paradoxes of Iberian science after the Grand Narratives. Histry Sci. **55**(2), 133–147 (2017)
53. Dhondt, R.: Triptico de la infamia by Pablo Montoya as a Baroque Painting. Mitologias Hoy-Revista de Pensamiento, Crítica y Estudios Literarios Latinoamericanos **16**, 307–319 (2017)
54. Soto, I.: Black Atlantic (Dis)Entanglements: Langston Hughes, Richard Wright, and Spain. Zeischrift fur Anglistik und Amerikanistic. **65**(2), 203–217 (2017)
55. Valdeon, R.A.: Bartolome de las Casas and the Spanish-American War. Transl. Interpreting Stud. **12**(3), 367–382 (2017)
56. Fernandez Sebastian, J.: A distorting mirror: the sixteenth century in the historical imagination of the first Hispanic liberals. History Eur. Ideas **41**(2), 166–175 (2015)
57. Burcar, L.: Interwoven Constructs of Gender and Race in Disney's Adaptations of Canonized Literary Works for Children. Primerjalna Knjizevnost **38**(1), 19(45) (2015)
58. Bazzano, N.: The leyenda negra continues: the sardinia of viceroys in the sardinian fiction between the late twentieth cetury and the new millenniun. Mediterranea-Recerche Historice **37**, 353–374 (2016)
59. Videogame 'Black Legend'. https://www.blacklegendgame.com/
60. 'Black Legend' yacht. https://www.superyachttimes.com/yachts/black-legend-50m
61. Denisova, N.: Filosofía de la historia de América: los cronistas de Indias en la historia del pensamiento español. Fundación Academia Europea e Iberoamericana de Yuste, Madrid (2019)

The Rural Information Penalty

Jean Hardy[⊠] [iD]

Department of Media and Information, Michigan State University, East Lansing, MI 48824, USA
jhardy@msu.edu

Abstract. This paper articulates the concept of rural information penalty, or the accumulation of rural disadvantages that lead to lower quality of information, disparate understandings of information, and increased barriers to information for rural people. Drawing inspiration from rural public health and economic development literature, I bring together research from information studies and human-computer interaction to build a framework for understanding the rural information penalty.

Keywords: Digital divide · Geography · Rural computing · Rural penalty

1 Introduction

There is an accumulation of rural disadvantages that greatly impact the use of information. These disadvantages, which range from infrastructural to cultural, lead to lower quality of information and increased barriers to information for rural people, especially when it comes to digital information and the use of information and communication technologies (ICTs). It is the goal of this paper to articulate the disadvantages in the form of what I am calling the *rural information penalty*. Drawing inspiration from rural health literature and the idea of the "rural mortality penalty," as well as the "rural penalty" in economic development literature, I bring together research from information studies and human-computer interaction to build up a framework for understanding the rural information penalty, and identify a path forward for better understanding its impact through empirical and theoretical research.[1]

This is not the first paper to consider the role of rurality on information. Prior work documents the importance of Internet infrastructure in rural communities and how different infrastructures result in different experiences of information [3, 6], as well as the place of libraries and other local institutions as key components of information infrastructure [38]. Geography, both urban and rural, plays an important role in information access. For example, prior research shows how access to health information is mediated by resource scarcity (e.g., limited health providers) as a result of location in rural communities [41]. Recent research by Lee and Butler on information deserts [22] foregrounds the role of materiality of information, meaning information's material form and

---

[1] I do not define rurality in this paper due to the complexity and diverging definitions of what rural means depending on geographic context. For further discussion of rurality in the computing context see [17].

structure in physical communities, to understand how information is fragmented and spread across space and time, negatively impacting information access in communities without diverse and centralized models of information access. Further, while there's little to no foundational research to my knowledge on the impact of rurality on information literacy, prior research encourages an understanding of information literacy as socially enabled rather than purely mediated by information sources [16, 24]. Bringing the above together, we can see the impact of place on information, as well as the mediating role of material, infrastructural, and social forms on information access and literacy.

While these topics are indeed important, the goal of this short paper is to step back from the specifics of topics like information access, digital infrastructure, and information literacy to take in a birds-eye view of what contributes to a much broader and more complex rural information penalty. While the digital divide literature has evolved greatly since the 1990s to understand that digital access isn't merely about Internet access, but has to deal with a host of issues related to technology access and maintenance [12], there is still a need to understand what penalties or barriers exist in the rural context beyond basic access and maintenance. Further, previous research on information poverty in rural places [13, 40] shows what happens when information is simply not available, or is available but the skills or ability to navigate it are inadequate. The framing of the rural information penalty focuses on when the information exists, but there are compounded barriers and material realities (borrowing from [22]) that impede information quality and understanding. The rural information penalty that I put forward here is indeed exacerbated by a digital divide, though one that is multimodal, both infrastructural and cultural. In other words, the rural information penalty is a cultural process as much as it is a process of understanding access to information via Internet and information institutions. This project reframes this conversation as one of a penalty, rather than a divide or poverty, to understand how different kinds of digital access and literacies, embedded in economic, geographic, and cultural contexts, result in different understandings of information.[2]

2   The Rural Information Penalty

The rural information penalty is *the accumulation of rural disadvantages that lead to lower quality of information, disparate understanding of information, and increased barriers to information for rural people*, especially when it comes to digital information and the use of information and communication technologies (ICTs). In this section I give a brief overview of the inspiration for this concept and then present a series of disadvantages coming out of research in information studies and human-computer interaction that contribute to the formation of the penalty.

The rural information penalty is inspired by the concept of the rural mortality penalty out of public health and the rural penalty from economic development literature. The

---

[2] I focus primarily on the American context in this paper. This is not to say that the rural information penalty is not a useful tool for understanding other international contexts, but merely to acknowledge that, as presented here, it reflects a particular geography and perspective. To utilize this concept outside of the American context, researchers should first seek a broader understanding of what rurality means in their particular context.

rural mortality penalty is the term given to the divergence of metropolitan versus non-metropolitan death rates starting in the mid-1980s [7, 8], with metropolitan areas seeing larger overall declines in heart disease and cancer death rates [9]. This rural mortality penalty is further exacerbated by type of rural area, race, poverty, access to medical care, and other factors [7, 19, 20]. The rural penalty is a term used in rural development literature to articulate the impact that low population density and distance to markets, information, and labor have on the economic development of rural communities [25]. Drawing from earlier theoretical work in rural development on the impact of remoteness on rural economies [18], Edward Malecki uses the rural penalty to explain the urban-rural digital divide and why broader efforts for digital infrastructure development continually trail behind that of urban areas [25]. Taken together, this research allows us to sense how "penalty" might be a helpful way to understand the impact rural geography has on information.

In what follows, I draw out a handful of influences that make up the rural information penalty. These influences are not meant to be exhaustive or totalizing, but are merely a first step towards conceptualizing and drawing out the disadvantages (and their relationships) that accumulate into the rural information penalty. These include: infrastructure, information institutions, information literacy, technology access and maintenance, population density, values and networks, and perceived outsider status.

2.1 Infrastructure

Infrastructure is a classic concern in information studies, especially with respect to Internet infrastructure. There have been decades of research on the digital divides between urban and rural communities that come as a result of lack of Internet infrastructure [e.g., 6, 44] and its compounding and cascading effects [36]. Beyond telecommunications infrastructure, rural communities in the United States face other infrastructural gaps, such as lack of access to public transportation [37], which contribute to additional barriers to accessing geographically diverse information sources and/or accessing local and regional institutions (e.g., libraries) that may offer more opportunities for information access and literacy.

2.2 Information Institutions

What I am calling "information institutions" are the place-based institutions such as libraries, museums, newspapers, colleges, and governmental entities (e.g., public health departments) that serve as key local information nodes in their locality. For example, prior research shows the importance of libraries in rural communities for accessing diverse information sources [27, 28, 39]. Information institutions writ large are essential *local* institutions that interface with everyday people in various information transactions. While information institutions might have easier access to individuals in rural areas, given lower population densities, that does not necessarily mean engagement and trust in information institutions. For example, prior research from the Pew Center found that library non-users were disproportionately located in rural areas [32]. Further, a decline in trust of governmental institutions in rural areas [4] means that information from those organizations is more likely to be viewed with distrust (something that has been increasingly clear during the COVID-19 pandemic). Lastly, the collapse of local journalism since the 1990s in the United States has hit rural communities particularly hard, resulting in vast rural news deserts throughout the country [1].

2.3 Information Literacy

Information literacy is broadly the process through which people access, make sense of, and internalize information sources. While there is little research specifically on the impact of rurality on information literacy [16], prior research in library and information science argues that contextual factors, such as culture, are key to understanding an individual's information literacy [23, 24, 29]. Though, information literacy has largely been relegated to official information institutions rather than cultural environments [16]. Information literacy, both as the end goal of literacy and the *process* of gaining literacy about a specific type of information, is negatively impacted by rurality through much of what is discussed above. With fewer information institutions, increased distrust in information sources, and lower access to information through libraries or the Internet, people living in rural areas have a much more complex task of gaining information literacy. For example, prior research on information literacy related to identity-based information for rural LGBTQ people found that rurality was a key mediator for understanding generational differences in information literacy [16]. While I am framing rurality as a key component of the information penalty, there are likely other ways that rurality improves information literacy in other topics. For example, given the unique relationship to land that rural people have, there is likely an increased information literacy in areas such as agriculture, gardening, hunting, and other related topics.

2.4 Technology Access and Maintenance

Technology access and the resulting maintenance of technology is a key component to understanding the rural information penalty. In the United States, rural areas have had consistently lower rates of home broadband adoption and smartphone, tablet, and computer ownership compared to urban and suburban areas [42]. When technology access is achieved, maintenance adds further complexity to rural people's ability to access information. As Amy Gonzales argues, low-income technology users often struggle with what she calls "dependable instability," or the normalization of disconnection or disruption in the ability to access the Internet [12]. Given the higher proportion of low-income people in rural areas compared to urban and suburban areas of the United States [21], in addition to the distinct difference in Internet infrastructure and access between urban and rural areas, it is safe to assume that technology maintenance is a more pronounced issue in rural areas.

2.5 Population Density

Population density and size are key to understanding and are the most frequently cited indicators of rurality in official definitions [17]. Population density is particularly important in understanding the rural information penalty because it is a broader determinant of other information penalties. For example, internet infrastructure development and internet service providers have historically benefited urban areas because more paying customers means more money for their business. Low population density in combination with long distances between places makes developing infrastructure much more expensive, and therefore unsustainable unless subsidized by state and federal governments (the major way that these infrastructures have been funded).

2.6 Values and Networks

The localization of values and trust are important aspects of rural society [14], but can often lead to distrust of outsiders, such as immigrants [33] or government officials [4, 10]. While a universal set of rural values does not exist [30], rural Americans view themselves as being more "neighborly" than urban Americans [43], and tend to be more religious [5]. Tight-knit communities are often seen as a defining feature of rural areas [15]. In fact, the density of social networks is higher in rural areas than in urban communities, with rural people more likely to have family and local ties in their social networks than urban people [11, 26, 34]. This means that rural networks are likely less diverse, and therefore more susceptible to filter bubbles in accessing information [31]. This is particularly important regarding our current understandings of the role that networks play in perpetuating misinformation [28]. Taken together we can see that values and networks can be both positive and negative influences on information access and quality. In some ways, information might flow more quickly, but in the post-truth age of COVID-denialism, we can also see how values and networks greatly influence and penalize a broader information ecosystem through its homogeneity, allowing less diverse and fewer authoritative sources of information gain the most trust.

2.7 Perceived Outsider Status

The final component of the rural information penalty I'd like to discuss is what I'm calling perceived outsider status. This disadvantage is an amalgamation of other disadvantages (e.g., values) alongside an understanding of the increased political and economic polarization between rural and urban communities in America. Katherine Cramer's *Politics of Resentment* looked at the rural-urban political divide in Wisconsin that led to the rise of ultra-conservative Governor Scott Walker and later President Trump [10]. What she found was an intense sense of distrust of political outsiders in rural communities, particularly those politicians from state or federal levels that were perceived as being out of touch with rural communities and therefore outsiders and fundamentally unable to serve rural places effectively. This was especially the case when it came to purported values and the allocation of resources between urban and rural areas. This distrust, while reflecting complex and sometimes false perceptions of disparities (e.g., in many cases rural areas actually receive a higher per capita proportion of state funds), resulted nonetheless in perpetuating the lived experience of the urban-rural divide from both sides of the geographic spectrum. Further work from Jennifer Sherman and others on the growth of amenity-based tourism in rural communities [35, 45] also demonstrates how rural communities can often get the real feeling that they are merely there to serve urban outsiders. This perpetuates a sense of regional and political divide while rural communities across the United States continue to lag behind urban communities more than a decade after the Great Recession [2]. The consequences of this perceived outsider status are likely impactful for not only the trust of information that originates from urban communities, but also reinforces filter bubbles and perpetuates an embrace of certain types of misinformation.

3   Conclusion and Future Work

What I have summarized here is a first look at what I am calling the *rural information penalty*, or the accumulation of rural disadvantages that lead to lower quality of information, disparate understanding of information, and increased barriers to information for rural people. The rural information penalty forefronts the role of geography in understanding the accumulative sociotechnical aspects of American rural areas that impact information. In doing so, I go beyond the comparative approach of the digital divide and offer a different and potentially more complex framework than information poverty, one that centers knowledge and perspectives from rural studies, development, and public health.

What is proposed here is merely that, a proposal for understanding the creation, transmission, storage, and use of information and how those processes are impacted by rurality. What is have outlined is not meant to be a totalizing or complete framing of the rural information penalty, merely the disadvantages that are at the forefront of contemporary information studies and human-computer interaction research when it comes to the intersection of rurality and technology. In particular, there are some notable elements that are missing including: the economic impacts of ICTs in rural communities; education deserts and the different types of education valued in rural places; and the role of identity and culture in the rural information penalty. Further, as characterized the information penalty is inherently negative. There is likely an inverse opportunity to highlight, as I did in my section on information literacy, the positive traits of rural places that lead to information advantages.

In addition to working to understand all of the disadvantages that accumulate to make up the rural information penalty, future work should also take an empirical approach to understanding the rural information penalty. How might we utilize measurements of information literacy, access to information institutions and technology, and the role of local values and the social capital, among other things, to generate a better understanding of how the rural information penalty changes across geography or which disadvantages impact it the most? The rural information penalty, as a framework, is also likely well situated for helping us understand the increasing role of ICTs in rural society and the expectations of connection that are imposed upon people, no matter their geography.

References

1. Penelope Muse Abernathy: News Deserts and Ghost Newspapers: Will Local News Survive? UNC Hussman School of Journalism and Media (2020)
2. Olugbenga Ajilore: Economic Recovery and Business Dynamism in Rural America. Center for American Progress (2020). https://www.americanprogress.org/issues/economy/reports/2020/02/20/480129/economic-recovery-business-dynamism-rural-america/

3. Ali, C.: The politics of good enough: rural broadband and policy failure in the United States. Int. J. Commun. **14**, 5982–6004 (2020)
4. Ashwood, L.: For-Profit Democracy: Why the Government Is Losing the Trust of Rural America. Yale University Press, New Haven (2018)
5. Baylor Religion Surveys: American Values, Mental Health, and Using Technology in the Age of Trump. Baylor University (2017)
6. Burrell, J.: Thinking relationally about digital inequality in rural regions of the U.S. First Monday **23**, 6 (2018). https://doi.org/10.5210/fm.v23i6.8376
7. Cosby, A.G., et al.: Growth and persistence of place-based mortality in the United States: the rural mortality penalty. Am. J, Public Health **109**(1), 155–162 (2019). https://doi.org/10.2105/AJPH.2018.304787
8. Cosby, A.G., et al.: Preliminary evidence for an emerging nonmetropolitan mortality penalty in the United States. Am. J. Public Health **98**(8), 1470–1472 (2008). https://doi.org/10.2105/AJPH.2007.123778
9. Cossman, J.S., James, W.L., Cosby, A.G., Cossman, R.E.: Underlying causes of the emerging nonmetropolitan mortality penalty. Am. J. Public Health **100**(8), 1417–1419 (2010). https://doi.org/10.2105/AJPH.2009.174185
10. Cramer, K.J.: The Politics of Resentment: Rural Consciousness in Wisconsin and the Rise of Scott Walker. University of Chicago Press, Chicago (2016)
11. Freudenburg, W.R.: The density of acquaintanceship: an overlooked variable in community research? Am. J. Sociol. **92**(1), 27–63 (1986). https://doi.org/10.1086/228462
12. Gonzales, A.: The contemporary US digital divide: from initial access to technology maintenance. Inf. Commun. Soc. **19**(2), 234–248 (2016). https://doi.org/10.1080/1369118X.2015.1050438
13. Haider, J., Bawden, D.: Conceptions of "information poverty" in LIS: a discourse analysis. J. Documentation **63**(4), 534–557 (2007). https://doi.org/10.1108/00220410710759002
14. Halfacree, K.H.: Locality and social representation: space, discourse and alternative definitions of the rural. J. Rural. Stud. **9**(1), 23–37 (1993). https://doi.org/10.1016/0743-0167(93)90003-3
15. Halfacree, K.H.: Talking about rurality: social representations of the rural as expressed by residents of six English parishes. J. Rural. Stud. **11**(1), 1–20 (1995). https://doi.org/10.1016/0743-0167(94)00039-C
16. Hardy, J.: Queer information literacies: social and technological circulation in the rural Midwestern United States. Inf. Commun. Soc. **24**(1), 102–117 (2021). https://doi.org/10.1080/1369118X.2019.1635184
17. Hardy, J., Wyche, S., Veinot, T.: Rural HCI research: definitions, distinctions, methods, and opportunities. In: Proc. ACM Hum. Comput. Interact. **3**(CSCW 196), 1–33 (2019). https://doi.org/10.1145/3359298
18. Hite, J.: The Thunen model and the new economic geography as a paradigm for rural development policy. Rev. Agric. Econ. **19**(2), 230–240 (1997). https://doi.org/10.2307/1349738
19. James, W.L.: All rural places are not created equal: revisiting the rural mortality penalty in the United States. Am. J. Public Health **104**(11), 2122–2129 (2014). https://doi.org/10.2105/AJPH.2014.301989
20. James, W., Cossman, J.S.: Long-term trends in black and white mortality in the rural United States: evidence of a race-specific rural mortality penalty. J. Rural Health **33**(1), 21–31 (2017). https://doi.org/10.1111/jrh.12181
21. Kyzyma, I.: Rural-urban disparity in poverty persistence. Focus **34**(3), 13–19 (2018)
22. Lee, M., Butler, B.S.: How are information deserts created? A theory of local information landscapes. J. Am. Soc. Inf. Sci. **70**(2), 101–116 (2019). https://doi.org/10.1002/asi.24114

23. Lloyd, A.: Framing information literacy as information practice: site ontology and practice theory. J. Documentation **66**(2), 245–258 (2010). https://doi.org/10.1108/00220411011023643

24. Lloyd, A.: Information literacy as a socially enacted practice: sensitising themes for an emerging perspective of people-in-practice. J. Documentation **68**(6), 772–783 (2012). https://doi.org/10.1108/00220411211277037

25. Malecki, E.J.: Digital development in rural areas: potentials and pitfalls. J. Rural. Stud. **19**(2), 201–214 (2003). https://doi.org/10.1016/S0743-0167(02)00068-2

26. McKnight, M.L., Sanders, S.R., Gibbs, B.G., Brown, R.B.: Communities of place? new evidence for the role of distance and population size in community attachment. Rural. Sociol. **82**(2), 291–317 (2017). https://doi.org/10.1111/ruso.12123

27. Mehra, B.: Mobilization of rural libraries toward political and economic change in the aftermath of the 2016 Presidential election. Libr. Q. **87**(4), 369–390 (2017). https://doi.org/10.1086/692303

28. Mehra, B.: Information ACTism in "Trumping" the contemporary fake news phenomenon in rural libraries. Open Inform. Sci. **3**(1), 181–196 (2019). https://doi.org/10.1515/opis-2019-0013

29. Montiel-Overall, P.: Information literacy: toward a cultural model. Can. J. Inform. Libr. Sci. **31**(1), 43–68 (2007)

30. Newby, H.: Locality and rurality: the restructuring of rural social relations. Reg. Stud. **20**(3), 209–215 (1986)

31. Pariser, E.: The Filter Bubble: What the Internet is Hiding from You. Penguin Books, London (2011)

32. Pew Research Center: From Distant Admirers to Library Loves: A typology of public library engagement in America (2014). https://www.pewresearch.org/internet/2014/03/13/library-engagement-typology/

33. Sacchetti, M., Guskin, E.: In rural America, fewer immigrants and less tolerance. Washington Post (2017). https://www.washingtonpost.com/local/in-rural-america-fewer-immigrants-and-less-tolerance/2017/06/16/7b448454-4d1d-11e7-bc1b-fddbd8359dee_story.html. Accessed 1 Apr 2019

34. Sampson, R.J.: Local friendship ties and community attachment in mass society: a multilevel systemic model. Am. Sociol. Rev. **53**(5), 766–779 (1988)

35. Sherman, J.: Dividing Paradise: Rural Inequality and the Diminishing American Dream. University of California Press, California (2021)

36. Stern, M.J., Adams, A.E., Elsasser, S.: Digital inequality and place: the effects of technological diffusion on internet proficiency and usage across Rural, Suburban, and Urban Counties. Sociol. Inq. **79**(4), 391–417 (2009). https://doi.org/10.1111/j.1475-682X.2009.00302.x

37. Stommes, E.S., Brown, D.M.: Transportation in Rural America: issues for the 21st Century. Commun. Transp. **20**, 4 (2002)

38. Strover, S., Whitacre, B., Rhinesmith, C., Schrubbe, A.: The digital inclusion role of rural libraries: social inequalities through space and place. Media Cult. Soc. **42**(2), 242–259 (2020)

39. Vavrek, B.: Rural information needs and the role of the public library. Lib. Trends **44**(1), 21–48 (1995)

40. Veinot, T.: A lot of people didn't have a chance to support us because we never told them Stigma management, information poverty and HIV/AIDS information/help networks. Proc. Am. Soc. Inform. Sci. Technol. **46**(1), 1–20 (2009). https://doi.org/10.1002/meet.2009.1450460273

41. Veinot, T.C.: Regional HIV/AIDS information environments and information acquisition success. Inform. Soc. **29**(2), 88–112 (2013). https://doi.org/10.1080/01972243.2012.757261

42. Vogels, E.: Some digital divides persist between rural, urban and suburban America. Pew Research Center (2021). https://www.pewresearch.org/fact-tank/2021/08/19/some-digital-divides-persist-between-rural-urban-and-suburban-america/. Accessed 8 Sept 2021
43. Washington Post.: Survey of Rural America. Survey of Rural America (2017). http://apps.washingtonpost.com/g/page/national/washington-post-kaiser-family-foundation-rural-and-small-town-america-poll/2217/. Accessed 1 Apr 2018
44. Whitacre, B.E., Mills, B.F.: Infrastructure and the rural—urban divide in high-speed residential internet access. Int. Reg. Sci. Rev. **30**(3), 249–273 (2007). https://doi.org/10.1177/0160017607301606
45. Winkler, R.: Living on lakes segregated communities and inequality in a natural amenity destination. Sociol. Q. **54**(1), 105–129 (2013). https://doi.org/10.1111/tsq.12002

Predicting the Usage of Scientific Datasets Based on Article, Author, Institution, and Journal Bibliometrics

Daniel E. Acuna[✉] , Zijun Yi, Lizhen Liang , and Han Zhuang

School of Information Studies, Syracuse University, Syracuse, NY 13244, USA
deacuna@syr.edu

Abstract. Scientific datasets are increasingly crucial for knowledge accumulation and reproducibility, making it essential to understand how they are used. Although usage information is hard to obtain, features from the publications that describe a dataset can provide clues. This article associates dataset downloads with the authors' h-index, institutional prestige, journal ranking, and the references used in the publication that first introduces them. Tens of thousands of datasets and associated publications from figshare.com are used in our analysis. We found that a gradient boosting model achieved the highest performance against linear regression, random forests, and artificial neural networks. Our interpretation results suggest that journal ranking is highly predictive of usage while the author's institutional prestige and h-index are less critical. In addition, we found that publications with a long but focused body of references are associated with more dataset downloads. We also show that prediction performance decays rapidly the farther we estimate downloads into the future. Finally, we discuss the implications of our work for reproducibility and data policies.

Keywords: Dataset usage · Prediction · Prestige · Science of science · Bibliometrics

1 Introduction

Datasets are essential for reproducibility and have become crucial for journals, funding agencies, and other scientists. While publications have multiple scientometric signals available [4, 8, 11], datasets are comparatively poorly tracked and understood [16]. For example, little is known about the factors predicting dataset usage if we compare it to how much we know about publication citation prediction [1, 14]. Understanding the factors predictive of dataset usage can allow us to advertise, disseminate, and store them better.

Scientific resources of many kinds are increasingly open, shared, and modified by the community. In the past, the primary source of knowledge was the articles themselves. Today, articles share datasets, code, and computational infrastructure. One of the main drivers of this trend is the exponential decay in storage and computational costs

M. Smits (Ed.): iConference 2022, LNCS 13192, pp. 42–52, 2022.
https://doi.org/10.1007/978-3-030-96957-8_5

[7] and the increased understanding that science depends on others' work to move forward. These trends have percolated into science. Resources are now commonly shared in authors' websites and special-purpose websites such as Figshare.com, Zenodo, and Harvard Dataverse [2]. These new services open unprecedented opportunities to study how resources are shared and what makes them popular.

We can begin to understand the relationship between resources and their usage by analyzing the publications that first introduce them. Because publications are still the standard medium for knowledge dissemination, they are also the standard medium for sharing resources [16]. Therefore, linking resource usage to factors we can extract from the publications that introduce datasets is logical. For example, are author, institution, and journal characteristics predictable of usage? Or does it depend only on the article itself, such as the references it has? Understanding the dynamics of downloads of datasets can allow us to better allocate the supporting mechanisms for these kinds of scientific artifacts. For example, we could allocate better Content Delivery Networks (CDNs) for resources that we predict will be used worldwide. Answers to these questions can shed light on why dataset usage happens and how it can be increased.

In this article, we analyze how datasets are used based on the publications that introduce them. Our result suggests there is a significant relationship between the publication characteristics and its dataset downloads. Most used datasets are those from lower-ranked journals with a large but focused set of citations. Surprisingly, we found that the academic ranking and authors' seniority/prestige, signaled by the h-index, did not matter.

2 Dataset and Publication Metadata

2.1 Dataset Metadata

Figshare is an open access online repository for researchers to upload and share any scientific resource, including publications, images, datasets, and experimental results. Figshare.com offers an official REST API[1] to query and fetch the metadata of resources. We use the following process to extract sample datasets from figshare.com and metadata corresponding to the publications that first introduce them:

1. **Sample random datasets.** The API does not allow us to do random sampling. Therefore, we retrieve datasets from random time slices from 2015 to 2021. For each of these slices, we obtained the first 1,000 datasets. After this, we only kept the datasets that had publications associated with them.
2. **Extract download information about a dataset.** We use another figshare.com API to access cumulative download information for each dataset.
3. **Match dataset with publication.** Because we only kept datasets with a publication associated, we could match a dataset with a publication using the DOI. In particular, we use the Microsoft Academic Graph (MAG) to obtain information about the dataset. The metadata includes resource type (only dataset), submission time, and the download number (at the query time).

---

[1] https://docs.figshare.com/.

We removed some of the publications if the MAG meta-data was incomplete. This processing left us with 18,183 datasets associated with 7,192 publications. There are more datasets than publications because some publications introduce multiple datasets at once. We acknowledge that there might not be a direct relationship between usage and downloads. We use downloads as a reasonable proxy for usage.

2.2 Publication Metadata

Microsoft Academic Graph, or MAG, was introduced by Microsoft Corp. in 2015 [15]. It is a large database that contains extensive information about publications, authors, affiliations, and publishing venues. It includes identifiers to disambiguate entities with similar names. The database also includes computed rankings of institutions, journals, and authors. With citation and reference information, we constructed the citation network and derived helpful features such as self-citation and authors' h-index at the time of a publication.

2.3 Computed Bibliographic Features, Data Preprocessing, and Model Evaluation

Bibliometric Features. To establish a statistical relationship between a dataset and the publication that first introduced it, we explored several features from the publication (Table 1). These features can be broadly grouped into article features (e.g., references), author features (e.g., h-index), institution features (e.g., ranking), and journal features (e.g., ranking). The dependent variable for our analysis is the logarithm of the total number of downloads to date plus one. We take the logarithm to improve the normality of such a long-tail distribution. In addition, to control for the apparent accumulation of downloads over time, we include the dataset age as part of our analysis.

Table 1. Bibliometric features extracted from MAG and figshare.com

Feature group	Feature set
Article references	1) # references; 2) # authors referenced; 3) # affiliations referenced; 4) # journals referenced; 5) # author self-reference(s); 6) # affiliation self-reference(s); 7) # journal self-reference(s); 8) Average year of publications referenced; 9) Minimum year of publications referenced; 10) Maximum year of publications referenced
Authors' prestige/seniority/impact	11) Average h-index of author(s); 12) H-index of the first author; 13) H-index of the last author; 14) Average h-index of middle author(s); 15) # unique affiliation(s)
Institution prestige	16) Affiliation Rank
Journal prestige	17) Journal Rank
Dataset metadata	18) Dataset Age
Dependent variable	Downloads

Data Preprocessing. We wanted to focus on the most common types of datasets by removing outliers. We removed 93 datasets with three or more standard deviations higher downloads than the average. This removal left us with 18,087 datasets and 7,134 associated publications.

Model Evaluation. We evaluated our models with cross-validation or adjusted performance to the degrees of freedom (e.g., adjusted R-squared). For held out dataset, we compute the R-squared as follows

$$R^2 = 1 - \frac{Residual\ variance}{Total\ variance} \tag{1}$$

where *residual variance* is the variance of predicted value minus the actual value. The actual downloads for a given model, and total variance is simply the variance of the actual downloads. We cross-validated using five-fold cross-validation.

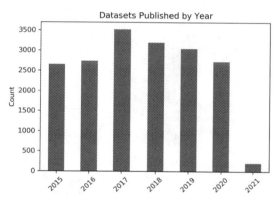

Fig. 1. Distribution of dataset year in figshare.com. Most datasets analyzed are from around five years ago.

3 Results

3.1 Characteristics of the Data

We found 18,087 datasets matched to 7,134 (unique) publications. The popularity of figshare.com seems to be stable across the seven years frame of our analysis (Fig. 1). We do not know if the dip in 2021 results from API delays or lower popularity in figshare.com.

We wanted to understand how our bibliometric features and the dataset downloads correlate (Fig. 2). The first-order trend of the correlation analysis is that reference and prestige (author, institution, journal) are all correlated within groups, in blocks. Also, we found a significant correlation between the co-author's h-index and the rate of self-citations. Finally, we found that the dataset age negatively correlates with the references and journal and affiliation ranking. These age correlations suggest that newer datasets have more references and higher-ranked journals on average.

3.2 Predictive Performance

We then wanted to evaluate a predictive model that would take all bibliometric features into account when predicting dataset downloads, effectively controlling for partial correlations in Fig. 2. In particular, we analyze models in increasing levels of flexibility and decreasing levels of interpretability: multivariate linear regression model, random forest model, gradient boosting model, and multi-layer perceptron model (Fig. 3).

Linear Regression. Using multivariate linear regression, we found an adjusted R^2 of 0.116.

Random Forest Model. Random forest relies on a bootstrapped aggregation of decision trees where the features are also sampled [5]. It aims at reducing the variance in the estimation. We use 500 trees to obtain a cross-validated $R^2 = 0.159$.

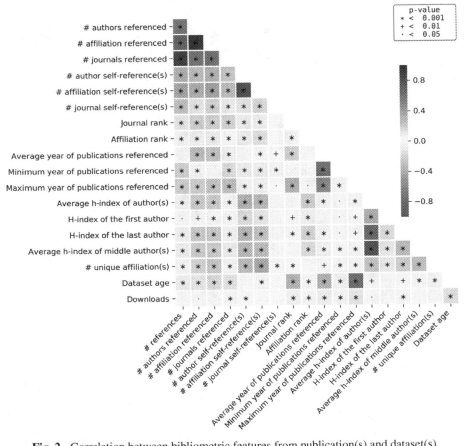

Fig. 2. Correlation between bibliometric features from publication(s) and dataset(s).

Gradient Boosted Tree Model. Gradient boosting tree is based on the sequential combination of decision trees, each meant to reduce the residuals of the previous tree [5]. GBT aims at reducing the bias in the estimation. We found a performance of $R^2 = 0.173$ with 100 estimators.

Multi-layer Perceptron. Multi-layer perceptrons (MLP) are models with a sequence of full-connected layers in an artificial neural network. Each unit has a sigmoid function inside [5]. We use three layers with 10, 10, and 5 neurons each and a limited-memory BFGS optimizer. We achieved a cross-validated $R^2 = 0.0001$. Notice that on cross-validation, r squares could go below zero.

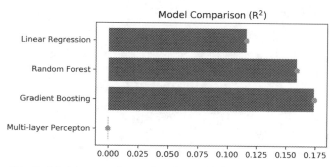

Fig. 3. Model comparison using the coefficient of determination.

3.3 Model Interpretation

Even though gradient boosting offered the best predictive performance, the method is significantly more complex to interpret than linear regression [5]. Therefore, we use a combination of the weights and directions of linear regression (Table 2) and combine them with the feature importance given by gradient boosting (Table 3). In this analysis, the most critical feature for our prediction is journal ranking (Tables 2 and 3). Journal ranking has a positive coefficient, suggesting that less prestigious journals are more likely to have more used datasets (Table 2). We also found that authors' prestige as captured by the h-index and the institutional prestige as captured by ranking have small effect sizes or are not significant. Finally, we found that the references in the article are essential as more references (more paper references in Table 2) and focused references (fewer journals referenced) predict higher downloads. Finally, it appears as if the fresher the publications (given by average year of publications referenced, Table 2 and 3), the more downloads are predicted.

Table 2. Ordinary least squares regression analysis

Predictors	Log (Downloads +1)		
	Estimates Z-score	CI	p
# References	0.09	0.08 – 0.09	**<0.001**
# Authors referenced	0.00	0.00 – 0.00	0.823
# Affiliation referenced	−0.01	−0.01 – −0.01	0.474
# Journals referenced	−0.08	−0.08 – −0.07	**<0.001**
# Author self-reference(s)	0.03	0.03 – 0.04	**0.003**
# Affiliation self-reference(s)	−0.04	−0.04 – −0.03	**0.001**
# Journal self-reference(s)	−0.03	−0.04 – −0.02	**<0.001**
Journal rank	0.25	0.25 – 0.25	**<0.001**
Affiliation rank	−0.00	−0.00 – −0.00	0.678
Average year of publications referenced	−0.02	−0.03 – −0.02	**0.040**
Minimum year of publications referenced	0.02	0.02 – 0.03	**0.011**
Maximum year of publications referenced	−0.03	−0.04 – −0.02	**0.023**
Average h-index of author(s)	−0.02	−0.02 – −0.02	0.213
H-index of the first author	0.00	0.00 – 0.01	0.632
H-index of the last author	0.03	0.03 – 0.03	**0.005**
Average h-index of middle author(s)	−0.00	−0.01 – −0.00	0.775
# Unique affiliation(s)	−0.02	−0.03 – −0.01	**0.004**
Dataset age	0.30	0.28 – 0.31	**<0.001**
Observations	18087		
R^2/R^2 adjusted	0.116/0.116		

Table 3. Top 5 feature importance from gradient boosted tree regression.

Feature	Feature importance
Journal Rank	0.408
Dataset Age	0.269
The number of author reference(s)	0.079
The number of affiliation reference(s)	0.032
The average year of publications referenced	0.029

3.4   Predictive Performance Decay into the Future

We then wanted to understand how the best predictor performs with more extended prediction periods. To accomplish this, we estimated the coefficient of determination for different dataset ages. Not surprisingly, the older the dataset, the harder it becomes to predict (Fig. 4).

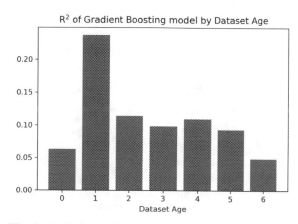

Fig. 4. Predictive performance as a function of dataset age.

4   Discussion

In this work, we wanted to understand whether it is possible to predict the usage of datasets with machine learning. Therefore, we gather information, including the prestige of authors, institutions, and journals about publications that share one or more datasets, along with features about publications themselves. Our results suggest that journal prestige is the most crucial factor, and that author and affiliation prestige are surprisingly irrelevant. We also found that if the work cites a disproportionately large number of publications, it is associated with higher usage only if the citations focus on fewer journals. We reason that this fact is related to work that does not just cite other work indiscriminately, but rather tailors the dataset being shared towards a specific community.

   In previous work, scientists have tried to make this prediction by relying on models of citations such as DataRank [17]. In our work, we are not making strong assumptions and simply make a direct prediction of downloads. However, while we obtain higher performance than model-based predictions (e.g., compared to [17], we achieved 16% higher R^2 from 0.1 to 0.116), models can be helpful if we want to understand the mechanisms behind usage (e.g., see [12]). In the future, we will adapt both model-based and data-based predictions.

We found that higher-ranking journals are predicted to have fewer downloads. We think there are several possible explanations. One explanation is that more prestigious journals might not be the ones where datasets are usually "advertised." Therefore, the community is not used to accessing datasets there. Another explanation is that higher ranked journals tend to be non-open, which we believe affects the usage of datasets as well. Also, datasets are not first-class citizens of science, and therefore not well appreciated compared to publications. However, there are some promising trends, such as the new journal Scientific Data by the Nature Research Group, solely dedicated to publishing and disseminating datasets. Finally, we measure dataset download rather than actual usage. It is entirely possible that real usage is more common in higher-profile journals but less accessible to our kinds of analyses. We plan to investigate these issues in the future by controlling for the kinds of data sharing practices of particular journals and the kinds of work scientists publish in them.

Improve Dataset Usage Tracking. Datasets could have advantages for tracking their usage compared to publications. For example, software packages could report back how often datasets are read or transformed when used in computational pipelines. This tracking already happens in some popular software package distribution systems, such as the Python Package Index (PyPI) through its preferred installer program (pip)[2] and the Comprehensive R Archive Network (CRAN)[3]. Previous research has found that easing dataset usage and recombination increases use in a virtuous cycle [6]. Nevertheless, resources shared in this way could add to a better appreciation and measurement of the impact of datasets.

The Benefit of Tracking and Sharing Datasets. Scientific knowledge is produced by a community of scientists building on each other's work. Therefore, a usual first step in building new knowledge is replicating others' results by reusing their resources. Also, datasets can be reuse and recombined to create new knowledge. Unfortunately, recent research has shown that this reproducibility has not been achieved to the extent that we thought [3]. For example, the Open Science Collaboration group showed that 32 percent of famous psychological experiments were not reproducible [10]. One of the issues is that the datasets and software for these experiments were not openly shared [9]. Furthermore, shared resources might be usable [13]. Therefore, data sharing and usage are essential parts of successful scientific knowledge reproduction.

Limitations. It could be desirable to extract information about the infrastructure for reusing datasets. Our analysis is limited in that we are only using the website that figshare.com produces for the projects without exploring whether figshare.com does an appropriate job at making datasets searchable and usable. After all, figshare started as a company to share *figures* rather than datasets. Future research will explore whether other websites with similar functions have higher or lower chances of making resources easier to reuse (e.g., Zenodo, the Dataverse project). Another limitation of our work is that we assume that the downloads equate to "usage." Continuous integration systems or ingestion systems automatically download datasets, inflating "usage." Conversely,

---

[2] https://pypistats.org/top.
[3] https://cranlogs.r-pkg.org/.

some datasets are downloaded once but used many more times behind closed doors. We will explore other ways of analyzing usage while also understanding the privacy and intellectual property limitations.

5 Conclusion

This paper develops and interprets a model to predict dataset downloads based on the publication that first advertises them. We found it possible to predict such downloads based on journal ranking and references of the article. However, we found that the author's and institution's prestige seem to be irrelevant.

There are many other avenues for exploration in the future. One is to have a much broader set of datasets to analyze beyond figshare.com. Also, we should analyze how datasets are being described and made available. For example, a detailed web page with code examples in different languages would improve usage significantly. Also, we should explore larger datasets from other regions of the world, such as those related to European funding agencies, Japan, and China. Finally, there are datasets that are not associated with a publication, and it would be worth thinking about how to predict their usage based on other factors about the author, institution, and method of sharing.

In the future, work like ours could increase the visibility of other non-traditional artifacts of science. With the advent of cheaper and faster storage, and more connected scientists, there is little reason to justify only keeping track of citations among publications. Instead, we should be keeping track of all usage, across all of science, and across all the time.

Acknowledgements. DEA, ZY, LL, and HZ were funded by the National Science Foundation grants #1800956 and #1933803, the US Office of Research Integrity grants ORIIR190049-01-00 and ORIIR200062-01. The authors wish to thank Hanlin Zhang for his invaluable help during preliminary data preparation and analysis.

References

1. Acuna, D.E., Allesina, S., Kording, K.P.: Future impact: predicting scientific success. Nature **489**, 201–202 (2012). https://doi.org/10.1038/489201a
2. Birnholtz, J.P., Bietz, M.J.: Data at work: supporting sharing in science and engineering. In: Proceedings of the 2003 International ACM SIGGROUP Conference on Supporting Group Work, pp. 339–348 (2003). https://doi.org/10.1145/958160.958215
3. Christensen, G., Miguel, E.: Transparency, reproducibility, and the credibility of economics research. J. Econ. Lit. **56**(3), 920–980 (2018)
4. Cronin, B., Sugimoto, C.: Beyond Bibliometrics. The MIT Press, Cambridge (2014). https://mitpress.mit.edu/books/beyond-bibliometrics
5. James, G., Witten, D., Hastie, T., Tibshirani, R.: An Introduction to Statistical Learning, vol. 112. Springer, New York (2013). https://doi.org/10.1007/978-1-4614-7138-7
6. Macneil, R., Hardeman, M.: RSpace & Figshare: Towards an integrated reearch data workflow (2017). https://era.ed.ac.uk/handle/1842/23360

7. Mearian, L.: CW@ 50: Data storage goes from $1 M to 2 cents per gigabyte. Computerworld (2017)
8. Moed, H.F., Halevi, G.: Multidimensional assessment of scholarly research impact. J. Assoc. Inform. Sci. Technol. **66**(10), 1988–2002 (2015). https://doi.org/10.1002/asi.23314
9. Nosek, B.A., Errington, T.M.: Making sense of replications. ELife **6**, e23383 (2017). https://doi.org/10.7554/eLife.23383
10. Open Science Collaboration: Estimating the reproducibility of psychological science. Science **349**(6251), aac4716 (2015)
11. Priem, J., Groth, P., Taraborelli, D.: The altmetrics collection. PLOS ONE **7**(11), e48753 (2012). https://doi.org/10.1371/journal.pone.0048753
12. Sinatra, R., Wang, D., Deville, P., Song, C., Barabási, A.-L.: Quantifying the evolution of individual scientific impact. Science **354**(6312), aaf5239 (2016)
13. Thelwall, M., Kousha, K.: Figshare: a universal repository for academic resource sharing? Online Inf. Rev. **40**(3), 333–346 (2016). https://doi.org/10.1108/OIR-06-2015-0190
14. Wang, D., Song, C., Barabási, A.-L.: Quantifying long-term scientific impact. Science **342**(6154), 127–132 (2013). https://doi.org/10.1126/science.1237825
15. Wang, K., et al.: A review of microsoft academic services for science of science studies. Front. Big Data **2**, 45 (2019). https://doi.org/10.3389/fdata.2019.00045
16. Zeng, T., Shema, A., Acuna, D.E.: Dead science: most resources linked in biomedical articles disappear in eight years. In: Taylor, N.G., Christian-Lamb, C., Martin, M.H., Nardi, B. (eds.) iConference 2019. LNCS, vol. 11420, pp. 170–176. Springer, Cham (2019). https://doi.org/10.1007/978-3-030-15742-5_16
17. Zeng, T., Wu, L., Bratt, S., Acuna, D.E.: Assigning credit to scientific datasets using article citation networks. J. Inform. **14**(2), 101013 (2020)

Library, Information Science, and Archives Doctoral Research Trends in Australia

Mozhdeh Dehghani(✉) ⓘ, Steven Wright ⓘ, and Tom Denison ⓘ

Monash University, Caulfield, VIC, Australia
{Mozhdeh.dehghani1,steven.wright,Tom.Denison}@monash.edu

Abstract. Research in the fields of the LIS, Archives and Recordkeeping sectors faces challenges as a result of course closures, which could have an impact on the number of future "academic-research-trained LIS professionals" and consequently the volume and quality of future research in Australia. This short paper aims to introduce a project currently underway in Australia to identify emerging trends in related PhD research, identify community needs and provide a summary of relevant background literature.

Keywords: Library and information science · LIS research · Archives research · Research trends · Subject trends · Topics trends

1 Introduction

Research in LIS, Archives and Recordkeeping in Australia has faced and is currently facing many challenges. First, as a result in recent years of declining enrolments and a decision by many universities to focus on higher volume disciplines with a greater rate of financial return to the institution [1], there have been a significant number of course closures in the fields of Library and Information Science (LIS) and Archives. These include the undergraduate program offered by Curtin University, and the postgraduate programs offered by Queensland University of Technology, the University of Technology Sydney, RMIT and Monash University [1].

Second, there is a certain "lack of incentive for doing a PhD in Australia because very few jobs have this as a requirement" [2]. Third, communication between scholarly research and practice is flawed within the field of LIS [3]. As a result, practice does not always benefit from formally defined research, nor is such research always informed by the experience of practitioners. This is a primary concern of the ALIA's Research Advisory Committee, a body that is dedicated to seeing LIS practice-based research flourish in Australia.

Of particular concern is the impact these challenges will have on the number of future academic-research-trained LIS professionals coming into the sector, and consequently the quality of future research. This problem had already been recognised by Macauley et al., who in 2010 noted that "the sustainability of LIS research and research training for the next generation in Australia is under threat" [4]. If anything, the trends noted in 2010 appear to have accelerated over the past decade. A further issue, as noted by Christine

M. Smits (Ed.): iConference 2022, LNCS 13192, pp. 53–60, 2022.
https://doi.org/10.1007/978-3-030-96957-8_6

Mackenzie (then President of IFLA) at the 2018 RAILS Conference held at Monash University, is that there appears to be a significant disagreement between practitioners and academics about the nature of research and the needs of the sector [5].

The project "Library, Information Science, Archives and Recordkeeping Doctoral Research trends in Australia[1]" is one response to this gap. The project aims to update previous studies of LIS and related research, notably those by Macauley, Evans and Pearson [4] and the environmental scan of Australian Library and Information Studies (LIS) research undertaken on behalf of ALIA by Middleton and Yates [6]. As with those studies, it is designed to assist with the development of a future research agenda, advocacy, and funding.

In particular, the project aims to:

1. Identify recent trends in LIS and Archives and recordkeeping related research by analysing theses completed since 2014 and those in progress
2. Identify emerging areas of research in LIS and Archives and recordkeeping, including those of potential interest to researchers in other disciplines, and
3. Identify priority areas for future research of interest to both academics and practitioners.

The research, which is currently underway, involves three stages:

1. Identification of relevant PhD theses completed or commenced since 2014, together with a content analysis based on their abstracts. Theses will be identified using the National Library of Australia's TROVE service. The initial focus will be on the output of the known university faculties. In order to identify relevant theses from other disciplines, keyword searches and searches based on relevant Australian and New Zealand Standard Research Classification (ANZSRC) codes will also be undertaken. It will include only doctoral theses that have appeared in the national databases and individual university databases.
2. A series of interviews (8–10) with academics and representatives of professional associations, is being undertaken in order to gain an in-depth understanding of needs and future directions. A small number of additional interviews may be added if it appears that key individuals have been missed.
3. Once Steps 1 & 2 have been completed, an online survey of academics and practitioners will be undertaken, using Survey Monkey. It is intended to provide an opportunity for a broader validation of the results, particularly in relation to areas of future research. This will be promoted through social media and the professional associations.

In what follows, we will provide a review of existing literature, from Australian and other sources, concerning doctoral research in LIS and related fields. But first, the circumstances that prompted the project will be examined.

---

[1] Both ALIA and RIMPA have endorsed the need for this research, and that it is funded by the Whyte Fund, Monash university.

2   Why is This Research Needed in an Australian Context?

The motivation for this research is based on discussion from ALIA's Research Advisory Committee regarding the shrinking LIS presence within academia, including a reduction in the number of LIS educators/researchers in Australia. Given these circumstances, we see the proposed project as relevant and timely, potentially holding considerable value to library and information services in Australia. We believe that the findings can a) prove of direct relevance to a number of ongoing projects within the sector, b) help support strategic planning for LIS research, including cross-disciplinary research, and c) feed into areas of ongoing work - including ALIA's major Professional Pathways project, which concerns the future of professional recognition for the library and information service profession.

As the Records and Information Professionals of Australasia (RIMPA) has likewise recently raised concerns about the future of available education for the information, records and archives industries, it is hoped that our proposed research will add value to RIMPA's Education Portfolio by providing up to date information for future projects.

From a practical perspective, research such as this study can motivate discussion about progress in LIS, Archives and Recordkeeping areas, and promote further growth. The project will suggest research guidelines aligning research needs with those arising from community needs, and which should help in the design of new, more targeted, research projects in an era of shrinking budgets and fewer library schools.

Last but not least, we anticipate that helping to identify recent research trends will prove useful for relevant professional associations in deciding how to allocate their own research funds.

3   Literature Review

There have been a number of mappings of outputs in the LIS field that address the published literature on the topic [7–14]. However, in this study we focus only on studies that examine PhD theses in LIS, beginning with what can be learned from the experience of other countries.

Franklin and Jaeger [15] investigated 34 doctoral dissertations completed at 13 US LIS schools over a ten-year period (1993–2003), identifying five main subject categories: issues related to librarians and librarianship (47%); information issues, including information literacy, information overload, information behaviour, and information retrieval (21%); literature with a specific focus on African American perspectives (15%); technological themes (12%), and educational issues (6%). Also in North America, Prebor [16] studied research trends at a number of information science departments worldwide between 2002–2006. She identified 228 doctoral dissertations and 107 master's theses published mainly in USA and Canada via the ProQuest Digital Dissertations database, with the most important research topics being: user studies (29%), information economics and management (14%), data organization and retrieval and information/learning society (both 13%), and foundation of information science and information technology (both 12%).

In another study, Shu, Larivière, Mongeon, Julien and Piper [17] performed an analysis of the evolution of research topics and interdisciplinarity in 3450 LIS doctoral dissertations between 1960 and 2013 in North America. Information science, library science, computer science, educational technology, and higher education were identified as the top 5 topical terms used, with information science becoming the dominant research topic. The study also found that most of LIS theses are interdisciplinary.

Two large surveys have been conducted in China. Song, Zhu and Shu [18] categorised 1018 LIS doctoral dissertations completed between 1994 and 2018 in three areas: information science, archive studies, and library science. They found no significant changes in topics over that period, suggesting that the academic background of library and information science doctoral advisors does not affect the interdisciplinarity of their students' doctoral dissertations. They identified knowledge management, informetric and research evaluation, corporation and government services, resource construction, networks and community, and innovation as the main themes. Similarly, Zong, Shen, Yuan, Hu, Hou and Deng [19] mapped the research topics of 640 doctoral dissertations in Library and Information Science in China, awarded between 1994 and 2011. They found the most popular topics to include: knowledge management, digital library, Network, ontology, and Information service.

In India, Singh and Babbar [20] studied doctoral research carried out by LIS departments, tracing the development of LIS research in India since the award of the first PhD in 1950, through to 2012. Data was collected by questionnaire from 81 departments located in the 22 states of India. They found that the volume of LIS research by PhDs has been continuously increasing since the 1970s, due to improved research infrastructure, and having a PhD becoming an essential qualification for higher positions both in libraries and LIS departments. They further discovered that only a limited number of studies had explored the theoretical aspects of LIS, with research topics dominated by surveys of emerging areas such as: web resources, search engines, open access, E-learning, and total quality management. Finally, they reported that the outcomes/suggestions of these studies were not normally communicated to libraries.

Several other Indian studies covering roughly the same period were also identified. Chatterjee, Rath and Poddar [21] examined 212 PhD theses completed between 1950 and 1993, and found academic libraries, bibliometric/citation studies, cataloguing, classification, and indexing to be popular research areas in LIS during this period. Lahiri [22], studying 255 PhD thesis from 1950–1995 found a similar list of topics: bibliometrics, academic libraries, information needs and user studies. Manjunatha and Shivalingaiah [23] reported the same broad areas, but also included information systems design. Finally, Maity and Hatua [24] analysed 1058 PhD theses awarded by various Indian universities from 1950–2012. Popular subject areas included ICT applications, and studies of specific libraries, and scholarly communication.

In a more recent study, Madasamy and Alwarammal [25] looked at 171 theses completed between 2003 and 2008, and reported that topics such as library information sources and services, user studies, library and information management, and bibliometrics continued to be dominant.

Topics like bibliometrics, user studies, planning and management topics were dominant research topics between 1950 and 1992 in Chandrashekara and Ramasesh [22] study who studied 802 doctoral theses awarded between 1957 and 2008.

As for Pakistan, Samdan and Bhatti [26] analysed 28 LIS PhD theses to provide comprehensive and current information about all the doctoral degrees awarded by various universities inside and outside that country between 1947 and 2010. They reported significant growth in terms of numbers of theses, university programs and subject areas over the period, with academic libraries, archives, bibliometric studies, cataloguing, and collection development being identified as significant research areas.

Tveit [27] investigated which research topics have been of interest in Nordic LIS institutions, studying 79 doctoral dissertations published between 2005 to 2014, by 13 research institutions in Norway, Denmark, Finland and Sweden. The five categories of research topics identified in the study were:

- Information behaviour including information seeking, information sharing, reference work, information practice and information and learning
- Knowledge organization and information retrieval including cataloguing, classification, other metadata issues, information systems and information architecture, generally emphasizing the system.
- Information and society including a variety of studies related to social sciences, for instance politics of libraries and information, library and information management, including library & information organisations' planning, staff, economy, decision-making and communication.
- Sociology of culture/literature including studies mainly related to humanities and the social sciences, like library and book history, cultural politics, sociology of literature, as well as mediation and promotion of literature, cultural studies and general (not scholarly) publishing.
- Scholarly communication including bibliometrics, webometrics, studies of communication genres, systems of communication among scholars and scholarly publication

Of these, information behaviour was the focus of the biggest group of dissertations (29%), followed by knowledge organization (23%), sociology of culture/literature (20%), scholarly communication (18%) and the relationship between information and society (10%). Only seven theses used quantitative methods, 15 used mixed methods, with the most frequently used qualitative methods being document analyses, interviews and observations.

In Australia, Macauley, Evans and Pearson [4] analysed 114 theses from LIS schools or completed by LIS educators, researchers or practitioners in non-LIS schools from 1948 to 2006. ANZSRC schema was used for coding of the subset of 114 LIS PhDs. Dominant research topics were library and information studies, librarianship, information retrieval and web search, organisation of information and knowledge resources, human information behaviour, records and information management, informatics, information systems. An interesting finding showed that the proportion of educators with PhDs increased during the study period, however, the proportion of practitioners with PhDs decreased because LIS practitioners in Australia who receive a PhD move into academia shortly afterwards. The generation and production of LIS knowledge is reduced because of the diversity and commitment to research outside the LIS field, which in turn dilutes the strength from within the field. Since a number of the authors of the 114 theses were overseas students who returned to their home countries upon graduation, the diversity combined with low numbers of LIS graduations already at this point in time indicated some challenges for future LIS research.

In the ALIA LIS research environmental scan conducted by Middleton and Yates [6], which focused on the period 2005–2013, 115 dissertations were identified of which 95 (83%) were at the doctoral level. This study was in turn a partial follow-up to earlier work that reported Australian LIS thesis output up to 2006 [4]. Of the 115 dissertations identified, 72 (63%) of all the dissertations were supervised by LIS schools in universities and colleges. Amongst these, 27 (23%) identified library and information science as the major topic, with information behaviour (28%), information literacy (14%), and management (13%) comprising other significant research topics. That study also looked at the methodologies used, reporting that while interviews were employed 43 times (37%), surveys or questionnaires were used in 19% of cases, and case studies in 14%. A small number drew upon grounded theory (5%), historical/historiography (4%), and phenomenography (4%) as methodological frameworks [6]. Sample table for the main topics identified (Table 1).

Table 1. Summary of literature review

Research topic	Countries	Studies
Knowledge management	China, Nordic countries	Song, Zhu and Shu [18], Zong, Shen, Yuan, Hu, Hou and Deng [19], Tveit [27]
Information management	USA, Canada, Australia	Middleton and Yates [6], Prebor [16]
Library and Information Studies	Australia, India	Macauley, Evans and Pearson [4], Madasamy and Alwarammal [25]
librarians and librarianship	USA, Australia	Franklin and Jaeger [15], Macauley, Evans and Pearson [4]
Information science and related issues including information behavior, information literacy, information overload, and information retrieval	USA, Canada, Nordic countries, Australia	Franklin and Jaeger [15], Tveit [27], Middleton and Yates [6]
User studies	USA, Canada	Prebor [16]
Web resources	India	Singh and Babbar [20]
Academic libraries	India, Pakistan	Chatterjee, Rath and Poddar [21], Lahiri [22], Samdan and Bhatti [26]
ICT applications	India	Maity and Hatua [24]
Bibliometric/citation studies	India	Chandrashekara and Ramasesh [28], Chatterjee, Rath and Poddar [21], Lahiri [22]

These previous studies have largely investigated dominant research topics, predominant research techniques and methodological frameworks in the library, information science, and archives via quantitative methods based on knowledge of research going on in the studied countries. Since the position of LIS is different across the world, there is a need to get a broader understanding of the range of research topics in different countries based on quantitative and qualitative methods to motivate discussion about progress in the area and find future directions.

4 Conclusion

There has been an increased interest in recent years in studying the trends of research in LIS in different countries. The studies discussed above have, for the most part, considered the quantitative output, growth pattern, and popular areas of research. While such studies typically concluded that more doctoral research needed to be carried out in particular areas - for example, digital libraries and ICT applications - there has often been less follow-up to chart the response to their concerns.

The above-mentioned studies provided useful information, but it was noted that most of the studies are limited to quantitative methods, they do not provide the latest information about doctoral studies in the Australian context. Thus, the need was felt for a study like this, which seeks to explore the current state of PhD research through a mixed methods approach. On the quantitative front, our study will aim to identify relevant PhD theses both through a content analysis and an online survey of academics and practitioners. On the qualitative front, we will continue to interview a relevant sample of academics/representatives and/or nominees of the professional associations across Australia, in pursuit of an in-depth understanding of research needs, possible current problems and disconnects, and desirable future directions. Through undertaking this research, we hope to supplement previous studies based on current actual needs, to plot the similarities and differences between research trends in Australia and those elsewhere.

References

1. Australian Library Information Association: The future of library and information science education in Australia: discussion paper (2020)
2. Howard, K.: The future of research in the Australian LIS profession. In: INCITE, vol. 42, p. 20. Australian Library and Information Association Sydney, NSW (2021)
3. Haddow, G., Klobas, J.E.: Communication of research to practice in library and information science: closing the gap. Libr. Inf. Sci. Res. **26**, 29–43 (2004)
4. Macauley, P., Evans, T., Pearson, M.: Australian PhDs by LIS educators, researchers and practitioners: depicting diversity and demise. Libr. Inf. Sci. Res. **32**, 258–264 (2010)
5. Mackenzie, C.: Where research and practice meet (or don't). Research Applications in Information and Library Studies (RAILS). Monash University, Melbourne (28–30 Nov 2018)
6. Middleton, M., Yates, C.: ALIA LIS research environmental scan report. Canberra ACT: The Australian Library and Information Association. Retrieved January 22, 2017 (2014)
7. Dora, M., Kumar, H.A.: National and international trends in library and information science research: a comparative review of the literature. IFLA J. **46**, 234–249 (2020)

8. Dorner, D.G.: Knowledge Creation from Australasian LIS Journals: A Content Analysis (2001)
9. Liu, P., Wu, Q., Mu, X., Yu, K., Guo, Y.: Detecting the intellectual structure of library and information science based on formal concept analysis. Scientometrics **104**(3), 737–762 (2015). https://doi.org/10.1007/s11192-015-1629-z
10. Moahi, K.H.: Library and information science research in botswana: an analysis of trends and patterns. Afr. J. Libr. Arch. Inf. Sci. **18**, 11–22 (2008)
11. Mokhtarpour, R., Khasseh, A.A.: Twenty-six years of LIS research focus and hot spots, 1990–2016: a co-word analysis. J. Inf. Sci. **47**(6), 794–808 (2020). https://doi.org/10.1177/016555 1520932119
12. Olmeda-Gómez, C., Ovalle-Perandones, M.-A., Perianes-Rodríguez, A.: Co-word analysis and thematic landscapes in Spanish information science literature, 1985–2014. Scientometrics **113**(1), 195–217 (2017). https://doi.org/10.1007/s11192-017-2486-8
13. Onyancha, O.B.: Forty-five years of LIS research evolution, 1971–2015: an informetrics study of the author-supplied keywords. Publ. Res. Q. **34**, 456–470 (2018)
14. Paul-Hus, A., Mongeon, P., Shu, F.: Portraying the Landscape of Canadian Library and Information Science Research= Portrait de la recherche en bibliothéconomie et sciences de l'information au Canada. Can. J. Inf. Libr. Sci. **40**, 332–346 (2016)
15. Franklin, R.E., Jaeger, P.T.: A decade of doctorates: An examination of dissertations written by African American women in library and information studies, 1993–2003. J. Educ. Libr. Inf. Sci. 187–201 (2007)
16. Prebor, G.: Analysis of the interdisciplinary nature of library and information science. J. Librariansh. Inf. Sci. **42**, 256–267 (2010)
17. Shu, F., Larivière, V., Mongeon, P., Julien, C.-A., Piper, A.: On the evolution of library and information science doctoral dissertation topics in North America (1960–2013). J. Educ. Libr. Inf. Sci. **57**, 131–142 (2016)
18. Song, Y., Zhu, L., Shu, F.: On the evolution of library and information science doctoral dissertation topics in China. J. Librariansh. Inf. Sci. **53**, 298–306 (2021)
19. Zong, Q.-J., Shen, H.-Z., Yuan, Q.-J., Hu, X.-W., Hou, Z.-P., Deng, S.-G.: Doctoral dissertations of library and information science in China: a co-word analysis. Scientometrics **94**, 781–799 (2013)
20. Singh, S.P., Babbar, P.: Doctoral research in library and information science in India: trends and issues. DESIDOC J. Libr. Inf. Technol. **34**, 170–180 (2014)
21. Chatterjee, A., Rath, P.N., Poddar, A.: Research trends in library and information science in India. Ann. Libr. Inf. Stud. **42**(2), 54–60 (1995)
22. Lahiri, R.: Research in library science in India (1950–95): an account of Ph.D. programme. Ann. Libr. Sci. Documentation **43**, 59–68 (1996)
23. Manjunatha, K., Shivalingaiah, D.: Library & information science (LIS) research 1987–1997: a decade of development. Ann. Libr. Inf. Stud. **45**, 137–155 (1998)
24. Maity, B.K., Hatua, S.R.: Research trends of library management in LIS in India since 1950–2012. Scientometrics **105**(1), 337–346 (2015). https://doi.org/10.1007/s11192-015-1673-8
25. Madasamy, R., Alwarammal, R.: Doctoral degrees in library and information science in India during 2003–2008: a study. Ann. Libr. Inf. Stud. **56**, 262–266 (2009)
26. Samdan, R.A., Bhatti, R.: Doctoral research in library and information science by Pakistani professionals: an analysis. Libr. Philos. Pract. **649**, 1–16 (2011)
27. Tveit, Å.K.: A celebration of diversity: LIS research in the Nordic countries as shown by PhD dissertations 2005–2014. J. Educ. Libr. Inf. Sci. **58**, 64–76 (2017)
28. Chandrashekara, M., Ramasesh, C.: Library and information science research in India. In: Asia–Pacific Conference on Library and Information Education and Practice, pp. 530–537 (2009)

Elapsed Collective Memory: Looking for the Forgotten Classic Works in Library and Information Science

Yujia Zhai[1]([⊠]) [iD], Alec McGail[2] [iD], and Ying Ding[3] [iD]

[1] Tianjin Normal University, Tianjin 300387, China
[2] Cornell University, Ithaca, NY 14850, USA
am2873@cornell.edu
[3] The University of Texas at Austin, Austin, TX 78705, USA
ying.ding@ischool.utexas.edu

Abstract. Collective memory of scientists shapes the foundation of the discipline. References in the scientific literature delineate the boundaries of the disciplines and also documented their history. However, due to the two mechanisms of preferential attachment and temporal decay, many articles that were frequently cited in the past are no longer cited. So, is the collective memory of library and information science partly gone? Which classic documents have been forgotten, and what caused the forgottenness? In this study, we analyzed the references of major publications in the Library and Information Science (LIS) field, and found that many famous works have been forgotten in the past few decades. Through calculating the differences in citations over decades, we find the top 2% forgotten publication list, and summarize the main reasons for the forgotten scientific literature, which are obliteration by incorporation, loss of fashion, short timeliness and replaced by new knowledge. Our findings provide a preliminary understanding of the establishment process of the collective memory.

Keywords: Collective memory · Citation analysis · History of LIS · Forgotten publication

1 Introduction

The collective memory of a scientific field is primarily documented by a collection of academic publications. All of these works are produced on the basis of a large number of scientific discoveries, which are recorded in the form of references [1]. Therefore, those references established a solid theoretical and methodological foundation and provided guidance for its future development of a research field as well.

For an academic community, the collective memories are all the memories, knowledge, and information sustained by scientists that at the same time shape communities' identities [2]. In order to understand the collective memory, we must first explore what forgetting is and what have been forgotten. The dynamics of collective memory is mainly driven by two mechanisms, preferential attachment and temporal decay [3]. Preferential

M. Smits (Ed.): iConference 2022, LNCS 13192, pp. 61–68, 2022.
https://doi.org/10.1007/978-3-030-96957-8_7

attachment is reflected in the increasing number of people that attend to a given publication and temporal decay refers to the habituation or competition from other research works that makes the same paper less likely to be cited as time goes on. Both mechanisms explain why we forget the early classic works in the long run history of an academic field.

Scientists keep forgetting something that is very obvious and are still surprised when it is brought to their attention [4]. It is obvious that science is a collective enterprise. For centuries, scientists have been answering some repetitive questions, and good solutions have been discovered repeatedly. This phenomenon is concentrated in the fact that certain articles are no longer cited. A possible explanation is the research has been completely incorporated into the field, known as obliteration by incorporation [5]. In addition, it may be that the development of the field has experienced major twists and turns, and the original knowledge system has been broken.

In the long history of Library and Information Science (LIS), a large number of documents have been cited. While some are enduring and some are no longer cited after a period of time. Finding classic documents which were popular in the past but suddenly lost their appeal can help us review the evolution of LIS and discover those potential underlying questions. In this article, we used a new method proposed by [6] to obtain a list of the most intense losses of recognition ("biggest falls") in journal citations in LIS field, and provides some preliminary explanations of these forgotten works.

2   Dataset and Methodology

2.1   Publications in LIS

As of Sept 2021, there were 86 journals indexed by Web of Science in the category "Information Science & Library Science". Many of these journals have not been fully indexed by Web of Science. A sudden drop-out of journals will produce spurious academic deaths for references which were primarily cited in those journals. Some journals have truly stopped producing papers, but some apparent journal deaths in WoS do not match reality. We limit our focus here to the journals which consistently publish articles with references Web of Science is able to (and chooses to) extract and index. This leaves 77 journals. According to this list, we download all the articles' metadata, including title, year, authors, and references, etc.

Within the 77 journals, 71,987 articles published between 1946 and 2022 have 2.8M citations in total. Of the 1.4M distinct cited works cited in these articles, 76% received only a single citation, 18% received between 2 and 4 citations, and 6% received at least 5 citations. However, 42% of citations are to the 7% of cited works which receive at least 5 citations. Typographic errors, alternate spellings, smudges of ink, and quirks of the algorithm will register as a totally separate cited work, so this number of once-cited works is an overestimate. But if it is even remotely accurate, it shows that the relatively uncited gets about as much attention as the relatively cited. The rest of this paper focuses only on cited works that received at least 5 citations total, disregarding the totally ignored.

2.2 Finding the Forgotten Pieces

A big fall is when a publication reaches the top tier in citations received in some decades, and subsequently drops to a very low number of yearly citations for a significant amount of time [6]. First, we make a list of any works which were cited in the top 2% in any decade 1930–1940 to 1995–2005. These are the "top cited" relative to their contemporaries, they are cited works which have at some time made them "big." To define a "fall," for each year Y from the work's first citation until 2005, we compare the average yearly citations before Y and the average yearly citations for ten years after Y. If the ratio of average citations in the ten years after Y to the average citations before Y is less than 1/10, we identify the cited work as having "fell" in recognition.

3 Results

3.1 Dataset Summary Statistics

Journal Of The Association For Information Systems produces the most citations per article, at 49.1. Meanwhile *Scientist* produces just 1.3 citations per article. Web of Science provides the most citations for the journals *Scientometrics* (93,773), *Information & Management* (56,828), *International Journal of Information Management* (47,820), *Mis Quarterly* (46,720), and *Journal Of Knowledge Management* (36,688). Together these five journals comprise 26% of all citations (18% of documents) in this dataset.

Only 116 articles were published in 6 journals from 1950–1959 (2.1 citations per article), compared to 13,410 articles in 67 journals from 2000–2009 (13.9 citations per article). In 2019 alone, there were 3,663 articles published. Of the 67,898 authors who published in this dataset, 44,821 only published a single time (66%). 683 authors have published more than 20 papers, and just 199 published more than 40. The top ten publishing first authors are Y. Chen (267), J. Lee (242), M. Thelwall (230), Y. Zhang (215), Y. Wang (213), J. Kim (211), Y. Liu (210), S. Kim (201), X. Li (193) and S. Lee (179). It is no accident that "Smith" shows up regularly in this list, a reminder that author names are not disambiguated.

We have already filtered cited works with less than five citations, so all 30,463 cited authors in this dataset have at least five citations. Of these, 4,660 (15%) were cited less than 10 times, 1,713 (6%) were cited at least 100 times and 40 were cited at least 1,000 times in this dataset. The top authors cited in this dataset were C. Fornell (2,422 citations), J. Hair (2,345 citations), V. Venkatesh (2,204 citations), D. Van (2,141 citations), F. Davis (2,086 citations), E. Garfield (1,861 citations), W. Orlikowski (1,737 citations), P. Podsakoff (1,728 citations), W. Chin (1,721 citations), D. Gefen (1,590 citations), T. Davenport (1,551 citations), L. Leydesdorff (1,542 citations), W. Glanzel (1,537 citations), R. Yin (1,461 citations), I. Nonaka (1,457 citations), M. Porter (1,433 citations), K. Eisenhardt (1,433 citations), I. Ajzen (1,415 citations), E. Rogers (1,401 citations) and J. Nunnally (1,356 citations).

All 72,602 cited works in this dataset have at least five citations. Of these, 13,174 (18%) were cited less than 10 times, 815 (1%) were cited at least 100 times and 9 were cited at least 1,000 times in this dataset. The top cited works in this dataset were Fornell's *J Marketing Res,V18,P39* (2237), Davis's *Mis Quart,V13,P319* (1594), Podsakoff's

J Appl Psychol,V88,P879 (1362), Hair's *Multivariate Data An* (1297), Venkatesh's *Mis Quart,V27,P425* (1241), Glaser's *Discovery Grounded T* (1202), Rogers's *Diffusion Innovation* (1166), Yin's *Case Study Res Desig* (1085), Hirsch's *P Natl Acad Sci Usa,V102,P16569* (1084) and Eisenhardt's *Acad Manage Rev,V14,P532* (952) (Fig. 1).

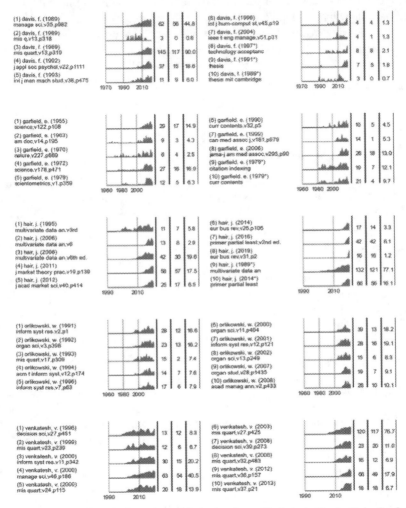

Fig. 1. The top 10 cited works from the top 5 cited authors: Venkatesh, Davis, Hair, Garfield, and Orlikowski.

3.2 Top 20 Cited Works in Each Decade

The following figures shows the citation life-courses of 134 works that show up in the top-20 list in some decade (Fig. 2).

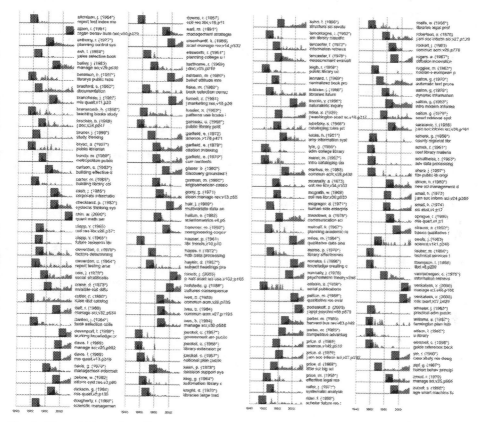

Fig. 2. These 134 cited works were in the top 20 in some decade between 1940 and 2015. The shaded region marks the first decade the work was in the top 20.

From the above results, we can find that the life cycle of these top works can be divided into three categories. The first is to reach the peak of citations at the very beginning, and then quickly disappear. Typical examples are Rougherty, R. (1969)[1] and Downs, R. (1957)[2]. This phenomenon is particularly prominent in the literature of library science, showing the rapid replacement iteration of the library science research. The second one is that the research work has been continuously cited since it appeared. The citation has maintained a good momentum of development, and there is no sign of abating. For example, Salton, G. (1983)[3] and Garfield. E. (1979)[4]. Information retrieval and bibliometrics have always been the popular topics in information science, and these

---

[1] Dougherty, R. M., & Heinritz, F. J. (1969). Scientific management of library operations (No. Z678 D6).

[2] Downs, R. B. (1957). The current status of university library staffs. College & Research Libraries, 18(5), 375–385.

[3] Salton, G., & McGill, M. J. (1983). Introduction to modern information retrieval. mcgraw-hill.

[4] Garfield, E., & Merton, R. K. (1979). Citation indexing: Its theory and application in science, technology, and humanities(Vol. 8). New York: Wiley.

two articles are the fundamental works in these two fields. The third is that it did not attract widespread attention at the beginning, but it has attracted more and more attention from scholars. For example, Kuhn, T. (1966)[5] and Rogers, E. (1967)[6]. These articles and books have provided a deep theoretical foundation for many subsequent studies, and are very forward-looking and predictive.

3.3   References Lost Memory in Highly Cited Articles

Most works are forgotten, even famous ones! 61% of works that got at least 5 citations between 1970 and 1980 went at least a decade without being cited. 43% were not cited whatsoever between 2005 and 2015.

The lifespan of a cited work is well described in aggregate by a lognormal distribution. The work reaches its maximum after a few years, declines slowly for 5–10 years, eventually receiving its last citation.

A few statistics should be sufficient to illustrate that cited works are almost surely headed to the grave, never to be revived. There were 1,816 works cited for the first time in the years 1970 to 1980. 13% of these would not receive a single citation after 1990. 72% of works cited in the 70s has gone at least a decade without being cited at all. And only 13% received at least 1 citation per year on average between 2005 and 2015. For comparison, 88% of works were first cited between 2005 and 2015 received a yearly average of at least 1 citation in that decade.

72,602 works in this dataset were cited at some point between 1980 and 1990. The top 1% consists of 746 cited works which have at least 7.0 citations in this decade. Of these only 64.1% got at least 1 citation in 2015–2020.

3.4   The Top 2% Forgotten Works

779 cited works were in the top 2% of citations in some decade between 1960–1970 and 2005–2015. Of these 779, just 124 (16%) experienced a decline to 10% their average yearly citations for a decade.

Among the first 2% of the forgotten works, most of the decline was around the turning point of the century, and a large part of them were books rather than journal articles. The development of emerging technologies has led to the transformation of LIS to digitalization and intelligence.

We further analyzed the content and citation methods of these documents, and found that the main reasons they stopped being cited can be divided into the four categories, which are obliteration by incorporation [5], loss of fashion, short timeliness and replaced by new knowledge.

For obliteration by incorporation, Van Rijsbergen(1979)'s book [7], "Information Retrieval", which has the largest decrease in citations, introduced the concepts and methods in information retrieval. In previous citations, scholars would cite this work when introducing certain concepts, such as "The performance of a retrieval algorithm is

---

[5] Kuhn, T. (1966). The structure of scientific revolutions (pp. 176–177). Princeton University Press.

[6] Rogers, E. M. (1967). Diffusion of innovations. Simon and Schuster.

often evaluated in terms of its recall and precision". And the book by Kerlinger (1964) [8] explained the process of the survey method in information behavior research, including the survey steps and sampling methods, which were also cited a lot in the early days. But these concepts and methods have become the standard knowledge of the discipline and are fully integrated into the collective memory of our field.

For loss of fashion, Haitun(1982) [9] introduced stationary scientometric distributions, and often used to support the existence of power law when referring to Zipf distributions and Lotka's law. But now there is very little research on these theorems, research on this topic has stalled.

In term of short timeliness, Dickson, Leitheiser, Nechis, and Wetherbe (1984) [10] conducted a Delphi study on behalf of the Society for Information Management (SIM) of top IS managers to identify the most critical issues they faced. This is the first reported an annual survey of practice and focused on the questions in 1980. However, various authors have replicated this study annually under SIM sponsorship.

And finally, for replaced by new knowledge, Rockart and Flannery (1983) [11] first introduced the phenomenon of end-user-computing which received much attention during the diffusion of visual interfaces in the 1980s and 1990s. During that time, many empirical studies focused on the association between the factors of usefulness, ease of use, and satisfaction. However, end-user-computing has faded into obscurity later and replace by end-user engineering [12].

4 Conclusion

In this study, we analyzed the references of major publications in the LIS field, and found that many famous works have been forgotten in the past few decades. Through the methods proposed in a previous research [6], we got the top 2% forgotten publication list, and explored the main reasons for the forgotten scientific literature, which are obliteration by incorporation, loss of fashion, short timeliness and replaced by new knowledge.

This study itself has some limitations in the part of the data analysis. We did not perform the disambiguation on the metadata such as author names and titles, which causes bias in the results.

This is the first step for us to understand the forgotten history of the LIS field, and it is also the initial result of exploring the process of shaping the collective memory of our discipline. In the future, we will further cleanse the data, think about the mechanism of forgotten works, and try to answer whether these classic publications can bring us more new inspirations.

References

1. Li, X., Yao, Q., Tang, X., Li, Q., Wu, M.: How to investigate the historical roots and evolution of research fields in China? a case study on imetrics using rootcite. Scientometrics **125**(2), 1253–1274 (2020). https://doi.org/10.1007/s11192-020-03659-3
2. Hirst, W., Manier, D.: Towards a psychology of collective memory. Memory **16**(3), 183–200 (2008)
3. Candia, C., Jara-Figueroa, C., Rodriguez-Sickert, C., Barabási, A.-L., Hidalgo, C.A.: The universal decay of collective memory and attention. Nat. Hum. Behav. **3**(1), 82–91 (2019)

4. Merton, R.K.: On the Shoulders of Giants: The Post-Italianate Edition. University of Chicago Press (1993)
5. McCain, K.W.: Mining full-text journal articles to assess obliteration by incorporation: Herbert A. S imon's concepts of bounded rationality and satisficing in economics, management, and psychology. J. Assoc. Inf. Sci. Technol. **66**(11), 2187–201 (2015)
6. McGail, A.: Lost & forgotten: an index of the famous works which sociology has left behind. Am. Sociol. **52**(2), 304–340 (2021)
7. Braslavski, P., et al. (eds.): RuSSIR 2015. CCIS, vol. 573. Springer, Cham (2016). https://doi.org/10.1007/978-3-319-41718-9
8. Kerlinger, F.N.: Foundations of Behavioral Research. Holt, Rinehart and Winst (1973)
9. Haitun, S.: Stationary scientometric distributions: part I. Differ. Approximations Scientometrics **4**(1), 5–25 (1982)
10. Dickson, G.W., Leitheiser, R.L., Wetherbe, J.C., Nechis, M.: Key information systems issues for the 1980's. MIS Q. 135–59 (1984)
11. Rockart, J.F., Flannery, L.S.: The management of end user computing. Commun. ACM **26**(10), 776–784 (1983)
12. Barricelli, B.R., Cassano, F., Fogli, D., Piccinno, A.: End-user development, end-user programming and end-user software engineering: a systematic mapping study. J. Syst. Softw. **149**, 101–137 (2019)

Putting Community-Based Learning and Librarianship into Practice

Alex H. Poole$^{(\boxtimes)}$ iD

Department of Information Science, College of Computing and Informatics, Drexel University,
Philadelphia, PA 19104, USA
ahp56@drexel.edu

Abstract. Based on a qualitative, exploratory case study, this research pivots around a three course, twelve credit, one year post-baccalaureate certificate (PBC) centering on community-based learning (CBL). We unpack the experiences and elicit the insights of our first cohort of Fellows (2020–2021). Interviewees discussed their motivations for applying; their project-based CBL work in three courses (data science, design thinking/UX, and a capstone) performed individually or in teams; their community competencies development (communication, technical, design, and community needs analysis); the ways in which the PBC enhanced their career opportunities (pursuing the Master's degree, tying in their PBC work with their current jobs, and its salutary impact on their career prospects); and how the certificate promoted diversity, equity, and inclusion (DEI) through targeted recruitment, a cohort structure, and community engagement. We discuss and reflect on lessons learned, the ways in which our research extends and complicates the existing literature, and suggestions for future research.

Keywords: LIS pedagogy · Community-based learning · Diversity, equity and inclusion (DEI)

1 Introduction

The Institute of Museum and Library Services-funded "Integrating Community-Based Learning into LIS Education" (2019–2022) centers on a three course, twelve credit postbaccalaureate certificate (PBC). Steeped in data science and design thinking/UX as well as Library and Information Science (LIS), the PBC enhances twelve Fellows' (six in 2020–21, and six in 2021–222) abilities to design, implement, and manage community-based data-driven projects.

In service of equitable opportunity, Fellows receive full tuition support for the certificate; moreover, they may transfer credits to Drexel University's ALA-accredited Master of Science in Information (MSI). Local partners include Drexel's Lindy Center for Civic Engagement, the Dornsife Center for Neighborhood Partnerships, and the Free Library of Philadelphia [1].

Featuring robust representation from marginalized groups, the first cohort of six Fellows (2020–2021) included five people of color (four Black and one Latinx). Testifying to their passion for community engagement, five of six Fellows worked in public libraries at the time of their PBC application.

This project's recruitment strategy, its course-based experiential project work, and its emphasis on developing community competencies successfully promoted civic engagement and diversity, equity, and inclusion (DEI). We first review the salient literature. Next, we explicate our qualitative methodological approach. Third, we set forth our findings. Fourth, we discuss how our findings extend and complicate the existing literature. We conclude with directions for future research.

2 Literature Review

This paper brings together literature on diversity, equity, and inclusion (DEI) in LIS, community-based learning (CBL), and community competencies. First, scholars lament the longstanding lack of LIS educational and professional diversity, equity, and inclusion [2]. IMLS therefore encouraged LIS programs to recruit paraprofessionals, provide cohort-based financial aid, and consider alternative credentialing [3]. The PBC accommodates all three recommendations.

Second, community-based learning (CBL) and librarianship represent a fresh opportunity for LIS programs [1, 4]. In CBL, students learn with and in communities, as opposed to a traditional classroom setting. Enriching established service learning principles and practices, CBL foregrounds common stewardship vis-à-vis local space and place [5]. Overall, CBL amalgamates academic learning, civic responsibility, and community engagement. Experiential, reciprocal, and reflective, it nourishes equitable partnerships among faculty, staff, students, and community organizations.

CBL's payoffs include, first, augmented learning and understanding. Students may leverage course material for practical, quotidian application. This seeds more rewarding learning experiences, just as serving community needs and constructing meaningful deliverables buoys motivation [6–15].

Second, CBL spurs professional development and ultimately, lifelong learning [16–19]. CBL socializes students into LIS professional practice, identity, and values [8, 20–22]. Students refine career goals, network, and enhance their professional prospects [6, 23].

Third, CBL facilitates skills development, for example leadership and management, teamwork, interpersonal, problem-solving, critical thinking, technical, and citizenship [6, 7, 9, 11, 13, 21, 22, 24–28].

Fourth, CBL ideally stirs LIS programs to (re)evaluate their curricula to engage the pressing needs of practitioners and community partners [7, 21, 23]. Pari passu, CBL may strengthen relationships between universities and surrounding communities [6, 7, 9, 15].

In line with its commitment to local communities, finally, CBL surfaces a commitment to DEI, social justice, and cultural competence [6, 7, 9–13, 20, 26, 29, 30].

Community-based learning concentrates on what IMLS called "community competencies" [3, p. 9]. Such competencies involve community-rooted information services, user- and community-centric leadership and management, culturally competent problem-solving and critical thinking, and sensitive, equitable, and reciprocal communication and collaboration. More broadly, CBL is an ideal space for community-based *librarianship*.

3 Methods

This paper centers on a qualitative case study that considers current, in-depth, complex, detailed, real-world phenomena [31]. Purposively sampling to ensure we obtained an insider perspective, we conducted semistructured interviews with five of the six 2020–2021 CBL Fellows [32]. Combining flexibility and control, semistructured interviews allowed us to understand perspectives, meanings, and experiences, and to reconstruct events describing social and political processes and discern how they change over time [33, 34]. Our coding progressed from initial to focused through a constant comparative strategy [35]. Indebted to Constructivist Grounded Theory, our analysis was inductive [33, 36]. Promoting credibility and trustworthiness, our research also relied on documentary evidence such as student work and published scholarly literature [37].

4 Findings

Findings concentrated on students' motivations to pursue the certificate, experiences in the certificate's three courses, community competencies development, pursuing the Master of Science (MSI) degree, and diversity, equity, and inclusion (DEI).

4.1 Pursuing the Certificate

All five Fellows had long considered pursuing their MLIS. The certificate appealed to them because it offered an effectively risk-free and economical entry into the field. As P1 summed up, "It was an easy decision."

4.2 Coursework

The three CBL courses brought together experiential learning, LIS, and cognate fields of burgeoning importance, namely data science [38] and design thinking/UX [39–41].

Data Analytics for Community-Based Data and Service

In Data Analytics for Community-Based Data and Service, groups of students (both of which CBL and Master's of Science in Information [MSI] students) collaborated with local non-profit organizations of their choosing. Through information needs analysis, each group plumbed urban civic engagement, democratic participation, and community evolution.

Though planned as an in-person community hybrid course [42], Data Analytics was reconfigured because of the pandemic; it took place remotely and asynchronously. Students collaboratively learned tools such as Excel, R Studio, and Tableau for data analysis as well as Slack for discussion and teamwork.

All five participants applauded the course. P4 reflected enthusiastically, "I really was looking at data and manipulating it, trying to figure out how I can make the data in service of the vision."

Data Analytics for Community-Based Data and Service hinged on project-based group work. One group worked with the Philadelphia Student Union (PSU), the other with Oak Lane Community Action Association (OLCAA).

P2, P3, and P4 formed a one based on their common interest in and experience working with underserved youths and anti-violence community organizations. Focusing on the police presence in schools, the group chose the Philadelphia Student Union, which had led social justice protests during the summer of 2020. The group subsequently examined the district's schools' budgets and funding allocations.

P4 began the project most interested in the near-complete lack of school librarians in the district. But her group's report showed "not just severe underfunding of school librarians but also mental health counselors and even nurses," as well as the presence of (and resources devoted to) a disproportionate number of police personnel. Of her work's significance, P3 marveled, "we have that anecdotal information, but seeing it in the data is a completely different thing." The group's final report provided PSU with data to inform the latter's social justice work.

The second group worked with Oak Lane Community Action Association (OLCAA). In this majority-Black neighborhood, the Refuge Evangelical Baptist Church wanted to build an affordable living space a four-story building comprising (40 apartments) for seniors on an adjacent plot of land it owned. The OLCAA, however, overwhelmingly opposed the development, and the PBC group marshalled data on OLCAA's behalf.

Design Thinking for Digital Community Service
Grounded in design thinking/UX principles and practices, Design Thinking for Digital Community Service broached problem-based community information needs assessment and analysis. It was planned as a side-by-side course [42] in which MSI and CBL students and community members, namely Free Library of Philadelphia paraprofessionals, would share perspectives, knowledge, and experiences. But Design Thinking for Digital Community Service was also rejiggered as a result of Covid-19; it met weekly remotely. Those able to attend synchronously did so; those unable to attend worked asynchronously.

In addition to the Fellows and MSI students, the course included seven FLP paraprofessionals (four people of color). Their perspectives proved particularly valuable to P1, P2, and P3. "I was inspired to work with [the paraprofessionals]," P2 reflected, "because I was inspired by the work that they've already done, so it was good to hear ideas from people that were doing awesome things."

Students chose whether to undertake course projects individually, in pairs, or in groups. Largely because of their work schedules, P1, P4, and P5 chose the former. Based on her own work experience, P1 developed basic computer literacy classes. She recalled, "jobseekers come into the library constantly for help to apply for jobs, doing resumes and they'll see a class and will be like, 'oh resume class,' and they'll come in and they don't know how to use [computers], they can't type, they've never used a mouse." P5 worked with her local public library director "to design a space for teenagers because in the library we don't really have a space for them and they're always being told to be quiet, or go outside and hang out."

By contrast, both P2 and P3 worked with the course's paraprofessionals. P2 developed a "top lending library," an outdoor safe space for library staff and patrons. Complementing her daily responsibilities with her library's afterschool program, P3's project focused on engaging teen groups who could no longer meet in person because of the pandemic; she successfully piloted a Discord channel.

Capstone

Fellows polished off their certificate work with a capstone project that built on their first two courses and furthered the Fellows' professional skills and their self-efficacy more broadly [43, 44]. P1, P2, P3, and P4 completed the capstone. P1 found the capstone deeply worthwhile; without it, her library branch would lack outdoor programming such as bilingual story times. Collaborating with her local public library, P2 conducted an equity, inclusion, and diversity audit. P3 worked to restart the library's staff mentoring program, which Covid had abrogated. Last, P4 partnered with her new employer to develop programming focused on educating youths about abolition and anti-Blackness.

4.3 Community Competencies

Each of the five participants improved four community competencies, namely communication, technical, design, and community needs analysis.

Communication

For example, conducting research to varied public library stakeholders increased P1's confidence. P4 also found it "nice to have a framework of how to approach different community leaders," that is, "How to just let them know that you're not there trying to profit off of them…but help with the work."

Technical

Leveraging her new technical skills, P2 discussed determining "the best way of presenting this information…so it would be readily accessible and useful to [community partner], and also useful to me." P4 also found new confidence. As she put it, "once I actually have a program, how do I measure who's coming, how successful it is, how do I quantify everything that I'm thinking about." Tableau she thought especially valuable as it helped illuminate "where things are located in Philadelphia, who's coming from where in Philadelphia, which neighborhoods are predominantly Black, predominately white, where's the poverty levels."

Design

P1 underlined her design skills development. She insisted "you really need to step outside of what you think the right procedure or the right program may be, and talk to the community." P2 similarly claimed, "The way that I see design thinking working the best is working within the community, not just with it."

Community Needs Analysis

P4 described improving her data analysis skills with social media content—"scanning through all of these posts, going months and months back whether it's Facebook, Twitter, Instagram, analyzing who's liking these things—is it mostly students, is it mostly older people, are they sharing things on their stories, or are they getting likes, or are people going to these events that they say they're having online?".

4.4 Career Development

Pursuing the MSI
All five participants found the certificate a segueway to the full-fledged MSI: four enrolled in the Master's program. P5 called her experience a fruitful "test run," and P1 felt more confident in handling the graduate school workload. For P4, the PBC proved "a good kick in the ass" to get reoriented to formal academic work.

Current Work
All five Fellows connected their PBC work directly to their current job roles and responsibilities. P3, for example, appreciated meeting and collaborating with fellow library employees who offered insightful institutional perspectives. She elaborated, "I have a little more of a leg up now, when I'm wanting to approach someone in a higher position of power to say, 'Hey, I worked on this project, and I think that we can really do xyz.'" P5 looked forward to returning to her library post-pandemic and implementing PBC lessons learned in new teen spaces. Last, skills developed during the PBC stimulated P4 "to think about how I can grow within my institution but also if I can't, how I can take this work and the skills elsewhere."

Career Enhancement
All five interviewees claimed their certificate work buoyed their career prospects. Most immediate, PBC courses counted officially toward P3's administrative development with the Free Library. Skills developed in CBL work meanwhile augmented P1's and P5's resumes. Not only did P2 overhaul her vita but she posted her PSU report, her DEI audit, and her top lending library PowerPoint on LinkedIn. Similarly, P4 suggested that the PBC boosted her job possibilities.

4.5 Diversity, Equity, and Inclusion

According to P3, the certificate promoted DEI because of the IMLS funding for students unable to afford the program. For P1, the PBC encouraged people of color to use it as a "steppingstone" to the MSI. P4 found the certificate an essential promoter of DEI. She explained, "when you're from an underrepresented group, especially in library science, where it's like 95% white, it can be really intimidating to just go into the Master's." "Even if you have some experience, you might feel like it's the wrong experience or that everyone else has all these other opportunities," she confessed. Certificate work tangibly developed students' skills and stamped them with the institution's imprimatur.

Three Fellows underscored the importance of seeing and working with other people in the program who looked like them. P2 reflected, "When I see other fellow Black people pursuing this field, it makes me feel drawn to them." She found her cohort-mates P3 and P4 "really inspiring." Similarly, P3 foregrounded the meaningfulness of "just having somebody that looks like you [who] can understand what you're saying culturally." Such diversity as represented by the Fellows, P4 asserted, "feels like what we need in the [LIS] field."

P5 also welcomed the opportunity to work with other people of color. Programs such as the PBC augured well for serving diverse communities. "I speak English and Spanish," she noted, "but you have certain communities where…if you only speak Spanish and the librarian only speaks English, there's a problem." P5 thus advocated for hiring bilingual or Spanish-speaking librarians. "You want to feel as though you are being understood," she concluded—a sentiment that surely applied to all interviewees.

5 Discussion

This research both extends and complicates current scholarship. First, this cohort's experiences indicates success in targeted DEI recruitment, as well as the value of cohort development and of an alternative credential such as a PBC both by itself and as an onramp to the MSI. Second, certificate work socialized Fellows into both community and professional practice, identity, and values. Third, by fusing theory and community practice, the PBC helped Fellows understand course content more deeply. What was more, the Fellows' previous work and life experiences and responsibilities paid clear intellectual, community, and professional dividends. Just as the Fellows built off previous work and life experiences to underpin their coursework and its interplay with their current professional and community work, so too did they plan to extend and enrich the projects developed and refined during the PBC into current or future work roles and responsibilities, a robust example of lifelong learning. Fourth, Fellows appreciably developed and refined their community competencies. Their project-based experiential learning in both individual and group work in data analysis, design thinking, and the capstone anchored this skills development. Fifth, the PBC fostered a closer relationship between the department and the Free Library, a quintessential community anchor.

Fellows' experiences also complicate current scholarship. First, while scholars suggest that CBL may nurture closer relationships between institutions and community partners, after just one year it is too soon to determine whether "Integrating Community-Based Learning into LIS Education" has made sustainable progress in this regard. Second, whether the PBC hints at a broader curriculum shift likewise remains open to debate. Third and most notable, the pandemic's impact cannot be overstated; it materially affected the pedagogy, groupwork, community partner work, and capstone project work. The inability to meet in person for coursework or by and large for community partnership work militated against robust communication, coordination, and relationship-building between students and community members such as Free Library paraprofessionals and between students and community partners.

6 Conclusion

P4 thought the certificate showed that Drexel University's Department of Information Science "has its ears to the ground" in valuing DEI and community engagement. Future research might consider three questions. First, in what other settings besides urban ones might community-based librarianship bear fruit? Second, what other types of CBL courses might prove promising? Third, this project developed an incipient community-competent pedagogy. How can stakeholders refine and expand such a pedagogy further?

In spite of COVID-19, Drexel's community-based learning post-baccalaureate certificate enjoyed an propitious first year. P2 put it well: "I'm proud of everything that I went through and I'm happy about everything I learned."

Acknowledgement. This project was made possible in part by the Institute of Museum and Library Services (RE-17-19-0006-19).

References

1. Poole, A.H., Agosto, D.E., Lin, X., Yan, E.: Librarianship as citizenship: the promise of community-based learning in North American library and information science education. J. Educ. Libr. Inf. Sci. **63**(2) (2022). https://doi.org/10.3138/jelis-2020-0090
2. Poole, A.H., Agosto, D., Greenberg, J., Lin, X., Yan, E.: Where do we stand? Diversity and social justice in North American library and information science education. J. Educ. Libr. Inf. Sci. **62**(3), 258–286 (2021). https://doi.org/10.3138/jelis-2020-0018
3. Sands, A.E., Toro, S., DeVoe, T., Fuller, S., Wolff-Eisenberg, C.: Positioning Library and Information Science Graduate Education for 21st Century Practice. Institute of Museum and Library Services, Washington, D.C. (2018). https://www.imls.gov/sites/default/files/publications/documents/imlspositioningreport.pdf
4. Poole, A.H.: Promoting diversity, equity, and inclusion in library and information science through community-based learning. In: iConference 2021, vol. 12645, pp. 529–540 (2021)
5. Tönnies, F.: Community and Civil Society. Cambridge University Press, Cambridge (2001). https://doi.org/10.1007/978-3-030-71292-1_41
6. Ball, M.A., Schilling, K.: Service learning, technology and LIS education. J. Educ. Libr. Inf. Sci. **47**(4), 277 (2006). https://doi.org/10.2307/40323821
7. Becker, N.J.: Service learning in the curriculum: preparing LIS students for the next millennium. J. Educ. Libr. Inf. Sci. **41**(4), 285–293 (2000)
8. Cooper, L.Z.: Student reflections on an LIS internship from a service learning perspective supporting multiple learning theories. J. Educ. Libr. Inf. Sci. **54**(4), 286–298 (2013)
9. Eyler, J.: Reflection: linking service and learning-linking students and communities. J. Soc. Issues **58**(3), 517–534 (2002). https://doi.org/10.1111/1540-4560.00274
10. Hatcher, J.A., Bringle, R.G., Hahn, T.W. (eds.): Research on Student Civic Outcomes in Service Learning: Conceptual Frameworks and Methods, 1st edn. Stylus Publishing LLC, Sterling (2017)
11. Hughes-Hassell, S., Vance, K.: Examining race, power, privilege, and equity in the youth services LIS classroom. In: Cooke, N.A., Sweeney, M.E. (eds.) Teaching for Justice: Implementing Social Justice in the LIS Classroom, pp. 103–137. Library Juice Press, Sacramento (2016)
12. Mehra, B., Singh, V.: Library leadership-in-training as embedded change agents to further social Justice in rural communities: teaching of library management subjects in the iTRl and iTRl2. In: Cooke, N.A., Sweeney, M.E. (eds.) Teaching for Justice: Implementing Social Justice in the LIS Classroom, pp. 247–286. Library Juice Press, Sacramento (2016)
13. Overall, P.M.: The effect of service learning on LIS students' understanding of diversity issues related to equity of access. J. Educ. Libr. Inf. Sci. **51**(4), 251–266 (2010)

14. Roy, L.: Service learning connecting diverse communities and LIS students and faculty. In: Meyers, A., Jensen, K., Roy, L. (eds.) Service Learning: Linking Library Education and Practice, pp. 73–82. American Library Association, Chicago (2009)

15. Yontz, E., de la Peña McCook, K.: Service-learning and LIS education. J. Educ. Libr. Inf. Sci. **44**(1), 58–68 (2003)

16. Bishop, A., Bruce, B., Jeong, S.: Beyond service learning: toward community schools and reflective community learners. In: Meyers, A., Jensen, K., Roy, L. (eds.) Service Learning: Linking Library Education and Practice, pp. 16–31. American Library Association, Chicago (2009)

17. Mehra, B., Robinson, W.C.: The community engagement model in library and information science education: a case study of a collection development and management course. J. Educ. Libr. Inf. Sci. **50**(1), 15–38 (2009)

18. Melaville, A., Berg, A.C., Black, M.J.: Community-based learning: engaging students for success and citizenship. Partnerships/Community **40** (2006). https://digitalcommons.unomaha.edu/slcepartnerships/40

19. Rickards, C.: Examining 21st-Century Skill Acquisition as a Result of Democratic Engagement within a Side-by-Side Community-Based Learning Course. Ph.D., Drexel University, Philadelphia, PA (2015)

20. Ball, M.A.: Practicums and service learning in LIS education. J. Educ. Libr. Inf. Sci. **49**(1), 70–82 (2008)

21. Huggins, S.: Practice-based learning in higher education. Libr. Trends **66**(1), 1–12 (2017). https://doi.org/10.1353/lib.2017.0024

22. O'Brien, H., Freund, L., Jantzi, L., Sinanan, S.: Investigating a peer-to-peer community service learning model for LIS education. J. Educ. Libr. Inf. Sci. **55**(4), 322–335 (2014)

23. Coleman, J.G.: The role of the practicum in library schools. J. Educ. Libr. Inf. Sci. **30**(1), 19 (1989). https://doi.org/10.2307/40323496

24. Albertson, D., Whitaker, M.S., Perry, R.A.: Developing and organizing a community engagement project that provides technology literacy training to persons with intellectual disabilities. J. Educ. Libr. Inf. Sci. **52**(2), 142–151 (2011)

25. Albertson, D., Whitaker, M.S.: A service-learning framework to support an MLIS core curriculum. J. Educ. Libr. Inf. Sci. **52**(2), 152–163 (2011)

26. Caspe, M., Lopez, M.E.: Preparing the next generation of librarians for family and community engagement. J. Educ. Libr. Inf. Sci. **59**(4), 157–178 (2018). https://doi.org/10.3138/jelis.59.4.2018-0021

27. Gilliland, A.J.: Pluralizing archival education: a non-zero-sum proposition. In: Caldera, M.A., Neal, K.M. (eds.) Through the Archival Looking Glass: A Reader on Diversity and Inclusion, pp. 235–272. Society of American Archivists, Chicago (2014)

28. Kimmel, S.C., Howard, J.K., Ruzzi, B.: Educating school library leaders for radical change through community service. J. Educ. Libr. Inf. Sci. **57**(2), 174–186 (2016). https://doi.org/10.3138/jelis.57.2.174

29. Chu, C.M.: Working from within: critical service learning as core learning in the MLIS curriculum. In: Meyers, A., Jensen, K., Roy, L. (eds.) Service Learning: Linking Library Education and Practice, pp. 105–123. American Library Association, Chicago (2009)

30. Cuban, S., Hayes, E.: Perspectives of five library and information studies students involved in service learning at a community-based literacy program. J. Educ. Libr. Inf. Sci. **42**(2), 86 (2001). https://doi.org/10.2307/40324022

31. Yin, R.: Case Study Research: Design and Methods, 4th edn. SAGE, Los Angeles (2009)

32. Pickard, A.J.: Sampling. In: Pickard, A.J. (ed.) Research Methods in Information, 2nd edn., pp. 59–69. Facet, London (2013)

33. Charmaz, K.: Constructing Grounded Theory, 2nd edn. Sage, Thousand Oaks (2014)

34. Rubin, H.J., Rubin, I.: Qualitative Interviewing: The Art of Hearing Data, 2nd edn. Sage Publications, Thousand Oaks (2005)
35. Saldaña, J.: The Coding Manual for Qualitative Researchers, 2nd edn. SAGE, Los Angeles (2013)
36. Pickard, A.J.: Qualitative analysis. In: Pickard, A.J. (ed.) Research Methods in Information, 2nd edn., pp. 267–281. Facet, London (2013)
37. Shenton, A.K.: Analysis of existing, externally created material. In: Pickard, A.J. (ed.) Research Methods in Information, 2nd edn., pp. 251–261. Facet, London (2013)
38. Poole, A.H.: LEADING the way: a new model for data science education. Proc. Assoc. Inf. Sci. Technol. **58**, 525–531 (2021)
39. Clarke, R.I.: Innovative library and information services: the design thinking process. In: Hirsh, S. (ed.) Information Services Today: An Introduction, 2nd edn. Rowman & Littlefield, Lanham (2018)
40. Clarke, R.I.: Toward a design epistemology for librarianship. Libr. Q. **88**(1), 41–59 (2018). https://doi.org/10.1086/694872
41. Bell, S.: Design thinking. Am. Libr. **39**, 44–49 (2008)
42. Lindy Center for Civic Engagement: Review of Community-Based Learning at Drexel University Provost Report, June 2018
43. Bossaller, J.S.: Service learning as innovative pedagogy in online learning. EFI **32**(1), 35–53 (2016). https://doi.org/10.3233/EFI-150962
44. McGuinness, C., Shankar, K.: Supporting reflection in the MLIS through a professionally-oriented capstone module. EFI **35**(2), 173–178 (2019). https://doi.org/10.3233/EFI-190256

Testing the Keystone Framework by Analyzing Positive Citations to Wakefield's 1998 Paper

Amulya Addepalli[1,3] , Karen Ann Subin[2,3] , and Jodi Schneider[3(✉)]

[1] William Fremd High School, Palatine, IL, USA
[2] Naperville North High School, Naperville, IL, USA
[3] University of Illinois at Urbana Champaign, Champaign, IL, USA
jodi@illinois.edu

Abstract. Science is constantly developing as new information is discovered. Papers discredited by the scientific community may be retracted. Such papers might have been cited before they were retracted (as well as afterwards), which potentially could spread a chain of unreliable information. To address this, Fu and Schneider (2020) introduced the keystone framework for auditing how and whether a paper fundamentally depends on another paper, and proposed that an alerting system be developed to flag papers that fundamentally depend on retracted papers. The need for expert labor is the main challenge of such alerting in such systems. This paper tests whether a flowchart process for non-experts could accurately assess dependencies between papers, reducing the need for expert assessment. We do this by developing such a process and testing it on citations to one highly cited retracted paper. In our case study, non-experts using our process can resolve the question of dependency in about half the cases. Two annotators had 92.9% agreement on 85 papers annotated, with 100% agreement after discussion. In future work we will assess the reliability of non-experts' decisions as compared to experts, and identify possibilities for automation.

Keywords: Retracted papers · Knowledge maintenance · Keystone citations · Wakefield · Misinformation in science

1 Introduction

Modern science evolves through the centuries, moving along the dual path of reforming and reinventing; it builds itself on trial and error. Papers discredited by the scientific community may be retracted when they are found to be in error or even fraudulent; about 1 paper in 2500 is retracted [1]. Such papers might have been cited before they were retracted (as well as afterwards), which potentially could spread a chain of unreliable information to a wide body of literature. Ideally, scientific information that becomes retracted would also be removed from or updated in earlier publications, and current guidelines specify that "Articles

M. Smits (Ed.): iConference 2022, LNCS 13192, pp. 79–88, 2022.
https://doi.org/10.1007/978-3-030-96957-8_9

that relied on subsequently retracted articles in reaching their own conclusions... may themselves need to be corrected or retracted," [4]. However, in practice, no such auditing process is in current use, even though papers are commonly cited after they are retracted [3,10]. This can allow disproven information to spread among the scientific community creating a domino effect which could invalidate the argument of a new paper written. But are there any corrective measures?

Recently, Fu and Schneider introduced the keystone framework [7], which aims to determine how a paper is affected when relying upon unsound findings. It is an approach for auditing how and whether existing papers depend on a particular paper, through the use of argumentation theory and citation context analysis. In particular, a keystone citation is defined as a citation that a paper heavily bases its argument or knowledge around. Fu and Schneider proposed that an alert system could selectively notify authors whose work significantly depended on a retracted paper. Although alerting is promising, a key limitation is that the proposed approach requires slow, laborious work done best by experts. Ideally, some of this work could be scaffolded by an expert, creating a process that a group of non-experts could apply, to reduce the expert labor required.

In this paper, our goal is to explore the effectiveness of a system which can accurately assess the dependency of a paper on unreliable data, using non-experts. This is accomplished by testing the process on a single highly cited retracted paper, which we introduce next.

2   Case Study

To analyze the impact a retracted paper can have on work that cited it, we focused on a paper written in 1998 by Andrew Wakefield and colleagues called Ileal-lymphoid-nodular hyperplasia, non-specific colitis, and pervasive developmental disorder in children [12]. Not long after its publication in *The Lancet*, the paper came under fire [6]. Wakefield's paper was partially retracted in 2004 and fully retracted in 2010. The main claim of the paper, which has been fully discredited [5], is that the measles, mumps and rubella (MMR) vaccine causes children to be more susceptible to behavioral regression and a form of autism called pervasive developmental disorder. The Wakefield paper contributed to mistrust of vaccines and low vaccination rates, setting the stage for measles outbreaks in the UK, US, and Canada [6]. The Wakefield paper is a good case for us to study keystone citations because citing papers that were published before the retraction, between 1998–2004, could not have known that it would be retracted.

3   Related Work

In 2019, scholarly communications librarian Elizabeth Suelzer and her team conducted a study to inspect the features of citations that mention Wakefield's 1998 paper. They found 1153 papers in English that cite Wakefield [11]. Suelzer's team used a stepwise approach to group the articles into categories such as negative, perfunctory, affirmative, and assumptive [8]. Alongside the abundance of affirmative citations, Suelzer and her team discovered a number of authors who didn't record the Wakefield paper as retracted.

More recently, Ivan Heibi and Silvio Peroni [8] analyzed open citations to Wakefield's paper found in COCI, the OpenCitations Index of Crossref DOI-to-DOI citations [9]. They annotated in-text citations and used both citation intent analysis and topic modeling to understand how Wakefield's paper has been cited. Over time, more papers mentioned the retraction, with the largest percentage (61%) of mentioning papers in the most recent (2017) publication year in their dataset. Following the partial retraction, publications beyond medicine became more prominent, with an increase in citations from social sciences papers and from new areas such as economics and environmental sciences.

4 Methods

4.1 Our Dataset

Our study focused on papers that cited and used information from the Wakefield article in an affirmative light: we hypothesized that these articles would be the most problematic since they were more likely to depend on the Wakefield paper. Starting with the dataset that Suelzer [11] provided, we retained papers matching the following criteria: 2004/2010 retractions were not referenced, classified as affirmative, published in any year (pre- or post-retraction). This gave us 89 papers that cite Wakefield's 1998 paper positively and fail to acknowledge the partial or full retraction. The subset was created to have a reasonable number of papers: large enough for any trends/patterns in the articles to be identified and yet small enough that we could analyze the dataset multiple times if needed as our theories developed. We used Zotero to store and organize the full-text of the articles we were analyzing; in the study period we did not find the full-text of 4 papers. Hence, ultimately our dataset was 85 papers.

4.2 Annotation Design

The goal of the annotation process was to operationalize the keystone framework, in order to enable non-experts to identify keystone citations to Wakefield's retracted 1998 paper. That is, the objective was to be able to distinguish whether or not a paper that cites the Wakefield paper can stand without the support of the information from the Wakefield paper. One person (AA) iteratively designed the annotation process in consultation with the larger group. During the initial, year-long process, one annotator manually used a systematic data analysis methodology, first categorizing the papers manually on an Excel spreadsheet without using a guideline. After recognizing the common steps taken to group each paper, a nuanced method of analyzing each paper was created which is represented the annotation manual excerpted in Fig. 1, available in our data deposit [2]. The process guides the annotator using questions such as "Does the article title correlate with the ideas presented in Wakefield?" and "How many times was Wakefield mentioned in the paper?". Using this process a non-expert should be able to determine if a paper is independent of the cited paper, dependent on it, or should be shown to a professional to make that determination.

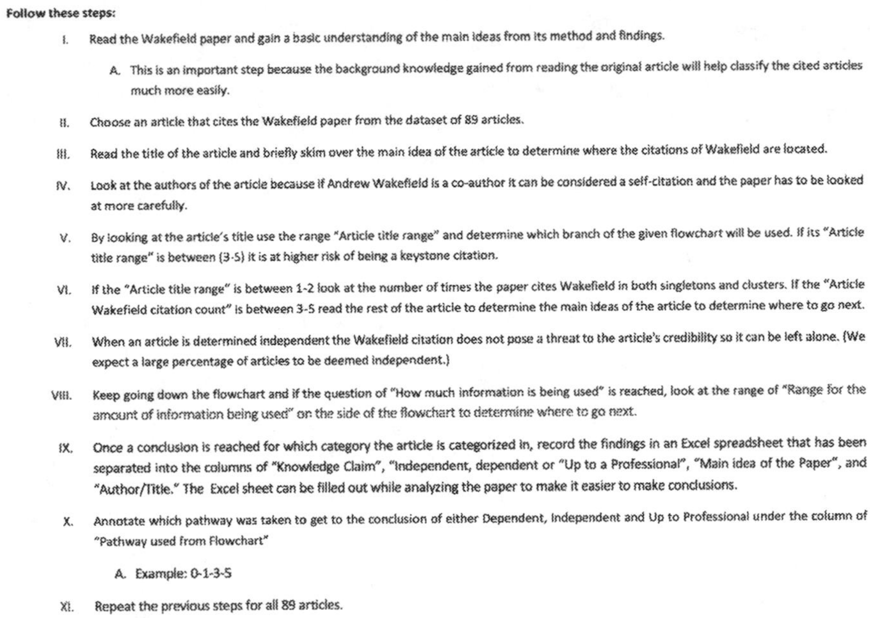

Follow these steps:

I. Read the Wakefield paper and gain a basic understanding of the main ideas from its method and findings.

    A. This is an important step because the background knowledge gained from reading the original article will help classify the cited articles much more easily.

II. Choose an article that cites the Wakefield paper from the dataset of 89 articles.

III. Read the title of the article and briefly skim over the main idea of the article to determine where the citations of Wakefield are located.

IV. Look at the authors of the article because if Andrew Wakefield is a co-author it can be considered a self-citation and the paper has to be looked at more carefully.

V. By looking at the article's title use the range "Article title range" and determine which branch of the given flowchart will be used. If its "Article title range" is between (3-5) it is at higher risk of being a keystone citation.

VI. If the "Article title range" is between 1-2 look at the number of times the paper cites Wakefield in both singletons and clusters. If the "Article Wakefield citation count" is between 3-5 read the rest of the article to determine the main ideas of the article to determine where to go next.

VII. When an article is determined independent the Wakefield citation does not pose a threat to the article's credibility so it can be left alone. (We expect a large percentage of articles to be deemed independent.)

VIII. Keep going down the flowchart and if the question of "How much information is being used" is reached, look at the range of "Range for the amount of information being used" on the side of the flowchart to determine where to go next.

IX. Once a conclusion is reached for which category the article is categorized in, record the findings in an Excel spreadsheet that has been separated into the columns of "Knowledge Claim", "Independent, dependent or "Up to a Professional", "Main idea of the Paper", and "Author/Title." The Excel sheet can be filled out while analyzing the paper to make it easier to make conclusions.

X. Annotate which pathway was taken to get to the conclusion of either Dependent, Independent and Up to Professional under the column of "Pathway used from Flowchart"

    A. Example: 0-1-3-5

XI. Repeat the previous steps for all 89 articles.

Fig. 1. A part of our annotation manual [2] which is intended to provide a replicable process for non-experts to recognize keystone citations to Wakefield's paper.

4.3   Testing the Annotation

To test our annotation manual [2], we recruited a second annotator (KAS) to provide suggestions on how to make the manual more understandable to a wider range of people and help locate areas of concerns on specific pathways on the flowchart. After comparing the analysis of each paper, we were able to agree on specific trends found in the results from the flowchart and made revisions to the flowchart accordingly. The final annotation was stored in Excel spreadsheets [2], completed independently by two annotators (AA, KAS), with some discussions regarding the level of expertise needed to make determinations of up to a professional articles. For instance, after seeing a number of articles using the same pathway (0-2-12-13), we updated the flowchart to classify these as independent; this pathway selects articles whose main topic autism, gastrointestinal problems, or the specific disorder (2); which include information about the Wakefield article (12); but which cite it outside the methods section (13). We compared the decisions, resolved disagreements, and came to a final determination for each article. We computed the percentage agreement and we analyzed the disagreements in an error analysis.

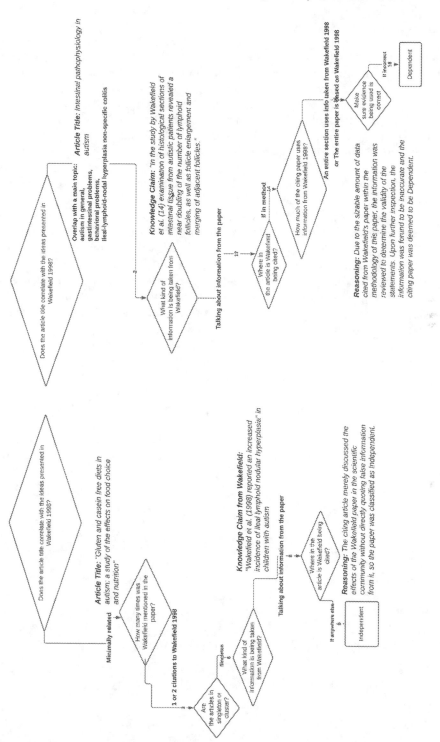

Fig. 2. Determining that an article was (a) independent (left) or (b) dependent (right).

4.4   Annotator Background

The annotators were high school students with honors biology coursework and a strong interest in science. A deep professional/scientific background in biomedicine or a related area, including up-to-date biomedical knowledge and knowledge of medical terminology, would be needed to fully understand the research papers annotated. Our focus was on the triage process, to determine which papers needed further vetting from a professional in order to determine the validity of a paper's scientific arguments and dependence on the Wakefield paper.

Figure 2 illustrates the annotation process for two articles from our subset. In each case, each annotator answered a series of questions, recording the pathway taken through the flowchart by noting the sequence of numbers encountered. First, the annotator read through the article and determined the most important points of the article. Second, the annotator examined how reliant each citation was on the Wakefield paper.

The paper classified as independent, shown on the left in Fig. 2, mentioned the Wakefield paper just once and the annotator judged that, since the citing article simply referenced the consequences of the Wakefield paper on the scientific community, it could be classified as independent.

The paper classified as dependent, shown on the right in Fig. 2, cited Wakefield multiple times. The annotator deemed that the paper directly cited data from the Wakefield paper, and in sizable amounts as well. Since the annotator assessed that a portion of the evidence taken from the Wakefield paper was mentioned in the methodology of the citing paper, and noted that substantial section of the paper referenced the Wakefield article. To check the validity of the statements, the annotator researched the topics discussed and determined that the information cited was inaccurate. Consequently, the paper was categorized as dependent on Wakefield's paper.

5   Results

From the annotation spreadsheets [2], we calculated the number of articles which had been classified into each category. Two annotators had 92.9% agreement on 85 papers annotated, with 100% agreement after discussion. All 6 disagreements are shown in Table 1. As seen in Fig. 3, using our process, we were able to classify 89.4% of the articles as "independent", meaning that they take a minimal to no amount of information from the Wakefield paper and it doesn't damage their paper's credibility. Only 2.4% of the articles were classified as "dependent",

Table 1. Error analysis

ID	Error	Final annotation	Annotator 1	Annotator 2	Pathway 1	Pathway 2	Comment
Deisher 2015	Different pathways	Up to a professional	Up to a professional	Independent	0-1-4-6-8-10	0-2-11	Public health-related analysis, talks extensively about the "Wakefield Scare" and the relationship between the MMR vaccine and autism prevalence
Levy 2007	Different pathways	Up to a professional	Up to a professional	Independent	0-1-4-6-8-10	0-1-4-6-8-9	Seeks to determine whether gastrointestinal symptoms are related to diets, comparing autistic and non-autistic children
Cohly 2005	Recording error	Independent	Up to a professional	Independent	0-2-12-13	0-2-12-13	Immunological findings in autism
Kawashima 2000	Flowchart evolution	Up to a professional	Up to a professional	Independent	0-2-12-14-15	0-2-12-14-15	Similar to Wakefield's study in that the children all had ileal lymphoid nodular hyperplasia and nonspecific colitis
Sabra 1998	Flowchart evolution	Up to a professional	Up to a professional	Independent	0-2-12-14-15	0-2-12-14-15	Mechanisms similar to that of ileal-lymphoid-nodular hyperplasia
Horton 1998	Flowchart insufficient	Up to a professional	Up to a professional	Independent	0-2-12-14-16-17	No current classification	"We did not prove an association between measles, mumps, and rubella vaccine and the syndrome described"

meaning that they use the Wakefield paper in a fundamental way. And 8.2% of the articles were classified into the "up to a professional" category, meaning that they need further review. Table 2 shows examples of some of the deciding factors in making these determinations.

Table 2. Examples of key indicators that helped categorize papers

Decision	Reason	Description	Paper ID
Independent	Cluster citation	There is only one citation to Wakefield, which supports the same information as multiple different papers: "Preliminary evidence has suggested that some children with autism and other PDDs may experience gastrointestinal problems (Horvath, Papadimitriou, Rabsztyn, Drachenberg, and Tildon, 1999; Lightdale et al., 2001; Wakefield et al., 1998; Williams et al., 2000)"	Kerwin, 2005
Up to a professional	Multiple uses, including in the methods and results section	Used Wakefield's paper as part of their background, method and results. The paper was released shortly after Wakefield's and constantly mentions the fact that the new study was done based on the findings of Wakefield	Sabra, 1998
Up to a professional	The paper uses Wakefield to make a conclusion about a medical phenomenon that we don't have the expertise to determine whether or not it is correct	"Wakefield et al. have introduced strong data to support our hypothesis that FA is the pivotal causative factor that produces the lesions in the terminal ileum that consist of greatly enlarged lymphoid nodules containing large collections of lymphocytes in the GI lymphoid tissues adjacent to Peyer patches"	Bellanti, 2003

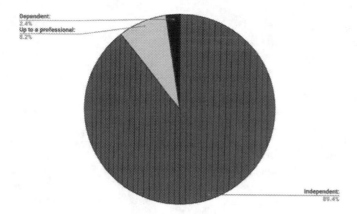

Fig. 3. The percentage of articles from our subset that we classified as dependent on versus independent of Wakefield's 1998 paper.

6   Discussion and Conclusion

In this paper, we explore and analyze how current research builds on previous work for one specific retracted paper. According to our analysis, only 9 out of the 85 papers we analyzed have a significant chance of needing correction due to the Wakefield retraction. This greatly reduces the number of papers that would need attention from authors or from editors in order to avoid the spread of scientific misinformation. Further work is needed to check whether experts would agree with our assessment.

Our future work lies in three areas. First, we need to validate our approach against an expert's view, particularly to determine whether the papers that we deemed dependent and up to a professional are in fact more likely to require correction than those that we deemed independent of Wakefield. Second, we would like to generalize this process, in order to determine how to handle any paper that cites any retracted paper. This is likely to require some domain analysis based on the topics, but perhaps not the full argumentation analysis proposed in the keystone framework [7]. Ultimately, we hope to help researchers determine the credibility of papers, since there are no guidelines for authors or editors to follow when a retracted paper has already been cited, and no systematic analysis of which papers might need reexamination. Third, we hope to create a computer algorithm that can go through the steps of our flowchart to avoid manual work and minimize human error. This would have the advantage of scaling the work so that it could be used in practice to support knowledge maintenance in digital libraries.

Data Availability

The annotation manual and flowchart, and annotated data are available at [2].

Acknowledgements. Liz Suelzer, Nathan D. Woods, Madelyn Sanfilippo, Information Quality Lab, Yuanxi Fu. Alfred P. Sloan Foundation G-2020-12623.

References

1. Tis but a scratch: Zombie research haunts academic literature long after their supposed demise. Economist **439**(9251), 89 (2021)
2. Addepalli, A., Subin, K.A., Schneider, J.: Dataset for testing the keystone framework by analyzing positive citations to Wakefield's 1998 paper (2022). https://doi.org/10.13012/B2IDB-2532850_V1
3. Bar-Ilan, J., Halevi, G.: Post retraction citations in context: a case study. Scientometrics **113**(1), 547–565 (2017). https://doi.org/10.1007/s11192-017-2242-0
4. COPE Council: Retraction guidelines (November 2019). https://doi.org/10.24318/cope.2019.1.4
5. Dudley, M.Z., et al.: Do vaccines cause autism? In: The Clinician's Vaccine Safety Resource Guide, pp. 197–204. Springer, Cham (2018). https://doi.org/10.1007/978-3-319-94694-8_26
6. Eggertson, L.: Lancet retracts 12-year-old article linking autism to MMR vaccines. Can. Med. Assoc. J. (CMAJ) **182**(4), E199–E200 (2010). https://doi.org/10.1503/cmaj.109-3179
7. Fu, Y., Schneider, J.: Towards knowledge maintenance in scientific digital libraries with the keystone framework. In: Proceedings of the ACM/IEEE Joint Conference on Digital Libraries in 2020, Virtual Event China, pp. 217–226. ACM (August 2020). https://dl.acm.org/doi/10.1145/3383583.3398514
8. Heibi, I., Peroni, S.: A qualitative and quantitative analysis of open citations to retracted articles: the Wakefield 1998 et al.'s case. Scientometrics **126**, 8433–8470 (2021). https://doi.org/10.1007/s11192-021-04097-5
9. Heibi, I., Peroni, S., Shotton, D.: Software review: COCI, the OpenCitations Index of Crossref open DOI-to-DOI citations. Scientometrics **121**(2), 1213–1228 (2019). https://doi.org/10.1007/s11192-019-03217-6
10. Hsiao, T.K., Schneider, J.: Continued use of retracted papers: temporal trends in citations and (lack of) awareness of retractions shown in citation contexts in biomedicine. Quant. Sci. Stud. **2**(4), 1144–1169 (2021). https://doi.org/10.1162/qss_a_00155
11. Suelzer, E.M., Deal, J., Hanus, K.L., Ruggeri, B., Sieracki, R., Witkowski, E.: Assessment of citations of the retracted article by Wakefield et al. with fraudulent claims of an association between vaccination and autism. JAMA Netw. Open **2**(11), e1915552 (2019). https://doi.org/10.1001/jamanetworkopen.2019.15552
12. Wakefield, A., et al.: RETRACTED: Ileal-lymphoid-nodular hyperplasia, non-specific colitis, and pervasive developmental disorder in children. Lancet **351**(9103), 637–641 (1998). Retracted in https://doi.org/10.1016/S0140-6736(10)60175-4

Information Governance and Ethics

Online "helpful" Lies: An Empirical Study of Helpfulness in Fake and Authentic Online Reviews

Alton Y. K. Chua[1](✉) and Xiaoyu Chen[2]

[1] Wee Kim Wee School of Communication and Information, Nanyang Technological University, Singapore, Singapore
altonchua@ntu.edu.sg
[2] Department of Library, Information and Archives, Shanghai University, Shanghai, China
xiaoyu-chen@shu.edu.cn

Abstract. Some fake online reviews may have overlapping textual features with authentic reviews. This paper explores the nuanced differences between helpful and unhelpful reviews, as well as fake and authentic reviews. Four textual features—polarity, subjectivity, readability, and depth—are used for the investigation. Results suggest that subjectivity, readability and depth help to distinguish between helpful and unhelpful reviews but not between fake and authentic ones. However, polarity offers a clue to differentiate between helpful fake and helpful authentic reviews. Specifically, for positive entries, helpful fake reviews contain more contents indicative of surprise while helpful authentic had more expectation-confirmed words like satisfaction. For negative entries, helpful fake reviews contained more contents indicative of anger while authentic helpful ones carried more anxiety.

Keywords: Authentic online reviews · Fake online reviews · Review helpfulness

1 Introduction

Online user-generated reviews have now become a convenient information source which consumers rely on when making purchase decisions. In a study, more than 70% of consumers regarded online reviews as trustworthy, while some 90% of shoppers acknowledged their purchase behavior could be influenced [1]. Given their strategic importance commercially, businesses are seeking ways to leverage online reviews in marketing and product improvement efforts.

In parallel, online reviews have attracted much scholarly attention. Existing literature revolves around a few distinctive streams. The classic theme considers the relationship between online reviews and purchase behaviors [e.g., 2, 3]. Another seeks to differentiate between authentic and fake reviews. Findings suggest that review authenticity can be discerned using the linguistic cues of comprehensibility, specificity, exaggeration, and negligence [e.g., 4, 5]. A third stream examines features that make a helpful review. These commonly include review polarity, subjectivity, readability and depth [e.g., 6, 7].

Yet, little research has been devoted to the study of helpful but fake reviews. Such reviews are particularly deleterious because they misrepresent truth but perfectly fulfill the intended role of bona fide entries. Scholars suggest that these fake reviews share overlapping textual features with helpful and authentic entries [3].

Current works on the textual features of review helpfulness have identified four primary constructs: polarity, subjectivity, readability, and depth. Polarity refers to the content valence of an online review, which is typically classified into positive and negative [8]. Subjectivity refers to the extent to which an online review is laden with personal emotions, opinions, and judgments [5]. Readability refers to the extent to which an online review is clear and easy to understand [9]. Depth refers to the amount of open-ended textual content an online review provides [6]. However, as a collection, these features have yet to be empirically tested to differentiate between helpful and unhelpful reviews. More interestingly, the question of whether they could be used to distinguish between fake and authentic reviews remains open. For this reason, this paper proposes the following:

RQ: *To what extent can polarity, subjectivity, readability, and depth be used to distinguish between (i) helpful and unhelpful reviews and (ii) fake and authentic reviews?*

To address the question, this paper uses supervised learning algorithms based on the four textual features to analyze a publicly available dataset comprising the following categories of reviews: helpful fake reviews, unhelpful fake reviews, helpful authentic reviews, and unhelpful authentic reviews.

This paper has both theoretical and practical contributions. On the theoretical front, the findings of this paper can serve as a significant dovetailing effort to the literature on distinguishing between helpful and unhelpful as well as fake and authentic reviews. On the practical front, readers and operators of review platforms may lean on the findings to conjecture which helpful reviews are likely to be fake and which are probably authentic. This could help potential consumers make more informed purchase decisions, thwarting business malpractices of online review manipulation [10].

2   Methods

2.1   Data Collection

This study used a publicly available dataset shared by University of Colorado, also known as "Boulder Lies and Truths Corpus" (BLT-C) [11]. BLT-C is one of the most extensive shared multidimensional corpora including attributes used to assess the authenticity and helpfulness of online reviews. The dataset contains 1,581 reviews on hotels and electronics collected via crowdsourcing on Amazon Mechanical Turk. Among them, 790 reviews are about hotels and 791 reviews are about electronics. Meanwhile, 1,203 reviews are fake while 478 reviews are authentic. Review helpfulness was manually scored by three coders. They scored the helpfulness of each review from 0 to 5, 0 being the least helpful and 5 being the most helpful. Each coder scored independently to minimize biases. The helpfulness metric was assessed using the Kendall Consistency Coefficient (KCC) to ensure inter-coder reliability. After checking for consistency, each review's helpfulness scores across the three coders were summed and averaged. The result was fairly consistent (KCC = 0.68). Informed by prior literature [9], we used the median split to divide the reviews into two groups. A review was marked as unhelpful if the score was lower than 3.3 and helpful otherwise (Table 1).

Table 1. Dataset description across four categories.

	Fake reviews	Authentic reviews	Total
Labeled as "helpful"	606 (38.33%)	336 (21.25%)	942 (59.58%)
Labeled as "unhelpful"	497 (31.44%)	142 (8.98%)	639 (40.42%)
Total	1,103(69.77%)	478(30.23%)	1,581(100%)

Note: a percentage in respective parenthesis denotes the proportion in the total sample

2.2 Operationalization of Textual Features

Four textual features, namely, polarity, subjectivity, readability and length, were extracted from the dataset. A python API known as "TextBlob" was used to operationalize the polarity and subjectivity of each review text. Based on the API, the polarity ranges from -1.0 to $+1.0$, indicating extreme negative valence to extreme positive valence, while the subjectivity ranges from 0 to 1, indicating the absence of personal views to one which is highly personal. The readability was measured by the automated readability index (ARI) [12]. The depth was measured by two indicators: word count and part-of-speech tags (POS tag). Word count is the number of words of a review. POS tag can categorize words in a text based on a particular part of speech, depending on the definition of the word and its context.

Term frequency-inverse document frequency (TF-IDF) was employed as an additional analysis to uncover fine-grained differences among the four categories of online reviews. TF represents the times a word appears in a document, while IDF specifies the number of documents containing a specific word.

2.3 Data Analysis

The description of the textual feature of online reviews in the dataset is presented in Table 2. A correlation test was employed to assess the associations among the feature variables, as shown in Fig. 1. The results showed that readability (ARI), subjectivity, word count, and POS tags slightly correlated with the authenticity of reviews. However, polarity seemed to have an insignificant correlation with both categorical variables.

We used three widely-used supervised learning algorithms: Logistic Regression, Support Vector Machine and Random Forest, based on Python scikit-learn API to train online reviews in the dataset. Thereafter, we validated and compared the accuracy between the algorithms in classification. Due to the imbalance dataset from the merging of fake reviews, we randomly sampled 478 fake reviews of the 1,103 fake reviews to match the 478 accurate reviews in the dataset. The dataset was then further randomly split into 80–20 training and testing sets. The training data was fed into the machine learning algorithms and the trained model was used to validate the testing set.

Table 2. Textual features of online reviews across four categories.

Category of reviews	Sample size	Polarity	Subjectivity	Readability	Depth
Fake + Helpful	606	Mean: 0.181	Mean: 0.55	Mean: 7.26	Mean: 120.20
		Min: −0.63	Min: 0.23	Min: 1	Min: 38
		Max: 0.78	Max: 0.88	Max: 33	Max: 546
Fake + Unhelpful	497	Mean: 0.15	Mean: 0.55	Mean: 6.42	Mean: 66.64
		Min: −1	Min: 0	Min: 0	Min: 4
		Max: 1	Max: 1	Max: 23	Max: 220
Authentic + Helpful	336	Mean: 0.16	Mean: 0.53	Mean: 7.83	Mean: 138.44
		Min: −0.45	Min: 0.25	Min: 2	Min: 43
		Max: 0.73	Max: 0.90	Max: 31	Max: 581
Authentic + Unhelpful	142	Mean: 0.14	Mean: 0.54	Mean: 6.53	Mean: 69.21
		Min: −0.70	Min: 0	Min: 0	Min: 14
		Max: 0.84	Max: 0.95	Max: 18	Max: 207

There were 942 helpful reviews and 639 unhelpful reviews. Likewise, to balance the dataset, we randomly sampled 639 out of 942 helpful reviews and combined them with unhelpful reviews to build the dataset for training. The proportion of training set and testing set remains at 80–20 for consistency.

Finally, for the joined labels, we balanced the dataset using the same approach. 336 reviews (fake and helpful) were randomly sampled from the original 497 reviews, and together with the 336 reviews (authentic and helpful), were used to build the dataset for training. The proportion of training set and testing set remains consistent at 80–20.

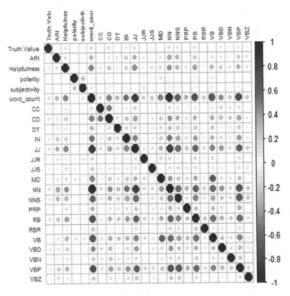

Fig. 1. Correlation plot of the variables

3 Results

A summary of the performance of the machine learning models with the fake and authentic reviews is shown in Table 3. An area under curve ROC (AUC-ROC) graph was drawn to assess the model's ability to distinguish between classes shown in Fig. 2. AUC value of 0.5 suggests that the model does not contain any separation ability. In contrast, a value of 1.0 suggests that it has perfect class label separation. The best performing model was the SVM at 75% accuracy but a slightly lower AUC at 0.84 than the logistic regression at 0.85. This is perhaps due to the over-prediction of authentic reviews from SVM.

Table 3. Performance of each model predicting fake vs. authentic reviews.

Logistic Regression				
	Precision	Recall	F1-score	Support
Fake reviews	0.76	0.72	0.74	130
Authentic reviews	0.72	0.76	0.74	126
Accuracy			0.74	256
Support Vector Machine				
Fake	0.80	0.72	0.75	137
Authentic reviews	0.71	0.79	0.75	119
Accuracy			0.75	256
Random Forest				
Fake	0.78	0.71	0.74	136
Authentic reviews	0.70	0.78	0.74	129
Accuracy			0.74	256

A summary of the performance of the machine learning models with the helpful and unhelpful reviews is shown in Table 4 and the AUC-ROC graph is in Fig. 3. The best performing model seems to be the SVM, with an accuracy of 77% and an AUC of 0.85. However, it does seem that the models differ in their performance only minimally.

A summary of the performance of the machine learning models with the helpful fake reviews and helpful authentic reviews is shown in Table 5 and the AUC-ROC graph is in Fig. 4. The best performing model here was the logistic regression model, but with a low accuracy score of 60%. The overall classifier for all three models only obtained about 60% accuracy, which is not optimal. Hence, TF-IDF was used to delve deeper. The results showed significant differences of discrete emotions in review polarity between the helpful fake reviews and helpful authentic reviews. Specifically, for positive reviews,

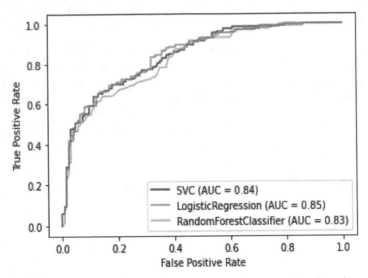

Fig. 2. AUC-ROC curve of 3 models predicting fake vs. authentic reviews.

Table 4. Performance of each model predicting helpful vs. unhelpful reviews.

Logistic Regression				
	Precision	Recall	F1-score	Support
Helpful reviews	0.76	0.73	0.74	91
Unhelpful reviews	0.76	0.79	0.77	108
Accuracy			0.76	199
Support Vector Machine				
Helpful reviews	0.76	0.75	0.76	93
Unhelpful reviews	0.79	0.79	0.79	106
Accuracy			0.77	199
Random Forest				
Helpful reviews	0.72	0.73	0.72	91
Unhelpful reviews	0.77	0.76	0.76	108
Accuracy			0.74	199

helpful fake reviews contained more contents indicative of surprise while authentic helpful ones had moderate emotion words like satisfaction. For negative reviews, helpful fake reviews contained more contents indicative of anger while authentic helpful ones had more anxiety.

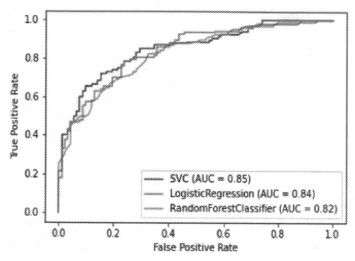

Fig. 3. AUC-ROC curve of 3 models predicting helpful vs. nonhelpful reviews.

Table 5. Performance of each model predicting helpful fake vs. helpful authentic reviews.

Logistic Regression

	Precision	Recall	F1-score	Support
Helpful fake reviews	0.63	0.60	0.61	102
Helpful authentic reviews	0.57	0.60	0.58	90
Accuracy			0.60	192

Support Vector Machine

	Precision	Recall	F1-score	Support
Helpful fake reviews	0.63	0.59	0.61	104
Helpful authentic reviews	0.55	0.59	0.57	88
Accuracy			0.59	192

Random Forest

	Precision	Recall	F1-score	Support
Helpful fake reviews	0.57	0.58	0.57	95
Helpful authentic reviews	0.58	0.57	0.57	97
Accuracy			57	192

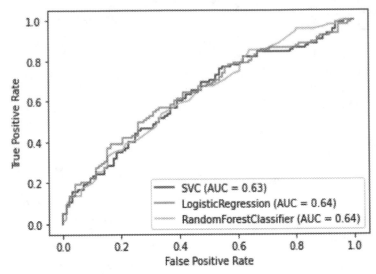

Fig. 4. AUC-ROC curve of 3 models predicting helpful fake vs. helpful authentic reviews.

4   Conclusions

This paper compared the differences between helpful and unhelpful reviews as well as fake and authentic reviews using four textual features: polarity, subjectivity, readability and depth. We examined the performance of three machine learning models containing the four features in three comparisons (helpful vs. unhelpful, fake vs. authentic, and helpful fake vs. helpful authentic). Two important findings can be gleaned from the data analysis.

First, the performance assessments based on three supervised learning algorithms showed that even for fake online reviews, textual features of helpfulness still apply. In particular, subjectivity, readability, and depth help distinguish between helpful and unhelpful reviews. However, it is challenging to distinguish fake helpful ones from a collection of helpful reviews solely based on textual features. This indicates that apart from the review content, who wrote the review also matters [1, 9]. In reality, online reviews are often linked to their reviewers' profiles. Therefore, in assessing fake helpful and authentic helpful online reviews, it is advisable to check the source.

Second, TF-IDF was used to delve deeper into the word differences between helpful fake and helpful authentic reviews. This helped uncover specific frequent words used. The findings suggested that helpful fake reviews were more likely to use harsh words to express emotions such as "surprise" and "angry." In contrast, helpful authentic reviews tended to be modest in emotional expressions, using words such as "satisfaction" or "anxiety." In line with existing literature, fake online reviews are commonly found to be more exaggerated than authentic ones [5, 13].

This paper holds implications for theory and practice. Theoretically, it contributes to the literature in two ways. First, it shows how both fake and authentic reviews can be helpful, thus making them hard to be distinguishable simply based on textual features. Second, the subtle differences in word choices in discrete emotions of the review text could offer telltale signs. Helpful fake reviews are likely to contain more contents indicative of surprise or anger. In terms of practical value, the findings from this paper provide guidance to readers and operators of review platforms to filter out helpful reviews that are likely to be fake.

Some limitations need to be acknowledged. First, the data were drawn from a publicly available secondary dataset [11]. Future research should consider collecting more data with fake and authentic reviews evenly distributed. Second, more features such as reviewer self-disclosure information, review rating, and writing style can be included to yield more interesting findings. In sum, this short paper suggests that although it could be challenging to differentiate between helpful fake and helpful authentic reviews solely using textual features, the review polarity may offer a clue.

Acknowledgments. The authors would like to thank Tengtao Lin, Sung Yang Ho, and Fangyi Shen for their help in data collection and analysis.

References

1. Wu, P.F.: Motivation crowding in online product reviewing: a qualitative study of amazon reviewers. Inf. Manag. **56**, 103163 (2019)
2. Duan, W., Gu, B., Whinston, A.B.: Do online reviews matter?—An empirical investigation of panel data. Decis. Support Syst. **45**, 1007–1016 (2008)
3. Li, X., Hitt, L.M.: Self-selection and information role of online product reviews. Inf. Syst. Res. **19**, 456–474 (2008)
4. Banerjee, S., Chua, A.Y.K.: A theoretical framework to identify authentic online reviews. Online Inf. Rev. **38**, 634–649 (2014)
5. Banerjee, S., Chua, A.Y.K., Kim, J.-J.: Don't be deceived: using linguistic analysis to learn how to discern online review authenticity. J. Assoc. Inf. Sci. Technol. **68**, 1525–1538 (2017)
6. Chua, A.Y.K., Banerjee, S.: Understanding review helpfulness as a function of reviewer reputation, review rating, and review depth. J. Assoc. Inf. Sci. Technol. **66**, 354–362 (2015)
7. Chua, A.Y.K., Banerjee, S.: Helpfulness of user-generated reviews as a function of review sentiment, product type and information quality. Comput. Hum. Behav. **54**, 547–554 (2016)
8. Kuan, K., Hui, K.-L., Prasarnphanich, P., Lai, H.-Y.: What makes a review voted? An empirical investigation of review voting in online review systems. J. Assoc. Inf. Syst. **16**, 48–71 (2015)
9. Ghose, A., Ipeirotis, P.G.: Estimating the helpfulness and economic impact of product reviews. IEEE Trans. Knowl. Data Eng. **23**, 1498–1512 (2011)
10. Dellarocas, C.: Strategic manipulation of internet opinion forums: implications for consumers and firms. Manag. Sci. **52**, 1577–1593 (2006)
11. Salvetti, F.: Boulder lies and truth. https://doi.org/10.35111/tj47-sd65. Accessed 13 Sept 2021
12. Kincaid, J.P., Delionbach, L.J.: Validation of the automated readability index: a follow-up. Hum. Factors: J. Hum. Factors Ergon. Soc. **15**, 17–20 (1973)
13. Banerjee, S.: Exaggeration in fake vs. authentic online reviews for luxury and budget hotels. Int. J. Inf. Manag. **62**, 102416 (2022)

Setting up a Checkpoint for Research on the Prevalence of Journal Data Policies: A Systematic Review

Jian-Sin Lee(✉) (iD)

National Taiwan University, Taipei, Taiwan
jslee19@ntu.edu.tw

Abstract. Openly sharing research data helps ensure research transparency and reproducibility, thus advancing scientific discoveries. As a pivotal player in the scholarly publishing ecosystem, more and more journals adopt data policies to encourage data sharing. Many previous studies have investigated the prevalence of journal data policies (JDPs). However, prior work usually focuses on the policy prevalence in certain disciplines at a specific time. To provide a comprehensive understanding of how JDPs have evolved across scientific areas over time, a systematic literature review was conducted. This study takes a content analysis approach to review 42 empirical studies that examine the prevalence of JDPs and their respective policy emphases. An upward trend was observed in the proportion of journals having data policies over the past two decades. The present study also reveals the policy emphases repeatedly discussed in the literature such as policy strength and suggested data sharing methods. The coding results and a reusable coding frame were made publicly available as a data package via the Open Science Framework (OSF) platform.

Keywords: Journal data policies · Research data sharing · Open science · Systematic literature review

1 Introduction

Scientific discoveries are driven by analyses of data. Openly sharing data generated during the research process enables data reusability, research reproducibility, criticism, and collaboration, thus advancing scientific research [1, 2]. The release of research data also reduces scientists' questionable research practices by enhancing transparency, verifiability, and accountability [3–5]. In spite of such benefits, data sharing remains limited due to a number of barriers, such as insufficient technical support and additional efforts needed [6–9].

To encourage data sharing, since the 2000s and especially in the 2010s, a broad range of stakeholders (e.g., funding agencies, professional societies, institutions, and journal publishers) have established all kinds of guidelines, standards, and even mandates to ensure the accessibility of research data. Some well-known examples include the mandates from the U.S. National Institutes of Health (NIH) and National Science

Foundation (NSF) [10] and the requirements of the International Committee of Medical Journal Editors (ICMJE) [11].

Among these efforts, journals and publishers play a particularly important role owing to the importance of journal publications to academic promotion and tenure. As indicated in Lin and Strasser's work, publishers 'occupy a leverage point in the research process' and can potentially 'effect change by requiring data to be openly and freely available' [12]. Munafò et al. also deemed journals a key player in providing incentives to reward reproducible practices [13].

As more and more journal data policies (JDPs) have been developed, scientists started probing into the nature, adoption, and influences of these policies. For example, Jones et al. explored two leading academic publishers' experience in establishing data policies for their journals and communicating the policies to authors given different disciplinary cultures [14]. Through interviews with journal editors and other scholarly publishing stakeholders in ecology, Scholler et al. indicated that consensus was hardly achieved regarding the enforcement of data archiving policies [15]. Nuijten et al. found that journals' data policies were effective in enabling data sharing but not necessarily associated with fewer reporting inconsistencies in psychology [16].

A lot of these studies revealed the *prevalence* of JDPs, namely the proportion of journals that have data policies in a given context. Such knowledge matters because it sheds light on the roles of journals and publishers in making contributions to a more open scientific community. The landscape of disciplinary norms and progress regarding data sharing practices can be better mapped as well.

However, previous studies often looked into the existence of JDPs in certain disciplines at a specific time. Few studies have unfolded changes in the prevalence of JDPs over time and drawn comparisons among different scientific areas in terms of the evolution of JDPs. Also, given the heterogeneity in data policies provided by different journals, it is unclear about the various approaches applied to analyze and interpret these JDPs and their temporal patterns of change. Filling up these gaps can be undoubtedly essential to inform the future development of better JDPs.

While Rousi and Laakso summarized 14 prior studies investigating the prevalence and a few characteristics of JDPs [17], journal policies on code, algorithms, and supplementary materials were excluded from their scope of analysis. Nonetheless, the importance attached to the release of source code and supplementary materials has continuously increased in recent years [18, 19]. A systematic literature review of research on JDPs in a broad sense is thus considered crucial to provide a comprehensive understanding of the extent to which journals adopt different kinds of data policies and the policy emphases that interest researchers. Accordingly, this study proposes the following research question:

What does the literature on JDPs reveal about 1) the policy prevalence in different disciplines over time, and 2) other patterns in the policy emphases or changes?

To address the research question, this study reviews 42 empirical studies that focus on the prevalence and various policy emphases of JDPs. The Preliminary Results section reports not only the disciplinary and temporal trends captured from the sampled publications, but also the most discussed policy aspects in these publications in terms of their research findings, recommendations to JDP stakeholders, and suggested future work for researchers. Additionally, in an attempt to facilitate similar studies that keep track of progress in implementing JDPs, this study makes its data package available as an Open Science Framework (OSF) project[1]. The data package can serve as an extensible toolkit for researchers to incorporate more relevant publications and perform further analysis. Details about the data released are elaborated in the Methods section.

2   Literature Review

2.1   Coverage, Types, and Sources of Journal Data Policies

In response to the concern that it is suboptimal for researchers to self-police [20], more and more journals and publishers have introduced data policies that fit their communities. Such bottom-up efforts resulted in varied coverage of JDPs, e.g., policy stringency, modes of data sharing, and many other policy aspects [21]. Hrynaszkiewicz et al. proposed JDPs' 14 features, including definitions of research data, embargoes, exceptions to policies, data citation, peer review of data, and so on [22]. The higher the number of features a policy covers, the stronger this policy is considered.

Different names of data policies were also observed, which often reflect the policies' respective foci on their data-related requirements. In their work, Butler and Currier indicated the differences between journals' data availability policies and data preservation policies, where the latter involves more details about long-term preservation such as persistent identifiers and restrictions on file size [23]. Savage and Vickers focused on data sharing policies and found that few journals have explicitly explained their policy enforcement [24]. Cummings et al. used open data policies as an umbrella term referring to those developed by both journals and research organizations [25]. Data archiving policies were found mentioned in studies that examined ecology and evolution journals [26, 27]. In other cases, previous studies cover discussions on data citation policies [28, 29], as well as policies that center on supplementary materials [30, 31] and the inclusion of data availability statements [32, 33].

A relatively special type of JDPs is replication policies, which are more frequently seen in political science, economics, psychology, and quantitative sociology [34]. Alvarez et al. discussed one of the first social science journals that launched replication policies in the mid-1990s and its shift from a voluntary option to a requirement in 2012 [35]. Dafoe recommended journals a series of replication policies with minimal costs [36]. Ishiyama proposed three models for journals to manage replication data and illustrated the debates over sharing data for replication purposes as individual or community responsibilities [34].

It is worth noting that while journals are described to adopt 'data policies', in many cases their data-related requirements are embedded in instructions for authors, submission guidelines, or other general editorial policies, instead of an independent data policy. FAIRsharing (https://fairsharing.org/) is a registry that keeps thousands of records of standards, repositories, and data policies [37]. As of late August 2021, 97 records can be found in its list of JDPs, where most of them are not dedicated data policies.

---

[1] https://osf.io/8bquy/.

By rolling out open science standards and guidelines, stakeholders such as academic societies, journal editors, and working groups from government agencies play a part in encouraging the development of JDPs as well. For example, the National Information Standards Organization (NISO) launched a standard to make policy recommendations on online supplemental journal article materials in 2013 [38]. The Transparency and Openness Promotion (TOP) Guidelines have now been widely used to assess journals' transparency requirements in their policies [39]. The focus group initiating the FAIR Principles actively collaborated with journal editors and publishers in improving their policies [40]. Many journals have also endorsed or complied with the Joint Data Archiving Policy (JDAP) [41] in ecology and evolution, the Data Access and Research Transparency (DA-RT) statement [42] in political science, the ICMJE requirements [11] in medicine, and the commitment of Coalition on Publishing Data in the Earth and Space Sciences (COPDESS) [43], respectively.

2.2 The Implementation of Journal Data Policies

With the many JDPs established, studies have emerged in respect of whether and to what extent JDPs are effective in facilitating data sharing practices. Prior studies provided both positive and negative results. On one hand, strong requirements were found useful for improving access to research data. According to Vines et al., in biological sciences, journal policies that demand the inclusion of a data availability statement in the submissions could increase the odds of discovering the data almost a thousandfold in comparison with having no policies [27]. Key found that in political science, it is 24 times more likely to access replication materials of an article in journals with mandatory policies than in those with no requirements [20]. Similar results were derived by scientists in cognitive science and phylogeny [2, 44].

On the other hand, a study conducted by Alsheikh-Ali et al. in the early 2010s reported that a high proportion of articles published in high-impact journals did not fully stick to the corresponding data availability policies [45]. Gorman's work in 2020 indicated that data sharing was rare in high-impact addiction journals with data sharing policies [46]. Two other studies in biomedicine also observed unsatisfactory data accessibility in articles of which the journals have strong data sharing policies [47] and in preprints with data availability statements, respectively [48].

Some studies have been interested in the incentives that drive researchers to comply with JDPs. Despite the significant association found between data availability and an increased citation rate [49], all kinds of inhibitors exist for researchers to share their data, as discussed in previous work [50, 51]. Consequently, an effective reward system supported by journals can be particularly important. In recent years, a few journals have acknowledged open science practices by offering 'badges' to their published articles, e.g., badges for open data, open materials, and preregistration [52, 53]. It is nonetheless worth reporting that Rowhani-Farid et al. did not find badges noticeably motivating researchers' data sharing behaviors [54]. Besides, van Elk et al. emphasized that badges do not guarantee scientific research's quality and merits [55]. There are also more explorations of journals' possible measures that might ensure researchers' willingness to adhere to data-related requirements, such as the inclusion of data authorship [56] and the use of data registration agencies that enable data citation [57].

3   Methods

3.1   Sampling Procedure

In order to retrieve the greatest number of publications that investigate the prevalence of JDPs, a systematic literature search was first conducted in the following four databases on April 2, 2021: Web of Science, Scopus, ACM Digital Libraries, and PubMed. The first two provide a broad range of publications across various disciplines, while the other two are expected to index the JDP-related publications in computational sciences and biomedicine, where data sharing and reproducibility issues have been rapidly growing topics in recent years [58, 59]. As the fifth source, Google Scholar ensures the comprehensiveness of the publications this study sampled.

Modified from Kitchenham's guidelines on systematic literature review [60], the sampling process of the present study consists of four stages: identification of research, selection of studies, eligibility check, and inclusion, as detailed in the following subsections.

Identification of Research. Given the varying coverage and types of JDPs discussed in the Literature Review section, I developed three search queries that respectively involve the following three themes: openness, reproducibility, and data stewardship. After a few search tests using keywords related to the three themes, the queries were finalized as shown in Table 1. All queries contain the keyword *journal polic**, given the most common wording identified in previous studies.

Table 1. The three queries used in the literature search process.

Themes	Search queries
Openness	(journal polic*) AND (data OR code OR supplementa* materia*) AND (availability OR sharing OR open)
Reproducibility	(journal polic*) AND (data OR code OR supplementa* materia*) AND (reproducibility OR replication)
Data stewardship	(journal polic*) AND ("data archiving" OR "data preservation" OR "data deposit" OR "data management")

The query for the theme *openness* helps to retrieve publications focusing on JDPs that address data accessibility and data sharing practices. The theme *reproducibility* centers on JDPs that encourage reproducible research or the provision of replication materials. Queries for both of these themes take into account different types of research data by including 'data, code, and supplementary materials' as search terms. The third theme, *data stewardship*, integrates several phrases beginning with 'data' and covering management or preservation issues. During the search process, the queries might have been slightly adjusted with different search tips and syntax for the five databases.

For each of the total 15 searches, bibliographic information of the top 100 results sorted by relevance was exported, generating a sampling pool of 1,060 records, given that the numbers of some queries' search results were less than 100.

Selection of Studies. At this stage, I preliminarily scanned the 1,060 records' titles and abstracts to determine their relevance. After discarding those publications with obviously irrelevant topics and those adopting methods other than really looking into journals' policy statements or author guidelines (e.g., those interviewing journal editors about their perceptions of the prevalence of JDPs), ninety-two publications were found potentially suitable for further examination. Most of these records (n = 85) were retrieved from Web of Science, Scopus, and Google Scholar. Forty-eight duplicate records were identified and thus removed. Next, I used the snowballing technique by screening the remaining 44 publications' reference lists, aiming to reach a broader range of relevant publications. Finally, I incorporated 14 additional resources, which resulted in a sample of 58 publications for the eligibility check.

Eligibility Check and Inclusion. This study follows two exclusion criteria to ensure the final sampled publications' quality. The first criterion considers a publication's research focus. Only when the main focus or a healthy proportion of a publication involved the prevalence of JDPs in specified subject areas was the publication kept. Given this criterion, 10 out of the 58 records were excluded due to their limited attention to the referred topics.

The second criterion makes sure that the sampled publications clearly documented their research protocol with sufficient descriptions of the methods used. Specifically, a study was expected to provide details about how the authors selected the journals surveyed, what policies or information they accessed to locate the JDPs, and so on. By applying this criterion, I excluded four publications due to their lack of method descriptions.

After removing two more publications found to be the other two sampled journal articles' conference version, 42 publications were included by this study as its final sample, which is listed in Table S1. Figure 1 shows the aforementioned four-stage sampling process.

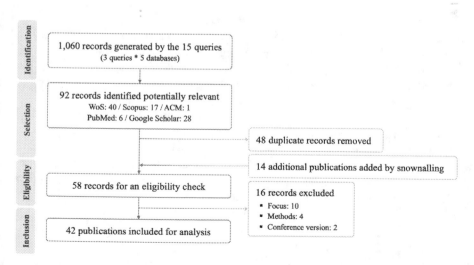

Fig. 1. Stages of the sampling process.

3.2 Data Extraction

This study adopts a content analysis approach to map the landscape of existing research on the prevalence of JDPs. Text in the sampled publications was coded into a number of content categories to identify trends in the development of JDPs over time.

As mentioned previously, the coding results and accompanying materials are openly available as a data package on the OSF platform. Comprising 1) a coding frame with the coding results, 2) a list of variable descriptions, and 3) a set of excerpts extracted from the sampled publications, this data package can be considered an extensible toolkit for future studies to conduct further analysis by incorporating new publications or variables portraying more characteristics of JDPs. The following subsections illustrate the three components of the data package.

Coding Frame. The coding frame consists of 82 fields (i.e., variables) in total if excluding the publication IDs assigned by this study. These variables were categorized into six groups based on their nature. Table 2 demonstrates all the variable names and their associated groups (A to F).

For all the 42 sampled publications, their basic bibliographic information (e.g., title and authors) was first coded into the fields in group A. Variables in group B address the publications' study information, such as sample size (B10), disciplines (B11), and the open science standards (B15) and data repositories (B16) mentioned in a publication. Variables in group C reveal method-related information of the publications, e.g., brief descriptions of how each study's surveyed journals were selected (C17), when the JDPs were collected (C20), and whether the study's research data are available (C22). Variables in groups A, B, and C help to provide background information of each publication so users of the data package can perform different analyses as appropriate and easily know how to interpret the results.

Groups D, E, and F contain binary variables that indicate whether the corresponding policy emphases was discussed in a publication as research results, recommendations, or future work. For example, the variable 'data accessibility' (D28) refers to whether research results concerning journals' expectations of data access were mentioned in a publication, and the variable 'collaboration' (E48) is about whether a publication proposes recommendations on collaboration among JDP stakeholders. Built on the common structure of research articles, variables were categorized into these three groups to respectively reflect the sampled publications' findings, suggestions made for various actors in the scholarly publishing ecosystem, and agendas proposed for future studies.

Using Dedoose, a qualitative data analysis tool, the content-based variables in groups D, E, and F were created with the following coding process. I first carefully went through the sampled publications and once a key policy emphasis was identified, added a *node* to indicate the potential theme associated with the excerpt. In most cases, excerpts were located in publications' Results, Discussion, and Conclusion sections. Until no more new themes could be identified from the text, the nodes were then further clustered or broken up into the final 60 variables in groups D, E, and F.

Table 2. List of the 82 variables.

Groups	Variable names
A. Bibliographic information	1. authors; 2. publication-year; 3. title; 4. resource-type; 5. venue; 6. citation-count; 7. bibliographic-citation
B. Study information	8. author-keywords; 9. objects-of-study; 10. sample-size; 11. disciplines; 12. number-of-disciplines; 13. subject-categories; 14. team-nationality; 15. standards-mentioned; 16. repositories-mentioned
C. Methods	17. sample-selection; 18. sampling-references; 19. index-years; 20. collection-date; 21. journal-info-referenced; 22. data-available
D. Results	23. association-analysis; 24. benefits-of-sharing; 25. compliance; 26. copyright-or-licensing; 27. disciplinary-comparison; 28. data-accessibility; 29. data-citation; 30. data-file-size; 31. data-formats; 32. data-reuse; 33. data-types; 34. documentation; 35. exceptions-to-policies; 36. for-peer-review; 37. guidance-on-data-sharing; 38. how-long-to-be-retained; 39. language-or-terminology; 40. location-of-policies; 41. policy-sources; 42. policy-strength; 43. prevalence; 44. reproducibility; 45. sharing-methods; 46. when-to-deposit-or-share
E. Recommendations	47. benefits-of-sharing; 48. collaboration; 49. compliance; 50. copyright-or-licensing; 51. data-accessibility; 52. data-citation; 53. data-file-size; 54. data-formats; 55. data-reuse; 56. data-types; 57. documentation; 58. exceptions-to-policies; 59. for-peer-review; 60. guidance-on-data-sharing; 61. language-or-terminology; 62. location-of-policies; 63. policy-sources; 64. policy-strength; 65. reproducibility; 66. sensitive-data; 67. sharing-methods; 68. standardization; 69. when-to-deposit-or-share
F. Future work	70. association-analysis; 71. compliance; 72. disciplinary-comparison; 73. data-accessibility; 74. data-types; 75. documentation; 76. for-peer-review; 77. guidance-on-data-sharing; 78. perspectives-and-practices; 79. policy-sources; 80. policy-strength; 81. reproducibility; 82. sharing-methods

Variable Descriptions. Along with the coding frame, a list of variable descriptions was compiled into the data package. The list presents the explanations of all the 82 variables, as well as the group and unique identifier assigned to each of them.

Excerpts. The third component of the data package is a spreadsheet containing the excerpts extracted from the sampled publications. These excerpts show the corresponding text in a publication when a certain variable in groups D, E, or F associated with this publication was coded as 1 (i.e., the publication has discussed the policy emphasis to which the variable refers).

4   Preliminary Results

In this section, I first present a descriptive overview of the 42 sampled publications shown in Table S1. The second, third, and fourth subsections then respectively reveal the three most high-frequency variables in groups D, E, and F, i.e., the three most discussed aspects of the publications' 1) research findings regarding the policy prevalence and emphases, 2) recommendations for JDP stakeholders, and 3) suggested future work for researchers.

4.1   Overview of the Sample

A majority of the 42 publications are journal articles (n = 35) and were published after 2012 (n = 36). Half of the studies (n = 21) were conducted by research teams from the U.S., 18 from Europe (five from Germany and Spain each), and three from the Asia-Pacific region.

In the coding frame, the 'subject categories' field (i.e., the B13 variable displayed in Table 2) was used to record in which subject areas the journal policies were investigated, according to the publications' descriptions of their surveyed journals. This study categorized all the disciplines mentioned in the publications into four subject areas: arts & humanities (AH), biomedicine (BM), sciences (SC), and social sciences (SS). Within the sample, 25 publications study data policies of biomedical journals, 19 of social sciences, 14 of sciences, and two of arts & humanities. Note that there are 13 publications simultaneously surveying JDPs in more than one subject area.

In terms of sampling methods, nearly two-thirds (n = 26) of the publications referred to the Journal Citation Reports (JCR) as a criterion to sample their journals. Some other criteria include self-compiled journal lists as well as citation indices and journal directories from other services. Beyond the existing lists, 17 publications further built subsets of journals using rankings, impact factors, and citation counts.

Regarding data availability, more than half (n = 22) of the publications have provided a link to their research data, despite the three with an invalid link or missing data files.

4.2   Findings on the Prevalence and Policy Emphases of JDPs

Figure 2 is a scatter plot that shows the prevalence of JDPs (i.e., the D43 variable) over time revealed by each of the sampled publications. The identifiers listed in the dots are directed to the corresponding publication IDs within the coding results and the index numbers in this study's reference list [P1–P42]. The color of a dot represents the subject area where the journals surveyed in a sampled publication are.

The prevalence (i.e., the y-axis) in Fig. 2 was calculated by deducting the proportion of journals that have no data policies from 100%. In other words, journals that only implicitly encourage data sharing were also treated as those with data policies. Considering possible publication delays, the year values on the x-axis were estimated based on facts such as when the authors collected the JDPs and when the referred journal lists were released. A publication's assigned year value presented in the figure might thus be inconsistent with its publication year. More details are provided through the notes attached in the figure.

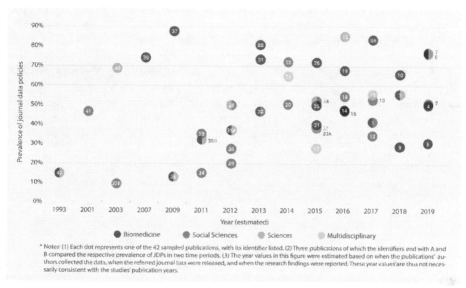

Fig. 2. An overview of the prevalence of JDPs derived from the 42 publications. A full version of this figure that contains more information is available in the OSF project.

Overall, an upward trend in the prevalence of JDPs can be observed in both social sciences and sciences. Biomedical journals were found to have set the highest benchmark over the years. The three most frequently discussed aspects of JDPs in the 42 publications' findings are presented as follows, along with the variable IDs and the numbers of publications mentioning the aspects.

D42. Policy Strength (n = 30). Unlike the pattern in Fig. 2 showing that more biomedical journals adopt JDPs when compared with other subject areas, there is no notable difference between biomedicine and social sciences (i.e., the two subject areas with sufficient sample size addressing the D42 variable) concerning policy strength. In most cases, the proportion of journals with strong data policies varies by discipline and more conditions set in individual studies. A few publications in the sample, however, did point out that biomedical journals tend to have stronger data policies than social science and science journals do [P1, P3, P5]. Additionally, in social sciences, it seems that economics and political science journals are more likely to have strong data policies [P13, P23, P34, P36], especially in comparison to journals in sociology [P13, P32].

D45. Sharing Methods (n = 28). In biomedicine, journals usually suggest researchers deposit data into public (or institutional in some cases) data repositories (n = 10), e.g., [P6, P25, P26]. Frequently mentioned generalist data repositories include Dryad, Figshare, and Mendeley Data. Domain-specific data repositories in biomedicine such as GenBank and Gene Expression Omnibus (GEO) are more common than those in social sciences, where ICPSR serves as a representative. Social science (especially economics) journals sometimes recommended journal-hosted websites or data archives instead [P18, P29, P36]. Deposition into institutional or personal websites and data sharing upon request are rarely encouraged in general [P8, P23]. Overall, journals' requirements concerning data sharing methods in all the subject areas seem to gradually converge towards using public data repositories instead of journal-hosted platforms.

D23. Association Analysis (n = 27). The sampled publications also substantially focused on the associations between different journal characteristics (e.g., journal quality, publishers, access types, age, language, regions, and mentions of reproducibility and analogous concepts) and the presence of JDPs. Among the 23 publications paying attention to journal impact factors (Ifs) and rankings, 15 found that high-IF or highly ranked journals are more likely to have some kinds of data policies, e.g., [P11, P29, P36]. Eight studies concluded that IFs or rankings are positively associated with the strength of JDPs, e.g., [P6, P18, P37], while there is also a study suggesting that business journals with stricter data policies tend to have lower Ifs [P2]. Regarding types of publishers, studies after 2012 reported that major publishers such as Elsevier and Wiley are more likely to implement JDPs [P3, P6, P33, P35], but in the early years, academic societies performed better [P39, P42].

4.3   Recommendations for JDP Stakeholders

On top of their research findings, the sampled publications have proposed a number of recommendations for JDP stakeholders (mostly publishers, journals, and researchers) to achieve better implementation of JDPs and data sharing practices. Followed are the three most commonly seen policy aspects of those recommendations.

E67. Sharing Methods (n = 14). Half of the publications that made suggestions on data sharing methods (n = 7) focused on social science journals. By and large, nine out of the 14 publications explicitly recommended establishing or adopting dedicated data repositories as a desired solution, e.g., [P5, P33, P34]. Some mentioned data journals [P14] and emphasized institutional data repositories as an essential option for long-term access and data citation [P25]. Other relevant recommendations include taking into account data repositories' quality, usability, and derived efforts for users [P15, P18, P29], providing lists of recommended repositories by journals [P17, P32], and making clear statements in JDPs on where and how to share data [P19, P28].

E64. Policy Strength (n = 12). Eleven out of these 12 publications suggested journals make data sharing mandatory, e.g., [P10, P11, P36]. Two of them even recommended data sharing to be a condition for publishing papers in journals [P21, P34]. These kinds of measures were considered helpful given that researchers rarely volunteer to share their data [P38]. As an exception, Sturges and colleagues [P28] proposed a model JDP and stated that such policies should address exemptions, procedures for closed access, and so on for certain types of data (e.g., sensitive ones) by reasonably allowing journals to merely encourage data sharing.

E49. Compliance (n = 11). To make sure that authors satisfactorily comply with JDPs, a quarter of the sampled publications recommended journals to deliver clear instructions on expectations for policy compliance in JDPs [P1, P7, P28], develop mechanisms to check whether JDPs are consistently followed during the editorial processes [P24, P33, P36, P37], or introduce sanctions against noncompliance with JDPs [P28]. Two studies even encouraged continuous audits of JDP enforcement, which might serve as a better indicator beyond impact factors to evaluate journal quality [P4, P6].

4.4 Suggested Future Work for Researchers

More than half of the sampled publications (n = 24) suggested future work for researchers interested in JDPs. The three most frequently recommended areas for future studies are shown below.

F78. Perspectives and Practices (n = 16). These publications recommended future studies to explore the perspectives and practices of two groups of JDP stakeholders: authors/researchers and journals/editors/publishers, as displayed in Table S2.

F71. Compliance (n = 10). These publications sought to probe into researchers' compliance with JDPs by 'narrowing the analytical focus from journals to individual articles' [P34]. Specifically, six studies suggested examining the actual data sharing practices at the article level after JDPs were implemented [P2, P17, P20, P34, P35, P39]. There are also studies attached great importance to understanding whether stronger policies really ensure compliance better [P3, P17, P22] as well as to what extent publishing entities enforce JDPs and pay attention to noncompliant submissions [P34, P42].

F70. Association Analysis (n = 7). One-sixth of the sampled publications suggested exploring more factors that might influence the prevalence and strength of JDPs. Five of them emphasized that journal characteristics such as publishers, languages used, and the number of empirical studies published in a journal could potentially affect the existence or strictness of JDPs [P3, P18, P35, P39, P42]. Other factors mentioned include IFs and rankings [P2, P42], disciplines of journals [P35, P39], and funding agencies' requirements [P26].

5 Discussion

5.1 Trends, Shifts, and Heterogeneity in JDPs

Based on prior work investigating the prevalence of JDPs over the past two decades, an upward trend can be observed in the proportion of journals adopting JDPs, especially those in social sciences and sciences. An average higher prevalence of JDPs has been noted in biomedical journals and well echoed the relatively advanced data sharing culture in biomedicine [61]. More than 85% of the sampled publications were published after 2012, which could be an indicator of the growing policy movement and the increasing awareness of having researchers share research data when publishing papers in journals since the 2010s.

Several shifts identified in the characteristics of JDPs are worth mentioning. In particular, the verb 'allow' used in Schaffer and Jackson's work [P40] implies journals' attitudes toward the submitted supplementary materials in the early 2000s when compared with the verbs 'require' and 'encourage' used in other studies afterward. Regarding data sharing methods, Hrynaszkiewicz and colleagues [62] considered data repositories an alternative to journal-hosted platforms for depositing data in the late 2000s, while the former serves as a more common solution nowadays.

Despite the seemingly promising progress summarized above, insufficient prevalence of JDPs can still be noted in certain disciplines, e.g., dentistry [P9]. Studies on this topic also face challenges in mapping a clear landscape of JDPs due to substantial heterogeneity found in these policies. The heterogeneity is often reflected by different policy characteristics such as policy names, definitions of 'research data', criteria for a 'strong' policy, and data types involved. For example, there are JDPs using the umbrella term 'supplementary materials' [P25], whereas there are also those dedicated to specific kinds of research outputs, such as program code [P35] or microarrays data [P39].

Even researchers have different understandings and perspectives on the JDPs they surveyed. A notable example is that most of the sampled publications focused on policies concerning only 'data' other than the derived manuscripts, while Aleixandre-Benavent and colleagues considered both article content and raw data when scoping 'open-data policies' as their object of study [P8, P15, P20, P30]. All these discrepancies reveal a long way to go for reaching a shared understanding of JDPs and the fruitful results they can bring to the scientific community.

5.2 Policy Implications

A number of frequently discussed policy issues in the sample have the following implications for improving how JDPs are developed.

Clearly Communicate What Happens if Authors Do Not Comply with JDPs. Most of the publications paying attention to compliance issues indicated that JDPs seldom specify the consequences of noncompliance [P6, P28, P33]. Beyond simply including data-related instructions, detailed statements in JDPs on the monitoring mechanisms and sanctions against noncompliance would be beneficial to authors. Exceptions to policy are also important, such as when explanations for not sharing data are acceptable. For better enforcement of all such measures, journals are suggested to consider more about building a sustainable model to minimize the derived costs.

Follow Best Practices and Avoid Language Ambiguity in JDPs. Standardization issues such as imprecise or loosely interpreted requirements [P10] and vague policy language [P1] are also considered common obstacles to the execution of JDPs. When drafting or refining JDPs, more clarity and uniformity could be achieved by referring to the best practices and policy templates from publishers, professional associations, and data repositories with successful experiences in implementing similar policies. Direct collaboration with these stakeholders helps as well, such as integrating repositories' deposit procedures and services into the submission process or building dedicated editorial teams for specific topics in open science.

Consider Researchers' Perspectives and Academic Incentives When Developing JDPs. The mere existence of JDPs does not guarantee more open science practices in the scientific community. As indicated by Anagnostou et al., scientists' own awareness and expectations may complement stakeholders' policies and lead to higher sharing rates [63]. To enhance researchers' voluntary adherence to JDPs, during the policy design or refinement process, journals should better understand the incentives and challenges that respectively drive and impede researchers' willingness to share data. Such a goal might be achieved by regularly distributing surveys to reveal authors' satisfaction and expectations toward a journal's data policies.

5.3 Limitations

This study did not analyze journal policies that address other themes in open science such as preregistration, clinical trial registration, and reporting guidelines, although these themes were sometimes examined together with research data and may involve the collection, processing, and presentation of data [64–66]. The visualization in Fig. 2 should be carefully interpreted due to the estimated year values explained previously and the sampled publications' different definitions and inclusion criteria for JDPs. Users of the data package might find it necessary to refer back to the source text when visiting the excerpts because of the lack of context in some cases. Lastly, introducing a second coder to collectively perform the content analysis would establish stronger reliability of the coding results.

6 Concluding Remarks and Future Work

This study reviews 42 publications concerning the prevalence of journal data policies, unfolding the disciplinary and temporal patterns of these policies over the past two decades. The analysis shows journals' increasing adoption of data policies across different subject areas. The strictness of JDPs and the recommended data sharing methods were found to be the two most frequently discussed policy emphases in the sampled publications. By and large, literature on the prevalence of JDPs suggested more subsequent studies on JDP stakeholders' perspectives and practices. Additionally, this study provides a data package that allows more investigators to conduct further analysis of the existing literature or develop their own research agenda based on the coding frame.

Beyond the existence of JDPs, actual compliance matters as well. Moving forward, future directions of this study include regularly incorporating the latest literature on policy prevalence into the data package and following the same protocol to review the literature on researchers' compliance with JDPs at the article level. Another interesting application could be developing classifiers to automatically identify different types of JDPs, such as those with greater strength or involving various open science-related requirements.

Acknowledgements. I thank Dr. Carole Palmer for providing consultation on the journal data policy literature and content analysis process and all the reviewers for their valuable feedback. This work was partially supported by the Ministry of Science and Technology (MOST) in Taiwan, under MOST 111-2636-H-002-004-.

Appendices

Table S1. List of the 42 publications sampled in this study.

ID	Publication
P1	Christian, T. M., Gooch, A., Vision, T., Hull, E.: Journal data policies: Exploring how the understanding of editors and authors corresponds to the policies themselves. PLoS ONE 15(3), e0230281 (2020)
P2	Dosch, B., Martindale, T.: Reading the fine print: A review and analysis of business journals' data sharing policies. Journal of Business & Finance Librarianship 25(3–4), 261–280 (2020)
P3	Kim, J., Kim, S., Cho, H. M., Chang, J. H., Kim, S. Y.: Data sharing policies of journals in life, health, and physical sciences indexed in Journal Citation Reports. PeerJ 8, e9924 (2020)
P4	Lombard, N., Gasmi, A., Sulpice, L., Boudjema, K., Naudet, F., Bergeat, D.: Research transparency promotion by surgical journals publishing randomised controlled trials: A survey. Trials 21(1), 1–7 (2020)
P5	Rousi, A. M., Laakso, M.: Journal research data sharing policies: A study of highly-cited journals in neuroscience, physics, and operations research. Scientometrics 124(1), 131–152 (2020)
P6	Siebert, M., Gaba, J. F., Caquelin, L., Gouraud, H., Dupuy, A., Moher, D., Naudet, F.: Data-sharing recommendations in biomedical journals and randomised controlled trials: An audit of journals following the ICMJE recommendations. BMJ open 10(5), e038887 (2020)
P7	Wiley, C.: Data sharing: An analysis of medical faculty journals and articles. Science & Technology Libraries 40(1), 104–115 (2020)

(continued)

Table S1. (*continued*)

ID	Publication
P8	Aleixandre-Benavent, R., Sapena, A. F., Ferrer, S. C., Peset, F., García, A. G.: Policies regarding public availability of published research data in pediatrics journals. Scientometrics 118(2), 439–451 (2019)
P9	Almaqrami, B. S., Hua, F., Liu, Y., He, H.: Research waste-related editorial policies of leading dental journals: Situation 2018. Oral diseases 26(3), 696–706 (2019)
P10	Nutu, D., Gentili, C., Naudet, F., Cristea, I. A.: Open science practices in clinical psychology journals: An audit study. Journal of Abnormal Psychology 128(6), 510 (2019)
P11	Resnik, D. B., Morales, M., Landrum, R., Shi, M., Minnier, J., Vasilevsky, N. A., Champieux, R. E.: Effect of impact factor and discipline on journal data sharing policies. Accountability in Research 26(3), 139–156 (2019)
P12	Butler, C. R., Currier, B. D.: You can't replicate what you can't find: Data preservation policies in economic journals. In: The 2017 Annual International Association for Social Science Information Services & Technology (IASSIST) Conference (Presentation). Lawrence, KS (2018). Available at http://doi.org/10.17605/OSF.IO/HF3DS
P13	Crosas, M., Gautier, J., Karcher, S., Kirilova, D., Otalora, G., Schwartz, A.: Data policies of highly-ranked social science journals. SocArXiv (2018). Available at https://doi.org/ https://doi.org/10.31235/osf.io/9h7ay
P14	Johnson, J. N., Hanson, K. A., Jones, C. A., Grandhi, R., Guerrero, J., Rodriguez, J. S.: Data Sharing in neurosurgery and neurology journals. Cureus 10(5), e2680 (2018)
P15	Vidal-Infer, A., Tarazona, B., Alonso-Arroyo, A., Aleixandre-Benavent, R.: Public availability of research data in dentistry journals indexed in Journal Citation Reports. Clinical Oral Investigations 22(1), 275–280 (2018)
P16	Wiley, C.: Data sharing and engineering faculty: An analysis of selected publications. Science & Technology Libraries 37(4), 409–419 (2018)
P17	Castro, E., Crosas, M., Garnett, A., Sheridan, K., Altman, M.: Evaluating and promoting open data practices in open access journals. Journal of Scholarly Publishing 49(1), 66–88 (2017)
P18	Höffler, J. H.: Replication and economics journal policies. American Economic Re-view 107(5), 52–55 (2017)
P19	Vasilevsky, N. A., Minnier, J., Haendel, M. A., Champieux, R. E.: Reproducible and reusable research: Are journal data sharing policies meeting the mark?. PeerJ 5, e3208 (2017)
P20	Aleixandre-Benavent, R., Moreno-Solano, L. M., Sapena, A. F., Pérez, E. A. S.: Correlation between impact factor and public availability of published research data in In-formation Science and Library Science journals. Scientometrics 107(1), 1–13 (2016)
P21	Barbui, C.: Sharing all types of clinical data and harmonizing journal standards. BMC medicine 14(1), 1–3 (2016)
P22	Blahous, B., Gorraiz, J., Gumpenberger, C., Lehner, O., Ulrych, U.: Data policies in journals under scrutiny: Their strength, scope and impact. Bibliometrie-Praxis und Forschung 5, bpf269 (2016)

(*continued*)

Table S1. (*continued*)

ID	Publication
P23	Herndon, J., O'Reilly, R.: Data sharing policies in social sciences academic journals: Evolving expectations of data sharing as a form of scholarly communication. In: Kellam, L., Thompson, K. (eds.) Databrarianship: The academic data librarian in theory and practice. Association of College and Research Libraries, Chicago, IL (2016)
P24	Naughton, L., Kernohan, D.: Making sense of journal research data policies. Insights 29(1), 84–89 (2016)
P25	Williams, S. C.: Practices, policies, and persistence: A study of supplementary materials in crop science journals. Journal of Agricultural & Food Information 17(1), 11–22 (2016)
P26	Charbonneau, D. H., Beaudoin, J. E.: State of data guidance in journal policies: A case study in oncology. International Journal of Digital Curation 10(2), 136–156 (2016)
P27	Fear, K.: Building outreach on assessment: Researcher compliance with journal policies for data sharing. Bulletin of the Association for Information Science and Technology 41(6), 18–21 (2015)
P28	Sturges, P., Bamkin, M., Anders, J. H., Hubbard, B., Hussain, A., Heeley, M.: Research data sharing: Developing a stakeholder-driven model for journal policies. Journal of the Association for Information Science and Technology 66(12), 2445–2455 (2015)
P29	Vlaeminck, S., Herrmann, L. K.: Data policies and data archives: A new paradigm for academic publishing in economic sciences?. In: Proceedings of the 19th International Conference on Electronic Publishing, pp. 145–155. IOS Press BV (2015)
P30	Aleixandre-Benavent, R., Vidal-Infer, A., Alonso Arroyo, A., Valderrama Zurian, J. C., Bueno Cañigral, F., Ferrer Sapena, A.: Public availability of published research data in substance abuse journals. International Journal of Drug Policy 25(6), 1143–1146 (2014)
P31	Hoffmann, T., English, T., Glasziou, P.: Reporting of interventions in randomised trials: An audit of journal instructions to authors. Trials 15(1), 1–6 (2014)
P32	Zenk-Möltgen, W., Lepthien, G.: Data sharing in sociology journals. Online Information Review 38(6), 709–722 (2014)
P33	Borrego, Á., Garcia, F.: Provision of supplementary materials in library and information science scholarly journals. Aslib Proceedings: New Information Perspectives 65(5), 503–514 (2013)
P34	Gherghina, S., Katsanidou, A.: Data availability in political science journals. European Political Science 12, 333–349 (2013)
P35	Stodden, V., Guo, P., Ma, Z.: Toward reproducible computational research: An empirical analysis of data and code policy adoption by journals. PLoS ONE 8(6), e67111 (2013)
P36	Vlaeminck, S.: Data management in scholarly journals and possible roles for libraries–Some insights from EDaWaX. Liber Quarterly 23(1), 48–79 (2013)
P37	Alsheikh-Ali, A. A., Qureshi, W., Al-Mallah, M. H., Ioannidis, J. P.: Public availability of published research data in high-impact journals. PLoS ONE 6(9), e24357 (2011)
P38	Weber, N. M., Piwowar, H. A., Vision, T. J.: Evaluating data citation and sharing policies in the environmental sciences. In: Proceedings of the American Society for Information Science and Technology 47(1), 1–2 (2010)

(*continued*)

Table S1. (*continued*)

ID	Publication
P39	Piwowar, H., Chapman, W.: A review of journal policies for sharing research data. Nature Precedings (2008). Available at http://precedings.nature.com/documents/1700/version/1
P40	Schaffer, T., Jackson, K. M.: The use of online supplementary material in high-impact scientific journals. Science & Technology Libraries 25(1–2), 73–85 (2004)
P41	Gleditsch, N. Metelits, C.: Replication in international relations journals: Policies and practices. International Studies Perspective 4, 72–79 (2003)
P42	McCain, K. W.: Mandating sharing: Journal policies in the natural sciences. Science Communication 16(4), 403–431 (1995)

Table S2. Suggested future work on JDP stakeholders' perspectives and practices.

	Authors/Researchers (n = 13)	Journals/Editors/Publishers (n = 9)
Perspectives (n = 8)	• Researchers' perceived incentives and barriers concerning data sharing and reuse [P7, P8, P15, P30, P34, P42] • Researchers' understanding of key concepts related to data sharing such as accessibility, reusability, and preservation [P7, P8, P15, P30] • Researchers' views and awareness of JDPs [P26, P38] • Researchers' attitudes towards data sharing requirements and information needs for data access [P42]	• Journal editors' views on data policies and data sharing [P26, P42]
Practices (n = 15)	• Researchers' practices regarding data sharing, accessibility, reusability, preservation, and so on [P8, P20, P30, P34] • How and to what extent JDPs change authors' and researchers' behaviors [P16, P26, P38, P39] • the nature and open science-related features of published data [P4, P20] • Experiences of and challenges faced by researchers who shared or did not share data and who acted as data requesters [P24, P42] • Authors' expected target audience and their corresponding data sharing practices [P7]	• How journals actually enforce their data policies and interact with the submitted data [P8, P15, P16, P38, P40] • The reasons why journals (do not) implement or change their data policies and the impact [P16, P35] • Whether improvements in JDPs really make policy implementation more effective [P1] • The proportion of journals that mandate data sharing in certain disciplines [P42]

References

1. Resnik, D.B., et al.: Effect of impact factor and discipline on journal data sharing policies. Account. Res. **26**(3), 139–156 (2019)
2. Hardwicke, T.E., et al.: Data availability, reusability, and analytic reproducibility: evaluating the impact of a mandatory open data policy at the journal cognition. Roy. Soc. Open Sci. **5**(8), 180448 (2018)
3. Aguinis, H., Ramani, R.S., Alabduljader, N.: What you see is what you get? Enhancing methodological transparency in management research. Acad. Manag. Ann. **12**(1), 83–110 (2018)
4. Glick, J.L., Shamoo, A.E.: A call for the development of "Good Research Practices" (GRP) guidelines. Account. Res. **2**(4), 231–235 (1993)
5. Sijtsma, K.: Playing with data—Or how to discourage questionable research practices and stimulate researchers to do things right. Psychometrika **81**(1), 1–15 (2016)
6. Tedersoo, L., et al.: Data sharing practices and data availability upon request differ across scientific disciplines. Sci. Data **8**(1), 1–11 (2021)
7. Tenopir, C., et al.: Data sharing, management, use, and reuse: Practices and perceptions of scientists worldwide. PLoS ONE **15**(3), e0229003 (2020)
8. Sayogo, D.S., Pardo, T.A.: Exploring the determinants of scientific data sharing: understanding the motivation to publish research data. Gov. Inf. Q. **30**, S19–S31 (2013)
9. Yan, A., Huang, C., Lee, J.S., Palmer, C.L.: Cross-disciplinary data practices in earth system science: Aligning services with reuse and reproducibility priorities. Proc. Assoc. Inf. Sci. Technol. **57**(1), e218 (2020)
10. Keralis, S.D., Stark, S., Halbert, M., Moen, W.E.: Research data management in policy and practice: the DataRes project. In: Research data management: Principles, practice, and prospects, pp. 16–38. Council on Library and Information Resources Publication, Washington, DC (2013)
11. Taichman, D.B., et al.: Data sharing statements for clinical trials: a requirement of the international committee of medical journal editors. Ann. Intern. Med. **167**(1), 63–65 (2017)
12. Lin, J., Strasser, C.: Recommendations for the role of publishers in access to data. PLoS Biol. **12**(10), e1001975 (2014)
13. Munafò, M.R., et al.: A manifesto for reproducible science. Nat. Hum. Behav. **1**(1), 1–9 (2017)
14. Jones, L., Grant, R., Hrynaszkiewicz, I.: Implementing publisher policies that inform, support and encourage authors to share data: two case studies. Insights **32**(11), 1–11 (2019)
15. Sholler, D., Ram, K., Boettiger, C., Katz, D.S.: Enforcing public data archiving policies in academic publishing: A study of ecology journals. Big Data Soc. **6**(1), 1–18 (2019). 205395171983-6258
16. Nuijten, M.B., et al.: Journal data sharing policies and statistical reporting inconsistencies in psychology. Collabra: Psychol. **3**(1), 31 (2017)
17. Rousi, A.M., Laakso, M.: Journal research data sharing policies: a study of highly-cited journals in neuroscience, physics, and operations research. Scientometrics **124**(1), 131–152 (2020)
18. McKiernan, E.C., et al.: Point of view: how open science helps researchers succeed. eLife **5**, e16800 (2016)
19. Price, A., Schroter, S., Clarke, M., McAneney, H.: Role of supplementary material in biomedical journal articles: Surveys of authors, reviewers and readers. BMJ Open **8**(9), e021753 (2018)
20. Key, E.M.: How are we doing? Data access and replication in political science. PS: Polit. Sci. Polit. **49**(2), 268–272 (2016)

21. Jones, S.: Research data policies: principles, requirements and trends. In: Pryor, G. (eds.) Managing Research Data, pp. 47–66. Facet Publishing (2012)
22. Hrynaszkiewicz, I., Simons, N., Hussain, A., Grant, R., Goudie, S.: Developing a research data policy framework for all journals and publishers. Data Sci. J. **19**(1), 5 (2020)
23. Butler, C.R., Currier, B.D.: You can't replicate what you can't find: data preservation policies in economic journals. In: The 2017 Annual International Association for Social Science Information Services & Technology (IASSIST) Conference (Presentation), Lawrence, KS (2018). https://doi.org/10.17605/OSF.IO/HF3DS
24. Savage, C.J., Vickers, A.J.: Empirical study of data sharing by authors publishing in PLoS journals. PLoS ONE **4**(9), e7078 (2009)
25. Cummings, J.A., Zagrodney, J.M., Day, T.E.: Impact of open data policies on consent to participate in human subjects research: discrepancies between participant action and reported concerns. PLoS ONE **10**(5), e0125208 (2015)
26. Whitlock, M.C.: Data archiving in ecology and evolution: best practices. Trends Ecol. Evol. **26**(2), 61–65 (2011)
27. Vines, T.H., et al.: Mandated data archiving greatly improves access to research data. FASEB J. **27**(4), 1304–1308 (2013)
28. Lammey, R.: How publishers can work with crossref on data citation. Sci. Ed. **6**(6), 166–170 (2019)
29. Federer, L.: Measuring and mapping data reuse: findings from an interactive workshop on data citation and metrics for data reuse. Harv. Data Sci. Rev. (2020). https://doi.org/10.1162/99608f92.ccd17b00
30. Krawczyk, M., Reuben, E.: (Un)available upon request: field experiment on researchers' willingness to share supplementary materials. Account. Res. **19**(3), 175–186 (2012)
31. Kenyon, J., Sprague, N.R.: Trends in the use of supplementary materials in environmental science journals. Issues Sci. Technol. Librariansh. **75**, 72–75 (2014)
32. Federer, L.M., et al.: Data sharing in PLoS ONE: an analysis of data availability statements. PLoS ONE **13**(5), e0194768 (2018)
33. Grant, R., Hrynaszkiewicz, I.: The impact on authors and editors of introducing data availability statements at nature journals. Int. J. Digit. Curation **13**(1), 195–203 (2018)
34. Ishiyama, J.: Replication, research transparency, and journal publications: Individualism, community models, and the future of replication studies. PS: Polit. Sci. Polit. **47**(1), 78–83 (2014)
35. Alvarez, R.M., Key, E.M., Núñez, L.: Research replication: practical considerations. PS: Polit. Sci. Polit. **51**(2), 422–426 (2018)
36. Dafoe, A.: Science deserves better: the imperative to share complete replication files. PS: Polit. Sci. Polit. **47**(1), 60–66 (2014)
37. Sansone, S.A., et al.: FAIRsharing as a community approach to standards, repositories and policies. Nat. Biotechnol. **37**(4), 358–367 (2019)
38. NISO RP-15-2013, Recommended Practices for Online Supplemental Journal Article Materials. http://www.niso.org/publications/niso-rp-15-2013-recommended-practices-online-supplemental-journal-article-materials. Accessed 06 Sept 2021
39. Nosek, B.A., et al.: Promoting an open research culture. Science **348**(6242), 1422–1425 (2015)
40. Wilkinson, M.D., Sansone, S.A., Schultes, E., Doorn, P., da Silva Santos, L.O.B., Dumontier, M.: A design framework and exemplar metrics for FAIRness. Sci. Data **5**(1), 1–4 (2018)
41. Baker, C.S.: Journal of heredity adopts joint data archiving policy. J. Hered. **104**(1), 1 (2013)
42. European Political Science Association: Data Access and Research Transparency (DA-RT): a joint statement by political science journal editors. Polit. Sci. Res. Methods **3**(3), 421 (2015)

43. Commitment statement in the earth, space, and environmental sciences. http://www.cop dess.org/enabling-fair-data-project/commitment-to-enabling-fair-data-in-the-earth-space-and-environmental-sciences/. Accessed 06 Sept 2021

44. Magee, A.F., May, M.R., Moore, B.R.: The dawn of open access to phylogenetic data. PLoS ONE **9**(10), e110268 (2014)

45. Alsheikh-Ali, A.A., Qureshi, W., Al-Mallah, M.H., Ioannidis, J.P.: Public availability of published research data in high-impact journals. PLoS ONE **6**(9), e24357 (2011)

46. Gorman, D.M.: Availability of research data in high-impact addiction journals with data sharing policies. Sci. Eng. Ethics **26**(3), 1625–1632 (2020)

47. Naudet, F., et al.: Data sharing and reanalysis of randomized controlled trials in leading biomedical journals with a full data sharing policy: survey of studies published in The BMJ and PLoS Medicine. BMJ **360**, k400 (2018)

48. McGuinness, L.A., Sheppard, A.L.: A descriptive analysis of the data availability statements accompanying medRxiv preprints and a comparison with their published counterparts. PLoS ONE **16**(5), e0250887 (2021)

49. Piwowar, H.A., Day, R.S., Fridsma, D.B.: Sharing detailed research data is associated with increased citation rate. PLoS ONE **2**(3), e308 (2007)

50. Borgman, C.L.: The conundrum of sharing research data. J. Am. Soc. Inform. Sci. Technol. **63**(6), 1059–1078 (2012)

51. Zuiderwijk, A., Shinde, R., Jeng, W.: What drives and inhibits researchers to share and use open research data? A systematic literature review to analyze factors influencing open research data adoption. PLoS ONE **15**(9), e0239283 (2020)

52. Kidwell, M.C., et al.: Badges to acknowledge open practices: a simple, low-cost, effective method for increasing transparency. PLoS Biol. **14**(5), e1002456 (2016)

53. Schweitzer, B., Schulz, J.B.: Open science badges in the journal of neurochemistry. J. Neurochem. **147**, 132–136 (2018)

54. Rowhani-Farid, A., Aldcroft, A., Barnett, A.G.: Did awarding badges increase data sharing in BMJ Open? A randomized controlled trial. Roy. Soc. Open Sci. **7**(3), 191818 (2020)

55. van Elk, M., Rowatt, W., Streib, H.: Good dog, bad dog: Introducing open science badges. Int. J. Psychol. Relig. **29**(4), 230–245 (2018)

56. Bierer, B.E., Crosas, M., Pierce, H.H.: Data authorship as an incentive to data sharing. N. Engl. J. Med. **376**, 1684–1687 (2017)

57. Mongeon, P., Robinson-Garcia, N., Jeng, W., Costas, R.: Incorporating data sharing to the reward system of science: linking DataCite records to authors in the Web of Science. Aslib J. Inf. Manag. **69**(5), 545–556 (2017)

58. Beam, A.L., Manrai, A.K., Ghassemi, M.: Challenges to the reproducibility of machine learning models in health care. JAMA: J. Am. Med. Assoc. **323**(4), 305–306 (2020)

59. Riccardi, E., Pantano, S., Potestio, R.: Envisioning data sharing for the biocomputing community. Interf. Focus **9**(3), 20190005 (2019)

60. Kitchenham, B.: Procedures for performing systematic reviews. Keele University, Keele, UK (2004). http://www.elizabete.com.br/rs/Tutorial_IHC_2012_files/Conceitos_RevisaoSi stematica_kitchenham_2004.pdf

61. Pampel, H., Dallmeier-Tiessen, S.: Open research data: from vision to practice. In: Bartling, S., Friesike, S. (eds.) Opening science, pp. 213–224. Springer, Cham (2014). https://doi.org/ 10.1007/978-3-319-00026-8_14

62. Hrynaszkiewicz, I., Norton, M.L., Vickers, A.J., Altman, D.G.: Preparing raw clinical data for publication: guidance for journal editors, authors, and peer reviewers. BMJ **340**, c181 (2010)

63. Anagnostou, P., et al.: When data sharing gets close to 100%: what human paleogenetics can teach the open science movement. PLoS ONE **10**(3), e0121409 (2015)

64. Krypotos, A.M., Klugkist, I., Mertens, G., Engelhard, I.M.: A step-by-step guide on preregistration and effective data sharing for psychopathology research. J. Abnorm. Psychol. **128**(6), 517–527 (2019)
65. Institute of Medicine: The clinical trial life cycle and when to share data. In: Sharing clinical trial data: Maximizing benefits, minimizing risk, pp. 91–137. The National Academies Press, Washington, DC (2015)
66. Simera, I., Moher, D., Hoey, J., Schulz, K.F., Altman, D.G.: A catalogue of reporting guidelines for health research. Eur. J. Clin. Invest. **40**(1), 35–53 (2010)

Internet Access and Bridging the Digital Divide: The Crucial Role of Universal Service Obligations in Telecom Policy

David McMenemy[1,2](✉) 🆔

[1] Strathclyde iSchool Research Group, University of Strathclyde, Glasgow, Scotland
David.McMenemy@glasgow.ac.uk
[2] Information Studies, University of Glasgow, Glasgow, Scotland

Abstract. With Internet access increasingly a vital element of day to day life, this paper explores the concept of the universal service obligation (USO) in telecommunications law and policy, and considers the arguments for it to be expanded in the digital age to include access to broadband as a fundamental right. It considers aspects of United States, European Union, and United Kingdom policy to consider the digital inclusion limitations of a legal concept that was created in an analogue time. Highlighting the increasing use of broadband and mobile telephony, the paper argues for a broader concept of universal service to emerge to help connect the digitally excluded and let them take their rightful place as digital citizens.

Keywords: Telecommunications policy · Broadband · Universal service · Equity of access

1 Introduction

The concept of universal service with regards to access to critical utility services emerged to ensure that essential services were available to all in a basic package and that all in society would be able to reap the benefits of emerging utilities. In other words "to ensure access to services that had become fundamental social and economic tools" was easily available to all [1, p. 152]. The key to universal service is understanding the notion that the benefits to society and individuals that arise out of access to such services, "outweigh the cost of provision" [2, p. 469]. This might mean that the market may have to be governed by increased state regulation to ensure a minimum level of service is guaranteed to at an affordable price. In that context, universal service obligations (USO) have been applied to policy goals in several utility service markets such as electricity and gas, water, mail, as well as telecommunications. As Simon informs us, the concept of universal service "is grounded in different legal and economic traditions on either side of the Atlantic" [3, p. 138]. This difference in approach on a global basis is clearly evident with regards to the range of views that can be seen on the importance of including broadband and mobile services within the definition of universal service [4]. However, the EU has rightly recognized that ICTs provide immense possibilities for economic and social growth, with "power for the transformation of economic, social and political life" [5, p. 25].

This paper will begin by exploring the components of universal service in telecommunications policy and what they seek to achieve. It will then examine how that concept as a policy dynamic is played out, and consider whether current definitions of universal service are fit for purpose in the modern era, or whether we need to expand our commitment to new and emerging technologies within the remit of the term.

2 The Scope of Universal Service

Universal access was first defined as a concept in the US telecommunications market in 1910 when the AT & T President called for a universal and extensive telephony system for all, before being confirmed in US law in the *Communications Act 1934*. More specifically in the modern era, it relates to a "diverse set of initiatives to subsidize communications services in contexts where such services would otherwise not be provided at all" [6, p. 295]. The prohibitive nature of providing services in these contexts is usually economic: high costs in delivering the infrastructure that cannot realistically be recouped, and/or not enough of a customer base to justify the expenditure.

This leads to a key policy element of universal access, namely that providing it usually entails government subsidy to incentivize the telecommunications companies to undertake infrastructural projects that support it. As we will see, policymakers see telecommunications policy as a vital arm in enhancing many aspects of public policy, and the cases we will discuss in this paper highlight the diversity and importance of universal access in fulfilling key government policy objectives.

2.1 Examples from the United States

The *Telecommunications Act 1996* affirmed the importance of universal access in the minds of American policy-makers. Section 254 (b) of the Act focuses on the principles of universal access, and states 6 key principles that underpin it:

1. Quality and rates
2. Access to advanced services
3. Access in rural and high-cost areas
4. Equitable and non-discriminatory contributions
5. Specific and predictable support mechanisms
6. Access for schools, health care, and libraries

For the purposes of this paper, principle 3 states, "Consumers in all regions of the Nation, including low-income consumers and those in rural, insular, and high-cost areas, should have access to telecommunications and information services... that are reasonably comparable to those services provided in urban areas" [7]. Written into policy, these principles compelled the Federal Communications Commission (FCC) to implement several programs to achieve them:

- The federal Lifeline and Link-Up programs: needs-based subsidy programs for low-income households. Lifeline, established in 1985, provides a $9.25 monthly discount for eligible subscribers, with up to $34.25 a month for eligible subscribers on tribal lands. This was extended to cell phone services in 2005.
- The High-Cost fund: a non-needs based fund aimed at keeping consumer costs low in mostly rural areas] set up in 1997
- The E-rate program which was initiated in 1997 and provided funding for broadband facilities in schools and libraries. This was expanded in 2014 to promote wi-Fi in schools and libraries
- A similar program to E-rate for rural health care facilities launched in 1997 [6, p. 296].

Nuechterlein and Weise evaluated the *High-Cost* fund, which by 2010 had accounted for $4.6 billion dollars in government investment, and highlighted two key concerns. Firstly, that for much of the period between 1996 and 2010 it focused on subsidising telephone lines rather broadband, a policy they considered anachronistic. Secondly that due to an over-emphasis on competition, multiple service providers were supported to provide services in rural areas, rather than focusing all subsidies on one company to keep costs down [6, p. 296]. The program was re-evaluated and re-launched in 2012 as the *Connect America Fund* with a re-definition of its mission as to include voice and broadband services in its strategic focus. Its renewed focus including 5 key universal service obligations:

- Preserve and Advance Voice Service
- Ensure Universal Availability of Voice and Broadband to Homes, Businesses, and Community Anchor Institutions
- Ensure Universal Availability of Mobile Voice and Broadband where Americans Live, Work, or Travel
- Ensure Reasonably Comparable Rates for Broadband and Voice Services
- Minimize Universal Service Contribution Burden on Consumers and Businesses [8].

Latest statistics indicate that nationally across the United States, 96% of households have a fixed lined telephony connection, and 77% of households have a high-speed broadband connection. The re-emphasis of the program, then, does seem valid if universal service around broadband access is to come close to that of fixed lined telephony.

Hauge et al. examined the Lifeline program aimed at low-income households and found it wanting. Their data revealed that low-income households were increasingly moving towards mobile telephony for their communications and information needs, while the subsidized programs such as Lifeline were over- focused on fixed telephony services. As they suggest, this is a problem because "US universal service policy has not changed to reflect the rise in mobile penetration" [9, p. 130]. Since the Telecommunications Act states that universal service should be to consider, "an evolving level of telecommunication services that the FCC shall establish periodically…taking into account advances in telecommunications and information technologies and services" there was scope here to expand the definitions of universal service beyond old paradigms of fixed telephony services. This occurred in March 2016 with the restructuring of the program to include broadband access within the Lifeline initiative [10]. The initiative was now to provide support for mobile or fixed broadband as standalone services, without the need to include telephony services. Importantly it also specified minimum universal service standards for both mobile broadband and mobile telephony services. Given the findings of Hauge et al. that the voice needs of consumers were increasingly being met by mobile telephony, the inclusion within the program of mobile services seemed both logical and timely.

The E-rate program to provide a universal service to schools and libraries has arguably been a great success, however. In 1996 when the initiative began, only 14% of schools were connected to the Internet, and now "virtually all" are connected [11]. Even here, however, we can see the impact of notions of what universal service should encompass evolving. As technology improves the need for schools and libraries to access super speed lines is of paramount importance if modern learning technologies are to be adopted; yet this progress is largely hindered if the institutions' access is via traditional copper cabling and not fiber optic cabling. The statistic that "31% of urban public schools and 41% of rural public schools do not have access to fiber facilities" highlights that the limitations of the old telephonic infrastructure arguably hinder progress and development [12].

2.2 Reflection on Global Universal Service Obligations

While this paper focused on the USA, UK, and EU, it is important to note that the case for universal service reform is not one that is universally agreed upon among countries around the globe. In a recent report, the OECD dealt with the debates around the inclusion of broadband coverage within universal obligations specified by countries [4]. In its summary of the worldwide commitments to universal service, it emphasized that "In some cases, the inclusion of mobile telephony in the scope of universal service obligations could lead to better coverage and reception" [4, p. 5]. In a hint too that an update to the concept of universal service was perhaps overdue, it suggested that reflections on it were aiming to, "establish whether some of the services currently guaranteed through universal service obligations no longer need to be supported through this means, and vice versa" [4, p. 5].

Nevertheless, the complexity of the global situation was well summarized by Garcio Calvo in her 2013 report:

A number of countries including the United States, Israel, Finland, Malta, Spain and Switzerland have already taken steps to include broadband Internet service as part of their existing universal service obligations. Other countries like Korea, Japan, the United Kingdom and Australia have developed strategies to ensure broadband "availability for all" through other universal service policies. A third group including, Denmark, Norway, Germany, The Netherlands and Ireland has opted not to support broadband through either inclusion in universal service obligations or other commitments to provide broadband for all [4, p. 16].

This global complexity does not negate the fact that essentially the requirements of universal service as specified pre the internet revolution no longer satisfy the requirements and the needs of consumers. If rural and disadvantaged communities are to benefit from the development of the new technologies, then the costs wasted on installing an old infrastructure must be weighed against the costs of providing one for the needs of the 21st century. This may entail news ways of thinking, for as Garcio Calvo highlights, many initiatives "were designed to cover relatively small gaps derived from fulfilling universal service obligations over existing networks, not to deploy new infrastructure" [4, p. 4].

The context of universal service in European telecommunications policy is laid out in Directive 2002/22/EC (Universal Service and Users' Rights Directive) and the updated 2009/136/EC (Citizens' Rights Directive). Article 8 of 2002/22/EC states that the "fundamental requirement of universal service is to provide users on request with a connection to the public telephone network at a fixed location, at an affordable price" [13]. Article 10 allows Member states some latitude with regards to defining the affordable price based on specific conditions within the member state. The focus in 2002/22/EC is also related to the availability of public payphones, as well as ensuring disability is considered regarding accessibility.

2.3 The Key Elements of Universal Service

Garcia Calvo discusses universal service in an international context in a report for OECD, and she summarizes the key elements of USO in the telecommunications sector as:

- Availability: that the level, price and quality of service is equivalent wherever a person lives or conducts business so that residing in a rural or remote area does not affect a person's ability to access communication services.
- Affordability: that maintaining and using the service does not place an unreasonable burden on consumers, particularly vulnerable or disadvantaged consumers.
- Accessibility: that a person with a disability can use the service so that a person's level of physical and mental ability does not exclude them from access to communication services [4, p. 9].

These goals are largely economic, and the social inclusivity aspects of them primarily relate to accessibility and access issues, without exploring the wider societal elements; arguably they focus on process rather than any grander notions of the use citizens can put the systems to. Milne and Feijoo offer three policy elements that they believe underpin the concept of universal service:

- economic (promoting economic efficiency and growth),
- social (achieving or maintaining social cohesion), and
- political (offering all citizens equitable opportunities) [14, p. 166].

We will see these elements occur throughout the paper as we discuss European experiences, but it is important to note this expanded aspect of universal service as encompassing both social and political elements in addition to the economic. Therefore, from the citizen perspective, we can elicit from our discussion of the concept of universal service two key elements that underpin it. These are:

7. Facilitating Communication and Inclusion
8. Enhancing the Economy

We will utilize these aspects in our discussion of emerging services to decide if universal service definitions need to be expanded.

3 Emergence of New Telecommunications Services

We will now move on to discuss the European dimension to universal service in a broader sense, with a focus on the particular situation in the UK. As OFCOM have observed, efficient and speedy Internet access "is already necessary for social and economic cohesion, and will become increasingly important as more services move online and new applications come to the market" [15].

The key issue with regards reconsidering the USO around telecommunication services is the convergence of services that has occurred in the information society [16]. The infrastructure and technologies that were designed to carry voice services have been revolutionized and now carry data. This simple explanation hides a multitude of complexity: data services have evolved from simple text-based services that emerged in the 1970s and 1980s to now include multimedia and entertainment services, and e-government and social media services. As Batura has argued, "the infrastructure which carries information and enables communication has become much more of a valuable asset than ever before and an indispensable precondition for success and development in the information society" [5, p. 24]. There is, thus, an argument for saying that a USO that guaranteed voice access no longer embraces the complexity of the kinds of access and potential that telecommunications services offer.

3.1 The United Kingdom Experience

Statistics from the Office of National Statistics reveal that UK citizens have embraced new technologies and Internet applications with great gusto. In 2020, 96% of the UK population had access to the Internet, with 46.6% using it daily. 70% used the access to access news, while 60% used it to access health information [17]. Meanwhile, the 2010s has been dubbed the "decade of the smartphone" [18] with 78% of the UK population claiming use of a smartphone in 2018, compared to 27% in 2011. Also in 2018, 76% of mobile phone users utilize the handsets to access the Internet, consuming an average of 1.9 GB of data per month [18].

These statistics present a picture of a telecommunications infrastructure that is changing regarding its usage; the idea of a landline for telephony purposes is increasingly becoming a thing of the past, and it is the broadband aspect that is increasingly becoming a crucial element of digital inclusion. Other recent research in the UK supports this notion and has indicated that consumers believe the ability to do away with the cost of paying for a landline for Internet access would be a money-saver for them, a net saving of around £2 a week. The respondents in the research concluded that the need for a landline was vastly diminishing and the need for telephony services and Internet access could be met via a mobile phone and Internet dongle.

The UK government has recently moved to expand the USO to include broadband access. A consultation was launched in the spring of 2016 aimed at eliciting views of citizens and organisations on how best to move forward with the idea. However, the government clearly stated its desire to develop a minimum USO of 10 MBPS: "10 Mbps enables full participation in our digital society - watching video on demand, listening to internet radio or streamed music, using social media, accessing Government services, shopping online and working from home" [19]. The list of services provided in the quote from the DCMS consultation indicates the aspects of life the government recognizes broadband access as supporting:

- Entertainment: increasingly entertainment services are streamed, including BBC and ITV players, in addition to Netflix, Amazon Prime and the like. Even when consumers do not subscribe to commercial services, they finance BBC services like iPlayer through the license fee and thus has a legitimate expectation to be able to utilise the service.
- Social interaction: social media, VOIP, Skype and the like are facilitated by good broadband access, and the ability of broadband to significantly enhance the communicative aspects of telecommunication services is significant
- Interaction with government: e-government allows services to be accessed online, but also enables interaction with elected representatives and officials. Such vital services such as applying for benefits are now exclusively online
- E-commerce: both as consumer and provider, the ability of citizens to undertake their buying and selling online is a fundamental aspect of economic development. Broadband allows new business to emerge where access is sufficient, as will be highlighted below
- Teleworking: capacity to work from home and continue to undertake business supports the economy, as well as taking pressure off transport infrastructure, and enables connectedness with the family and community

These services can be argued to be important aspects of digital citizenship, and thus there is a substantial justification for expanding USO to enable them to occur.

In a Scottish context, there is a critical focus on expanding broadband access to rural areas and other socially excluded groups. While telecommunications policy remains a reserved issue dealt with by the Westminster government, there is also a need for the Scottish Government to focus on the expansion of digital infrastructure within Scotland to aid inclusion and growth. The Digital Scotland initiative focuses on four key themes:

- Connectivity
- Digital economy
- Digital participation
- Digital public services [20].

To that end, it follows closely the key issues of universal service defined earlier by Mile and Feijoo. Nevertheless, a USO for broadband could be an expensive undertaking in areas like the Highlands of Scotland, and speeds of 10 MBPS as suggested by the UK government would likely rely on significant state subsidy, let alone the 30 MBPS recommended by the EU Digital Agenda. In the feedback to OFCOM related to the UK government consultation in 2016, it was clear the broadband industry were concerned about a USO obligation that was economically onerous [15]. A USO that was able to include rural and highland areas suitably, then, would need to be looked at carefully for economic viability.

Some major initiatives have been seen to promote inclusive connection programs within the UK. Programs like Digital Glasgow aim to build both infrastructure and skills within the community to enable society to benefit from the technological revolution, and aspects of it include initiatives like citywide free Wi-Fi [21]. Programs like this are replicated throughout the UK and usually work as a partnership between public, private and third sectors. The potential issues on relying on such initiatives to facilitate universal access to internet services is the reliance on what can often be a sub-standard network. While free citywide Wi-Fi provides a safety net for citizens, and an incentive for tourists and visitors, the public nature of it raises issues of security and privacy for users. It is important that any safety net services do not compromise on privacy and they, therefore, do not provide a suitable proxy for a USO aimed at individual citizens.

4   Justification for the Expansion of Universal Service

The emergence of new telecommunications services such as broadband and mobile telephony has clearly transformed society, and the telecommunications industry. We have already discussed the experiences in the UK, and we can posit a strong argument that universal service should be expanded to include the array of emerging services that are continuously evolving into the digital marketplace. As Feijoo and Milne argue, "The current model revolving around the provision of well-defined "services" (e.g. fixed voice) appears in need of fundamental re-thinking" [22, p. 4].

Revisiting our earlier categories that underpinned the concept of universal service, we will now attempt to justify the argument for expansion of USOs to broadband services by providing a discussion around the concepts of facilitating communication and inclusion, and enhancing the economy. The original vision for universal service for telephone services was deemed important to enable citizens to have access to a technology that allowed them to communicate with each other across regions, countries, and continents. This noble goal is clearly one that high-speed Internet access transforms exponentially since it allows communication to be undertaken in numerous ways. While voice remains straightforward, whether via the existing fixed line or as VOIP, the ability add video communications enhances the communication experience significantly. The evolution of new communication mediums such as social media services has enabled interactions in previously unexplored ways, even allowing celebrities and politicians to be able to communicate with their fans and electors.

Whether in the form of re-connecting families and friends, or facilitating business interaction, the communicative elements of broadband transcend what is possible via fixed telephone lines and on their own could arguably justify the expansion of the USO to broadband services.

4.1 Facilitating Communication and Inclusion

The original vision for universal service for telephone services was deemed important to enable citizens to have access to a technology that allowed them to communicate with each other across regions, countries, and continent. This noble goal is clearly one that high-speed Internet access transforms exponentially since it allows communication to be undertaken in numerous ways. While voice remains straightforward, whether via the existing fixed line or as VOIP, the ability add video communications enhances the communication experience significantly. The evolution of new communication mediums such as social media services has enabled interactions in previously unexplored ways, even allowing celebrities and politicians to be able to communicate with their fans and electors.

Whether in the form of re-connecting families and friends, or facilitating business interaction, the communicative elements of broadband transcend what is possible via fixed telephone lines and on their own could arguably justify the expansion of the USO to broadband services.

4.2 Enhancing the Economy

The economic benefits of high-speed broadband services are many-faceted. As identified by the UK government in its proposal to expand the USO obligation, the digital economy presents significant opportunities for the emergence of new companies and services. The ability for new services to emerge is heavily reliant on the capacity to do business online in an efficient manner, and many companies rely on high bandwidth to achieve this. While this might not be an issue in areas covered by high-speed networks, the ability for rural areas to expand their economies within the digital economy remain restricted if high-speed access is not made available to them.

The UK case study dubbed Cybermoor provides a good picture of the potential for high-speed broadband to transform a rural area. Utilising a long-range radio-based broadband solution, the community of Alston Moor was able to provide high-speed access of 10MB plus to all in the community, enabling skills and educational benefits as well as economic. As the case study states:

In a perfect example of how broadband connectivity can empower people to change their economic status, one resident moved his business from the South East of England to Alston Moor. Due to the extremely low cost of office space and connectivity, he was able to cost-effectively run a global business from a refurbished farm [23].

Notwithstanding the benefits to the individuals who was able to run his business by moving more effectively, the opportunity also allowed business types that were previously not able to be based in the area to thrive there.

The faster the broadband access in rural and excluded areas, the more diverse opportunities that can manifest regarding economic benefits. The connection of the village of Exminster in Devon to high-speed broadband allowed a local photographer to transform his business and be able to transmit and download large file sizes that are the basic stuff of digital image work [24]. He can email clients images quickly, and can access any software downloads he needs to undertake his work in a fast and cost-efficient way.

4.3   Keeping the Status Quo?

The status quo with regards to USO in telecom services no longer seems an option. As Cave and Hatta argue, "the spread of mobile technologies is displacing the traditional fixed network as the natural or only means of discharging USO, and this justifies full technological neutrality in allocating and discharging USO" [25]. It simply no longer seems plausible to argue that the wide diffusion of broadband access within developed countries, and the services that rely on broadband access to be viable, does not constitute a prima facie case for the expansion of a USO to broadband. While this growth has been exponential, it remains the case that the penetration of broadband and the design of increasingly bandwidth-hungry services to utilize its benefits result in those without access to high-speed networks being excluded from large swathes of modern society. Whether this USO fixes on fixed line solution, or more realistically a mixed solution incorporating fixed line, mobile, and satellite services, the need for a USO that guarantees high-speed access to all is long overdue.

Nevertheless, Simon offered some words of caution when discussing the potential of developing broadband access as a USO in 2008:

Lessons of history clearly show that the deployment of a network requires considerable time and that during this period there is an enduring discrepancy between social but theoretical goals and the reality of what the market can provide under normal economic conditions. To try to close the gap by adding social obligations and redistributing revenues may have some political appeal but will add extra costs as well as negative incentives [3, p. 146].

There is a *real politick* element, in that commitment to the admirable goal of a full USO around adequate high-speed access for all is not something that can be achieved overnight. Commitment from both a political and an industry standpoint is an absolutely vital element in expanding broadband services, and expectation management within rural communities may also need to be handled sensitively. There are real challenges in providing access to some remote or challenging locations that may need innovative solutions to overcome.

4.4   Other Considerations: Spectrum Allocation and Net Neutrality

While the space does not exist in this paper to discuss them in detail, other telecommunications issues also impact on equity of access and need to be given due consideration. As argued by Cave and Matta, the importance of spectrum management in mobile telecommunications is a vital aspect of any potential mobile USO [25, p. 63]. Spectrum allocation relates to the management of mobile telephony spectrums within countries and regions, and usually involves those countries or regions auctioning off mobile network space to telecom companies to use and charge consumers. These licenses to use the spectrum are usually enormously expensive, therefore an argument can be made that if the companies are seeking to recoup these costs, a compelled USO may well lead to companies not wishing to bid for the licenses and/or invest in innovative new services. One solution to this is, of course, for governments to subsidize companies who provide a USO for mobile services, but the dangers of this are clear from the point of view of ensuring that any mobile USO is not a second-class service due to lack of investment or high quality companies providing them.

Similarly the concerns over net neutrality are also a consideration for a comprehensive USO policy in the digital age. Net neutrality is the principle that an internet service provider should provide access to all contents without fear or favor, and not prioritize their own market interests in delivering content. Yet Glass and Tardiff highlight that notions of a separation between telecommunications services and information services is an outdated way of looking at the world in the modern era [26, p. 201]. It is no accident that telecommunications companies increasingly became buyers of digital content creators throughout the 1990s and into the modern age, and also began to create their own content to deliver via their networks, with a view to enticing subscribers to their own networks. In the UK, for instance, BT launched a BT Sport channel in 2013, free to their own subscribers. In a move from the opposite end of the room, satellite broadcaster Sky Television got into the telecom business in 2005 by buying the Internet Service Provider EasyNet. Such moves are typical of those seen across other countries and are designed to be able to package content and telephony services in one package while privileging their own subscribers. Such moves are clearly a concern in terms of a USO spirit, and need to be monitored closely to ensure digital citizens do not see themselves disenfranchised from key services because they cannot afford the services of a particular telecom provider.

5   Conclusions

This paper has explored the concept of universal service in policy terms and argued that the concept needs to be expanded to include emerging mobile and broadband services and that existing commitments to fixed telephony USOs should be regularly re-evaluated in the light of the significant reduction in usage of such services. If a genuinely inclusive information society is to emerge, and the benefits of the telecommunication services that are developing are to be for the advancement of all, then we must seek to ensure that old technologies and policy commitments to them, however noble, are updated for the modern era. Batura argues that:

> A comprehensive examination of different electronic communications services is necessary in the context of their importance for the life and participation in the Information Society. It needs to be taken into account that in the Information Society process of communication and access to means of communication become disproportionally decisive for all societal activities [5, p. 31].

As we have discussed, the concept of universal service was defined in an era before the Internet was conceived as a tool for citizens to communicate. The universal service concept was relatively static for decades, as telephony itself remained a simple issue of voice services over a fixed telephone line. In that vein, Milne and Feijoo offer that:

We are no longer talking just about plain old telephones, but also about personal digital assistants, multifunctional mobile phones, computers, digital televisions – and their associated networks, modes of connectivity and skills. Any universal service regulation has to take account of these varying preferences [14, p. 167].

The emerging services we have seen on the Internet, and technologies needed to access them, have grown exponentially, and it may be the case that the policy principles that underline 21st century USOs need to be revisited on a much more regular basis than in the past. The logistical and policy-formulation elements of this present a challenge, but it is one that governments have to address if citizens are to be able to take their place in and benefit from the Information Society. As has been observed, the expansion of Internet services and the technologies that support them are "regarded by OECD policy makers as a critical foundation for sustainable economic growth and prosperity" [4]. Such a recognition needs to be met by governments with increased focus on action, to cement affordable access to such services as a cornerstone of modern USOs and to enhance digital citizenship and economic development within communities.

Policies relating to universal access are now focusing more on broadband and mobile services to efficiently harness both the advantages of the emerging technologies, and the significant investments made by governments. The recent commitments from both the US and the UK governments to develop a universal service obligation for broadband is a welcome step towards a re-definition of the concept for the 21st century.

References

1. Blackman, C., Forge, S.: The future of universal service in Europe. Info **10**, 152 (2008)
2. Wild, C., et al.: Electronic and Mobile Commerce Law: An Analysis of Trade, Finance, Media and Cybercrime in the Digital Age, p. 469. University of Hertfordshire Press (2011)
3. Simon, J.P.: Universal service: between socio-political mythology and economic reality – an international cross comparison EU-USA of the regulatory-economic framework. Info **10**, 138 (2008)
4. Garcia Calvo, A.: Universal Service Policies in the Context of National Broadband Plans (OECD Digital Economy Papers, No. 203) (2013)
5. Batura, O.: Universal service in the EU information society policy. Info **16**, 24–34 (2014)
6. Nuechterlein, J.E., Weise, P.J.: Digital Crossroads: Telecommunications Law and Policy in the Internet Age, p. 295
7. Telecommunications Act 1996
8. Connect America Fund Portal. https://www.fcc.gov/general/connect-americfund-progress-portal
9. Hauge, J.A., Chiang, E.P., Jamison, M.A.: Telecommun. Policy **33**, 129–145 (2009)
10. FCC Modernizes Lifeline Program for the Digital Age. https://apps.fcc.gov/edocs_public/att achmatch/DOC-338676A1.pdf
11. Universal Service Program for Schools and Libraries (E-Rate). https://www.fcc.gov/general/universal-service-program-schools-and-libraries-e-rate
12. Wireline Competition Bureau and Office of Strategic Planning and Policy Analysis. https://apps.fcc.gov/edocs_public/attachmatch/DOC-330505A1.pdf
13. Directive 2002/22/EC of the European Parliament and of the Council of 7 March 2002 on universal service and users' rights relating to electronic communications networks and services (Universal Service Directive)

14. Milne, C., Feijoo, C.: Re-thinking universal service policy for the digital era: editors' conclusions. Info **10**, 166 (2008)
15. OFCOM, Designing the broadband universal service obligation: summary of responses to the calls for inputs (2016)
16. Xavier, P.: From universal service to universal network access? Info **10**, 20 (2008)
17. Office for National Statistics. Internet access – households and individuals, Great Britain (2020)
18. OFCOM, Communications Market Report (2018)
19. Davis, A., Hirsch, D., Padley, M.A.: Minimum Income Standard for the UK in 2014, p. 18. Joseph Rowntree Foundation (2014)
20. Digital Scotland: Scotland's Digital Future. http://www.gov.scot/Topics/Economy/digital
21. Digital Glasgow. https://www.glasgow.gov.uk/index.aspx?articleid=17711
22. Feijoo, C., Milne, C.: Re-thinking universal service policy for the digital era: setting the scene – an introduction to the special issue on universal service. Info **10**, 4 (2008)
23. Cybermoor. http://www.ukbroadband.com/case-studies-remote-areas
24. Connecting Somerset and Devon – Case Studies. https://www.connectingdevonandsomerset.co.uk/faster-broadband-for-business/case-studies/
25. Cave, M., Hatta, K.: Universal service obligations and spectrum policy. Info **10**, 62 (2008)
26. Glass, V., Tardiff, T.: A new direction for the net neutrality debate. Telecommun. Policy **43**(3), 199 (2019)

Toward a Practice-Based Approach to Privacy Literacy

Priya C. Kumar[✉] [iD]

Pennsylvania State University, University Park, PA 16802, USA
priya.kumar@psu.edu

Abstract. Children play, communicate, create, learn, and socialize with networked digital technologies. These activities generate data about what children do, where they go, and with whom they interact, raising questions about children's privacy. To help children understand and navigate such questions, information scholars and professionals advocate for privacy literacy efforts. Prior work builds on Nissenbaum's contextual integrity framework to define *what* privacy literacy is. In this paper, I link this prior work with theories of practice-based learning to begin explaining *how* educational efforts can help strengthen children's privacy literacy. Drawing on an example of a challenging incident described by an 11-year-old boy, I propose a practice-based approach to privacy literacy. I contend that educational efforts grounded in this approach will not only help children develop the skills they need to navigate privacy concerns, but also help them internalize the value of privacy.

Keywords: Children · Contextual integrity · Education · Online safety · Privacy

1 Introduction

Children play, communicate, create, learn, and socialize with networked digital technologies. These activities generate data about what children do, where they go, and with whom they interact, raising questions about children's privacy. To help children understand and navigate such questions, information scholars and professionals advocate for privacy literacy efforts [1–3]. In that vein, I have articulated privacy literacy as "the practice of enacting appropriate information flows within sociotechnical systems" [4]. I used the concepts of literacy as a social practice [5] and privacy as the appropriate flow of information [6, 7] as a foundation for defining *what* privacy literacy is. In this paper, I link that work with theories of practice-based learning [8] to begin explaining *how* educational efforts can help strengthen children's privacy literacy. Drawing on an example of a challenging incident described by an 11-year-old boy, I propose a practice-based approach to privacy literacy. I contend that educational efforts grounded in this approach will not only help children develop the skills they need to navigate privacy concerns, but also help them internalize the value of privacy.

© The Author(s), under exclusive license to Springer Nature Switzerland AG 2022
M. Smits (Ed.): iConference 2022, LNCS 13192, pp. 135–142, 2022.
https://doi.org/10.1007/978-3-030-96957-8_13

2   Practice-Based Learning and Privacy Literacy

To develop literacy, one must learn. Learning involves acquiring knowledge, and effective education entails tapping into learners' motivations and fostering their ability to transfer knowledge to new situations [8]. Greeno et al. [8] describe three perspectives of learning that influence education. The behavioral/empiricist view treats learning as the transmission of information and skills that is reinforced through rewards and punishments. The cognitive/rationalist view considers learning as an intrinsically driven process of understanding concepts and developing abilities, such as problem solving. The situative/pragmatist-sociohistoric view regards knowledge as distributed across individuals, artifacts, and communities. Here, learning is a shared practice to which people contribute and through which they build identity. When people develop strong practice-linked identities, that is, when they have opportunities to connect closely with a practice, take on integral roles within it, and express themselves through it, they are more likely to actively engage with the practice [9]. One means of cultivating practice-linked identities is to craft experiences relevant to learners' everyday lives. For instance, designing and conducting food-related experiments with children can foster their identities as scientists and more actively engage them in science learning [10]. The situative/pragmatist-sociohistoric view is the most difficult for educators to put into practice, so to speak. But the upshot is learning experiences through which individuals connect knowledge to their own lives to the extent that it influences how they define themselves—a powerful educational outcome.

The purpose of privacy literacy efforts is to help children learn about privacy. Existing efforts embody the different perspectives of learning that Greeno et al. [8] articulate. What I have previously identified as the knowledge-based approach to privacy literacy [4] focuses on increasing people's awareness about institutional data management practices and teaching them to do things like change their privacy settings. Here, privacy literacy means knowing a set of facts, and the motivation for learning those facts is to gain the reward of protecting one's privacy (or risk losing it). In this way, the knowledge-based approach embodies a behaviorist/empiricist perspective of education. In contrast, researchers and practitioners in library and information studies have adopted a process-based approach to privacy literacy, which focuses on developing people's understanding of the contexts and implications of disclosing information online [3, 11]. Here, privacy literacy means thinking critically about a particular situation and making an informed choice. As such, the process-based approach aligns with the cognitive/rationalist perspective of education.

By defining privacy literacy as a practice of enacting appropriate information flows, I move privacy literacy toward the situative/pragmatist-sociohistoric perspective [4]. Practices are everyday routines embedded in particular contexts and often involving groups of people [12]. Practices are not just cognitive, but also social and cultural. When privacy is a practice, privacy is not a fact someone knows or a thought process in which someone engages, but an action someone does, often without conscious effort. Recognizing privacy as a practice aligns with broader shifts in privacy scholarship that treat privacy as a social, rather than individual, matter [6, 7].

Approaching privacy as a practice also complements sociotechnical shifts in the study of information literacy [12, 13]. Information literacy is not simply a set of discrete skills and competencies pertaining to seeking and using information, but a social and cultural practice of meaning-making. The development of skills cannot be separated from the context in which it occurs, the social interactions that foster it, and the technologies that shape it. For instance, children gain privacy knowledge and skills from formal and informal learning environments, including school lessons and interactions with parents, siblings, relatives, and friends [2].

Indeed, while information literacy and online safety efforts often charge parents with monitoring or controlling children's online activities, parents are also a key source of support and guidance for children [14, 15]. Teachers and librarians are also well-positioned to incorporate privacy knowledge and skills into their interactions with children, which can reinforce and strengthen children's privacy literacy [1, 16]. Children can hone their data literacy, which includes recognizing the privacy implications of data collection, by participating in communities of practice. For example, children in the online programming community Scratch observed that the system displayed information about previous projects, reminding children of the persistence of information that in many cases they explicitly chose to display publicly [17]. In comments on projects and forum posts, children grappled with the privacy implications of such design decisions. Importantly, they engaged in these discussions on their own, unprompted by an adult trying to teach them a lesson [17]. This research on Scratch demonstrates how communities of practice offer meaningful opportunities to develop data literacy.

In summary, grounding privacy literacy in the situative/pragmatist-sociohistoric perspective of learning can yield educational efforts that not only help children develop practices to enact privacy in their everyday life, but also to help them internalize the value of privacy. To explain how, I draw on an example of challenging incident recounted by an 11-year-old boy and his mother and show how the experience can inform the development of a practice-based approach to privacy literacy.

3   Incident: Scammers on Instagram

As part of a larger project on how elementary school-age children conceptualize privacy online, I interviewed 18 families (23 parents and 26 children ages 5–11) about children's experiences with digital technologies [14]. When children described a situation that implicated privacy, I inquired further to explore how the child interpreted and handled the circumstances. One participant recounted a particularly salient experience. Ryan (a pseudonym) was 11 years old at the time of the interview and enjoyed playing mobile games such as Clash Royale. When asked if he had ever seen anything where people said things that made him feel uncomfortable or confused, he said, "I used to have Instagram and I saw some things. But, but those weren't inappropriate [things]. There were just people trying to get me to buy stuff…and they were, like, acting like my friend, like a kid or something."

A few years ago, when Ryan was 8 or 9, his family had returned to the U.S. after living abroad. Ryan set up an Instagram account to keep in touch with his friends. He said his Instagram profile was "open," and his mother added, "I knew nothing about Instagram then 'cause I wasn't on it, so I didn't know how to change the settings." Ryan and his friends enjoyed playing FIFA mobile soccer games, and Ryan posted about FIFA on his Instagram. He explained that once, "I had gotten a good thing. So, I posted on my page the person I got. And then, so, like, so, a few FIFA scammers who wanted, like, coins and stuff. Yeah, they joined my thing. And they were talking to me like kids." They asked for his Xbox password, and though he didn't have an Xbox at the time, Ryan said, "I thought there might have been a password that my mom maybe…set up. So, I asked [my mom]."

His mother explained, "He just goes, 'Mom, Mom, can you give me the password of my Xbox and all these things, 'cause these people are going to give me cards.' And I was like, 'hold on a minute. Let's change your settings and, um, whatever.' But they were literally just trying to get information." When asked if he thought he would have disclosed the password, had he known it, Ryan replied, "Well, maybe when I was that age…I stopped completely sharing password when, like, I was around 10." Ryan's mother agreed, saying, "He would have given it [the password] in a heartbeat had he known it."

Later in the interview, Ryan's mother said that after the interaction, she discussed with Ryan that "these people aren't, you know, aren't probably being honest, and they're maybe trying to steal some information or money or buy things or you know, hack into your box, so, we never give the information out." She said she uses these organically arising moments to talk with her children about navigating online activities.

4   Understanding How Privacy Manifests in Children's Lives

To develop a practice-based approach to privacy literacy, it is important to understand how privacy manifests in children's everyday lives. Only then can information scholars and professionals craft privacy literacy efforts that truly resonate with children. I analyze the Instagram incident through the two theoretical frameworks that underpin a practice-based approach to privacy literacy: contextual integrity (CI) [6, 7] and situative/pragmatist-sociohistoric learning [8]. I specifically highlight how these frameworks attune adults to approach children's practices as valid, rather than flawed, even if they may lead to questionable outcomes. This attitude is critical because it frames privacy literacy as something adults can help children strengthen, rather than something adults need to fix in children.

CI contends that privacy arises when a given information flow follows the norms appropriate to its context. A privacy violation is then a misalignment between an information flow and the norms that it followed. Privacy norms are shaped by five parameters: information type, sender, recipient, subject, and transmission principle [7]. In the Instagram incident, the information type in question is the Xbox password. The sender would have been Ryan, and the recipient, the "FIFA scammers." The subject is the person to whom the information belongs, which in this case would have been Ryan's mother or whomever took ownership over the Xbox information. The transmission principle refers to the constraints that circumscribe an information flow. For example, Ryan believed that if he disclosed the Xbox password, his interlocutors would "give me cards," or materials useful for his FIFA gaming. In his mind, he would be offering a piece of information in return for useful materials, which suggests a transmission principle of exchange. However, his mother believed the people were "just trying to get information," potentially to steal money or break into systems, suggesting a transmission principle of exploitation.

Different transmission principles point to different outcomes—Ryan wanted to proceed with the information flow and his mother did not. Though it is impossible to know the true motives of the "FIFA scammers," Ryan's mother drew the more plausible conclusion that disclosing the password would result in harm. The Instagram incident supports conventional wisdom that parents should hide important passwords from children. However, this is not to suggest that Ryan's thinking was flawed.

When children and adults express conflicting desires, analysts are quick to attribute the differences to children's developmental immaturity and naïveté [18]. In this line of thinking, children do not yet possess the skills or life experience to make responsible decisions, but with time and guidance, they will hopefully learn to do so. This mindset is apparent in Ryan's own comments, as he noted that stopped sharing passwords as he grew older.

CI offers an alternative frame, one that does not approach children from a position of lack. Many adults would interpret Ryan's willingness to take the "FIFA scammers" at their word as demonstrating his lack of good judgment. Yet when the five parameters of the information flow, especially the transmission principle, are considered in context, his thinking becomes easier to understand. Ryan used Instagram as a way to keep in touch with his friends and participate in their shared interest of FIFA mobile gaming. For Ryan, Instagram operated in the context of friendship, where information often flows mutually and fosters close interpersonal bonds. This was the frame of reference through which Ryan interpreted the requests from the "FIFA scammers," and it explains why he perceived the requests as benign. In contrast, Ryan's mother recognized that Instagram also operates as a global interaction space where unfamiliar actors can intrude. She knew to approach unsolicited requests with skepticism and explained to Ryan that some people act with bad intentions. She predicted that the information flow, if allowed to occur, could violate privacy, and she used the incident as an opportunity to help her son understand what constitutes responsible online behavior.

Analyzing the Instagram incident through the CI framework provides insight into how seemingly risky actions can make sense to children. I now consider the incident through the situative/pragmatist-sociohistoric perspective of learning to illustrate why children might be motivated to engage in seemingly risky actions. This perspective approaches learning as a shared practice of building identity in community with others. Developing privacy literacy efforts from this perspective requires understanding:

- What are the social practices involved in navigating privacy?
- How do children participate in these practices?
- What identities do children develop through these practices?

Ryan used Instagram in the context of friendship, which involved engaging in the social practices of information disclosure and self-expression. Ryan and his friends connected over a shared enjoyment of FIFA, and he posted about his accomplishments in its mobile games. This not only informed his friends about his progress in the games, but also represented an aspect of his identity.

Ryan participated in these practices by leveraging the affordances of Instagram. He followed his friends and posted content relevant to them. As long as his friends also followed him, his content would automatically appear on their feeds. This reduced the effort he had to expend to share information with his friends, but it also meant that he had less awareness of who precisely saw what he posted. Since Instagram only recently began defaulting youth users to a private profile [19], Ryan likely did not consciously decide to make his content publicly visible. But the consequence was that he, perhaps unwittingly, opened himself up to interactions with people beyond his friends.

Ryan said "a few FIFA scammers... joined my thing. And they were talking to me like kids." This suggests that people began following his account and trying to communicate with him, either by commenting on his posts or sending him direct messages. According to Ryan, the messages appeared to be coming from other children and offered him game perks in exchange for an Xbox password. The messages tapped into both aspects of identity development linked to Ryan's Instagram use—his identity as a friend and as a FIFA gamer—which can explain why the requests to share his password resonated with Ryan.

5   Future Directions for Developing Practice-Based Privacy Literacy

Analyzing the Instagram incident through the theoretical frameworks of CI and pragmatist-sociohistoric learning demonstrate how practices that seem obviously risky to adults can make sense to young children. This is important because it frames children's actions as valid, rather than naive or wrong. Practice-based privacy literacy focuses on equipping children to understand and reflect on their actions in the context of social, rather than purely individual, well-being. Here, enacting privacy is not simply about protecting oneself, but about contributing positively to a community of practice. For example, in the Instagram incident, Ryan's mother could have emphasized that a compromised Xbox could have put Ryan's friends and fellow FIFA gamers at risk by bringing unauthorized parties into their games.

Given the importance of community and identity in practice-based learning, privacy literacy efforts will need to be grounded something other than privacy. For example, Clegg et al. [10] promoted science learning by creating a program about cooking and embedding scientific concepts into the activities. Similarly, educators could promote privacy literacy by creating programs that appeal to children's interests (e.g., creating a successful YouTube channel), and embedding privacy concepts into the program content.

Practice-based privacy literacy does not seek to instruct children about the correct ways to interact online nor to prevent children from experiencing challenging situations. It aligns with Wisniewski's [20] resilience-centered approach to online safety, which moves away from parental control and prioritizes helping youth develop self-regulation strategies to cope with risky situations when they inevitably encounter them. One way that educational efforts can promote resilience is by leveraging the persuasive power of stories. People regularly share stories when interacting with friends and family, and when such stories involve security-related decisions, hearing them can shape how people think and act when they encounter a situation that implicates their security [21]. Children already glean privacy knowledge from friends and family [2], so a privacy literacy effort could help children use their experiences (or those they hear from others) to craft and exchange privacy-related stories. To embed this effort within a community of practice, researchers could partner with an after-school coding club or a makerspace, work with children to identify how privacy manifests in their coding or making practices, and help children craft and present stories about their experiences navigating privacy.

I invite information scholars and professionals, along with experts in privacy, learning science, education, and child development, to build on this foundation and design educational experiences that help children understand and navigate privacy questions. Specifically, future work should identify the communities of practice children engage in and the identities they develop within these communities, explore how the practices in these communities implicate privacy, and devise meaningful activities, including but certainly not limited to storytelling, that truly resonate with children's lives.

Acknowledgements. I thank Tammy Clegg for introducing me to the learning sciences and for inspiring my thinking in this paper.

References

1. Chi, Y., Jeng, W., Acker, A., Bowler, L.: Affective, behavioral, and cognitive aspects of teen perspectives on personal data in social media: a model of youth data literacy. In: Chowdhury, G., McLeod, J., Gillet, V., Willett, P. (eds.) iConference 2018. LNCS, vol. 10766, pp. 442–452. Springer, Cham (2018). https://doi.org/10.1007/978-3-319-78105-1_49

2. Subramaniam, M., Kumar, P., Morehouse, S., Liao, Y., Vitak, J.: Leveraging funds of knowledge to manage privacy practices in families. Proc. Assoc. Inf. Sci. Technol. **56**, 245–254 (2019). https://doi.org/10.1002/pra2.67

3. Wissinger, C.L.: Privacy literacy: from theory to practice. Commun. Inf. Lit. **11**, 378–389 (2017)

4. Kumar, P.C., Subramaniam, M., Vitak, J., Clegg, T.L., Chetty, M.: Strengthening children's privacy literacy through contextual integrity. Media Commun. **8**, 175–184 (2020). https://doi.org/10.17645/mac.v8i4.3236

5. Scribner, S., Cole, M.: The Psychology of Literacy. Harvard University Press, Cambridge (1981)

6. Nissenbaum, H.: Privacy in Context: Technology, Policy, and the Integrity of Social Life. Stanford University Press, Stanford (2010)

7. Nissenbaum, H.: Contextual integrity up and down the data food chain. Theoret. Inq. Law. **20**, 221–256 (2019). https://doi.org/10.1515/til-2019-0008

8. Greeno, J.G., Collins, A.M., Resnick, L.B.: Cognition and learning. In: Berliner, D.C., Calfee, R.C. (eds.) Handbook of Educational Psychology, pp. 15–46. Macmillan Library Reference USA, Simon & Schuster Macmillan; Prentice Hall International, New York, London (1996)

9. Nasir, N.S., Hand, V.: From the court to the classroom: opportunities for engagement, learning, and identity in basketball and classroom mathematics. J. Learn. Sci. **17**, 143–179 (2008). https://doi.org/10.1080/10508400801986108

10. Clegg, T.L., Gardner, C.M., Kolodner, J.L.: Playing with food: moving from interests and goals into scientifically meaningful experiences. In: Proceedings of the 9th International Conference of the Learning Sciences, pp. 1135–1142. International Society of the Learning Sciences (2010)

11. Rotman, D.: Are you looking at me?—Social media and privacy literacy. In: Proceedings of the iConference 2009, pp. 1–3. iSchools, Chapel Hill (2009)

12. Tuominen, K., Savolainen, R., Talja, S.: Information literacy as a sociotechnical practice. Libr. Q. **75**, 329–345 (2005). https://doi.org/10.1086/497311

13. Lloyd, A.: Information Literacy Landscapes: Information Literacy in Education, Workplace and Everyday Contexts. Chandos, Oxford (2010)
14. Kumar, P., Naik, S.M., Devkar, U.R., Chetty, M., Clegg, T.L., Vitak, J.: "No telling passcodes out because they're private": understanding children's mental models of privacy and security online. Proc. ACM Hum.-Comput. Interact. 1(CSCW), 1–21 (2017). https://doi.org/10.1145/3134699
15. Subramaniam, M., Valdivia, C., Pellicone, A., Neigh, Z.: Teach me and trust me: creating an empowered online community of tweens and parents. In: Proceedings of the 2014 iConference, pp. 244–258 (2014). https://doi.org/10.9776/14078
16. Kumar, P.C., Chetty, M., Clegg, T.L., Vitak, J.: Privacy and security considerations for digital technology use in elementary schools. In: Proceedings of the 2019 CHI Conference on Human Factors in Computing Systems, CHI 2019, pp. 1–13. ACM Press, Glasgow (2019). https://doi.org/10.1145/3290605.3300537
17. Hautea, S., Dasgupta, S., Hill, B.M.: Youth perspectives on critical data literacies. In: Proceedings of the 2017 CHI Conference on Human Factors in Computing Systems, pp. 919–930. ACM, New York (2017). https://doi.org/10.1145/3025453.3025823
18. Castañeda, C.: Figurations: Child, Bodies, Worlds. Duke University Press, Durham (2002)
19. Instagram: Giving Young People a Safer, More Private Experience (2021). https://about.instagram.com/blog/announcements/giving-young-people-a-safer-more-private-experience
20. Wisniewski, P.: The privacy paradox of adolescent online safety: a matter of risk prevention or risk resilience? IEEE Secur. Priv. 16, 86–90 (2018). https://doi.org/10.1109/MSP.2018.1870874
21. Rader, E., Wash, R., Brooks, B.: Stories as informal lessons about security. In: Proceedings of the Eighth Symposium on Usable Privacy and Security – SOUPS 2012, p. 1. ACM Press, Washington, D.C. (2012). https://doi.org/10.1145/2335356.2335364

Good Governance and National Information Transparency: A Comparative Study of 117 Countries

Mahmood Khosrowjerdi[✉] 🆔

Inland Norway University of Applied Sciences, 2418 Elverum, Norway
mahmood.khosrowjerdi@inn.no

Abstract. Information transparency is a major building block of responsible governments. We explored factors influencing the information transparency of 117 world nations. After controlling for the effects of confounding variables of wealth (GDP per capita), corruption rate, population density, human capital, and telecommunication infrastructure, we found that the good governance indices (democracy, economy, and management) were strong and stable predictors of information transparency of world nations.

Keywords: Information transparency · Information policy · Information quantity · Information quality · Access to information · Democracy · Culture · Cross-national study

1 Introduction

Transparency (as a general term) is defined as "the quality of being done in an open way without secrets" (Cambridge Dictionary, n.d.), and, the transparency of "a process, situation, or statement" has been termed as "the quality of being easily understood or recognized… in a clear way" [12].

Although transparency is a prevalent concept in religious texts [34], the academic research on transparency dates to 1980s [5]. Transparency have been differently conceptualized and studied in many fields, but three dimensions of *availability*, *quality*, and *clarity* could be common in those conceptions. This is in accordance with the recent perceptions of transparency as "the degree of openness in conveying information" [5]. Transparency could be used in different contexts. The transparency of nations/governments could be categorized into two dimensions: 1) the information transparency (the amount, quality, and flow of information in a society) and, 2) the accountability (e.g. fiscal transparency, free media, etc.) [37]. The focus of current study is on the first dimension, that is, the information transparency.

Information transparency is a major antecedent of effectiveness of decision-makings of public institutions [5]. Information transparency contributes to quality of public services [6, 33], increases trust in governments [17, 32], and it is an important perquisite of international relations and collaborations [27].

M. Smits (Ed.): iConference 2022, LNCS 13192, pp. 143–160, 2022.
https://doi.org/10.1007/978-3-030-96957-8_14

The dissemination of credible and fast information is very necessary for citizens of all societies to properly response to global health crises [3, 4]. A recent study shows that the level of information transparency is strongly associated with the number of COVID-19 death cases of 108 nations [3].

1.1 Factors Influencing Information Transparency of Nations

Previous studies show that many variables could influence the information transparency of nations.

Of the sociodemographic factors, the wealth of the nations [37], the education level of citizens [24], the corruption perception [30], the technological infrastructures such as access to internet [2], the governance style [9, 19, 22, 23] and the population density of nations [24] have been shown as correlators of national information transparency.

Williams [37] revealed a statistically significant, positive and linear relationship of wealth of countries with the information transparency. The researcher showed that wealthy countries (operationalized by GDP per capita) had higher national information transparency than others. Kumar et al. (2021) investigated the relationships of national cultural values with the e-government development of 78 countries. They revealed the positive effects of wealth (GDP per capita), the positive effects of five cultural dimensions of individualism, uncertainty avoidance, long-term orientation, and indulgence, and the negative effect of power distance, on the e-government development in noted countries.

Transparency can reduce corruption [21], and the higher corruption have been prevalent in non-democratic societies with lower transparencies in public institutions or central governments [30]. Previous research shows that the corruption level in a society has a negative relationship with information transparency. Agyei-Mensah [1] studied the information disclosure behavior of 174 businesses in two countries of Botswana and Ghana and revealed that the firms in countries with lower corruption rate (Botswana) had higher information disclosure rate than businesses in countries with higher corruption rate (Ghana). Similarly, Brusca et al. [9], as a part of a larger research, explored the relationships of information transparency and corruption level of 75 countries, and found that higher transparency of societies were associated with lower corruption level in noted societies. Furthermore, the researchers revealed that the democratic societies were more likely to have lower corruption and higher transparency level (measured by budget openness of the countries).

Population density have been shown as positive correlators of transparency of nations. In other words, the larger the population of nation, the higher the information needs of citizens of the nation could be. Lowatcharin and Menifield [24] studied the influences of various governance features of 816 Midwest counties of 12 local governments of USA on their websites' transparency. The researchers found that the total land area (in square miles), the population density (persons per square mile), percentage of minorities (non-white population), education level (percent of population with a bachelor's degree and beyond), and the governance style (council-manager form) were statistically significant predictors of provided online information transparency of counties.

The countries which have enriched their information and communication technologies (ICT), are more likely to provide citizens with the required information, than those who lack those technological infrastructures. For instance, Alcaraz-Quiles et al. [2] investigated the predictors of transparency of sustainability information of 17 regional governments in Spain, and revealed that of several socioeconomic variables, the population density, access to internet, and education levels of population had positive correlations with the transparency of sustainability information.

The governance style of nation could be a correlator of information transparency. For instance, Guillamón et al. [18] researched the financial information transparency of 100 largest Spanish municipalities and found that the information transparency was dependent to political factors (ideology), collected taxes by municipalities, and received transfers by municipalities. Explicitly, the researchers found that the left-wing parties were more likely to provide higher transparent information than the right-wing parties.

Rodríguez Bolívar et al. [30] published a meta-analysis on the predictors of public information disclosures. The researchers summarized, at least, four conclusive results of previous studies. First, the financial situation of public institutions had a positive effect on their information transparency, and this effect was moderated by the type of national governance, that is, the effect of financial situation of firms on information disclosure was higher in institutions of Anglo-Saxon countries which could have efficient governance cultures. Second, the political competitions were a positive predictor of information disclosure. In other words, politicians in national institutions were more likely to be under pressure to disclose information than those working in local institutions. Third, because of getting funds and grants from central governments, the local authorities were more likely to publish public information than central government institutions. Finally, the information transparency was a governance dependent factor, that is, the information transparency was higher in nations with stronger oppositions and political parties. In other words, the higher the national political competitions, the higher the need for information disclosures.

Liu et al. [23] studied the information disclosure patterns of 516 businesses in Taiwan and found that the type of governance was associated with information transparency of firms. They found that family-owned businesses (which possibly had more autonomy and freedom) were more likely to have higher degrees of information disclosures than other businesses.

Kachouri and Jarboui [19] investigated the degree of openness of 28 corporates in Tunisia and found that the governance style of corporates (i.e. the "ownership concentration") had negative effect on information transparency of the corporates.

1.2 Rationale for This Study

The review of current literature shows that the research on information transparency, with a couple of exceptions, has been focused on counties/firms/businesses of a single nation, and the current knowledge is not inclusive for cross-country comparisons.

The previous studies have focused on several types of information transparency (e.g. public, financial, etc.), used numerous measures to assess the transparency (e.g. number of websites, publication of general information, publication of financial information, and so on), used data from various sources, and researched different layers of information transparency (e.g. counties, firms, businesses, regional governments, and so on). Thus, the current literature does not provide us with an inclusive cross-country comparison of information transparency of world nations. This research is going to fill these gaps.

We base our analysis on nations (as a macro layer of information transparency). In our research, the information transparency is operationalized as "the amount, quality, and flow of information in a society and study". We include several variables which have been correlated with information transparency in previous studies, that is, the GDP (per capita), Human Capital, Telecommunication Infrastructure, Corruption Perception, Population Density, and the Governance Style (Democracy, Economy, and Management). In order to have an inclusive research design and to have most of nations in the study, we use the open access data for all nations for year 2008. This would contribute to a general picture of antecedents of information transparency of world nations.

In summary, our research aims to a cross-country analysis of 117 nations which could reveal the antecedents of information transparency of world nations.

2   Methods

The study follows quantitative research methodologies, has a secondary data analysis approach, and explores the antecedents/correlators of information transparency of nations. The (open access) data for this study is collected from multiple sources.

After a list-wise alignment of the datasets on included variables in this research, 117 countries were included in the final analyses. The included nations in this study is listed in Appendix 1.

2.1   Description of Included Variables in This Study

In this study, we included those variables which were shown as correlators with information transparency of nations.

The description of each included variable in this research, and the data source(s) for noted variable is drawn in Table 1.

The national information transparency data was extracted from Williams [37] for year 2008. Williams [37] developed this index based on data from various sources mostly from United Nations, World Bank, and the International Monetary Fund (IMF).

Table 1. The descriptions of included variables/datasets in this study and their original sources

Variable	Description	Source
GDP per capita	GDP per capita (current, US dollar)	World Bank [38]
Population density	A nation-level indicator that shows the population density (The midyear population of a nation divided by land area in square kilometers) of world countries	World Bank [39]

(*continued*)

Table 1. (*continued*)

Variable	Description	Source
Corruption perception	A nation-level, aggregate index that lists world countries according their score on corruption perception among citizens. The index has a scale of 0–10 (0 equals the highest level of perceived corruption and 10 equals the lowest level of perceived corruption)	Transparency International [35]
Human capital	A nation-level, aggregate index based on two variables, that is, 1) adult literacy: "the percentage of people aged 15 years and above who can, with understanding, both read and write a short simple statement on their everyday life", and 2) Gross enrolment ratio: "the total number of students enrolled at the primary, secondary and tertiary level, regardless of age, as a percentage of the population of school age for that level". The index has a scale of 0 (the worst score) to1 (the best score)	United nations [36]
Telecommunication infrastructure	A nation-level, aggregate index that is composed of five variables: "1) estimated internet users per 100 inhabitants; 2) number of main fixed telephone lines per 100 inhabitants; 3) number of mobile subscribers per 100 inhabitants; 4) number of wireless broadband subscriptions per 100 inhabitants; and 5) number of fixed broadband subscriptions per 100 inhabitants." The index has a scale of 0 (the worst score) to1 (the best score)	United nations [36]
Governance	*Democracy Status.* A nation-level, aggregate index based on following variables: the state-ness, political participation, rule of law, stability of democratic institutions, and political and social integration. The index has a scale of 0 (the worst score) to1 (the best score)	Bertelsmann Stiftung [8]

(*continued*)

Table 1. (*continued*)

Variable	Description	Source
	Economy Status. A nation-level, aggregate index composed of "the level of socioeconomic development, the organization of market and competition, monetary and fiscal stability, private property, welfare regime, economic performance, and sustainability. The index has a scale of 0 (the worst score) to1 (the best score)	
	Management Status: This nation-level, aggregate index included subdimensions like the level of difficulty, steering capability, resource efficiency, consensus-building, and international cooperation of nations. The index has a scale of 0 (the worst score) to1 (the best score)	
National information transparency	The aggregate data for Information transparency of nations based on three sub-dimensions of information quantity (e.g. amount of social, economic, and financial information available for public), information quality (e.g. the dissemination and disclosure of economic and social information in accordance with international standards), and information infrastructure (e.g. access to information, online information users, etc.). The index has a scale of 0 (the worst score) to100 (the best score)	Williams [37]*

Note for Table 1:
*The information transparency data was extracted from noted source for year 2008.

The developed national information transparency index has been used in different academic fields such as politics [25] public administration [7, 26], economics [10, 16], and media studies [14].

3 Results

In order to investigate the relationships of included variables in this study with the national information transparency we used Pearson's' correlation analysis.

We explored assumptions of Pearson's' correlation analysis [31] based on the level of measurement (i.e. continuous values of included variables in the study), absence of outliers, normality of variables, linearity, and homoscedasticity. The included variables in this study were either ratio or interval, and they were labeled as scale (i.e. continuous). The data had no outliers (-3.29 *standard devistioins* $<$ *the mean value of variables* $<$ $+3.29$ *standard devistioins*) and the variables had normal distributions ($-1 <$ *skewness* $< +1$). Linearity and homoscedasticity refer to the shape of the values formed by the scatterplots (see Fig. 1). The shape of values formed by the scatterplots were relatively straight line (linearity assumption met) and the distance between the points to that straight line was very close, and relatively tube-like in shape (homoscedasticity assumption met).

Table 2 shows the results of Pearson's correlation analysis. As it is shown, there were positive and significant correlations between GDP (per capita), human capital, telecommunication infrastructure, corruption perception, and the three dimensions of good governance (democracy, economy, and management) with the information transparency of countries. Of the included variables in this study, the three dimensions of good governance have relatively the strongest relationships with the national information transparency.

Because of relatively strong correlations of the three dimensions of good governance with the national information transparency, we calculated the Partial Pearson's correlation coefficients (see Table 3) to explore if those correlations are stable after controlling for the effects of other (confounding variables), that is, GDP (per capita), Human Capital, Telecommunication Infrastructure, Corruption Perception, and the Population Density.

As it is visible in Table 3, the three dimensions of good governance (democracy, economy, and management) were stable predictor of national information transparency, and the statistically significant correlations of those three dimensions with the national information transparency did not vanished but moderated.

Tables 2 and 3 show the statistically significant relationships of some variables with national information transparency, but they do not reveal the nature of those relationships. In order to explore the pattern of relationships of included variables with the national information transparency, the scatterplots of relationships of all variables with the national information transparency are drawn (see Figs. 2, 3, 4, 5, 6, 7, 8 and 9). The scatterplots help to see both the values of individual data points (i.e. nations), and the patterns when the data are taken as a whole (i.e. whether the nations with similar scores on one variable have relatively close scores on national information transparency).

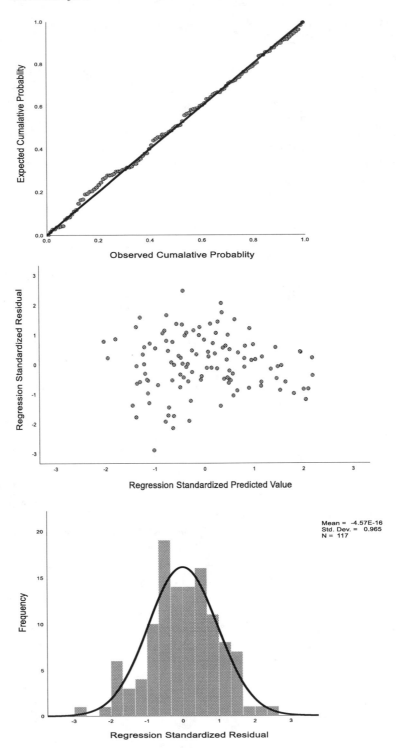

Fig. 1. Exploring the assumptions of Pearson's' correlation analysis

Table 2. The Pearson's' correlation coefficients

		Information transparency
GDP (per capita)	Pearson correlation	.339
	Sig. (2-tailed)	.000
Human capital	Pearson correlation	.564
	Sig. (2-tailed)	.000
Telecommunication infrastructure	Pearson correlation	.652
	Sig. (2-tailed)	.000
Corruption perception	Pearson correlation	.521
	Sig. (2-tailed)	.000
Population density	Pearson correlation	.101
	Sig. (2-tailed)	.279
Democracy	Pearson correlation	.708
	Sig. (2-tailed)	.000
Economy	Pearson correlation	.785
	Sig. (2-tailed)	.000
Management	Pearson correlation	.618
	Sig. (2-tailed)	.000

Note for Table 2: *Dependent variable*: Information Transparency. *Independent variables*: GDP (per capita), Human Capital, Telecommunication Infrastructure, Corruption Perception, Population Density, Democracy, Economy, and Management.

Table 3. The Partial Pearson's' correlation coefficients

		Information transparency
Democracy	Correlation	.527
	Significance (2-tailed)	.000
	df	110
Economy	Correlation	.525
	Significance (2-tailed)	.000
	df	110
Management	Correlation	.437
	Significance (2-tailed)	.000
	df	110

Note for Table 3: *Dependent variable*: Information Transparency. *Independent variables*: Democracy, Economy, and Management. *Control variables*: GDP (per capita), Human Capital, Telecommunication Infrastructure, Corruption Perception, and Population Density.

The relationships of wealth of countries (measured by GDP per capita) and the information transparency of nations, which is shown in Fig. 2, do not seem linear. Enough wealth seems a perquisite for good information transparency, but those countries which are among the richest in the world (e.g. Arabic nations) do have a moderate information transparency level.

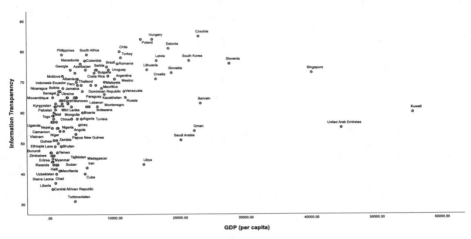

Fig. 2. Scatterplot of the correlation between GDP (per capita) and the information transparency of nations

Figure 3 illustrates the relatively strong and positive correlations of human capital (measured by adult literacy and the studentship enrollment ratio) and the information transparency of nations. The figure shows that most of countries which have better human capital are scattered in top-right section of the figure and have higher information transparency scores. However, the previous colonies of Soviet Union (Tajikistan, Uzbekistan, and Turkmenistan) which have relatively high human capital, do have very low information transparency.

The linear associations of telecommunication infrastructure and national information transparency of nations are drawn in Fig. 4. Those nations which have low ICT infrastructure (e.g. Liberia, Chad, Turkmenistan, and so on) are scattered at the bottom-left of the figure and are more likely to have lower information transparency. The nations with excellent ICT infrastructures (e.g. Singapore, South Korea, Estonia, Czechia, and so on) are grouped at top-right of the figure and have high information transparency too.

The relationships of corruption of included nations in this study and their information transparency are scattered in Fig. 5. The figure shows a moderate correlation between mentioned two variables. Countries with high corruption and low information transparency (e.g. Chad, Haiti, Myanmar, Turkmenistan, and Uzbekistan) are scattered in bottom-left of the figure, and the nations with low corruption and high information transparency (e.g. Singapore, Slovenia, and Estonia) are clustered in top-right of the figure.

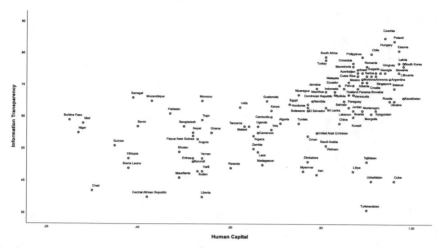

Fig. 3. Scatterplot of the correlation between human capital and the information transparency of nations

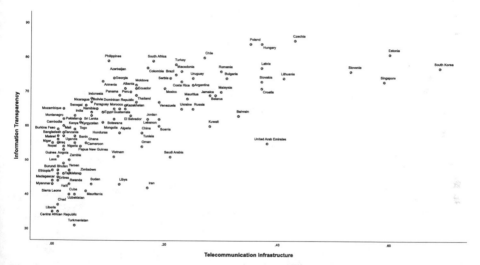

Fig. 4. Scatterplot of the correlation between telecommunication infrastructure and the information transparency of nations

Figure 6 illustrates the positions of including nations in this study according to their scores on population density and information transparency. The relationships of noted variables was not statistically significant, and this is confirmed via the scatterplot too.

Figure 7 shows the nations' scores on two variables of democracy and national information transparency via a scatterplot. The figure shows a sharp linear relationship of mentioned variables. The democratic nations (those which have highest scores on this dimension) are clustered in top-right of the figure. Nations such as Slovenia, Chechia, Chile, Hungary, and Poland are in this cluster. The non-democratic nations such as

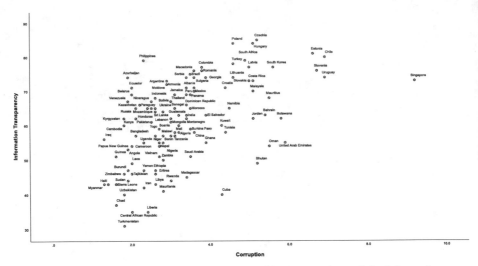

Fig. 5. Scatterplot of the correlation between corruption perception and the information transparency of nations

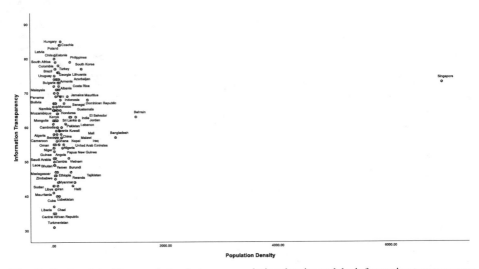

Fig. 6. Scatterplot of the correlation between population density and the information transparency of nations

Turkmenistan, Chad, and Myanmar are clustered in bottom-left of the figure and they have very high information transparency scores too. This pattern is similar for other countries (e.g. Kyrgyzstan, Russia, Bangladesh, and Sri Lanka) which have average scores on both variables.

Figure 8 demonstrates the strong linear relationships of two variables of economy and information transparency of nations. Countries such as Singapore, Chile, South Korea, Costa Rica, and all European nations have high scores on both economy and information transparency and are clustered in top-right of the figure, and nations which have low scores on both economy and information transparency (e.g. Liberia, Zimbabwe, and Myanmar) are grouped together in bottom-left of figure.

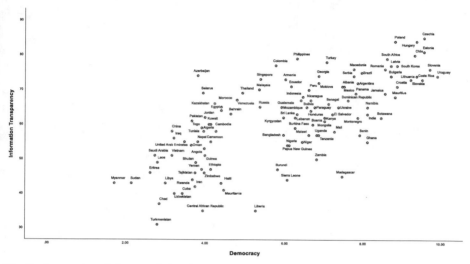

Fig. 7. Scatterplot of the correlation between democracy and the information transparency of nations

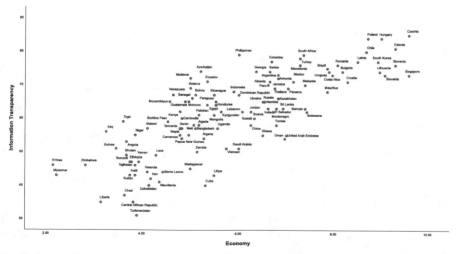

Fig. 8. Scatterplot of the correlation between economy and the information transparency of nations

The strong links of two variables of management and information transparency of nations are depicted in Fig. 9. The figure shows that those nations which have high scores on both management and information transparency variables (e.g. the European nations, South Africa, South Korea, and Chile) are gathered together in top-right of the figure, and those countries with weak management and low scores on information transparency (e.g. Turkmenistan, Uzbekistan, Chad, and Myanmar) are congregated in bottom-left of the figure.

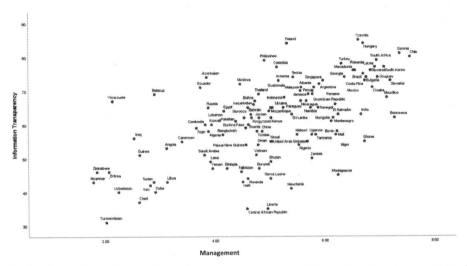

Fig. 9. Scatterplot of the correlation between management and the information transparency of nations

4   Discussions and Conclusion

The aim of this study was to empirically investigate the information transparency of world nations. Our findings provided evidence that seven variables of GDP (per capita), human capital, telecommunication infrastructure, corruption perception, democracy, economy, and management are important correlators of the information transparency of nations.

The wealth of countries (as operationalized by GDP per capita in this study) had a positive and linear relationships with the national information transparency. It means that enough money could be regarded as a perquisite to deliver transparent information to citizens, and the transparency of information could flourish the national economy.

This is in accordance with previous findings of Williams [37] which reveals that the wealthy nations were more likely to have better information transparency, or the results of studies which highlight the information transparency as a positive predictor of economic performance [11].

However, wealth could be an antecedent for many other variables in this study, for instance, telecommunication infrastructures and human capital.

The relationships of human capital (measured by literacy and studentship ratio) with the national information transparency was statistically significant in this study. In other words, the literacy of citizens plays an important role in disseminating transparent information. The transparency of governments does not automatically generate informed citizens. The citizens should have enough literacy to communicate with the authorities, and to understand/give feedback on the delivered information to them. As correctly highlighted by Lindstedt and Naurin [21], "the reforms focusing on increasing transparency should be accompanied by measures for strengthening citizens' capacity to act upon the available information".

The strong correlations of telecommunication infrastructure with information transparency of nations in this study is in accordance with the previous findings of researchers. For example, Alcaraz et al. [2] showed that those local governments which had better technological infrastructures were more likely to be more transparent in delivering information to citizens. The Public's access to information is a hinderance for corruption too [13].

Our findings show that the corruption level in societies have negative effects on information transparency. In corrupted societies, the information transparency could be regarded as disclosure risk for authorities, and the information and communication channels would be more controlled. In other words, the ICT could provide citizens a tool for monitoring the process, and finally, could result in reduced corruption of public institutions [13].

The last major finding of this study is the strong relationships of good governance (democracy, economy, and management) with the information transparency of nations. The statistical analyses in this study revealed that the good governance dimensions was a stable predictor of national information transparency and this association was statistically significant after controlling for the effects of five confounding variables, that is, the GDP (per capita), human capital, telecommunication infrastructure, corruption perception, and population density. The three indicators of good governance, that is, economy status, governance status, and democracy status were among the strongest predictors of national information transparency. This shows to somewhat that information transparency is a cultural-dependent variable. In democratic societies, the trust is accelerator of using public information systems [29], the governments are more responsible, and the citizens are very informed and engaging [28].

This research has limitations that should be noted. First, the included nations in this research is wide-ranging but not complete. Some countries (e.g. USA and UK) are not included in this study because the data for at least one of investigated variables in this study was not available for them. Second, from the methodological point of view, the included variables in this study are not inclusive. In could exist many other relevant variables which could influence information transparency of nations. For example, it would be interesting to see whether feminine societies which are characterized by high concerns with the quality of life would have better positions in information transparency indices. Another important variable which is not included in this study is the national culture. There is evidence [15, 20] that cultural values could influence information access and use of citizens, and it could possibly influence the information transparency of world nations too.

Appendix 1. Included nations in this study

Albania, Algeria, Angola, Argentina, Armenia, Azerbaijan, Bahrain, Bangladesh, Belarus, Benin, Bhutan, Bolivia, Bosnia, Botswana, Brazil, Bulgaria, Burkina Faso, Burundi, Cambodia, Cameroon, Central African Republic, Chad, Chile, China, Colombia, Costa Rica, Croatia, Cuba, Czechia, Dominican Republic, Ecuador, Egypt, El Salvador, Eritrea, Estonia, Ethiopia, Georgia, Ghana, Guatemala, Guinea, Haiti, Honduras, Hungary, India, Indonesia, Iran, Iraq, Jamaica, Jordan, Kazakhstan, Kenya, Kuwait, Kyrgyzstan, Laos, Latvia, Lebanon, Liberia, Libya, Lithuania, Macedonia, Madagascar, Malawi, Malaysia, Mali, Mauritania, Mauritius, Mexico, Moldova, Mongolia, Montenegro, Morocco, Mozambique, Myanmar, Namibia, Nepal, Nicaragua, Niger, Nigeria, Oman, Pakistan, Panama, Papua New Guinea, Paraguay, Peru, Philippines, Poland, Romania, Russia, Rwanda, Saudi Arabia, Senegal, Serbia, Sierra Leone, Singapore, Slovakia, Slovenia, South Africa, South Korea, Sri Lanka, Sudan, Tajikistan, Tanzania, Thailand, Togo, Tunisia, Turkey, Turkmenistan, Uganda, Ukraine, United Arab Emirates, Uruguay, Uzbekistan, Venezuela, Vietnam, Yemen, Zambia, Zimbabwe

References

1. Agyei-Mensah, B.K.: The relationship between corporate governance, corruption and forward-looking information disclosure: a comparative study. Corp. Gov. **17**(2), 284–304 (2017). https://doi.org/10.1108/CG-11-2015-0150
2. Alcaraz-Quiles, F.J., Navarro-Galera, A., Ortiz-Rodríguez, D.: Factors influencing the transparency of sustainability information in regional governments: an empirical study. J. Clean. Prod. **82**, 179–191 (2014)
3. Annaka, S.: Political regime, data transparency, and COVID-19 death cases. SSM-Popul. Health **33**, e13359 (2021). https://doi.org/10.1016/j.ssmph.2021.100832
4. Arora, G., et al.: Solidarity and transparency against the COVID-19 pandemic. Dermatol. Ther. (2020). https://doi.org/10.1111/dth.13359
5. Ball, C.: What is transparency? Public Integr. **11**(4), 293–308 (2009)
6. Bauhr, M., Carlitz, R.: When does transparency improve public services? Street-level discretion, information, and targeting. Public Adm. **99**(3), 500–516 (2020). https://doi.org/10.1111/padm.12693
7. Bauhr, M., Czibik, Á., de Fine Licht, J., Fazekas, M.: Lights on the shadows of public procurement: transparency as an antidote to corruption. Governance **33**(3), 495–523 (2020)
8. Bertelsmann Stiftung: Bertelsmann Transformation Index (BTI) 2008. Gütersloh: Bertelsmann Stiftung (2008). https://bti-project.org/content/en/downloads/data/BTI%202003-2014%20Scores%20(old%20methodology).xlsx. (Internet Archive https://web.archive.org/web/20210818080811/https://bti-project.org/en/meta/downloads.html)
9. Brusca, I., Manes Rossi, F., Aversano, N.: Accountability and transparency to fight against corruption: an international comparative analysis. J. Comp. Policy Anal.: Res. Pract. **20**(5), 486–504 (2018)
10. Challe, E., Lopez, J.I., Mengus, E.: Institutional quality and capital inflows: theory and evidence. J. Int. Money Financ. **96**, 168–191 (2019)
11. Cimpoeru, M.V., Cimpoeru, V.: Budgetary transparency–an improving factor for corruption control and economic performance. Procedia Econ. Financ. **27**, 579–586 (2015)
12. Collins Dictionary. Transparency. https://www.collinsdictionary.com/dictionary/english/transparency

13. DiRienzo, C.E., Das, J., Cort, K.T., Burbridge, J.: Corruption and the role of information. J. Int. Bus. Stud. **38**(2), 320–332 (2007)

14. George, C.: 24. Journalism, censorship, and press freedom. In: Journalism, pp. 473–492. De Gruyter Mouton (2018)

15. Gong, W., Li, Z.G., Stump, R.L.: Global internet use and access: cultural considerations. Asia Pac. J. Mark. Logist. **19**(1), 57–74 (2007). https://doi.org/10.1108/13555850710720902

16. Goodell, J.W., Goyal, A.: What determines debt structure in emerging markets: transaction costs or public monitoring? Int. Rev. Financ. Anal. **55**, 184–195 (2018)

17. Grimmelikhuijsen, S.G.: Transparency and trust. An experimental study of online disclosure and trust in government. Utrecht University (2012). http://dspace.library.uu.nl/bitstream/han dle/1874/218113/Grimmelikhuijsen.pdf?sequence=1&isAllowed=y

18. Guillamón, M.-D., Bastida, F., Benito, B.: The determinants of local government's financial transparency. Local Gov. Stud. **37**(4), 391–406 (2011)

19. Kachouri, M., Jarboui, A.: Corporate governance and information transparency: a simultaneous equations approach. Asian Econ. Financ. Rev. **7**(6), 550–560 (2017). https://doi.org/10.18488/journal.aefr.2017.76.550.560

20. Khosrowjerdi, M., Sundqvist, A., Byström, K.: Cultural patterns of information source use: a global study of 47 countries. J. Am. Soc. Inf. Sci. **71**(6), 711–724 (2020). https://doi.org/10.1002/asi.24292

21. Lindstedt, C., Naurin, D.: Transparency is not enough: making transparency effective in reducing corruption. Int. Polit. Sci. Rev. **31**(3), 301–322 (2010)

22. Liu, Y., Liyuan, Z.: The influence of corporate governance structure on the accounting information transparency: based on the empirical evidence from manufacturing listing corporation. In: 2016 13th International Conference on Service Systems and Service Management (ICSSSM), pp. 1–6 (2016). https://doi.org/10.1109/ICSSSM.2016.7538503

23. Liu, Y., Valenti, A., Chen, Y.J.: Corporate governance and information transparency in Taiwan's public firms: the moderating effect of family ownership. J. Manag. Organ. **22**(5), 662–679 (2016). https://doi.org/10.1017/jmo.2015.56

24. Lowatcharin, G., Menifield, C.E.: Determinants of Internet-enabled transparency at the local level: a study of Midwestern county web sites. State Local Gov. Rev. **47**(2), 102–115 (2015)

25. Lührmann, A., Marquardt, K.L., Mechkova, V.: Constraining governments: new indices of vertical, horizontal, and diagonal accountability. Am. Polit. Sci. Rev. **114**(3), 811–820 (2020)

26. Ma, L., Zheng, Y.: Does e-government performance actually boost citizen use? Evidence from European countries. Public Manag. Rev. **20**(10), 1513–1532 (2018)

27. McCarthy, D.R., Fluck, M.: The concept of transparency in international relations: towards a critical approach. Eur. J. Int. Rel. **23**(2), 416–440 (2017)

28. Milner, H.: Civic Literacy: How Informed Citizens Make Democracy Work. UPNE, Lebanon (2002)

29. Pérez-Morote, R., Pontones-Rosa, C. Núñez-Chicharro, M.: The effects of e-government evaluation, trust and the digital divide in the levels of e-government use in European countries. Technol. Forecast. Soc. Change **154**, 119973 (2020)

30. Rodríguez Bolívar, M.P., Alcaide Muñoz, L., López Hernández, A.M.: Determinants of financial transparency in government. Int. Public Manag. J. **16**(4), 557–602 (2013). https://doi.org/10.1080/10967494.2013.849169

31. Schober, P., Boer, C., Schwarte, L.A.: Correlation coefficients: appropriate use and interpretation. Anesth. Analg. **126**(5), 1763–1768 (2018)

32. Song, C., Lee, J.: Citizens' use of social media in government, perceived transparency, and trust in government. Public Perform. Manag. Rev. **39**(2), 430–453 (2016)

33. Stirton, L., Lodge, M.: Transparency mechanisms: building publicness into public services. J. Law Soc. **28**(4), 471–489 (2001)

34. Taufiq, I.: Transparency and accountability in the Qur'an and its role in building good governance. Int. J. Bus. Econ. Law **6**(4), 73–81 (2015)
35. Transparency International. Corruption Perceptions Index (2008). https://www.transparency.org/en/cpi/2008
36. United nations (UN). E-Government development Index (2008). https://publicadministration.un.org/egovkb/en-us/Data-Center
37. Williams, A.: A global index of information transparency and accountability. J. Comp. Econ. **43**(3), 804–824 (2015). https://doi.org/10.1016/j.jce.2014.10.004
38. World Bank. GDP per capita (current, US dollar) (2008a). https://data.worldbank.org/indicator/NY.GDP.PCAP.CD?end=2008&start=2008
39. World Bank. Population density (2008b). https://data.worldbank.org/indicator/EN.POP.DNST?end=2008&start=2008

Involve Humans in Algorithmic Fairness Issue: A Systematic Review

Dan Wu[1,2](✉) [ID] and Jing Liu[1] [ID]

[1] School of Information Management, Wuhan University, Wuhan 430072, China
woodan@whu.edu.cn
[2] Center of Human-Computer Interaction and User Behavior,
Wuhan University, Wuhan 430072, China

Abstract. With the increasing penetration of technology into society, algorithms are more widely used in people's lives. The intentional or unintentional bias brought about by algorithms may affect people's lives and even affect the destiny of certain groups of people, which raises concerns about algorithmic fairness. We aim to systematically explore the current research of human-centered algorithmic fairness (HAF) research, understand how to involve human in algorithmic fairness issue and how to promote algorithmic fairness from the human perspective. This review followed the procedure of systematic review, identifying 417 articles of algorithmic fairness ranging from the years 2000 to 2020 from 5 target databases. Application of the exclusion criteria led to 26 included articles, which are highly related to human-centered algorithmic fairness. We classified these works into 4 categories based on their topics and concluded the research scheme. Methodological conclusions are presented from novel dimensions. Besides, we also summarized 3 patterns of human-centered algorithmic fairness. Research gaps and suggestions for future research also be discussed in this review based on the findings of current research.

Keywords: Algorithmic fairness · Human-centered · Systematic review · Algorithmic bias

1 Introduction

Fueled by the ever-growing development of artificial intelligence (AI) technology, algorithms are often embedded in a wide variety of systems and are increasingly employed to make consequential decisions for human subjects. However, the algorithmic bias/discrimination issues have aroused a lot of concern recently due to their potential impact on human lives.[1] believe that algorithm might be inherently biased since it learns and preserves historical biases. Algorithmic bias was found in various scenarios. For instance, in the field of criminal justice, some studies showed the algorithm used by the criminal justice system (COMPASS) has a preference for white people since it falsely predicted future criminality among African-American [2]. Another example is advertisement. It was shown that Google's ad-targeting algorithm proposed higher-paying job advertisements for men than for women. [3].

M. Smits (Ed.): iConference 2022, LNCS 13192, pp. 161–176, 2022.
https://doi.org/10.1007/978-3-030-96957-8_15

Luckily, a lot of scholars have explored how to develop fairer algorithms from a technical perspective. They proposed different definitions of algorithmic fairness, including disparate impact [4], demographic parity [5], equalized odds [6], equal opportunity [6], and individual fairness [7]. Each definition has its own formula and metrics that can help evaluate whether the algorithm is fair. But it's impossible to satisfy multiple notions of algorithmic fairness simultaneously [8, 9]. Indeed, many studies support the existence of trade-off between fairness and accuracy from both theoretical and empirical perspectives [10]. Thus, how to achieve a model that allows for higher fairness without significantly compromising the accuracy or other alternative notion of utility still needs to be explored.

However, in addition to the technical perspective, we believe that algorithmic fairness research should also be conducted from a human perspective. The reasons are: (i) Algorithms serve human beings, and some algorithmic decisions may even have a lifelong impact on humans. Therefore, human feelings and cognitions of algorithmic fairness should also be considered. (ii) Compared to technical data training, human can evaluate fairness and utility more directly based on their own needs, which may provide a different solution for developing algorithms that balance fairness and utility. (iii)In fact, it has become the consensus of many scholars that algorithmic fairness is not only a technical problem but should be regarded as a sociotechnical issue [11].

Motivated by this, we conducted this systematic review to explore how to involve humans in algorithmic fairness issue. To be more specific, what can be done, what methods could be used, and how to accompanist technical research.

To the best of our knowledge, there is no systematic literature review to date investigating algorithmic fairness from the human perspective. It's helpful to emphasize the importance of human on algorithmic fairness and provide some research clues for scholars interested in this topic.

2   Methodology

We put forward and define human-centered algorithmic fairness (HAF) as "exploring algorithmic fairness from the human point of view." To be more specific, HAF regard human as an important part of algorithm development and emphasizing the impact of human (including users, developers, practitioners, etc.) on algorithmic fairness.

A systematic review focuses on the detailed research question and aims to provide evidence of a subject or research area [12]. To conduct this study, we follow the four-element framework put forward by [13], which including a) set up the review question(s); b) mapping and scoping the review space; c) reviewing, evaluating, and synthesizing extant research base, and d) devising systematic empirical evidence drawn from the reviewed articles.

We proposed our detailed research questions based on the research goal put forward in the introduction part and established our research protocol. We designed the research questions as follows:

RQ1: What are the research topics and the research scheme of HAF research?
RQ2: What kinds of research methods are appropriate for HAF research?
RQ3: How to involve humans in the whole process of algorithm development?

2.1 Search Terms and Retrieval Strategy

Although we focus on articles that explore algorithmic fairness, the occurrence of algorithmic bias has led to discussion among society on the topic of algorithm fairness. We believe that there is a twin relationship between algorithmic bias and algorithmic fairness. Thus, we also include algorithmic bias as search terms. We expanded the search terms based on "algorithmic fairness" and "algorithmic bias" and developed a Boolean search string as follows: (algorithm* AND (fairness OR equity OR bias OR discrimination)). We adopt this search string in the article title, abstract, and keywords. We limited the time to "2000–2020" and the language to "English".

The strategy above was applied to the following five databases: WOS, ACM digital library, APA, Wiley online library, and Elsevier ScienceDirect. The search for databases was modified to fit the specific settings for each database due to the different characteristics of databases, such as adjustment of thesaurus keywords and limitation settings.

The initial search was conducted on November 23, 2020. All data were imported into Endnotes for management, and duplications were then removed.

2.2 Selection Strategy

Two rounds of screening were conducted to select relevant articles.

The first round of screening is the title and abstract screening. In this part, we aimed to filter out the articles related to the topic of algorithm fairness. Based on this, we used the following four selection criteria for article exclusion in this phase:

- Non-English articles.
- Domain irrelevant: Articles unrelated to algorithms.
- Topic irrelevant: Articles unrelated to algorithm fairness.
- Low topic relevance: Articles briefly mention algorithm fairness, but algorithm fairness is not the main content of its research.

This round of screening was conducted by a trained reviewer according to the criteria. The screening is performed twice and at intervals of one month. If there is a difference between the two times, a second person is brought into judge, ultimately reaching a final consensus of the coding and article inclusion. We regard articles left after the first round of screening as potentially eligible.

The second round of screening is full-text screening. In order to ensure articles included are fit to our research goals and RQs, we set up another 2 criteria to limit the inclusion of articles:

- Not focuses on human perspective: As we mentioned at the beginning of this section, this study focuses on Human-centered perspective, that is, emphasizing the impact of human (including users, developers, practitioners, etc.) on algorithmic fairness or using methods of user study. Articles that do not meet this qualification will be excluded.

– Articles with low quality. We evaluate the quality of the articles based on three aspects:
(i) whether the research is complete, (ii) whether the method is appropriate, and (iii)
whether the conclusion is representative.

2.3   Data Extraction Strategy

A top-down code of articles' content was developed for data extraction. We captured general information (author, title, publication year) and methodology components (methods, sample size, and sample group background) of included articles.

We also conducted a content analysis of the included articles in terms of research topics, research methods, and research patterns by browsing through the full text.

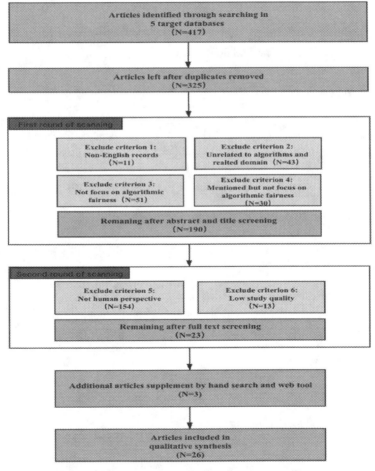

Fig. 1. Flow diagram of the studies selection.

3 Results

Through the search strategy developed earlier, we have retrieved 417 articles in 5 target databases distributed as follows: WOS 235, ACM digital library 93, APA 14, Wiley online library 33, and Elsevier ScienceDirect 42. Removing duplicates resulted in 325 articles.

After two rounds of screening based on the criteria we set, 23 documents were included. Indeed, 3 articles were included through web tools based on references provided in articles included before. Of these, 26 eligible articles were included. Figure 1 summarizes the process of study identification and selection.

Although 26 included articles seem to be relatively small, it's reasonable. Because the topic of algorithm fairness has only been widely concerned in recent years, the number of studies is generally tiny. What's more, studying algorithmic fairness from the human perspective is a branch of algorithmic fairness, which is a new research topic.

The reasons we use 26 articles for this systematic review are: 1) It has high value to conduct a systematic review of algorithmic fairness from a human perspective due to increasing attention to it. It's worth analyzing their content. 2) Research on this topic is still in its infancy. It is necessary to conduct a review to form systematic cognition to help with follow-up research.

Besides, [14] and [15] conducted their systematic reviews based on 25 and 19 included articles. This means conducted a systematic review with a small number of included articles is practical.

3.1 General Information About the Papers

We reported the qualitative analysis of the included studies with publishing time and paper type.

(1) Publishing time. Although our time limit in the search process is 2000–2020, the included articles' year of publication ranged between 2017–2020. The number of articles published from 2017–2020 are 3, 4, 13, 7. The time distribution of included article could indicate that HAF is a relatively new topic of algorithmic fairness. And there is also an increasing trend in the number of articles in 2017–2019, which means that more and more attention is being paid to algorithm fairness related topics from the human-centered perspective.

(2) Paper type. There are 20 conference papers, like ACM SIGCHI Conference on Human Factors in Computing Systems (CHI) and The International World Wide Web Conference (WWW), there are 6 journal papers, and 4 of them were published in 2020. It reflects the transformation of outcome in HAF research from conference to journal, indicating that the relevant research gradually matured.

3.2 RQ1: Topics and Schemes

Through a content analysis of the 26 articles included in this review, we summarized the research topics of each article and finally excavated 12 research topics (some articles contain more than one topic, and there is an uneven distribution of these topics.). We sorted these topics into 4 categories to present the scheme of HAF research: phenomena and sources of algorithmic bias, users' perception of algorithmic fairness, promoting algorithmic fairness, the related concepts of algorithmic fairness (see Fig. 2). These topics indicated the research scheme of HAF research: social phenomenon appears → question perception → question solution → topic expansion.

– **Category I: Phenomena and sources of algorithmic bias**

The social demand for algorithmic fairness comes from the discovery and confirmation of algorithm discrimination/bias phenomenon. The exploration of algorithmic fairness begins with the study of algorithm discrimination/bias. Topics in this category include phenomena of algorithmic bias and sources of algorithmic bias.

Phenomena of algorithmic bias were detected by data collection and analysis in specific situations. Studies focus on this topic explore both intentional or unintentional bias in algorithm usage. Scholars revealed the phenomenon of algorithmic in multiple situations, like advertising [17], social media [21, 34], justice [26] and so on. This topic does not appear as the only topic of the article, but often with sources detecting algorithmic bias or promoting algorithmic fairness together.

Studies detecting sources of algorithmic bias usually analyze the causes of algorithm bias. Although different studies express the source of algorithm bias from different aspects, there are three main sources: 1) data collection bias. Engineers may use biased data during algorithm development without taking data representation into account [20]. 2) bias in data labeling. Some biases from the real world were brought into the data labeling process [36]. 3) attributes selection. Programmers may use attributes that might lead to bias, like population attributes, as they develop algorithms [24].

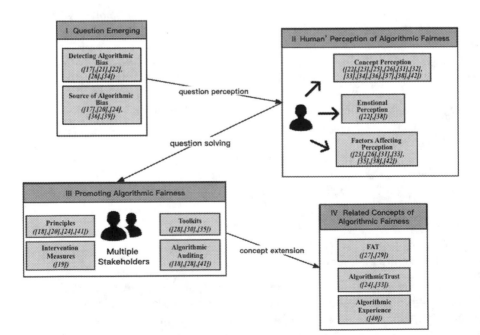

Fig.2. Topics and scheme of HAF research.

– Category II: Human' perception of algorithmic fairness

The human's understanding of fairness may deviate from technical knowledge. Some scholars have studied algorithm fairness from human perception. There are three topics in this category: concept perception, emotional perception, and influencing factors of human perception.

On topics of concept perception, scholars summarize the popular definition of algorithmic fairness from the technical perspective. Participants are allowed to choose concepts they regard as fairer in experiments or questionnaires [22, 36]. Articles in this topic have a context characteristic, which means specific scenarios are usually setting for users to understand. For example, [25] set a credit loan scenario in their study for interviewees to make a loan decision.

Emotional perception refers to the emotional reflection of people's understanding of different algorithmic fairness definitions. For instance, [38] found that people with the strongest comprehension of demographic parity express the most negative sentiment toward it.

Influencing factors of human perception explore factors that influence human judgment of algorithmic fairness. Scholars have studied factors like the definition style of algorithmic fairness [23], personal experience of algorithmic bias [33], demographic characteristics [42], and so on. Especially, Wang et al. [35] explored situation factors and found that participants consider accuracy more important than equality when stakes are high.

– Category III: Promoting algorithmic fairness

This category mainly focuses on exploring measures to promote algorithmic fairness. Articles in this category were characterized by taking multiple stakeholders into account, including users, experts in related fields, industry practitioners, programmers, and so on. There are four topics in this category: developing principles for fair algorithm development, interventions of algorithm development, developing toolkits for algorithmic fairness, auditing of the algorithm.

The topic of developing principles for fair algorithm development aims to guide the practitioners to develop a fair algorithm by moral constraints. Some principles, like require engineers to select representative data and beware trade-offs, were put forward [20]; Interventions of algorithm development refer to giving developers some tips or help to assist engineers in developing fair algorithms. For example, [19] found that both representative data and interventions effectively promote algorithmic fairness based on control experiment; Some stakeholders suggest that toolkits for algorithmic fairness are needed, like processes and tools for fairness-focused debugging [28]; Besides, conducting algorithmic audits has also become recognized by stakeholders. They call for more proactive auditing processes and more holistic auditing methods [28].

– Category IV: Related concepts of algorithmic fairness

Articles in this category linked algorithmic fairness to concepts like algorithm trust, FAT (Fairness, Accountability, and Transparency), and algorithmic experience. Although topics of this category are scattered, algorithmic fairness is generally linked to other related concepts, which is beneficial for exploring algorithmic fairness.

Algorithm trust is a concept that refers to whether human trust algorithms, AI, or machine learning technics. As far as algorithm trust is concerned, studies were conducted to explore the relationship between algorithmic fairness and algorithm trust [27, 29]. [33] claim that algorithmic fairness might affect users' trust in algorithms and even affect their attitude towards companies and their products; FAT topic explores algorithmic accountability and transparency, bringing algorithmic fairness into a larger concept [40]. Conference on Fairness, Accountability, and Transparency have been held since 2018 to discuss FAT issues. Usually, scholars regard transparency and accountability of algorithms as an essential part of promoting algorithm fairness [24]; Algorithm experience refers to how users experience and perceive algorithms. Shin, [40] regarded algorithmic fairness as an essential index to measure users' algorithm experience.

3.3   RQ2: Methodologies Identified

We usually classify research methods into qualitative and quantitative methods. However, to answer RQ2, we noticed that acquiring human behavior and thoughts in human interaction with algorithms is one of the foundations of studies to explore algorithmic fairness from the human perspective. Based on the mindset of human-centered, we summarize the research methods of included articles from the two original dimensions: behavior collection and thought collection (see Table 1).

Table 1. Methods of HAF.

Dimension	Methods	Definition	Advantages
Behavior collection	Interventional behavior collection	Collecting behavior data in a laboratory environment	- Systematic observation of the participants' behavior - Control experiments have great flexibility
	Non-interventional behavior collection	Collecting behavior data through technical means without being detected by participants	- Observing participants in a natural state - Reduce the interference of external factors
Thoughts collection	Independent self-expression	Participants independently reported their personal feelings and thoughts	- Understanding user's authentic response by individual self-report - Participants think without influence from others

(*continued*)

Table 1. (*continued*)

Dimension	Methods	Definition	Advantages
	Group heuristic expression	Participants share their personal thoughts with other participants	- Participants could inspire each other about the topics - Opinions from different perspectives can be collected in a group

In the dimension of behavior collection, the methods used include interventional behavior collection and non-interventional behavior collection. Interventional behavior collection usually carries out laboratory experiments, setting scenarios (i.e., Criminal justice, credit lending, medical treatment, etc.) to guide the participants to complete relevant tasks and collecting the behavior data during them complete experimental tasks. Based on the characteristic of algorithmic fairness, scholars also add some technics in computer science into user experiments, such as setting up the user interface (UI) [20, 30], using algorithms to calculate the minimum number of tasks required for different participants [32], using some material made by algorithms [36] and so on. These technics could help participants record their choices and understanding of algorithmic fairness in a timely manner. The use of these new intervention methods provides new ideas for collecting user behavior in laboratory environments. Non-interventional behavior collection allows scholars to collect user behavior data in a natural state of participants. This method is often used to collect data on mainstream social media, such as Twitter and YouTube. Scholars use API to collect data to detect algorithmic discrimination [21, 22] and understand users' attitudes towards algorithmic fairness [37].

When it comes to thoughts collection, methods used in HAF research including independent self-expression and group heuristic expression. Independent self-expression collects individual self-feedback through questionnaires or one-on-one interviews. This method is generally used to express the participants' understanding of algorithmic fairness [23] and their opinions on promoting it [28]. Group heuristic expressions often use workshops or focus groups which allow participants to discuss as a group. This method could be used in studies which focus on a particular group, like potential affected by algorithmic bias [33]. It also is used to explore the measurements of promoting algorithmic fairness from the multi-stakeholder perspective [18, 40].

3.4   RQ3: Research Patterns of HAF Based on the Process of Algorithm Development

To answer RQ3, we try to conclude research patterns to explain what's human could do in the whole process of algorithm development. [16] concluded three types of mechanisms to enhance fairness in machine learning algorithms based on the timeline. Inspired by this, we summarized the general process of algorithm development first, including algorithm research, algorithm design, and algorithm application. And then we concluded 3 research patterns of HAF: pre-process pattern, in-process pattern, and post-process pattern (see Fig. 3).

Pre-process pattern focuses on the stage before algorithms are developed. It is necessary to fully investigate the algorithm on the applicable scenarios and target users before developing it. Pre-process pattern aims to get a comprehensive understanding of algorithmic fairness in a specific context. The object of these studies is the user of algorithm. It focuses on algorithmic bias detection, users' perception of algorithmic fairness definition, and their fair needs.

In-process pattern focuses on finding measures to promote algorithmic fairness during the process of algorithm design. Studies in this pattern usually focus on the staff involved in the development of the algorithm. For example, [19] tested the impact of interventions on the fairness of algorithms by adding interventional measures in the laboratory experiment.

Post-process pattern refers to the research pattern of testing the adaptability and fairness of users after designing an algorithm. This pattern aims to identify problems through actual usage.

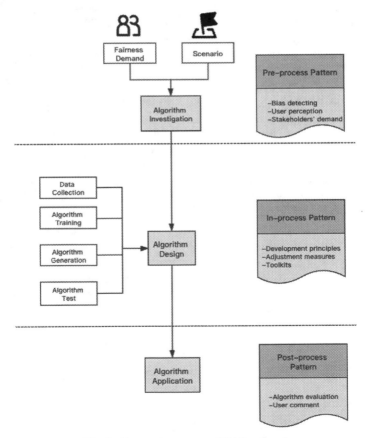

Fig. 3. Research patterns of HAF research.

4   Discussion

In this section, we focus on the relationship between these findings and future research, trying to find the research gaps and summarizing recommendations and implications for future research.

4.1   Taking Advantage of Human Research

Technical research and social research are complementary to each other. Technical research promotes algorithmic fairness through dataset testing, metrics conditioning, and model training. However, research from a human perspective has many advantages. One of the most common advantages is the ability to deeply understand the behavior and ideas of the algorithmic service recipients. Compared to deal with data, direct face-to-face contact with users through experiments or interviews could provide a more direct and in-depth understanding of users' needs and avoid the potential risk of algorithmic bias. Another advantage is that human research makes it easier to collect feedback in real-world use to assist programmers in finding problems. It will reduce the times of adjusting parameter for programmer. Therefore, it is necessary to integrate a human perspective in the whole process of algorithm development and conduct human-centered algorithm fairness research.

In Sect. 3 we summarized three pattern of HAF research. Future research could be conducted with this in mind, and here are some recommendations based on the three patterns.

Pre-process Pattern: Future research could explore human perception and demand for algorithmic fairness through more extensive questionnaires or interviews. Although the perception of algorithm fairness is variable in a different group of people, some universal demand could be extracted. Based on this, scholars could construct an evaluation index of algorithmic fairness from user and algorithm developer perspectives independently and achieving the standard expression and collection mode of the fair demand of the algorithm.

In-process Pattern: This pattern is mainly focused on the developers and practitioners in the field of algorithms. Some achievements of algorithmic fairness have been made at the technical level. These outcomes could combine with user research in the future, which could be more practical. For example, scholars could conduct user experiments to test different toolkits, adjustment measures designed by technical scholars and further summarized a systematic solution for promoting algorithmic fairness.

Post-process Pattern: Future research could collect large-scale user feedback for real-life usage scenarios, which depends on deeply explores the relationship between user behavior and user algorithm fair perception. Of course, it is also possible to capture the direct expression of the user through user experiments. The advantage of the experiment is that scholars could compare users' perception change between the pre-use stage and post-use stage, finding the gap between human need and actual usage and solutions for the gap.

4.2 Topic Expansion and Content In-Depth Mining

We analyzed 12 topics of HAF research and divided them into 4 categories which reflect the overall research scheme. It shows that HAF research has the characteristics of a wide range of topics and content coverage. However, we also noticed that HAF research has an uneven distribution of topics. The research gaps we found are as follows:

- Few scholars have systematically studied the consequences of algorithmic discrimination from the level of user behavior (e.g., burnout behavior, deprecation behavior, etc.).
- Current studies focus on the concept perception of a few special contexts like hiring, criminal justice, and medicine. In the future, more attention should be paid to context perception. The research scenario needs to be expanded. Therefore, we believe that Category II should focus more on contextual perception rather than concept perception in future studies.
- Current studies have explored users' perceptions of algorithmic fairness and its influencing factors. These factors are mainly focused on demographic characteristics. More factors and the relationship between factors still need to be discovered.
- The measures to promote algorithmic fairness are relatively fragmented, and no systematic solution has been developed.

Based on these gaps, we give some research recommendations from the topic level (see Table 2).

Table 2. Research recommendations of HAF research.

Category	Topic expansion	Detail
Category I: phenomena and sources of algorithmic bias	Human behavior when encounter algorithmic bias	The consequence of algorithmic bias: - Burnout behavior - Avoidance behavior - Deprecation behavior
Category II: human' perception of algorithmic fairness	Context perception	- Explore more practical context - Multi-contextual comparison
	Emotion perception	- Fine-grained emotional analysis - Connection of emotion perception and user behavior

(*continued*)

Table 2. (*continued*)

Category	Topic expansion	Detail
	Influencing factors of human perception	- Background of human (knowledge of algorithm, prior experience of algorithmic bias/discrimination) - Situational factors (risks of context) - Quantitative study of influencing factors - Interaction between the influencing factors
Category III: promoting algorithmic fairness	Theoretical construction	- Fusion of multi-disciplinary theory - The mechanism of system-pushing algorithm fairness
	HCI (Human Computer Interaction)	- UI design for algorithmic bias - User study of interaction between human and algorithm
	multi-stakeholders	- Gambling between multi-stakeholders - Finding systematic solutions
Category IV: related concepts of algorithmic fairness	Algorithm trust, FAT, Algorithmic experience	Deeper relationship exploration between each other

4.3 Physiological Signals: The Breakthrough Point of Research Methods

Research on HAF requires humans to be an important research object. This systematic review divided the research methods into four research methods from the two dimensions of human behavior collection and human thought collection in Sect. 3.

However, technological development has provided new support for the development of HAF research. In the future, scholars could also incorporate the collection of human physiological signals. Eye-tracking experiments and brain-computer interfaces can be used to collect more diverse data. For example, by collecting data like movement trajectory, gaze duration and frequency of eye-tracking, users' gaze interest areas could be found. It could help us to design user interfaces that cultivate users' algorithmic fairness perception. Besides, lectroencepha-lography (EEG) data could also be beneficial for scholars to explore user's cognitive burden of algorithmic fairness concept in different situations.

5 Conclusion and Limitation

As a socio-technical issue, algorithmic fairness not only requires technical exploration but also requires people to be included as important research objects. Algorithm fairness is a frontier topic in both computer science and social science, and HAF is a new trend in algorithmic fairness research. The articles included in this systematic review revealed that HAF research is gradually attracting more and more attention of scholars, and the number of articles is increasing year by year. Results show a trend from conference to periodical in article types. However, we also noticed that HAF research is still in the preliminary stage of exploration.

Our main contributions including (i) Presentation of an overview of existing research in exploring algorithmic fairness from the human perspective; (ii) Identified the research topics and scheme of HAF research, summarized the research methods based on the idea of human-centered, and concluded 3 research patterns; (iii) Concluded possible gaps in this field and summarized future research directions which could provide suggestions for future research.

There are, of course, limitations to our study. First, although we selected five mainstream databases, some articles that is written in English or not included in our target database may have been omitted. Second, limited by the topic of this review, we finally included only 26 articles for analysis, so this article could only provide a systematic overview of the initial stage of HAF research, which is time-sensitive.

Acknowledgement. This work is sponsored by Major Projects of the National Social Science Foundation: 19ZDA341.

References

1. Kleinberg, J., Mullainathan, S., Raghavan, M: Inherent trade-offs in the fair determination of risk scores. In: 8th Innovations in Theoretical Computer Science Conference. Berkeley, Article No. 43, p. 43:1–43:2 (2017)
2. Chouldechova, A.: Fair prediction with disparate impact: a study of bias in recidivism prediction instruments. Big Data **5**(2), 153–163 (2017)
3. Datta, A., Tschantz, M.C., Datta, A.: Automated experiments on ad privacy settings. Proc. Priv. Enhanc. Technol. **2015**, 92–112 (2015)
4. Feldman, M., Friedler, S.A., Moeller, J., Scheidegger, C., Venkatasubramanian, S.: Certifying and removing disparate impact. In: Proceedings of the 21th ACM SIGKDD International Conference on Knowledge Discovery and Data Mining, Sydney, pp.259–268 (2015)
5. Calders, T.: Verwer, S: Three naive Bayes approaches for discrimination-free classification. Data Min. Knowl. Disc. **21**(2), 277–292 (2010)
6. Hardt, M., Price, E., Srebro, N.: Equality of opportunity in supervised learning. In: Advances in Neural Information Processing Systems, Barcelona, pp.3315–3323 (2016)
7. Kallus, N., Mao, X., Zhou, A.: Assessing algorithmic fairness with unobserved protected class using data combination. In: Conference on Fairness, Accountability, and Transparency 2020, Barcelona, p.110 (2020)
8. Berk, R., Heidari, H., Jabbari, S., Kearns, M., Roth, A.: Fairness in criminal justice risk assessments: the state of the art. Sociol. Methods Res. Article number: 0049124118782533 (2018)
9. Corbett-Davies, S., Pierson, E., Feller, A., Goel, S., Huq, A.: Algorithmic decision making and the cost of fairness. In: Proceedings of the 23rd ACM SIGKDD International Conference on Knowledge Discovery and Data Mining. Halifax, pp.797–806 (2017)

10. Friedler, S.A., Scheidegger, C., Venkatasubramanian, S., Choudhary, S., Hamilton, E.P., Roth D.: A comparative study of fairness-enhancing interventions in machine learning. In: Proceedings of the Conference on Fairness, Accountability, and Transparency. New York, pp.329–338 (2019)
11. Rosenbaum, H., Fichman, P.: Algorithmic accountability and digital justice: a critical assessment of technical and sociotechnical approaches. Proc. Assoc. Inf. Sci. Technol. **56**, 237–244 (2019)
12. Moher, D., Liberati, A., Tetzlaff, J., Altman, D.G.: Preferred reporting items for systematic reviews and meta-analyses: the PRISMA statement. J. Clin. Epidemiol. **62**(10), 1006–1012 (2009)
13. Gough, D., Oliver, S., Thomas, J.: An Introduction to Systematic Reviews. Sage, Thousand Oaks (2016)
14. Tian, L., Kirsten, H.: Making professional development more social: a systematic review of librarians' professional development through social media. J. Acad. Librariansh. **46**(5) Article number: 102193 (2020)
15. Sørensen, K.M.: The values of public libraries: a systematic review of empirical studies of stakeholder perceptions. J. Doc. **76**(4), 909–927 (2020)
16. Pessach, D., Shmueli, E: Algorithmic Fairness (2020). arXiv:2001.09784 [cs.CY]

List of selected studies

17. Lambrecht, A., Tucker, C.: Algorithmic bias? An empirical study of apparent gender-based discrimination in the display of STEM career ads. Manag. Sci. **65**(7), 2947–3448 (2019)
18. Koene, K., et al.: Algorithmic fairness in online information mediating systems. In: WebSci 2017, New York (2017). https://doi.org/10.1145/3091478.3098864
19. Cowgill, B., Dell-Acqua, F., Deng, S., Hsu, D., Verma, N., Chaintreau, A.: Biased programmers? Or biased data? A field experiment in operationalizing AI ethics. In: Proceedings of the 21st ACM Conference on Economics and Computation, Virtual Event, pp.679–681 (2020)
20. Rantavuo, H.: Designing for intelligence: user-centred design in the age of algorithms. In: Proceedings of the 5th International ACM In-Cooperation HCI and UX Conference, Indonesia, pp.182–187 (2019)
21. Salminen, J., Jung, S., Jansen, B.J.: Detecting demographic bias in automatically generated personas. In: Conference on Human Factors in Computing Systems 2019, Scotland (2019). https://doi.org/10.1145/3290607.3313034
22. Abul-Fottouh, D., Song, M.Y., Gruzd, A.: Examining algorithmic biases in YouTube's recommendations of vaccine videos. Int. J. Med. Inform. **148** Article number: 104385 (2019)
23. Dodge, J., Liao, Q.V., Zhang, Y.F., Bellamy, R.K.E., Dugan, C.: Explaining models: an empirical study of how explanations impact fairness judgment. In: Proceedings of the 24th International Conference on Intelligent User Interfaces, pp.275–285 (2019)
24. Veale, M., Kleek, M.V., Binns, R.: Fairness and accountability design needs for algorithmic support in high-stakes public sector decision-making. In: Proceedings of the 2018 CHI Conference on Human Factors in Computing Systems, Canada, pp.1–14 (2018)
25. Saxena, N.A., Huang, K., DeFilippis, E., Radanovic, G., Parkes, D.C., Liu, Y.: How do fairness definitions fare? Examining public attitudes towards algorithmic definitions of fairness. In: Proceedings of the 2019 AAAI/ACM Conference on AI, Ethics, and Society, Honolulu, pp.99–106 (2019)
26. Grgić-Hlača, N., Redmiles, E.M., Gummadi, K.P., Weller, A.: Human perceptions of fairness in algorithmic decision making: a case study of criminal risk prediction. In: Proceedings of the 2018 World Wide Web Conference, Lyon, pp.903–912 (2018)

27. Williams, A., Sherman, I., Smarr, S., Posadas, B., Gilbert, J.E.: Human trust factors in image analysis. In: Boring, R. (ed.) AHFE 2018. Advances in Intelligent Systems and Computing, vol. 778, pp. 3–12. Springer, Cham (2019). https://doi.org/10.1007/978-3-319-94391-6_1

28. Holstein, K., Vaughan, J.W., Daumé III, H., Dudík, M., Wallach, H: Improving fairness in machine learning systems: what do industry practitioners need. In: Proceedings of the 2019 CHI Conference on Human Factors in Computing Systems, Glasgow, pp.1–16 (2019)

29. Araujo, T., Helberger, N., Kruikemeier, S., de Vreese, C.H: In AI we trust? Perceptions about automated decision-making by artificial intelligence. AI Soc. **35**, 611–623 (2020)

30. Zhang, Y., Bellamy, R.K.E., Varshney, K.R.: Joint optimization of AI fairness and utility: a human-centered approach. In: Proceedings of the AAAI/ACM Conference on AI, Ethics, and Society, New York, pp. 400–406 (2020)

31. Loukina, A., Madnani, N., Zechner, K: The many dimensions of algorithmic fairness in educational applications. In: Proceedings of the Fourteenth Workshop on Innovative Use of NLP for Building Educational Applications, Florence, pp.1–10 (2019). https://doi.org/10.18653/v1/W19-4401

32. Srivastava, M., Heidari, H., Krause, A: Mathematical notions vs. human perception of fairness: a descriptive approach to fairness for machine learning. In: Proceedings of the 25th ACM SIGKDD International Conference on Knowledge Discovery & Data Mining, Anchorage, pp.2459–2468 (2019)

33. Woodruff, A., Fox, S.E., Rousso-Schindler, S., Warshaw, J: A qualitative exploration of perceptions of algorithmic fairness. In: Proceedings of the 2018 CHI Conference on Human Factors in Computing Systems, Montréal, pp.1–14 (2018)

34. Eslami, M: Understanding and designing around users' interaction with hidden algorithms in sociotechnical systems. In: Companion of the 2017 ACM Conference on Computer Supported Cooperative Work and Social Computing (CSCW), Portland, pp.57–60 (2017)

35. Wang, Q., Xu, Z., Chen, Z., Wang, Y., Liu, S., Qu, H: Visual analysis of discrimination in machine learning. IEEE Trans. Vis. Comput. Graph. **27**(2), 1470–1480 (2020)

36. Barlas, P., Kyriakou, K., Kleanthous, S., Otterbacher, J.: What makes an image tagger fair. In: Proceedings of the 27th ACM Conference on User Modeling, Adaptation and Personalization, Larnaca, pp. 95–103 (2019)

37. Burrell, J., Kahn,Z., Jonas, A., Griffin, D: When users control the algorithms: values expressed in practices on the Twitter platform. In: Proceedings of the ACM on Human-Computer Interaction, Article number: 138 (2019). https://doi.org/10.1145/3359240

38. Saha, D., Schumann, C., McElfresh, D.C., Dickerson, J.P., Mazurek, M.L., Tschantz ICSI, M.C: Human comprehension of fairness in machine learning. In: Proceedings of the AAAI/ACM Conference on AI, Ethics, and Society, New York (2020). https://doi.org/10.1145/3375627.3375819

39. Johnson, G.M: Algorithmic bias: on the implicit biases of social technology. Synthese (2020). https://doi.org/10.1007/s11229-020-02696-y

40. Shin, D., Zhong, B., Biocca, F.A: Beyond user experience: what constitutes algorithmic experiences. Int. J. Inf. Manag. **52**, Article number: 102061 (2019)

41. Lee, M.K., Kim, J.T., Lizarondo, L: A human-centered approach to algorithmic services: considerations for fair and motivating smart community service management that allocates donations to non-profit organizations. In: Proceedings of the 2017 CHI Conference on Human Factors in Computing Systems, Denver, pp. 3365–3376 (2017)

42. Pierson, E.: Demographics and discussion influence views on algorithmic fairness (2018). arXiv:1712.09124 [cs.CY]

Tensions Between Intellectual Property Law and Freedom of Expression: A UK Perspective

David McMenemy[1,2](✉) (iD)

[1] Strathclyde iSchool Research Group, University of Strathclyde, Glasgow, Scotland
[2] Information Studies, University of Glasgow, Glasgow, Scotland
david.mcmenemy@glasgow.ac.uk

Abstract. This short paper explores the tensions inherent in intellectual property law and freedom of expression from a UK perspective. It considers the barriers IP law puts in place to creative ideas and free expression, and the impact of the changes in UK law in 2014 that enhanced exceptions for key areas such as criticism, and parody and pastiche. It considers some key case law that tested the boundaries of the law in relation to free expression, and considers whether the 2014 exceptions favor a broader approach to freedom of expression.

Keywords: Intellectual property · Freedom of expression · Fair dealing · Copyright

1 Introduction

By its nature as a property right, copyright protection limits some other freedoms, such as freedom of expression, since in protecting the interests of a copyright holder, limitations are placed on what can be done by others with copyrighted material. Additonally, as technology has improved, the ability to undertake new activities with copyrighted materials has increased, and with it the capacity to open up new ways of working with and delivering content. Such concerns were considered as part of two fundamental reviews of intellectual property law in the UK [1, 2]. Recent amendments to copyright law in the UK regarding exceptions have attempted to bring clarity.

2 Defenses to Copyright Infringement

As a property right, copyright provides a rights holder with very specific and powerful legal rights. Critics of the traditional Anglo-American copyright tradition challenge what they see as a privilege that is not in the interests of wider society. Wheeldon [3] identifies a contested narrative of copyright whereby the prevailing discourse identifies a natural right that should be respected by all, whereby the critical discourse identifies a state-bestowed privilege that is to the detriment of wider society. Craig [4, p. 67] argues that, "the language of property and entitlement pervades copyright rhetoric." Considered in this vein, we can interpret copyright as a barrier that prevents wider society from benefitting from creative works.

The allowed uses of copyrighted material are clearly set out within the *Copyright, Designs and Patents Act 1988* (henceforth CDPA) and are known as permitted acts. Outwith the permitted acts as specified, people or organisations are able to negotiate with rightsholders for any uses that do not fall under these categories, and such use can be granted a license permitting the use to be authorized.

2.1 Public Interest

The defense of public interest is not explicitly defined in the CDPA, instead "the public interest defense is based on the court's inherent jurisdiction to refuse an action for infringement of copyright in cases in which the enforcement of copyright would offend against the policy of law" [5, p. 295]. This is specified in s.171 (3) which deals with rights and privileges under other enactments or the common law and states that nothing in the Act prevents the role of law enforcing or restricting, "the enforcement of copyright, on grounds of public interest or otherwise" [6]. Bainbridge defines public interest as "a nebulous concept" [7, p. 216] and at its heart it involves judges determining whether the wider public interests necessitates copyrights being overruled. Torremans offers that, "the circumstances in which the court could invoke its inherent jurisdiction depend on the work at issue, rather on the issue of ownership of the work" [5, p. 295]. To that end public interest can incorporate a range of issues, such as public safety, national security, or matters related to public accountability, as well as issues of immorality, illegality, or scandal.

Freedom of Expression

Freedom of expression has been clearly codified as a human right under Article 10 of the *Human Rights Act 1998* (HRA). Copyright and freedom of expression provide us with a clear potential for conflict in terms of individual rights. Craig charges that the "clash between copyright owners' rights to control expression and citizens' rights to express themselves cannot be adequately resolved" [4, p. 204]. These rights have been reconciled by applying specific tools:

- The idea-expression dichotomy – ideas are not protected, and the same idea can be expressed differently
- The fair dealing defence (to be discussed below)
- The public interest defence (as discussed above) [5]

Torremans suggests that these tools work in most cases to resolve the clashes between the competing rights, however as we will see in the case law, they do not cover all eventualities.

Parody, Pastiche, and Caricature

Parodies can be a controversial element in copyright cases, as they constitute potential breaches of both economic rights and moral rights. For instance, if the parody in question copies excessively from the original in terms of content or structure, there is a potential objection that can be made with regards to economic impact on the copyright holder; but equally under the CDPA the moral rights of the author include the ability to object to derogatory treatments of work. The right to parody, then, was not a straightforward one under UK law, despite the presence of it as a feature in EU law. Both the Gowers and Hargreaves reviews in the UK stressed the importance of an exception to parody being constituted. For Hargreaves the issue was not merely one of freedom of expression, but also of economic importance too: "Video parody is today becoming part and parcel of the interactions of private citizens, often via social networking sites, and encourages literacy in multimedia expression in ways that are increasingly essential to the skills base of the economy [2, at 5.35].

2.2   Fair Dealing

Fair dealing operates on the basis that the usage of some parts of a copyright work are allowable if they fall within the definition of fair. Unless the fair dealing has been clearly specified by virtue of contract, such as through a rights agency like the Copyright Licensing Agency, what is deemed to be fair when accused of infringement will have to be clarified by the court. How much of a copyrighted work that is fair to use is not merely a matter of quantity, it can also be about quality. Six key factors apply when considering if the use of an item could be considered fair dealing, and these are:

- Purpose
- Proportion
- Motive
- Status of other work
- Extent of use
- Prejudice to the copyright owner [7, p. 224]

This is similar in scope to the PNAM test that was part of the USA via the *Copyright Act 1976*. The **purpose** and character of use, the **nature** of the copyrighted work, the **amount** and sustainability of the portion used, and the **market** impact of the copying.

2.3   Updates to the Law – The 2014 Exceptions

Significant amendments were made to exceptions to copyright in 2014 in the UK, introducing new elements to the permitted acts that enhance freedom of enquiry and expression. The "new copyright exceptions for private copying, parody and quotation marked an important milestone in the government's efforts to make UK law 'fit for purpose' for the digital age" [8, p. 1002]. Notable amongst the changes was a new parody exception which situated parody as an issue requiring the fair dealing approach to be applied with regards to deciding on the legality [9]; however, the exception also left the moral rights remedies in place for authors, meaning that creators of parodies still required to be aware of potential derogatory treatment that could be actionable by the original copyright holder. While what parody should be considered to be was not clearly delineated within the exception, the guidance from the Intellectual Property Office grounds the definitions in EU law, specifically *Deckymyn v Vanderstten* which highlighted that to be recognized as parody a work had "to evoke an existing work, while being noticeably different from it, and to constitute an expression of humour or mockery" [10].

Other relevant amendments related to the new exception for text and data mining, for non-commercial research purposes only, and only where legal access to the data concerned had already been obtained [11]. Additionally, exceptions were added with regards to quotation from copyright materials, as well as the ability to present digital copies of copyright materials on terminals within educational establishments and libraries. These exceptions, then, enhanced freedom of enquiry, but narrowly, to non-commercial research.

3   Relevant Case Law

This section will explore cases that explore the themes discussed above in more detail.

3.1   Public Interest

The use of public interest in a defense is a case of weighing up competing interests [7, p. 217]. In *Lion Laboratories Ltd v Evans* [12] two ex-employees of the plaintiff, a manufacturer of devices that police officers used to measure intoxication levels in suspected drink-drive cases, provided a newspaper with internal company documents that indicated faults in some of the machines may render a positive result even when the subject was not over the prescribed drink-drive limit. Initially successful in obtaining an injunction against the ex-employees and Express newspapers on the basis of breach of confidence and copyright, the appeals judges took the position that public interest in the case applied to both the confidence and copyright elements. Breach of confidence and the press had been visited previously in several cases, including *Initial Services v Putterill* [13] where, again, an ex-employee had leaked to a newspaper confidential company information that was deemed to be in the public interest.

In *Ashdown v Telegraph Group Ltd* [14] the issue at stake was the publication of a private memo of a meeting between politicians Paddy Ashdown and Tony Blair and others. Rather than merely summarize the contents of the memo, the defendant published substantial extracts of the memo itself. Ashdown was successful in arguing that his copyright had been breached from the point of view of his human rights. The clash in the case was between what could be perceived to be the public interest in terms of a significant political meeting, albeit a private one, versus Ashdown's rights to his own private property.

Public interest can also be satisfied by *not* enforcing copyright in a work. This is an example of the state reversing the privilege it bestows on a rights holder by removing said rights. A key example of this relates to the 1980s *Spycatcher* controversy, where in *Attorney General v Guardian Newspapers* [15] the House of Lords decided not to enforce copyright in the book, meaning anyone could copy, republish, or otherwise use the content and not face any sanction. This was an interpretation of public interest by the House of Lords as being damaged by the actions of the author, since in revealing secrets regarding the national security apparatus, he had arguably harmed the country.

This premise can be extended to any situation where someone seeks to use copyright law to benefit from a criminal act. Torremans suggests, "courts are authorized to use the public interest principle to grant an injunction" against any such use of copyright law [5, p. 297]. However, in a recent case the Duchess of Sussex successfully sued the *Mail on Sunday* for both misuse of private information, and breach of copyright for publishing a letter she had sent to her estranged father [16].

3.2 Fair Dealing

Fair dealing is the concept that some uses of copyrighted material can be defended if they are deemed to be reasonable. What constitutes fair dealing is often at the mercy of the courts, but it does not always equate to a significant portion of the work in terms of a percentage of the total. In *Hawkes & Sons (London) Ltd v Paramount Film Service* [17] 20 s of a four-minute musical composition used in a newsreel was deemed to be substantial, since it formed the most recognizable part of the melody (in this case, the march "Colonel Bogey"). If even a small part of a work becomes instantly identifiable in the public mind as representing the whole, then there is an argument for stating that the quality of the material used overrides any concern with the quantity, in copyright terms. The value of the item itself may largely be in that identifiable section, and therefore the rights of the copyright holder would not be served by ignoring this vital.

In *Ladbroke (Football) Ltd v William Hill (Football) Ltd* [17] this important aspect of fair dealing was further explored. In the case, the complainant was seeking redress over the defendant's copying of a football fixed-odds betting coupon, and although some aspects of the original coupon were not copied in their entirety, enough was copied for the court to deem the copying to be substantial. Pearce J offered that:

> Whether a part is substantial must be decided by its quality rather than its quantity. The reproduction of a part which by itself has no originality will not normally be a substantial part of the copyright and therefore will not be protected [18].

The issue of quality as a factor in deciding on infringement issues continues to be of concern with regards to case law and fair dealing. In *England and Wales Cricket Board Ltd –v Tixdaq Ltd* [19] the defendant claimed that the use of 8 s summaries of cricket matches qualified under the exemption in the CDPA for reporting current news or events. In this case the court decided that the usage did not qualify under this exemption, since the use was not for the purposes of informing regarding current events, but was instead a reward for activity on a mobile phone application. In addition, the court applied the quality test, and considered the 8 s clips to contain much of the important elements of the matches concerned, which prejudiced the broadcaster who had paid significant monies for the broadcast rights.

3.3 Review and Criticism

A significant case related to review and criticism had obvious freedom of expression implications. In *Hubbard v Vosper* [20] the defendant had reviewed a book by Scientology founder and leader L Ron Hubbard, and within the review itself had made extensive quotations from the book and, in addition, criticism of the underlying philosophy of the religion. The case was important because it clarified that fair dealing not only can encompass the use of significant parts of a text for review and criticism, but that the critique of the morality and ethos of the underlying philosophy that informed the work was also to be able to call on a fair dealing defense. As Lord Denning states in the decision:

> A literary work consists, not only of the literary style, but also of the thoughts underlying it, as expressed in the words. Under the defense of 'fair dealing' both can be criticized [19].

Here we see a clear example of what Bainbridge summarizes as, "the desire of the courts to protect free speech, particularly as with regards the press, or in a political, or quasi-political sphere" [7, p. 225].

4   Discussion

Do the available defenses to copyright infringement suitably mitigate the threats it poses to freedom of enquiry and freedom of expression? To answer this, we will utilize the three categories summarized earlier by Torremans to facilitate our discussion, namely:

- The idea-expression dichotomy
- The fair dealing defence
- The public interest defence

We will also consider whether free enquiry can be considered to be limited by copyright law.

4.1   The Idea-Expression Dichotomy

As ideas themselves cannot be copyrighted, anyone objecting to how another has expressed a specific idea is free to challenge that idea in their own words. This seems a basic, logical right that is at the heart of free expression in a civilized society.

A flavor of the idea can be found in the case *Baigent v Random House* [20] where the author of a book called *Holy Blood, Holy Grail* had sued Dan Brown, author of *The Da Vinci Code* for using ideas expressed in the former. Brown had created a fictionalized version of Baigent's work, and the appeals judges concluded that what had been inspired from the original text amounted to "generalised propositions at too high a level of abstraction to qualify for copyright protection because it was not the product of the application of skill and labour by the authors of the former book in the creation of their work" [21]. Within the scope of copyright law, then, the opportunity exists to build on existing ideas as long as the execution of them is original in form.

4.2 The Fair Dealing Defense

In terms of fair dealing, one of the largest barriers to freedom of expression is the concept reconfirmed in *England and Wales Cricket Board Ltd –v Tixdaq Ltd* that the issue of fair dealing must be considered not merely in its quantitative terms but also its qualitative terms. This becomes increasingly challenging in the social media age, where highlights of sporting events can be shared via Twitter of Facebook at the click of a mouse. The highlights of such events may well singularly be the goals, or the runs, or tries; therefore, should rights holders who pay many millions of pounds for the rights to broadcast such events not be entitled to protect the most valuable aspects of the broadcasts? Conversely, the restrictions on viewing such events that occurs when media companies purchase rights is a restriction on access, since often only subscribers to that service are able to view the sporting events concerned. There is an argument for stating that restrictions on access to highlights of such events is a block on freedom of access to information, yet it is difficult to justify a wide-ranging fair dealing exemption for content that is so economically valuable.

4.3 The Public Interest Defense

The courts have drawn the defense of public interest narrowly, meaning that only very specific uses of the defense are likely to be successful, which we have seen reinforced in the recent Duchess of Sussex case [16]. Importantly, the areas where the defense is likely to succeed support the free expression and free enquiry categories. The press is able to utilize the defense in key areas related to public safety and the other similar considerations, meaning that matters where the wider public concern is important are likely to see successful defenses from a public interest perspective.

5 Conclusions

The copyright exceptions introduced in 2014 have updated the law in key areas related to free enquiry and freedom of expression. To that end, it is difficult not to argue that the threats to free expression and enquiry have been mitigated to an acceptable extent, both in the historical conception of copyright legislation, the subsequent case law, and the revisions of statute. The balance in protecting the interests of copyright holders and the wider social benefits that accrue from as free an access to knowledge as possible will always be a precarious one, however.

References

1. Gowers, A.: Gowers review of intellectual property. The Stationery Office (2006). https://www.gov.uk/government/uploads/system/uploads/attachment_data/file/228849/0118404830.pdf. Accessed 30 Apr 2021
2. Hargreaves, I.: Digital opportunity: a review of intellectual property and growth: an independent report. (2011). https://www.gov.uk/government/uploads/system/uploads/attachment_data/file/32563/ipreview-finalreport.pdf. Accessed 30 Apr 2021

3. Wheeldon, J.: Patrons, Curators, Inventors and Thieves. Palgrave, London (2014). https://doi. org/10.1057/9780230306677

4. Craig, C.J.: Copyright, Communication and Culture. Edward Elgar MUA, Cheltenham (2012)

5. Torremans, P.: Holyoak and Torremans Intellectual Property Law, 7th edn, Oxford University Press, Oxford (2013)

6. Copyright, Designs and Patents Act 1988

7. Bainbridge, D.I.: Intellectual Property, 9th edn. Pearson, London (2012)

8. Cameron, A.: Copyright exceptions for the digital age: new rights of private copying, parody and quotation. J. Intellect. Prop. Law Pract. **9**, 1002 (2014)

9. Copyright and Rights in Performances (Quotation and Parody) Regulations 2014

10. Johan Deckmyn and Vrijheidsfonds VZW v Helena Vandersteen and Others C-201/13, EU:C:2014:2132

11. The Copyright and Rights in Performances (Research, Education, Libraries and Archives) Regulations 2014 No. 1372

12. Lion Laboratories Ltd v Evans [1985] QB 526

13. Initial Services v Putterill [1968] 1 QB 396

14. Ashdown v Telegraph Group Ltd [2001] RPC 34

15. Attorney General v Guardian Newspapers [1988] 3 All ER 567

16. Duchess of Sussex v Associated Newspapers Ltd [2021] EWHC 273 (Ch)

17. Hawkes & Sons (London) Ltd v Paramount Film Service [1934] Ch 593

18. Ladbroke (Football) Ltd v William Hill (Football) Ltd [1964] 1 W.L.R. 273

19. England and Wales Cricket Board Ltd –v Tixdaq Ltd [2016] EWHC 575 (Ch)

20. Hubbard v Vosper [1972] 2 QB 84

21. Baigent v Random House [2007] EWCA Civ 247

An Annotation Schema for the Detection of Social Bias in Legal Text Corpora

Ece Gumusel[1(✉)], Vincent Quirante Malic[1], Devan Ray Donaldson[1],
Kevin Ashley[2], and Xiaozhong Liu[1]

[1] Indiana University Bloomington, Bloomington, USA
egumusel@iu.edu
[2] University of Pittsburgh, Pittsburgh, USA

Abstract. The rapid advancement of artificial intelligence in recent years has led to an increase in its use in legal contexts. At the same time, a growing body of research has expressed concerns that AI trained on large datasets may learn and model undesirable social biases. In this paper, we investigate the extent to which such social biases are inherent in a real-world legal corpus. We train a *word2vec* word embedding model on case law data and find evidence that NLP methods make undesirable distinctions between legally equivalent entities that vary only by race. Since legal AI applications that model such distinctions risk perpetuating these inequalities when used, we argue that the development of such applications must incorporate a means to detect and mitigate such biases. To this end, we propose an annotation schema that identifies and categorizes deviations from legal equivalence, so that debiasing may be more systematically incorporated into legal AI development. Future directions for research are discussed.

Keywords: Artificial intelligence · Information ethics · Machine learning · Natural language processing

1 Introduction

Legal artificial intelligence (AI) is playing an increasingly important role in addressing different kinds of legal needs to assist clients, lawyers, and judges with accessing, understanding, predicting, and generating legal domain knowledge [16]. Applying AI within the legal domain can be more challenging than its use in other Natural Language Processing (NLP) disciplines. Some prior research suggests that when applying AI in the legal domain, the risks may outweigh the benefits [2]. Therefore, legal AI and its concomitant automation technologies should be carefully inspected for fairness and trustworthiness. For example, the existence of the appellate court system and of judgements split into majority and dissenting opinions highlights the fact that while judges are expected to make decisions based only upon legal reasoning, preexisting biases can produce differing interpretations, and subsequently influence legal outcomes.

M. Smits (Ed.): iConference 2022, LNCS 13192, pp. 185–194, 2022.
https://doi.org/10.1007/978-3-030-96957-8_17

While prior research has focused on identifying and removing biases in machine learning (ML) models [3,5,10], more recent research concentrates on the problem of bias in legal settings [13]. Our paper addresses two primary research questions. First, we ask "What properties of undesirable social bias are unique to legal text corpora and to the application of AI to the legal setting?" We train a *word2vec* word embedding model on a legal corpus consisting of historical case law data and find that undesirable non-equivalences intrinsic to the text are reflected in the model. Our second research question is "How can data be annotated to better allow the development of unbiased legal AI applications?" We present a legal data annotation schema to better enable the detection and mitigation of undesirable social bias in the development of legal AI. In addition, this data annotation schema advances research by systematically defining what undesirable bias is and what makes it unique when understood in a legal context. We ground this schema on a principle we introduce in this paper called *legally equivalent entities*, which posits that any two people or groups of persons who are equivalent except for a property such as gender, race, or age should be modeled as equivalent in any AI that is trained on legal data. References to such distinctions are potentially harmful in their capacity to bias legal decision makers. The goal in introducing our annotation schema is twofold: (1) to encourage more research on the unique properties of bias in legal areas, and (2) to enable the creation of datasets that can train ML algorithms on the task of finding biases in legal data used by legal AI applications.

2   Related Work

Rapid development of ML NLP methods has prompted researchers to investigate different avenues for use in real-world tasks, including the legal work conducted by judges, lawyers, legal scholars, and jurors [16]. Katz et al. [9] achieve over 70% accuracy in predicting the behavior of Supreme Court judges from case features and descriptions. Teruel et al. [14] present both an annotated corpus and a suite of classifiers trained to perform named entity recognition and argument mining. Duan et al. [8] use an expert-annotated corpus of Chinese judiciary documents to train high-performing element extraction models, while Chalkidis et al. [6] apply neural network models to cases from the European Court of Human Rights. We expect growth in legal AI research to continue alongside the rapid advancement of general NLP methods.

As more practical applications employ ML methods trained on large datasets, recent research has focused on how these methods absorb undesirable cultural and social biases from the data they use, thus perpetuating these biases. To date, most legal AI applications rely specifically on NLP methods [8,9,14–16], which research has shown may contain biases. Bolukbasi et al. [3] find gender biases in the embedding method used in this paper, while Caliskan et al. [5] uncover multiple forms of gender and racial bias in a similar embedding method.

3   Legally Equivalent Entities

Any examination of undesirable social bias in NLP models must draw from criteria formulated outside of the model and the corpus itself. Prior research involves intervention to mitigate or remove undesired associations, such as stereotypical assignments of genders to careers [3] or unacceptable links between races and negative terms [5,13]. While considering what external standards training corpora and NLP models should be held to, we assert that in the legal field such standards can be further elucidated. Due to the protections afforded by the US Constitution, its amendments (particularly the Fourth Amendment), and landmark legislation such as the Civil Rights Act of 1964, all individuals and communities should be considered what we call *legally equivalent entities* regardless of their race, gender, age, sexual orientation, etc. In fact, the only case where such characteristics should be mentioned are in instances where these equality guarantees are not met, as in cases involving discrimination, hate crimes, or equal opportunity violations. This is specific to legal corpora and legal AI, as in more general corpora there may be cases where positive, acceptable distinctions of race, gender, or age may be modeled.

The American legal system, in its most idealized form, should treat all legal parties as equivalent regardless of their race, and this equivalence should be reflected in any legal AI applications trained on documents produced by this system. We regard deviations from this equivalence to be *prima facie* undesirable bias specific to legal corpora and AI.

4   Case Study: Legal (Non-)Equivalence in *word2vec*

4.1   Method

We conducted a preliminary investigation of this legal equivalence concept by training a *word2vec* [12] word embedding model on the Harvard Case Law dataset [1], which contains 6.7 million unique cases across all US jurisdictions spanning from 1658 to 2018. We preprocessed the text so that every instance of the adjectives `white` and `black` when used to signify race were merged with the nouns that followed them to ensure that we generate word embeddings for legal entities that vary only by race.

To observe the principle of legal equivalence in the learned model, we note how similar each pair of differently-prefixed nouns are to each other. We use the cosine similarity metric [4,11] to measure the similarity of word pairs. A cosine similarity of 1 indicates semantic equivalence, while a cosine similarity of 0 indicates that the two embeddings have no shared components of meaning. Thus, in an absolutely ideal legal setting, we would expect $s_{cos}(\texttt{black\_man}, \texttt{white\_man}) = 1$. In practice, this is not the case, and we are interested in discovering the degree to which this ideal is departed from.

w_1	w_1 Freq.	w_2	w_2 Freq.	Similarity
black_male	23,865	white_male	17,489	0.89
black_males	10,688	white_males	5260	0.89
black_man	13,564	white_man	13,614	0.86
black_men	5611	white_men	5561	0.86
black_woman	2928	white_woman	5198	0.78
black_female	5541	white_female	6177	0.72
black_women	1520	white_woman	1570	0.71
black_females	1334	white_females	1140	0.69
black_people	4017	white_people	3994	0.66
black_persons	4628	white_persons	5541	0.60
black_person	3019	white_person	4976	0.54

Fig. 1. Similarity of equivalent entities in the *word2vec* model

4.2   Results and Analysis

Figure 1 shows the cosine similarity of entity pairs of interest. The similarity values for all pairs are greater than 0.50, indicating that the American legal system, as reflected in this corpus of case law, has seen some success in treating equivalent entities differing in race as equal. Word embeddings are ultimately derived from co-occurrence statistics, so the data above may be interpreted as showing that black/white variations of noun phrases tend to appear in similar contexts. For instance, whether a given man is Black or White, we expect the phrases black_man AND white_man to serve similar semantic roles in eyewitness testimonies.

At the same time, any cosine similarity score that is less than 1 indicates that the two entities being compared are semantically *dissimilar* in some fashion. Even with a score as high as 0.89, there are still instances of black_male being used in different contexts than white_male. Furthermore, the variation of scores in Fig. 1 show that the noun in the noun phrase interacts with the racial adjective in differing ways. Relative similarity between race is preserved across the four nouns indicating the male gender (e.g. man, male, etc.), while dissimilarity grows when the entities under consideration are female (e.g. woman, female, etc.). Finally, the non-gendered terms people, person, and persons show the largest dissimilarity across race.

We further explore the dissimilarities across race by finding which words in the vocabulary are significantly more similar to noun phrases of one race than the other. We iterate through each term in the vocabulary, determine its mean similarity with the black versions of the 11 nouns in Fig. 1, and subtract this from its mean similarity with the 11 white versions. This results in a final *racial skew* score, adapted from Rice et al. [13], which, if negative, indicates a closer association with `black` noun phrases, while a positive score means a closer association with `white` entities.

`black` associated	`white` associated
talesmen -0.128, venire -0.110, peremptories -0.105, holdout - 0.096, panelist -0.094, alternates -0.085, gunshots -0.065, juror - 0.063, robber -0.053, prowler - 0.053, racially -0.050, shots -0.050, gunman -0.05, underrepresentation -0.049, systematically -0.048, bullets -0.042, plainclothes -0.041, caller -0.040, suspects -0.038, spectators -0.038, vials -0.036, baggies -0.035, rounds -0.035, shooter - 0.031, eyewitnesses -0.031, bandit -0.029	mulatto 0.144, natives 0.141, naturalized 0.131, indians 0.130, native 0.130, nations 0.121, slavery 0.118, heterosexual 0.115, nazi 0.109, seduced 0.109, cohabiting 0.108, jews 0.107, slave 0.106, immigrants 0.106, enemies 0.105, lesbian 0.105, lover 0.096, teenage 0.094, catholics 0.093, foreigner 0.090, traditions 0.089, paramour 0.089, ravished 0.088, families 0.088, virtuous 0.088, believers 0.088, sin, 0.087, strangers 0.087, communists 0.086, homosexual 0.086

Fig. 2. A sample of words with high racial skew scores

The words in Fig. 2 are outliers in that they are more strongly associated with noun phrases of one race over another. Examining these outliers allows us to gain a preliminary understanding of the ways in which Black entities differ from White entities in the case law corpus, and how these differences are learned by the word embedding model. For example, words like `talesmen`, `venire`, `panelist`, `alternate`, `underrepresentation`, and `juror` show that jury selection and composition play a significant role in distinguishing Black legal entities from White ones. Rather surprisingly, a number of generically "criminal" words like `gunshots`, `robber`, `suspects`, and `eyewitnesses` showed a skewed association with Black entities. This merits further investigation, though we tentatively propose that this may be due to discussion of the details of criminal cases explicitly referring to Black parties as Black (e.g., *witnessed the black suspect*), while a White party is less likely to be labeled outright as such (e.g., *witnessed the suspect*).

Many of the White-skewed words reflect an emphasis on racial, sexual, and ideological purity. Associated sets of words include references to race and citizen status (`mulatto`, `natives`, `naturalized`, `immigrants`, `foreigner`), religion and virtue (`jews`, `catholics`, `virtuous`, `believers`, `sin`), and relationships (`heterosexual`, `homosexual`, `cohabiting`, `lesbian`, `lover`). As with our analysis of Black-skewed words we are curious to know why some words that would be expected to be racially-neutral, such as those describing relationships, turn out to be White-skewed in the word embedding model. Terms such as `mulatto`, `indians`, `slavery`, and `communists` suggest the explicit use of `white_noun` phrases may be linked to particular historical contexts. Some of these terms are legally and culturally obsolete, while others draw attention to specific periods of American history, such as the era of institutional slavery or the fear of communist infiltration during the Red Scare. Furthermore, the skewness scores for `white` associated words tend to be slightly higher than those for `black` associated words, suggesting that "whiteness" tends to be evoked in comparatively more specific and specialized contexts in the corpus.

A major concern about the presence of social bias in language models is their potential to perpetuate unwanted biases from the past by replicating them in practical application. This presents a particularly unique challenge in legal AI. On one hand, in a legal system steered by precedence, it is vital to expose legal AI to texts spanning a long period of time. On the other hand, our analysis shows that doing so exposes models to the complex concept of race, which has been highly problematic in the past and continues to evolve. Although recent trends in NLP research have attained considerable progress by increasing the quantity of training data, in some domains, such as the legal one, it is vital for such data to be contextualized in a way that is visible to the model. Only then can a legal AI understand the obsolescence of racial concepts such as *mulatto* or the illegality of homosexuality while retaining the same concepts for the purposes of historicity and precedence.

The purpose of this preliminary analysis was to establish that entities in the case law corpus which varied only in being Black/White are not fully equivalent, falling short of the standard the US legal system holds itself to. Furthermore, this non-equivalence is captured by a word embedding model trained on this corpus, verifying that precedents established in recent research hold when considering the legal context. We suggest that undesirable bias in legal corpora and its manifestation of legal AI is worthy of investigation on its own terms, taking uniquely legal standards into account. To aid in this investigation, we propose a legal equivalence schema for the annotation and creation of legal text datasets.

5   Legal Data Annotation

In a society with a perfect legal system, no distinction would exist between a Black and White legal entity. Our investigation above reveals, however, that this is not the case in practice. Legal AI applications trained on historical data will inevitably learn these distinctions, which threaten to perpetuate them further as their use becomes more widespread. We therefore urge caution when out-of-the-box NLP methods are used directly on legal corpora to serve some applied function in legal settings.

As is the case with all debiasing methods, intervening in an NLP algorithm to remove undesired social bias requires an intervention from researchers and engineers [3,5]. We propose that, in the legal AI setting, this intervention be based on our proposed principle of *legally equivalent identities*. To this end, we present our preliminary efforts in annotating a legal dataset using this principle, with the aim of training AI applications themselves to recognize and classify social bias markers before being trained to carry out some specific legal task.

5.1 Legal Equivalence Schema

The principle of legal equivalence consists of three assertions:

1. Legal equivalence is the base standard to which all distinctions of race in the legal setting should be held against. Except when absolutely necessary, the initial inclination of any AI should be to ignore such distinctions.
2. Identification on the basis of appearance has become an undesirable but necessary element of the American justice system. Eyewitness testimony that a suspect was a certain race, gender, or age does not determine a suspect's guilt, but does play a role in the determination of judges and juries. We call these non-equivalences *substitutable*. An AI application may be permitted to learn a person of race x was witnessed by a bystander, but need not know which specific race it was.
3. US citizens can use legal channels to assert their right to fair representation. Over the course of these challenges, the legal system will generate documents that draw attention to racial, gender, and age distinctions. These constitute necessary instances of non-equivalence. In order to guarantee equivalence, the legal system and its participants must speak in detail of existing non-equivalence. A socially sensitive legal AI must be aware of these instances of "necessary" distinction.

5.2 Annotation Method

Our data annotation process is as follows: first, we manually assemble a set of words indicative of racial or ethnic distinction. This includes official Census-designated terms, such as `caucasian`, `african-american`, and `hispanic`; common cultural terms such as `white` and `black`; geographical terms and demonyms that reliably indicate race such as `asian`, `mexican`, and `jamaican`; and finally we add a set of racial slurs which appear in both older cases as well as testimony in more recent ones. We then iterate through the Harvard Caselaw Access Project's [7] comprehensive corpus of case law texts and isolate those which involve criminal and procedural and contain an appearance of these words.

In order to detect bias and enable bias removal our expert annotators examine the case texts and assign additional labels. We isolate the section of the cases' natural language text which indicates the legal outcome: affirmed, dismissed, denied, or remanded to a lower court. Then, we examine the case details and label which party was negatively affected by the aggregate decisions of the judges. Taking into account all the details obtained during the review and annotation of the case, we assign each explicit racial reference one of three labels: *unnecessary*, *substitutable*, or *necessary*. Two examples of our ongoing annotation process are presented in Fig. 3.

Case Title	United States v. Wenxia Man
Citation	891 F.3d 1253
Date	June 6, 2018
Jurisdiction	US Court of Appeals for the 11th Circuit
Location	FL
Category	Criminal & Procedure
Outcome	Affirmed
Negative Outcome Party	Defendant

After Liu confirmed to Man that he was "Chinese," Man explained that she was looking for military engines.	substitutable
Man also told Liu that Zhang was "a tech spy," expressed concern about detection by the "many federal agents [who are] investigating and arresting many Chinese people," and directed Liu not to "get [her] involved"	substitutable

Case Title	State v. McNeill
Citation	90 N.C. App. 257
Date	May 17, 1988
Jurisdiction	North Carolina Court of Appeals
Location	NC
Category	Criminal & Procedure
Outcome	Dismissed
Negative Outcome Party	Defendant

She became lost and asked a black man how to get to 705 North East Street. The man told her he would take her to where she wanted to go. He directed her, and they went to an apartment, where the victim and the man saw another black man, William Yates.	unnecessary
Yates told officers that defendant, Alphonzo McNeill, had come to the apartment with a white woman and said "he was going to rob that old white lady."	substitutable

Fig. 3. Annotation examples

6   Discussion

NLP methods inevitably model both the semantic meaning and intrinsic social associations of the terms contained in their training texts. This is particularly problematic when such methods are used to design legal AI applications, as legal contexts have much higher standards for fairness and legal equivalence. We therefore argue that detection of legal non-equivalence should be an explicit component of the development process.

Our initial investigation of legal equivalence in a *word2vec* model shows, however, that in order to challenge and combat systemic legal inequality, it is necessary to highlight such inequality during legal procedures. Therefore, a modeling of legal non-equivalence is acceptable in certain contexts. We acknowledge this subtlety with our proposed annotation schema, which categorizes all markers of distinction as *necessary*, *unnecessary*, or *substitutable*. By explicitly annotating these distinctions in training data with these categories, the learning process for legal AIs can account for and model distinctions in a more transparent and fair fashion.

This study only used one embedding algorithm, and was conducted without considering the date or the location of the case. Going forward, our research will investigate differences in legal non-equivalence that may be attributed to when and where a case took place. To date, we have annotated a total of 272 cases. Future work will utilize a larger sample of the annotated dataset to train legal AI to identify and categorize instances of legal non-equivalence.

7   Conclusion

In this paper, we propose the concept of *legally equivalent entities* as a framework for understanding, identifying, and mitigating undesirable bias in corpora used to train legal AI. We found that equivalent entities that differ solely by being Black or White are semantically modeled by the *word2vec* algorithm in an undesirably different fashion. In an effort to prevent this from occurring in real-world legal AI applications, we propose an annotation framework for the identification of undesirable racial references in legal texts that can be removed, modified, or mitigated before use as training data.

Acknowledgments. This research is supported by a grant from the Indiana University Racial Justice Research Fund.

References

1. Caselaw Access Project (2018). https://case.law/
2. Angwin, J., Larson, J., Mattu, S., Kirchner, L.: Machine bias. ProPublica **23**(2016), 139–159 (2016)
3. Bolukbasi, T., Chang, K.W., Zou, J., Saligrama, V., Kalai, A.: Man is to computer programmer as woman is to homemaker? Debiasing word embeddings. arXiv arXiv:1607.06520 [cs, stat] (July 2016)
4. Bullinaria, J.A., Levy, J.P.: Extracting semantic representations from word co-occurrence statistics: a computational study. Behav. Res. Meth. **39**(3), 510–526 (2007)
5. Caliskan, A., Bryson, J.J., Narayanan, A.: Semantics derived automatically from language corpora contain human-like biases. Science **356**(6334), 183–186 (2017). https://doi.org/10.1126/science.aal4230. arXiv arXiv:1608.07187
6. Chalkidis, I., Androutsopoulos, I., Aletras, N.: Neural legal judgment prediction in English. arXiv preprint arXiv:1906.02059 (2019)

7. Chang, F., McCabe, E., Lee, J.: Mining the Harvard Caselaw Access Project. SSRN Scholarly Paper ID 3529257, Social Science Research Network, Rochester, NY (September 2020). https://doi.org/10.2139/ssrn.3529257. https://papers.ssrn.com/abstract=3529257

8. Duan, X., et al.: CJRC: a reliable human-annotated benchmark dataset for Chinese judicial reading comprehension. In: Sun, M., Huang, X., Ji, H., Liu, Z., Liu, Y. (eds.) CCL 2019. LNCS (LNAI), vol. 11856, pp. 439–451. Springer, Cham (2019). https://doi.org/10.1007/978-3-030-32381-3_36

9. Katz, D.M., Bommarito, M.J., Blackman, J.: A general approach for predicting the behavior of the Supreme Court of the United States. PLoS ONE **12**(4), e0174698 (2017)

10. Kurita, K., Vyas, N., Pareek, A., Black, A.W., Tsvetkov, Y.: Measuring bias in contextualized word representations. arXiv preprint arXiv:1906.07337 (2019)

11. Lapesa, G., Evert, S.: Evaluating neighbor rank and distance measures as predictors of semantic priming. In: Proceedings of the 4th Annual Workshop on Cognitive Modeling and Computational Linguistics (CMCL), pp. 66–74 (2013)

12. Mikolov, T., Chen, K., Corrado, G., Dean, J.: Efficient estimation of word representations in vector space. arXiv preprint arXiv:1301.3781 (2013)

13. Rice, D., Rhodes, J.H., Nteta, T.: Racial bias in legal language. Res. Polit. **6**(2), 2053168019848930 (2019)

14. Teruel, M., Cardellino, C., Cardellino, F., Alemany, L.A., Villata, S.: Legal text processing within the MIREL project. In: 1st Workshop on Language Resources and Technologies for the Legal Knowledge Graph, p. 42 (2018)

15. Tsurel, D., Doron, M., Nus, A., Dagan, A., Guy, I., Shahaf, D.: E-commerce dispute resolution prediction. In: Proceedings of the 29th ACM International Conference on Information & Knowledge Management, pp. 1465–1474 (2020)

16. Zhong, H., Xiao, C., Tu, C., Zhang, T., Liu, Z., Sun, M.: How does NLP benefit legal system: a summary of legal artificial intelligence. arXiv preprint arXiv:2004.12158 (2020)

Selling Political Data: How Political Ad Tech Firms' Discourses Legitimate Microtargeting

Kelley Cotter(✉) 📵

The Pennsylvania State University, University Park, PA 16802, USA
kcotter@psu.edu

Abstract. In spite of mounting concerns about the use of microtargeting in politics and attendant regulatory pressure, spending on digital advertising and ad tech has significantly increased over the past decade. In this article, I explore how political ad tech firms pursue continuity for the high stakes business of political microtargeting. Specifically, I present findings from a discourse analysis of the websites of 34 political ad tech firms who have developed microtargeting tools. Applying van Leeuwen's framework for legitimation in discourse to this analysis, I find that the firms legitimate microtargeting through four key discourses: Rationalization ("Microtargeting is the Right Approach"), mythopoesis ("Microtargeting is How you Win"), moral evaluation ("Microtargeting is the Democratic Thing to Do"), and Authorization ("Everybody's Doing It"). I argue that these discourses offer insight for understanding and contextualizing ongoing discussions about the future of microtargeting in politics.

Keywords: Political ad tech · Microtargeting · Political campaigning · Political communication

1 Introduction

Microtargeting, or tailoring strategic appeals to specific audience segments, has become increasingly central to political campaigns [1–4]. In response to this trend, ahead of the U.S. presidential election in 2020, multiple bills were introduced to ban microtargeting in political advertising [5]. These bills, alongside the establishment of data protection rules in European countries [4] and efforts to do so in the U.S. [6], decisions by big tech platforms to curb political ad targeting in 2020 [7], and criticism from activists, scholars, and journalists [4, 8–10], position political microtargeting as highly contentious. Yet, in spite of political microtargeting's contentiousness—as undergirded by mounting concerns about surveillance, privacy, inequality, and representation [3, 4, 8, 9, 11–18]—political ad tech spending has increased significantly over the last decade [2, 19].

In this article, I explore how political ad tech firms pursue continuity for the high stakes business of political microtargeting. Specifically, I present findings from a discourse analysis of the websites of 34 political ad tech firms who have developed microtargeting tools. Applying van Leeuwen's framework for legitimation in discourse [20] to

M. Smits (Ed.): iConference 2022, LNCS 13192, pp. 195–208, 2022.
https://doi.org/10.1007/978-3-030-96957-8_18

this analysis, I find that the firms legitimate microtargeting through four key discourses: Rationalization ("Microtargeting is the Right Approach"), mythopoesis ("Microtargeting is How you Win"), moral evaluation ("Microtargeting is the Democratic Thing to Do"), and Authorization ("Everybody's Doing It"). I argue that these discourses offer insight for understanding and contextualizing ongoing discussions about the future of microtargeting in politics.

2 Background

2.1 Microtargeting and Democracy

Targeted advertising is by no means new. Political campaigns have relied on targeted appeals since the radio age [21]. Yet, in the digital age, targeted advertising has become dramatically more granular and complex with advances in computation, as well as decreasing attachment to political parties [18]. "Microtargeting" is now used to "activate" narrow segments of the public who are likely to take action with the nudge of tailored messaging [8, 9]. For example, George W. Bush's 2004 presidential campaign produced microtargeting segments of Michigan voters, such as "Archie in the Bunker," "Flag & Family Republicans," and "Wageable Weak Democrats" [13]. This approach allows campaigns to direct resources towards individuals deemed most likely to act in ways that supports campaign goals—whether that is winning an election, passing a ballot measure or legislative proposal, or generating grassroots support for an issue.

Microtargeting has the potential to optimize labor and resources, help campaigns reach hard-to-reach and politically disinterested populations, increase the relevance of messages, diversify political campaigns, and augment political knowledge among voters about certain issues [4]. Yet, in spite of the promises of political microtargeting, some argue that it also poses various threats to democracy [4, 8, 18]. Some have suggested microtargeting may give rise to "political redlining" [1], wherein campaigns "ignor[e] individuals they model as unlikely to vote, such as unregistered, uneducated, and poor voters" [3]. Because political interest and engagement tend to vary according to socioeconomic background, there is concern that microtargeting reinforces and compounds inequalities in political involvement and knowledge [8]. Relatedly, some have suggested that microtargeting erodes participatory democracy by focusing attention on a small minority of the public, rather than encouraging broad engagement [8, 9, 22]. Others still have pointed to the "consumerization of the political" and an erosion of self-determination critical for a healthy democracy [18].

At the same time, there is also considerable doubt about just how precise machine classification and modelling actually are. Though headlines often stoke fear of AI capable of predicting a variety of complex behaviors, traits, and opinions that matter for campaigns, in reality, these claims may be overblown [23, 24]. In fact, perhaps the more legitimate concern about data-centric technologies in politics is the way they err. As was famously seen in the 2016 U.S. presidential election, the models predicting voter behavior and beliefs, and resultant campaign outcomes, are by no means perfect [7]. Indeed, concerns about the flawed, overvalued nature of targeted advertising have even resulted in comparisons to the pre-recession housing bubble [25].

More broadly, campaign technology acts as an "exostructure" of political life, "the material embodiment of social choices in the writing of behavioral routines, scripts, and protocols" [1]. As an increasingly integral part of this exostructure, the AI that underlies microtargeting has the potential to harden political power structures in different ways. First, AI frequently reenacts structural inequalities as a result of human biases embedded in data and developers' choices, which contributes to marginalization of the working poor, people of color, and women [14–17], among other marginalized groups. Indeed, algorithmic classification for microtargeting is political. As one study found, Facebook's classification of users' political "interests" for ad targeting prioritizes the interests of the socially and economically powerful through the categories produced [11].

Beyond bias, AI cannot effectively capture the full richness of people's political preferences. Algorithms are good at predicting what we will click on, watch, and/or purchase [2]. Algorithms are less good at predicting the complex emotions (e.g., guilt, pride, disgust) that coincide with such behavioral patterns or our closely held values that give rise to such reactions [2]. Further, algorithms cannot always effectively discern issues of interest (or concern) to a minority of a population, i.e. "long tail" interests [11]. Moreover, available political data has many blind spots, most reliably representing known voters, rather than would-be voters [26]. Given these shortcomings, machine-modelled microtargeting segments may omit or downplay important political features of the populace, particularly those associated with minoritized communities. In other words, microtargeting may reinforce the stratification of social problems in mainstream political discourse [27].

2.2 Technology and the Political Consulting Industry

Political consulting firms are largely responsible for developing and deploying microtargeting tools and services in campaigns. This industry has long played a broader, important role in constructing public opinion and orchestrating patterns of political participation [2]. Political consultants act as "critical intermediaries in the democratic process, standing between the voters and those who endeavor to represent them" [21]. Indeed, political consultants shape what political work looks like and how practitioners think about and appeal to the populace, particularly as mediated by data analytics [28]. As key elements of the infrastructure of political work [28], it is important to understand how political consulting firms conceptualize and sell the (data-centric) tools and services that shape the nuts and bolts of democracy and citizenship.

"Technology-intensive campaigning" is the bread and butter of the contemporary political consulting industry [28]. While present day political tech is the natural progression of decades of efforts to apply computation and mathematical modelling to voter behavior and public opinion [29], tech spending has vastly increased in recent years [19]. Technological innovation in campaigning has been afforded largely by the political consulting industry's lucrative nature [19, 21]. Its lucrative nature, in turn, has been propelled by the U.S.'s relatively lax regulation of political advertising, the lack of a general data protection law, and the watershed Citizens United decision, which greatly expanded flows of financial resources [21]. This is why microtargeting and ad spending in the U.S. far exceed that of other countries [4], although other countries have followed suit [18]. Additionally, a partisan arms race in political tech development in the U.S. has also brought additional infusions of cash, with both Democratic and Republican venture capital firms entering the scene [30].

2.3   The Legitimation of Microtargeting in Politics

In order to continue to be accepted in the face of the mounting concerns described above, political microtargeting requires ongoing legitimation by stakeholders, particularly the political ad tech firms that stand to profit from it. The institutionalization of industry practices grows not only from pragmatic imperatives, but also as a result of cultural norms and beliefs [31]. In the ongoing investment in microtargeting in politics, what matters is not (just) the merits of the underlying technology or the needs it satisfies, but the discourses that legitimate it. Here, I define legitimacy according to Suchman's definition: "a generalized perception or assumption that the actions of an entity are desirable, proper, or appropriate within some socially constructed system of norms, values, beliefs, and definitions" [31].

According to van Leeuwen [20], discourses construct legitimation and do so in four key ways: authorization (references to figures and objects of authority), moral evaluation (reference to value), rationalization (reference to instrumentality) and mythopoesis (reference to moral and cautionary tales). As political consulting firms sell their ad targeting tools and services to politicians, interest groups, and others, the discourses they employ to legitimate these tools and services are part of interested "sociotechnical imaginaries" [32] of what big data and AI mean and afford. Understanding and acknowledging these discourses can help disentangle the promises, possibilities, and demonstrated effects of political microtargeting.

In the remainder of this article, I offer insights on how ad tech firms in the political consulting industry discursively position microtargeting in ways that suggest responses to rhetorical "why's"—why, in spite of the risks [4], should democratic societies rely on microtargeting for mobilizing support for political candidates and causes? Why, in spite of doubts about its supreme efficacy [24], should campaigns enlist microtargeting? Why, in the face of potential threats to statutes of freedom of expression [4] and self-determination [18], should microtargeting remain largely unencumbered (thus far, in many places) by regulation? Through a discourse analysis of the websites of 34 political ad tech firms with microtargeting offerings, I describe how these firms mobilize van Leeuwen's four categories of discursive legitimation.

3   Method

To identify political ad tech firms for this analysis, I reviewed listings provided by trade publication Campaign & Elections and the American Association of Political Consultants' member directory. I also identified some firms via reference by other political consulting firms (including a list of more than 500 firms compiled by Higher Ground Labs).[1] Firms were included in the analysis if they met all of the following criteria: 1) have developed tools for microtargeting (e.g., targeting software, self-serve platforms),

---

[1] https://airtable.com/shrgc1cEc4FQzhhbD/tblBLLNHWBxRs7g0L.

2) serve political advertisers (candidates and/or causes), and 3) have an active, publicly accessible website. From these lists and criteria, I identified 34 firms to include in analyses. Of these, 11 were bipartisan or non-partisan, seven were Republican or conservative, and 16 were Democrat or progressive (see Table 1).

For each website, I navigated through all of the main pages, identifying pages relevant to political microtargeting. I took screenshots of each relevant page. Some firms published case studies and white papers on their websites in the form of PDF files, which I also downloaded. All files were imported into NVivo for analysis. Data collection took place between February 2021 and September 2021.

I approached each firm's website as a discursive text. From a Foucauldian perspective, I focused on how the firms' language and imagery constructed a system of representation that gave meaning to political microtargeting [33]. The analysis followed two cycles of iterative coding [34]. In the first cycle, I conducted initial coding to gain a provisional understanding of how the firms represented and assigned meaning to political microtargeting, as well as supporting work and technologies (data science, machine classification and modelling, technical interfaces, etc.). Initial coding included both coding for action (e.g., "Highlighting efficiency") and values (e.g., "It's for everyone"). In the second cycle of coding, I conducted pattern coding to identify higher-level categories and axial coding to explore how categories and subcategories related to one another [34]. Then, I conducted elaborative coding [34] to analyze categories through van Leeuwen's framework of discursive legitimation, which prompted further axial coding.

Table 1. List of ad tech firms

Firm	Website	Ideology
a4 Media	https://a4media.com/solution/politics	Non-partisan
AdVictory	https://advictory.com	Right-leaning*
Aristotle	https://www.aristotle.com	Non-partisan
Blue State Digital	https://www.bluestate.co	Democrat & progressive
Call Time	https://www.calltime.ai	Democrat
Campaign Ad-Cloud	http://www.campaignadcloud.com	Non-partisan
CampaignUprising.com	https://campaignuprising.com	Non-partisan
Catalist	https://catalist.us	Democrat & progressive
Civictech	https://civitech.io	Progressive
Civis	https://www.civisanalytics.com	Progressive
Cygnal	https://www.cygn.al	Republican
Data Trust	https://thedatatrust.com	Republican & conservative

(continued)

Table 1. (*continued*)

Firm	Website	Ideology
Deck	https://www.deck.tools	Democrat
Deep Roots Analytics	https://www.deeprootanalytics.com	Right-leaning*
DSPolitical	http://www.dspolitical.com	Democrat
El Toro	https://www.eltoro.com	Bipartisan
EveryAction	https://www.everyaction.com	Progressive
Grow Progress	https://growprogress.ai	Progressive
IQM Corporation	https://www.iqm.com	Non-partisan
L2	https://l2-data.com	Non-partisan
NationBuilder	https://nationbuilder.com	Non-partisan
NGPVAN	https://www.ngpvan.com	Democrat & progressive
Numinar	https://numinar.com	Right-leaning*
Outfox A.I	https://www.outfox.ai	Left-leaning*
Point Blank Political	https://www.PointBlankPolitical.com	Conservative***
Political Data Inc	https://www.politicaldata.com	Democrat
PredictWise	https://www.predictwise.com	Progressive
Speakeasy	https://www.speakeasypolitical.com	Left-leaning*
TargetSmart	https://targetsmart.com	Democrat & progressive
topplr	http://www.topplr.com	Non-partisan
Tru Optik Political Data Cloud	https://www.truoptik.com	Non-partisan**
Unearth	https://www.unearthcampaigns.com	Non-partisan**
VoteMAP	www.thevotemap.com	Democrat & progressive
Voter Gravity	https://votergravity.com	Conservative

Notes: Ideology was determined from explicit declarations on firms' websites, with the below exceptions:
*Ideology inferred from past clientele
**Firms were listed as non-partisan by default when no ideology was evident
***Ideology as determined by Campaigns & Election's directory

4 Findings

In the following sections, I describe the discourses political ad tech firms in the sample enlist to legitimate the practice of microtargeting and underlying technologies. First, I describe the most prominent discourses in which firms urge legitimation through rationalization, namely by emphasizing the appropriateness of microtargeting for the means and ends of winning campaigns. Second, I describe how firms urge legitimation through mythopoesis, or narratives wherein microtargeting pays off with winning campaigns. Third, I describe how firms legitimate microtargeting through moral evaluation, by gesturing to its democratizing force. Fourth, I describe how firms legitimate microtargeting through authorization, naturalizing its use among campaigns of all sizes and as accepted across multiple sectors.

4.1 Rationalization: Microtargeting is the Right Approach

All of the firms investigated described microtargeting and technologies that support it with reference to utilitarian and pragmatic claims about its efficiency, precision, and efficacy. For example, Deep Roots Analytics stated that the firm "provides greater efficiency, effectiveness and accountability so your media buying decisions can be deeply rooted in data." Discussing a campaign targeting voters at risk of losing health care, DSPolitical wrote that "smart campaigns and organizations should be looking at innovative ways to speak with the very people these cuts will hit hardest—and there is simply no more precise and efficient way to do exactly that than with digital advertising." HaystaqDNA simply proclaimed in all capitals "WE LOOK FORWARD TO HELPING YOU USE YOUR RESOURCES MORE EFFICIENTLY." Such claims about efficiency, precision, and efficacy commonly revolve around cost, implying that microtargeting will reduce "wasteful" spending. For example, in a blog post, Boulder Strategies paired an image of six burning $100 USD bills with the claim that by using a CTV/OTT ad targeting platform, campaigns' ad dollars "will almost certainly go further in reaching your target audience" (see Fig. 1). With these kinds of statements, the firms constructed a sense that microtargeting is the smart approach. As TargetSmart succinctly put it, "we believe that good data makes you smarter."

Fig. 1. Screenshot from a Boulder Strategies blog post

In addition to emphasizing the ways microtargeting improves campaigning, nearly all firms also made reference to well-established tropes of technological progress. This discourse communicated a sense that integrating big data and AI are simply the way of the future (or bringing the future to the present), with descriptors like "disruptive," "cutting-edge," and "trailblazing." Boulder Strategies, for example, self-referentially declared: "Behind the magic, there's a revolutionary technology platform." Aristotle explained: "[T]oday's modern political campaign must be supported by a relational database, with online and multi-channels accessibility (via web-browser, mobile-optimized web application, or a native smart-phone app) an absolute must." Many firms also contrasted their cutting-edge approaches with traditional methods. For example, in a webinar trailer, Campaign Ad-Cloud proclaimed "Outdated tactics reflect outdated messaging" and "Digital is taking over politics with or without you." In a blog post titled "13 Ways Digital Ads Outperform Political Mailers," the firm illustrated its argument with an image of an individual typing on a laptop, while depositing a campaign mailer in the trash (see Fig. 2). Mirroring this, HaystaqDNA wrote on its website: "Traditional marketing wastes time and money reaching people who aren't interested." Likewise, in relation to their IP targeting tools, Online Candidate exhorted campaigns to "Avoid the waste and inefficiency of traditional advertising."

Fig. 2. Screenshot of a Campaign Ad-Cloud blog post

Through these discourses, the firms position microtargeting as the means to an end. They make a case for microtargeting by emphasizing its utility and the sense that it is the best and, indeed, *right* way to approach campaigning in the present and going forward.

4.2 Mythopoesis: Microtargeting is How You Win

Most firms in the sample shared case studies of past successful clients, namely campaigns that won an election, passed a ballot measure, met a donation goal, and so on. These narratives offered data-supported moral tales that present a compelling example of how microtargeting helps campaigns win. A common trope throughout these tales is what I refer to as "David (armed with data) vs. goliath." Take, for example, AdVictory's recap of Doug Burgum's successful campaign for the North Dakota Office of the Governor:

> When Doug entered the race in February the campaign began at a 49 point polling deficit and was dealt a blow in April when Doug's opponent received the official endorsement and support of North Dakota's Republican Party. North Dakota columnist and radio host Mike McFeeley framed the race nicely in a piece written just before Election Day. According to McFeeley, "…if Burgum pulls the upset, it'd be a victory for the ages. It'd also be a defeat of epic proportions for Stenehjem, who'd be left to answer how he blew a 49-point lead." That is exactly what happened. Also, Burgum won by 19 points.

As AdVictory went on to explain, the firm achieved this win via "an aggressive, calculated, and coordinated voter contact effort across all fronts." This story, like many other put forth by firms, could be read as either a moral or a cautionary tale [20]. In the former case, we see that Burgum was rewarded for his use of AdVictory's microtargeting tools and services. Yet, we can also see how the story might suggest that Burgum's opponent fumbled his 49-point lead *because* he failed to employ the same strategies.

Many firms also explicitly articulated the moral of these kinds of tales. For example, Boulder Strategies boasted "We're proud to have racked up a 92% win rate," while Unearth declared an 85% win rate. Alternately, VoteMap proclaimed on their homepage, "It's what we do with our data that win campaigns," while the bold, prominent text on Numinar's homepage reads, "We turn your data into votes." Point Blank Political simply features a "Get Elected" button on their homepage.

These promises of a happy ending present a clear model of action: *microtargeting is how you win political campaigns.* The stories and statements put forth by the firms establish clear risks and rewards related to whether or not campaigns employ microtargeting. In doing so, the firms legitimate microtargeting as an essential campaign practice.

4.3 Moral Evaluation: Microtargeting is the Democratic Thing to Do

Beyond linking microtargeting to winning, many firms additionally positioned microtargeting as resonant with—sometimes upholding—democratic principles. For example, SpeakEasy framed microtargeting as a means of supporting participatory democracy, writing on their homepage that the firm "democratizes the campaign process to put you in control of your messaging, targeting and delivery." Similarly, in a blog post that quoted the firm's CEO, IQM wrote: "'Algorithms and data mining have already revolutionized our consumer experiences. It's time to apply these best practices to voting and the political arena.' The public policy stakes are too high and it's the only way our democratic institutions can endure." L2 showed an image of the U.S. Constitution next to a statement declaring the firm to be "the chosen data provider for members of the U.S. Congress conducting constituent outreach" (see Fig. 3). Others, like Aristotle and Political Data, Inc., respectively, described their missions as "further[ing] the democratic process" and "strengthen[ing] the democratic process by providing political candidates and organizations with the best data and innovative tools supporting effective voter communications." Of their self-serve targeted advertising platform, DSPolitical's CEO shared, "We're excited to be disrupting and democratizing the voter targeted digital ad space with DemocraticAds.com by putting the power of our unrivaled data and near universal reach into the hands of local Democratic campaigns and progressive causes." Likewise, VoteMap described their work as "democratizing data and bringing enterprise-level innovation to progressive campaigns of all sizes," while Numinar describes their work as "building the future of data-driven democracy."

Fig. 3. Screenshot of a L2 "Customers" webpage

Through these statements, firms configured microtargeting tools and services as associated with the moral value of democracy. In this, microtargeting becomes abstracted from actual practices, particularly any shortcomings or consequences, to foreground its natural fit with democratic principles of freedom and equality.

4.4 Authorization: Everybody's Doing It

As some of the statements in the last section hint, many firms emphasized the widespread use of microtargeting in politics. By highlighting its widespread use, particularly among authorities in political advertising and other domains, the firms naturalized microtargeting as standard practice. For example, Resonate states on its website: "Hundreds of consumer brands, ad agencies, and political and advocacy organizations are using Resonate's consumer insights to make better connections with their customers and yours. Don't let your competition get ahead." In a blog post titled "Political Campaigning 101: Building a list of Target Voters and Supporters," Speakeasy offered a reference group for upward comparison: "Big campaigns spend lots of time on targeting (choosing which voters to communicate with) and you will hear a lot about this if you are talking to consultants." Here, Speakeasy implied that "big campaigns," who know the ropes, rely on targeting and that one should expect to encounter talk of targeting.

Beyond references to microtargeting's widespread use in political campaigning, firms also frequently referenced other sectors' affinity for microtargeting or the data and technologies underlying it. For example, Aristotle noted that "Universities and research institutions across the United States nationwide call on us for quick analysis and reporting.

Many Researchers routinely tap into our national voter file for large, complex queries." Yet, more often than not, the sector firms referenced was the private sector, which was presented as a role model of sorts for public sector marketing. For example, in an infographic titled "How Much Does It Cost to Buy the Presidency," El Toro presented bar graphs depicting digital spending across commercial and political sectors, noting "[P]olitical is still trailing the private sector. For digital ads $1 billion campaign investment in digital [among political campaigns] only amounts to 9.5% of total ad spending, but 38–50% is allocated by many other industries" (see Fig. 4). In a blog post, IQM similarly stated,

> Large scale marketing now uses a combination of e-commerce tools, creative services, data analytics, and artificial intelligence to deliver messages to a targeted audience. The days are [sic] creating high-end print ads published in a glossy magazines [sic] have dwindled--and some industries, such as politics have been slower to adapt than others.

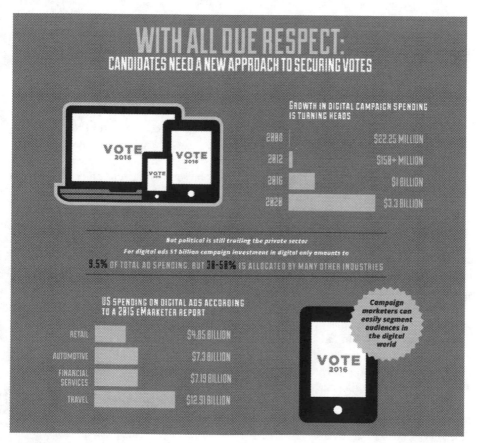

Fig. 4. Excerpt of El Toro's infographic, "How Much Does It Cost to Buy the Presidency"

Likewise, Grow Progress explained: "Predictive modeling has revolutionized how corporations message and advertise to audiences—and our algorithm brings that innovation directly to campaigns and progressive organizations." Throughout the firms' websites, references like this to the broader marketing industry seem designed to persuade political campaigns that microtargeting had already been sanctioned by the marketing industry, and those who resist its use lack insider expertise.

By invoking figures of authority in politics and marketing, the firms presented microtargeting as an already well-established practice. In a sense, the firms communicated that those who do not embrace microtargeting risk being labeled a luddite. In associating the use of microtargeting with industry expertise, the firms legitimized it via the logics of institutional hierarchies of authority.

5   Discussion

Through an analysis of political ad tech firms' websites, I have demonstrated four ways these firms construct discourses that legitimize the use of microtargeting (and its underlying technologies) in politics. Specifically, the firms analyzed urged the legitimation of microtargeting through positioning microtargeting as pragmatic, a "no brainer" approach (rationalization); with moral tales, wherein they link microtargeting to winning campaigns (mythopoesis); by presenting microtargeting as furthering or upholding democracy (moral evaluation); and by aligning microtargeting with expert-sanctioned best practices (authorization).

As spending on digital advertising continues to rise, these discourses of legitimation grant insight into the ongoing naturalization of microtargeting in U.S. political campaigning at all levels. They further grant insight on why and how microtargeting could be naturalized elsewhere. For example, while microtargeting is not currently as central to political campaigns in European countries, campaign practices in the U.S. often inspire practices abroad [4]. Moreover, the discourses help explain how microtargeting has proliferated in the face of concerns about its negative impacts on democracy—including new proposed legislation in the U.S.—and doubts about the hype that surrounds it. It is difficult to pinpoint the exact techniques that make a difference in campaign outcomes [21]. The discourses described in this study strategically elided this point, while seeking to mount a compelling case for the use of microtargeting.

As we continue to debate the risks and rewards of political microtargeting, the discourses laid out in previous sections offer insight into the arguments that are being and could be used to sustain the practice. Importantly, I do not accept these discourses as ground truth. Rather, the discourses represent the engine of the interested sociotechnical imaginaries [32] being actively constructed around microtargeting within the political ad tech space. As in other domains, a deeply held belief in the power of data science and data-centric technology urges increasing investment in them (van Dijck 2014) and enjoins us to look beyond their so-called unintended consequences [35]. By identifying these discourses of legitimation, I offer a means of recognizing the technoutopian norms and values being constructed around political microtargeting that both help explain its continued and largely unimpeded use (at least in the U.S.) and warrant further investigation. Moreover, because political ad tech firms' clientele happen to be those most closely involved in shaping, if not making, policy around data protection and use, it will be important to attend to whether/how these discourses of legitimation permeate other areas of the public sphere increasingly enlisting big data. Future work might examine how political ad tech firms' discourses about microtargeting identified in this study travel and evolve among different actors in the political sphere and with what effect.

This study has limitations. All of the firms in the sample constructed are based in the U.S. Although this bias is somewhat unavoidable given that the U.S. has become the center of gravity for political microtargeting, findings should be understood as bounded by the political, legal, and social landscape of the U.S. Second, a plurality of firms in the sample were left-leaning. While this is consistent with historical trends in the political consulting industry [28], this further bounds the analysis. Third, there are many other political consulting firms that offer microtargeting services, but do not develop their own microtargeting tools. These firms may employ other discourses to legitimate political microtargeting, or may even articulate a more sober take on their utility. Finally, per an interpretivist lens, the analysis presented should be considered but one reading, among other possible interpretations, of ad tech firms' communications about microtargeting.

References

1. Howard, P.N.: New Media Campaigns and the Managed Citizen. Cambridge University Press, Cambridge (2006)
2. Karpf, D.: Analytic Activism: Digital Listening and the New Political Strategy. Oxford University Press, New York (2016)
3. Kreiss, D.: Yes we can (profile you): a brief primer on campaigns and political data. Stanf. Law Rev. Online **64**, (2012)
4. Zuiderveen Borgesius, F.J., et al.: Online political microtargeting: promises and threats for democracy. ULR **14**, 82 (2018). https://doi.org/10.18352/ulr.420
5. Cox, K.: Proposed bill would ban microtargeting of political advertisements. https://arstechnica.com/tech-policy/2020/05/proposed-bill-would-ban-microtargeting-of-political-advertisements/. Accessed 12 Sep 2021
6. Larson, B.N., Schmit, C., Kum, H.-C.: Data privacy laws in the US protect profit but prevent sharing data for public good – people want the opposite. http://theconversation.com/data-privacy-laws-in-the-us-protect-profit-but-prevent-sharing-data-for-public-good-people-want-the-opposite-166320. Accessed 14 Sep 2021
7. Ryan-Mosley, T.: The technology that powers the 2020 campaigns, explained. https://www.technologyreview.com/2020/09/28/1008994/the-technology-that-powers-political-campaigns-in-2020-explained/. Accessed 12 Sep 2021
8. Kim, Y.M.: Algorithmic opportunity: digital advertising and inequality in political involvement. Forum **14** (2016). https://doi.org/10.1515/for-2016-0034
9. Barocas, S.: The price of precision: voter microtargeting and its potential harms to the democratic process. In: Proceedings of the first edition workshop on Politics, elections and data - PLEAD 2012, p. 31. ACM Press, Maui (2012). https://doi.org/10.1145/2389661.2389671
10. Ortutay, B., Seitz, A.: How microtargeted political ads are wreaking havoc on our elections (2020). https://www.latimes.com/business/technology/story/2020-02-01/how-microtargeted-political-ads-are-wreaking-havoc-on-our-elections
11. Cotter, K., Medeiros, M., Pak, C., Thorson, K.: "Reach the right people": the politics of "interests" in Facebook's classification system for ad targeting. Big Data Soc. **8**, 1–16 (2021). https://doi.org/10.1177/2053951721996046

12. Gandy, O.H.: The panoptic sort: a political economy of personal information. Westview, Boulder, Colo (1993)
13. Gorton, W.A.: Manipulating citizens: how political campaigns' use of behavioral social science harms democracy. New Polit. Sci. **38**, 61–80 (2016). https://doi.org/10.1080/07393148. 2015.1125119
14. Benjamin, R.: Race After Technology: Abolitionist Tools for the New Jim Code. Polity, Medford (2019)
15. Eubanks, V.: Automating Inequality: How High-Tech Tools Profile, Police, and Punish the Poor. St. Martin's Press, New York (2017)
16. Noble, S.U.: Algorithms of Oppression: How Search Engines Reinforce Racism. New York University Press, New York (2018)
17. O'Neil, C.: Weapons of math destruction: how big data increases inequality and threatens democracy. Crown, New York (2016)
18. Bennett, C.J.: Trends in voter surveillance in western societies: privacy intrusions and democratic implications. SS **13**, 370–384 (2015). https://doi.org/10.24908/ss.v13i3/4.5373
19. Higher Ground Labs: 2020 Political tech landscape report (2020)
20. Van Leeuwen, T.: Legitimation in discourse and communication. Discourse Commun. **1**, 91–112 (2007). https://doi.org/10.1177/1750481307071986
21. Sheingate, A.D.: Building a Business of Politics: The Rise of Political Consulting and the Transformation of American Democracy. Oxford University Press, New York (2016)
22. Schier, S.E.: By invitation only: the rise of exclusive politics in the United States. University of Pittsburgh Pre (2000)
23. Baldwin-Philippi, J.: The myths of data-driven campaigning. Polit. Commun. **34**, 627–633 (2017). https://doi.org/10.1080/10584609.2017.1372999
24. Karpf, D.: Preparing for the Campaign Tech Bullshit Season. https://civichall.org/civicist/pre paring-campaign-tech-bullshit-season/
25. Hwang, T.: Subprime attention crisis advertising and the time bomb at the heart of the internet. Farrar Straus and Giroux, New York (2020)
26. Hersh, E.D.: Hacking the Electorate: How Campaigns Perceive Voters. Cambridge University Press, New York (2015)
27. Hilgartner, S., Bosk, C.L.: The rise and fall of social problems: a public arenas model. Am. J. Sociol. **94**, 53–78 (1988)
28. Kreiss, D.: Prototype Politics: Technology-Intensive Campaigning and the Data of Democracy. Oxford University Press, New York (2016)
29. McKelvey, F.: The other cambridge analytics: early "artificial intelligence" in American political science. Roberge, J., Castelle, M. (eds.) The Cultural Life of Machine Learning an Incursion into Critical AI Studies, pp. 117–142. Springer, Cham (2021). https://doi.org/10.1007/978-3-030-56286-1_4
30. Isenstadt, A.: Republicans launching innovation fund to match Democrats. https://politi.co/2OUySoP. Accessed 12 Sep 2021
31. Suchman, M.C.: Managing legitimacy: strategic and institutional approaches. Acad. Manag. Rev. **20**, 571–610 (1995)
32. Jasanoff, S.: Future imperfect: science, technology, and the imaginations of modernity. In: Dreamscapes of Modernity: Sociotechnical Imaginaries and the Fabrication of Power. University of Chicago Press, Chicago (2015)
33. Hall, S.: Foucault: power, knowledge and discourse. In: Wetherell, M., Yates, S., Taylor, S. (eds.) Discourse Theory and Practice: A Reader, pp. 72–81. SAGE, Thousand Oaks (2001)
34. Saldaña, J.: The Coding Manual for Qualitative Researchers. Sage Publications Ltd., London (2009)
35. Parvin, N., Pollock, A.: Unintended by design: on the political uses of "unintended consequences." Engag. Sci. Technol. Soc. **6**, 320–327 (2020). https://doi.org/10.17351/ests2020.497

Data Science

A Brief Typology of Time: Temporal Structuring and Dissonance in Service Provision for People Experiencing Homelessness

Stephen C. Slota[1]([⊠]) [iD], Kenneth R. Fleischmann[1] [iD], and Sherri R. Greenberg[2]

[1] School of Information, University of Texas at Austin, Austin, TX 78712, USA
stephen.slota@austin.utexas.edu
[2] LBJ School of Public Affairs, University of Texas at Austin, Austin, TX 78712, USA

Abstract. How does time matter in applied data science, and how do the different temporal rhythms of various stakeholders and organizations impact how cities accomplish data-intensive work? This paper explores the role of time in collaborations oriented around leveraging data toward issues of key social concern. This paper builds upon the literature of critical infrastructure studies and organizational studies of time. Data collection included thirty-one interviews with stakeholders involved in service provision to people experiencing homelessness. Key findings included identifying two main types of temporal dissonance, interpersonal (involving stakeholders) and infrastructural (involving data). The result is a refined typology that draws from, and builds upon, prior literature in infrastructure and organizational studies. Understanding the factors that contribute to temporal dissonance can help organizations identify and resolve tensions between meeting immediate goals and work toward a broader vision.

Keywords: Critical infrastructure studies · Organizational studies · Temporality

1 Introduction

Our visions of the future are often closely tied to the problems of the present. Politically, infrastructure is often presented as both an idealized future and the means towards achieving that future (Larkin 2013). This becomes even more visible in current discussion of smart cities, which often present algorithmic governance, expansive data collection and sensing regimes, and other means of deploying data infrastructure to support the development, management, and progress of cities (van Ooijen et al. 2019). This utopian vision of knowledge-informed governance supporting community engagement built upon regimes of data collection and analysis (Ismagilova et al. 2019; Kurzweil and Grossman 2010) often insufficiently accounts for the practices required for data analysis and the infrastructures that support it.

More specifically, smart cities are future-oriented, operating on the assumption that the technologies of the future will displace the problems of the present. However, especially in the context of 'big data' applications, where data are often used outside the

© The Author(s), under exclusive license to Springer Nature Switzerland AG 2022
M. Smits (Ed.): iConference 2022, LNCS 13192, pp. 211–224, 2022.
https://doi.org/10.1007/978-3-030-96957-8_19

context of their initial collection, the temporal aspects of data collection, analysis, and deployment are often considered apart from the ever-changing circumstances and environments that they first represented. In this paper, we present a set of 'temporal dissonances' that emerged from an ongoing, mixed-method, study of the City of Austin's collaborative work towards ending homelessness. These temporal dissonances remind us that time does indeed matter, and that the deployment of data in the name of progress must consider the temporal aspects of that data to effectively make use of it.

2   Related Work

Emerging knowledge infrastructures (Edwards et al. 2013) have a complex temporality. Infrastructure projects exist in the "long now", where future use is consistently in tension with present needs (Ribes and Finholt 2009). Infrastructure is not static and unchanging, rather it needs repair, maintenance, and ongoing support to maintain a degree of homeostasis in operation (Jackson 2014). Collected data, in the view of algorithmic or knowledge-driven governance, is infrastructural to the knowledge work that supports the evaluation of policies and inter-organizational collaboration. Remembering that there is no such thing as 'raw data' (Bowker 2013), the impact of time on data becomes vital to understanding how knowledge might be deployed and used as cities grow increasingly 'smart'.

The discourse on smart cities and algorithmic governance, similarly, invokes a narrative where historical aspects of a city are displaced by novel technologies. In contrast, Olmstead (2021) proposes that these histories, while they do not produce a singular narrative of progression through technology, still "[diffract] through the present in ways that both inform and constrain possibility" (p. 260). Hence, a conception of governance through novel technology and computational analysis must grapple with its embedded practices and concepts of temporality, and this produces significant tensions when the present and future seek to wholly displace the past. Mills (2000) points out that data carry temporal elements and demonstrates that data work often seeks to account for the past in the present. Similarly, predictive analyses propose an indistinct relationship between the past, present, and future where the future is assumed to be to some extent determined by the past and present. These 'datafied' perceptions of time often obscure the lived experience of time and have inconsistent temporal dynamics that require context and localization to be effectively understood (Ladner 2012). Data evolve over time (Letondal et al. 2009), and the temporality of data is not limited to descriptions of time within data, but also, how the context and quality of data evolve with changing circumstances and environments.

Büthe (2002) argues that temporality is a central consideration for social scientists engaged in the study and modeling of history, and that narrative accounts work to test models of history against their specific contexts. But the importance of temporality is not limited to the study of what has already happened. Reactive uses of data, such as in those responding to disaster, are often situated in an ongoing present, where an orientation that considers future change and history as well, might be more appropriate (Compton 2020). Pink and Lanzeni (2018) demonstrate the need for temporal commitment in the ethical use of data, particularly at the forefront of 'big data' interventions, which have relatively short histories and indeterminate futures.

Studies of time had been long entrenched in the distinction between subjective and objective time (Adam 1995), but Orlikowski and Yates (2002), and Jackson et al. (2011) both reject this distinction to varying degrees. In the case of Orlikowski and Yates, this distinction is rejected in favor of considering how sociomaterial practices structure temporal aspects of organizations, and how individual and organizational behaviors constitute different temporalities of work and collaboration. In the case of Jackson et al., the distinction between objective and subjective time is not considered. Rather, they present four distinct temporal registers, or rhythms, that produce dissonance that must be resolved in conducting collaborative knowledge production. For Jackson et al., this also involved not being solely concerned with the practices giving rise to these temporal registers but considering how temporal rhythms of natural phenomena (phenomenal register), personal narratives (biographical register), supportive systems (infrastructural register), and organizations (organizational register) must be resolved as part of producing knowledge about the world.

Jackson et al., propose that "this makes rhythmic disjuncture or dissonance a frequent and under-examined tension within distributed scientific forms – and the complex art of rhythmic alignment a much-understudied category of organizational work." (Jackson et al. 2011, p. 249). Rather than focusing on how organizational practice structures concepts of time, they extend the concept of sociomaterial practices of temporality to considerations of how collaborations necessarily engage across organizations, and across the temporal registers they identify. This is a natural expansion of the concept of temporal structuring as it exceeds the boundaries of a single organization and provides leverage for understanding time as it impinges upon knowledge work both within and outside the academy. In this paper, we draw upon Jackson et al. (2011) to structure our understanding of the conflicting rhythms of work in ending homelessness in the City of Austin. We explore 'the complex art of rhythmic alignment' through the dissonances produced as participating members of the collaborative Continuum of Care seek to direct their work with data, while still addressing immediate needs of people experiencing homelessness.

3   Methods

This work occurred as part of an ongoing mixed-method collaboration between our research team and the City of Austin, regarding making more effective use of data collected for the City's mission of ending homelessness. The City of Austin has invested substantially in the process of more effectively using its data – a key example is the Affordable Housing Search Tool, which resulted from the 2019 Code for America Summit (City of Austin 2020). The City of Austin collaborates with a Continuum of Care (CoC), including numerous nonprofits and governmental offices to address and end homelessness in the City of Austin and Travis County. This portion of the study was conducted the as part of an exploratory study of the data and collaboration practices of those participating in the CoC in the context of an ongoing interdisciplinary study that will leverage social and data scientific research toward refining the City of Austin's approach to ending homelessness.

For this portion of the study, we interviewed 31 stakeholders within the CoC, drawing primarily from those directly engaged with providing services or information to people experiencing homelessness. Initially, we selected interviewees following recommendations from key collaborators in the City of Austin government. Then, we used snowball sampling among this initial group to effectively leverage the social knowledge of our participants to identify further potential informants (Noy 2008). Of these participants, 4 were from ECHO, 14 from nonprofit organizations, 12 from collaborating local or state governmental roles, and 1 participant who was primarily in an academic role.

We conducted hour-long interviews with each participant, structured according to critical incident technique (Flanagan 1954) to ground these interviews in the lived experience of participants. In these interviews we addressed data practices, collaborations, and outcome measures to better understand how knowledge and data directed and structured service provision. We analyzed interviews according to thematic analysis (Braun and Clarke 2006), which we selected for its flexibility in conducting both inductive and deductive analyses of rich qualitative data sets. We first transcribed and coded the data inductively, developing a set of themes that we presented to the larger team. After identifying temporality and time as key themes, we drew upon the theoretical framework presented by Jackson et al. (2011) to interpret these themes according to their disjunct and dissonant temporal registers.

In this paper, we present four tensions created through differing temporal rhythms of work, expectation, collaboration, and assessment, and explore how these tensions structure, inhibit, or otherwise impact knowledge work undertaken within and among stakeholder organizations in the CoC. First, we will consider the tensions arising from the desire to effectively document, represent, and record, compared to the perceived need to enact rapid interventions among those experiencing homelessness, and how these concerns impact data quality. Second, we consider temporal dissonance arising from the coverage of data and its use in supporting inter-organizational collaboration. Third, we present tensions arising between disjunct rhythms of collaboration, funding, and intervention. Finally, we consider the tension between daily work and long-term organizational goals.

4 Findings

Through these interviews, the key theme that emerged was the role of temporal dissonance in disrupting activity and creating tensions among stakeholders. We observed several tensions arising from the negotiation of differing temporal aspects related to organizational goals and the use of data in structuring, assessing, or planning activities. Time, and timing, was, indeed, an important factor of how work was imagined and conceived. Temporal aspects themselves varied, and in that variation, they often produced tensions. Additionally, concerns of time and timing were key components of how collaborations were negotiated, how incremental work was understood to contribute to long-term goals, and how data were deployed, interpreted, and understood.

4.1 The Infrastructural Register: Documenting in Tension with Acting

A consistent trend within these interviews is the notion that data work is, indeed, work. However, many of the service providers had few people doing such work. For many of the interviewed organizations, one person was responsible for managing, analyzing, and representing data. Data collection, though, was an expectation for nearly all employees engaged in active interventions. A significant portion of ongoing data collection about those experiencing homelessness was performed through a coordinated assessment process, where new clients of the system completed a standardized assessment known as the VI-SPDAT (Vulnerability Index – Service Prioritization Decision Assistance Tool). While we have previously explored some of the implications of this tool (*citation removed*), for this analysis, we emphasize the disconnect, embodied by this tool, between documentary work and service provision.

Our interviews revealed that often the expectations for documentation and other forms of data collection were in tension with other expected outcomes. When tension arose between data collection and the daily work, most often, it was the data collection that suffered, as in the below quote from a manager working with survivors of domestic violence:

> "The amount of paperwork that's required in this project is burdensome to the frontline staff. And it takes away from direct services to the clients and the time that you're able to provide face to face...it's an arduous amount of paperwork that's required case managers [to] spend...a quarter of their time at least. It's a resource burden for the organization."

Here we see two aspects of temporal structuring of data use in its initial collection. First, time itself is a resource for these organizations, and a limited one. Second, the bureaucratic requirements that rely on consistent collection of data, documentation of activities, etc. were in tension with the requirements of daily work. Managing the collection of data for internal evaluation, as well as those data intended for external sharing, was seen as a burdensome interference with the expressed goals of many of the organizations providing services to people experiencing homelessness. This was a concern of the following participant, who worked in the management of public watersheds:

> "...we relied heavily on our service providers to do the distribution. In terms of data and how that's looked, again, it goes back to we're asking the service providers to self-report the data when they're out in the field, and to tell us where they're going. And so, there's some challenges in that, that we want to honor our service providers, and desire to protect the people that they're caring for... So, the challenge [is], how do we encourage staff to give us all the data that we need, but also walk that line?"

According to interviewees, data quality issues arose, in part, from data practices such as sharing, metadata, and other aspects of data structure. However, data quality was often linked to the practice of requiring people engaged in direct intervention to split their time between data collection and the more immediate goals of their organizations. And here, we see an additional implication of this tension: data collection in many ways supported long-term goals of organizations and even collaborations, but it was somewhat remote from more short-term activities. Thus, data in the short term becomes a living resource: its viability and accuracy were perceived to evolve over time, according to changing circumstances of both individuals and the environment.

4.2   The Infrastructural Register: Planning in Tension with Acting

While it was largely expected that data could be used to understand trends, its utility in directing work was closely tied to its temporality. Thus, ineffectiveness in resolving these temporal differences becomes an exercise in ensuring that data sharing agreements, data quality, and data fit all receive the necessary attention to ensure utility over time. Some data sharing agreements, as referenced in the below quotes, required ongoing commitment and collaborations from participating organizations. This was tied to ongoing support and funding of these activities, and similarly to being able to demonstrate their effectiveness. Barriers in sustaining these arrangements – what might also be thought of as the inability to resolve the rhythms of resources, action, and long vs. short term goals – led to the end of collaborations, and the 'expiry' of data shared and collected for them:

> "Well, yeah, and that we couldn't, we couldn't determine how to make it sustainable. Okay, so that kind of makes it all... we just weren't able to identify a way to do that, at a large scale on an ongoing basis."

The above quote refers to a collaborative data analysis project that sought to both demonstrate the impact of organizational actions to the community, and to provide 'data matching', ensuring that one set of records refers to the same individual as another set of records in a different system. With both goals, issues of ongoing funding, prioritization of work in a collaboration, and other tensions related to limited resources and the time-sensitive nature of the data, served as barriers to project sustainability – a highly-desired goal (and measure of success or failure) among our participants. Service providers related their participation in ongoing plans and goals, but often questioned how effective these long-term goals were for current efforts:

> "And we have had a 30-year plan called Imagine Austin. But as you might imagine, a 30-year plan doesn't really have implementation or specific sort of short-term goals or activities."

The above member of a nonprofit organization seeking to end homelessness went on to relate that looking a bit less far in the future was more tractable in structuring their efforts:

> "...And so, this... strategic direction 2023 plan really is supposed to be a three-to-five-year plan. And homelessness was identified as the top priority."

Planning assumes temporal structuring of activities, and reapportions resources according to long-term goals, rather than short-term intervention. Present needs and future goals are often in tension. Service providers weighed pressure to produce tangible results quickly against future needs. Here, data begins to play a much more visible role in resolving tensions between present work and future directions. Time remained a key axis for understanding and structuring work, and trend data and information was vital in understanding the population being served. According to interviewees, outcome measures have both short-term components and long-term goals, according to organizational and professional priorities:

> "...outcome measures are very much around safety, immediate and ongoing safety. But they're also around, getting a home, maintaining a home, being able to have an income that allows you to sustain the home, and also to be able to have supports in place that you can rely on when things go south."

Similarly, client issues were not seen as being resolved after immediate intervention. Goals for clients were phrased in the long term, even as short term needs similarly structured daily work:

> "But it's disappointing to me when I see some of these people that are back out on the streets after, you know, one month or two months, or sometimes even longer, and some of them on multiple occasions... Because you see somebody, how excited they were when they were moving in, and, you know, you find out you see him on the street, sometime later and find out that they've been kicked out..."

This emerges as a dynamic in the City's mission of ending homelessness because many of the potential harms of homelessness happen in the short term, rather than in the long term:

> "I think [an] important thing for funders and the public [to] understand is that when you subject a young child to homelessness, both the transience of what's happening to that child, it's baked in. And it also normalizes that sort of life, and it doesn't give them some of the opportunities that you would hope would happen for children. So, I think if you look at the earliest stages of prevention, you want to make sure that kids--any child's time being homeless is extraordinarily brief. And best prevented on the front end."

Therefore, the constraints of strategic planning were in tension with the short-term nature, and long-term impact, of potential harms to more vulnerable populations. Similarly, the data were subject to the tensions between planning and acting, often due to the transient nature of the population being served:

> "I think it's good that as a community, we have this snapshot in time, but the data is fuzzy, at best, it's imperfect. [It] depends on the weather. It depends on the HUD definitions that year."

4.3 Biographical and Organizational Registers

Service provision among the CoC was often a collaborative effort, engaging multiple service providers, each of whom created data for both internal tracking and intended for system-wide sharing. These data often did not significantly overlap, as many service providers saw the need to adjust data formatting and description for sharing to be a burden on their limited time. Direct service provision often required rapid intervention, in part due to the more transient nature of people lacking access to consistent housing. This inability to engage over time was seen as problematic:

"I think the transient nature of the population we're working with makes it a difficult population to try and come up with any sort of real hard conclusions on..."

Similarly, diffusion of effort due to limited time emerges again:

"And I think just things, you know, tend to, you know, pop up, and I think that, like, the attention span, that's focused on that effort, you know, tends to wane or get shifted in a different direction. So focus gets taken off of that, and resources have to be allocated somewhere else that, you know, possibly a higher priority. And so that's really one of the big, the biggest issues or barriers, right now."

Some aspects of service provision became very short-term as the constraints of organizational engagement required some steps to happen before others, such as the need for legal identification prior to applying for housing:

"And that the ID issue...[is] kind of time sensitive in the next, you know, 30 to 60 days. But really, it's not even developed into anything as of yet, but that is going to be a time sensitive thing. A lot of those, as I mentioned, a lot of these people don't have IDs currently. And that's one of those one of the requirements that you have to have an ID in order to move into a lot of these housing opportunities."

What we saw in this theme was a tension between the rapid intervention that was seen as necessary to avoid further harm, and the organizational need to track, represent, and understand served communities. Inconsistent living arrangements of people in need of services required that intervention be rapid to avoid losing track of those entering the system, but bureaucratic and organizational constraints often led to a 'hurry up and wait' scenario. In these scenarios, those who were not rated as significantly vulnerable were often left waiting for limited resources to become available. In one specific set of cases related by participants, expected aspects of personal development became much more evident in structuring how people in need of services engaged with the system. In the case of homeless youth, and youth who have aged out of the foster system, the natural progression of gaining maturity through life experience led to some tension in moving these youth out of the system into more permanent housing:

"...there is a very high rate of rehousing for youth...I think it is currently about 32% of youth are not successful in their first apartment and need another need to be rehoused...you might experience that as, okay, this, this huge failure of the organization not to anticipate needs, but as we have collected data and let it play out, it's actually looking more like this is actually kind of part of the developmental journey. So…in a sense, seeing them make that first stumble is a is a learning opportunity…that almost seems to be necessary for some of them…[to] learn to be successful in the next placement."

Here the concerns of service provision take on a very biological aspect, one that was initially quite frustrating to those providing services. The quantity of youth requiring rehousing, while in tension with organizational goals to resolve the need for services, could be seen as a fundamental aspect of aging and maturing – something that often occurs with a familial or community safety net, allowing for safe exploration and growth. Absent that safety net, this growth becomes another temporally situated concern to be negotiated against more short-term organizational goals and outcome measures.

4.4 Phenomenal and Organizational Registers

Due to the nature of the community of people experiencing homelessness, and the shifting landscape of regulation, funding, and long-term priorities, collected data became less useful as the time period they accounted for became more distant. Some organizations related periods where data about service users had to be assessed and updated to ensure its accuracy over time:

"I've been able to access the system data and do a couple of rounds of what we call targeted assertive outreach, where we contact everybody in the system to engage to clean up the data to discharge youth who no longer need services, and to update and in some cases reassess youth whose circumstances have changed"

Some data were structured, formatted, and standardized for sharing, while other data were used for internal tracking and outcome measurement, and were structured according to organizational needs and capacity. To this, we add another 'pot' of data: data collected to meet requirements of funders and complete grant proposals, as expressed by the below affordable housing developer.

"we're very focused on the rules of the game to win the tax credit funding and that funding it's often two thirds half to two thirds of the funding for a new community."

These data bore a substantially different temporality than the other forms, though there were overlaps in coverage between these different datasets. Data used to apply for and manage funding were structured around the requirements of those funders, which operated along their own organizational timelines, and projects were often related to end or be considered temporary in line with expectations of ongoing funding. In this case, the needs of current work and organizational infrastructure did not meld well with funding requirements, which require a more concentrated effort. Despite the time limitations of funding, there was a perceived expectation that demonstrating improvement over time and across grant cycles was vital for further funding:

"So utilizing our board and also the feedback from the citizens, residents, and businesses, we really began to develop a story around what it would take for us to evolve and provide more intensive services and also shift…to being proactive and engaging in an outreach…and be more preventative…we started gaining more resources from counsel, after the first sort of round of resources, [because we were] able to show that we could be successful and stabilizing…the frequent utilizers of our court."

In the above quote, from an employee of a community court focused on homelessness outreach, there are two key temporal aspects. The first is the aforementioned focus on demonstrating effectiveness across budgetary cycles, but the second is the negotiation between proactive and reactive engagement, or prevention and correction. It is here that we see the tension produced by the need to react to changing circumstances and policy environments in tension with organizational requirements to achieve longer-term outcomes desired by the organization as well as their funders. Resolving existing cases fits outcome measures much more effectively than the analytic work required to similarly demonstrate preventative activities, leading to further tensions between present- and future-oriented work. Demonstrating effective preventative work was a goal related in these interviews:

"[We wanted to] really clearly say… if I house Bri, based on…a brief history in our healthcare system, and our criminal justice system, and even our…shelter system, that…Bri cost our community X amount of money…and that by providing the intervention of housing and supportive services, we can now clearly demonstrate from data… how much money essentially was being saved as a system."

However, this was slow, data-intensive, work, requiring significant coordination between organizations, and the resolution of numerous barriers to data sharing and coordination:

"…it was complex in the amount of data that had to be shared in the entities that we needed to share. So, lots of…fully HIPAA compliant organizations…and…trying to gather data from our criminal justice system, which is incredibly hard to do, ironically, harder than our healthcare system…I still don't understand that."

In this effort to develop a social impact model that would demonstrate effective preventative use of resources (which, ultimately, was not fully realized), the pace of data work limited ongoing collaborations and the effective use of the analysis that was performed. The level of effort necessary to coordinate, use, and reason from this data was in tension with the need to rapidly respond, and to demonstrate effectiveness of these methods to funders in such a way as to fit their funding cycles. Here, responsiveness to changing circumstances was in tension with the slower pace of large-scale data analysis, both internally as organizational outcome measures and externally according to the requirements of funding. As such, the ability to coordinate and collaborate in a future-oriented manner was consistently limited by the need to conform to funding and evaluation cycles.

5   Discussion

Throughout these findings, the notion of time as both a limited resource and constraint on activities emerges. Following Jackson et al. (2011), the varying temporal rhythms of knowledge production in the sciences were paralleled in the knowledge work the City of Austin and the CoC employed in their goal of ending homelessness. We found evidence that, much as in the sciences, knowledge work in this area involved resolving dissonance and tension between the differing temporal registers identified by Jackson et al. While much of these concepts of time were rooted in sociomaterial practice (Orlikowski and Yates 2002), adjusting that practice, especially along biographical and phenomenal registers, becomes a task of significant complexity. Our research confirms the proposition of Jackson et al. (2011) substantially, but as we go forward, we see in our findings a further elaboration of the dynamics of the infrastructural register.

In Fig. 1, we present the temporal dissonances we observed through this study. We found that there were both interpersonal and infrastructural temporal dissonances, and that the 'interpersonal' aspect closely aligned to three temporal registers presented in Jackson et al. (2011) - those of phenomenal, organizational, and biographical rhythms. We found, in this environment, that most tensions occurred between organizational and other registers, and clustered these moments of dissonance under the 'interpersonal' category. We also found that the infrastructural register exhibited dissonance within itself, where various aspects of maintaining, supporting, and growing infrastructural resources were in tension with their uses and capacity to serve as infrastructure - i.e., to underpin those activities that are the primary focus of work (Slota and Bowker 2017).

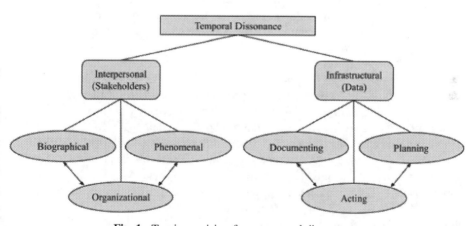

Fig. 1. Tensions arising from temporal dissonance.

We did not find a singular set of temporal dynamics that might be considered as the 'infrastructural register'. Rather, our analysis indicates that the infrastructural register itself comprises several rhythms endogenous to infrastructural work. Similarly, planning data analysis was temporally dissonant with the ability to act upon that insight due to changes in the policy landscape and circumstances of those reflected in the data. Hence, we propose that the infrastructural register itself accounts for a heterogeneity of dissonant rhythms related to the management, deployment, and development of information resources and systems.

A key novel aspect of these findings is that data itself often rose and fell in viability and accuracy as it moved into and out of alignment with phenomenal, biographical, and organizational registers. This finding confirms Olmstead's (2021) notion of 'biodegradable data' in its recognition of the changing value of data over time when those data are used to inform policy. In doing data-intensive work, or seeking toward better knowledge-informed policy, this research indicates a need to resolve these temporal rhythms with the scope of coverage of the data, and local, organizational, context. Knowledge itself is temporally situated, and practices are embedded in an understanding of time borne of normative expectations or external rhythms. Negotiating temporal scales, thus, becomes a fundamental factor in knowledge work, and something that requires an understanding of the temporal registers of that work.

Organizations consider the needs of the present alongside their longitudinal goals, an aspect of their work that resonates with the 'long now' of infrastructure development (Ribes and Finholt 2009). And while the themes presented here did not focus exclusively on the infrastructural aspects of work, this study does indicate that the temporal dimensions of knowledge infrastructures (Edwards et al. 2013) bear significant impact on the utility and effectiveness of data-informed policy. A key gap in the findings presented here, however, is in our lack of accounting for the experiences of service users, except second-hand through experiences related by service providers. Ongoing work in this study will engage people experiencing homelessness through open surveys, interviews, and/or focus groups to further develop our understanding of this environment and its dynamics. In future work, attention to temporal structuring and dissonance could help to understand and refine data and collaborative practice in a wide variety of contexts beyond those considered in this study.

As Ansell and Gash (2008) argue, the increasing scope and specialization of knowledge, alongside increasingly complex collaborative infrastructures, has led to a growing focus on collaboration in public service provision. In supporting such collaborative growth, these findings also point to the need to identify not only areas of temporal dissonance, or tensions arising from differing temporal registers, but also to seek out and identify areas of temporal coordination where the rhythms of work productively align across organizations. In doing so, moments in time where significant change and particularly effective use of data might be more effectively identified. As our findings indicate, temporal aspects of data impacted the efficiency of service provision and coordination as well as the ability for people experiencing homelessness to gain access to those services and their attendant resources.

In many ways, temporal structuring works to resolve the tension between imagination and action. If time were not a limited resource, we would be paralyzed, perpetually frozen in imagination – the danger would then be to endlessly ponder without acting. The need to manage time structures work in a significant way, both within and presumably without the environment we studied, as a limited, non-negotiable resource. Improved temporal coordination could potentially lead to more efficient access to and use of grant funding, lead to more coherent, individualized, and responsive tracking of individuals seeking services, and ultimately has the potential to better optimize the use of limited resources, including time itself.

6   Conclusion

In this paper, we explored temporal dissonances arising within the collaborative work of the City of Austin and the Travis County CoC towards ending homelessness. While time and temporality often structure our approach to working, living, and understanding the world, the impact of temporality on data work and governance is an area of research that calls for much more in-depth investigation. Throughout this paper, we discussed how temporal dissonance along the four registers proposed by Jackson et al. (2011) impacted the provision of services for people experiencing homelessness within the Travis County CoC. We found significant, and impactful, moments of dissonance arising between organizational, biographical, and phenomenal registers that would need to be resolved to ensure sustainable collaborative arrangements and high data quality.

We also found the infrastructural register to be substantively complex, operating along multiple rhythms and with internal temporal dissonance all its own. It is likely that an in-depth investigation into any of these registers will find similar complexity and heterogeneity. When drawing upon data to support governmental decision-making and assessment, the context (spatial, temporal, social) of data is an issue of vital concern. Temporality, for both the scope of data being analyzed and the temporal rhythms of data as infrastructure, represents a key aspect of this context, and one that is often underexplored or assumed. Recognizing temporal dissonance and seeking moments of temporal coordination could enable a more effective resolution of the tension between work undertaken towards immediate goals, and that supporting long-term development.

Acknowledgements. This work was supported by Good Systems, A UT Grand Challenge #Y2P11: "Smart Cities Should Be Good Cities: AI, Equity, and Homelessness." The authors wish to thank our collaborators Min Kyung Lee, Ishan Nigam, Michelle Surka, Keyanna Evans, Tara Zimmerman, Destiny Moreno, David Cruz, James Snow, Sarah Rodriguez, Khalil Bholat, Divya Rathanlal, and Jonathan Tomko for their organizational, methodological, and conceptual contributions to this project. The authors acknowledge all of our study participants, including those who chose to be named and credited for their intellectual contributions to this study: Patricia Barrera, Bill Brice, Veronica Buitron Camacho, Samantha Campbell, Sarah Garvey, Shontell Gauthier, Alex Graham, David Gomes, Mark Hilbelink, Andy Hoffmeister, Vella Karmen, Robert Kingham, Audrey Kuang, Nora Linares-Moeller, Allison Mabbs, Susan McDowell, Walter Moreau, Jo Kathryn Quinn, Katie Rose, Lisa Ruiz, Julia Spann, Whitney Thurman, Pete Valdez, Soleece Watson, Bree Williams, and the seven participants who chose to remain anonymous.

References

Adam, B.: Timewatch: The Social Analysis of Time. Polity Press, Cambridge (1995)

Ansell, C., Gash, A.: Collaborative governance in theory and practice. J. Public Adm. Res. Theory **18**(4), 543–571 (2008). https://doi.org/10.1093/jopart/mum032

Büthe, T.: Taking temporality seriously: modeling history and the use of narratives as evidence. Am. Polit. Sci. Rev. **96**(3), 481–493 (2002). https://doi.org/10.1017/S0003055402000278

Bowker, G.C.: Data flakes: an afterword to "Raw Data" is an oxymoron. In: Gitelman, L. (ed.) "Raw data" is an oxymoron. MIT Press (2013). https://doi.org/10.7551/mitpress/9302.001.0001

Braun, V., Clarke, V.: Using thematic analysis in psychology. Qual. Res. Psychol. **3**(2), 77–101 (2006). https://doi.org/10.1191/1478088706qp063oa

City of Austin: Austin announces new online affordable housing search tool (AHOST) (2020). http://www.austintexas.gov/news/austin-announces-new-online-affordable-housing-search-tool-ahost

Compton, C.: The temporality of disaster: data, the emergency, and climate change. Anthr. – Hum. Inhuman, Posthuman **1**(1), 14 (2020). https://doi.org/10.16997/ahip.24

Edwards, P., et al.: Knowledge infrastructures: intellectual frameworks and research challenges (2013). https://escholarship.org/uc/item/2mt6j2mh

Flanagan, J.C.: The critical incident technique. Psychol. Bull. **51**(4), 327–358 (1954). https://psycnet.apa.org/doi/10.1037/h0061470

Ismagilova, E., Hughes, L., Dwivedi, Y.K., Raman, K.R.: Smart cities: advances in research—an information systems perspective. Int. J. Inf. Manage. **47**, 88–100 (2019). https://doi.org/10.1016/j.ijinfomgt.2019.01.004

Jackson, S.J.: Rethinking repair. In: Gillespie, T., Boczkowski, P.J., Foot, K.A. (eds.) Media Technologies: Essays on Communication, Materiality, and Society, pp. 221–239. MIT Press (2014)

Jackson, S.J., Ribes, D., Buyuktur, A., Bowker, G.C.: Collaborative rhythm: temporal dissonance and alignment in collaborative scientific work. In: Proceedings of the ACM 2011 Conference on Computer Supported Cooperative Work, pp. 245–254 (2011)

Kurzweil, R., Grossman, T.: Bridges to life. In: Fahy, G.M., West, D.M.D., Coles, L.S., Harris, S.B. (eds.) The Future of Aging, pp. 3–22. Springer, Dordrecht (2010). https://doi.org/10.1007/978-90-481-3999-6_1

Ladner, S.: Ethnographic temporality: using time-based data in product renewal. Ethnogr. Prax. Ind. Conf. Proc. **2012**(1), 30–38 (2012). Blackwell Publishing Ltd. https://doi.org/10.1111/j.1559-8918.2012.00005.x

Larkin, B.: The politics and poetics of infrastructure. Annu. Rev. Anthropol. **42**, 327–343 (2013). https://doi.org/10.1146/annurev-anthro-092412-155522

Letondal, C., Tabard, A., Mackay, W.E.: Temporal data and data temporality: time is change, not only order. In: CHI 2009 Workshop on Interacting with Temporal Data, April 2009, Boston, United States (2009). http://www.lii-enac.fr/~letondal/Papers/LetondalTabard-temporal-CHI09-v10x.pdf. Accessed 15 Sep 2021

Mills, M.: Providing space for time: the impact of temporality on life course research. Time Soc. **9**(1), 91–127 (2000). https://doi.org/10.1177/0961463X00009001006

Noy, C.: Sampling knowledge: The hermeneutics of snowball sampling in qualitative research. Int. J. Soc. Res. Methodol. **11**(4), 327–344 (2008). https://doi.org/10.1080/13645570701401305

Olmstead, N.A.: Data and temporality in the spectral city. Philos. Technol. **34**(2), 243–263 (2019). https://doi.org/10.1007/s13347-019-00381-8

van Ooijen, C., Ubaldi, B., Welby, B.: A data-driven public sector: enabling the strategic use of data for productive, inclusive and trustworthy governance. OECD Working Papers on Public Governance, no. 33. OECD Publishing (2019). https://doi.org/10.1787/09ab162c-en

Orlikowski, W.J., Yates, J.: It's about time: temporal structuring in organizations. Organ. Sci. **13**(6), 684–700 (2002). https://doi.org/10.1287/orsc.13.6.684.501

Pink, S., Lanzeni, D.: Future anthropology ethics and datafication: temporality and responsibility in research. Soc. Media + Soc. **4**(2), 1–9 (2018)

Ribes, D., Finholt, T.A.: The long now of technology infrastructure: articulating tensions in development. J. Assoc. Inf. Syst. **10**(5), 375–398 (2009). https://doi.org/10.17705/1jais.00199

Slota, S.C., Bowker, G.C.: How infrastructures matter. In: Felt, U., Fouché, R., Miller, C.A., Smith-Doerr, L. (eds.) The Handbook of Science and Technology Studies, pp. 529–554. MIT Press (2017)

Exploiting Transformer-Based Multitask Learning for the Detection of Media Bias in News Articles

Timo Spinde[1]([⊠])(iD), Jan-David Krieger[2](iD), Terry Ruas[1](iD), Jelena Mitrović[3](iD), Franz Götz-Hahn[4](iD), Akiko Aizawa[5](iD), and Bela Gipp[1](iD)

[1] University of Wuppertal, Wuppertal, Germany
`timo.spinde@uni-wuppertal.de`
[2] University of Konstanz, Konstanz, Germany
`Jan-David.Krieger@uni-konstanz.de`
[3] Institute for Artificial Intelligence Research and Development of Serbia,
University of Passau, Passau, Germany
`jelena.mitrovic@Uni-Passau.de`
[4] University of Kassel, Kassel, Germany
`franz.goetz-hahn@uni-kassel.de`
[5] NII Tokyo, Tokyo, Japan
`aizawa@nii.ac.jp`

Abstract. Media has a substantial impact on the public perception of events. A one-sided or polarizing perspective on any topic is usually described as media bias. One of the ways how bias in news articles can be introduced is by altering word choice. Biased word choices are not always obvious, nor do they exhibit high context-dependency. Hence, detecting bias is often difficult. We propose a Transformer-based deep learning architecture trained via Multi-Task Learning using six bias-related data sets to tackle the media bias detection problem. Our best-performing implementation achieves a macro F_1 of 0.776, a performance boost of 3% compared to our baseline, outperforming existing methods. Our results indicate Multi-Task Learning as a promising alternative to improve existing baseline models in identifying slanted reporting.

Keywords: Media bias · Text analysis · Multi-task learning · News analysis

1 Introduction

Media bias, i.e., slanted news coverage, has the potential to drastically change the public opinion on any topic [31]. One of the forms bias can be expressed by is by word choice, e.g., depicting any content in a non-neutral way [22]. Detecting and highlighting media bias might be relevant for media analysis and mitigate the effects of biased reporting. To date, only a few research projects focus on the detection and aggregation of bias [6,16]. One of the reasons that make the

M. Smits (Ed.): iConference 2022, LNCS 13192, pp. 225–235, 2022.
https://doi.org/10.1007/978-3-030-96957-8_20

creation of automated methods to detect media bias a complex task is often the subtle nature of media bias, which represents a challenge for quantitative identification methods [10,16,29,32]. While many current research projects focus on collecting linguistic features to describe media bias [11,22,28,33], we propose a Transformer-based [38] architecture for the classification of media bias. Similar models have recently shown to achieve performance increases in the media bias domain, e.g., sentence-level bias detection [6,12,26,31]. However, so far, they rely on very limited resources. Data sets with bias gold standard annotations are, to date, only scarcely available, and exhibit various weaknesses, such as low inter annotator agreement, small size, or no information about the annotator background [30,31,35]. Additionally, state-of-the-art neural language models usually require large amounts of training data to yield meaningful representations [9,23], which are incompatible with the size of current media bias data sets [10,34]. To mitigate the lack of suitable data sets, our model incorporates Multi-Task Learning (MTL) [23], which allows for increasing performance by sharing model representations between related tasks [13,18,36]. The use of cross-domain data sets in our model is particularly relevant for the media bias domain as multiple sources can provide a more robust model. To the best of our knowledge, the MTL paradigm has not been explored in existing work on media bias. Our research question is therefore to assess whether MTL can improve models to classify media bias automatically.

The main contribution of this paper is to incorporate Transformer-based MTL into a system to identify sentence-level media bias automatically. We exploit MTL in the media bias context by computing multiple models based on different combinations of auxiliary training data sets (Sect. 2). All our models, data, and code are publicly available on https://bit.ly/3cmiQgB.

2   Related Work

While there are multiple forms of media bias, e.g., bias by personal perception or by the omission of information [27], our focus is on bias by word choice, in which different words refer to the same concept [22]. We will first summarize available media bias data sets and then present automated methods to identify bias as well as MTL.

The concept of media bias is covered by many data sets [1,6,10,17,34]. However, they all exhibit specific deficiencies, such as (1) a low number of topics [16,17], (2) no annotations on the word level [17], (3) low inter-annotator agreement [1,16,17,34], (4) no background check for its participants (except [34]), and (5) only article-level annotations [6]. Also, some related papers focus on framing rather than on bias [1,10], or on Wikipedia instead of news[12], and results are only partially transferable. To the best of our knowledge, the most extensive and precise data set was presented recently [31]. The data set consists of 3700 sentences annotated by expert raters on sentence-level with an inter-annotator agreement of 0.40 measured by Krippendorff's α [15], which is higher than for all other available data sets.

Several studies tackle the challenge of identifying media bias automatically [6,11,12,22,33]. Most of them use hand-crafted features to detect bias [11,33]. For example, [33] identify and evaluate a wide range of linguistic, lexical, and syntactic features serving as potential bias indicators. The existing work on neural models is based on the data sets mentioned above, which exhibit the described weaknesses [6,12]. Most media bias models focus on sentence-level bias [6,10–12,22]. Therefore, we follow the standard practice and construct a sentence-level classifier.

MTL approaches have shown to be helpful when high-quality data sets in the domain are scarce, but text corpora covering general related concepts are available [13,18,36,37,39]. For example, [13] report that MTL applied on BERT yields an accuracy increase of 1.03% compared to the baseline BERT in a subjectivity detection task. MTL might be a suitable training paradigm for media bias identification systems since sufficiently sized bias corpora with qualitative hand-crafted annotations do not exist. Therefore, we propose the first neural MTL media bias classifier composed of inter-domain and cross-domain data sets.

3 Methodology

We explore how fine-tuning a language model via MTL can improve the performance in detecting media bias on the sentence level. Computational costs are an important consideration for us since we train multiple large-scale MTL models. For this reason, we employ a distilled modification of BERT [9], called DistilBERT [25], which achieves a 40% reduction in size while simultaneously accelerating the training process by 60% and retaining 97% of language understanding capabilities on NLP benchmark tasks [39]. DistilBERT represents an appropriate architecture, keeping resource consumption and performance balanced. The incorporation of larger models trained via MTL is left to future research.

Our MTL technique is based on *hard parameter sharing* in which all hidden model layers are shared between auxiliary training tasks [23]. Task-specific layers are added on top of the last hidden state, accounting for the label structure of auxiliary data sets. The MTL paradigm we propose is architecture-independent and can be adjusted to future NLP architectures.

For our training procedure, we distinguish between models trained on in-domain and cross-domain data sets. For in-domain data sets, the creation process included concepts related to media bias, such as subjectivity [20]. Conversely, cross-domain data sets include data points that are not directly annotated for or related to media bias, but are retrieved from tasks that bear some connection to it. The auxiliary data sets we use comprise a diverse set of NLP tasks requiring two different losses for the learning process - the Cross-Entropy (CE) loss [8] and the Mean Squared Error (MSE) loss [24]. The origin and number of the data used for the training of our models, as well as their respective original tasks and used loss functions, are shown in Table 1. We use in-domain (ID) and cross-domain (CD) data sets used in other MTL studies within the language processing domain [13,18,36].

Table 1. Auxiliary data sets incorporated in the MTL models (n = number of instances)

Data set	Domain	n	Task	Loss	Description
Reddit data set (Reddit) [4]	ID	6861	Single sentence regression	MSE	Reddit comments labeled on a continuous scale ranging from 0 (supportive) to 1 (discriminatory)
Subjectivity data set (Subj) [20]	ID	10000	Single sentence classification	CE	Movie reviews labeled as *objective* or *opinionated*
IMDb [19]	ID	50000	Single sentence classification	CE	Movie reviews containing positive and negative sentiment labels
Wikipedia data set (Wiki)[a] [21]	ID	180000	Single sentence classification	CE	Neutral and biased sentence pairs from articles going against Wikipedia's NPOV rule
Semantic Textual Similarity Benchmark (STS-B) data set [5]	CD	10943	Pairwise sentence similarity	MSE	Multilingual and cross-lingual sentence pairs labeled in terms of similarity
Stanford Natural Language Inference (SNLI) corpus[a] [2]	CD	570000	Pairwise sentence classification	CE	Sentence pairs labeled for linguistic relations within the labels *entailment*, *neutral*, or *contradiction*

[a]We only use 50000 text instances from these corpora in our MTL approach to keep the size of training sets balanced.

Figure 1 outlines our in-domain MTL model consisting of DistilBERT's encoder, whose parameters are shared across tasks, and the added task-specific layers[1]. The represented model is based on the maximum number of possible data sets within the approach. In our experiments on MTL, we try various combinations, including at least three in-domain and five cross-domain data sets, respectively.

For preprocessing and MTL training, we took the same approach as [18]. Initially, pre-trained parameters are loaded from *huggingface*[2]. We split up data for a fixed-size subset of tasks into batches, and batches are merged and shuffled to guarantee the model does not train on too many subsequent batches of a single task. The preprocessing step is repeated every epoch. Batches are then passed on by the data loader one by one to the model, which outputs task-specific predictions and the respective loss. Finally, the loss is backpropagated, and parameters are updated.

4   Experiments

To investigate the benefit of MTL to identify media bias on a fine-grained linguistic level, we train ten models using MTL, which we compare to five baseline models. As a consequence of a lack of robust guidelines for selection criteria for

---

[1] The cross-domain model is not shown due to lack of space but is published at the repository mentioned in Sect. 1.

[2] https://huggingface.co/transformers/model_doc/distilbert.html.

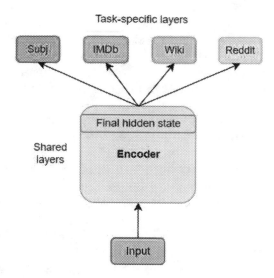

Fig. 1. Outline of in-domain MTL model consisting of a shared encoder block and task-specific layers. *Note*: We implement multiple MTL models based on different combinations of the presented data sets.

auxiliary corpora, we choose a variety of auxiliary tasks to fine-tune the DistilBERT model via MTL that have previously been used successfully in MTL studies [13, 18, 36]. Each of our MTL models is trained using a different combination of a sample of six popular data sets, where IMDb [19], Subj [20], Wiki [21], and Reddit [4] are considered in-domain data sets, and STS-B [5], and SNLI [2] comprise examples of cross-domain data sets[3].

The in-domain models are based on bias-related data sets[4]. Combining the in-domain corpora yields five different models (Table 2, M1–M5): four use triple combinations, and one model relies on all in-domain data sets. The cross-domain models extend the pool of experiments by adding the STS-B and SNLI data sets to each of the five in-domain models (Table 2, M6–M10). The approaches are oriented on the MTL fine-tuning approaches applied in [36]. In their experiments based on BERT, the authors apply MTL on domain-related and domain-unrelated data yielding a performance boost for sentiment classification.

All experiments are performed on a *Google Colab NVIDIA Tesla K80*[5]. We choose the *AdamW optimizer* [14] and a batch size of 32. All downstream task layers are based on a hidden state dimensionality of 768. All performance metrics are calculated based on 5-fold cross-validation [3]. Thus, we divide the final bias data set containing 1700 instances into five different train and tests[6]. The

---

[3] A detailed description of the data sets is published at the repository mentioned in Sect. 1.

[4] IMDb, Subj, Wiki, Reddit.

[5] https://colab.research.google.com/notebooks/intro.ipynb.

[6] We use a subset of BABE [31], introduced in Sect. 2, to evaluate the MTL models.

models are then iteratively trained on all five training sets and evaluated on the respective held-out test set. Finally, the performance metrics on the test sets are averaged, yielding the cross-validated model performance. Each respective model is trained over four epochs with an early stopping criterion based on validation CE loss. In many cases, the model stops learning after two epochs. The MTL fine-tuning is based on a learning rate of $5 \cdot 10^{-5}$.

As far as we know, there are no related works applying MTL in the media bias domain. Therefore, we compare the performances of our MTL approaches to a set of baseline models (Table 2; B1–B5). We report the performance scores achieved from pre-trained DistilBERT provided by *huggingface* (B1). Furthermore, we train four DistilBERT models on each of the in-domain data sets (B2-B5). Thus, we can observe whether the assumed performance boost of our MTL models results from MTL rather than domain-relatedness of the training data.

We expect that fine-tuning via MTL leads to an improvement of DistilBERT's bias identification power. Mainly, we want to analyze whether the MTL technique yields a substantial performance boost compared to simple Transfer Learning (TL) approaches training the model on only a single data set. Therefore, we run several experiments.

5   Results and Discussion

We show the performance indicators of our model on our expert-labeled media bias data set in Table 2, according to F_1, precision, recall, and loss. Since the highest macro F_1 score does not necessarily match with the lowest loss, we elaborate on the results from the perspective of both metrics.

Among all MTL-trained models the highest F_1 score is achieved from the in-domain M4 model with 0.776. The best cross-domain model regarding macro F_1 is reached by M8 with 0.771. Compared to DistilBERT, M4 achieves a 3% increase in macro F_1, while B5 achieves the highest macro F_1 for TL-based models at 0.782, which is not surpassed by any MTL approach. Although all MTL models outperform DistilBERT, the highest macro F_1 score of all MTL models is 0.6% lower than that of B5. Overall, MTL improves the B1 baseline macro F_1 score in a range from 0.3% (M9) to 3% (M4). When considering the models from a loss-based perspective, the performance ranks change slightly: M4 remains as the best in-domain MTL model, but M7 (the second to last in terms of macro F_1 performance) reaches the lowest loss within the cross-domain approaches. Compared to DistilBERT, M4 shows a decrease in loss of 4.9%. B5 prevails as the best TL model with a CE loss of 0.466. In contrast to the macro F_1-based perspective, however, M4 achieves the lowest overall loss, outperforming B5 by 0.2%.

In general, our MTL approaches surpass the baseline methods. However, the best overall model based on macro F_1 was a TL model trained on a data set containing revised Wikipedia excerpts (B5). Based on CE loss, only one MTL model slightly outperform this TL model. Thus, we cannot state whether Transformer-Based MTL improves media bias detection on the sentence level.

Table 2. Results for all baseline models, i.e., the *huggingface* model or models obtained by TL, as well as the models trained using MTL considering only in-domain data sets or also incorporating cross-domain data. For each metric we have denoted the best performance in bold.

	Model	Subj	IMDb	Reddit	Wiki	STS	SNLI	Macro F_1	Micro F_1	Binary F_1	Precision	Recall	CE loss
TL	B1	*huggingface* DistilBERT						0.746	0.750	0.711	**0.805**	0.640	0.513
	B2	✓						0.744	0.744	0.730	0.744	0.716	0.545
	B3		✓					0.761	0.762	0.746	0.770	0.725	0.491
	B4			✓				0.743	0.746	0.709	0.790	0.646	0.497
	B5				✓			**0.782**	**0.782**	**0.7695**	0.785	0.754	0.466
ID MTL	M1	✓	✓	✓				0.768	0.768	0.753	0.778	0.731	0.482
	M2	✓	✓		✓			0.760	0.760	0.746	0.766	0.729	0.495
	M3	✓		✓	✓			0.773	0.774	0.762	0.777	0.755	0.482
	M4	✓	✓	✓	✓			0.776	0.777	0.759	0.794	0.727	**0.464**
	M5	✓	✓	✓	✓			0.772	0.771	0.757	0.778	0.737	0.473
CD MTL	M6	✓	✓	✓		✓	✓	0.766	0.766	0.758	0.756	0.763	0.492
	M7	✓	✓		✓	✓	✓	0.765	0.765	0.751	0.770	0.735	0.474
	M8	✓		✓	✓	✓	✓	0.771	0.771	0.762	0.765	0.761	0.491
	M9		✓	✓	✓	✓	✓	0.749	0.750	0.759	0.714	**0.812**	0.499
	M10	✓	✓	✓	✓	✓	✓	0.769	0.770	0.751	0.789	0.720	0.480

We assume that the strong performance of B5 results from the relatedness of the underlying data set to our bias corpus. The Wikipedia data set contains biased and neutral sentences extracted from revised Wikipedia passages. Hence, the data set is similar to our bias corpus[7]. The only difference to our fine-tuning data set is the source from which the data is extracted. Pre-training a Transformer-based model on a highly bias-related corpus seems to hinder MTL's relative performance improvement. Furthermore, we assume that our selection of auxiliary data sets might not have been sufficiently comprehensive. In our MTL approaches, updating DistilBERT's parameters only required the computation and back-propagation of binary CE loss and MSE loss. [23] argues that well-performing MTL approaches must be trained on NLP tasks, including multiple loss functions.

Existing MTL studies [13,18,36] do not report diverse TL baseline models. The MTL approaches are primarily compared to a pre-trained baseline model provided by model libraries. Future research should incorporate a comprehensive set of baseline models allowing for a more robust analysis. Comparing our best MTL model to DistilBERT, the effect of MTL is similar as in [13].

Considering our MTL-based media bias research, future work should include more comprehensive sets of bias-related auxiliary data sets with multiple loss functions. Possible tasks could, for example, comprise the detection of bias-inducing linguistic features such as negative sentiment [33]. In this way, deep learning techniques could benefit from other types of tasks, such as classifying

---

[7] Let us point out that **none** of the instances from the Wikipedia data set are contained in our target media bias data set.

linguistic features. Moreover, future MTL approaches could benefit from larger transformer models (e.g., XLNet [40], ELECTRA [7]). Our approach based on DistilBERT is the first step towards balancing cloud-computing costs and performance. We note that a follow-up experiment about an improved model and a larger exploratory data analysis are already in progress and will be published in the future.

6 Final Considerations

This work proposes a Transformer-based MTL approach to identify media bias by word choice in news articles. The motivation for selecting the training technique results from our observation that the size of available media bias data sets is not compatible with the requirements of state-of-the-art neural language models. We train ten MTL models based on different combinations of six auxiliary data sets and compare them to five baseline models. Our results show that the best performing MTL model partly surpasses the baseline models in terms of macro F_1 loss and CE loss. Yet, we can not ascertain a significant superiority of the MTL approach in classifying media bias instances. The main limitation of our work is the restricted inclusion of auxiliary tasks. In future work, we plan to incorporate more tasks based on bias-inducing linguistic features. We have to emphasize that any successful MTL implementation in the context of media bias identification could decrease financial burdens emerging from the collection of hand-crafted training data. Yet, at the same time, cloud computing requires substantial financial resources. Costs of using larger models should therefore be properly evaluated. We believe the MTL approach to be promising in the area and aim to continue the research on MTL in connection with media bias identification in the future.

References

1. Baumer, E., Elovic, E., Qin, Y., Polletta, F., Gay, G.: Testing and comparing computational approaches for identifying the language of framing in political news. In: Proceedings of the 2015 Conference of the North American Chapter of the Association for Computational Linguistics: Human Language Technologies, pp. 1472–1482. Association for Computational Linguistics, Denver, Colorado (May–Jun 2015). https://doi.org/10.3115/v1/N15-1171. https://www.aclweb.org/anthology/N15-1171
2. Bowman, S.R., Angeli, G., Potts, C., Manning, C.D.: A large annotated corpus for learning natural language inference. In: Proceedings of the 2015 Conference on Empirical Methods in Natural Language Processing. pp. 632–642. Association for Computational Linguistics, Lisbon, Portugal (September 2015). https://doi.org/10.18653/v1/D15-1075. https://www.aclweb.org/anthology/D15-1075
3. Browne, M.W.: Cross-validation methods. J. Math. Psychol. **44**(1), 108–132 (2000). https://doi.org/10.1006/jmps.1999.1279. https://doi.org/10.1006/jmps.1999.1279
4. Cabot, P.H., Abadi, D., Fischer, A., Shutova, E.: Us vs. them: a dataset of populist attitudes, news bias and emotions. CoRR abs/2101.11956 (2021). https://arxiv.org/abs/2101.11956

5. Cer, D., Diab, M., Agirre, E., Lopez-Gazpio, I., Specia, L.: Semeval-2017 task 1: semantic textual similarity multilingual and crosslingual focused evaluation. In: Proceedings of the 11th International Workshop on Semantic Evaluation, SemEval-2017 (2017). https://doi.org/10.18653/v1/s17-2001. http://dx.doi.org/10.18653/v1/S17-2001

6. Chen, W.F., Al Khatib, K., Wachsmuth, H., Stein, B.: Analyzing political bias and unfairness in news articles at different levels of granularity. In: Proceedings of the 4th Workshop on Natural Language Processing and Computational Social Science, pp. 149–154. Association for Computational Linguistics (2020). https://doi.org/10.18653/v1/2020.nlpcss-1.16. https://www.aclweb.org/anthology/2020.nlpcss-1.16

7. Clark, K., Luong, M.T., Le, Q.V., Manning, C.D.: ELECTRA: pre-training text encoders as discriminators rather than generators. arXiv:2003.10555 [cs] (March 2020)

8. De Boer, P.T., Kroese, D.P., Mannor, S., Rubinstein, R.Y.: A tutorial on the cross-entropy method. Ann. Oper. Res. **134**(1), 19–67 (2005)

9. Devlin, J., Chang, M.W., Lee, K., Toutanova, K.: BERT: pre-training of deep bidirectional transformers for language understanding. In: Proceedings of the 2019 Conference of the North American Chapter of the Association for Computational Linguistics: Human Language Technologies, Volume 1 (Long and Short Papers), Minneapolis, Minnesota, pp. 4171–4186. Association for Computational Linguistics (June 2019). https://doi.org/10.18653/v1/N19-1423. https://www.aclweb.org/anthology/N19-1423

10. Fan, L., et al.: In plain sight: media bias through the lens of factual reporting. In: Proceedings of the 2019 Conference on Empirical Methods in Natural Language Processing and the 9th International Joint Conference on Natural Language Processing (EMNLP-IJCNLP), Hong Kong, China, pp. 6343–6349. Association for Computational Linguistics (November 2019). https://doi.org/10.18653/v1/D19-1664. https://www.aclweb.org/anthology/D19-1664

11. Hube, C., Fetahu, B.: Detecting biased statements in Wikipedia. In: Companion Proceedings of the the Web Conference 2018, WWW 2018, Republic and Canton of Geneva, CHE, pp. 1779–1786. International World Wide Web Conferences Steering Committee (2018). https://doi.org/10.1145/3184558.3191640

12. Hube, C., Fetahu, B.: Neural based statement classification for biased language. In: Proceedings of the 12th ACM International Conference on Web Search and Data Mining, WSDM 2019, New York, NY, USA, pp. 195–203. Association for Computing Machinery (2019). https://doi.org/10.1145/3289600.3291018

13. Huo, H., Iwaihara, M.: Utilizing BERT pretrained models with various fine-tune methods for subjectivity detection. In: Wang, X., Zhang, R., Lee, Y.-K., Sun, L., Moon, Y.-S. (eds.) APWeb-WAIM 2020. LNCS, vol. 12318, pp. 270–284. Springer, Cham (2020). https://doi.org/10.1007/978-3-030-60290-1_21

14. Kingma, D.P., Ba, J.: Adam: a method for stochastic optimization. In: Bengio, Y., LeCun, Y. (eds.) 3rd International Conference on Learning Representations, ICLR 2015, Conference Track Proceedings, San Diego, CA, USA, 7–9 May 2015 (2015). http://arxiv.org/abs/1412.6980

15. Krippendorff, K.: Computing Krippendorff's alpha-reliability. Departmental Papers (ASC); University of Pennsylvania (2011). https://repository.upenn.edu/cgi/viewcontent.cgi?article=1043&context=asc_papers

16. Lim, S., Jatowt, A., Färber, M., Yoshikawa, M.: Annotating and analyzing biased sentences in news articles using crowdsourcing. In: Proceedings of the 12th Language Resources and Evaluation Conference, Marseille, France, pp. 1478–1484. European Language Resources Association (May 2020). https://www.aclweb.org/anthology/2020.lrec-1.184

17. Lim, S., Jatowt, A., Yoshikawa, M.: Understanding characteristics of biased sentences in news articles. In: CIKM Workshops (2018). http://ceur-ws.org/Vol-2482/paper13.pdf

18. Liu, X., He, P., Chen, W., Gao, J.: Multi-task deep neural networks for natural language understanding. In: Proceedings of the 57th Annual Meeting of the Association for Computational Linguistics, Florence, Italy, pp. 4487–4496. Association for Computational Linguistics (July 2019). https://www.aclweb.org/anthology/P19-1441

19. Maas, A.L., Daly, R.E., Pham, P.T., Huang, D., Ng, A.Y., Potts, C.: Learning word vectors for sentiment analysis. In: Proceedings of the 49th Annual Meeting of the Association for Computational Linguistics: Human Language Technologies, Portland, Oregon, USA, pp. 142–150. Association for Computational Linguistics (June 2011). https://www.aclweb.org/anthology/P11-1015

20. Pang, B., Lee, L.: A sentimental education: sentiment analysis using subjectivity summarization based on minimum cuts. In: Proceedings of the 42nd Annual Meeting on Association for Computational Linguistics, ACL 2004, USA, p. 271. Association for Computational Linguistics (2004). https://doi.org/10.3115/1218955.1218990. https://doi.org/10.3115/1218955.1218990

21. Pryzant, R., Diehl Martinez, R., Dass, N., Kurohashi, S., Jurafsky, D., Yang, D.: Automatically neutralizing subjective bias in text. In: Proceedings of the AAAI Conference on Artificial Intelligence, vol. 34, no. 01, pp. 480–489 (April 2020). https://doi.org/10.1609/aaai.v34i01.5385. https://ojs.aaai.org/index.php/AAAI/article/view/5385

22. Recasens, M., Danescu-Niculescu-Mizil, C., Jurafsky, D.: Linguistic models for analyzing and detecting biased language. In: Proceedings of the 51st Annual Meeting of the Association for Computational Linguistics (Volume 1: Long Papers), pp. 1650–1659 (2013). https://www.aclweb.org/anthology/P13-1162.pdf

23. Ruder, S.: An overview of multi-task learning in deep neural networks. CoRR abs/1706.05098 (2017). http://arxiv.org/abs/1706.05098

24. Mean squared error. In: Sammut, C., Webb, G.I. (eds.) Encyclopedia of Machine Learning. Springer, Boston, MA (2011). https://doi.org/10.1007/978-0-387-30164-8_528

25. Sanh, V., Debut, L., Chaumond, J., Wolf, T.: Distilbert, a distilled version of BERT: smaller, faster, cheaper and lighter. CoRR abs/1910.01108 (2019). http://arxiv.org/abs/1910.01108

26. Spinde, T.: An interdisciplinary approach for the automated detection and visualization of media bias in news articles. In: 2021 IEEE International Conference on Data Mining Workshops (ICDMW) (2021). https://media-bias-research.org/wp-content/uploads/2021/09/Spinde2021g.pdf

27. Spinde, T., Hamborg, F., Donnay, K., Becerra, A., Gipp, B.: Enabling news consumers to view and understand biased news coverage: a study on the perception and visualization of media bias. In: Proceedings of the ACM/IEEE Joint Conference on Digital Libraries in 2020, JCDL 2020, Virtual Event, China, pp. 389–392. Association for Computing Machinery (2020). https://doi.org/10.1145/3383583.3398619

28. Spinde, T., Hamborg, F., Gipp, B.: Media bias in German news articles: a combined approach. In: ECML PKDD 2020 Workshops: Workshops of the European Conference on Machine Learning and Knowledge Discovery in Databases (ECML PKDD 2020): INRA 2020, Ghent, Belgium, 14–18 September 2020, Proceedings, vol. 1323, pp. 581–590 (2020). https://doi.org/10.1007/978-3-030-65965-3_41. https://www.ncbi.nlm.nih.gov/pmc/articles/PMC7850083/

29. Spinde, T., Kreuter, C., Gaissmaier, W., Hamborg, F., Gipp, B., Giese, H.: Do you think it's biased? How to ask for the perception of media bias. In: Proceedings of the ACM/IEEE Joint Conference on Digital Libraries (JCDL) (September 2021)

30. Spinde, T., Krieger, D., Plank, M., Gipp, B.: Towards a reliable ground-truth for biased language detection. In: Proceedings of the ACM/IEEE Joint Conference on Digital Libraries (JCDL) (September 2021)

31. Spinde, T., Plank, M., Krieger, J.D., Ruas, T., Gipp, B., Aizawa, A.: Neural media bias detection using distant supervision with BABE - bias annotations by experts. In: Findings of the Association for Computational Linguistics, EMNLP 2021, Dominican Republic (November 2021)

32. Spinde, T., Rudnitckaia, L., Hamborg, F., Gipp, B.: Identification of biased terms in news articles by comparison of outlet-specific word embeddings. In: Proceedings of the iConference 2021 (March 2021)

33. Spinde, T., Rudnitckaia, L., Mitrović, J., Hamborg, F., Granitzer, M., Gipp, B., Donnay, K.: Automated identification of bias inducing words in news articles using linguistic and context-oriented features. Inf. Process. Manage. **58**(3), 102505 (2021). https://doi.org/10.1016/j.ipm.2021.102505

34. Spinde, T., Rudnitckaia, L., Sinha, K., Hamborg, F., Gipp, B., Donnay, K.: MBIC - a media bias annotation dataset including annotator characteristics. In: Proceedings of the iConference 2021. iSchools (2021). https://doi.org/10.5281/zenodo.4474336

35. Spinde, T., Sinha, K., Meuschke, N., Gipp, B.: TASSY - a text annotation survey system. In: Proceedings of the ACM/IEEE Joint Conference on Digital Libraries (JCDL) (September 2021)

36. Sun, C., Qiu, X., Xu, Y., Huang, X.: How to fine-tune BERT for text classification? In: Sun, M., Huang, X., Ji, H., Liu, Z., Liu, Y. (eds.) CCL 2019. LNCS (LNAI), vol. 11856, pp. 194–206. Springer, Cham (2019). https://doi.org/10.1007/978-3-030-32381-3_16

37. Sun, Y., et al.: ERNIE 2.0: a continual pre-training framework for language understanding. In: Proceedings of the AAAI Conference on Artificial Intelligence, vol. 34, pp. 8968–8975 (April 2020). https://doi.org/10.1609/aaai.v34i05.6428

38. Vaswani, A., et al.: Attention is all you need. In: Guyon, I., et al. (eds.) Advances in Neural Information Processing Systems, vol. 30. Curran Associates, Inc. (2017). https://proceedings.neurips.cc/paper/2017/file/3f5ee243547dee91fbd053c1c4a845aa-Paper.pdf

39. Wang, A., Singh, A., Michael, J., Hill, F., Levy, O., Bowman, S.R.: Glue: a multitask benchmark and analysis platform for natural language understanding. arXiv preprint arXiv:1804.07461 (2018)

40. Yang, Z., Dai, Z., Yang, Y., Carbonell, J., Salakhutdinov, R., Le, Q.V.: XLNet: generalized autoregressive pretraining for language understanding. arXiv:1906.08237 [cs] (June 2019)

Data Analytics Usage, Absorptive Capacity and Sharing Economy Innovation Performance

Alton Y. K. Chua[(⊠)] [iD], Hattie Liew [iD], and Liuyu Huang

Wee Kim Wee School of Communication and Information, Nanyang Technological University, Singapore, Singapore
{altonchua,hattie.liew,lyhuang}@ntu.edu.sg

Abstract. This study investigates the usage of data analytics and absorptive capacity and its relationship to innovation performance in the context of the sharing economy. 127 survey responses from participants who held managerial positions or higher in organizations operating within the sharing economy were collected. A hierarchical regression analysis was conducted to assess the relationship between data analytic usage and absorptive capacity with innovation performance. Findings show that both data analytics usage and absorptive capacity are important to organizations operating in the sharing economy, with data analytic usage accounting for a higher variance in innovation performance.

Keywords: Data analytics · Absorptive capacity · Innovation performance · Sharing economy

1 Introduction

1.1 Background

The sharing economy has recently emerged as a strong economic and cultural force. It is characterized by its heavy reliance on digital technology, peer-to-peer sharing of idle resources, and the economic logic of access instead of ownership [1]. Its worth has been projected to be USD 335 billion by the year 2025 [2].

At its core, the sharing economy is a knowledge-based economy where the management of knowledge drives innovation, as well as day-to-day operations such as data-driven decision making [3]. As disruptive innovators, organizations in the sharing economy must learn continually to adopt new business and organizational practices [4] so that they are responsive to socio-cultural-economic conditions and users' changing needs.

1.2 Data as Knowledge and Organization Absorptive Capacity for Innovation

The sharing economy is part of digital platform economy and relies heavily on data analytics to develop product and services (e.g. dynamic pricing). Data analytics refers to a technologically enabled processing of large volumes and varieties of data with

M. Smits (Ed.): iConference 2022, LNCS 13192, pp. 236–243, 2022.
https://doi.org/10.1007/978-3-030-96957-8_21

velocity [5]. With the prevalence of digitalization, it has now become an important means through which organizations gain insights to tweak their processes and offerings in fast, innovative ways that benefit both users and the organization [6]. For example, supply chains use data analytics to remain resilient in the face of market volatility [5].

Amid fierce competition and an ever-evolving business environment, thriving organizations are those that possess absorptive capacity. This is the ability to assess the value of external knowledge, and thereafter, internalize and apply it [7, 8]. Organizations with absorptive capacity are able to transform the information gained, including through data analytics, into actionable knowledge. Extant literature has studied absorptive capacity in practice in various forms, though mostly in the research and development context [9]. Having absorptive capacity is particularly important to organizations in the sharing economy, as it facilitates innovation and keeps them agile [10].

A key output of using data analytics and building absorptive capacity is innovation performance, or the success in creating new processes and products [11]. As such, the clever use of information not only adds to an organization's bottom line but contributes to innovation. Beyond launching a better product or service, innovative performance translates to cultural shifts and it can facilitate larger goals such as sustainability. The sharing economy itself represents a collective innovation performance at the sectoral level by focusing on access over ownership to reduce consumers' overall consumption and subsequent resource use [12].

1.3 Research Gaps and Objective

Given that data analytics usage and absorptive capacity are intangible capabilities leading to value creation and organizational success, they are expected to be intertwined. However, existing studies largely use different approaches due to varying scholarly traditions. Data analytics in the literature tends to be driven by technology and techniques [13] while the theme on absorptive capacity revolves around the human factor in sensemaking [12]. Even though existing literature has provided a basic understanding on how an organization's use of data analytics and its absorptive capacity are associated with its performance, few studies have considered them together. This study argues that integrating both yields a more comprehensive understanding of innovation performance than addressing only one side of the phenomenon. For these reasons, the purpose of this paper is to investigate the role of data analytic usage and absorptive capacity in influencing innovation performance of organizations in the sharing economy.

1.4 Significance

To the authors' knowledge, there has not been a paper that studies the use of data analytics and absorptive capacity in the context of the sharing economy. Given the high reliance on digital technology and the emphasis on innovation in this sector, the sharing economy serves as an ideal ground to study these topics. Additionally, this paper is the first to examine the interdependent relationship between data analytics usage, absorptive capacity and innovation performance. In terms of its practical implications, findings from this paper offer insights on how data analytics usage and absorptive capacity jointly build innovative products and services that are sensitive to users' needs and changing business environments.

2 Theoretical Framework and Hypotheses

The Information Processing Theory (IPT) which has been used widely in studying organizations and management, and more recently, in studying big data [14] forms the theoretical underpinning of this study. According to the classic Galbraith's Information Processing Theory [15], organizations must organize and use information effectively, particularly in high uncertainty situations. Consequently, organizations will have to increase their information processing capacities. However, data analytics usage alone does not automatically lead to better decisions and performance [16]. An organization's absorptive capacity is required in assessing what data to capture and analyze.

Given the strong associations found in previous studies on data analytics usage, absorptive capacity and innovation performance outcomes in existing research [17–19], it is expected that each of these individually would influence innovation performance. Hence, the first two hypotheses are formulated:

H1: Data analytics usage has an influence on the innovation performance of the organization.
H2: Absorptive capacity has an influence on the innovation performance of the organization.

Simultaneously, it has been argued that having information alone does not necessarily lead to increased organizational outcomes [16], including innovation performance. It is thus expected that absorptive capacity would be more important to an organization's innovation as it helps to turn information into useful knowledge. Hence, the third hypothesis is formulated:

H3: Absorptive capacity has a stronger influence than data analytics usage on a firm's innovation performance.

3 Research Design

3.1 Research Sample

Data for this study, which is part of a larger project, was collected via survey. The study's population was derived from the member list of the Sharing Economy Association (Singapore) and via web searches of other entities that were not members of the association. Two inclusion criteria were applied to potential participants for this paper. Firstly, respondents have to be full-time employees working in corporate offices of organizations operating within the sharing economy in Singapore, regardless of whether Singapore was an operating (e.g. Grab) or non-operating market (e.g. Uber). Secondly, only participants who held managerial positions or higher were included, to gain insights on their organization's innovation performance.

Out of 600 participants who responded, a total 127 senior managers and directors participated in the survey, yielding a response rate of 21.17%. Though a relatively small sample size, it meets the absolute minimum number of participants for the statistical procedures to work effectively and the estimates of regression coefficients, variance and standard errors produced to be unbiased and accurate [20–23].

3.2 Measurements

A seven-point Likert-type scale format was used to measure participants' assessments of each item. All scales used were derived from previously established measures. Table 1 provides the details.

Table 1. Measures

Variable	Definition
Data analytics usage (DATA)	Adopted from [24]. Data analytics utilization refers to the practice of using data analytics to describe the current situation, predict the future and prescribe future action. Items = 11 (Cronbach α = .944). Assessed on a seven-point Likert scale labeled 1 = strongly disagree to 7 = strongly agree
Absorptive capacity (ACAP)	Adopted from [25]. Items = 3 (Cronbach α = .788). Refers to the transformation and assimilation of knowledge and technology. Assessed on a seven-point Likert scale labeled 1 = strongly disagree to 7 = strongly agree
Innovation performance (INNOV)	Adopted from [24]. Refers to relative competitiveness in introducing innovation to the markets. Items = 5 (Cronbach α = .820). Assessed on a seven-point Likert scale labeled 1 = strongly disagree to 7 = strongly agree

3.3 Reliability and Multicollinearity Tests

Cronbach reliability tests were conducted to measure the internal reliability of the three constructs. All Cronbach's alpha values were acceptable, surpassing the threshold of α = 0.7 [26], as shown in Table 1. Thus, the scales showed internal consistency.

The correlated matrix is shown in Table 2. Prior to the analysis, to test for multicollinearity, three items were checked. First, the zero-order correlations were examined for correlations of about .80 or larger. Second, the variance inflation factors were examined for scores of 10 or greater, and third, a condition index greater than 30 [15, 27, 28]. Specifically, all of the correlation coefficients were smaller than 0.70, the variance inflation factors (VIF) were within 3, and the condition indices were 27.985 for innovation performance as dependent variable. Thus, the results suggested that multicollinearity is not a concern.

Tabulated in Table 3 are the results of the hierarchical regression. Model 1 is the base model with only control variables, firm age and firm size. It could explain only 1.5% of the variance in innovation performance. Model 2 includes data analytics usage, and it could explain an additional 19.5% of the variance in innovation performance. Moreover, there is a significant positive relationship between data analytics usage and innovation performance (β = .896, p < .001), lending support for H1. Model 3 includes absorptive capacity, and it could now explain 20.2% of the variance innovation performance.

Table 2. Correlation matrix

	Mean	SD	1	2
DATA	5.068	.917		
ACAP	5.302	.944	.665**	
INNOV	4.981	.999	.580**	.404**

** p < .01

There is a significant positive relationship between data analytics usage and innovation performance ($\beta = .508$, p $< .001$), lending support for H2. Model 4 which combines both independent variables further increases the overall explanatory power to 26.8%. However, the partial correlation coefficient of absorptive capacity ($\beta = .330$, p $< .01$) is less than that of data analytics usage ($\beta = .555$, p $< .01$). Thus, H3 is not supported.

4 Findings

The proposed hypotheses were tested by hierarchical linear regression analysis. The results are presented in Table 3.

Table 3. Hierarchical regression results

	Model 1		Model 2		Model 3		Model 4	
	Coeff	SE	Coeff	SE	Coeff	SE	Coeff	SE
Firm age	−.008	.007	−.005	.006	−.002	.006	−.002	.006
Firm size	.004	.080	−.024	.073	−.031	.073	−.047	.071
DATA			.896***	.003			.555**	.002
ACAP					.508***	.080	.330**	.007
ΔR^2 (%)	1.5		19.5		20.2		25.3	
Total R^2 (%)	1.5		21.0		21.7		26.8	
F value	.957		30.38***		31.75***		9.517***	

*** p < .001, ** p < .01

Tabulated in Table 3 are the results of the hierarchical regression. Model 1 is the base model with only control variables, firm age and firm size. It could explain only 1.5% of the variance in innovation performance. Model 2 includes data analytics usage, and it could explain an additional 19.5% of the variance in innovation performance. Moreover, there is a significant positive relationship between data analytics usage and innovation performance ($\beta = .896$, p $< .001$), lending support for H1. Model 3 includes absorptive capacity, and it could now explain 20.2% of the variance innovation performance. There is a significant positive relationship between data analytics usage and innovation performance ($\beta = .508$, p < .001), lending support for H2. Model 4 which combines both independent variables further increases the overall explanatory power to 26.8%. However, the partial correlation coefficient of absorptive capacity ($\beta = .330$, p < .01) is less than that of data analytics usage ($\beta = .555$, p < .01). Thus, H3 is not supported.

5 Conclusion

Overall, findings reveal that both data analytics usage and absorptive capacity are important to organizations operating in the sharing economy, with data analytic usage accounting for a higher variance in innovation performance. An overall improvement in innovation performance in the sharing economy would contribute to the advancement of several objectives. This includes both economic objectives such as customer satisfaction and market performance [11], and social objectives such as sustainability and inclusivity [12, 29].

Companies should thus develop these two abilities in practice. Interestingly, for sharing economy organizations, data analytics usage was more important than having absorptive capacity, which is contrary to some existing findings in other industries, such as healthcare and hospitality [10]. Perhaps one of the reasons is that the speed of new products emerging in the sharing economy is too high [30], and the sharing economy is volatile by nature [31], making the absorptive capacity not as salient. As such, organizations in the sharing economy potentially represent a new breed of organization in terms of their knowledge practices, and are worth further investigation.

This study is not without limitations. Firstly, the research was conducted in Singapore. It is a highly urbanized city with an educated population that is digitally literate and proficient users of the sharing economy. The results may differ in other contexts. Future studies can replicate the study in other sociocultural contexts and ascertain how contextual differences may produce varying efficacies of data analytic use and absorptive capacity on innovation performance. In addition, apart from data analytics usage and absorptive capacity, other factors such as employee innovativeness [32] and human resource incentive system [11] can be considered. Secondly, this study assumes that all innovation is beneficial to society, despite studies highlighting the pitfalls of some practices of the sharing economy. For example, the contribution of the sharing economy to sustainability has been questioned [33] and it has been critiqued for its perpetuation of social inequality [34]. As such, future studies can distinguish between different types of innovations through an assessment of their organizational and societal outcomes.

References

1. Trenz, M., Frey, A., Veit, D.: Disentangling the facets of sharing. Internet Res. **28**(4), 888–925 (2018). https://doi.org/10.1108/intr-11-2017-0441
2. PwC: Sharing or Paring? Growth in the Sharing Economy (2015). https://www.pwc.com/hu/en/kiadvanyok/assets/pdf/sharing-economy-en.pdf
3. Sax, M.: Big data: finders keepers, losers weepers? Ethics Inf. Technol. **18**(1), 25–31 (2016). https://doi.org/10.1007/s10676-016-9394-0

4. Gazzola, P.: Behind the sharing economy: innovation and dynamic capability. In: Vătămănescu, E.-M., Pînzaru, F.M. (eds.) Knowledge Management in the Sharing Economy. KMOL, vol. 6, pp. 75–94. Springer, Cham (2018). https://doi.org/10.1007/978-3-319-66890-1_5

5. Srinivasan, R., Swink, M.: An investigation of visibility and flexibility as complements to supply chain analytics: an organizational information processing theory perspective. Prod. Oper. Manag. 27(10), 1849–1867 (2017). https://doi.org/10.1111/poms.12746

6. Karaboga, T.: big data analytics and firm innovativeness: the moderating effect of data-driven culture (2019). https://doi.org/10.15405/epsbs.2019.01.02.44

7. Cohen, W.M., Levinthal, D.A.: Absorptive capacity: a new perspective on learning and innovation. Adm. Sci. Q. 35(1), 128 (1990). https://doi.org/10.2307/2393553

8. Khan, Z., Lew, Y.K., Marinova, S.: Exploitative and exploratory innovations in emerging economies: the role of realized absorptive capacity and learning intent. Int. Bus. Rev. 28(3), 499–512 (2019). https://doi.org/10.1016/j.ibusrev.2018.11.007

9. Yun, J.J., Zhao, X., Hahm, S.D.: Harnessing the value of open innovation: change in the moderating role of absorptive capability. Knowl. Manag. Res. Pract. 16(3), 305–314 (2018). https://doi.org/10.1080/14778238.2018.1471328

10. Darwish, T.K., Zeng, J., Rezaei Zadeh, M., Haak-Saheem, W.: Organizational learning of absorptive capacity and innovation: does leadership matter? Eur. Manag. Rev. 17(1), 83–100 (2018). https://doi.org/10.1111/emre.12320

11. Inkinen, H.T., Kianto, A., Vanhala, M.: Knowledge management practices and innovation performance in Finland. Balt. J. Manag. 10(4), 432–455 (2015). https://doi.org/10.1108/bjm-10-2014-0178

12. Božič, K., Dimovski, V.: Business intelligence and analytics for value creation: the role of absorptive capacity. Int. J. Inf. Manag. 46, 93–103 (2019). https://doi.org/10.1016/j.ijinfomgt.2018.11.020

13. Mikalef, P., Pappas, I.O., Krogstie, J., Giannakos, M.: Big data analytics capabilities: a systematic literature review and research agenda. Inf. Syst. e-Bus. Manag. 16(3), 547–578 (2017). https://doi.org/10.1007/s10257-017-0362-y

14. Song, M., Zhang, H., Heng, J.: Creating sustainable innovativeness through big data and big data analytics capability: from the perspective of the information processing theory. Sustainability 12(5), 1984 (2020). https://doi.org/10.3390/su12051984

15. Galbraith, S.: Galbraith, Jay R.: Master of organization design – recognizing patterns from living, breathing organizations. In: The Palgrave Handbook of Organizational Change Thinkers, pp. 1–20 (2020). https://doi.org/10.1007/978-3-319-49820-1_39-3

16. Müller, O., Junglas, I., vom Brocke, J., Debortoli, S.: Utilizing big data analytics for information systems research: challenges, promises and guidelines. Eur. J. Inf. Syst. 25(4), 289–302 (2016). https://doi.org/10.1057/ejis.2016.2

17. Hao, S., Zhang, H., Song, M.: Big data, big data analytics capability, and sustainable innovation performance. Sustainability 11(24), 7145 (2019). https://doi.org/10.3390/su11247145

18. Popescu, D.I., Ceptureanu, S.I., Alexandru, A., Ceptureanu, E.G.: Relationships between knowledge absorptive capacity, innovation performance and information technology. Case study: the Romanian creative industries SMEs. Stud. Inform. Control 28(4), 463–476 (2019). https://doi.org/10.24846/v28i4y201910

19. Yu, S.-H.: Social capital, absorptive capability, and firm innovation. Technol. Forecast. Soc. Chang. 80(7), 1261–1270 (2013). https://doi.org/10.1016/j.techfore.2012.12.005

20. Dielman, T., Pfaffenberger, R.: Least absolute value regression: necessary sample sizes to use normal theory inference procedures. Decis. Sci. 19(4), 734–743 (1988). https://doi.org/10.1111/j.1540-5915.1988.tb00298.x

21. Harris, R.J.: A primer of multivariate statistics (2001). https://doi.org/10.4324/978141060 0455
22. Maas, C.J.M., Hox, J.J.: Sufficient sample sizes for multilevel modeling. Methodology **1**(3), 86–92 (2005). https://doi.org/10.1027/1614-2241.1.3.86
23. Wilson Van Voorhis, C.R., Morgan, B.L.: Understanding power and rules of thumb for determining sample sizes. Tutor. Quant. Methods Psychol. **3**(2), 43–50 (2007). https://doi.org/10.20982/tqmp.03.2.p043
24. Hussinki, H., Kianto, A., Vanhala, M., Ritala, P.: Assessing the universality of knowledge management practices. J. Knowl. Manag. **21**(6), 1596–1621 (2017). https://doi.org/10.1108/jkm-09-2016-0394
25. Szulanski, G.: Exploring internal stickiness: impediments to the transfer of best practice within the firm. Strateg. Manag. J. **17**(S2), 27–43 (1996). https://doi.org/10.1002/smj.425017 1105
26. Legum, S.E.: Jum C. Nunnally, Introduction to statistics for psychology and education. New York: McGraw Hill, 1975. Lang, Soc. **6**(2), 225–227 (1977). https://doi.org/10.1017/s00474 04500007272
27. Belsley, D.A., Kuh, E., Welsch, R.E.: Regression diagnostics. Wiley Ser. Probab. Stat. (1980). https://doi.org/10.1002/0471725153
28. Pelled, L.H., Xin, K.R.: Down and out: an investigation of the relationship between mood and employee withdrawal behavior. J. Manag. **25**(6), 875–895 (1999). https://doi.org/10.1177/014 920639902500605
29. Caldecott, S.: The age of access: how the shift from ownership to access is transforming modern life, by Jeremy Rifkin. Chesterton Rev. **29**(1), 186–189 (2003). https://doi.org/10.5840/chesterton2003291/225
30. Chalmers, D., Matthews, R.: Good to be bad: should we be worried by the sharing economy? Strateg. Chang. **28**(6), 403–408 (2019). https://doi.org/10.1002/jsc.2295
31. Anwar, S.T.: Growing global in the sharing economy: lessons from Uber and Airbnb. Glob. Bus. Organ. Excell. **37**(6), 59–68 (2018). https://doi.org/10.1002/joe.21890
32. McDowell, W.C., Peake, W.O., Coder, L., Harris, M.L.: Building small firm performance through intellectual capital development: exploring innovation as the "black box." J. Bus. Res. **88**, 321–327 (2018). https://doi.org/10.1016/j.jbusres.2018.01.025
33. Martin, C.J.: The sharing economy: a pathway to sustainability or a nightmarish form of neoliberal capitalism? Ecol. Econ. **121**, 149–159 (2016). https://doi.org/10.1016/j.ecolecon.2015.11.027
34. Schor, J.B., Attwood-Charles, W.: The "sharing" economy: labor, inequality, and social connection on for-profit platforms. Sociol. Compass **11**(8), e12493 (2017). https://doi.org/10.1111/soc4.12493

Cross-Regional Analysis of the Aging Phenomenon of Biomedical Scholars

Tongyang Zhang[1] , Jiexun Wu[1] , Zhiwei Ye[1], Ying Ding[2] , and Jian Xu[1(✉)]

[1] School of Information Management, Sun Yat-Sen University, Guangzhou, Guangdong, China
issxj@mail.sysu.edu.cn
[2] School of Information, University of Texas at Austin, Austin, TX, USA

Abstract. Comparing the aging of scholars in different regions is critical to have an integrative understanding of its causes and effects on academic performance. Using descriptive statistics and comparative analysis methods, we categorize aging trends in four types and find correlations between aging and academic performance by regression analysis. Findings show that: (1) Aging phenomenon is widespread in different regions, but their aging trends are obviously different at the regional level. Aging types include: Tending towards youth, tending towards maturity, maintaining maturity, and tending towards senility; (2) the type of aging largely depends on the variation in the proportion of scholars in different age groups; (3) aging can be further categorized into positive and negative ones based on the academic performance across of a region. The research is of great significance for understanding aging mechanism, solving problems it brings and informing decision-making for policy-makers.

Keywords: Aging phenomenon · Aging of scholars · Regional analysis

1 Introduction

In recent years, as the degree of social aging around the world is on the rise, the aging phenomenon has been valued by the academic community worldwide [1, 2]. Some scholars attribute the aging of scholars to higher education policy, the rapid growth of universities over the last few years, etc. [2, 3]. However, the effects and significant level of aging are complex, affected by policies, research environment, and state-of-the-art research situation across different geographical areas.

In order to reveal differences in variation trends of aging across different regions and explore the effect of aging on academic performance, descriptive statistics and comparative study methods were used to analyze literature and author data provided by PubMed Knowledge Graph (PKG) [4], a high-quality self-constructed dataset disambiguating author names, extracting entities, identifying affiliation data, and supplementing author information based upon PubMed. Regression analysis is used during analyzing the relevance of aging formation factors to academic performance and aging characteristics of scholars across different regions. The study aims to provide valuable information for relevant decision-making and scientific research development plans in various regions by exploring factors related to the formation and effects of aging.

M. Smits (Ed.): iConference 2022, LNCS 13192, pp. 244–254, 2022.
https://doi.org/10.1007/978-3-030-96957-8_22

2   Literature Review

Studies on the aging phenomenon of scholars can be traced back to the 1950s [5]. These studies have primarily focused on the following aspects: (1) Exploring associations between the age of researchers and their scientific output, including finding the peak age for academic productivity or comparing academic productivity in different age groups [6–9]. For instance, Ray Over studied the relationship between productivity and age through comparing publication rates of researchers across various age groups [9]; (2) discussing effects of contextual factors such as region and age on research output [10–12]. For instance, James Feyrer examined how the aggregate productivity relates with workforce demographics [10]; (3) proving the existence of aging phenomenon of researchers and then analyzing its cause and influences [13–16]. For instance, Benjamin Jones discovered Nobel Prize winners are more likely to produce great achievements at old ages [15].

Previous studies basically focused on scholars who made great achievements as research objects. Limited by the number of samples on a single type, they are insufficient in large-scale investigations on a large group of scholars, which exactly contributes insight into the formation and effects of aging a on academic performance. Therefore, this study seeks to reveal the underlying age group characteristics of scholars in different geographical regions, so as to understand the relevance of aging to academic performance.

3   Data and Methodology

3.1   Data Description

We chose the top ten most productive countries to represent the most influential countries in the medical field among 200 countries around the world. They all have an output volume exceeding 250 thousand articles and are divided into ten regions based on geographical characteristics. Among them, we collectively refer to European Union (EU) countries including German, France, Italy, Spain, Sweden, and the neutral state Switzerland as European countries. Consequently, the main regions to be studied include: America, European countries, England, Japan, Australia, Canada, Korean, India, China, and Brazil. In order to remove abnormal data, we only collected articles falling into the geographical range and having not exceeding 10 authors as research objects in case of an inordinate number of authors of a single article result the inordinate number of authors of a region. Since some of the articles before 1988 have not been completely recorded by PubMed, and the output of authors is relatively small during that time, we eventually locate over 23.64 million articles spanning from 1988 to2017 to extract usable statistical information of academic performance of scholars.

3.2   Methodology

Definition of Academic Age.   In previous studies, there are basically two kinds of methods to obtain ages of researchers. One is to extract detailed information on physical age with census data [17], while the other one is to take academic age as the substitution of physical age [18]. The academic age refers to the time that a scientist has entered the research field and remains active in publishing articles. It is computed by the year span from the first published work to the present, as shown in Formula (1):

$$\text{Academic Age}_i = \text{Current Year} - \text{First Publication Year}_i + 1 \tag{1}$$

Compared with physical age, academic age is much easier to access and can better explain the impact of aging on research output as the calculation of it is closely related to publications of scholars. In this study, we take academic age as the aging analysis indicator and denote the term "academic age" as "age" in order to simplify the subsequent expression.

Author Disambiguation. In order to obtain good effect in author disambiguation, PKG was constructed with author names disambiguated through integrating two existing author name disambiguation (AND) datasets Author-ity [19] and Semantic Scholar [20]. This is a self-built dataset completely covered by PubMed articles. The recall of the author disambiguation is estimated at ~98.8%. Lumping affects ~0.5% of clusters, whereas splitting affects ~2% of articles.

Age Group. We divided scholars into three groups: young scholars, middle-aged scholars, and elderly scholars based on the distribution of research output throughout their academic careers from 1988 to 2017.

We respectively counted the total number of publications of representative scholars who published more than 30 papers from 1988 to 2017 by age. In order to exclude the impact of the disruption caused by a circumstance that most scholars are limited to a certain group, the number of publications of all scholars were also counted by age.

As seen in Fig. 1, the distribution of publications of representative scholars conforms an inverted U-shaped curve. The number of publications is growing fast before the age of 8 and reaches its peak between 8 and 17. Then it gradually declines after the age of 18. Furthermore, the three intervals of academic output divided by 8 and 17 are approximately equal. Given the distribution pattern above, we define three age groups as follows: young scholar, aged between 1 and 7; middle-aged scholar, aged between 8 and 17; and elderly scholar, aged above 17. Ages above 45 are ignored as outliers.

Bias Ratio. The study introduces an important indicator Bias Ratio (BR) to measure the degree of bias between the average academic age of scholars of a certain region in year i and the expected age, which is calculated as:

$$BRi = (AVi - IV)/IV \times 100\% \tag{2}$$

where *Actual Value* (AVi) is the actual average academic age of scholars in year i and *Ideal Value* (IV) is the expected academic age of scholars over all years. The expected age is selected to be the average age at which the number of normalized citations of all scholars' research work in a region reach its highest among all other regions over all years.

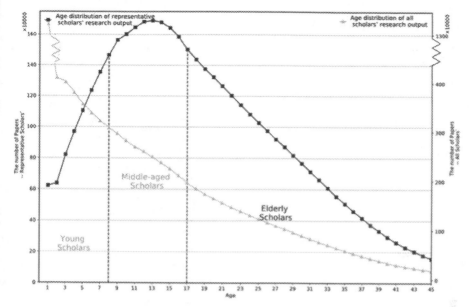

Fig. 1. Distribution of publications of all scholars and representative scholars at different ages

Normalized Citation. For the purpose of quantitatively measuring the quality of scholarly work, the study uses normalized citation as an evaluation indicator. Although it has been proven by many scholars that citations as a performance indicator can reflect the impact and quality of a scholarly work [21–23], the timing of publication can make a difference to the number of citations received. The normalized citation index uses citations of papers published in the same year with the target article to mitigate the problem of accumulative advantage by age, which is calculated as:

$$NCyi = \frac{Citation_i - CitationMean_y}{CitationStanDev_y} \tag{3}$$

where $NC_{y}i$ is the number of the normalized citations of an article i in year y, $Citation_i$ is the number of citations of article i, $CitationMean_y$ is the average number of citations of all articles in year y, $CitationStanDev_y$ is the standard deviation of the number of citations of all articles in year y.

4   Empirical Study and Preliminary Results

The study analyzes age characteristics of scholars in different regions, including observing the average age of first authors and that of all authors, as well as variation in the proportion of different groups of scholars, in combination of aging trend analysis with the change of time. In addition, we conducted a regression analysis to explore the relevance of BR to academic performance of scholars from different regions.

4.1 Basic Overview of Aging in Various Regions

Overall Situation of Aging Phenomenon in Different Regions. Considering that the first author is supposed to be the representative author who made the most contribution to an article, we focus on examining variation patterns of the average ages of the first authors over years across different regions.

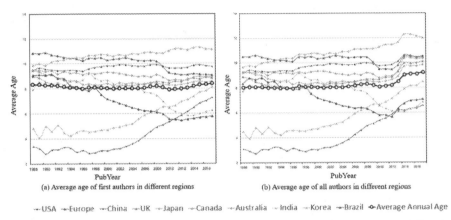

(a) Average age of first authors in different regions   (b) Average age of all authors in different regions

--USA --Europe --China --UK --Japan --Canada --Australia --India --Korea --Brazil --Average Annual Age

Fig. 2. Yearly Distribution of the average ages of the first authors and average ages of all authors in different regions

As shown in Fig. 2, significant differences in the degree of growth of age exist among different countries. As seen in Fig. 2(a), China and Korean present obvious aging trend, transforming from youth toward maturity gradually (tending towards maturity); the aging trend in Japan goes from maturity toward senility gradually (tending towards senility); the average ages of first authors in Europe, America and Australia constantly remain at a maturity level (maintaining maturity). Contrary to the most above, the trend in Brazil and India goes from maturity to getting younger (tending towards youth).

4.2 Analysis of Variation in the Proportion of Young, Middle-Aged and Elderly Scholars

The yearly proportion (the percentage of the number of scholars of a certain age group in the number of scholars of all age groups) distribution pattern of different types of scholars varies across different regions as follow: (1) In Japan, the pattern of all age groups tend to deviate from the average line of the proportions, indicating that tending towards senility relates to the rising proportion of the elder group and the decreasing proportion of the youth group; (2) in China and Korea, the pattern of all age groups tend to approach the average line of the proportions, indicating that tending towards maturity relates to the rising proportion of the elder group and the decreasing proportion of the youth group; (3) In India and Brazil, the pattern of all age groups tend to deviate from the average line of the proportions, indicating tending towards youth relates to the rising proportion of the youth group and the decreasing proportion of the elder group (Fig. 3).

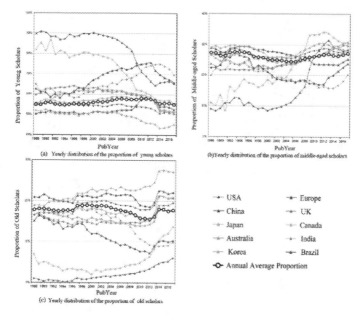

Fig. 3. Yearly proportion distribution of scholars in different age groups.

Academic Performance. With the research output and normalized citation as indexes, academic productivity, and impact of scholars in different regions can be quantitatively measured.

Figure 4(a) and (b) show that: In aspects of the quantity and proportion of publications, Japan, the scholars' ages of which have been in the stage of the transition from maturity to senility, is at a distinct disadvantage; China and Korea, the scholars' ages of which have been in the stage of the transition from youth to maturity, is on an upward trajectory; India and Brazil, the scholars' ages of which have showed younger trend, is on the way up but lower-leveled.

Bias Ratio between Expected Age and Average Age. Figure 5(a) shows the corresponding academic age of the maximum average normalized citations per scholar on the vertical axis is 9.43, which can be used as IV in formula (2). Based on formula (2), the yearly distribution of the average BR in different regions is shown in Fig. 5(b).

As shown in Fig. 5(b), the annually average BR in Europe, America, Australia, etc. keep stabilized around the x-axis; in Japan the annual average of BR keeps greater than zero and steadily rising; in China and Korea the annual average of BRs keeps less than zero and steadily rising to zero; in India and Brazil the annual average of BRs keeps less than zero and remains stable at a big absolute value after the drop. Given the patterns of BR evolution in different regions, the next step is to examine the correlation between BR and academic performance. The purpose for the examination is to answer questions about whether performance has a dependency on the degree of deviation from the expected age and how the two are related.

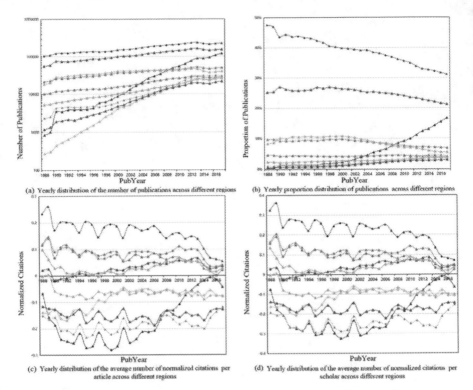

(a) Yearly distribution of the number of publications across different regions

(b) Yearly proportion distribution of publications across different regions

(c) Yearly distribution of the average number of normalized citations per article across different regions

(d) Yearly distribution of the average number of normalized citations per scholar across different regions

Fig. 4. Yearly distribution of academic performance of different regions.

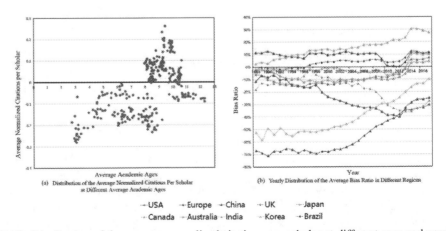

(a) Distribution of the Average Normalized Citations Per Scholar at Different Average Academic Ages

(b) Yearly Distribution of the Average Bias Ratio in Different Regions

— USA   — Europe   — China   — UK   — Japan
— Canada   — Australia   — India   — Korea   — Brazil

Fig. 5. Distribution of the average normalized citations per scholar at different ages and yearly distribution of bias ratio in different regions.

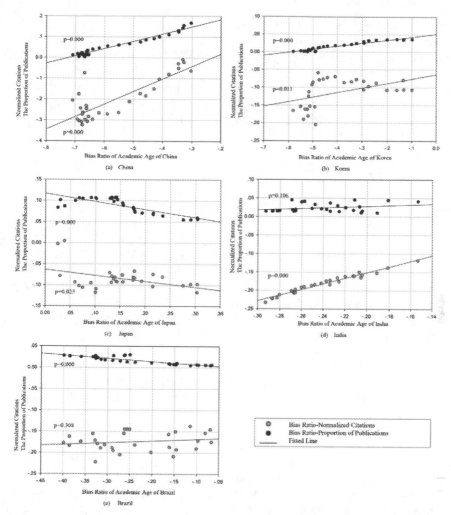

Fig. 6. Distribution of the average normalized citations per scholar at different ages and yearly distribution of bias ratio across different regions. (Note: The blue dots indicate the proportion of publications of the country in the total number of publications of all countries. The red dots indicate the average normalized citations of the country.) (Color figure online)

Relationship between Academic Age and Academic Performance. As shown in Fig. 6(a), (b) and (c), when scholars in a region are at the stage of growing elder, variations in academic age are associated with academic performance. For Japan, China, and Korea, as the average academic age goes closer to the expected age, the trends of both the quantity and quality of publications are upwards, and vice versa. Among them, China and Korea are at the stage of growing towards to the expected age, and Japan is at the stage of deviating from the expected age.

As shown in Fig. 6(d) and (e), when scholars in a region are at the stage of tending towards youth, the quantity and quality of research output do not necessarily reduce as the average academic age of the region deviate from the expected age. Specially the proportion of publications tend to increase with micro amplitudes while the trend of average normalized citations is still not positive as deviating from the expected age. Therefore, we speculate that the deviation from the expected age of the getting younger trend is not in favor of enhancing academic performance.

5   Discussion

The aging trend of scholars needs in-depth exploration of its formation and diverse impacts across different regions. Compared with previous studies that putting primary focus on academic awards winners, this study introduced the concept of academic age and conducted large-scale investigations on a large group of scholars. Specially the study is based on combining regional characteristics with patterns of aging and explore effects of different types of aging patterns on academic performance. Results show that age changes have relevance to academic performance.

Comparing various yearly distribution patterns of the average ages of representative authors across different regions, we categorize aging phenomenon of scholars into four different types: (1) Tending towards maturity (e.g., China and Korea), transforming from youth toward maturity; (2) Tending towards senility (e.g., Japan), transforming from maturity toward senility; (3) Maintaining maturity (e.g., Europe, America, Australia), remaining at a maturity level; (4) Tending towards youth (e.g., Brazil and India), transforming from maturity to getting younger. We relate the aging pattern in different regions with their respective changing patterns of the various yearly proportion distribution patterns of each age group: (1) in Japan, aging is related to the rising proportion of the elder group and the decreasing proportion of the youth group; (2) in China and Korea, the maturity trend is related to the rising proportion of the elder group and the decreasing proportion of the youth group; (3) In India and Brazil, the younger trend is related to the rising proportion of the youth group and the decreasing proportion of the elder group.

With research output and normalized citation as indexes, we quantitatively measured the academic productivity and impact of scholars in different regions, further subdividing aging into positive aging and negative aging. As for regions at the stage of growing elder, the approach of IV is positively associated with academic performance. Among them, Japan at the stage of deviating from IV performs negatively while China and Korea at the stage of approaching IV perform positively. As for regions at the stage of tending towards youth, the approach or deviation of IV is not associated with academic performance.

6   Conclusion and Future Work

The study categorizes and analyzes the aging of medical scholars across various regions, examining the relevance of aging to academic performance from the aspects of the quantity and quality of research output. For different regions, the aging pattern can be used as a reference for avoiding negative aging, formulating research policies, and making strategies of adjusting talented persons' enrollment. For instance, when Japan is in a negative aging stage due to the rising proportion of the elder group and the decreasing proportion of the youth group, universities can implement the strategy of importing more young talents to moderate the negative influence of aging on academic performance. For countries that are in a positive aging stage, how to keep the average academic age stable at the expected value and avoid getting stuck in negative states is also a challenge. The policy of encouraging young scholars to enter the medical field in India [24] is a pretty good guide for other countries.

In the future, we would like to broaden the coverage of scholars' backgrounds and compare aging in various subject areas, exploring effects of regional characteristics on the development of diverse academic subjects.

Acknowledgement. This work was supported by National Social Science Fund of China [18BTQ076].

References

1. Stroebe, W.: The graying of academia: will it reduce scientific productivity? Am. Psychol. **65**(7), 660–673 (2010)
2. Kaskie, B., Walker, M., Andersson, M.: Efforts to address the aging academic workforce: assessing progress through a three-stage model of institutional change. Innov. High. Educ. 1–13 (2016)
3. Hugo, G.: Demographic trends in Australia's academic workforce. J. High. Educ. Policy Manag. **27**(3), 327–343 (2005)
4. Xu, J., Kim, S., Song, M., et al.: Building a PubMed knowledge graph. Sci. Data **7**(1), 205 (2020)
5. Dennis, W.: Age and achievement: a critique. J. Gerontol. **11**(3), 331–333 (1956)
6. Homer, K.L, Rushton, J.P., Vernon, P.: A. relation between aging and research productivity. Psychol. Aging (1), 319–324 (1986)
7. Mumford, M.D.: Age and outstanding occupational achievement_Lehman revisited. J. Vocat. Behav. **25**, 225–244 (1984)
8. Dennis, W.: Age and productivity among scientists. Science (1956)
9. Over, R.: Does research productivity decline with age? High. Educ. **11**, 511–520 (1982). https://doi.org/10.1007/BF00194416
10. Feyrer, J.: Demographics and Productivity. Dartmouth College, Hanover (2004)
11. Hamermesh, O.D.S.: Aging and productivity among economists. Rev. Econ. Stat. **80**(1), 154–156 (1998)
12. Carayol, N., Matt, M.: Individual and collective determinants of academic scientists' productivity. Inf. Econ. Policy **18**(1), 55–72 (2008)
13. Sabharwal, C.M.: Foreign-born academic scientists and engineers: producing more and getting less than their U.S.-born peers? Res. High. Educ. **48**(8), 909–940 (2007)
14. Bonaccorsi, A., Daraio, C.: Age effects in scientific productivity. Scientometrics **58**(1), 49–90 (2003)
15. Jones, B.F.: Age and great innovation. Rev. Econ. Stat. **92**(1), 1–14 (2010)
16. Matthews, K.R.W., Calhoun, K.M., Lo, N., Ho, V.: The aging of biomedical research in the United States. PLoS ONE **6**(12), e29738 (2011)

17. Blau, D.M., Weinberg, B.A.: Why the US science and engineering workforce is aging rapidly. Proc. Natl. Acad. Sci. USA **114**(15), 3879–3884 (2017)
18. Wang, W., Yu, S., Bekele, T.M., Kong, X., Xia, F.: Scientific collaboration patterns vary with scholars' academic ages. Scientometrics **112**(1), 329–343 (2017). https://doi.org/10.1007/s11 192-017-2388-9
19. Torvik, V.I., Smalheiser, N.R.: Author name disambiguation in MEDLINE. ACM Trans. Knowl. Discov. Data (TKDD) **3**(3), 1–29 (2009). https://doi.org/10.1145/1552303.1552304
20. Ammar, W., et al.: Construction of the literature graph in semantic scholar. In: Proceedings of the 2018 Conference of the NAACH-HLT, no. 3, pp. 84–91 (2018). https://doi.org/10.18653/ v1/N18-3011
21. Hirsch, J.E.: An index to quantify an individual's scientific research output. Proc. Natl. Acad. Sci. **102**(46), 16569–16572 (2005)
22. Tan, Z.Y.: The method and application of strategic discipline information research [学科战略情报研究方法与实践]. Libr. Inf. Ser. **50**(5), 14–19 (2006)
23. Du, J., Zhang, B., Li, Y., Tang, X.L., Xu, P.Y., Liu, X.T.: Optimization of the evaluation indicators of scholars' research impact and comparative analysis between national and international academic behaviors of researchers [学者学术影响力评价指标的优选与学术行为特点的国内外比较]. Libr. Inf. Ser. **55**(10), 98–102 (2011)
24. Tole, S., Vale, R.D.: Young leaders for biology in India. Science **329**(5998), 1441 (2010)

Practicing What is Preached: Exploring Reproducibility Compliance of Papers on Reproducible Research

Renata G. Curty[1], Jian-Sin Lee[2], Wayland Chang[2], Ting-Hsuan Kao[2], and Wei Jeng[2(✉)]

[1] University of California Santa Barbara, Santa Barbara, CA 93106, USA
[2] National Taiwan University, Taipei, Taiwan
wjeng@ntu.edu.tw

Abstract. Motivated by the growing importance of both scientific transparency and accountability in the open science context, this study examines a series of papers on the topic of reproducible research and its alignment with open and transparent practices that are critical for research reproducibility. We screened an initial pool of 250 documents retrieved from Google Scholar that resulted in a final corpus of 19 articles used for further analyses. We adopted a checklist developed based on the Transparency and Openness Promotion (TOP) Guidelines and thus reported the results following six TOP dimensions: 1) data citation; 2) data, code, and additional documentation transparency; 3) design and analysis transparency; 4) pre-registration of studies; 5) pre-registration of analysis plans, and 6) replication. Preliminary findings have shown that most papers have made the underlying data, code, and documentation altogether available for reuse, primarily through generalist repositories. Some authors have used disciplinary conventions to produce research reports for disclosing key aspects of the research design and data analysis. Contrariwise, we observe that there is still room for improvement in current data citation practices, given that most papers do not correctly attribute the datasets they reused.

Keywords: Open science · Transparency and Openness Promotion (TOP) Guidelines · Reproducible research · Scientific reproducibility

1 Background and Motivation

Unequivocally, reproducibility is an essential attribute for open science. Reproducibility's facilitating self-correcting science also underpins the scientific method. Rooted in rigorous and transparent scientific workflows, altogether along with the disclosure of data, documentation, and code that backup study findings, this meta-concept designates

Supplementary Information The online version contains supplementary material available at https://doi.org/10.1007/978-3-030-96957-8_23.

research that is made available for public scrutiny as a means to be fully understood, verifiable, and reusable.

Non-reproducibility issues have been enduring concerns in the modern scientific enterprise. Bastian (2016) outlined a few milestones responsible for arising the discussion on reproducible research since the 1950s that includes the notorious example involving U.S.-based pharmaceutical companies, which culminated with significant changes to the U.S. Food and Drug Administration's (FDA) reproducibility requirements and the codification of standard procedures for controlled clinical trials (Randal 1999).

Despite not being a new problem, the issue of the lack of reproducibility has undoubtedly become more evident in the early 2010s, as more research data has been made publicly available on the Web, either altruistically or pushed by the growing enforcement of publishers and funders' data-sharing mandates. New forms of data publishing, beyond auxiliary files and *ad hoc* provisions, such as those involving data repositories and data papers, have altogether opened up discussions about strategies for improving scientific integrity through more rigorous checks and balances and peer-reviewing of data, documentation, and code (Iorns and Chong 2014; Kratz and Strasser 2014).

The so-called "reproducibility crisis" and initiatives to mitigate this problem has gained even more traction after Baker (2016) published results from Nature's survey of over 1,500 scientists who reported that science has increasingly failed to produce scientific claims and conclusions verifiable through organized skepticism, a cornerstone of the scientific ethos. About 70% of participants were unable to reproduce other scientists' results. According to various respondents in Baker's study (2016), some primary sources for irreproducible research included selective reporting, flawed analysis, poor research design and methods, code, and data unavailability.

Following the reproducibility crisis, the recognition that science needs some restructuring in the publishing and reward systems to promote the alignment of scientific principles with open science practices and guarantee the fundamental principle that publicized discoveries are reproducible has brought together multiple research communities to discuss the adoption of tools, policies, and recommendations. One example has been the Transparency and Openness Promotion (TOP) Guidelines[1] that had been developed by the Center of Open Science (COS) in collaboration with editors, funders, and scientific societies, which establishes standards toward a more transparent and reproducible science. In short, the TOP Guidelines assess journals according to eight standards of transparency, openness, reproducibility, and different endorsement levels (Nosek et al. 2016). The TOP Factor, directly derived from the TOP Guidelines, offers a journal-level metric that demonstrates the venue's effort to implement reproducibility practices, valuable to the different actors involved in the scientific enterprise. For example, potential authors who want to submit a manuscript to the venue can make a more informed decision about where to submit their papers with the underlying data, documentation, codes, and scripts and know ahead of time what to expect. Thus, both editors and publishers can overview current best practices for specific disciplines, researcher communities, and specific journals and benchmark them. At the same time, funders can encourage funded projects to publish in journals conforming to desirable open science practices. Yet, how

---

[1] https://www.cos.io/initiatives/top-guidelines.

are these reproducibility standards being adopted at the paper level, specifically among papers claiming the importance of reproducible research?

To answer this question, this study presents preliminary findings of an ongoing study investigating whether empirical papers from various fields concerned with scientific reproducibility and which recognize the value of the TOP Guidelines have adopted reproducible principles through open and transparent practices for sharing their respective delivered research products. Based on the initial analysis of a small corpus of papers, we seek not only to explore the level of compliance of these papers with reproducible standards, but more importantly, explore the different strategies that have been adopted by researchers for recording, referencing, and providing underlying data, documentation, and code, with the expectation to demonstrate practical examples of reproducible ideals. By untangling their various relationships and dissimilarities with the expectation to provide unambiguous operational criteria for these terms, this research expects to contribute to the still bewildering conceptualization of other "R" terms associated with reproducibility.

2   Untangling the Conflicting "R" Terminology

The terminology associated with reproducible research remains puzzling and still unsettled across disciplines (Goodman et al. 2016; Gundersen 2021; Peng and Hicks 2021; Plesser 2018). Frequently reusability, reproducibility, replicability, and repeatability are used interchangeably or even in conflicting ways given their subtle differences and intertwinement.

To recap and summarize the differences and similarities among these terms, we present an adapted version of Ryan and Duke's (2021) scheme for quality evidence attributes, as depicted in Table 1.

Table 1. The "R" terms and attributes

Terms (attributes)	Research question	Researchers	Data	Procedures/methods	Results
Reusability (reusable)	Same or different	Same or different	Same (part or whole)	Same or different	Same or different
Repeatability (repeatable)	Same	Same	Same	Same	Same
Reproducibility (reproducible)	Same	Different	Same	Same	Same
Replicability (replicable)	Same	Same or different	Similar	Same	Similar

To contribute to this terminological debate, we present our views of these four respective core terms and how they represent in a relatable manner. Still, yet other desirable research attributes with the goals to produce more reliable and robust science. Most of these attributes are only achievable in highly controlled and experimental environments dependent on computationally intensive methods that explain their more common application in the hard sciences.

2.1 Reusability

Reusability is an umbrella term that generally describes the potential for any new use of the data and evidence generated by the original study. According to Thanos (2017), reusability encompasses "the ease of using data for legitimate scientific research by one or more communities of research (consumer communities) that is produced by other communities of research (producer communities)." Hence, the data should be made available along with enough contextual information and documentation to allow its use partially or entirely by the same researcher(s) or by other parties not involved in the original study to answer similar or even different research questions than those asked by the primary investigators. Thus, reusability does not necessarily imply that identical or similar results will be achieved. Examples of various data reuse approaches recognized by the Evolutionary Informatics Working Group (EvoIO) (2011) include:

- Re-analysis: follows the same analytical process employed by the original study for verification purposes to refute or confirm previous findings.
- Integration: combines data from disparate data sources linked by one or more related variables to both enrich the data analysis and explore new relationships in the data.
- Repurposing: explores existing datasets in new ways to answer research questions not necessarily anticipated by the primary investigators.
- Aggregation: gathers data from multiple existing sources to form a unique dataset to answer new research questions.
- Meta-analysis: merges analyses (not raw data) from multiple independent sources to produce actual results.

2.2 Repeatability

Repeatability can be understood as "the consistency with which an observer measured a set of objects" (Harper 1994). A study or experiment is considered repeatable when it is performed again by the same researcher(s), following the exact same procedures, materials, and methods, leading to identical outcomes. Thus, repeatability implies that the quality of being repeated precisely like the original study (sameness) to internal validation and consistency checking. In short, it can be considered the measure of the likelihood that a researcher can conduct the same trial with the same setup and will ultimately achieve the same outcomes.

2.3 Reproducibility

For a study to be considered reproducible, a different researcher should perform the same processes and analyses to produce an identical result as the first researcher. Original researchers have to make available the study's associated data, documentation, and code pipelines and workflows in a way that is sufficiently self-explanatory and well-documented so that independent investigators can reproduce/recreate the original study under the same conditions, using identical materials and procedures, and ultimately achieve consistent results and render equal outcomes. According to Ryan and Duke (2021), "reproducibility requires that the process is fully-specified, generally in both human-readable and computer-executable form such that no study decisions are left to the discretion of the investigator." Hence, it requires original investigators to produce rich and detailed documentation for themselves and others.

2.4 Replicability

A replicable study refers to its ability to be recreated by original researchers or even investigators who were not involved in the original research, using the same methods and procedures to answer similar questions, with similar data, which will ultimately yield very similar outcomes. Along these lines, NSF (2016) states that replicability means "the ability to duplicate the results if the same procedures are followed, but new data are collected."

3 Methods

To explore existing practices within empirical studies about reproducible research, we adopted a sampling strategy that took into account journal papers indexed by Google Scholar and which explicitly acknowledged the existence of reproducibility standards such as the TOP Guidelines.

In April 2021, we searched with the following query: *empirical AND (reproducibility OR replicability OR repeatability OR reanalysis) AND ("Transparency and Openness Promotion" OR "TOP guidelines" OR "TOP guideline")* that yielded a total of 500 results. The first 250 results were reviewed by two independent coders to select eligible papers for further analysis. A total of 19 articles were considered after removing topic-irrelevant items, other types of publications, duplicated items, non-empirical studies, papers published in languages other than in English, and papers written by authors involved in this study to avoid conflicts of interest. Most papers were published in 2020 (n = 8) and are from Biomedicine (n = 7). One article was published in the journal *Science* (5Y-IF: 44.374), while the remaining 18 papers were published in 15 different journals with an average 5-year impact factor of 5.029. From the 16 distinguished journals, six are indexed by the TOP Factor and have scores ranging from 3 (*Journal of Consulting and Clinical Psychology*) to 11 (*PLoS Biology*, *PLoS One*, and *Science*).

The TOP Guidelines encompasses eight standards (GS1–8) for assessing journals' reproducibility practices (Nosek et al. 2016), which inspired the development of a checklist[2] comprised six dimensions (CS1–6) (Mellor et al. 2016), broken down into 15 items

---

[2] https://osf.io/hcnme/.

(CI1–15) in this study to assess the level of reproducibility compliance of the selected sample[3], as described in Table 2. Three coders analyzed each of the 19 papers and each coder spent an average of 50–60 min coding them independently. When needed, a fourth researcher served as an auditor to reconcile potential disagreements.

Table 2. Coding scheme overview

TOP guidelines standards (for journals)	TOP guidelines checklist standards (for journal papers)	Checklist items	Example question items
GS1. Citation standards	CS1. Citation	CI1x–CI2x	CI1x. Are the data, program code, and other methods from other studies appropriately cited within the text and listed in the reference section? If so, how?
GS2. Data transparency GS3. Analytic methods (code) transparency GS4. Research materials transparency	CS2. Data, analytical methods, code, and research materials transparency	CI3–CI4	CI3. Have the authors indicated whether the data, methods used in the analysis, and materials used to conduct the research will be made available?
GS5. Design and analysis transparency	CS3. Design and analysis transparency	CI5x–CI6x	CI5x. Did the authors mention any reporting guidelines or reproducibility-related standards that they followed for disclosing key aspects of the research design and data analysis?
GS6. Study pre-registration	CS4. Pre-registration of studies	CI7–CI9	CI7. Did the authors, in acknowledgments or the first footnote, indicate if they did or did not pre-register the research in an independent, institutional registry?
GS7. Analysis plan pre-registration	CS5. Pre-registration of analysis plans	CI10–CI14	

(*continued*)

---

[3] The coding worksheet template, the version history of our coding schemes, and the list of sampled papers can be found at: https://osf.io/5atyq/.

Table 2. (*continued*)

TOP guidelines standards (for journals)	TOP guidelines checklist standards (for journal papers)	Checklist items	Example question items
GS8. Replication	CS6. Replication	CI15	CI15. Is this study a replication of a previously published study?

4 Preliminary Findings and Discussion

We reviewed 19 papers and checked their level of compliance with a pre-established checklist. This section highlights key findings, corresponding to the dimensions CS1–CS6 in Table 2.

Lack of Proper Citation/Attribution of the Data. Data citation (CS1) is a crucial practice to lower data sharing withholding and to promote open, transparent and reproducible science. Yet, our analysis revealed that 11 papers (58%) reused other studies' data or methods, but none of them provided proper attribution to all the data or methods they reused. By adequate attribution, we mean a complete citation, following the style adopted by the journal, containing all required citation components to allow readers to easily identify the authorship, title, age, provenance, and location of the cited item.

One paper justified the inexistence of attribution due to confidentiality restrictions, and the other was limited to offering the URL to the study's Open Science Framework (OSF) project without more information about the study. Six (33%) papers provided in-text citations to the data- or method-related studies and subsequently added them to the reference list. Surprisingly, only one citation included a DOI. This finding demonstrates the need to extend the discussion towards the *Joint Declaration of Data Citation*[4] and the importance of its core eight principles.

The Underlying Data is Oftentimes Made Available for Reuse. For dimension CS2, the majority of the papers in our sample (89.5%, n = 17) explicitly stated that the data, methods, code/scripts, supplementary materials, and documentation (e.g., protocols, notes, survey instruments) were openly available for inspection and reuse. Most of them shared the DOI or the link to the data accessible via a generalist repository (n = 9), including Zenodo, Figshare, OSF, Mendeley Data, and GitHub. Five papers shared their underlying data and documentation via the journal website, two made data available simultaneously through a generalist repository and the journal website, and the remaining one shared data via an institutional data repository. We did not observe any disciplinary patterns with regard to preferred data availability means.

Some Use Disciplinary Reproducibility Standards. About half of the papers (52.6%) did not explicitly mention the use of guidelines to report the research design and the data

---

[4] https://www.force11.org/datacitationprinciples.

analysis (CS3). However, the remaining papers in our sample acknowledged the use of disciplinary reproducibility-related standards, including the Institute for Computational and Experimental Research in Mathematics (ICERM) standard, the International Committee of Medical Journal Editors (ICMJE), and the Companion Guidelines on Replication & Reproducibility in Education Research.

Study Pre-registration is Not as Standard Practice and is Less Adopted to Document Analysis Plans. The dimensions *of* pre-registration (i.e., CS4 and CS5) can be understood as the act of planning and documenting the research project, and the analysis (or set of analyses) procedures before any data are collected (sources). The advantage of adopting pre-registration is that researchers have to specify and roster their respective study plan to eliminate research misconducts, especially regarding data, e.g., data fabrications and falsifications. Researchers could also get credits for their thoroughly planned analyses (Simmons et al. 2021). We found only three (15.8%) out of the 19 papers have pre-registered their study in an independent registry and indicated it in the text. All pre-registrations protocols identified were made via the OSF, and only one of these papers has also preregistered the analysis plan.

Replication, When Performed, was Acknowledged. For the dimension CS6, four (21%) out of the 19 articles examined explicitly indicated that the study intended to replicate previous research, meaning that the same research questions were explored following the same procedures with the same data. Table 3 shows the compliance observed in each of the six dimensions:

Table 3. Levels of compliance by TOP dimensions

Dimension	Percentage
CS1. Appropriate citation	0%
CS2. Data, analytical methods, code, and research materials transparency	89.5%
CS3. Design and analysis transparency	52.6%
CS4. Pre-registration of studies	15.8%
CS5. Pre-registration of analysis plans	5.26%
CS6. Replication	21%

In sum, our preliminary results reveal that there are still some opportunities for papers to improve formal data citation practices and to adopt pre-registration procedures as means to further scientific reproducibility. More importantly, there is a need to encourage data citation at the same level as publications by including all required elements to make them stand the most, be more discoverable and accurately count towards scholarly impact metrics. In general, our sampled publications were sensitive to the practices of data availability and research transparency. The great majority of them openly provided the underlying dataset and supplementary documentation for future reuse.

5   Concluding Remarks

We recognize that the exploratory and small-scale nature of the study prevents us from making generalizations or drawing any firm conclusions about the *status quo* of the adoption of open and transparent practices which contribute to reproducibility compliance of academic papers about reproducible research.

Moving forward, we plan to refine the proposed coding scheme and checklist items for deepening the examination of authors' choices and approaches to addressing their research reproducibility. We also expect to interview primary authors from the sample and understand better what guided their decisions and the factors that may prevent them from complying with reproducibility standards. Additionally, we plan to explore journals' policies and guidelines to establish better comparisons concerning the different approaches adopted by authors to address scientific reproducibility. Future work will also consider a larger sample size for a broader range of publications regarding reproducibility and developing mechanisms to automate the coding process.

Acknowledgements. This work was financially supported by the Ministry of Science and Technology (MOST) in Taiwan, under MOST 111-2636-H-002-001- and MOST 111-2634-F-002-045, and the Center for Research in Econometric Theory and Applications (Grant no. 111L900204) from The Featured Areas Research Center Program within the framework of the Higher Education Sprout Project by the Ministry of Education (MOE) in Taiwan.

References

Bastian, H.: Reproducibility crisis timelines: milestones in tackling research reliability. PLoS Blogs: Absolutely maybe, 5 December 2016. https://absolutelymaybe.plos.org/2016/12/05/reproducibility-crisis-timeline-milestones-in-tackling-research-reliability/

Baker, M.: 1,500 scientists lift the lid on reproducibility. Nature **533**, 452–454 (2016). https://doi.org/10.1038/533452a

Data Citation Synthesis Working Group: Joint Declaration of Data Citation Principles—Final. Force 11 (2014). www.force11.org/datacitation

EvoIO Working Group: Reuse Cases (2011). http://www.evoio.org/wiki/Reuse_Cases. Accessed 5 Sept 2021

Gundersen, E.O.: The fundamental principles of reproducibility. Philos. Trans. Roy. Soc. A **379**(2197) (2021). https://doi.org/10.1098/rsta.2020.0210

Goodman, S.N., Fanelli, D., Ioannidis, J.P.: What does research reproducibility mean? Sci. Transl. Med. **8**(341), 341ps12 (2016). https://doi.org/10.1126/scitranslmed.aaf5027

Harper, D.G.C.: Some comments on the repeatability of measurements. Ringing Migr. **15**(2), 84–90 (1994). https://doi.org/10.1080/03078698.1994.9674078

Iorns, E., Chong, C.: New forms of checks and balances are needed to improve research integrity. F1000Research **3**, 119 (2014). https://doi.org/10.12688/f1000research.3714.1

Kratz, J., Strasser, C.: Data publication consensus and controversies. F1000Research **3** (2014). https://doi.org/10.12688/f1000research.3979.3

Mellor, D.T., Esposito, J., DeHaven, A.C., Stodden, V.: TOP resources - evidence and practices (2016). http://osf.io/kgnva

Nosek, B.A., et al.: Transparency and Openness Promotion (TOP) Guidelines, 5 October 2016. https://doi.org/10.1126/science.aab2374

National Science Foundation (NSF): Dear Colleague Letter: Robust and Reliable Research in the Social, Behavioral, and Economic Sciences (NSF 16–137) (2016). http://nsf.gov/pubs/2016/nsf16137/nsf16137.jsp. Accessed 13 Sept 2021

Peng, R.D., Hicks, S.C.: Reproducible research: a retrospective. Annu. Rev. Publ. Health **42**, 79–93 (2021). https://doi.org/10.1146/annurev-publhealth-012420-105110

Plesser, H.E.: Reproducibility vs. replicability: a brief history of a confused terminology. Front. Neuroinform. **11**, 76 (2018). https://doi.org/10.3389/fninf.2017.00076

Randal, J.: Austin Bradford Hill: a pioneering force behind clinical trials. JNCI: J. Natl. Cancer Inst. **91**(1) (1999). https://doi.org/10.1093/jnci/91.1.11

Ryan, P., Duke, J.: Evidence quality. In: Observational Health Data Sciences and Informatics, The Book of OHDSI. OHDSI (2021). https://ohdsi.github.io/TheBookOfOhdsi/EvidenceQuality.html

Simmons, J.P., Nelson, L.D., Simonsohn, U.: Pre-registration: why and how. J. Consum. Psychol. **31**(1), 151–162 (2021)

Thanos, C.: Research data reusability: conceptual foundations, barriers and enabling technologies. Publications **5**(1), 2 (2017)

A Higher Purpose: Towards a Social Justice Informatics Research Framework

Jasmina Tacheva[✉], Sepideh Namvarrad, and Najla Almissalati

Syracuse University, Syracuse, NY, USA
ztacheva@syr.edu

Abstract. In today's complex information environment, marked by deepening societal divides and growing inequality, issues of equity and justice are no longer the exclusive domain of the humanities and a handful of humanities-driven social scientists in the fields of information and technology. Instead, a growing number of researchers are seeking to make the intersection of information and technology on the one hand, and human flourishing and liberation, especially with respect to marginalized communities, on the other, the central focus of their teaching and research. Rather than trying to pigeon-hole these efforts as a distinct stream of research in the field of information and technology, this paper argues that centering questions of justice ought to be considered as the foundation of the field and therefore should permeate any epistemological agenda within in. To this end, we offer six actionable principles to help guide information researchers interested in justice-focused work which we refer to as *social justice informatics*.

Keywords: Social justice informatics · Critical theory · Data justice

1 Introduction

The deep societal divisions information and communication technologies (ICTs) help induce leave little doubt about the moral responsibility of anyone studying online discourse to not only call out and critically investigate the pernicious effects of propagating divisive (mis)information, but also to seek theoretical and practical ways to uphold human dignity, flourishing, and liberation. There has been a long tradition of humanist criticality in the information field, dating back to the origins of feminist technoscience in the 70's and 80's [1], and even earlier, to Alice Hilton's (1964) concept of cyberculture [2]. However, advances in computational techniques, as well as the exponential growth of user-generated data in the last decade have enabled the development of a new line of research which, while informed by the critical epistemological framings of its precursors, goes a step further to mobilize technology, information, and computational analysis in the praxis of social justice. Due to its simultaneous origination in several distinct fields such as information science, computer science, communication studies, rhetorical studies, and the digital humanities, this research direction is perhaps better viewed as a *transfield* permeating many different theoretical domains, rather than a discrete body of knowledge and practice neatly situated in a particular discipline. Nonetheless, there are

M. Smits (Ed.): iConference 2022, LNCS 13192, pp. 265–271, 2022.
https://doi.org/10.1007/978-3-030-96957-8_24

several key aspects that research examples of what we refer to as *social justice informatics* (SJI) have in common which we believe can serve as earmark properties of SJI studies.

This analysis seeks to conceptualize these defining characteristics of SJI and offer a set of principles which can guide the work of researchers in information science and beyond. By proposing a dynamic collection of principles to serve as the foundation of SJI research, we hope to give interested scholars and practitioners not so much a codified list of norms to follow in social justice-oriented research and community projects but rather an initial set of guiding questions to aid their learning, and, more importantly – *unlearning*, of ideas, methods, and practices in information-based contexts to ensure a more just development of the scientific fields they are a part of. To this end, the remainder of this paper is organized as follows: in Sect. 2, we provide an overview of the multisource origins of SJI which can be traced back to concurrent developments in several different scholarly domains. Section 3 seeks to delineate the properties of SJI research and offer a necessarily incomplete definition of SJI. In Sect. 4, we provide a collection of principles to help introduce anyone interested in doing SJI research to an emergent framework for this type of scholar-activist work. Section 5 concludes the paper by summarizing the key aspects of SJI research and offering avenues for further exploration.

2 From Criticality to Justice: SJI's Multi-source Origins

One of the key contributions of critical theory is its attention to *concepts*, or *Begriffe*, in Hegel's philosophy [3]. Through concepts, critical disciplines arm us with the ability to make sense of the world, especially in the case of oppressive practices, since injustice cannot be fought unless it can be named. Information-centered critical literature across multiple scholarly domains has given us an indispensable plethora of concepts which helps us reconstruct the complex landscape of our information environment, understand existing and potential sources of oppression, and chart paths towards collective liberation.

In this context, early tech industry activists and pioneers in the field of critical data studies danah boyd and Kate Crawford give us the concept of *data interpretation*, arguing that from the moment we pose the question, "What does this data mean?," we are already engaged in a subjective process of interpretation and therefore, data can never be objective, neutral, or said to speak for itself [4]. The way data interacts with black-boxed artificial intelligence algorithms to perpetuate racial bias, on the other hand, has been called by computer science scholar Joy Buolamwini the *coded gaze* [5] to capture the way computer vision "sees" selectively. Political scientist Virginia Eubanks extends this line of concern to the automation of public housing programs [6] and business school professor emerita Shoshana Zuboff studies how the process of automation, combined with the ubiquity of personal data, leads to the creation of a new model of capitalist accumulation and control she calls *surveillance capitalism* [7]. African and African Diaspora Studies Professor Simone Browne reminds us however, that despite the new multicore processor packaging, surveillance is by no means a new occurrence and is intimately connected with the dark history of transatlantic slavery [8]. Critical race and sociology scholar Ruha Benjamin aptly refers to this algorithmic modality of oppression as the "New Jim Code" to capture the danger of algorithms not just covering historical fault lines of racism but also streamlining discrimination [9]. Intersectional feminist thought helps elucidate at least one possible reason for this pernicious development: in their book *Data Feminism*, Urban Science and Planning professor Catherine D'Ignazio and English professor Lauren Klein attribute the proliferation of bias in algorithms to what they call the *privilege hazard*, or the lack of lived experience people from dominant groups experience which renders them incapable of understanding, or even allowing for the possibility of, ethical risks technology may pose to minoritized communities [10].

We argue that this bricolage of critical concepts enables researchers, activists, and the public to acquire what Paulo Freire (1973) calls *critical consciousness* – the adoption of a critical mindset capable of understanding and seeking to resist various forms of oppression, power, marginalization, privilege, and dominance [11]. As Freire points out, becoming aware of these interconnected systems of oppression is just the first step; the real work of critical consciousness happens when we start counteracting these systems in the pursuit of justice [11].

3   Towards a Social Justice Informatics Research Framework

The enormous potential for harm resulting from the ubiquity of ICTs combined with the processes of datafication and dataveillance [12] demonstrates that *social justice*, or the view that everyone deserves equal economic, political and social rights and opportunities [13], ought not to be a separate stream of research within the field of information studies, but rather an ethical bedrock for all research examining the generation, use, and sharing of information.

While it is important to be mindful of the constraining status of any definitional attempt seeking to capture the "true essence" or "authenticity" of a phenomenon [14], before proposing a research framework informed by and informing social justice principles, we would like to offer a necessarily incomplete and incipient definition of SJI. Specifically, we define SJI as the application of *critical theory*, where the term is necessarily plural to encompass the many criticalist schools present in different fields [15], to the study of information and technology and their effects on society, on various groups of peoples within society, on other-than-human animals, and the environment. Albeit broad, this attempt at a definition places humanistic methods at the core of SJI, since working towards justice is only possible if one is aware of the various forms of injustice taking place in society and how these forms are related, which is the central epistemological task of critical theory [16]. We further argue for a suprahuman definition of social justice of the kind philosopher Iris Marion Young puts forth, which contends that as long as an inhabitant of this world suffers institutional domination and oppression, they are a legitimate subject of justice [17]. While the use of computational methods is not antithetical to this definition, SJI should be seen as a body of scholarship and pedagogical practices where humanistic methods are given due respect when used in a study, rather than invoked in name only or as an afterthought.

Broader than a methodology, the SJI research framework is more properly understood as a *research architecture* rather than a method. This architecture sees knowledge not as an academic abstraction divorced from practice (not so much the practice of coding or applied data science for example, but rather the practice of day-to-day lived experiences, both on- and off-line) but as a collection of orientations and implicit understandings which operate as comportments to the world and which we, the pursuers of knowledge, may not always be aware of [18]. This embodied view of knowledge also suggests an awareness of oppressive regimes acting along the interpenetrating axes of race, ethnicity, class, caste, gender, sexuality, and ability which informs, and is in turn informed by, the analysis of data and information produced by the networked artifacts under examination such as the analysis of user-generated content. This iterative and recursive quality of SJI research assumes neither a purely deductive research approach nor an inductive one but rather their non-purist synthesis [19], and considers writing an active, generative, theory-, and world-building part of the research process rather than a passive summary of the results of the computational or qualitative technique used [20].

4 Doing SJI Research: A Framework of Guiding Principles

We contend that more important than teasing out the inferential status of SJI research – deductive, inductive, or a combination of the two – is the shared understanding of the following foundational principles pertaining to the problems of social justice in an information environment.

Principle 1: SJI research pursues freedom and justice, not merely the mechanistic production of self-serving knowledge.
    The co-primacy of theory and method in SJI research implies a focus on the rigor of humanistic theorization on the one hand and a critical awareness of the shortcomings of the computational or qualitative technique in use on the other. The first ensures the research project is not simply sprinkling humanistic concepts on top of social-scientific modeling without deeply reflecting on how these concepts came to be and how they relate to other phenomena in the information environment and the broader cultural ecosystem we live in [12]. SJI scholars ought to remember that adopting a particular concept such as *intersectional feminism* or *decolonization* has more than metaphorical meaning [21] and is never an innocent gesture because of the actionable power of concepts and their influence on methodology [22]. Similarly, critically engaging the assumptions and simplification moves any research technique necessarily employs ensures SJI researchers are doing their part to avoid both the "anything goes" pitfall of qualitative research [23] and the "enchanted determinism" of quantitative methodology, especially in its computational variety which is often spoken of as an unprecedented, almost magical, force of accuracy and perceptiveness in pattern discovery [24]. Ensuring an agenda of maximizing freedom and justice rather than personal advancement also means pursuing research questions not because they are "in vogue" or represent "hot research topics" but rather because they have the potential to positively benefit vulnerable communities beyond the confines of institutionalized academic spaces.

Principle 2: SJI research seeks to undo positivist dichotomies such as the divide between researchers and research subjects or learners and educators.
    The clear demarcation between who leads a study and who the study focuses on, as well as who has the expertise and who the expertise is imparted on, is part of science's Enlightenment legacy which still haunts information and technology studies. This false

dichotomy plagues our field by flattening the meaning and effort we invest in community-focused research such as participatory action research (PAR). Specifically, although we subscribe to PAR's principles in theory, there is of yet no effective mechanism to ensure our research practices are not merely extractive and that we acknowledge the agency, but also the indigenous knowledges, of the communities we work with. SJI researchers are advised to keep in mind the epistemological origins of PAR, rooted in the critical pedagogy of Paulo Freire and the liberatory education model of Miles Horton, and be aware of how their positionality may not only not help the communities they conduct research in, but actually harm them through what has become known as a "culture of handouts" where "experts" feel they need to intervene in "communities of need" both at home and abroad, and impart their "superior knowledge" [25].

Principle 3: *Liberatory education is a key component of SJI research which impacts not only learners in the classroom but also members of the communities of study and researchers themselves.*

Informed by critical theory, SJI research sees students not simply as passive empty vessels waiting to receive the instructor's knowledge and expertise, but rather as active participants in the co-creation of knowledge. This dynamic process leads to, and is in turn governed by, the coming together of individual students and the instructor as a *community* – a community of thinkers and doers. Relatedly, neither students, nor instructors are "brains in a vacuum." Rather, we each bring our unique body, identity, experiences, insights, traumas, and dreams to the research lab, classroom, or field site and we cannot pretend these do not exist or do not matter. Teaching in an information field ought not to be primarily about technical expertise but rather about trying to bridge our multifaceted worlds and arrive at a collective understanding of how data and algorithms impact us collectively, individually, and within our personal communities. This type of resolutely liberatory education is a key component of SJI since as critical educators, we should not forget that we have a responsibility to teach for a more just world for all.

Principle 4: *Just as there is no such thing as raw, neutral, or small data, there is no neutral or objective method either.*

The central lesson of critical data studies is the need to always contextualize and localize data since any attempt to take it out of context already results in deleterious loss of meaning [4]. However, the same considerations apply to the qualitative and quantitative methods we choose to use in our research. It is, for example, easy to focus on the newness of a statistical technique for the classification of data, but SJI research prompts us to think carefully and critically about the problematic history of classification as a process of determining what counts and what doesn't; what is normal and what isn't, dating at least as far back as Linnaeus' 18th c. classificatory system which has been developed in an undeniably colonial historical context and has been applied not just to the classification of plant and animal species, but to humans as well [10].

Principle 5: *AI and ICTs are developed by humans and therefore it is unrealistic to expect that algorithmic biases can be effectively countered without critical consciousness.*

Since there is no objective or neutral method, and because algorithms are methods developed by human actors situated in particular contexts [10], a merely computational or logical intervention to "correct" an algorithm and "debias" it may temporarily allevi-ate the problem at hand but ultimately does little to change the technocratic, seemingly apolitical and agnostic, weltanschauung of algorithmic regulation. Exuberant calls from techno-enthusiasts to "improve algorithms because we cannot improve humans" are bla-tantly oblivious of the fact that algorithms are human creations and that the technological progress we admire algorithms for ought to be accompanied by societal improvement, through interacting with diverse communities and unlearning deeply-entrenched false beliefs instead of hoping that algorithms would relieve us of the moral responsibility to take an ethical stance.

Principle 6: If the harms exceed the social benefits from AI and ICTs, discontinuing their use is not off-limits.

Because of the resolutely human-centered ethos of SJI, information researchers inter-ested in issues of justice should accept the basic premise that our primary task is not so much to save the computational infrastructure AI and ICTs rely on but rather to defend society, in its suprahuman definition discussed earlier. This last principle is perhaps the one that most definitively distinguishes SJI from other critical information and technol-ogy domains such as ethical AI which, with its very name, privileges AI systems over communities.

5 Conclusion

This paper seeks to provide an initial glimpse into the effort to consolidate the mani-fold epistemological engagements with justice-related issues across scientific disciplines focused on the social aspects of information and technology. By examining critical infor-mation and technology concepts from a variety of fields beyond informatics, we aimed to demonstrate the multisource origins of the growing body of work we describe as social justice informatics (SJI). We further provided a working definition of SJI, along with six foundational principles to help ground SJI research. Future work could focus on developing a step-by-step guide for the application of SJI principles to empirical work in the field, especially when it comes to the use of computational methods. The viability of key computational tools and techniques such as data scraping in SJI research needs to be examined and guidelines for the ethical use of such techniques should be provided.

References

1. Haraway, D.: Situated knowledges: the science question in feminism and the privilege of partial perspective. Fem. Stud. **14**(3), 575–599 (1988)
2. Hilton, A.M.: An ethos for the age of cyberculture. In: Proceedings of the April 21–23, 1964, Spring Joint Computer Conference (1964)
3. Hegel, G., Brockmeyer, H., Harris, W.: The phenomenology of spirit. J. Specul. Philos. **2**(3), 165–171 (1868)
4. Boyd, D., Crawford, K.: Critical questions for big data: provocations for a cultural, technological, and scholarly phenomenon. Inf. Commun. Soc. **15**(5), 662–679 (2012)
5. Buolamwini, J.: InCoding–in the beginning was the coded gaze. MIT Media Lab (2016)

6. Eubanks, V.: Automating Inequality: How High-Tech Tools Profile, Police, and Punish the Poor. St. Martin's Press, New York (2018)
7. Zuboff, S.: The Age of Surveillance Capitalism: The Fight for a Human Future at the New Frontier of Power: Barack Obama's Books of 2019. Profile Books, London (2019)
8. Browne, S.: Dark Matters: On the Surveillance of Blackness. Duke University Press, Durham (2015)
9. Benjamin, R.: Race after technology: abolitionist tools for the new JIM code. Soc. Forces **98**, 1–3 (2019)
10. D'ignazio, C., Klein, L.F.: Data Feminism. MIT Press, Cambridge (2020)
11. Freire, P.: Education for Critical Consciousness, vol. 1. Bloomsbury Publishing, London (1973)
12. Cheney-Lippold, J.: We are Data. New York University Press, New York (2017)
13. Assembly, N.D.: Code of ethics of the national association of social workers (2008)
14. Bhabha, H.K.: The Location of Culture. Routledge, Abingdon (2012)
15. Kincheloe, J.L., McLaren, P., Steinberg, S.R.: Critical pedagogy and qualitative research. In: The SAGE Handbook of Qualitative Research, pp. 163–177 (2011)
16. Kincheloe, J.L., McLaren, P.: Rethinking critical theory and qualitative research. In: Key Works in Critical Pedagogy, pp. 285–326. Brill Sense, Paderborn (2011)
17. Young, I.M.: Five Faces of Oppression. Rethinking Power, pp. 174–95 (2014)
18. Pohlhaus Jr., G.: Knowing without borders and the work of epistemic gathering. In: Decolonizing Feminism: Transnational Feminism and Globalization, pp. 37–54 (2017)
19. Dershowitz, N., Reddy, U.S.: Deductive and inductive synthesis of equational programs. J. Symb. Comput. **15**(5–6), 467–494 (1993)
20. Braun, V., Clarke, V.: Using thematic analysis in psychology. Qual. Res. Psychol. **3**(2), 77–101 (2006)
21. Tuck, E., Yang, K.W.: Decolonization is not a metaphor. In: Decolonization: Indigeneity, Education & Society, vol. 1, no. 1 (2012)
22. Pawlicka, U.: Data, collaboration, laboratory: bringing concepts from science into humanities practice. Engl. Stud. **98**(5), 526–541 (2017)
23. Antaki, C., et al.: Discourse analysis means doing analysis: a critique of six analytic shortcomings (2003)
24. Campolo, A., Crawford, K.: Enchanted determinism: power without responsibility in artificial intelligence. Engag. Sci. Technol. Soc. **6**, 1–19 (2020)
25. Mohanty, C.T., Carty, L.: Feminist Freedom Warriors: Genealogies, Justice, Politics, and Hope. Haymarket Books, Chicago (2018)

XCoref: Cross-document Coreference Resolution in the Wild

Anastasia Zhukova[1]([✉])(iD), Felix Hamborg[2,4](iD), Karsten Donnay[3,4](iD),
and Bela Gipp[1,4](iD)

[1] Data and Knowledge Engineering, University of Wuppertal, Wuppertal, Germany
{zhukova,gipp}@uni-wuppertal.de
[2] Department of Computer Science, University of Konstanz, Konstanz, Germany
felix.hamborg@uni-konstanz.de
[3] Department of Political Science, University of Zurich, Zurich, Switzerland
donnay@ipz.uzh.ch
[4] Heidelberg Academy of Sciences and Humanities, Heidelberg, Germany
https://dke.uni-wuppertal.de/en/

Abstract. Datasets and methods for cross-document coreference resolution (CDCR) focus on events or entities with strict coreference relations. They lack, however, annotating and resolving coreference mentions with more abstract or loose relations that may occur when news articles report about controversial and polarized events. Bridging and loose coreference relations trigger associations that may expose news readers to bias by word choice and labeling. For example, coreferential mentions of "direct talks between U.S. President Donald Trump and Kim" such as "an extraordinary meeting following months of heated rhetoric" or "great chance to solve a world problem" form a more positive perception of this event. A step towards bringing awareness of bias by word choice and labeling is the reliable resolution of coreferences with high lexical diversity. We propose an unsupervised method named *XCoref*, which is a CDCR method that capably resolves not only previously prevalent entities, such as persons, e.g., "Donald Trump," but also abstractly defined concepts, such as groups of persons, "caravan of immigrants," events and actions, e.g., "marching to the U.S. border." In an extensive evaluation, we compare the proposed XCoref to a state-of-the-art CDCR method and a previous method TCA that resolves such complex coreference relations and find that XCoref outperforms these methods. Outperforming an established CDCR model shows that the new CDCR models need to be evaluated on semantically complex mentions with more loose coreference relations to indicate their applicability of models to resolve mentions in the "wild" of political news articles.

Keywords: Cross-document coreference resolution · News analysis · Media bias

1 Introduction

Coreference resolution (CR) is a set of techniques that aim to resolve mentions of entities, often in a single text document. CR is an essential analysis component in a broad

© The Author(s), under exclusive license to Springer Nature Switzerland AG 2022
M. Smits (Ed.): iConference 2022, LNCS 13192, pp. 272–291, 2022.
https://doi.org/10.1007/978-3-030-96957-8_25

spectrum of use cases, e.g., to identify potential targets in sentiment analysis or as a part of discourse interpretation. While CR focuses on single documents, *cross-document coreference resolution* (CDCR) resolves concept mentions across a set of multiple documents. Compared to CR, CDCR is a less-researched task, although more challenging due to a larger search space and much required to facilitate content understanding of multiple articles. Further, many use cases require CDCR of more varying concepts than just entities typically resolved within CR, e.g., events or abstract entities.

Although the CDCR research has been gaining attention, the annotation schemes and corresponding datasets have infrequently explored a mix of identity and loose coreference relations and lexical diversity of the annotated chains of mentions. We explore CDCR in a particularly challenging use case, i.e., to identify bias by word choice and labeling. Such bias occurs due to substantial variance in the words and loose coreference relations that yield possibly biased interpretations of events or entities. For example, coreferential mentions of "direct talks between U.S. President Donald Trump and Kim" such as "an extraordinary meeting following months of heated rhetoric" or "great chance to solve a world problem" form a more positive perception of this event.

Resolution of identity relations (i.e., coreference resolution) and resolution of more loose relations (i.e., bridging) are typically split into two separate tasks [18]. Resolution and evaluation of entity and event mentions of the mixed relations remain a research gap in general CDCR research. Hamborg et al. [13] first explored CDCR in a particularly challenging use case, i.e., to identify bias by word choice and labeling in news articles. Their proposed approach, called TCA, resolved mentions with strong lexical diversity.

In this paper, first, we revisit TCA and propose XCoref, an unsupervised sieve-based method that jointly resolves mentions of strict and loose identity relations into coreferential chains[1]. Methods of such design have been successfully used to resolve mentions of identity relation in events and entities [19,23], and bridging relations in entities [15].

Second, we conduct an extensive evaluation where we compare XCoref with TCA and one of the state-of-the-art methods for CDCR [2]. We evaluate the annotated mentions of varying coreference strength jointly as one task of set identification and calculate the results with the standard CoNLL metrics in (CD)CR [39]. We discuss a direction of the CDCR evaluation to address the complexity of coreferential chains annotated on politically diverse news articles, i.e., in the "wild." The political news articles may suffer from framing by polarized word choice when journalists report on the same event from multiple perspectives and use strongly divergent words [12].

2   Related Work

Coreference resolution (CR) and cross-document coreference resolution (CDCR) are tasks that aim to resolve coreferential mentions in one or multiple documents, respectively [45]. (CD)CR approaches tend to depend on the annotation schemes of the CDCR datasets that specify the definition of mentions and coreferential relations [4].

Most (CD)CR datasets contain only strict identity relations, e.g., TAC KBP [28, 29], ACE [1,21], MEANTIME [27], OntoNotes [47], ECB+ [3,9]. Less commonly

---

[1] Code is available at https://github.com/anastasia-zhukova/XCoref.

used (CD)CR datasets explore relations beyond strict identity. For example, NiDENT [41,42] is a CDCR dataset of entities-only mentions that was created by reannotating NP4E. NiDENT explores coreferential mentions of more loose coreference relations coined near-identity that among all included metonymy, e.g., "White House" to refer to the US government, and meronymy, e.g., "US president" being a part of the US government and representing it. Reacher Event Description (RED), a dataset for CR, contains also more loose coreference relations among events [33].

Mentions coreferential with more loose relations are more difficult to annotate and automatically resolve than mentions with identity relations [40]. Bridging relations occur when a connection between mentions is implied but is not strict, e.g., a "part-of" relation. Bridging relations, unlike identity relations, form a link between nouns that do not match in grammatical constraints, e.g., gender and number agreement, and allow linking noun and verb mentions, thus, constructing abstract entities [18]. The existing datasets for identification of bridging relations, e.g., ISNotes [15], BASHI [43], ARRAU [37], annotate the relations only of noun phrases on a single-document level and solve the problem as antecedent identification problem rather than identification of a set of coreferential anaphora [15]. Definition identification in DEFT dataset [46] focuses on annotating mentions that are linked with "definition-like" verb phrases (e.g., "means," "is," "defines," etc.) but does not address linking the antecedents and definitions into the coreferential chains.

To our knowledge, only one dataset contains annotations of coreferential mentions with varying strength of coreferential relations. NewsWCL50 [13] contains annotations of concepts based on a minimum number of (coreferential) mentions across a set of news articles reporting on the same event. The dataset contains diverse concept types, such as actors, entities, events, geo-political entities (GPEs), and more complex types, such as actions or abstract entities. The dataset argues that in political news articles, more loose coreferential relations form links and associations to phrases that could bear bias by word choice and labeling, e.g., "DACA recipients" – "undocumented immigrants who came to the U.S. as children" – "illegal aliens" – "innocent kids." There are two approaches for event CDCR, easy-first and mention-pair [23]. Usually, easy-first approaches are unsupervised, whereas mention-pair are supervised. Most methods employ the easy-first approach and sequentially execute so-called sieves. Each sieve resolves mentions concerning specific characteristics. Earlier sieves target simple and generally reliable properties, such as heads of phrases. Later sieves address more complex or specialized cases and use special techniques, such as pair-wise scoring of the pre-identified concepts with binary classifiers, e.g., SVM [13,20,22,32]. Alternatively, a mention-pair approach uses a neural model trained to score the likelihood of a pair of the event- or entity-mentions to refer to the same semantic concept. The features to represent mentions are spans of text, contexts, and semantic dependencies [2].

Most CDCR methods focus on only events and resolve entities—if at all—as subordinate attributes of the events [2,7,10,16,17,22,23]. These a few CDCR methods resolve chains of both event and entity mentions with strict identity, and there is only one method the resolve concepts with more loose the identity and coreference relations [13]. The method named TCA [13], resolves mentions of varying identity levels, i.e., include strict and near-identity. Target Concept Analysis (TCA) is a sieve-based method that resolves concepts that represent entities, events, and aggregating categories, e.g., categories that include mentions referring to both a country and its governmental institutions to which they belong annotated with a name of a country [13]. Other sieve-based feature-engineering methods for mention resolution were successfully used for identification of entities and events with strict identity [19,23,32], and resolution of mentions with bridging relations [14, 15].

In conclusion, prior methods for CDCR suffer from at least one of two shortcomings, i.e., they (1) only resolve mentions interlinked with identity relations or (2) focus on event-driven narrowly defined coreferential mentions. The contributions of this paper are two-fold: first, we revisit the methodology of TCA because it is the only method that addresses the resolution of mentions with various identity relations [13]. Then, we propose XCoref, an unsupervised method that jointly resolves mentions with strict and loose anaphoric relations. Second, we evaluate the approach on a CDCR dataset with coreferential chains with varying identity relations, i.e., NewsWCL50, and compare the results to the previously proposed CDCR methods for these datasets using metrics established in the literature on (CD)CR, i.e., B3, CEAF_e, and MUC [30].

3 Methodology: XCoref

XCoref revisits Target Concept Analysis (TCA) proposed by Hamborg et al. [13]. XCoref consists of five sieves (see Fig. 1) and applies the "easy-first" principle, i.e., it first resolves mentions that belong to named entities (NEs), such as person, organization, and country, and are coreferential with identity relation [15]. Afterward, the method addresses chains coreferential with mixed identity and bridging relations, i.e., groups of persons, events, and abstract entities. TCA is a sieve-based method to resolve coreferential chains by addressing issues of the previously unresolved mentions. In contrast to TCA, XCoref resolves mentions of specific concept types in each sieve and analyzes combinations of phrases' modifiers to resolve mentions with varying coreference relations.

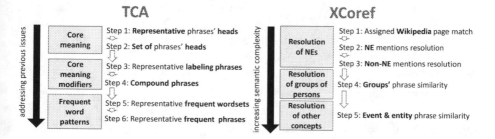

Fig. 1. Comparison of TCA to XCoref: TCA resolves mentions by addressing previous issues whereas XCoref first resolves coreferential chains of NEs with identity relations (S1–S3) and then resolve those chains with more loose coreferential relations (S4 and S5).

3.1 Preprocessing

Since each sieve of XCoref resolves specific concept types, we first need to identify these types. We distinguish nine types: person, group, country, misc, and their NE- and non-NE variations [13]. Further, each sieve S_i uses a comparison matrix cm_i, i.e., a manually created cross-type matrix, to determine which types x and y to compare for potential merging ($cm_{i,x,y} \geq 1$ allows comparison, 0 not).

To yield reliable concept type determination, we propose a type scoring based on WordNet sense ranking [11]. For a given concept, Hamborg et al. [13] proposed counting frequencies of WordNet senses assigned to all concept's heads', e.g., "president" is four times "noun.person." We propose an improvement to the counting by weighting the senses according to their rank in WordNet. Since highly ranked senses have more influence on the concept type score, the weighted scoring minimizes tilting of the final concept's type towards the rare meanings of its mentions.

An additional improvement to the preprocessing proposed by Hamborg et al. [13] is CoreNLP's coreference resolution on (virtually) concatenated documents. We observe that CoreNLP resolves more true mentions in concatenated texts than within single texts but is also prone to wrongly merging large coreferential chains, even when using the improved CR model [8]. Thus, we split chains by analyzing NEL results of each of their mentions, i.e., for each mention and its compound+head sub-phrases, we obtain its Wikipedia page name [24]. We split chains whose members are assigned to different Wikipages [27]. We attach a resolved Wikipage title to each cleared chain as a new property.

Each mention contains dependency and structure parsing subtrees. Structure subtrees are created by 1) parsing the sentences of mentions' origin, 2) mapping heads of mentions to the structure parsing trees, 3) taking the longest subtree but not larger than 20 tokens. The dependency subtree contains all the tokens as in the structure subtree. These subtrees play a role in the feature sources for the sieves.

S1: Named Entity Linking (NEL)

The first sieve, S1, leverages CoreNLP to mainly resolve mentions NE-containing chains, i.e., pronominal, nominal, and pronoun mentions. Specifically, S1 reused CoreNLP's coreference resolution on the concatenated documents and the assigned Wikipages. We resolve mentions by the winner-takes-it principle [15], i.e., we merge the smaller chains into the coreference chains that were pre-identified by CoreNLP if the chains have identical Wikipage titles.

S2: Head-Word and Compound Match of NEs

The second sieve, S2, merges the NE-containing chains, which mentions CoreNLP and NEL (in S1) failed to resolve. These typically smaller NE-containing chains of comparable types by cm_2 are merged into the larger NE-containing chains if they have identical NE heads (*"Kim"* – *"North Korean dictator Kim Jong Un"*) or have cross-overlapping NE heads and compounds (*"Donald"* – *"Donald Trump"*).

S3: Resolution of Non-NE Mentions

The third sieve, S3, merges any comparable NE-containing chain c_{ne} with a smaller chain with non-NE mentions c_{nn} if they match due to string or cosine similarity, e.g., "Teresa May" – "the prime minister." S3 uses dependency subtrees of the mentions and extracts head modifiers from the subtrees, e.g., adjective, compound, apposition, or noun. Such anaphora tend to be missed by CoreNLP. In S3, we merge chains if at least one of the conditions holds:

1) $r(c_{nn}) \subset r(c_{ne}) \wedge m(c_{nn}) \subset |r(c_{nn}) \cap r(c_{ne})|$, where $r(..)$ extracts representative phrases, i.e., phrases that contain heads of phrases and their direct modifiers (i.e., adjectival, noun, and compound) expanded with a list of all apposition modifiers, and $m(..)$ are modifiers (i.e., compounds and appositions) extracted from the chains' mentions,

2) $|c_{nn} \cap c_{ne}| \geq 2$ and at least one head of phrases from each chain belongs to this intersection,

3) $cos(v(c_{ne}), v(c_{nn})) \geq t_{nn}$, where $v(..)$ is a mean vector of the word vector representation of all unique non-stop-words from the concept's mentions, cos is cosine similarity and t_{nn} is a threshold derived during experiments.

S4: Identification of Groups of Persons

The fourth sieve, S4, resolves chains of mentions referring to the group of individuals, e.g., "illegal aliens" – "undocumented immigrants," and semantically related phrases to countries, e.g., "Trump administration officials" – "American government."

We incorporate a clustering approach of Zhukova et al. [48] that puts mentions into chains in the decreasing semantic similarity between mentions. The approach consists of six stages where the first identifies cluster cores and subsequent stages expand the clusters: (1) preprocessing, (2) identify cluster cores, (3) form cluster bodies, (4) add border mentions, (5) form non-core clusters, and (6) merge final clusters (see Fig. 2). The final clusters form coreference chains.

In summary, the approach of Zhukova et al. works as follows. First, it finds distinctive cluster cores, i.e., each core is a group of mentions that are highly semantically similar to each other as to two factors: 1) cosine similarity of word-vectorized mentions in a potential core and 2) the normalized number of other mentions to which mentions of a potential core are similar. Then, the approach tries to assign the remaining mentions to the cores based on the relaxed rules of one-level similarity, i.e., using only cosine similarity between unresolved mentions and the already clustered mentions into chains. Mentions must be left unresolved and converted into singleton-concepts if they do not meet similarity requirements, such as similarity to one of the core points. Lastly, because the annotation of GPEs include also mentions to the nations of the countries, we merge the country-NE-containing chains c_{ne} with the groups of people c_{gr} if $cos(v(h(c_{ne}), v(m(c_{gr})) \geq t_{gr}$, where $h(..)$ extracts heads of phrases, $m(..)$ extracts modifiers (i.e., NE-compounds and NE-adjectives) from chains' mentions, and t_{gr} is a threshold derived during experiments.

To improve the results in the intermediate cluster, we propose two "cleaning" steps: merge similar clusters and move alien points. After identification of cluster cores, forming cluster bodies, and non-core clusters, we check if there are clusters C that are similar enough to be merged or contain some points, i.e., alien mentions, that are different from the other cluster members and should be moved from one cluster to another.

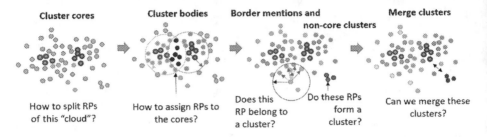

Fig. 2. Sieve S3: Identification of mention clusters proposed by Zhukova et al. [48].

Merge Intermediate Clusters. After each step, we check if there are multiple clusters, mentions of which share linguistic and semantic properties. The shared properties indicate that the clusters can be merged and improve the effectiveness of the following steps.

First, we calculate two cross-cluster similarity matrices: (1) a phrase-similarity matrix P where each cell P_{c_i,c_j} is a mean cosine similarity of the vectorized cluster representatives $r(c_i)$:

$$P_{c_i,c_j} = \frac{1}{|c_i| \cdot |c_j|} \sum_{rp_k \in r(c_i)} \sum_{rp_l \in r(c_j)} cos(v(rp_k), v(rp_l)), \qquad (1)$$

where $r(..)$ extracts representative phrases from cluster's mentions, i.e., heads of phrases and all modifiers such as adjective, noun, and compound, and $v(..)$ vectorizes words in word vector space.

(2) a head-similarity matrix H where each cell H_{c_i,c_j} is a mean cosine similarity of vectorized heads of phrases :

$$H_{c_i,c_j} = \frac{1}{|c_i| \cdot |c_j|} \sum_{h_k \in h(c_i)} \sum_{h_l \in r(c_j)} cos(v(h_k), v(h_l)) \qquad (2)$$

where $h(..)$ extracts heads of phrases.

Second, we construct a cross-cluster similarity matrix SM elements SM_{c_i,c_j} of which show how two clusters are similar to each other given head- and phrase-similarity levels and uses

$$SM_{c_i,c_j} = \begin{cases} 0, & \text{if } \exists rp_k \in r(c_i), \exists rp_l \in r(c_j) : NG_{ne(rp_k),ne(rp_l)} = 0 \\ w_p \cdot P_{c_i,c_j} + w_h \cdot H_{c_i,c_j}, & \text{else} \end{cases} \qquad (3)$$

where $w_p = 0.5$ is a phrase weight, $w_h = 0.5$ is a head weight, $ne(..)$ extracts named-entity tokens from a phrase, and NG is a named entity grid proposed by Zhukova et al. [48] that indicates relatedness across named entities extracted from ConceptNet knowledge graph. $NG_{ne(rp_k),ne(rp_l)} = 0$ means that named entities are not related, e.g., "Kremlin" is not related to "United States." The weighting of phrases and heads balances the mean clusters' position in the vector space towards the core meanings of the contained phrases, i.e., the heads of phrases.

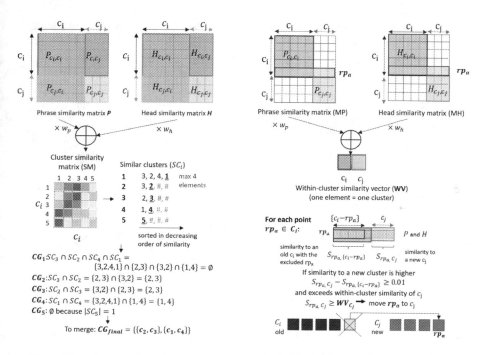

Fig. 3. Merge intermediate clusters.   **Fig. 4.** Move alien mentions across clusters.

Third, for each cluster c_i, we take a row of SM, and we sort indexes of the values in the decreasing order of the value. From each sorted list, we take all elements until the index of c_i (and including it), or maximum four elements, e.g., take c_3 and c_2 as the most similar for c_2 (see Fig. 3). To find cluster groups CG_i, we iterate over the similar clusters from the position of c_i (SC_i) and find which clusters are symmetrically similar to c_i, i.e., find in which clusters c_i is listed as a similar cluster:

$$\forall C_i \in C: \quad CG_i = \{ \bigcap_{sc \in SC_i} SC_{sc} \text{ if } |SC_i| > 1\} \tag{4}$$

$$CG_{final} = \{ \bigcup_{CG_a \in CG} CG_i \text{ if } CG_i \neq \emptyset\} \tag{5}$$

Finally, we collect all non-empty cluster groups CG_i, and indexes in these groups indicate which clusters need to be merged.

Move Alien Points. When forming clusters at each step, we might add a mention that was similar to the other mentions at the moment of that clustering step but not after a step was completed when combinations of mentions in clusters changed. In other words, some mentions could become *alien points* in a cluster by the completion of a step. To identify an alien point, we (1) calculate a cross-mention similarity value of a mention to other mentions in this cluster and a similarity value of a mention to other clusters, (2) move a mention to a cluster with a higher similarity score. Figure 4 depicts the process of moving a mention to a more suitable cluster.

First, for each cluster, we calculate a *within-cluster similarity vector* WV_{c_i} that determines how similar are the mentions within this cluster. WV_{c_i} will later be used as a threshold similarity value which an alien point from another cluster c_j should exceed to move from a cluster c_j to a cluster c_i.

$$WV_{c_i} = \begin{cases} P_{c_i}, \text{ if } \exists r(c_i) \in c_i : ne(r(c_i)) \in NG \\ w_p \cdot P_{c_i} + w_h \cdot H_{c_i}, \text{ else} \end{cases} \tag{6}$$

where $w_p = 0.4$ is a phrase weight, $w_h = 0.6$ is a head weight, $ne(..)$ extracts named-entity tokens from a phrase, NG is a named entity grid, P is a phrase similarity vector elements P_{c_i} of which are an average cosine similarity of vectorized representative phrases of a cluster c_i

$$P_{c_i} = \frac{1}{|c_i|^2} \sum_{rp_k \in r(c_i)} \sum_{rp_l \in r(c_i)} cos(v(rp_k), v(rp_l)) \tag{7}$$

and H is a head similarity vector elements H_{c_i} of which are an average cosine similarity of vectorized heads of phrases of a cluster c_i

$$H_{c_i} = \frac{1}{|c_i|^2} \sum_{h_k \in h(c_i)} \sum_{h_l \in h(c_i)} cos(v(h_k), v(h_l)) \tag{8}$$

Second, we iterate over all representative phrases of mentions in each cluster c_i and decide if a mention is an alien point, i.e., a mention needs to be moved to the more similar cluster c_j. We can move a mention from a cluster c_i into a cluster c_j only if there is no restriction by a named-entity grid NG between a mention's representative phrase rp_a and any representative phrases in c_j, i.e., $\forall rp_a \in c_i, \exists rp_l \in r(c_j) : NG_{ne(rp_a),ne(rp_l)} \neq 0$, where $ne(..)$ extracts named entity tokens from a phrase.

We estimate which cluster is more suitable for a mention rp_a (i.e., its representative phrase) for those clusters between which it is allowed to move the points. To find a better matching cluster, we calculate (1) a similarity value between rp_a and a cluster c_i without rp_a:

$$S_{rp_a,\{c_i-rp_a\}} = \frac{1}{|c_i|-1}(w_p \cdot \sum_{rp_l \in r(\{c_i-rp_a\})} cos(v(rp_a), v(rp_l)) \qquad (9)$$

$$+ w_h \cdot \sum_{h_l \in h(\{c_i-rp_a\})} cos(v(h(rp_a)), v(h_l))) \qquad (10)$$

(2) a similarity value between rp_a and a new cluster c_j:

$$S_{rp_a,c_j} = \frac{1}{|c_j|}(w_p \cdot \sum_{rp_k \in r(c_j)} cos(v(rp_a), v(rp_k)) \qquad (11)$$

$$+ w_h \cdot \sum_{h_k \in h(c_j)} cos(v(h(rp_a)), v(h_k)))) \qquad (12)$$

where

$$(w_p, w_h) = \begin{cases} (1.0, 0.0), & \text{if } \exists rp \in r(c_j) : rp \in NG \\ (0.6, 0.4), & \text{else} \end{cases} \qquad (13)$$

where $rp \in NG$ means that a representative phrase is contained in a named-entity grid NG.

Finally, we move an alien point rp_a from c_i to c_j if (1) a similarity of rp_a to a new cluster c_j is larger than to the old cluster c_i, i.e., $S_{rp_a,c_j} - S_{rp_a,\{c_i-rp_a\}} \geq 0.01$, and (2) a similarity of rp_a to a new cluster c_j is not worse than the internal similarity level of c_j, i.e., $S_{rp_a,c_j} \geq WV_{c_j}$.

S5: Events and Abstract Entities

The fifth sieve, S5, resolves mention chains of events and so-called abstract entities [37], i.e., actions, objects, events, etc., that contain mentions of noun phrases (NPs) and verb phrases (VPs), for example, "Trump-Kim *meeting*" – "*discussed* an issue". Such mentions are typically not resolved by CoreNLP: only identical mentions are resolved as coreferential. S5 vectorizes each concept c_i by (1) preprocessing chains, i.e., keeping the unique mentions within chains, removing stopwords, and lemmatizing words, and (2) using a weighting scheme of vectorizing chains $V(c_i)$ with word embedding vectors [48]:

$$V(c_i) = \frac{1}{|p(c_i)|} \sum_{l \in p(c_i)} k \cdot v(l) \qquad (14)$$

where $p(..)$ preprocesses a chain according to the step (1) and yields lemmas, and k depend on a status of a lemma, i.e., a lemma is a head of one of mentions in c_i or not:

$$k = \begin{cases} 2, & \text{if } \exists l \in h(c_j) \\ 1, & \text{else} \end{cases} \qquad (15)$$

i.e., we keep the original vectors for all lemmas except for the head lemma of the mentions. Such a weighting scheme allows emphasizing the core meaning of a mention while keeping the mention's context. Lastly, we form coreferential chains by clustering the mentions with hierarchical clustering [31] using cosine distance, average linkage, and a threshold t_{cl}. Hierarchical clustering commonly used in concept identification [6].

4   Evaluation

We compare XCoref to the established CDCR model of Barhom et al. [2] on NewsWCL50, i.e., a concept-driven CDCR dataset with a mix of identity and bridging relations. We evaluate the datasets containing coreference anaphora with bridging relations with the standard coreference metrics of CoNLL [39], although most of the bridging relations are not classified as a problem of set identification [15].

4.1   Dataset: NewsWCL50

Similar to [7], we do not evaluate the approaches on two separate lists of mentions for events and entities but consider the mentions of all mentions combined as if they formed abstract entities. If an approach requires input or separate event and entity mentions (e.g., Barhom et al. [2]), then we implement splitting of mentions into two lists based on the heads of phrases, i.e., VPs represent events whereas other part-of-speech tags represent entities.

We removed "ACTOR-I" category from NewsWCL50 due to a considerable level of abstractnesses [13]. Our manual inspection of the chains labeled with this category did not identify consistency in annotating mentions as coreferential by identity, near-identity, or bridging relations. Therefore, to focus only on the listed relations, we removed this category from the evaluation.

4.2   Methods and Baselines

We compare the performance of XCoref to a lemma baseline, an established event-entity CDCR model of Barhom et al. [2], and Target Concept Analysis method (TCA) of Hamborg et al. [13] to identify semantic concepts in NewsWCL50. Additionally, we perform an ablation study and evaluate modifications of XCoref. For all approaches, we use the same default parameters across topics, datasets, and run configurations to facilitate fair evaluation. We describe each method briefly in the following.

Lemma. Our baseline is a primitive CDCR approach that resolves mentions based on matching lemmas of the phrases' heads. This baseline was also used by Barhom et al. [2], thus, establishes a fair comparison to the other approaches in the evaluation.

EeCDCR. Barhom et al. [2] proposed a joint event and entity CDCR model (hereafter EeCDCR). EeCDCR is trained on ECB+ and resolves event and entity mentions jointly. To reproduce EeCDCR's performance, we use the model's full set of optional features: semantic role labeling (SRL), ELMo word embeddings [36], and dependency relations. Barhom et al. [2] used the output files of the SRL parser, SwiRL, which makes it impossible to apply EeCDRCR to the other datasets. Therefore, we used the most recent AllenNLP's SRL method [44] to make the feature extraction a part of the EeCDCR and applicable for all datasets. To resolve intra-document mentions, identical to the original setup, we use Stanford CoreNLP. We reused default parameters for the model inference.

TCA. Target Concept Analysis (TCA) is a method of identification of the reported concepts in the related news articles, the mentions of which are typically a subject of bias by word choice and labeling [13]. Based on the functionality of TCA, we can classify the method as CDCR focusing on the resolution of concepts with varying strength of cross-mention identity relations and mentions of high lexical diversity.

TCA uses six sieves to determine whether two candidate chains should be merged because they refer to the same semantic concept. Each sieve uses specific similarity measures, e.g., cosine similarity or string equality, and analyzes specific characteristics of the candidates' mentions, e.g., heads and their modifiers, i.e., adjective, noun, apposition, compound, and number. We use the reported TCA's default parameters for all datasets. For a word embedding model, we used a version of word2vec [26] that, unlike the original implementation, vectorizes out-of-vocabulary words [34].

Identical to Hamborg et al., we use TCA's default parameters for all datasets. We report the results of multiple variants of TCA. First, the original version as reported by Hamborg et al. Second, to facilitate comparability of TCA's sieves to the sieves of XCoref, we use the preprocessing steps of XCoref in TCA and also show the effectiveness of these steps to improve the performance. Additionally, we evaluate $\text{TCA}_{preproc}$ using three different word embeddings (see below).

Ablation Study. For the ablation study, we test two variants of XCoref with which we investigate the effectiveness of various word embedding models and the effectiveness of approaches identifying more loose anaphoric coreference relations.

First, an "intermediate" model named XCoref_{interm} uses sieves S1–S3 of XCoref, S4_{interm} is a baseline used by Zhukova et al. [48] with the same threshold parameters, and S5_{interm} is the second sieve adopted from TCA, i.e., cosine similarity of phrases' heads. Resolution with semantically similar heads can effectively resolve mentions of abstract entities, e.g., "meeting" – "talks." S4_{interm} and S5_{interm} resolve mentions of the same concept types as in XCoref. Using XCoref_{interm}, we test if the proposed methods for resolution of the bridging coreference anaphora outperform the simpler methods for the same coreference relations.

Second, we test for either XCoref and XCoref_{interm} how using state-of-the-art, non-contextualized word embeddings affects their performance: word2vec [26], fast-Text [25], and GloVe [35]. We use the model implementations that facilitate the representation of out-of-vocabulary (OOV) words [34], which is critical to address the inability of the default word2vec and GloVE models to represent OOV words.

4.3 Metrics

We report the established CoNLL metrics for (CD)CR, i.e., MUC, $B3$, $CEAF_e$, and an average of them as $F1_{CoNLL}$ [39]. Similar to Barhom et al. [2], we evaluate the methods with an official CoNLL scorer [38]. The CoNLL metrics evaluate the quality of coreference chains regarding multiple properties of coreference chains. MUC evaluates the combination of coreference links formed between mentions in predicted and annotated chains. $B3$ estimates the chains as sets and evaluates compositions of predicted sets of mentions compared to the annotated sets by overlapping these sets.

$CEAF_e$ aligns and calculates the goodness of fit of the predicted chains to the annotated chains, i.e., finds the best unique match of predicted to annotated chains.

Although NewsWCL50 contains mentions with varying coreference strength, i.e., from strict identity to loose synonyms and bridging relations, we do not distinguish between the strength of coreferential relations. We evaluate the coreferential chains as if their mentions had relations of identical strength.

Table 1. Evaluation of a lemma baseline, EeCDCR [2], TCA [13], XCoref$_{interm}$ (a version of XCoref with baseline methods for sieves S4 and S5), and XCoref on NewsWCL50 dataset with diverse strength of coreference chains.

Method	Word vectors	MUC			B3			CEAF$_e$			F1$_{CoNLL}$
		R	P	F1	R	P	F1	R	P	F1	
Lemma	–	75.7	93.8	83.8	36.8	88.8	52.0	63.1	7.8	13.9	49.9
EeCDCR [2]	GloVe	69.4	90.6	78.6	33.1	82.3	47.2	58.6	7.8	13.7	46.5
TCA [13]	word2vec	73.4	89.4	80.6	37.2	73.7	49.4	51.9	8.7	14.9	48.3
TCA$_{preproc}$	word2vec	72.9	89.5	80.3	38.4	75.6	50.9	54.5	9.1	15.6	48.9
	fastText	72.9	87.6	79.6	37.3	71.5	49.0	52.0	9.5	16.0	48.2
	GloVe	77.2	88.3	82.4	41.8	67.0	51.4	52.9	12.1	19.6	51.2
XCoref$_{interm}$	word2vec	68.4	90.3	77.8	37.7	84.0	52.0	63.0	8.4	14.8	48.2
	fastText	74.2	87.3	80.2	38.7	71.5	50.2	58.4	11.6	19.4	50.0
	GloVe	75.7	88.5	81.6	40.6	72.1	52.0	58.9	12.1	20.0	51.2
XCoref	word2vec	70.7	89.8	79.1	36.3	82.4	50.4	63.0	9.4	16.3	48.6
	fastText	78.6	90.0	83.9	43.1	70.5	53.5	60.4	13.7	22.4	53.3
	GloVe	79.3	90.8	**84.7**	44.4	72.2	**55.0**	61.1	13.9	**22.6**	**54.1**

Table 2. Comparison of XCoref's sieves to the intermediate version of XCoref$_{interm}$ in NewsWCL50 with GloVe word vectors. XCoref and XCoref$_{interm}$ share sieves S1–S3 and differ in the last sieves. S4 and S5 of XCoref outperform sieves of XCoref$_{interm}$.

Sieves	MUC			B3			CEAF$_e$			F1$_{CoNLL}$
	R	P	F1	R	P	F1	R	P	F1	
init$_{shared}$	28.6	89.8	43.4	15.6	96.0	26.8	41.4	2.1	4.1	24.7
S1$_{shared}$	40.2	92.3	56.0	22.9	95.0	36.9	49.7	3.1	5.8	32.9
S2$_{shared}$	42.2	92.5	58.0	24.6	94.6	39.1	51.2	3.3	6.2	34.4
S3$_{shared}$	45.7	91.0	60.8	27.3	91.3	42.1	51.6	3.6	6.7	36.5
S4$_{interm}$	52.7	90.2	66.6	29.1	87.5	43.6	51.5	4.2	7.8	39.3
S5$_{interm}$	75.7	88.5	81.6	40.6	72.1	52.0	58.9	12.1	20.0	51.2
S4	54.6	91.1	68.3	30.4	86.1	44.9	51.9	4.4	8.1	**40.4**
S5	79.3	90.8	84.7	44.4	72.2	55.0	61.3	13.9	22.7	**54.1**

Table 3. Comparison of S4 for resolution groups of persons between XCoref to the intermediate version of XCoref$_{interm}$.

Method	Word vectors	MUC			B3			CEAF$_e$			F1$_{CoNLL}$
		R	P	F1	R	P	F1	R	P	F1	
Lemma	–	74.8	71.7	73.2	17.4	68.8	27.8	53.8	5.3	9.7	36.9
EeCDCR [2]	GloVe	67.2	54.9	60.4	16.7	56.0	25.7	49.2	4.4	8.0	31.4
TCA [13]	word2vec	74.7	48.4	58.7	21.2	39.6	27.6	40.9	5.4	9.5	32.0
S3$_{interm}$	word2vec	60.0	75.5	66.9	13.8	75.0	23.3	46.1	3.5	6.5	32.2
	fastText	71.6	68.7	70.1	21.8	60.7	32.1	38.8	4.4	8.0	36.7
	GloVe	72.6	72.1	72.3	19.8	63.0	30.1	38.1	4.5	8.1	36.8
S3	word2vec	80.0	69.2	74.2	27.3	55.0	36.5	45.7	7.2	12.5	**41.1**
	fastText	81.5	60.1	69.2	33.2	42.7	37.4	34.1	6.1	10.3	39.0
	GloVe	81.7	63.3	71.3	28.4	49.7	36.2	38.0	6.7	11.4	*39.6*

4.4 Results and Discussion

The evaluation shows that XCoref, our multi-sieve feature-based unsupervised method, is capable of consistently resolving coreferential anaphora of mixed identity and bridging coreference relations with $F1_{CoNLL} = 54.1$ when using GloVe as word vectors.

Section 1 reports the $F1_{CoNLL}$ score typically used to evaluate (CD)CR approaches (named $F1$ in this section). We find that XCoref outperforms all methods on NewsWCL50 dataset ($F1 = 54.1$). XCoref performs better than a simple lemma-baseline by $F1_\Delta = 4.2$ and outperforms TCA, i.e., a previously used method for the concept identification in NewsWCL50 dataset, by $F1_\Delta = 5.8$. XCoref shows that the mentions of the mixed identity and bridging relations are resolved if treating all mentions without an upfront separation by the coreference strength of the anaphora. Moreover, learning context can substituted by feature engineering from the phrases' extracted nearest context, i.e., parsing subtrees.

When comparing TCA to its modification TCA$_{preproc}$, we see that the preprocessing steps employed in XCoref improve the overall performance, i.e., the improved identification of concept type and initial coreference resolution by CoreNLP on the combined documents instead on single documents. Using TCA with GloVe word vectors improves the performance of original TCA by $F1_\Delta = 2.9$. We assume that the concentration of the NE mentions in NewsWCL50 is high, and such a preprocessing step positively impacts the overall performance.

Section 2 compares the sieves of XCoref to the "intermediate" version XCoref$_{interm}$. Sieves S4 and S5 outperform S4$_{interm}$ and S5$_{interm}$ by $\Delta_{S4} = 1.1$ and $\Delta_{S5} = 1.8$ correspondingly. Additionally, we evaluate S4 on the mentions annotated as groups of persons. Section 3 shows that S4 in the original implementation by Zhukova et al. [48] with word2vec as word embedding performs best and the implementation with GloVe is second best. We assume that the thresholds of the proposed approach are better suited for word2vec and could be tuned for GloVe.

Table 4. Examples of mentions resolved by XCoref. The table shows the annotated concept names and only unique resolved mentions.

Name	Resolved mentions
PRK-USA Summit	The summit meeting, a potential meeting of the two leaders, an extraordinary meeting following months of heated rhetoric, meet with the North Korean dictator, discuss its nuclear weapons program, Kim's offer for a summit, a great chance to solve a world problem, won't even have a meeting at all, a once-unthinkable encounter between him and Mr. Kim, a one-on-one meeting with North Korea leader Kim Jong Un, direct talks between U.S. President Donald Trump and Kim, Mr. Kim's invitation to meet, the upcoming summit meeting with the North Korean leader, a great chance to solve a world problem, unwavering determination in addressing the challenge of North Korea
DNC's lawsuit	The process of legal discovery, a sham lawsuit about a bogus Russian collusion claim, a bogus Russian collusion claim, allegations of obstruction of justice, a desperate attempt to keep a collusion narrative going ahead of November mid-term elections, a new low to raise money, the DNC's move, the lawsuit to drum up donations for the party
Denucleari-zation	A deal to destroy only inter-continental missiles that could reach the United States, gives up nuclear weapons, months of heated rhetoric over Pyongyang's nuclear weapons program, to engage in a process headed toward an ambiguous goal, broad and "abstract " statements about the need for North Korea to "denuclearize", give up its nuclear program, yet to take any tangible steps to give up its nuclear arsenal, To address the threats posed by its nuclear and missile program
Coming into the US	Made their way to the U.S.-Mexico border, begun crossing into the U.S., the arrival of a caravan of Central American migrants, the arrival of a few hundred, crossing through a legal port of entry, driving families to flee, the caravan's steady approach to the U.S., to pass through into our country, several attempted illegal entries by people associated with the caravan, may be detained or fitted with ankle monitors and released, wait to be processed by U.S. authorities, to turn themselves in, a process that unfolds over several months or longer, made their way toward the border, a test of President Trump's anti-immigrant politics, a volatile flash point in the immigration debate ignited by Mr. Trump, headed north together as a form of protection, the final act of the caravan
Immigrants	No legitimate asylum-seekers, the asylum-seekers, the individual migrants planning to seek asylum, groups of the migrants with their children, migrant families that request asylum, unauthorized immigrants, the migrants in the caravan, a caravan of immigrants, members of the caravan, these large "Caravans" of people, a few hundred asylum seekers, refugees, those individuals, applicants, people who request protection, people traveling without documents, several groups of people associated with the caravan, undocumented immigrants, asylum-seeking immigrant "caravan", group of about 100 people

Section 4 shows multiple examples of how XCoref manages to resolve the annotated mentions that belong to the complex abstract entities. The table shows that some mentions form coreference relations only within a given context. For example, a mention "a great chance to solve a world problem," which describes the summit between Donald Trump and Kim Jong Un, forms a positive association "the summit = a great chance" via a context-specific bridging relation. A coreference link "a one-to-one meeting with North Korean leader Kim Jong Un" – "a once-unthinkable encounter between Trump and Mr. Kim" indicates similar positive bias via the chosen word choice.

NewsWCL50 dataset shows that CDCR datasets with a mix of identity and bridging, i.e., looser, coreference relations represent a challenge to the established models, such as EeCDCR (performs worst among all baselines). A new direction in CDCR research proposed Caciularu et al. [5] by training a cross-document language model to enable CDCR models to understand the broad and narrow context of the mentions. Such deep context learning will improve the representation of phrases' semantics and cross-phrase relations.

5   Conclusion

We propose XCoref, an unsupervised sieve-based method for cross-document coreference resolution (CDCR) that, unlike the state-of-the-art CDCR methods, resolves mentions of a mix of strict and loose coreference relations, e.g., "American steelmakers" – "shuttered plants and mills," and "the United States" - "Trump Administration officials." XCoref performs best among the evaluated approaches and also outperforms a previous approach for resolution of such complex coreferential chains by $F1_{CoNLL} = 5.8$. Further, a well-established CDCR model performs worse on NewsWCL50. Our findings suggest that CDCR models need to be tested on more diverse CDCR datasets that contain both strict identity and more loose bridging coreference relations. In political news articles, i.e., a challenging "wild" environment for the application of CDCR approaches, such relations might create a biased perception of reported entities and concepts. Therefore, resolution of mentions with context-specific coreference relations is a step towards bringing awareness of bias by word choice and labeling and increasing CDCR research's complexity and application.

References

1. Linguistic Data Consortium, et al.: ACE (automatic content extraction) English annotation guidelines for events. version 5.4. 3. ACE (2005). https://www.ldc.upenn.edu/sites/www.ldc.upenn.edu/files/english-events-guidelines-v5.4.3.pdf
2. Barhom, S., Shwartz, V., Eirew, A., Bugert, M., Reimers, N., Dagan, I.: Revisiting joint modeling of cross-document entity and event coreference resolution. In: Proceedings of the 57th Annual Meeting of the Association for Computational Linguistics. pp. 4179–4189. Association for Computational Linguistics, Florence, Italy, July 2019. https://doi.org/10.18653/v1/P19-1409, https://www.aclweb.org/anthology/P19-1409
3. Bejan, C.A., Harabagiu, S.: Unsupervised event coreference resolution with rich linguistic features. In: Proceedings of the 48th Annual Meeting of the Association for Computational Linguistics, pp. 1412–1422 (2010). https://aclanthology.org/P10-1143
4. Bugert, M., Reimers, N., Gurevych, I.: Generalizing cross-document event coreference resolution across multiple corpora. Computat. Linguis. **47**(3), 575–614 (2021). https://doi.org/10.1162/coli_a_00407, https://aclanthology.org/2021.cl-3.18
5. Caciularu, A., Cohan, A., Beltagy, I., Peters, M.E., Cattan, A., Dagan, I.: Cross-document language modeling. CoRR abs/2101.00406 (2021). https://arxiv.org/abs/2101.00406
6. Cambria, E., Poria, S., Bajpai, R., Schuller, B.: SenticNet 4: a semantic resource for sentiment analysis based on conceptual primitives. In: Proceedings of COLING 2016, the 26th International Conference on Computational Linguistics: Technical Papers, pp. 2666–2677 (2016). https://aclanthology.org/C16-1251

7. Cattan, A., Eirew, A., Stanovsky, G., Joshi, M., Dagan, I.: Cross-document coreference resolution over predicted mentions. CoRR abs/2106.01210 (2021). https://arxiv.org/abs/2106.01210

8. Clark, K., Manning, C.D.: Improving coreference resolution by learning entity-level distributed representations. In: Proceedings of the 54th Annual Meeting of the Association for Computational Linguistics (Volume 1: Long Papers), pp. 643–653. Association for Computational Linguistics, Berlin, Germany, August 2016. https://doi.org/10.18653/v1/P16-1061, https://www.aclweb.org/anthology/P16-1061

9. Cybulska, A., Vossen, P.: Using a sledgehammer to crack a nut? Lexical diversity and event coreference resolution. In: Proceedings of the Ninth International Conference on Language Resources and Evaluation (LREC 2014), pp. 4545–4552. European Language Resources Association (ELRA), Reykjavik, Iceland, May 2014. http://www.lrec-conf.org/proceedings/lrec2014/pdf/840_Paper.pdf

10. Cybulska, A., Vossen, P.: Translating granularity of event slots into features for event coreference resolution. In: Proceedings of the The 3rd Workshop on EVENTS: Definition, Detection, Coreference, and Representation, pp. 1–10. Association for Computational Linguistics, Denver, Colorado, June 2015. https://doi.org/10.3115/v1/W15-0801, https://www.aclweb.org/anthology/W15-0801

11. Fellbaum, C.: Wordnet and wordnets. In: Brown, K. (ed.) Encyclopedia of Language and Linguistics, pp. 665–670. Elsevier, Oxford (2005)

12. Hamborg, F., Donnay, K., Gipp, B.: Automated identification of media bias in news articles: an interdisciplinary literature review. Int. J. Digital Libr. **20**(4), 391–415 (2018). https://doi.org/10.1007/s00799-018-0261-y

13. Hamborg, F., Zhukova, A., Gipp, B.: Automated identification of media bias by word choice and labeling in news articles. In: Proceedings of the ACM/IEEE Joint Conference on Digital Libraries (JCDL), June 2019. https://doi.org/10.1109/JCDL.2019.00036

14. Hou, Y., Markert, K., Strube, M.: Global inference for bridging anaphora resolution. In: Proceedings of the 2013 Conference of the North American Chapter of the Association for Computational Linguistics: Human Language Technologies, pp. 907–917. Association for Computational Linguistics, Atlanta, Georgia, June 2013. https://aclanthology.org/N13-1111

15. Hou, Y., Markert, K., Strube, M.: Unrestricted bridging resolution. Computat. Linguis. **44**(2), 237–284 (2018). https://doi.org/10.1162/coli_a_00315

16. Kenyon-Dean, K., Cheung, J.C.K., Precup, D.: Resolving event coreference with supervised representation learning and clustering-oriented regularization. In: Proceedings of the Seventh Joint Conference on Lexical and Computational Semantics, pp. 1–10. Association for Computational Linguistics, New Orleans, Louisiana, June 2018. https://doi.org/10.18653/v1/S18-2001, https://www.aclweb.org/anthology/S18-2001

17. Keshtkaran, A., Yuhaniz, S.S., Ibrahim, S.: An overview of cross-document coreference resolution. In: 2017 International Conference on Computer and Drone Applications (IConDA), pp. 43–48 (2017)

18. Kobayashi, H., Ng, V.: Bridging resolution: a survey of the state of the art. In: Proceedings of the 28th International Conference on Computational Linguistics, pp. 3708–3721. International Committee on Computational Linguistics, Barcelona, Spain (Online), December 2020. https://doi.org/10.18653/v1/2020.coling-main.331, https://aclanthology.org/2020.coling-main.331

19. Lee, H., Peirsman, Y., Chang, A., Chambers, N., Surdeanu, M., Jurafsky, D.: Stanford's multi-pass sieve coreference resolution system at the CoNLL-2011 shared task. In: Proceedings of the 15th Conference on Computational Natural Language Learning: Shared Task, pp. 28–34. Association for Computational Linguistics (2011)

20. Lee, H., Recasens, M., Chang, A., Surdeanu, M., Jurafsky, D.: Joint entity and event corefer-ence resolution across documents. In: Proceedings of the 2012 Joint Conference on Empir-ical Methods in Natural Language Processing and Computational Natural Language Learn-ing, pp. 489–500. Association for Computational Linguistics, Jeju Island, Korea, July 2012. https://www.aclweb.org/anthology/D12-1045

21. Linguistic Data Consortium, et al.: ACE (automatic content extraction) English annotation guidelines for entities. Technical report, Linguistic Data Consortium (2008). https://www.ldc.upenn.edu/sites/www.ldc.upenn.edu/files/english-entities-guidelines-v6.6.pdf

22. Lu, J., Ng", V.: Event coreference resolution with multi-pass sieves. In: Proceedings of the Tenth International Conference on Language Resources and Evaluation (LREC 2016), pp. 3996–4003. European Language Resources Association (ELRA), Portorož, Slovenia, May 2016. https://aclanthology.org/L16-1631

23. Lu, J., Ng, V.: Event coreference resolution: a survey of two decades of research. In: Pro-ceedings of the Twenty-Seventh International Joint Conference on Artificial Intelligence, IJCAI-18, pp. 5479–5486. International Joint Conferences on Artificial Intelligence Organi-zation (2018). https://doi.org/10.24963/ijcai.2018/773

24. MediaWiki: MediaWiki – MediaWiki, the free wiki engine (2020). https://www.mediawiki.org/w/index.php?title=MediaWiki&oldid=3770840. Accessed 15 May 2020

25. Mikolov, T., Grave, E., Bojanowski, P., Puhrsch, C., Joulin, A.: Advances in pre-training dis-tributed word representations. In: Proceedings of the International Conference on Language Resources and Evaluation (LREC 2018) (2018)

26. Mikolov, T., Sutskever, I., Chen, K., Corrado, G.S., Dean, J.: Distributed representations of words and phrases and their compositionality. In: Burges, C.J.C., Bottou, L., Welling, M., Ghahramani, Z., Weinberger, K.Q. (eds.) Advances in Neural Information Processing Systems 26, pp. 3111–3119. Curran Associates, Inc. (2013)

27. Minard, A.L., et al.: MEANTIME, the NewsReader multilingual event and time corpus. In: Proceedings of the Tenth International Conference on Language Resources and Evaluation (LREC 2016), pp. 4417–4422. European Language Resources Association (ELRA), Por-torož, Slovenia, May 2016. https://www.aclweb.org/anthology/L16-1699

28. Mitamura, T., Liu, Z., Hovy, E.: Overview of TAC KBP 2015 event nugget track. In: TAC (2015)

29. Mitamura, T., Liu, Z., Hovy, E.H.: Events detection, coreference and sequencing: what's next? Overview of the TAC KBP 2017 event track. In: TAC (2017)

30. Moosavi, N.S., Strube, M.: Which coreference evaluation metric do you trust? A proposal for a link-based entity aware metric. In: Proceedings of the 54th Annual Meeting of the Asso-ciation for Computational Linguistics (Volume 1: Long Papers), pp. 632–642. Association for Computational Linguistics, Berlin, Germany, August 2016. https://doi.org/10.18653/v1/P16-1060, https://www.aclweb.org/anthology/P16-1060

31. Murtagh, F., Contreras, P.: Algorithms for hierarchical clustering: an overview. Wiley Inter-disc. Rev. Data Mining Knowl. Disc. 2(1), 86–97 (2012)

32. NLP Architect, Intel AI Lab: Cross document co-reference (2018). https://intellabs.github.io/nlp-architect/cross_doc_coref.html. Accessed 10 Jan 2021

33. O'Gorman, T., Wright-Bettner, K., Palmer, M.: Richer event description: integrating event coreference with temporal, causal and bridging annotation. In: Proceedings of the 2nd Work-shop on Computing News Storylines (CNS 2016), pp. 47–56. Association for Computational Linguistics, Austin, Texas, November 2016. https://doi.org/10.18653/v1/W16-5706, https://www.aclweb.org/anthology/W16-5706

34. Patel, A., Sands, A., Callison-Burch, C., Apidianaki, M.: Magnitude: a fast, efficient univer-sal vector embedding utility package. In: Proceedings of the 2018 Conference on Empiri-cal Methods in Natural Language Processing: System Demonstrations, pp. 120–126 (2018). https://doi.org/10.18653/v1/D18-2021, https://aclanthology.org/D18-2021

35. Pennington, J., Socher, R., Manning, C.: GloVe: global vectors for word representation. In: Proceedings of the 2014 Conference on Empirical Methods in Natural Language Processing (EMNLP), pp. 1532–1543. Association for Computational Linguistics, Doha, Qatar, October 2014. https://doi.org/10.3115/v1/D14-1162, https://www.aclweb.org/anthology/D14-1162

36. Peters, M., et al.: Deep contextualized word representations. In: Proceedings of the 2018 Conference of the North American Chapter of the Association for Computational Linguistics: Human Language Technologies, Volume 1 (Long Papers), pp. 2227–2237. Association for Computational Linguistics, New Orleans, Louisiana, June 2018. https://doi.org/10.18653/v1/N18-1202, https://www.aclweb.org/anthology/N18-1202

37. Poesio, M., Artstein, R.: Anaphoric annotation in the ARRAU corpus. In: Proceedings of the Sixth International Conference on Language Resources and Evaluation (LREC 2008). European Language Resources Association (ELRA), Marrakech, Morocco, May 2008. http://www.lrec-conf.org/proceedings/lrec2008/pdf/297_paper.pdf

38. Pradhan, S., Luo, X., Recasens, M., Hovy, E., Ng, V., Strube, M.: Scoring coreference partitions of predicted mentions: a reference implementation. In: Proceedings of the 52nd Annual Meeting of the Association for Computational Linguistics (Volume 2: Short Papers), pp. 30–35. Association for Computational Linguistics, Baltimore, Maryland (2014). https://doi.org/10.3115/v1/P14-2006, https://www.aclweb.org/anthology/P14-2006

39. Pradhan, S., Moschitti, A., Xue, N., Uryupina, O., Zhang, Y.: CoNLL-2012 shared task: modeling multilingual unrestricted coreference in OntoNotes. In: Joint Conference on EMNLP and CoNLL - Shared Task, pp. 1–40. Association for Computational Linguistics, Jeju Island, Korea, July 2012. https://www.aclweb.org/anthology/W12-4501

40. Recasens, M., Hovy, E., Martí, M.A.: A typology of near-identity relations for coreference (NIDENT). In: Proceedings of the Seventh International Conference on Language Resources and Evaluation (LREC 2010) (2010). http://www.lrec-conf.org/proceedings/lrec2010/pdf/160_Paper.pdf

41. Recasens, M., Hovy, E., Martí, M.A.: Identity, non-identity, and near-identity: Addressing the complexity of coreference. Lingua **121**(6), 1138–1152 (2011)

42. Recasens, M., Martí, M.A., Orasan, C.: Annotating near-identity from coreference disagreements. In: Proceedings of the Eighth International Conference on Language Resources and Evaluation (LREC 2012), pp. 165–172. European Language Resources Association (ELRA), Istanbul, Turkey, May 2012. http://www.lrec-conf.org/proceedings/lrec2012/pdf/674_Paper.pdf

43. Rösiger, I.: BASHI: a corpus of Wall Street Journal articles annotated with bridging links. In: Proceedings of the Eleventh International Conference on Language Resources and Evaluation (LREC 2018). European Language Resources Association (ELRA), Miyazaki, Japan, May 2018. https://aclanthology.org/L18-1058

44. Shi, P., Lin, J.: Simple BERT models for relation extraction and semantic role labeling. arXiv preprint arXiv:1904.05255 (2019)

45. Singh, S., Bhattacharjee, K., Darbari, H., Verma, S.: Analyzing coreference tools for NLP application. Int. J. Comput. Sci. Eng. **7**, 608–615 (2019). https://doi.org/10.26438/ijcse/v7i5.608615

46. Spala, S., Miller, N.A., Yang, Y., Dernoncourt, F., Dockhorn, C.: DEFT: a corpus for definition extraction in free- and semi-structured text. In: Proceedings of the 13th Linguistic Annotation Workshop, pp. 124–131. Association for Computational Linguistics, Florence, Italy, August 2019. https://doi.org/10.18653/v1/W19-4015, https://www.aclweb.org/anthology/W19-4015

47. Weischedel, R., et al.: OntoNotes release 4.0. LDC2011T03, Philadelphia, Penn.: Linguistic Data Consortium (2011)
48. Zhukova, A., Hamborg, F., Donnay, K., Gipp, B.: Concept identification of directly and indirectly related mentions referring to groups of persons. In: Toeppe, K., Yan, H., Chu, S.K.W. (eds.) iConference 2021. LNCS, vol. 12645, pp. 514–526. Springer, Cham (2021). https://doi.org/10.1007/978-3-030-71292-1_40

Impartial Predictive Modeling and the Use of Proxy Variables

Kory D. Johnson[1]([⊠]) [iD], Dean P. Foster[2], and Robert A. Stine[3]

[1] TU Wien, 1040 Vienna, Austria
kory.johnson@tuwien.ac.at
[2] Amazon, New York, New York, USA
dean.foster@gmail.com
[3] University of Pennsylvania, Philadelphia, PA, USA
stine@wharton.upenn.edu

Abstract. Fairness aware data mining (FADM) aims to prevent algorithms from discriminating against protected groups. The literature has come to an impasse as to what constitutes explainable variability as opposed to discrimination. This distinction hinges on a rigorous understanding of the role of proxy variables; i.e., those variables which are associated both the protected feature and the outcome of interest. We demonstrate that fairness is achieved by ensuring *impartiality* with respect to sensitive characteristics and provide a framework for impartiality by accounting for different perspectives on the data generating process. In particular, fairness can only be precisely defined in a full-data scenario in which all covariates are observed. We then analyze how these models may be conservatively estimated via regression in partial-data settings. Decomposing the regression estimates provides insights into previously unexplored distinctions between explainable variability and discrimination that illuminate the use of proxy variables in fairness aware data mining.

1 Introduction

Machine learning has been a boon for improved decision making. The increased volume and variety of data has led to a host of data mining tools for knowledge discovery; however, automated decision making using vast quantities of data needs to be tempered by caution. One goal in FADM is to provide suitably "fair" estimates of a response Y, given legitimate covariates $\mathbf{x}$, sensitive covariates $\mathbf{s}$, and suspect covariates $\mathbf{w}$. The primary distinctions between these categories concerns the ability of an individual to be morally responsible for their value: covariates in $\mathbf{s}$ are considered to be outside of one's control, e.g. race and gender, while $\mathbf{x}$ are those features for which an individual can be held accountable. The $\mathbf{w}$ group contains those covariates for which it is uncertain whether or not one ought to be held responsible for their value.

These covariate groups and the response Y are connected through an unknown, joint probability distribution $\mathbb{P}(Y, \mathbf{x}, \mathbf{s}, \mathbf{w})$, and our data consists of

M. Smits (Ed.): iConference 2022, LNCS 13192, pp. 292–308, 2022.
https://doi.org/10.1007/978-3-030-96957-8_26

n iid draws from this joint distribution. The standard statistical goal is to estimate the conditional expectation of Y given the covariates:

$$Y = \mathbb{E}[Y|x, s, w] + u$$

where u has mean zero and is uncorrelated with all functions of the covariates.

Our goal is to estimate a conditional expectation that is "fair" with respect to the sensitive covariates. Others have argued for penalizing discrimination during estimation [10,11,26], modifying the input data before supervised training takes place [5,18,33], or modifying objective functions with fairness criteria [19,20,24,39]. Conceptually closest to our work is [20], which explicitly discusses economic models of equality of opportunity and presents an optimization problem of maximizing utility subject to a constraint on prediction error. Their formulation incorporates the concept of "effort-based" utility to encode the effects of legitimate covariates.

From a technical perspective, [13,27,29,36] use similar path diagrams as those presented in Sect. 2 to describe fair estimation methods. Our focus, however, is different, as we concretely describe heretofore unknown distinctions between covariate groups. This understanding is crucial to correctly determining these groups, which are considered to be externally given in previous analyses. Other papers which address this issue include [1,34], though the present paper covers more settings (none, some, or all suspect covariates), broader use cases (extending to "black-box" models), and defends the disentanglement and partial omission of the proxy signal.

A simple example clarifies the issue of fairness. Consider a bank that wants to estimate the risk of a loan applicant via a credit score model. Such automated eligibility or pricing systems are ubiquitous both in banking and public assistance offices [14]. The concern is that personalized credit pricing could provide results which either reflect discrimination which is present in the training data or either intentionally or unintentionally discriminate based on race or gender etc. Fair lending law attempts to address this through "input scrutiny", in which "sensitive" or "protected" covariates such as race, gender, and age are barred from use [16]. The goal of input scrutiny is to model prices solely on the remaining "legitimate" covariates, i.e., the log of historical credit use. The use of big data in pricing models, however, has opened the door to non-standard data sources such as purchase history and online activities, which could allow for predatory or targeted pricing [22]. This highlights a third covariate group of "suspect" or "potentially discriminatory" covariates whose information content for establishing creditworthiness is uncertain and potentially serves only to establish "creditworthiness by association," i.e., by associating an applicant to a protected covariate [22]. The canonical example of such a proxy variable is the applicant's address. While location is not a protected characteristic such as race, it is often barred from use given the ability to discriminate using it.

FADM asks whether or not the estimates the bank constructs are fair and perhaps even what effect enforcing fairness has on profit [28]. This is different than asking if the data are fair or if the historical practice of giving loans was fair.

It is a question pertaining to the estimates produced by the bank's model, and thus necessarily would imply a shift in lending law to outcome-focused analysis [16]. This generates several questions. First, what does fairness mean for this statistical model? Second, what should the role of the sensitive covariates be in this estimate? Third, how do legitimate and suspect covariates differ? Lastly, how do we constrain the use of the sensitive covariates in black-box algorithms? These questions are addressed in the remainder of the paper.

A primary hurdle for FADM is to separate explainable variability from discrimination. Many authors have argued that input scrutiny is insufficient to achieve fairness [16,25,26]. Due to the relationships between race and other covariates, merely removing race can leave lingering discriminatory effects that permeate the data and potentially perpetuate discrimination. The use of covariates associated with s to discriminate is called "redlining", which originated in the United States to describe maps that were color-coded to represent areas in which banks would not invest. While policies were facially neutral and race blind, they were in-effect discriminatory. The advent of big data has given rise to what has been called technological or digital redlining [31], wherein similar demarcations can be made by, for example, only looking for housing close to high-quality schools. Conceptually, the core issue is the *misuse* of available information.

We improve upon previous discussions by providing a simple, tractable formulation of impartiality that addresses issues often encountered in real data; namely, that sensitive features often *do not appear* to be unrelated to the response. In what follows, we argue that this task is accomplished by creating impartial estimates. Intuitively, impartiality requires that the sensitive covariates do not influence estimates. For clarity, we will refer to this as the fairness assumption:

Fairness Assumption: Sensitive covariates ought not be a relevant source of variability or merit.

A clear objection to this assumption is that it is often not observed in the data, but this is precisely the point. To be explicit, consider a circumstance in which Y is an observed quantity realized by an agent in a "free" (non-coerced) way, e.g. credit history. To play devil's advocate in this case, a most fundamental question for FADM is: if models are intended to describe the world, and the fairness assumption is often inaccurate, why compromise predictive accuracy for fairness' sake? Instead of addressing this philosophically, we specify models in which fairness is the accurate statistical description of the world. Our fairness assumption is specified as an "ought" statement, as it embodies this often unrealized ideal.

Impartial estimates are fair because the covariate groups are chosen to be normatively relevant and are assumed to be provided externally. As such, the statistical task is disjoint from the normative task of identifying covariate groups. This project uses the term "impartial" to describe the statistical goal. This is done in order to separate our task from normative complications. That being said, the different covariate groups have normative significance and need to be differentiated.

The construction of our impartial estimates is motivated by distinctions in the philosophical literature on equality of opportunity, which analyzes the way in which benefits are allocated in society [2]. One way of understanding equality of opportunity is formal equality of opportunity (FEO), which requires an open-application for benefits (anyone can apply) and that benefits are awarded to those of highest merit. Merit will of course be measured differently depending on the benefit in question. There may, however, be cause for concern if discrimination exists in the analysis of merit or the ability of some individuals to be of high merit.

Substantive equality of opportunity (SEO) contains the same strictures as above, but is satisfied only if everyone has a genuine opportunity to be of high merit. In particular, suppose there are social restrictions or benefits that only allow one group to be of high merit. In this case, proponents of SEO claim that true equality of opportunity has not been achieved. While many countries lack a formal system to enforce this, some may argue that cycles of poverty and wealth lead to a similar regress in the reasons for the disparity between protected groups.

Identifying impartial estimates and fairness constructively has both philosophical and empirical support. The philosopher John Rawls discusses fair institutions as the method of achieving fairness [38]. Similarly, [9,17] explain the importance of process fairness as opposed to merely outcome fairness. Process fairness focuses on how people are treated throughout the process of a decision. The authors identify several examples in which firms attempt to layoff workers in a fair manner. Workers often feel that the decisions are fair when they are consulted frequently and the process is transparent, even if their severance packages are far worse. This points out the importance of fair treatment as fair use of information, not merely a measure of the outcome.

Our main contribution is a framework which allows for rigorous analysis of how the use of covariates changes when moving between FEO and SEO. We address the complications produced by the various viewpoints by introducing and demonstrating the importance of the suspect covariate group $\mathbf{w}$. After providing this framework, it will be clear how to both construct impartial estimates using simple procedures as well as correct black-box estimates.

Section 2 introduces various data generating models in order to construct mathematical models of impartiality. This section also draws connections to the literature on causal inference. Importantly, the claim that these are impartial requires a strict interpretation of the influence of sensitive covariates. Section 3 provides a simple procedure for constructing impartial estimates. The difference between achieving group fairness via FEO and SEO is demonstrated via a simple example in Sect. 4. Section 5 analyzes two data sets from criminology that consider the effect of race and sex. Impartial estimates are produced with an package R [35] that is available on github.com.

2   Mathematical Models of Impartiality

Fairness in modeling will be explained via path diagrams to conveniently represent conditional independence assumptions. While often used as a model to measure causal effects, we are explicitly not using them for this purpose. This stems from a different object of interest: in causal modeling, one cares about a casual parameter or direct effect of the covariate of interest whereas we care about the estimates produced by the model. Estimating a causal effect requires considering a counterfactual, such as a patient's outcome under the treatment even though they were part of the control group. See, for example, [30].

Our goal is to create impartial *estimates*, whereas the estimation of a causal effect would attempt to answer whether the historical data are impartial. Hence, we do not require the same type of causal interpretation, which is fraught with difficulties for attributes such as race [5,21]. Counterfactuals can be easily computed because it only requires producing an estimate for a modified observation, regardless of whether it exists in the data set. We do not need recourse to the interventionist or causal components of standard causal models [32] and can focus only on their predictive component. Path diagrams only represent the conditional independence assumptions made between variables as necessitated by the fairness assumption.

The rest of this section briefly introduces impartial estimates in stages via models in which the fairness assumption is tractable. We begin by enforcing FEO, which only uses sensitive and legitimate covariates. The goal in FEO is to have a best estimate of merit while satisfying the legal requirements of disparate treatment and disparate impact. Second, we consider a full SEO model, in which there are no legitimate covariates, only sensitive and suspect covariates. The total model case with sensitive, legitimate, and suspect covariates is considered last.

FEO is not concerned with potentially discriminatory covariates. Consider an idealized population model that includes all possible covariates: $\mathbf{x}_o$ contains the observed, legitimate covariates, and $\mathbf{x}_u$ contains the unobserved, legitimate covariates. Unobserved covariates could be potentially observable such as drug use, or unknowable such as future income. The data are assumed to have a joint distribution $\mathbb{P}(Y, \mathbf{s}, \mathbf{x}_o, \mathbf{x}_u)$, from which n observations are drawn. The fairness assumption requires that $\mathbf{s}$ is not predictive for the response given full information:

$$\mathbb{P}(Y|\mathbf{s}, \mathbf{x}_o, \mathbf{x}_u) = \mathbb{P}(Y|\mathbf{x}_o, \mathbf{x}_u).$$

It is important to posit the existence of both observed and unobserved legitimate covariates to capture the often observed relationship between sensitive covariates and the response. Specifically, observed data often show

$$\mathbb{P}(Y|\mathbf{s}, \mathbf{x}_o) \neq \mathbb{P}(Y|\mathbf{x}_o),$$

which violates the fairness assumption.

These assumptions are captured succinctly for various models using the path diagrams of Table 1. Single headed arrows show direct effects while dashed, double-headed arrows indicate correlations which are potentially unfair.

Table 1. Observationally Equivalent Data Generating Models: FEO (first row), SEO (second row), mixture (third row).

OBSERVED	UNRESTRICTED	FAIR
$\mathbf{x}_o$ s $\longrightarrow$ Y $\mathbf{x}_u$	$\mathbf{x}_o$ s $\longrightarrow$ Y $\mathbf{x}_u$	$\mathbf{x}_o$ s $\qquad$ Y $\mathbf{x}_u$
s $\longrightarrow$ Y w	s $\longrightarrow$ Y w $\leftrightarrow \mathbf{x}_u$	s $\qquad$ Y w $\leftrightarrow \mathbf{x}_u$
$\mathbf{x}_o$ s $\longrightarrow$ Y w	$\mathbf{x}_o$ s $\longrightarrow$ Y w $\leftrightarrow \mathbf{x}_u$	$\mathbf{x}_o$ s $\qquad$ Y w $\leftrightarrow \mathbf{x}_u$

Observed data are often only representable by a fully connected graph which contains no conditional independence properties. This observed distribution can be generated from multiple full-information models. The first possible representation of the full data is an unrestricted model. In this case, sensitive covariates are not conditionally independent of the response given full information. The fairness assumption is enforced by assuming that sensitive information is conditionally independent of the response given full information. Under the fair, full-information model, the apparent importance of sensitive information in the observed data is only due to unobserved covariates.

One objection to FEO is the assumption that all $\mathbf{x}$ covariates are legitimate. Thus, while the response may be explained in terms of $\mathbf{x}$ without recourse to $\mathbf{s}$, that is only because the covariates $\mathbf{x}$ are the result of structural discrimination. This class of "potentially illegitimate" or "suspect" covariates is denoted by $\mathbf{w}$ and can be used to estimate merit, but only in such a way that does not distinguish between groups in $\mathbf{s}$. This treats $\mathbf{w}$ as proxy variables for missing information. The setting for which all legitimate covariates are considered suspect is given in the second row of Table 1. Note again that the observed data model can be the result of multiple full-information models. The final row of Table 1 shows the fairness assumption in a model that includes both legitimate and suspect covariates.

3 Creating Impartial Estimates

In this section, we demonstrate one simple way to estimate the models of Section 2. We define impartiality with respect to the linear projection of Y on a set of covariates $\mathbf{v}$:

$$Y = \mathbf{v}'\beta + \epsilon,$$

where the error term ϵ satisfies

$$\mathbb{E}[\epsilon] = 0, \quad \mathrm{Cov}(\mathbf{v}, \epsilon) = \mathbf{0}.$$

This allows core ideas to be fully explained in a familiar setting as well as clear decompositions of covariate effects. While our definition uses linear projections, estimates are not required to be linear. Section 5 uses the notion of suspect covariates to correct "black box" estimates.

For clarity, we introduce the full estimation procedure in stages. Collect the observations into matrices $\mathbf{Y}$, $\mathbf{S}$, $\mathbf{X}$, and $\mathbf{W}$, and consider the *estimated* response given various subsets of covariate groups. Estimates will be decomposed into various components using projections. For a matrix M, $\mathbf{H_M}$ is the projection matrix onto the column-span of $\mathbf{M}$. We use bracket notation to indicate when two matrices are joined column-wise, e.g. $\mathbf{M} = [\mathbf{X}_o, \mathbf{W}]$ contains the columns of both $\mathbf{X}_o$ and $\mathbf{W}$. All covariates are assumed to have mean 0 as we include an intercept in our model. Covariate matrices of each covariate type are separated into the portion correlated with the others and the component which is orthogonal to them. We will refer to these as the "shared" and "unique" components, respectively. While the decomposition is standard, this is perhaps a non-standard presentation. It is important to note that the coefficient for each group is computed only from the unique component of that group in the model considered. For example, if all covariate groups are used, let $\mathbf{X}_{o,a} = (\mathbf{I} - \mathbf{H}_{[\mathbf{S},\mathbf{W}]})\mathbf{X}_o$ be $\mathbf{X}_o$ "adjusted" for the other covariates in the model. The least squares estimate of its parameter in this model is given by $\hat{\beta}_{x,t} = (\mathbf{X}'_{o,a}\mathbf{X}_{o,a})^{-1}\mathbf{X}'_{o,a}\mathbf{Y}$, provided the inverse exists. In what follows, we put additional subscripts on parameters which depend on the model considered. This highlights that parameters are different depending on the model in which they are estimated. Lastly, note that "hats" are used to indicate estimated values.

First, consider a model with only $\mathbf{S}$ and $\mathbf{X}$ as predictors (1) and the resulting decomposition of the estimates (2). This is the FEO model as all non-sensitive covariates are considered legitimate.

$$Y = \beta_{0,f} + \beta_{s,f}^{\top}\mathbf{s} + \beta_x^{\top}\mathbf{x}_o + \epsilon_f \tag{1}$$

$$\hat{Y}_f = \hat{\beta}_{0,f} + \underbrace{\mathbf{H_{X_o}}\mathbf{S}}_{di}\hat{\beta}_{s,f} + \underbrace{(\mathbf{I} - \mathbf{H_{X_o}})\mathbf{S}}_{dt}\hat{\beta}_{s,f} + \underbrace{\mathbf{H_S}\mathbf{X}_o}_{sd^+}\hat{\beta}_{x,f} + \underbrace{(\mathbf{I} - \mathbf{H_S})\mathbf{X}_o}_{u}\hat{\beta}_{x,f} \tag{2}$$

By decomposing the estimates as in Eq. (2), we can identify components which are of philosophical and legal interest. The term dt captures the disparate treatment effect: it is the component of the estimate which is due to the unique variability of $\mathbf{S}$. Given the data generating model in Table 1, we assume that the apparent importance of $\mathbf{S}$ (signified by the magnitude of $\hat{\beta}_{s,f}$) is due to excluded covariates; however, it is identified by $\mathbf{S}$ in the observed data. While this may be a "sufficiently accurate generalization" in that the coefficient may be statistically significant, this is considered to be illegal statistical discrimination [7]. The term di captures the disparate impact effect. We refer to it as the *informative* redlining effect (as it is due to an legitimately informative covariate) in order to contrast it with an effect identified shortly. Intuitively, it is the misuse of informative covariates and is the result of the ability to estimate $\mathbf{S}$ with other covariates. It is important that the adjustment is identified by variability in $\mathbf{S}$ instead of $\mathbf{X}_o$. If one merely ignores $\mathbf{S}$ completely in estimation, the term di will still be included in the final estimate, resulting in an estimate which is not impartial.

Previous discussions of redlining do not distinguish between the terms di and $sd+$ in Eq. (2) [25,26], because they are both due to the correlation between $\mathbf{X}_o$ and $\mathbf{S}$. It is clear that they are different, however, as $\mathbf{H}_{\mathbf{X}_o}\mathbf{S}$ is in the space spanned by $\mathbf{X}_o$ and $\mathbf{H}_{\mathbf{S}}\mathbf{X}_o$ is in the space spanned by $\mathbf{S}$. Furthermore, the coefficients attached to these terms are estimated from different sources. Intuition may suggest we remove all components in the space spanned by $\mathbf{S}$, but this is often incorrect. The term $sd+$ cannot be excluded in many settings because it accounts for the group means of $\mathbf{X}$. Excluding $sd+$ implies that the *level* of $\mathbf{X}$ is not important but that an individual's *deviation* from their group mean is. This makes group membership a hindrance or advantage and is inappropriate for a legitimate covariate. Therefore, in this model $sd+$ must be included.

Second, consider a model with only $\mathbf{S}$ and $\mathbf{W}$ as predictors (3) and the resulting decomposition of the estimates (4):

$$Y = \beta_{0,p} + \beta_{s,p}^{\top}\mathbf{s} + \beta_{w,p}^{\top}\mathbf{w} + \epsilon_p, \tag{3}$$

$$\hat{Y}_p = \hat{\beta}_{0,p} + \underbrace{\mathbf{H_W S}\,\hat{\beta}_{s,p}}_{di} + \underbrace{(\mathbf{I} - \mathbf{H_W})\mathbf{S}\,\hat{\beta}_{s,p}}_{dt} + \underbrace{\mathbf{H_S W}\,\hat{\beta}_{w,p}}_{sd-} + \underbrace{(\mathbf{I} - \mathbf{H_S})\mathbf{W}\,\hat{\beta}_{w,p}}_{u}. \tag{4}$$

In Eq. (4), $sd-$ addresses the concern that group differences in covariate $\mathbf{W}$ are potentially discriminatory, as contrasted with $sd+$ in (2). For example, if $\mathbf{W}$ is location, $sd-$ measures racial differences between neighborhoods. Given that proxy variables $\mathbf{W}$ are not considered directly informative, it is unclear what these differences can legitimately contribute. If there is racial bias in neighborhood demographics, using this information would perpetuate this discrimination. Ensuring that this does not occur requires removing $sd-$ from the estimates of Y. This identifies a new type of redlining effect that we call *uninformative* redlining (as it is due to a proxy variable); it is the sum of di and $sd-$. Uninformative redlining can be identified visually using the graphs in Table 1. Fairness constrains the information contained in the arrow $\mathbf{s} \to Y$ as well as information conveyed in the path $\mathbf{s} \to \mathbf{w} \to Y$. This is because $\mathbf{s} \to \mathbf{w}$ is potentially discriminatory. Therefore, impartial estimates with suspect or proxy variables only use the unique variability in $\mathbf{W}$. An important consequence of this SEO model is that average estimates are the same for different groups of $\mathbf{s}$. This is an alternate construction of the initial estimates used by [10].

Lastly, the final model includes all covariate groups $\mathbf{S}$, $\mathbf{X}$, and $\mathbf{W}$ as predictors (5) and the resulting estimates (6):

$$Y = \beta_{0,t} + \beta_{s,t}^\top \mathbf{s} + \beta_{x,t}^\top \mathbf{x}_o + \beta_{w,t}^\top \mathbf{w} + \epsilon_t. \tag{5}$$

$$\hat{\mathbf{Y}} = \hat{\beta}_{0,t} + \underbrace{\mathbf{H}_{[\mathbf{X}_o,\mathbf{W}]}\mathbf{S}}_{di}\,\hat{\beta}_{s,t} + \underbrace{(\mathbf{I} - \mathbf{H}_{[\mathbf{X}_o,\mathbf{W}]})\mathbf{S}}_{dt}\,\hat{\beta}_{s,t}$$

$$+ \underbrace{\mathbf{H}_{[\mathbf{S},\mathbf{W}]}\mathbf{X}_o}_{sd+}\,\hat{\beta}_{x,t} + \underbrace{(\mathbf{I} - \mathbf{H}_{[\mathbf{S},\mathbf{W}]})\mathbf{X}_o}_{u}\,\hat{\beta}_{x,t}$$

$$+ \underbrace{\mathbf{H}_{[\mathbf{X}_o,\mathbf{S}]}\mathbf{W}}_{sd-,sd+}\,\hat{\beta}_{w,t} + \underbrace{(\mathbf{I} - \mathbf{H}_{[\mathbf{X}_o,\mathbf{S}]})\mathbf{W}}_{u}\,\hat{\beta}_{w,t} \tag{6}$$

While the majority of the terms in the above display mirror the previous discussion, the suspect covariates display a more complex behavior. The unique component can still be considered additional information orthogonal to the sensitive covariates, but the component correlated with other covariates is labeled both $sd+$ and $sd-$ to indicate that this combines both legal and illegal forms of statistical discrimination. The notation $\mathbf{H}_{[\mathbf{X}_o,\mathbf{S}]}\mathbf{W}$ indicates that the shared component is the best linear estimate of $\mathbf{W}$ given both $\mathbf{S}$ and $\mathbf{X}$. As $\mathbf{W}$ is a suspect covariate, we can remove $sd-$ while retaining $sd+$ by producing an impartial estimate of $\mathbf{W}$. In this case, $\mathbf{W}$ has taken the place of $\mathbf{Y}$ as the response in an FEO model that only contains $\mathbf{S}$ and $\mathbf{X}_o$.

Removing the components labeled di, dt, and $sd-$ can be accomplished through the following procedure.

Definition 1 (Impartial Estimate). *Linearly impartial estimates are created with the following multi-step procedure, where "estimate" means "estimate via least-squares:"*

1. *Estimate the model (5) to produce $\hat{\beta}_0$, $\hat{\beta}_s$, $\hat{\beta}_x$, and $\hat{\beta}_w$.*
2. *Create an impartial estimate of each element of $\mathbf{w}$.*
   a. *Estimate $\mathbf{w} = \lambda_0 + \Lambda_s^\top \mathbf{s} + \Lambda_x^\top \mathbf{x}_o + \eta$.*
   b. *Set $\hat{\mathbf{w}} = \hat{\lambda}_0 + \hat{\Lambda}_x^\top \mathbf{x}_o$.*
   c. *Collect the estimates, $\hat{\mathbf{w}}$, as $\hat{\mathbf{W}}$.*
3. *Set $\hat{Y} = \hat{\beta}_0 + \mathbf{X}_o\hat{\beta}_x + \hat{\mathbf{W}}\hat{\beta}_w + (\mathbf{I} - \mathbf{H}_{[\mathbf{X}_o,\mathbf{S}]})\mathbf{W}\hat{\beta}_w.$*

4   Simple Example: FEO vs SEO

This section provides a simplified example to compare the estimates implied by FEO and SEO. Without a proper data-generation narrative, "fair" estimates can appear decidedly *unfair*. Consider a simple example of credit score modeling that has only two covariates: education level, $\mathbf{x}$, and sensitive group, $\mathbf{s}$. Suppose the data is collected on individuals who took out a loan of a given size, that higher education is indicative of better repayment, and that education is split into two categories: high and low. To see the relevant issues, $\mathbf{s}$ and $\mathbf{x}$ need to be associated.

Table 2. Simplified loan repayment data and estimated default probabilities.

Education ($\mathbb{P}(x)$)	Low (.6)		High (.4)			
Group ($\mathbb{P}(s\|x)$)	s_- (.75)	s_+	s_- (.25)	s_+	Total	
Default yes	225	60	20	30	335	
Default no	225	90	80	270	665	

	$\hat{\mathbb{P}}$(Default YES$\|x_i, s_i$)				DS	RMSE
Full model	.5	.4	.2	.1	$-.25$	13.84
Exclude s	.475	.475	.125	.125	$-.17$	13.91
FEO	.455	.455	.155	.155	$-.15$	13.93
SEO	.39	.535	.09	.235	0.00	14.37
Marginal	.35	.35	.35	.35	0.00	14.93

The two sensitive groups will be written as s_+ and s_- to indicate which group, on average, has higher education: the majority of s_- have low education and the majority of s_+ have high education. The response is the indicator of default, D.

Synthetic data and estimates are provided in Table 2, in which there exist direct effects for both s and x. This is consistent with the observed data graphs in Table 1. Five possible estimates are compared in Table 2: the full OLS model, the restricted regression which excludes s, the FEO model in which education is considered a legitimate covariate, the SEO model in which education is considered a suspect covariate, and the marginal model which estimates the marginal probability of default without any covariates. Estimates are presented along with the in-sample RMSE from estimating the true default indicator and the discrimination score (DS) [11]. While we have argued that "discrimination score" is at times a misnomer since it does not separate explainable from discriminatory variation, it provides a useful perspective given its widespread use in the literature. Furthermore, as one often discusses discrimination toward groups, it is nevertheless helpful to gauge the difference between estimates between groups.

Since education is the only covariate that can measure similarity, one would expect that estimates should be constant for individuals with the same education. This is easily accomplished by the legal prescription of input scrutiny by excluding s. If the information is not observed, it cannot lead to disparate treatment directly related to group membership. The FEO model satisfies this as well. As seen in Eq. (2), the only difference between the two estimates is the coefficient on x. Said differently, the term di in Eq. (2) lies in the space spanned by x. Therefore its removal only changes estimates for education groups. Excluding s permits redlining because it increases the estimated disparity between low- and high-education groups. This disproportionately effects those in s_- as they constitute the majority of the low education group. The FEO estimates result in some average differences between groups, but this is acceptable if the association between $\mathbf{x}$ and $\mathbf{s}$ is benign. This accurately measures the proportional differences desired by [4] for fair treatment.

The SEO estimates appear counter-intuitive: although $\mathbf{s}_+$ performs better in our data set even after accounting for education, these estimates predict the opposite. Understanding this requires accepting the world view implicit in the SEO estimates: average education differences between groups are the result of structural discrimination. Members of $\mathbf{s}_-$ in the high education group have a much higher education than average for $\mathbf{s}_-$. Similarly, members of $\mathbf{s}_+$ who are in the high education group have a higher education than average for $\mathbf{s}_+$, but not by as much. The magnitude of these differences is given importance, not the education level.

As an example where these deviations are given importance, consider the college admissions process in the United States and the two explanatory covariates "class rank" and "SAT score." The SAT is a standardized test commonly used in the United States to assess students' readiness for university, and it is under scrutiny for doing more to measure disparities in students' learning opportunities, e.g. wealth and race, than college preparedness [15,23]. The SAT score provides information on where an applicant lies in the national test score distribution, whereas class rank specifies their location in the local grade distribution. Considering class rank is equivalent to placing importance on the deviation between a student and others much more likely to be in a comparable situation. Similarly, the SAT score could be used to only measure differences *within* a group. Conceptually, this is what was done in the "Strivers" proposal, wherein students were termed "strivers" when they significantly outperformed the expected score based on socioeconomic and structural factors [12].

In our example, the SEO model balances the differences in education distributions, resulting in both groups having the same average estimated default. This is seen in the discrimination score of 0. Without claiming that education is partially the result of structural differences, the SEO estimates discriminate against $\mathbf{s}_+$. Other methods to achieve group fairness produce estimates relevantly similar to SEO in this regard. Furthermore, if the structural effects are not such that all $\mathbf{s}_+$ individuals are given a benefit or not all $\mathbf{s}_-$ individuals receive a detriment, then these models are merely approximations of the fair correction. An ideal protected or sensitive covariate $\mathbf{s}$ is exactly that which accounts for differences in the opportunity of being high merit. This is in line with Rawls' conception of equality of opportunity [37].

The SEO estimates show another important property: their RMSE is lower than that of the marginal estimate of default while still minimizing the discrimination score. Therefore, if a bank is required to minimize differences between groups in the interest of fairness, it would rather use the SEO estimates than the marginal estimate. SEO still acknowledges that education is an informative predictor and contains an education effect. Furthermore, equality of opportunity is not satisfied when marginal estimates are used because all merit information is ignored. See [2] for a more detailed discussion.

5   Data Illustrations with Black-Box Estimates

This section present results on two criminology data sets. For a detailed discussion of the trade-offs between different fairness measures in criminology see [6]. We show the performance of various procedures using the discrimination score (average predicted difference between groups), the root mean squared prediction error, as well as the positive and negative residual differences (PRD and NRD, respectively):

$$PRD := \left| \frac{1}{n_1} \sum_{i \in S_1} \max\{0, Y_i - \hat{Y}_i\} - \frac{1}{n_0} \sum_{i \in S_0} \max\{0, Y_i - \hat{Y}_i\} \right|$$

$$NRD := \left| \frac{1}{n_1} \sum_{i \in S_1} \min\{0, Y_i - \hat{Y}_i\} - \frac{1}{n_0} \sum_{i \in S_0} \min\{0, Y_i - \hat{Y}_i\} \right|.$$

These measures play the role of false positive and false negative rates for regression problems [10]. All statistics shown in the following subsections are computed out-of-sample using 5-fold cross-validation and averaged over 12 repetitions.

Lastly, to correct a "black-box" estimate, suppose that we have an estimate of the response, $Y^\dagger$, given by an unknown model with unknown inputs. The model may use sensitive information to be intentionally or unintentionally discriminatory. While potentially informative, there is no guarantee that the estimates are impartial. This identically matches the description of suspect covariates. Therefore, if we treat $Y^\dagger$ as a suspect covariate, its information can be used but not in a way that makes distinctions between protected groups. For simplicity, we only include estimates from a support vector regression [3] or random forest algorithm [8] as they are high-performing, off-the-shelf "black boxes." Furthermore, they are allowed to use s and w in order to demonstrate that estimates can be easily corrected.

We compare our models with the propensity score stratification methods of [10] as well as the convex optimization approaches of [19,20]. [19] is motivated by social welfare considerations, places an upper bound on prediction error, and controls the PRD and NRD. [20] requires a prespecified utility function to be defined for all groups and explicitly tries to maximize the utility for both groups while placing an upper bound on prediction error. These three methods will be referred to as *propensity*, *welfare*, and *utility*, due to the motivations for the frameworks. These methods are compared to impartial estimates that use various covariate specifications for s, x, and w. The *exclude* model merely excludes s during estimation, the *FEO* model treats all non-sensitive features as legitimate, the *SEO* model treats all non-sensitive features as suspect, and the *mixed* model treats some as legitimate and some as suspect. We separately consider each model when they are given additional black-box estimates which are treated as a suspect covariate (*_rf* or *_svr*).

In all data cases, **Y** is rescaled to lie in $[0, 1]$ and larger values correspond to better estimates, i.e. lower estimates of crime and fewer days jailed. This is required to use the utility function specified in [20]. As acknowledged therein, the choice of this function has large impact on estimates as seen below. The final example uses the same data set used in [20] to promote easier comparison. Rescaling in this way yields small baseline values for the mean difference in $\mathbf{Y}$ as well as the standard deviation of $\mathbf{Y}$. As such, small reductions in prediction error can still be sizable on a more natural scale.

The first data set contains information from parolees. The guiding question is whether men are more likely to do hard time holding constant age, the neighborhood in which the live, and prior record. In particular, the goal is to provide estimates of number of days in jail which are impartial with respect to sex. This data set contains information from approximately 83,000 individuals on probation after excluding observations that with zero previous jail days as well as minors. Covariate information includes age, sex, and prior record information such as the number of violent priors as an adult or juvenile. We also consider adding a random forest estimate that is not constrained in its use of covariate information. Lastly, as all covariates and the response exhibit long right tails, all variables are log transformed. The only covariate treated as suspect is age, as beyond attributing to prior record, it is unclear what direct information this could contain.

For this data set, the standard deviation of the transformed response is 0.227 with a mean difference of 0.05 between groups. Therefore, in general, men have served longer sentences without conditioning on prior record. Table 3 shows that the random forest estimates do not appreciably improve prediction in this setting. That being said, the models already perform as well as all competitors in terms of prediction error. While the differences are slight, we can see that driving the DS to zero again results in small increases in the PRD and NRD.

Table 3. Impartial estimates of jail days

Model	DS	PRD	NRD	RMSE
Exclude	0.02	0.02	0.01	0.14
FEO	0.02	0.02	0.01	0.14
SEO	**0.00**	0.03	0.02	0.14
Mixed	0.02	0.02	0.01	0.14
FEO_rf	0.02	0.02	0.01	0.13
SEO_rf	**0.00**	0.03	0.02	0.13
mixed_rf	0.02	0.02	0.01	0.13
Propensity	0.02	0.01	0.02	0.22
Utility	0.07	0.01	0.01	0.17
Welfare	0.02	0.00	0.02	0.14

Our second illustration uses the Crime and Communities data set also considered in [20]. This allows for a more direct comparison as the authors specify a utility function in this case, removing the largest open input to using the method.

The data set contains information on 1,994 communities such as demographic statistics (race, immigrant, and age distributions), law enforcement (budget, racial distribution of officers, etc.), economic (income, unemployment, home-ownership, etc.). In total, there are 100 predictive covariates which can be used to estimate the per capita number of violent crimes. Impartial estimates of crime in this case directly links back to the original redlining example presented in the introduction: lower estimates of crime provide more incentive for investment, etc.

Similar to [20], we label a community as a member of the protected group if more than 25% of the residents are black. Specifying the groups this way as opposed to merely non-Caucasian highlights an important concept behind the current work: it is possible to predict the proportion of black residents in a community using the other covariates. In fact, there are 14–20 covariates which can be used either separately or together to reduce the error sum of squares for predicting the proportion of black residents by 95%. As such, this data set provides our first sincere case with suspect covariates which fall into various categories. Examples of predictive economic indicators include the percentage of households with income from investments, social security, or from public assistance. Others include percentage of people born in the same state, or living in the same house as 5 years before, as well as number of people in shelters or on the street. The conceptual difficulty is that there may be some debate about whether these covariates are legitimate. For comparison, we consider all such covariates as suspect in the mixed model in Table 4.

Table 4. Impartial estimates of crime

Model	DS	PRD	NRD	RMSE
Exclude	0.30	0.04	0.04	0.14
FEO	0.28	0.02	0.05	0.14
SEO	**0.00**	0.08	0.23	0.19
Mixed	0.23	0.00	0.08	0.14
FEO_svr	0.28	0.01	0.04	0.11
SEO_svr	0.00	0.08	0.23	0.17
mixed_svr	0.23	0.01	0.07	0.11
Propensity	0.27	0.02	0.06	0.15
Utility	0.19	0.07	0.05	0.19
Welfare	0.30	0.01	0.02	0.14

We now see clear differences in performance of various impartial models. Importantly, the predictive performance of the mixed model matches that of the FEO model while reducing the mean difference between groups. Furthermore, there is also now a penalty in prediction for switching to a full SEO model which considers no legitimate covariates. As the mean difference in the transformed response is 0.31, it is clear that many models make little to no improvement in this regard. On the other hand, including the black box estimates improves predictive performance dramatically. While the welfare model does achieve good predictive performance, the mean difference is hardly changed. As a final note, we observe that the propensity model performs better, as it is no longer able to perfectly classify the protected groups based on the remaining legitimate covariates. That being said, if one wants the mean difference between groups to be small, the SEO models achieve this exactly.

6   Discussion

This paper provides a clear statistical theory of impartial estimation and explainable variability through the analysis of proxy variables. Covariate groups can only be specified for use in FADM if one has a clear understanding of the implications of the decisions. By considering full-data scenarios in which our fairness assumption is satisfied, we concretely describe the role of proxy variables and their allowable use in FADM. This also provides connections to legal concepts such as our newly identified "uninformative redlining" effect and distinctions between various types of statistical discrimination.

References

1. Adler, P., et al.: Auditing black-box models for indirect influence. Knowl. Inf. Syst. **54**(1), 95–122 (2017). https://doi.org/10.1007/s10115-017-1116-3
2. Arneson, R.: Equality of opportunity. In: Zalta, E.N. (ed.) The Stanford Encyclopedia of Philosophy. Summer 2015 edition (2015)
3. Awad, M., Khanna, R.: Support Vector Regression, pp. 67–80. Apress, Berkeley, CA (2015)
4. R. R. Banks: Race-based suspect selection and colorblind equal protection doctrine and discourse. UCLA Law Review, 48 (2001)
5. Benthall, S., Haynes, B.D.: Racial categories in machine learning. In: Proceedings of the conference on fairness, accountability, and transparency, pp. 289–298 (2019)
6. Berk, R., Heidari, H., Jabbari, S., Kearns, M., Roth, A.: Fairness in criminal justice risk assessments: the state of the art. Sociol. Meth. Res. **50**(1), 3–44 (2021)
7. Blank, R.M., Dabady, M., Citro, C.F. (eds.): Measuring Racial Discrimination. National Research Council (2004)
8. Breiman, L.: Random forests. Mach. Learn. **45**(1), 5–32 (2001)
9. Brockner, J.: It's so hard to be fair. Harv. Bus. Rev. **84**(3), 122 (2006)
10. Calders, T., Karim, A., Kamiran, F., Ali, W., Zhang, X.: Controlling attribute effect in linear regression. In: 2013 IEEE 13th International Conference on Data Mining (ICDM), pp. 71–80, December 2013
11. Calders, T., Verwer, S.: Three Naive Bayes approaches for discrimination-free classification. Data Min. Knowl. Disc. **21**(2), 277–292 (2010)
12. Carnevale, A.P., Haghighat, E.: Selecting the strivers: a report on the preliminary results of the ets "educational strivers" study. Hopwood, Bakke, and beyond: diversity on our nation's campuses, pp. 122–128 (1998)

13. Chiappa, S., Isaac, W.S.: A causal Bayesian networks viewpoint on fairness. In: IFIP International Summer School on Privacy and Identity Management, pp. 3–20. Springer (2018). https://doi.org/10.1007/978-3-030-16744-8_1
14. Eubanks, V.: Automating Inequality: How High-Tech Tools Profile, Police, and Punish the Poor. St. Martin's Press, New York (2018)
15. Geiser, S.: Norm-referenced tests and race-blind admissions: the case for eliminating the sat and act at the university of California. Center for Studies in Higher Education. Research and Occasional Paper Series (ROPS). CSHE 15 (2017)
16. Gillis, T.B.: The input fallacy. Minnesota Law Review 2022. Forthcoming (2022)
17. Grgic-Hlaca, N., Zafar, M.B., Gummadi, K.P., Weller, A.: The case for process fairness in learning: feature selection for fair decision making. In: NIPS Symposium on Machine Learning and the Law, vol. 1, pp. 2 (2016)
18. Hajian, S., Domingo-Ferrer, J.: A methodology for direct and indirect discrimination prevention in data mining. IEEE Trans. Knowl. Data Eng. 25(7), 1445–1459 (2013)
19. Heidari, H., Ferrari, C., Gummadi, K., Krause, A.: Fairness behind a veil of ignorance: a welfare analysis for automated decision making. In: Bengio, S., Wallach, H., Larochelle, H., Grauman, K., Cesa-Bianchi, N., Garnett, R. (eds.) Advances in Neural Information Processing Systems, vol. 31. Curran Associates Inc, 2018
20. Heidari, H., Loi, M., Gummadi, K.P., Krause, A.: A moral framework for understanding fair ML through economic models of equality of opportunity. In: Proceedings of the Conference on Fairness, Accountability, and Transparency, FAT* 2019, pp. 181–190, New York, NY, USA, 2019. Association for Computing Machinery (2019)
21. Holland, P.W.: Causation and race. ETS Research Report Series 2003(1), i–21 (2003)
22. Hurley, M., Adebayo, J.: Credit scoring in the era of big data. Yale JL & Tech. 18, 148 (2016)
23. Jencks, C., Phillips, M.: The black-white test score gap: an introduction. The Black-White test score gap 1(9), 26 (1998)
24. Kamiran, F., Calders, T., Pechenizkiy, M.: Discrimination aware decision tree learning. In: Proceedings of the 2010 IEEE International Conference on Data Mining, ICDM 2010, pp. 869–874, Washington, DC, USA, 2010. IEEE Computer Society (2010)
25. Kamiran, F., Zliobaite, I., Calders, T.: Quantifying explainable discrimination and removing illegal discrimination in automated decision making. Knowl. Inf. Syst. 35(3), 613–644 (2013)
26. Kamishima, T., Akaho, S., Asoh, H., Sakuma, J.: Fairness-aware classifier with prejudice remover regularizer. In: Flach, P.A., De Bie, T., Cristianini, N. (eds.) ECML PKDD 2012. LNCS (LNAI), vol. 7524, pp. 35–50. Springer, Heidelberg (2012). https://doi.org/10.1007/978-3-642-33486-3_3
27. Kilbertus, N., Carulla, M.R., Parascandolo, G., Hardt, M., Janzing, D., Schölkopf, B.: Avoiding discrimination through causal reasoning. In: Guyon, I., Luxburg, U.V., Bengio, S., Wallach, H., Fergus, R., Vishwanathan, S., Garnett, R. (eds.) Advances in Neural Information Processing Systems, volume 30. Curran Associates Inc, (2017)
28. Kozodoi, N., Jacob, J., Lessmann, S.: Fairness in credit scoring: assessment, implementation and profit implications. Eur. J. Oper. Res. 297(3), 1083–1094 (2021)
29. Kusner, M.J., Loftus, J., Russell, C., Silva, R.: Counterfactual fairness. In: Guyon, I., Luxburg, U.V., Bengio, S., Wallach, H., Fergus, R., Vishwanathan, S., Garnett,

R. (eds.) Advances in Neural Information Processing Systems, volume 30. Curran Associates Inc, (2017)

30. Morgan, S.L., Winship, C.: Counterfactuals and Causal Inference: Methods and Principles for Social Research. Analytical Methods for Social Research. Cambridge University Press, 2 edition (2014)

31. Noble, S.U.: Algorithms of Oppression. New York University Press, New York (2018)

32. Pearl, J.: Causality: Models, Reasoning and Inference. Cambridge University Press, Cambridge, 2 edition, September 2009

33. Pedreschi, D., Ruggieri, S., Turini, F.: Discrimination-aware data mining. In: Li, Y.B.L., Sarawagi, S. (eds.) KDD, pp. 560–568. ACM (2008)

34. Pope, D.G., Sydnor, J.R.: Implementing anti-discrimination policies in statistical profiling models. Am. Econ. J. Econ. Pol. **3**(3), 206–31 (2011)

35. R Core Team. R: A Language and Environment for Statistical Computing. R Foundation for Statistical Computing, Vienna, Austria (2019)

36. Ravishankar, P., Malviya, P., Ravindran, B.: A causal linear model to quantify edge flow and edge unfairness for unfairedge prioritization and discrimination removal. arXiv preprint arXiv:2007.05516 (2020)

37. Rawls, J.: Justice as Fairness: A Restatement. Harvard University Press, Cambridge (2001)

38. Wenar, L., Rawls, J.: In: Zalta, E.N. (ed.) The Stanford Encyclopedia of Philosophy. Winter 2013 edition (2013)

39. Zemel, R.S., Wu, Y., Swersky, K., Pitassi, T., Dwork, C.: Learning fair representations. In: ICML (3), volume 28 of JMLR Workshop and Conference Proceedings, pp. 325–333. JMLR.org (2013)

Human-Computer Interaction and Technology

Flexibility, Occupation and Gender: Insights from a Panel Study of Online Freelancers

Isabel Munoz[1]([⊠]) [iD], Michael Dunn[2] [iD], and Steve Sawyer[1] [iD]

[1] Syracuse University, Syracuse, NY 13210, USA
iimunoz@syr.edu
[2] Skidmore College, Saratoga Springs, NY 12866, USA

Abstract. We report findings and discuss implications from a panel study of 68 U.S.-based online freelancers. These findings emerge from analysis of two rounds of data collection: The first round straddled the arrival of COVID in 2020 and the ensuing pandemic-inspired economic downturn. The second round, from early 2021, provides insight into how online work changed in the following months. We see online freelancing as a window into one future of work, one where the market, not the organization, is the primary structure of the worker-employer interaction, mediated by digital platforms and relying on both algorithms and interaction between parties. Our purposive sampling framework, multiple sources of data, and longitudinal design provides for both empirical and conceptual insights into the occupational differences and arrangements of freelance workers. Findings make clear: 1) these workers value job flexibility even as workers experience diminishing flexibility; 2) occupation mediates worker's experiences; and 3) gender differences impact the outcomes of this form of work. These findings also highlight the precarity of online freelance work, raising questions about both online freelancing, and market-based labor structures more generally, as a sustainable source of work or viable career path.

Keywords: Freelance work · Platform work · Upwork · Precarity · Work flexibility · COVID-19 · Gender · Knowledge work

1 Introduction

We focus on how online labor platforms are helping to re-shape the future of work and advance our understanding of flexibility, occupation, and gender in platform-based labor. Online labor platforms such as Upwork, Fiverr, Freelancer.com and others provide us insight into one future of work: online freelancing. Online freelancing has emerged over the last two decades by leveraging technological advances, increased reliance on digital platforms, and increased demand of more flexible workforces [6, 12, 14]. Although it is difficult to estimate the number of online freelancers, the "Freelancing in America 2020" study reports that approximately 55 million people (37% of the U.S. workforce) take part in the economy as freelancers across a variety of platforms [22]. And, the effects of the COVID-19 pandemic has led many employers to hire more freelance workers globally [21].

M. Smits (Ed.): iConference 2022, LNCS 13192, pp. 311–318, 2022.
https://doi.org/10.1007/978-3-030-96957-8_27

We advance understanding of online freelancers by focusing on their experience as they adapt to market changes brought about by the ongoing pandemic, highlighting the role of flexibility and the effects of occupation and gender in this form of work. We draw on data from a longitudinal panel study consisting of surveying and interviewing online freelancers at two time periods. Multi-year panel data provide us an opportunity to understand patterns of adaptation among workers, employers, and the platforms. These data also allow for more explicit attention to ways in which occupation and gender mediate the experiences on online labor platforms. Our research questions are (1) What are the experiences and expectations of online freelancers in the face of rapid market changes? and (2) In what ways do responses differ by occupation and gender?

We focus on online freelancing, which is different from the platform-mediated work of GrubHub, AirBnB, Uber, Lyft, and others because it is not tied to location. Online freelancing also differs from micro-task work such as that done on Amazon Mechanical Turk (AMT) [10]. Both are cognitive efforts, but micro-tasks entails simple, broken down piece work, such as identifying a table in a picture or slang words in a caption [19]. Freelancing jobs are larger efforts, not easily decomposed into tasks. Freelance work also requires both specific expertise (web design, email marketing, etc.) and routine interaction with employers [7, 20].

Online freelancing is mediated by platforms like Upwork.com, creating a two-sided market between workers and employers. As such, online labor platforms are market-makers, supporting a form of labor that has evolved over the past 15 years [6, 12, 14]. The market-making ability of online labor platforms is centered on several human-computer interactions. Freelancers who sell their services and employers who seek services interact through the interfaces of these labor platforms. This means the platforms' features and functions are both the structure of the market and the negotiating space for participants. And these interfaces are evolving as data from interactions are used to adjust the features and functions offered. To succeed, freelancers must constantly adapt to the platform evolution. So, the platform interfaces serve both as a view into a labor market and the frame for negotiating employment: a dynamic playing out over time.

More broadly, we know that digital platforms are helping to transform the ways workers find new employment opportunities and carry out work tasks [16]. Platform-based freelance work is often touted for supporting flexibility, autonomy, and equality [15]. Digital platforms frame freelancing as empowering; giving workers the agency to set their own schedules, choose the clients they work with, and gain control of their work-life balance [4, 13]. And freelance workers are typically motivated by this notion of flexibility and autonomy [20].

Recently, scholars have been more critical of the perceived flexibility, autonomy and equality afforded to online freelance workers. Studies have begun to show that worker's access to flexibility and autonomy depends on several factors, including the availability of work, competition, deadlines, and other factors that may be imposed by the client or the broader market trends [9, 17]. Additionally, online platforms are often designed around traditional workflows, embedding known biases such as gendered occupational expectations [3]. Platforms also use rating and review data to drive recommendation and search results, which means they often rely on data with embedded social bias, resulting in systems that reproduce hiring and labor inequalities [11, 23]. We investigate these differential experiences among online freelance workers in a multi-year panel study described in the following section.

2 Methods

The study is designed as a longitudinal panel of freelancers and combines both interview and survey data. The advantage of the panel study is collecting data from the same people at routine points in time. The focus is on workers who pursue freelance work as a primary or secondary source of income, selected from one digital labor platform, Upwork, to minimize platform effects. Upwork was selected as it is the dominant platform and largest online labor market, accounting for more than 40% of online freelancing [14].

This panel study involves 68 total freelancers located in the United States, assembled to reflect a range of occupation types, skill levels, online experience, gender, and success online. To do this, the sample of online freelance workers is based on three criteria: 1) having completed work on Upwork over the past year, 2) engaged in knowledge-based work organized as temporary gigs or projects, and 3) demographic characteristics (such as gender and amount of experience). Participants in our sample range from 23 to 75 years old, with the median age being 36. The participants also reflect a range of experience on the Upwork platform from 0 to 11 years, the median being 2 years of experience in the first round and 3 years of experience in the second round of data collection. We also note that the household and family arrangements of our participants were diverse, with participants' household sizes ranging from 1 to 7 individuals, including from 0 to 5 children. Table 1 summarizes additional sample characteristics.

Table 1. Freelancer sample characteristics

		Round 1	Round 2
Gender	Female	41 (60%)	28 (56%)
	Male	27 (40%)	22 (44%)
Role of freelance work	Primary source of employment/income	33 (49%)	30 (60%)
	Secondary source of employment/income	35 (51%)	20 (40%)
Job classification	Administrative	29 (42.5%)	19 (38%)
	Technology	10 (15%)	7 (14%)
	Creative	29 (42.5%)	24 (48%)

The study includes two rounds of data collection, the first round ran from December 2019 through April 2020 and the second ran from December 2020 through March 2021. These timeframes reflect our longitudinal study design, in which we collect data in one-year intervals. Participants were hired and paid as they would for any job found on Upwork. This encourages participation, as we acknowledge that our sample is made up of people who get paid by the hour or project. Participants spent 15 min completing a survey that provided us an overview of working arrangements, experiences, and demographic information. Then, participants spent approximately 45 min being interviewed. The interview is based on semi-structured questions and was designed in consort with the survey. The study's longitudinal design and interview schedule provided us time to conduct interim analysis of the data and to reflect on changes and allowed for the inclusion of COVID-19-related data collection.

Interview and survey data were analyzed independently and then together. Interviews were transcribed and, in conjunction with detailed interview notes, were inductively coded but loosely guided by the stated research questions. We then used a thematic analysis to find patterns and common themes within the interview data. Initially, researchers individually reviewed all interview transcripts and developed reports on common patterns. Themes were shared in a group channel and discussed during weekly meetings, with careful note-taking and additional reading to develop a documented understanding of these themes and the data supporting them.

3 Findings: Flexibility, Occupation, and Gender

We report three primary findings from our analyses, which reflect our research questions. These finding focus on freelancing flexibility and differences experienced across participant occupations and genders.

3.1 Value of Flexibility vs. Actual Worker Flexibility

Our data aligns with prior work which finds flexibility is a core reason for pursuing freelance work. Our most recent round of data reveals that 54% of the freelancers in our panel report flexibility is critical to them, with another 44% saying it is useful or helpful. Participants tell us flexibility is important due to the autonomy in setting their working schedules, choosing types of projects/tasks, and being able to fit non-work tasks, including childcare and other household responsibilities, around their workdays. However, due to earnings uncertainty, increased competition, and the lack of protection for online freelance workers, we find the desire for flexibility is almost always an aspiration rather than reality for most workers [2].

Data suggest that worker-controlled flexibility in online freelancing is typically low, due to the need to continuously find new work and accept work and project rates that don't always align with workers' expectations. Worker-controlled flexibility also decreased amid the COVID-19 pandemic. Freelancers indicated significantly more competition, resulting in both a decrease in the number of proposals accepted and a marked decrease in compensation, likely stemming from increased competition. This decrease in flexibility was true for both long-term freelancers and new freelancers, and for both full-time and part-time freelancers.

3.2 The Role of Occupation in Freelancers' Experiences

Data show freelancers' experiences differ across occupations. For example, administrative workers face more competition; they report higher rates of weekly job bids, lower hourly wages, and lower earning predictability. However, during the COVID-19 pandemic downturn, administrative freelance workers had the smallest earnings decrease (−12%) as compared to that experienced by creative workers (−30%) and technology workers (−47%).

Analysis makes clear there are differences in the way workers from different occupational categories engage with the work. Creative workers, by a wide margin, report a greater dependency on the wages from gig work; for 66% of creative workers, freelancing was their primary source of income, as compared to 50% of technology workers and 42% of administrative workers in our sample. Furthermore, while our data showed that the majority (~59%) of workers did not have health benefits, 70% of the respondents in the creative occupations did not have health benefits. Given that the economic shock that workers are experiencing is driven by a virus-centered pandemic, the magnitude of precarity among these workers without health coverage is evident and likely leading to a greater feeling of desperation.

3.3 Gendered Experiences in Online Freelancing

We also find evidence that gender also mediates the experiences of freelance workers. In our sample, 65% of the administrative workers were women. This compounds with our earlier finding that administrative workers face more competition, lower wages, and lower earning predictability. As such, women are more likely to face precarious situations as freelance workers.

Across all occupations, women freelancers reported a lower average monthly income than men, despite having equal or more years of freelance experience than their counterparts. Women in our sample reported average monthly earnings from Upwork $659, while men reported $1,136. Data also show women report a higher percentage of their work being done on Upwork, with Upwork accounting for an average 43.5% of all work for women compared to 33% for men.

Analysis also makes clear that women were more likely to be affected negatively by the COVID-19 pandemic. Data show women were more likely than men to reduce working hours to help absorb the increased share of caregiving and other domestic responsibilities. Women's average hours worked per week dropped by 12.7 h since the start of the pandemic. This reduction in work hours is nearly double the rate of men's, whose work hours dropped by 6.45 h.

In addition to the reduction in hours worked, we also saw a gendered trend in the participants who dropped out completely from our study. As we pursued the second round of data collection, we lost 18 participants. In analyzing the participants who dropped out of the study we found that 13 of these participants were female (72%) and 5 were male (28%). These findings align with other work that has highlighted the impact of the COVID-19 pandemic on women, and especially women with children who are dealing with balancing increased household responsibilities and the continued uncertainty of school operations [5, 18].

4 Discussion: Implications and Future Work

Online freelance work is growing, and many see it as an important part of the future labor force, with more people turning to this form of work full- or part-time. Our study of Upwork freelancers highlights the experiences of these independent platform workers in the face of rapidly changing market conditions, including by the disruption enacted by the COVID-19 pandemic. We find that workers are clearly motivated by the perception of freelance work as being flexible, despite that this is more of an aspiration than reality for most. Our findings highlight that earnings uncertainty, increased competition, and the lack of labor protections for online freelance workers diminishes the perceived worker-controlled flexibility. Instead, workers are left to spend hours of unpaid work to find and compete for new work and take on less than desirable projects and tasks. The experiences of workers also vary by occupation and gender, with administrative workers and women facing some of the most precarious work conditions, including lower pay. This findings aligns with literature that shows women are overrepresented in certain occupations, namely those associated with lower earnings [8]. Foong et al. found that women across the entirety of the Upwork platform earned significantly less per hour than the median man on Upwork, even when controlling for key variables such as work experience, highest education level, and job category [8].

These findings highlight the precarity of online freelance work, raising questions about exacerbated challenges among certain population of workers, and market-based labor structures more generally, as a sustainable source of work or viable career path. Previous work has highlighted challenges of freelance work, including the lack of work and earnings security [1, 17, 24] and the constant need to be available despite a perception of "flexibility" [15, 24].

Computer Supported Cooperative Work (CSCW) and Human-Computer Interaction (HCI) scholars have also begun to highlight the ways gender and race may impact the experiences of workers in platform-mediated work arrangements, including online freelancing. Hannák et al. found that perceived gender and race can have significant negative consequences for an individual's search ranking results because existing biases can manifest in online labor markets [11]. Their study of TaskRabbit freelancers showed that White women received 10% fewer reviews than males of equal experience and Black workers received more negative evaluations than white workers [11]. This means that despite perceptions of neutrality, freelance work is mediated by worker's attributes, including gender and race, which exacerbate worker precarity.

Considering these implications, future work should continue to focus on the differential experiences of workers in the under-regulated space of online freelancing. We propose three primary areas for future work: 1) studies of gender and race in online freelancing, 2) studies of job quality and precarity of new freelance workers, and 3) studies of clients who are hiring freelancers on digital platforms. Addressing these three areas will allow us to develop a deeper understanding about the impact and challenges of online freelancing for all players in this form of labor.

We are beginning to explore these research needs in at least four ways. First, during the Summer of 2021, we began data collection to increase the diversity of our panel; we will add a subset of participants from minority races to better understand the impact of race within online freelancing. Second, we will explore the effect that experience has on our findings by including a subset of freelancers who are new to Upwork and online freelancing. Third, our study will incorporate a sample of Upwork clients to begin to gather the perspective of this player in the online freelance transaction. And, finally, we will be extending the panel timeframe to continue to survey and interview our participants annually to understand how they adapt to platform changes over time, and how the role of online freelancing evolves in participants' career strategies. Expanding this multi-year panel study will also allow us to learn more about the job quality of online freelancing and compare responses among participants of varying occupations, genders, and races.

Acknowledgements. This material is based upon work supported by the National Science Foundation under grant nos. 1665386, 2121624, 2121638. This research is also supported, in part, by grants from Syracuse University's office of the Vice President of Research and SOURCE. Any opinions, findings, and conclusions or recommendations expressed in this material are those of the author(s) and do not necessarily reflect the views of the organizations supporting our work.

References

1. Aroles, J., et al.: Mapping themes in the study of new work practices. New Technol. Work Employ. **34**(3), 285–299 (2019)
2. Barley, S., Kunda, G.: Gurus, Hired Guns, and Warm Bodies: Itinerant Experts in a Knowledge Economy. Princeton University Press, Princeton (2006)
3. Barzilay, A.: Discrimination without discriminating: learned gender inequality in the labor market and gig economy. Cornell J. Law Publ. Policy **28**(3), 545–568 (2019)
4. Churchill, B., Craig, L.: Gender in the gig economy: men and women using digital platforms to secure work in Australia. J. Sociol. **55**(4), 741–761 (2019)
5. Collins, C., et al.: COVID-19 and the gender gap in work hours. Gend. Work Organ. **28**(S1), 101–112 (2020)
6. Dunn, M.: Digital work: new opportunities or lost wages? Am. J. Manag. **17**(4), 10–27 (2017)
7. Dunn, M., et al.: Gender differences and lost flexibility in online freelancing during the COVID-19 pandemic. Front. Sociol. **6**, 166 (2021)
8. Foong, E., et al.: Women (still) ask for less: gender differences in hourly rate in an online labor marketplace. Proc. ACM Hum.-Comput. Interact. **2**(CSCW), 53:1–53:21 (2018)
9. Graham, M., et al.: Digital labor and development: impacts of global digital labor platforms and the gig economy on worker livelihoods. Transf. Eur. Rev. Labour Res. (2017). https://doi.org/10.1177/1024258916687250
10. Gray, M., Suri, S.: Ghost Work: How to Stop Silicon Valley from Building a New Global Underclass. Houghton Mifflin Harcourt, Boston (2019)
11. Hannák, A., et al.: Bias in online freelance marketplaces: evidence from Taskrabbit and Fiverr. In: Proceedings of the 2017 ACM Conference on Computer-Supported Cooperative Work and Social Computing, pp. 1914–1933 (2017)
12. Kalleberg, A.L.: Flexible firms and labor market segmentation: effects of workplace restructuring on jobs and workers'. Work Occup. **30**(2), 154–175 (2003)
13. Kalleberg, A.L., Dunn, M.: Good jobs, bad jobs in the gig economy. LERA Libr. **20**, 1–2 (2016)
14. Kässi, O., Lehdonvirta, V.: Online labour index: measuring the online gig economy for policy and research. Technol. Forecast. Soc. Change. **137**, 241–248 (2018)
15. Lehdonvirta, V.: Flexibility in the gig economy: managing time on three online piecework platforms. N. Technol. Work. Employ. **33**(1), 13–29 (2018)
16. Nash, C., Jarrahi, M.H., Sutherland, W., Phillips, G.: Digital nomads beyond the buzzword: defining digital nomadic work and use of digital technologies. In: Chowdhury, G., McLeod, J., Gillet, V., Willett, P. (eds.) iConference 2018. LNCS, vol. 10766, pp. 207–217. Springer, Cham (2018). https://doi.org/10.1007/978-3-319-78105-1_25

17. Pichault, F., McKeown, T.: Autonomy at work in the gig economy: analysing work status, work content and working conditions of independent professionals. N. Technol. Work. Employ. **34**(1), 59–72 (2019)
18. Reichelt, M., et al.: The impact of COVID-19 on gender inequality in the labor market and gender-role attitudes. Eur. Soc. **23**(sup1), S228–S245 (2021)
19. Ross, J., et al.: Who are the crowdworkers? Shifting demographics in Mechanical Turk. In: CHI 2010 Extended (2010)
20. Sawyer, S., et al.: Freelancing online during the COVID-19 pandemic (2020)
21. Stephany, F., et al.: Distancing bonus or downscaling loss? The changing livelihood of US online workers in times of COVID-19. Tijdschr. Econ. Soc. Geogr. (2020). https://doi.org/10.1111/tesg.12455
22. Upwork: Freelancing in America: 2019 Survey (2019). http://Upwork.com
23. Vyas, N.: Gender inequality - now available on digital platform': an interplay between gender equality and the gig economy in the European Union. Eur. Labour Law J. (2020)
24. Wood, A.J., et al.: Good gig, bad gig: autonomy and algorithmic control in the global gig economy. Work Employ. Soc. **33**(1), 56–75 (2019)

Causal Discovery and Knowledge Linkage in Scientific Literature: A Case Study in Biomedicine

Yujie Zhang, Rujiang Bai$^{(\boxtimes)}$, Qiming Chen, Yahui Zhang, and Mengying Feng

Institute of Information Management, Shandong University of Technology,
Zibo 255000, China
brj@sdut.edu.cn

Abstract. Scientific literature is the main carrier to express innovation thinking, and the discovery of laws of knowledge from the literature is the necessary basis for scientific research to achieve innovation development, but current knowledge mining methods still have deficiencies in logic and reasoning. And causality is a higher-order cognitive relationship with logical reasoning ability, so it is necessary how to mine causality from the literature and establish knowledge linkage based on causality. [Methods] This paper proposes to find causality from the scientific literature and make a knowledge linkage based on the causal events and take full-text data in the biomedical field as an example. Firstly, we design a causal event extraction method that sythetically employs rules and deep learning. Secondly, the causal events are connected globally to build a causal knowledge network. Then, based on the graph embedding, a feature representation of the causal knowledge network is performed. Finally, we analyze knowledge community differences and identified potential causal events. [Results] The results show that causal networks can realize medical knowledge logical association more comprehensively, and can correlate local information from single literature into global knowledge elements. Moreover, our study can discover the knowledge of potential medical causality, which provides an important reference for disease diagnosis and treatment and academic innovation.

Keywords: Knowledge mining · CausalAI · Biomedicine

1 Introduction

The academic literature is the most dominant form of scientific research, and most of the research results are presented in the form of literature, which bears researchers' intellectual logic and innovative thinking. Mining hidden knowledge from the literature is an important means to promote information transformation and knowledge innovation.

In recent years, the common practice of data mining from the vast amount of scientific literature is to use text mining tools and machine learning methods to

© The Author(s), under exclusive license to Springer Nature Switzerland AG 2022
M. Smits (Ed.): iConference 2022, LNCS 13192, pp. 319–328, 2022.
https://doi.org/10.1007/978-3-030-96957-8_28

analyze the subject matter, evolutionary features, and then perform tasks such as modeling, clustering, prediction [1–3]. However, these methods mainly suffer from the following deficiencies:

(1) These methods can only reflect correlations. Many methods rely on the prior art to fit a law from a large amount of literature data and analyze the correlation relationship of features, but the correlation is not equal to causality, the former is reversible and the latter is irreversible [4].
(2) Logical reasoning was insufficient. Knowledge mining modalities based on data fitting can be computed, analyzed quickly, but inferences about knowledge are difficult. For example, machines can extract information from the news that a plane has fallen, but they cannot deduce that a person on board might die.
(3) Knowledge is weakly correlated. Many methods are based on local information, so it is difficult to reflect the overall situation of the whole field or discipline. At present, the rapid progress of the knowledge graph provides a solution to this limitation, but how to deduce and recognize from knowledge graph needs to be further improved.

Knowledge system is a huge network, the transfer effect of academic research urges researchers to mine logical associations from this network to realize cognitive reasoning, and causality is a high-order cognitive relationship that can effectively reveal this process [5]. For example, in the biomedical field, *endothelial cell injury* would cause *systemic inflammatory response syndrome*, *systemic inflammatory response syndrome* would cause *multiple organ dysfunction syndromes*, and *metalloproteinase* would promote *attachment of endothelial cell injury*. Discovering a causal relationship between *endothelial cells* and *metalloproteinase* would be very helpful to resolve *endothelial cell injury* and *systemic inflammatory response syndrome*. Moreover, storing causal events in a structured manner, building knowledge associations from a single piece of literature to a global one, enables the teasing out and succession of knowledge from the medical field and enables the mining of causal knowledge that is artificially hard to discover, to promote medical progress.

Based on the above motivation, we propose to discover causal knowledge from the scientific literature of biomedicine, construct a global causal network, and use embedding techniques for the feature representation of causal networks, to comb the knowledge transmission context, excavate potential causal relationships, and finally provide new insight for disease diagnosis and academic innovation.

2   Dataset

This article takes the Biomedical field as an example to conduct research, which not only contains a large number of open access literature resources, but also is currently one of the most closely integrated disciplines with AI and Information Science, and the selection of this field as a research object is of great academic value and practical significance. Article data were derived from the PubMed

Central, and we selected 49021 full-text articles over the period 2007–2021 by random sampling. Data were stored in XML format using ElementTree and PubMed-parser to parse the full-text information including title, abstract, body, meanwhile, to obtain the basic information for each article such as year, journal, DOI, article ID.

3   Methodology

The methodology of this paper can be described as follows: Firstly, cause-effect phrase pairs are extracted from data using rule-based approaches. Secondly, combining with manual annotation of parts of the literature content, transformed it into the causal event recognition task of binary classification. Then, the causal events are connected globally and the causal network is constructed. Then, the feature representation of the causal knowledge network is carried out based on graph embedding. Finally, based on this representation, knowledge community differences in medical literature are analyzed and potential medical causality is explored.

3.1   Causality Extraction

We argue that causal events should be able to reflect the basic elements of literature causality and should have structural features. Therefore, causal events are expressed in the form of an SVO triplet, with S as the cause, O as the result, and V as the causal trigger word. Current Causality Extraction (CE) has made some progress, but the vast majority of work is based on sequence tagging approaches [6], which require extensive manual annotation of sequence data sets. This is difficult to achieve for a large amount of unannotated data in this paper. Therefore, the article adopts a rule that combine deep learning classification task-based method for causality extraction. The specific ideas are as follows:

(1) First, define the words and rules that express cause and effect,
(2) Second, extract sentences with causal trigger words from the text,
(3) Then, identify all the entities, phrases, and causal triggers in the sentence, construct SVO causal events,
(4) Finally, part of the data is manually annotated and converted into a binary classification task to obtain real causal events.

For the definition of causal rules, we refer to Wolff's work [7] and form trigger words such as lead to, cause, because to express causal relationship. We use existing medical entity recognition tools to identify medical entities, in which the causes and effects can be expressed by nouns, nouns + verbs, verbs + nouns, adjectives + nouns to form a more complete expression structure. In the fourth step, multiple causal pairs are first extracted from the sentence, such as $[(S_1, S_2, S_n), V, (O_1, O_2, O_n)]$, and then traversal matching is performed to form a single causal event with more clear meaning as a candidate, such as $[S_1 V O_1,$

S_1VO_2, S_1VO_n], Then the annotator will annotate part of the data according to the content of the article to determine whether the real causal relationship is expressed. After that, the mainstream deep learning model is selected for the classification experiment, and the model with the best effect is used to obtain all the real causal events.

3.2   Causal Knowledge Linkage

Based on the causal events obtained above, we can organize and correlate the causality to link the local causality of single literature into global causality on the whole biomedical field, construct into a causal network, and thus more further mine the logical relationship of knowledge in the medical field. Additionally, mapping this causal knowledge network into vector space enables the identification of inter knowledge community discovery versus potential causality through the calculation of vector distances. Here, we divide the knowledge association of causal events in the literature into three steps:

(1) Construct causal networks,
(2) To represent the feature of the network,
(3) Knowledge community discovery and potential causal identification based on causal network representation.

In the above steps, the causal knowledge network is composed of nodes and edges. Each node represents a cause or effect event, and each node contains several attributes of the corresponding article, such as DOI, affiliated journal, time, and the number of articles. The weight of the node is represented by the frequency of the node. The edge represents the direction of cause and effect, and the weight of the edge is represented by SVO frequency. It should be noted that the causal relationship between events is different from the correlation relationship, the direction is one-way and irreversible, and only the cause can lead to the effect. Therefore, the causal knowledge network is a weighted directed graph. Representation of causal knowledge networks we perform by graph embedding.

4   Results

4.1   Causality Extraction

First, sentences containing causal trigger words are extracted from the literature, and then all medical entities, medical phrases, and causal trigger words in the sentence are identified using ScispaCy and NLTK, and split with the position of trigger words as the boundary, with the former as the cause and the latter as the result. Multiple cause-effect phrase pairs in literature can be extracted based on this method. However, these multi-causation pairs are vague in meaning expression and not pointed, and some of them are real causation events while others are pseudo-causation relationships. We go through the causes and outcomes of these multiple causal pairs, got more definite single cause-effect phrase pairs.

Then, according to the content of the article, three annotators annotated the SVO expressing the true causality. Only when the results of at least two of the annotators are consistent can data take effect. We labeled 5000 true causal events and 5000 pseudo causal pairs as the training dataset. Then, five deep learning models, CNN, RNN, BiLSTM, Transformer and BioBERT, were selected for the classification experiment of causal events. After several parameter adjustments and iterative training, the accuracy of each model is shown in Table 1.

Table 1. Accuracy of each model.

Model	Accuracy
CNN	0.7500
RNN	0.7222
BiLSTM	0.7517
Transformer	0.7156
BioBERT	0.8260

It can be found that the BioBERT model pre-trained from large-scale medical data has better results in classification results, and then we classify causal events based on this model. In the end, 71781 causal events were obtained from the 49021 literature. We find that causal trigger words like *"lead to"*, *"have effect on"*, *"cause"*, *"evoke"* are more common, while some nouns and phrases such as *"sars-cov-2"*, *"coronavirus disease"*, *"cell death"*, *"insulin resistance"*, *"proliferation"*, *"pharmacological inhibition"*, *"tumor growth"*, *"oxidative stress"* were more frequent in both cause and effect. Partial SVO causal events are shown in Table 2.

4.2   Causal Network Construction

In order to make a global knowledge linkage of these causal events, we transformed them into graph structure and constructed a causal knowledge network. The node represents an event, the frequency of the node is taken as the weight value. The edge represents the causal trigger words, and the frequency of the whole SVO is taken as the weight of the edge. A total of 62503 event nodes and 71781 causal relationships are obtained.

We choose coherent and representative events for visualization, as shown in Fig. 1. These events include the relationships of single-cause & single-effect, single-cause & multiple-effects, multiple-causes & single-effects, and multiple-causes & multiple-effects. For example, from the causal network, we found *"coronavirus disease engenders severe respiratory syndrome"*, and also, *"Coronavirus disease provoked the rapid global spread"* (Fig. 1-A). From the timeline, there was a rapid increase in research on COVID-19 within a short period time, as well as a sharp rise in the number of articles, reflecting the importance people

Table 2. Partial SVO causal events.

SVO	Frequency
Fat accumulation **causes** *increased mortality*	12
Nicotinamide **lead to** *hepatotoxicity*	8
Hematopoietic stem cell transplantation **promotes** *patient recovery*	7
Coronavirus disease **lead to** *multiple organ failure*	6
Growth suppressor **arouse** *angiogenesis*	5
nonalcoholic fatty liver disease **bringing about** *fat accumulation*	5
Candidalysin **lead to** *liver disease*	4
Prolonged exposure **have effect on** *impaired pancreatic*	4
Physiological brain aging **lead to** *cognitive function reduced*	3
Adam proteolysis **evoke** *platelet receptor shedding*	3
Cd36-mediated fa uptake **provoke** *the fat accumulation*	3

attach to the virus. For another example, it can be found from the causal network that *"acute infection caused decreased cell viability"* and *"decreased cell viability result in cell death"* (Fig. 1-D). These events interact and interact with each other, and this complex causal relationship can be more intuitively reflected in the causal knowledge network.

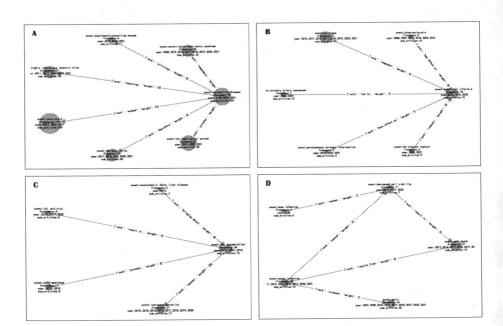

Fig. 1. Partial causal knowledge network.

4.3 Knowledge Community Analysis

In order to further discover the community relationship between events and dig the deeper causal relationship, we carry out the embedding-based causal representation of the network and map them to the continuous vector space, which is more conducive to calculation and analysis.

We use Node2Vec [8] to represent the causal knowledge network, where p(return parameter) determines the probability that the random walk goes back to the original node, and q (in-out parameter) determines the probability that the random walk goes to the farther literature node. Then, the causal sequence contains a more holistic network structure as much as possible through deep-first sampling and breadth-first sampling.

After that, in order to find the similarities and differences between events, the nodes are clustered based on K-means algorithm, the number of categories K has been adjusted several times, and the clustering effect is most obvious when set to 3. 1000 nodes are randomly selected, compressed into 2D based on t-SNE dimensionality reduction algorithm, and mapped into spatial coordinates with Matplotlib for visualization, the results are shown in Fig. 2-A. Events with the same or similar zodiac are closer in distance. For example, *"SARS-CoV-2 Infection", "COVID-19 pandemic"* and similar events show much closer proximity.

We can also find that among the three categories, the number of category-1 has an obvious advantage, mainly because the research related to COVID-19 occupies most of the category. We also map the relationship vector of causal events in category-1 to 2D coordinates, as shown in Fig. 2-B. It can be found that the causal relationship of events in category-1 is clustered, and the causal events in close clusters are more similar. Secondly, causation events for category-1 are mainly concentrated in 2019, 2020, and 2021 (Fig. 2-C), which is similar to the development trend of COVID-19.

4.4 Potential Causal Identification

To find out whether and how likely there is a causal relationship between unconnected events, we perform a potential causal discovery on the causal network. First, we used common neighbors and in-degree centrality to search for causal pairs with stronger associations and calculated the connectivity index of causal pairs (Fig. 3), from which we remove independent nodes, and then replace a subset of nodes from strongly associated nodes as spurious causal pairs without altering the structure of the causal network to balance the training data.

Afterward Multilayer Perceptron was used for training based on the features of nodes and edges that had been generated by Node2Vec before. The model was then migrated over the events of the testset, producing the results shown in Fig. 4, on the left is the generated confusion matrix between events, transforms them into causal networks, where the solid lines represent known causal events with both probabilities of 1, the dashed lines represent the discovered causal events that are likely to exist, and the size of the probability indicates the probability that these two events are causal. We found that in cases where

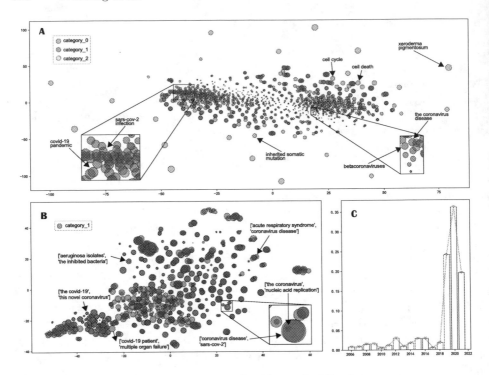

Fig. 2. Node embedding and relationship embedding in vector space.

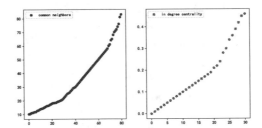

Fig. 3. common neighbors and in-degree centrality of nodes.

"arterial injury" is known to cause *"cell migration"*, *"cell migration"* may cause *"disrupts cytoskeleton"*, *"cell migration"* can also cause *"cancer cell invasion"*, which with 87% probability. This underlying knowledge of cause and effect can provide health care professionals and academics with a broader perspective to help diagnose and treat diseases.

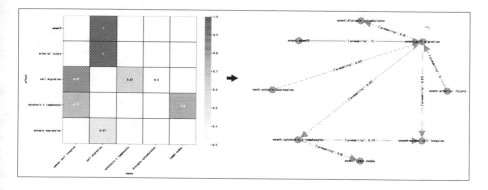

Fig. 4. Potential causal knowledge discovery.

5   Conclusion

This paper proposes to mine causality and construct causal knowledge linkage from the scientific literature, and conduct empirical studies using the field of biomedicine as an example. Causal events extracted from the literature can dominantly express logical associations of knowledge, mining out causal chains such as hcmv infection - > reduced cell viability - > cell death - > acute infection. Causal network-based knowledge associations enable the mining of community differences in medical knowledge. Meanwhile, through the link prediction of the network, it is able to discover the potential causal relationships in biomedicine and provide references for further innovative research and disease treatment. However, there are still several points that need to improve in this paper. It is still difficult to identify implicit causality, and the article has not extended to more fields to study the cause and effect between multidisciplinary discovery. In view of the above problems, we will conduct further research in the future.

References

1. Wang, X., Zhu, P., Liu, T., et al.: BioTopic: a topic-driven biological literature mining system. Int. J. Data Min. Bioinform. **14**(4), 373–386 (2016)
2. Wang, S.-H., et al.: Text mining for identifying topics in the literatures about adolescent substance use and depression. BMC Public Health **16**(1), 1–8 (2016)
3. Sosa, D.N., et al.: A literature-based knowledge graph embedding method for identifying drug repurposing opportunities in rare diseases. In: Pacific Symposium on Biocomputing 2020 (2019)
4. Pearl, J., Mackenzie, D.: The Book of Why: The New Science of Cause and Effect. Basic Books, New York (2018)
5. Guyon, I., Janzing, D., Schölkopf, B.: Causality: Objectives and Assessment. PMLR (2010)
6. Yang, J., Han, S.C., Poon, J.: A survey on extraction of causal relations from natural language text. arXiv preprint arXiv:2101.06426 (2021)

7. Wolff, P., Song, G.: Models of causation and the semantics of causal verbs. Cogn. Psychol. **47**(3), 276–332 (2003)
8. Grover, A., Leskovec, J.: node2vec: scalable feature learning for networks. In: Proceedings of the 22nd ACM SIGKDD International Conference on Knowledge Discovery and Data Mining (2016)

Facial Recognition Interaction in a University Setting: Impression, Reaction, and Decision-Making

Hengyi Fu[1]([⊠]) [iD] and Yao Lyu[2] [iD]

[1] School of Library and Information Studies, The University of Alabama,
Tuscaloosa 35401, USA
hfu4@ua.edu
[2] College of Information Sciences and Technology,
Pennsylvania State University, State College 16802, USA
yaolyu@psu.edu

Abstract. Facial recognition technology (FRT) is now being introduced across various aspects of public life. However, the controversial nature of FRT and improper uses often generate critical concerns and even resistance. Research on human interactions with FRT has focused principally on individual-level usage in private spaces, tending not to capture in-situ, nuanced human-surveillance technology interactions. To address this gap, we investigated users' lived experiences with a facial recognition system at a university in the United States, using semi-structured interviews. In this paper, we reported findings of participants' first impressions and initial reactions to FRT, whether and why their attitudes changed afterwards, and how they evaluated the administration that made the deployment decision. We found that besides issues of privacy, data security, and possible bias, the participants highlighted the idea that FRT might deconstruct the nature of community and connections between people as well as resulting in mass surveillance. In evaluating the deployment decision, the participants perceived control of and transparency in the decision-making process, the accuracy and timeliness of the information, and respect accorded to users in the process as equal in importance to the technology itself. Our findings also point to organizational issues associated with the administration of FRT and offer insights into controversial technology deployment from an organizational justice perspective.

Keywords: Human-computer interaction · Facial recognition system · User perceptions · Technology acceptability · Technology deployment

1 Introduction

The past few years have seen the deployment of facial recognition systems in a range of social realms. Many people are broadly welcoming of the various proclaimed benefits associated with such technology, which include more efficient and secure transactions, enhanced public safety, and highly developed commercial services. Nevertheless, concerns are growing in regard to the place of facial recognition technologies (FRT) in

M. Smits (Ed.): iConference 2022, LNCS 13192, pp. 329–343, 2022.
https://doi.org/10.1007/978-3-030-96957-8_29

democratic society ranging from invasion of privacy, compromised civil rights, hidden bias, and a lack of limits on the use of political power. As demonstrated in recent efforts to curtail the public use of facial recognition (such as the successful campaign to prohibit San Francisco public agencies from using facial recognition), these concerns have generated strong and successful resistance.

While rarely foregrounded in debates about FRT in society, the education sector is one of the public settings in which this technology is beginning to be taken up and implemented at scale. Prominent educational applications of FRT are campus security and attendance monitoring. Facial recognition has also been used in a number of virtual learning contexts and as a tool to measure student engagement. Indeed, a growing number of US school districts have either already implemented FRT or are in the process of doing so [1]. At the same time, there seems to be little sustained opposition to the implementation of FRT in schools—in contrast to more contentious discussions about the application of facial recognition in other areas of society. A recent survey in Australia showed high levels of approval for the deployment of FRT in schools for the purposes of "monitoring attendance and ensuring student safety" [2].

Facial recognition is an emerging technology that will transform our understanding and experiences of monitoring in a range of public and private spaces. However, most recent research of human interactions with FRT focused on individual-level usage in private spaces (e.g., face unlocking, face tagging) [3, 4] or general perceptions of the technology in specific scenarios [5, 6]. The few studies that do focus on users' perceptions of FRT in the workplace [7] are mostly quantitative and do not capture in-situ, nuanced human-surveillance technology interactions.

To fill the research gap, we ask: What are individuals' lived experiences of FRT in a university setting? To answer this question, we conducted a qualitative study at a public university in the United States using semi-structured interviews. The research took place immediately after the deployment of a facial recognition system at a makerspace reconstructed from a former library. Participants were asked about their experiences of interacting with the system, how they viewed the implementation of the system and how they reacted to the decision. To our best knowledge, this is the first empirical study focused on how users perceive and interact with FRT in a university setting. This study is expected to contribute to current literature by (1) providing empirical insights into people's interactions with an actual facial recognition system in a public space, (2) reflecting the controversy of FRT in a university setting, and (3) revealing organizational issues related to FRT deployment and offering insights into our future research in this direction from an organizational justice perspective.

2 Public Concerns Relating to FRT Implementation

Previous Research summarizes several controversial issues related to the deployment of FRT, including accuracy, bias, privacy, and security [5, 6].

Accuracy: Concerns over accuracy focus on the reliability of FRT in real-world scenarios. The past five years have seen repeated reports of facial recognition systems failing to recognize African American faces due to the racially skewed datasets the algorithms had been trained on [8]. Recent studies suggest that we are still far from having facial recognition systems that can accurately identify everyone in a large crowd [9] and that some systems continue to be more accurate for certain demographic groups than for others [10–12].

Bias: In addition to reliability problems, there are concerns that existing bias against certain groups may be amplified by FRT. Previous research showed that machine bias does exist in the form of systematic misrecognition on the basis of ethnic background. Such concerns are often associated with fears that FRT will be misused and lead to mistaken arrests by law enforcement [13, 14]. Even if these identifications are rendered more technically accurate, certain groups may still be more negatively impacted by FRT. For example, women were more likely to resist FRT in the workplace because they were not part of the group that would control it [7]. Although it's possible to use FRT surveillance as a tool against workplace sexual harassment, the application would be controlled by exactly those most likely to be the harassers due to the distribution of power.

Privacy and Security: The widespread use of FRT enables the creation of detailed databases about people's actions and whereabouts, raising a host of concerns about control over personal information and the uses to which it is put, especially when the technology is used by authoritarian governments and/or for commercial interests. Further, demographic and other private information can be revealed by unique facial features, leading to functional creep and intrusions of privacy [15]. As FRT develops, it is likely to treat people's faces not just as a form of biometric identification, but also as a new source of demographic and psychographic data. For example, employers are testing automated job interview systems that measure facial "micro-expressions" to screen potential employees. The lack of data collection, storage, and usage specifications of FRT applications further deepen public concerns in relation to violations of the citizenry's privacy. Moreover, research has shown that Deepfakes videos present great challenges to FRT, especially with the further development of face-swapping technology [16]. Harm that may result from DeepFakes include extortion, psychological abuse, sabotage of competitors' reputations, and weakened trust in institutions.

3   Research Setting

In January 2019, a facial recognition system was installed in a makerspace in a public university in the United States. It provided open access to university members. People who frequently used the makerspace included faculty, students, makerspace managers and other staff. The staff included graduate assistants and undergrad in-terns recruited as student employees.

Implemented with the support of the makerspace manager, the university administration, and the campus police. The system, according to the company, has high recognition accuracy and huge data storage space. The makerspace manager stated that the long-term plan is to replace the card-swipe system with this facial recognition system given that the new system can enhance campus security by detecting people who are not members of the university. Also scanning faces is more convenient and faster than swiping cards. The makerspace manager had the FaceEx system mounted on the card-swipe system. This meant that everyone entering the space with the exception of those using a wheelchair exposed their faces to the FaceEx system (Fig. 1). The FaceEx system automatically scanned their faces, matched facial information with records in database and showed the matching results on the screen.

Fig. 1. Interface of the FaceEx device (right) and the FaceEx device at the entry system (left). The facial recognition system is mounted on the card-swipe entry system.

4   Data Collection and Analysis

We conducted semi-structured interviews during the first two months (from January to March 2019) shortly after the FaceEx system had been installed. Recruiting messages were sent to makerspace staff and visitors using direct contact and snowball sampling. In total, nineteen participants were selected, comprising four faculty and staff members and fifteen students. Eight of the participants, i.e., one manager, two graduate assistants, and five undergraduate interns, were affiliated with the makerspace. Each participant was required to complete an online questionnaire reporting basic demographic information. The interviews lasted from 25 to 70 min with an average time of 45 min. All the interviews took place at least 2 weeks after the participants had first encountered the FaceEx system.

The interview guidelines were constructed based on previous research on users' reflections/concerns of facial recognition system, especially in school setting [17]. Interview questions covered multiple concerns including the participants' knowledge of and previous experience with facial recognition systems, their initial impressions of and reactions to the FaceEx system, their overall attitudes towards the system and the decision to install it, and if their opinions changed after initial interactions and why (if so).

All the interviews were audio-recorded, transcribed, and coded using NVivo 12 Pro. An open-coding approach [18] was used to code the interview data, and a constant comparison was performed in the coding process. To improve coding validity, two coders coded all the interview transcripts, with agreement reached at the level of 85.6%. Any discrepancies were resolved through extensive discussion.

5 Findings

5.1 Previous Knowledge of and Experience with FRT

All participants identified themselves as having basic knowledge of FRT, including the working mechanism, scenarios in which FRT is used, and the possible benefits and challenges of FRT. Two thirds of the participants reported that they had previous experience with FRT, including a face-unlocking iPhone, face tagging on social media, and identity verification in international travel. The information channels they drew on included class materials and discussion, research articles, sci-fi fiction and TV series (e.g., the Black Mirror series), and family and friends. We did not, however, find a relationship between the participants' knowledge of and previous experience with FRT and the extent to which they did/did not find the system to be acceptable.

5.2 First Impressions of and Reactions to FRT Deployment

Uncomfortable, Confused, Avoidance and Protesting

The participants' first impressions of the FaceEx system were diverse and can be loosely grouped into three categories: uncomfortable, confused, and curious. More than half of the participants (11 out of 19) described their initial feelings as "uncomfortable," "freaking out," or "wired." Some of them clearly linked such negative feelings to a particular concern:

> When I first saw it, I just started thinking about things like all the data they're collecting, they're probably sending data to advertisers or government. So at first, I just thought about, oh my god, they're doing this on purpose. (P6)

> That first time I walked up, I was trying to swipe my card, I didn't know that this thing was capturing me until I looked up...I didn't consent, obviously. I'm in a public space, I didn't authorize to be filmed in public spaces. You know, PRIVACY. (P7)

P7's experience suggests that she accepted providing ID card for access as the default setting. Her emphasis on privacy also indicates that she valued her facial information above the information stored on her ID card. She was irritated by the FaceEx system which scanned human faces without consents. Interestingly, according to the makerspace manager (P17), the FaceEx system is, in fact, a livestream device that does not film or record videos like a traditional surveillance camera. However, P7 was not aware of this fact.

Although they did not express strong negative feelings such as those described by P7, three other participants talked about being "confused" about or "having no idea" as to why the system had been installed. The main reason for this sense of confusion was that they did not know what the system was being used for, why the old card-swipe system had been replaced, and why they had not been informed of the decision. One participant described how she felt upon seeing the system for the first time:

It [FaceEx] caught me off guard. I don't know why it's there. I wasn't expecting to see this big square that lit up looking at me, because usually when you enter anything and if you just swipe your card, you're good to go. You don't have to interact with anybody. [The system] looks at yourself when you walk in. It was irritating. (P5)

The routine of entering the makerspace used to involve swiping an ID card without interacting with anyone. P5 emphasized that she was accustomed to the old routine. However, the facial recognition system had changed the process. She had to accept being watched by the system. The scrutiny induced emotional distress.

Similar to P5, most participants in those two categories immediately questioned the need for the system by comparing it with the existing card-swipe system. They argued it was questionable whether the claimed benefits outweighed the disadvantages in respect to invading users' privacy. They also questioned the explanation they later received from the makerspace staff, who claimed that the new system has improving campus security. The explanation met with skepticism from P15, who argued that there was no need to pay extra money for a technology to fulfill a need already being met.. Furthermore, the FaceEx system actually gave rise to a sense of powerlessness:

There's a big difference between you choosing to scan your card and you being recognized by a computer, right? One is an active process, and one is a passive process. If I walk up to the turnstile and I decide I don't want to scan, [so I] turn around and walk away, the turnstile doesn't know who I was. But I walk up to that camera and realize it has scanned my face, I'm stuck. I've been identified. I can't undo that. (P3)

On first encountering the system, these participants either talked with/complained to makerspace staff or tried to avoid/bypass the system. They asked for an explanation in regard to the system. However, they considered the information provided to be vague and/or inaccurate. For example, according to P15 and P19, they had been told the implementation was just a trial and that users' feedback could affect the final decision, although this was not the case:

When I first saw the technology, I asked R about it. He said it was a trial basically, said that overwhelmingly people didn't like it. So my attitude then was that this is temporary, and this is going away. Nobody [will] like this, so they'll actually listen to the people in the space and the students, cater [to] their feelings, and not move towards a shifting baseline model where they move it in during the summer. (P19)

Some participants talked with the makerspace staff to protest the implementation decision. P7 told the staff that she would no longer visit the makerspace if the system were not removed. This was the most extreme instance of avoiding the system.

Several participants commented that they had immediately decided to avoid the FaceEx system. They either went through the handicap gate or attempted to hide from the system by covering their faces:

I tested to see how far it could see me. I walked up, and it was about five feet. So, I was trying to maneuver around the camera to get inside ... I put my hat down. I walked through the gates. (P13)

Curious and Voluntarily Testing

Despite having doubts about the need for the system and related concerns, still some participants (5 out of 19) described their first impressions as "curious," "interested," or "feeling cool" given the novelty of the system. P2, for example, commented that he found the system's accuracy and speed impressive:

I was really surprised how quickly it was able to look at my face and identify who I was, like comparing it to my student ID, and that picture is from 2014 or 2015. Obviously, I probably look a little bit different and it quickly recognizes it [me]. So I was very impressed. It's very good technology. (P2)

Those participants were so curious about the FaceEx system that they reacted by exploring it in a way they found enjoyable. Some participants who responded in this way experimented with the technology, by, for example, trying out different facial expressions, covering half of their face, taking off their glasses, changing their hair styles. They concluded that interacting with the FaceEx system was smoother and more convenient. Some participants even found it interesting when the system made a mistake:

The first time I saw it, it was on J's [another student] Snapchat. And I was like, where is this at? He says it's in the makerspace. So, I went there, me and my friend. [And, when we are scanned,] it shows different people, so we laugh about that. We would like play around and be like "Oh what [will it] accept?" Like we put Beyonce [her picture] on the screen and see if it would accept it. Honestly, I was fascinated the first time, this technology is being placed into school, like saying that we're keeping up with the times and we're not staying behind or something. (P10)

Even though the system did not work as accurately as the makerspace staff claimed, P10 and her friend did not feel disappointed. The system's mistake even inspired them to explore more ways to play with it. They considered the novel FaceEx system to be a sign of "keeping up with the times" and thus felt proud of the university.

5.3 Overall Attitudes and Evaluations Over Time

Changed Attributes

None of the eleven participants who described their first impressions as negative had a change in respect to the deployment decision when this study was conducted. Some said that their concerns had evolved to become more serious in nature based on additional interactions with the system and discussions with others. In addition to their concerns over privacy and data security, they realized that surveillance was another important issue. P15 commented that the FaceEx system reminded him of a totalitarian scenario, a

"Big Brother" feeling, wherein individuals are stripped of their civil rights and subjected to mass surveillance. FaceEx had turned the makerspace from a place where he felt at home to one in which he felt ill at ease. Given this changed sense of space, he approached the question of the FaceEx system with the makerspace staff several times:

> *Because that [FaceEx] does actually create an oppressive environment. It changes my behavior, changes the way I walk into the building, changes how often I come, because I don't like being tracked. It's not just about the facial recognition technology, it's a very, very oppressive, very "BIG BROTHER" feeling. I immediately went to R (staff name). I asked him what the hell is up. (P15)*

Of the four participants who had initially held a middle position, three have a stronger sense of acceptance than had been the case originally. For example, after using the system for a month, P13 explained that he could see that it had advantages over the card-swipe system:

> *I don't know if it's just like because I've grown used to it, I guess I could see the benefits of being like a help rather than a hinder or an invasion of privacy. Because you're choosing to go there. I've just come to accept it. I think I just smile at it every time I go into work, like showing me with my face. (P13)*

However, this acceptance was mixed with, as P13 admitted, helplessness to some extent. Such mixed feelings were echoed by P16, who explained that his acceptance was largely based on the fact that the university already had his photograph and facial information:

> *At first I was confused, you know, for NSA or government tracking monitoring reasons, but I realized that they already had my face on file anyway. Yes, I figured out they already have my facial information. So there's nothing I can do at this point, but you know, if you can't beat them, try to reap the benefits. (P16)*

P14, on the other hand, took a different view. Having used the system for several weeks, he felt that it worked very well, and he appreciated not having to bring his card. He had come to see his initial hesitation as proceeding from a more generalized unwillingness to accept new technologies:

> *Because it's akin to when my dad doesn't trust the text messaging or when my mom like she doesn't want to face time or like my friend's dad does not do banking on the computer, which we can agree is a bit of a silly mindset. But the truth of the matter is he is unwilling to accept modern technology and now it's our turn. Are we gonna fight the current or go with it?*

Of the five participants who had initially expressed a sense of excitement about the deployment, three commented that their attitudes had gradually changed towards neutrality or slightly objecting. The reasons for these changes in attitude were diverse. One participant, an undergraduate intern in the makerspace, mentioned that he had seen several mismatching cases and for this reason had become concerned about the possibility that the system was inherently biased. He thought the system might generate more mismatches for minority groups and that such mismatches might result in them being questioned by the authorities and even disallowed entry. Therefore he felt installing a facial recognition system in a public space cannot be considered until risks of this nature are minimized. Further, two other participants commented that although they were not against the technology per se, now that their initial excitement had faded, they did not support the idea of investing additional money into the system in the makerspace.

Complaints about the Decision-Making Process

Our findings showed that the users' evaluations of the system were based not only on system performance but also involved a cost-benefit analysis and an assessment of the decision-making. Most participants (15 out of 19) complained about the decision-making process, considering it to be unfair to them. Such feeling even shared by those who supported the installation. Most complaints focused on the lack of transparency: users did not have a voice in the decision-making process; their consent was assumed. The university administration and the makerspace manager decided to implement it without consulting with other stakeholders such as staff members (e.g., graduate assistants and undergraduate student interns) and visitors. The participants felt that the university had failed to show respect for the majority of stakeholders, the students, in particular. The makerspace manager's reflections partly confirmed their feelings: Although the FaceEx company had provided information sessions, only the manager was arranged to attend. The lack of information confirmed participants in the opinion that they had not been considered in the decision to install the system. Even the student staff had not been apprised of the full picture of the installation decision. None reported that they had participated in an official training such that they did not know why the system was installed, how the decision was reached, or how the device functioned. After the installation, the makerspace manager had taken a resolutely technocratic and bureaucratic approach to explaining its presence. The approach was top-down and one-way, from manager to staff and then to visitors. Further, there was no indication that the manager had put any effort into determining whether the explanation provided was sufficient.

Attitudes Towards the University

Based on the perceptions of the system itself and the deployment decision-making process, our participants further judged the administration. They criticized the makerspace management team for providing an insufficient explanation of the FaceEx system and speculated given the apparently arbitrary decision to implement the system that it was a result of coercion from administration at the university level. This criticism and speculation contributed to the judgment that they had been treated unfairly by the university.

More than half of the participants (10 out of 19) reported they had turned to the makerspace staff for information at some point but had not received the information they had asked for. The insufficient explanations from staff generated frustration and complaints among visitors. the users of the makerspace:

When I first asked, there was nothing about the police department. I asked R (staff name) about it. R said there's nothing about the police department and he would forward me an email. I never got the email. And then progressively over time, I heard various other things. Eventually, somebody mentioned that the police are really interested in getting this thing hooked up so they can be tracking people across campus. I've been promised emails, and I haven't seen them. (P15)

In P15's case, the result of requesting resulted not in clarity but only in the anticipation of emails that would never arrive—with an increased level of frustration the predictable consequence. P15 turned to other sources and got conflicted information. He then suspected that the makerspace staff were intentionally deceiving him.

It should be noted, however, that the perspective of the makerspace staff was quite different. Some staff members felt that those visitors did not understand how the FaceEx system worked, and their concerns were unreasonable or even ridiculous. Thus, They did not bother to give detailed explanations. For example, P17, the makerspace manager, provided this account:

Other university libraries, they didn't want to [adopt FaceEx], because they would consider that as an invasion of privacy. So that's why this came in here [the makerspace]. We said, okay, we'll play the guinea pig of this experiment. [When explaining the system to people] primarily, I don't go into more detail. I just tell them this is a test. There are people who say that "Oh, I don't want to go in because this machine is recording my face," which they don't understand. First of all, it doesn't record anything, it just matches your face with the database that contains your picture. Because you've been associated with the university and your picture is taken and kept in there. And, people post way more personal data on any other social media. It is just ridiculous to me. (P17)

In the manager's view, privacy concerns in regard to the FaceEx system were not legitimate, and, indeed, this view paved the way for the installation. Aware of the users' concerns in relation to privacy, P17 compared using the FaceEx system to peoples' self-disclosures on social media and on that basis had concluded that the concerns were "ridiculous." According to the manager, users who argued against the system did not understand it such that their concerns were baseless. Yet, presumably, she could have addressed their concerns readily enough. However, she was unwilling to offer an explanation. Instead, she simply told the users that the system had been installed as a test.

Most participants (12 out of 19) further speculated that the installation was the result of coercion on the part of the university administration. Because the university administration had supported the implementation, some participants saw the system as an expression of the will of the university administration. In fact, some participants explicitly connected the installation with the university's surveillance infrastructure. For instance, P3, a faculty member, speculated that the university's goal was to use the system to track students and evaluate their performance accordingly.

In addition to speculating about the system in regard to specific functions, some participants perceived FaceEx as a symbol of the administration's pernicious attempts to regulate their actions:

And I think that's gonna hurt the division and the goals of the makerspace in the long term. I have seen through many summers, the university constantly making really large structural changes while the students are gone because they know that the students are against those activities. (P15)

P15's speculation was not based just on his observations and perceptions of the FaceEx system's implementation. Rather, he connected the implementation to the university's past practices pertaining to making structural changes. He considered the implementation of the FaceEx system as one of a series of malfeasances on the part of the university administration—i.e., yet another example of the abuse of power. Similar speculations actually hurt the participants' feelings in relation to their sense of themselves as members of the university community. For example, P7 expected that the university to be open to all community members and used to feel proud about it. However, the implementation of FaceEx had led P7 to feel disappointed and even "betrayed" by the university. The makerspace had been created in what had been a library and the community nature and connection of this public space had changed for the worse in P7's opinion. Thus, she had decided to avoid FaceEx by no longer visiting the makerspace.

With the exception of two cases of ongoing resistance (P7 and P15), most participants whether or not they were in favor of the system felt they had no choice but to accept it. For example, P11 noted that he believed the power of the administration to be unchallengeable. Challenging such a powerful administration was like "fighting with a current" to him. He did not think that the university administration would change their decision.

6 Discussion and Implementation

6.1 The Controversy Over FRT and the Need for Pre-deployment Communication and Education

According to our findings, facial recognition is a controversial technology that easily triggers strong and often negative responses in a university setting. In deciding whether or not to accept such a technology, the participants treated its features as "comparative rather than discrete [19]." Users spontaneously made sense of the decision by comparing it with other decisions. Through comparison, users construct standards and examine current decisions in reference to those standards. Specifically, in this study, the participants compared the facial recognition system with the card-swipe system in terms of cost, security performance, privacy risks, novelty, etc. They came to the conclusion overall that the FaceEx system was more invasive thus would hurt their privacy. They further questioned whether there was a need for the system.

Whereas most participants opposed the implementation, some appreciated the system's novelty. This matches previous research's claim that simply framing a controversial technology as innovative and cutting-edge may incentivize a certain segment of the population to adopt it [20]. However, general controversy surrounding FRT means that it can be difficult for an organization to mediate between its proponents and opponents and in particular to resolve opponents' concerns. Similar to previous studies, concerns of FRT included privacy, data security, and possible bias against minority groups. Our findings also highlighted issues pertaining to mass surveillance and possible abuse of authority as well as in regard to the destruction of community ties. None of those concerns were addressed by the university at any level, which was a major reason for the participants' initially negative impressions of the implementation and for a further deepening their antipathy toward university administration. Our findings also suggested first impressions counted: After encountering the technology over time, the participants overall generally expressed negative perceptions of it: Those who had initially opposed the technology continue to oppose it. Those who had supported the installation gradually became opposed to it. Only those who had initially taken a moderate position became somewhat more accepting of it though in most cases reluctantly so. No pre-deployment user education was provided: not only did the university administration and the makerspace manager fail to proactively provide information, they did not even notify users of the installation such that the latter had become aware of the system only upon directly encountering it for the first time. It is also the case that the makerspace manager and the other makerspace staff did not took users' questions or complaints seriously. They simply assumed that users would eventually accept the technology.

6.2 Social Perspective of Technology Acceptability

Although most participants expressed negative perceptions of FaceEx and did not support its implementation, the technology itself was not the only factor in eliciting this hostility. Other considerations had come into play, including the participants' perceptions of a lack of cost-effectiveness associated with the technology itself, the university administration's control of the decision-making process and a lack of transparency in that process, a lack of both accuracy and timeliness in relation to the information provided to the users, and a lack of respect shown to the users.

The decision-making process should have been participatory rather than persuasive and autocratic. However, by definition and design, it did include the stakeholders. The makerspace manager and the university administration had made the decision to implement the system without consulting other stakeholders such as other staff members and visitors. The administration did not take any steps to foster technology acceptance such as by communicating with stakeholders and offering opportunities to discuss risks and benefits in an open way before installing the technology. The administration also failed to provide transparency in terms of the algorithm governing the workings of the facial recognition system. As our findings showed, although the makerspace manager argued that the facial recognition system neither films people nor keeps a record of their movements, few participants were aware that. This lack of transparency led the participants to be distrustful of the facial recognition system, the makerspace staff, and the university.

The reflections shared by most of the participants show that neither the university administration nor the makerspace manager provided a sufficient rationale to justify the system's installation or an account of how the decision had been made, not even to all student staffs. We argue that it is not only the content but also the power structure that matters in terms of offering an explanation. Our findings show that there are several levels of power and authority: visitors; makerspace staff; the manager, and the university administration. (It was possible the police department had a role; however, it was unclear since they cancelled the scheduled interviews with us.) Although most of the users took some actions in terms of appealing against or resisting the installation, none of these actions were recognized by the university administration or the makerspace manager. Despite the fact that some staff members (e.g., P6, a student intern) shared similar privacy concerns and could have advocated for those concerns themselves, they chose to just repeat what the manager had told them to users. Thus participants had a difficult time obtaining proper explanations from any unit (unable to reach high-level administration and low-level student staff didn't have much information or unwilling to tell), as well as attributing responsibility to any single unit. To ensure a high level of technology acceptance, decision-makers should initiate communication and possible corrective measures, rather than waiting for people who are not decision makers in the institutional structure to fight for themselves.

As discussed above, the participants used a comparative approach to assessing the justifiability of the deployment decision. However, the reality is that whatever the results of their comparisons, their only choice was to refrain from visiting the makerspace. This fact highlights the powerless of the participants with just one exception, i.e., P17, the makerspace manager who in line with other library spaces on campus could have opposed the university administration. Further, when introducing a new technology, especially a controversial one, decisionmakers should not eliminate other possible choices and force people to adapt to the new system. In this case, mounting the new system over the old system in the main entry meant the visitors would inevitably expose their faces to the facial recognition system such that they were deprived of any choice in the matter.

7 Limitations, Future Work, and Conclusion

In this study, we investigated the participants' encounters with a facial recognition system in a university setting. We reported participants' first impressions and reactions, if and why their attitudes changed, concerns they have toward the implementation, and how they extended their judgements from the technology to the organization. However, the generalizability of this study is limited by the sample size and the snowball sampling technique used. We plan to collect more interview data in regard to matters such as how the decision was made, how the student staff members were trained, and how they and the users of the makerspace evaluated their explanations about the technology and the installation. Further, we will reframe the project from an organizational justice perspective. Quantitative data will also be collected via, for example, structured surveys administered to a broader range of users in order to verify and enhance the findings of the present study and create a basis for establishing whether or not over time a shift in terms of attitudes towards FRT technology has taken place. We argued that the implementation of technology in organizational settings could engender intense experiences of unfairness, especially when the technology has already generated controversy. Moreover, this issue extends far beyond just a few concerns raised by a small number of privacy-oriented people given that it has a direct effect on entire societies including in regard to the ways in which people move in physical spaces. Moving forward, as public criticism mounts and the use of facial recognition becomes more prevalent, considerably more research is needed if we are to understand the ways in which controversial technologies are implemented in institutional/organizational settings, the kinds of experiences they engender, and people's responses to those technologies and the process through which they are introduced.

References

1. Durkin, E.: New York school district's facial recognition system sparks privacy fears. The Guardian (2019)
2. Selwyn, N.: Digital lessons? Public opinions on the use of digital technologies in Australian schools (2019). https://www.monash.edu/data/assets/pdf_file/0008/1626236/Education-Futures-Research-Report-Digital-Lessons.pdf
3. Bhagavatula, R., Ur, B., Lacovino, K., Su, M.K., Cranor, L.F., Savvides, M.: Biometric authentication on iPhone and Android: usability, perceptions, and influences on adoption. Presented at the Workshop on Usable Security 2015, San Diego, CA (2015). https://ink.library.smu.edu.sg/sis_research/3967
4. Ellerbrok, A.: Playful biometrics: controversial technology through the lens of play. Sociol. Q. **52**(4), 528–547 (2011). https://doi.org/10.1111/j.1533-8525.2011.01218.x
5. Lai, X., Rau, P.-L.P.: Has facial recognition technology been misused? A public perception model of facial recognition scenarios. Comput. Hum. Behav. **124**, 106894 (2021). https://doi.org/10.1016/j.chb.2021.106894
6. Seng, S., Nasrullah Al-Ameen, M., Wright, M.: A first look into users' perceptions of facial recognition in the physical world. Comput. Secur. **105**, 102227 (2021). https://doi.org/10.1016/j.cose.2021.102227
7. Stark, L., Stanhaus, A., Anthony, D.L.: 'I don't want someone to watch me while I'm working': gendered views of facial recognition technology in workplace surveillance. J. Assoc. Inf. Sci. Technol. **71**(9), 1074–1088 (2020). https://doi.org/10.1002/asi.24342
8. Noble, S.U.: Algorithms of Oppression. New York University Press, New York (2018). https://doi.org/10.18574/9781479833641
9. Reilly, C.: Facial-recognition software inaccurate in 98% of cases, report finds. Cnet.com (2018). https://www.cnet.com/news/facial-recognition-software-inaccurate-in-98-of-metropolitan-police-cases-reports/
10. Buolamwini, J., Gebru, T.: Gender shades: intersectional accuracy disparities in commercial gender classification. In: Proceedings of the 1st Conference on Fairness, Accountability and Transparency, pp. 77–91 (2018). http://proceedings.mlr.press/v81/buolamwini18a.html?mod=article_inline
11. Hachim, E.K., Wechsler, H.: Face verification subject to varying (age, ethnicity, and gender) demographics using deep learning. J. Biom. Biostat. **7**(323) (2016). https://doi.org/10.4172/2155-6180.1000323
12. Klare, B.F., Burge, M.J., Klontz, J.C., Vorder Bruegge, R.W., Jain, A.K.: Face recognition performance: role of demographic information. Proc. IEEE Trans. Inf. Forensics Secur. **6**, 1789–1801 (2012). https://doi.org/10.1109/TIFS.2012.2214212
13. Allyn, B.: The computer got it wrong': how facial recognition led to false arrest of black man. NPR (2020). https://www.npr.org/2020/06/24/882683463/the-computer-got-it-wrong-how-facial-recognition-led-to-a-false-arrest-in-michig
14. Hill, K.: Another arrest, and jail time, due to a bad facial recognition match. New York Times (2020). https://www.nytimes.com/2020/12/29/technology/facial-recognition-misidentify-jail.html
15. Akhtar, Z., Rattani, A.: A face in any form: new challenges and opportunities for face recognition technology. Computer **50**(4), 80–90 (2017). https://doi.org/10.1109/MC.2017.119
16. Korshunov, P., Marcel, S.: Deepfakes: a new threat to face recognition? Assessment and detection (2018). https://arxiv.org/abs/1812.08685
17. Andrejevic, M., Selwyn, N.: Facial recognition technology in schools: critical questions and concerns. Learn. Media Technol. **45**(2), 115–128 (2020). https://doi.org/10.1080/17439884.2020.1686014

18. Charmaz, K.: Constructing Grounded Theory, 2nd edn. SAGE Publications, Thousand Oaks (2014)
19. Wolfe, K., Bjornstad, D.J., Russell, M., Kerchner, N.D.: A framework for analyzing dialogues over the acceptability of controversial technologies. Sci. Technol. Hum. Values **27**(1), 134–159 (2002). https://doi.org/10.1177/016224390202700106
20. Petrun, E.L., Iles, I., Roberts, H., Liu, B.F., Ackerman, G.: Diffusing controversial technology: barriers, incentives, and lessons learned. Rev. Commun. **15**(2), 140–160 (2015). https://doi.org/10.1080/15358593.2015.1058410

The Need for Transparent Demographic Group Trade-Offs in Credit Risk and Income Classification

Ananth Balashankar[1,2(✉)] and Alyssa Lees[1]

[1] Google AI, New York, USA
ananth@nyu.edu
[2] New York University, New York, USA

Abstract. Prevalent methodology towards constructing fair machine learning (ML) systems, is to enforce a strict equality metric for demographic groups based on protected attributes like race and gender. While definitions of fairness in philosophy are varied, mitigating bias in ML classifiers often relies on demographic parity-based constraints across sub-populations. However, enforcing such constraints blindly can lead to undesirable trade-offs between group-level accuracy if groups possess different underlying sampled population metrics, an occurrence that is surprisingly common in real-world applications like credit risk and income classification. Similarly, attempts to relax hard constraints may lead to unintentional degradation in classification performance, without benefit to any demographic group. In these increasingly likely scenarios, we make the case for transparent human intervention in making the trade-offs between the accuracies of demographic groups. We propose that transparency in trade-offs between demographic groups should be a key tenet of ML design and implementation. Our evaluation demonstrates that a transparent human-in-the-loop trade-off technique based on the Pareto principle increases both overall and group-level accuracy by 9.5% and 9.6% respectively, in two commonly explored UCI datasets for credit risk and income classification.

1 Introduction

In recent discussions of ethical ML algorithms, evaluating fairness has been frequently predicated on defining constraints based on specific protected attributes, such as race or gender [1,2]. These attributes should **not** demonstrate conditionally discriminative behavior while learning classification targets. If care is not taken in the construction of an ML model, works such as [3] and [4] have shown that inequalities in underlying data distributions can be amplified in the predicted output, leading to runaway feedback loops. Recent works [5] have argued that examining the intersectionality of multiple protected attributes is crucial for establishing coherent standards of fairness. However, real-world data sub-populations often display varying underlying sampling distributions, bias and noise. We argue that principles towards *fair* ML should encourage transparency

M. Smits (Ed.): iConference 2022, LNCS 13192, pp. 344–354, 2022.
https://doi.org/10.1007/978-3-030-96957-8_30

in the trade-offs between demographic group accuracy in a classification task and at a minimum be able to reflect their true underlying population distributions. At a fixed sample size, as the number of protected attributes increases, the intersectional subgroup populations tend to decrease in size. In these scenarios, it is evident that any classifier which does not perform worse on all groups can never be *fair* [6]. Hence, in this paper we aim to understand the research question of how the trade-offs between demographic groups affect the evaluation of different methodologies proposed that are aimed to improve classification accuracy. To quantify this, we look to the rich literature of "individual fairness" which defines fairness with respect to a similarity metric between two individuals and enforces that similar individuals are treated similarly, within an error bound [5,7,8]. We find this definition to be useful in allowing us to continue to ensure that minority demographic group populations perform at their best accuracy while ensuring that majority demographic groups do not suffer a large decrease in group-level accuracy.

Using this transparent Pareto-principle of Efficiency [9], popular in social welfare and economics, we argue that trade-offs between demographic group accuracy undertaken by ML algorithms in high-stakes applications like credit risk and income classification [10] should be made transparent in order to be examined against socio-technical norms in that application domain [11–13]. We have been motivated by the insight that many fairness problems in existing classification tasks for specific subpopulations can be remedied by controlled data collection, subject to ethical considerations [14,15]. As such, we suggest that in the spirit of achieving fair outcomes, when learning on datasets with varying demographic group sample sizes, how we weigh the loss suffered by each demographic group can be a critical choice and should be transparent.

In the domain of credit risk assessment, the trade-off between the accuracy of demographic groups has implications on financial justice across demographic groups. For example, older married male individuals have better accuracy than younger single female individuals for credit risk assessment. This means that even a seemingly group-blind ML algorithm can have significantly different accuracy across demographic groups. Similarly, in the income classification task, Caucasian male individuals have much better baseline accuracy than non-Caucasian female individuals in the United States. Therefore, to build transparent and fair ML systems, we show that the trade-offs between these demographic groups cannot be avoided, but rather should be an integral part of the transparent design of any socio-technical ML system. We illustrate one such transparent trade-off mechanism by arguing for efficiency based on the Pareto principle, where degradation in the accuracy of one group should not occur without improving another group's accuracy. In this paper, we compare our transparent Pareto-principle based trade-off with several other strict equality-based constraints and demonstrate an increase in 9.5% and 9.6% overall and group-level accuracy respectively on both the credit risk and income classification tasks.

2   Motivation: Trade-Offs in the Real World

COMPAS. A ML model (COMPAS tool) was used for determining the risk of recidivism in Broward County, Florida, USA. ProPublica [16] found in an independent investigation involving 18,610 people over 2 years that black males were twice as likely to be misclassified by the model as high risk as compared to white males. This scenario highlights the critical need for auditing existing decision-making systems (including the ones based on human experts) and understanding the trade-offs made in their design. In such a high stakes scenario, ideally, a decision-making system that achieves the highest group level metrics (such as accuracy) is required. By incorporating inductive biases based on racial and social justice, one could hope to achieve the end objective of improving the Pareto front transparently. If we do not attempt to evaluate and discover Pareto efficient classifiers, a domain expert choosing a classifier might end up making trade-offs of accuracy and fairness among inefficient classifiers.

Gender Shades. Certain image recognition models were discovered to have lower accuracy for one particular group (darker females) than other groups in the Gender Shades project [17]. The intervention undertaken to resolve this discrepancy involved collecting better data for the poor performing group (females with darker skin tone). The progress from such interventions amounts to discovering better group accuracies on the Pareto frontier, as opposed to restricting the models to strict equality among groups. Here too, the authors of the project, Buolamwini and Gebru, advocate for a complete ban of ML models for facial recognition tasks since these models are not advanced enough to perform with high accuracy on all groups independent of skin tone and gender, without encoding spurious correlations. Hence, a ML model needs to be transparent in the trade-offs that it implicitly makes to gain socio-technical acceptance in the real world.

3   Transparent Trade-Offs

The Pareto frontier has been used to characterize the trade-offs between more than one dimension in multiple objective learning [18,19]. It characterizes solutions such that no point on the Pareto curve dominates another point on all the dimensions across which we measure an objective. Evaluating the Pareto curve for any ML classifier can be critical in making transparent trade-offs between demographic groups [20].

3.1   Pareto Front in ML Based Models

In our analysis of the German Credit and Adult Census Datasets, we take an example of a feedforward neural network model with up to 3 layers with each layer containing 256, 128 and 64 hidden units respectively. We then perform a sweep of the hyperparameters by varying the depth of the neural network, learning rates and L1 and L2 regularization parameters [21], and the training data made available to train the network (specific demographic groups versus the entire dataset). Each network was trained multiple times with randomized seeds for initializing the parameters of the network. This gives us a wide range of group-level accuracies along each of the demographic groups we slice the accuracy of the model. We then constructed the Pareto front of these group-level accuracies after varying the hyper-parameters, with each group corresponding to a dimension of the Pareto front. Note that visualization of the Pareto front can be tricky, given that in most real-world applications, the demographic groups are more than three. Hence, we need a principled approach using which a domain practitioner can argue about their choice of a specific classifier on the Pareto front. In Fig. 1, we see that in simulated data with two demographic groups, a domain expert can trade-off one group's performance with another by choosing different points on the Pareto front. Also, we can see that a trade-off is inevitable unless we assume that the Pareto front exactly intersects with the hyperplane where all demographic groups perform equally (x = y in case of two dimensions).

3.2   Pareto Trade-Offs

Having established that a trade-off between group-level accuracy should be conducted on the Pareto front, we now provide an example where such a trade-off is transparent and based on a Pareto Efficient and fair principle. In this principle, a domain expert might choose a classifier where each group's performance sacrifices accuracy equally. For example, in the German Credit risk assessment task, older male individuals can achieve their best accuracy of 91% among all the points on the Pareto front, whereas younger female individuals can achieve only 73%. In this case, the Pareto-based trade-off would advocate for a classifier that achieves 89% and 71.4% on the two groups respectively, each of them about 2.2% below (Pareto Loss) their respective optimal choices on the Pareto front. This choice is different than the one a domain expert would choose based on the principle of strict equality or Demographic Parity [22] between the groups (both groups at 73%, i.e. zero Parity Loss). We acknowledge that both of these choices might be valid in different contexts based on the principles the corresponding algorithmic decision-making system prescribes. But, the choice needs to be transparent and cannot be masked behind the objective of minimizing overall classification error. This transparency allows people who apply for credit to contend the trade-offs and the corresponding principles in automated decision-making systems. Hence, with transparency, the people who were previously left out of the decision-making systems' design can be involved and provide them the ability to appeal the trade-offs made by such ML models.

4   Evaluation

4.1   Baselines

We compare our transparent trade-off approach with optimization techniques that use fairness constraints such as Equality Constraint [3], Adversarial [23],

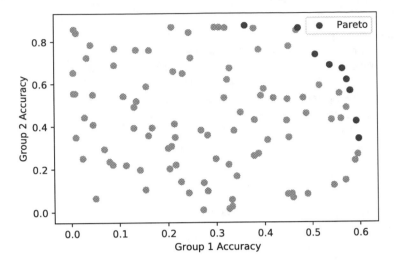

Fig. 1. An illustration of a two group-setting plotting group-level accuracy and its corresponding Pareto front (in blue) shows that demographic group trade-offs are implicit and unavoidable in ML systems. (Color figure online)

and Min-Max fairness [24]. Zhao et al. [3] aim to lower the sum of absolute discrepancy of all group accuracy from the overall accuracy (Parity loss), while Beutel et al. [23] adversarially attempt to nudge the classifier such that it cannot predict the protected attributes. Martinez et al. [24] aim to maximize the accuracy of the least performing demographic group.

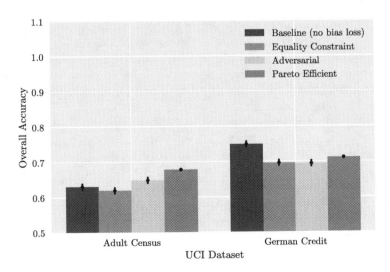

Fig. 2. Comparison for 2 UCI datasets showing that the pareto-based transparent trade-off achieves better overall accuracy than other fairness constrained classifiers.

4.2   UCI Adult Dataset

The UCI Census Adult dataset focuses on the prediction of income as a binary variable (>\$50K, <=\$50K) based on demographic information. Protected attributes selected are gender and race and are denoted as binary categorical variables. We consider the 4 groups at the intersection of the protected attributes, to overcome the limitations of group fairness as outlined in [25]. The dataset has 48,842 instances out of which 20% is held out as test data, while the remaining is used for training and cross-validation. There are 14 attributes out of which 6 are continuous and 8 variables are categorical. Table 1 shows the Pareto loss, i.e. how much each group deviates from the pseudo-optimal of the respective group for the UCI Census Adult dataset. Based on the Pareto principle, we were able to choose an optimal point on the Pareto front that ensured that each of the demographic groups perform optimally. In our transparent trade-off on the Pareto front, each of the groups has better individual accuracy than the other approaches and thus better overall accuracy as shown in Fig. 2. Figure 3 demonstrates that our approach arrives at a better classifier on all demographic groups. Some groups even exceed the baseline accuracy (computed using the average of all unconstrained optimization results) due to an extensive swap of the hyperparameters and transparently choosing the Pareto optimal classifier.

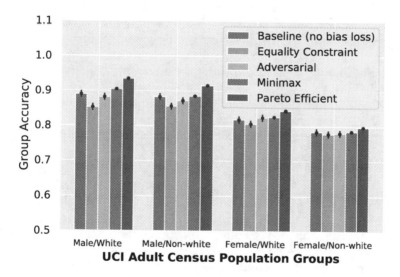

Fig. 3. Group accuracy comparison shows that we achieve Pareto dominating group level accuracy for all groups in UCI Adult dataset.

Table 1. Comparison of test losses in UCI Adult dataset - False Positive Rate (FPR), False Negative Rate (FNR), Parity and Pareto Losses. Our Pareto-based trade-off has no difference as compared to the Pareto optimal group-accuracy, while [3] minimizes Parity loss.

Model	FPR	FNR	Parity loss	Pareto loss
Baseline (no bias loss)	0.253	0.747	0.199	0.016
Equality constraint[3]	0.283	**0.712**	**0.167**	0.133
Adversarial [23]	0.224	0.769	0.226	0.077
Min-max [24]	0.202	0.773	0.218	0.075
Pareto efficient	**0.165**	0.830	0.250	**0.000**

4.3   UCI German Credit Dataset

The UCI German Credit risk assessment dataset involves predicting credit type as a binary label (good or bad) from demographic information where the protected attributes selected are age, gender and personal status. Each of these protected attributes is binarized and the intersection of these 3 attributes is considered as the groups in our study. There are 1000 instances in the dataset with a total of 20 categorical attributes. We hold out a random 20 % as test data over which we present the results. The evaluation of this dataset is determined by a cost matrix where the false positives are considered 5 times more costly than a false negative. The final accuracy reported takes this into account. Similar to the UCI Adult Dataset, in Fig. 4, we see that choosing a point based on our Pareto principle, we increase the group-level accuracies as compared to the equality constraints [22], adversarial loss [23] and minimax [24] optimization techniques. The 5 groups (out of the total 8) are shown in the UCI German Credit Dataset, as the rest of the groups do not have enough samples (<100).

4.4   Sample Size Inconsistencies

The use of explicit demographic attributes in real-world scenarios is sometimes a hard constraint. One example is legislation enforcing fairness around disparate impact [26,27]. In simplified examples, exploring the intersectionality of protected attributes may be appropriate. For example, in this paper, we explore two gender and two race subgroups in the evaluation of the UCI Adult dataset, which translates to four separate groups. It is conceivable that in a real-world application, the intersection of gender and race subgroups could extend into **many** different groups. As the intersectionality of groups grows, a group's sample size will likely be insufficient. In the case of the UCI German credit risk assessment dataset, the attribute - marriage status, with five possible values, is treated as a protected attribute along with gender and age. However, in the dataset, there were **no** samples containing both the attributes of young, female and being married.

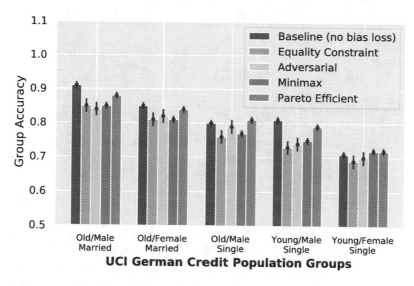

Fig. 4. Group accuracy comparison showing we achieve optimal group level accuracy for all groups in UCI German Credit dataset among constrained classifiers.

Despite the impossibility results of achieving fairness in the extreme case of subgroup sized one, there is still a need to highlight cases where simple (linear) models are inadequately applied in datasets with complex underlying subgroup distributions [16,28]. The ability to transparently argue about the trade-offs made in designing the required model along with the limitations of small sample sizes for certain demographic groups will guide the choices made by practitioners and ML researchers. Through our work, we see that even an ML model that does not explicitly perform a trade-off between demographic groups has already decided the trade-off implicitly.

Using the theory of sample complexity based on Rademacher complexity [29,30], if we assume all the hypotheses are linear with VC Dimension d, we can rank the hardness of learning the target for each demographic group, and order them (Table 2 - higher numbered rank has higher complexity values). The sample complexity to learn a PAC algorithm which achieves error of less than ϵ with probability δ in all k subgroups is lower bounded by m:

$$m = O(\frac{ln^2(k)}{\epsilon}((d + k)ln(\frac{1}{\epsilon}) + kln(\frac{1}{\delta}))) \tag{1}$$

In the UCI Adult Census dataset, the ordering of the actual subgroup sample sizes ($4 > 2 > 3 > 1$) reveals that new samples are needed to match the desired sample complexity ordering ($3 > 2 > 4 > 1$). Specifically, more samples for subgroup 3 (Female/White) need to be gathered than for subgroup 2 (Male/Non-white) to ensure the ordering of actual sample sizes aligns with that of the sample complexities. Similarly, in the German Credit Dataset, Table 2 shows disparity in the order of the actual sample sizes ($3 > 2 > 4 > 1$) as

Table 2. Comparison of sample complexity ranking for probably approximately metric fairness with actual subgroup sizes of subgroups

#	Group	Complexity rank	Sample size (rank)
	UCI adult dataset		
1	Male/White	1	2,129 (1)
2	Male/Non-white	3	8,642 (3)
3	Female/White	4	2,616 (2)
4	Female/Non-white	2	19,174 (4)
	UCI German credit dataset		
1	Old/Male	3	50 (1)
2	Old/Female	4	310 (3)
3	Young/Male	2	548 (4)
4	Young/Female	1	92 (2)

compared to desired sample complexity $(2 > 1 > 3 > 4)$. This implies that in the UCI German Credit dataset, more new samples from group 2 (Old/Female) than from group 3 (Young/Male) should be drawn for us to make a balanced and transparent choice while performing trade-offs. Similarly, more samples from subgroup 1 (Old/Male) need to be collected than from subgroup 4 (Young/Female) to remove any inversion in the ranking of complexities and actual group sample sizes to ensure that the trade-offs are not performed inefficiently due to insufficient sample sizes.

5   Conclusion

We advocate for transparency in the demographic group accuracy trade-offs in high-stakes real-world applications like credit risk and income classification tasks. We demonstrate that transparency in how we balance group-level accuracies can lead to better classifiers being explored on the Pareto front while improving overall accuracy too by 9.5%. Further, we caveat that trade-offs on demographic groups with smaller sample sizes should be taken into account and appropriate data collection exercises should be conducted. We argue that for the development of an ethical AI framework for policy and decision-makers, transparency in the group-level accuracy trade-offs is critical. Future work to extend this analysis to more complex ML models may provide principled standards for transparent trade-offs between groups in other application domains along with mechanisms to contest them.

References

1. Salamanca, C.D.J.R., et al.: A local law in relation to automated decision systems used by agencies (2018)

2. Bickel, P.J., Hammel, E.A., O'Connell, J.W.: Sex bias in graduate admissions: data from Berkeley. Science **187**(4175), 398–404 (1975)
3. Zhao, J., Wang, T., Yatskar, M., Ordonez, V., Chang, K.W., Reducing gender bias amplification using corpus-level constraints. In: EMNLP, Men also like shopping (2017)
4. Ensign, D., Friedler, S.A., Neville, S., Scheidegger, C.E., Venkatasubramanian, S.: Runaway feedback loops in predictive policing. CoRR, abs/1706.09847 (2017)
5. Kearns, M., Neel, S., Roth, A., Wu, Z.S.: Auditing and learning for subgroup fairness. In: ICML, Preventing fairness gerrymandering (2018)
6. Menon, A.K., Williamson, R.C.: The cost of fairness in binary classification. In: Proceedings of the 1st Conference on Fairness, Accountability and Transparency, volume 81 of Proceedings of Machine Learning Research, pp. 107–118. PMLR, New York, NY, USA, 23–24 Feburary 2018 New York, NY, USA, 23–24 Feburary 2018
7. Dwork, C., Hardt, M., Reingold, O., Zemel, R.S.: Fairness through awareness. In: ITCS, Toniann Pitassi (2012)
8. Dwork, C., Ilvento, C.: Fairness under composition. In: ITCS (2019)
9. Godfrey, P., Shipley, R., Gryz, J.: Algorithms and analyses for maximal vector computation. VLDB J. **16**(1), 5–28 (2007)
10. Dheeru, D., Taniskidou, E.K.: UCI machine learning repository (2017)
11. Selbst, A.D., Boyd, D., Friedler, S.A., Venkatasubramanian, S., Vertesi, J.: Fairness and abstraction in sociotechnical systems. In: FAT* 2019 (2019)
12. Grgic-Hlaca, N.: The case for process fairness in learning : Feature selection for fair decision making. In: NIPS Symposium on Machine Learning and the Law, vol. 1, pp. 2 (2016)
13. Madras, D., Creager, E., Pitassi, T., Zemel, R.: Fairness through causal awareness: learning causal latent-variable models for biased data. In: FAT* 2019 (2019)
14. Buolamwini, J., Gebru, T.: Gender shades: Intersectional accuracy disparities in commercial gender classification. In: FAT (2018)
15. Chen, I., Johansson, F.D., Sontag, D.A.: Why is my classifier discriminatory? CoRR, abs/1805.12002 (2018)
16. Angwin, S.M.A., Larson, J.E., Kirchner, L.: How we analyzed the compas recidivism algorithm.(2016)
17. Foster, D., Vohra, R.: An economic argument for affirmative action. Rationality Soc. **4**(2), 176–188 (1992)
18. Ali, J., Zafar, M.B., Singla, A., Gummadi, K.P.:. Loss-aversively fair classification. In: AIES 2019, pp. 211–218 (2019)
19. Rawls, J.: A Theory of Justice (1971)
20. Agarwal, A., Beygelzimer, A., Dudík, M., John, L., Wallach, H.M.: A reductions approach to fair classification. CoRR, abs/1803.02453 (2018)
21. Andrew, Y.N.: Feature selection, l_1 vs. l_2 regularization, and rotational invariance. In: Proceedings of the Twenty-First International Conference on Machine Learning, ICML 2004, p. 78. Association for Computing Machinery, New York, NY, USA (2004) , New York, NY, USA (2004)
22. Hardt, M., Price, E., Srebro, N.: Equality of opportunity in supervised learning. CoRR, abs/1610.02413 (2016)
23. Beutel, A., Chen, J., Zhao, Z., Hsin Chi, E.H.: Data decisions and theoretical implications when adversarially learning fair representations. CoRR, abs/1707.00075 (2017)
24. Martinez, N., Bertran, M., Sapiro, G.: A multi objective perspective. In: ICML, Minimax pareto fairness (2020)

25. Kearns, M., Neel, S., Roth, A., Wu, Z.S.: Preventing fairness gerrymandering: Auditing and learning for subgroup fairness. CoRR, abs/1711.05144 (2017)
26. Supreme Court of the United States. Griggs v. duke power co. (1971)
27. Feldman, M., Friedler, S.A., Moeller, J., Scheidegger, C., Venkatasubramanian, S.: Certifying and removing disparate impact. In: Proceedings of the 21th ACM SIGKDD International Conference on Knowledge Discovery and Data Mining, KDD 2015, pp. 259–268. ACM, New York, NY, USA (2015)
28. Chouldechova, A., G'Sell, M.: Fairer and more accurate, but for whom? 06 (2017)
29. Mohri, M., Rostamizadeh, A., Talwalkar, A.: Foundations of Machine Learning. MIT Press, Adaptive Computation and Machine Learning (2012)
30. Shawe-Taylor, J., Anthony, M., Biggs, N.: Bounding sample size with the vapnik-chervonenkis dimension. **42**, 65–73 (1993)

Data Capitalism, Microsoft's Planetary Computer, and the Biodiversity Informatics Community

Przemyslaw Matt Lukacz[✉]

New York, USA
pml2130@columbia.edu

Abstract. Joining the growing literature on the design of information infrastructures for the Anthropocene, this paper explores the Big Tech's efforts to support biodiversity informatics community. Drawing on the information infrastructure studies, political economy of science, and critical data studies, the paper aims to shed light on the reception of artificial intelligence and cloud computing on the part of a biodiversity data network. The preliminary interview findings reported here suggest a cautious optimism about the funding of biodiversity informatics, yet likewise underscore the importance of considering political-economy of infrastructures, both among their users and designers.

Keywords: Environmental information infrastructures · Political economy · Biodiversity informatics

1 Introduction

Information infrastructures are a key component of the humanity's response to environmental crises such as biodiversity loss and the sixth great extinction [1]. Yet, as a growing number of scholars note, environmental impact of computing [12, 15], environmental data [26, 27], and environmental knowledge infrastructures [16] are still on the periphery of research interests of information scholars. This trend is changing—the theme of 2020 iConference "Sustainable Digital Communities" is but one testament to the new ways of problematizing nature in information studies. Three trends in information infrastructure studies related to environment could be distinguished. First, there are studies posing questions about the environmental costs of computing infrastructures [19, 28]. Second, an emerging literature draws attention to the co-constitution of nature and infrastructures [38], or the analysis of data centers as a "techno-organic jungle" [53]. Third—and this is perhaps the longest-standing tradition—information scholars have studied the design and implementation of information infrastructure which serve environmental sciences [3, 43]. The following discussion draws on the third set of concerns by problematizing the interactions between biodiversity informatics community and the data analytics industry.

I frame my analysis within the broader concerns about the private-state hybridization and the processes of privatization of environmental observation infrastructures. Part

M. Smits (Ed.): iConference 2022, LNCS 13192, pp. 355–369, 2022.
https://doi.org/10.1007/978-3-030-96957-8_31

of this literature has focused on the post-Second World War influence of the national security concerns and its influence on the development of environmental monitoring and modelling [2, 8, 9, 14, 18], and the commercialization of environmental data [46, 49, 50]. I mobilize these intellectual currents to ask: What changes for environmental monitoring in the era of "surveillance capitalism"? This question builds on previous analysis of the design of information infrastructures in ecology [3, 4, 7, 43] and adds the focus on the new economic reality of data capitalism.

Two key queries of this paper are: what are the consequences of the public-private partnership for environmental data practices and information infrastructures? And what can biodiversity management look like in the era of surveillance capitalism? I unpack four distinct problems emerging as a result of Big Tech's support for environmental monitoring. The categorization of this themes emerged from oral interviews I have conducted, but they are all not without precedence in the information infrastructure studies. Based on my preliminary research with conservation data experts from the Global Earth Observatory Biodiversity Observation Network (GEO BON), I show that while the investment in environmental knowledge infrastructures coming from the data analytics industry is welcomed among this user community and has a potential to improve response to the biodiversity crisis, the tactics of such investment are imbricated with the public-facing performance of environmental stewardship. I argue that the members of the GEO BON secretariat are in a unique position to illuminate the role of data analytics industry for the biodiversity informatics community as first, the GEO BON-Microsoft partnership is among the first one if its kind, and second, as an organization, GEO BON is concerned with comprehensive array of activities of the wider biodiversity informatics community.

This paper responds to a call made by Megan Finn and Daniela K. Rosner in the 2019 iConference paper in which they "suggest that information scholars have a critical opportunity to remake next-generation computing fields by noticing the entanglements of world-building practices, bodies, and environments" [21]. Finn and Rosner argue that information studies scholars have a critical opportunity for "reintegrating a concern for nature into our analyses" [21]. In their syllabus also entitled "Troubled Worlds," Finn, Rosner and colleagues [22] articulate an environmentally oriented information studies, or the question of how to design "Knowledge Infrastructures for the Anthropocene," to use Paul Edwards' words [16]. As this paper shows, environmental knowledge infrastructures are increasingly imbricated in global politics and digital economy. Hence, I wish to draw a connection with the growing importance of nature and environment in information studies with the tradition of political economy in broader social studies of science. To this end, I build on the work of Finn and Rosner and the principles of ethnography of ecological information infrastructure [37]. Concurrently, I draw on the analytics of the co-production of life science and market forces [52].

2 Methods

The findings presented here are derived from my ongoing research on the history and ethnography of interactions between biodiversity science and computer science. I used the interview method to understand the perceptions of advanced computational tools provided by the data analytics industry on the part of an international biodiversity infor-matics consortium. I used snowball sampling and solicited interviews via email. All participants were either current or past members of the GEO BON secretariat, affiliates of the GEO BON, or recipients of the GEO BON-Microsoft grant. I conducted a total of 11 semi-structured interviews all in the range of 60 to 90 min. Audio was recorded and transcribed. I used inductive thematic analysis to code the interview material and divided the data into four main categories, discussed later. Furthermore, I have reviewed primary and grey literature from both GEO BON and Microsoft, participated in the 2020 conference of the Ecological Society of America titled "Harnessing the Data Revolu-tion," and transcribed and analyzed interviews with the Microsoft Chief Environmental Officer, Lucas Joppa.

3 Environmental Data in the Era of Data Capitalism

The interest of the data analytics industry in environmental stewardship can be considered a part of a larger landscape of "data for good" and "AI for Good" campaigns. "Data for Good" has become a popular, albeit contentious, slogan most often referring to the application of advanced computational methods such as machine learning to big data with the aim of helping a socially desirable cause. Sometimes such big data comes from the private sector, and in the process of what has been called "data philanthropy," data sets are "donated" to help address a variety of challenges. Yet often such campaigns do not deliver the promised outcomes. Communication scholars Maria Espinoza and Melissa Aronczyk [20] examined the implications and public constructions of "data philanthropy" in the realm of climate change to demonstrates that spearheaded by the United Nations project Data for Climate Action (D4CA) is primarily oriented towards the framing of the data sector as trustworthy. In this way, D4CA is more about legitimation and preservation of data-oriented business model rather than about offering meaningful opportunities for the use of big data in climate action. I argue that just like in the case of D4CA, Microsoft's environmental programs should be seen as "a strategy to legitimate extractive, profit-oriented data practices by companies [rather] than a means to achieve global goals for environmental sustainability" [20]. Yet, a claim that the totality of Microsoft's environmental initiatives can be explained by profit-seeking delivers only partial explanation. Therefore, I want to complicate this account.

The emerging scholarship on critical environmental data studies is concerned with the question of what is at stake when environmental data is subsumed into an informa-tion infrastructure with a particular politico-economic positionality? Drawing on this approach, I contend that the inquiry into Microsoft's environmental programs should encompass politics and ethics of cloud infrastructure, and the economy of the cloud and data sectors. It is therefore important to understand the logic of accumulation of data pervading the data analytics industry in the era of "surveillance capitalism" [55, 56] and "data capitalism" [54]. For this paper, I use Sara West's definition of "data capitalism," who defines it as.

"a system in which the commoditization of our data enables an asymmetric redis-tribution of power that is weighted toward the actors who have access and the capability to make sense of information. It is enacted through capitalism and justified by the association of networked technologies with the political and social benefits of an online community, drawing upon narratives that foreground the social and political benefits of networked technologies" [54].

Myers argues that data capitalism is about the "redistribution of power in the information age" [54]. In other words, those who can analyze, store, and predict the future based on data gain asymmetrically more power than actors without such capacities. As Mel Hogan and Tamara Shephard [30] show, the question of ownership of both information and the infrastructure on which it relies gains a new meaning in the emerging surveillance economy—this point is equally relevant in the context of environmental knowledge and its materiality. While Shoshana Zuboff offers a sweeping analysis of the "logic of accumulation" of data in the private sector, her study falls short of examining how data companies extend their reach beyond the realm of human culture and behavior. Zuboff writes that for the last three centuries humans have tried to dominate nature, and "now we are at the beginning of a new arc that I have called information civilization, and it repeats the same dangerous arrogance. The aim now is not to dominate nature but rather human nature" [56]. But is nature strictly outside of the curfew of surveillance capitalists? In another register, we can ask: at what point environment becomes perceived by data companies as just another big-data source on par with social media, internet transactions, communication metadata, etc.?

In grappling with these questions, the oeuvre of this paper is to embrace the critical data studies' spirit of "critique and contribute" [44]—or to highlight the areas for improvement instead of rejecting the private investment in environmental information infrastructures. I use the GEO BON-Microsoft partnership as a case study to inquiry into the processes of "overdetermination of environmental science by market forces" (Fortun, pers. Comm). If on the one hand I link Microsoft's environmental aspirations to the proliferation of "data capitalism," by no means am I dismissing this development as a priori a negative one.

4 Empirical Landscape

4.1 The Planetary Computer

Having situated my intervention within the literatures on environmental information infrastructures, critical data studies, and political economy of science, the article now transitions to the empirical section. There, I briefly describe the Microsoft's Planetary Computer, GEO and GEO BON, and the partnership between Microsoft and GEO BON. The article then returns to the problematization of the support for biodiversity monitoring, and later the four specific issues caused by this trend identified during the interviews. I begin by outlining the Planetary Computer initiative.

In 2017, Microsoft launched the "AI for Earth" initiative: a 50-million-dollar grant program promising to put "Microsoft's cloud and AI tools in the hands of those working to solve global environmental challenges" (AI for Earth website). Since its inception, the program has offered technical and financial support to a host of academic and nongovernmental organizations, focusing on creating partnerships between data and environmental scientists. Through AI for Earth, environmental scientists can collaborate with

AI experts and use storage and processing capacity via Microsoft's Azure infrastructure. In April of 2020, Microsoft introduced the second stage of its environmental program. The "Planetary Computer," as it is called, is a proposal for a centralized environmental knowledge infrastructure which combines cloud computation with environmental monitoring. The Planetary Computer program's technological backbone is the Microsoft cloud computing and storage service Azure. On the social level, the program intends to foster interdisciplinary exchange between environmental scientists and data and AI experts. Thematically, AI for Earth and the Planetary Computer are programs primarily concerned with sustainability and conservation. Microsoft Chief Environmental Officer, Lucas Joppa, described the Planetary Computer in this way:

> "Think of the Planetary Computer less as a giant computer in a stark white room and more of an approach to computing that is planetary in scale and allows us to query every aspect of environmental and nature-based solutions available in real-time."

While revealing, this statement is itself nonspecific. It is partly this ontological ambivalence about what the Planetary Computer is that makes it an object infused with a particular imaginary and promise for the GEO BON community. One of the GEO BON interviewees told me:

> if the planetary computer is what we think it is, which is some virtual place where you can put tools, and tools are coupled to data, we want to create tools that anybody can have access to, that are free, tools that are open. [Tools] you could even modify them yourselves if you wanted to.

When asked about Microsoft, most of my interlocutors did not see the company's environmental initiatives as unique. My interviewees reiterated the support for GEO BON from other big tech companies, notably Amazon, Google, Esri, and SAS. Another GEO BON member put it this way:

> [big tech companies] want to be able to tell a story about how they're saving the world. It is the same with Google Earth Engine, Esri gives us a ton of support. All these different technology companies are in the game for this sort of "Data for Good or AI-first" type thing. And not surprisingly, these companies and their spokespeople try to play that up as the ultimate solution.

As an infrastructure in the making, the Planetary Computer is a "technology of speculation" [31] enabling an anticipatory narrative which reconfigures what counts as the truth about nature. It is possible to see Microsoft and other Big Tech companies' actions as an example of corporate social responsibility (CSR) [42], or CSR's subset: corporate environmentalism [11]. Yet I want to use Microsoft's environmental programs as a case study political economy of environmental information infrastructures in the era of data capitalism.

Having outlined the discourse and premise of the Planetary Computer, I now shift to the background of the GEO BON consortium.

4.2   The Global Earth Observatory (GEO) and GEO Biodiversity Observation Network (GEO BON)

The GEO is an international scientific body created to foster earth data shareability and interoperability. The ultimate goal of the GEO is to inform political decision-making through comprehensive, global monitoring cooperation. The network consists of more than 100 national governments and another hundred participating organizations. The network's origins go back to the mid-90s discussions among space agencies—notably NASA, European and Japanese Space Agencies—about inter-agency data agreements. An underlying incentive for establishing the GEO was the promotion of satellite and other remote sensing technologies operated by the said space agencies and data exchange networks. The problem in the mid-90s was that not only data from individual agencies were siloed, but much of this data was also, for a variety of reasons, inaccessible to the broader scientific community.

One of the so-called Societal-Benefit Areas within the GEO is biodiversity. To support biodiversity data coordination, the GEO organized GEO Biodiversity Observation Network (GEO BON). As its website states, GEO BON is "A global biodiversity observation network that contributes to effective management policies for the world's biodiversity and ecosystem services." The interim committee for GEO BON was formed in January of 2008. GEO BON set out to consolidate the already existing elements of the biodiversity observation systems into a singular network. Thus, GEO BON belongs to a larger ecology of information infrastructures which together provide open biodiversity data. But the network's interest is not only in consolidating and standardizing raw data. As one document states, "The "value proposition" of GEO BON is to build on, coordinate and link existing major initiatives working with biodiversity data and information, to derive higher-level "value-added" analytical products not currently available through the existing activities when considered separately" [45]. I will return to this modelling aspect later in the paper.

4.3   GEO BON and Microsoft

One key liaison between Microsoft and the biodiversity informatics community, and GEO BON specifically, is a funding program with a $1M budget called "Essential Biodiversity Variables in the Cloud." The program provided in the Fall of 2020 five grantees with funding and Azure cloud credits specifically for, as its website states, "advancing research and applications that leverage cloud-scale computation to expand the geographical and temporal coverage of biodiversity information." Bonnie Lei, a founding member and Head of Global Strategic Partnerships for AI for Earth program presented the rationale behind the Microsoft-GEO BON partnership in the following way:

> "Over the past half century, human activity has decreased wildlife populations by more than two thirds. To protect and preserve the biodiversity of the world's ecosystems, we need a scientific-led and data-driven way to assess biodiversity and enable informed decision making in our global conservation efforts" [47].

Notably, the GEO BON-Microsoft partnership alters the expertise composition of biodiversity organizations by promoting teams with advanced computational skills. For example, one of the five grantees of the program is a team of researchers from the Songs of Adaptation project from Future Generations University. The team uses big data management capabilities of the Azure with machine learning to provide 1) "open-source tools and data for the GEO BON community", 2) "specific species insights for species in biodiversity hotspots in Nepal, Bolivia, USA, and Uganda." The Songs of Adaptation team partners with researchers from the Cloudera Foundation, a non-profit organization supported by a Cloudera—a US-based potentate on the data analytics market. Cloudera's "Data4Change" program supports "efforts that strengthen the conditions for the responsible nonprofit use of data." In sum, the Microsoft-GEO BON partnership exemplifies some of the key features of how data analytics industry spreads its imaginary of a data-driven decision making into environmental management, while at the same time promoting its tools as necessary to manage the environmental crisis. The scrutinization of the Microsoft-GEO BON program supports the thesis that the data analytics industry is invested in spreading its computational regime, and by advocating "cloud-scale computation," the company positions its products as an obligatory passage point for biodiversity informatics.

As Baker and Mayernick argue, it is imperative to disentangle the processes of data production and knowledge production in ecology [6]. In this vein, I want to highlight that GEO BON does not produce knowledge, but data products. Therefore, I will describe the role and potential of GEO BON's key data modelling product: "essential biodiversity variables" (EBVs) as means to further contextualize the GEO BON-Microsoft partnership.

GEO BON-Microsoft collaboration strives to develop a cloud-based support for biodiversity modelling through GEO BON data product EBV. The EBV, as an international data product, is modeled after the essential climate variables, an earlier data product with relevance for guiding climate change assessment and policy.[1] GEO BON, which strives to emerge as a leading political-scientific body for guiding biodiversity monitoring and assessment efforts, promotes the EBVs as one means for integrated, transnational (and yet locally relevant) legislation. To reiterate, GEO BON sets out to enhance the economic, scientific, and political value of "raw" biodiversity data through modeling and prediction. Yet to do so, GEO BON must coordinate not only data standards but also computing infrastructure—and such computing infrastructure is still lacking. A key paper explaining the EBVs published in the *Nature Ecology & Evolution* written by GEO BON members with a lead author Walter Jetz from Yale University stated:

"An informatics framework is needed that is strongly informed by research and is based on the incorporation of environmental sensor data, flexible modelling methodology that integrates data types and scalable computational statistical approaches and associated cloud-based data management. The infrastructure should form a community platform for the best possible development of standardized, scientifically rigorous and transparent SP EBVs" [33].

Funding for the EBVs on the Cloud program is the initial solution to the above recommendation for a novel informatics framework. Here, the support of the data analytics

---

[1] For the history of ECVs, see Edwards, 2010.

industry rises in relevance. Now I want to return to the main questions of this paper: what are the consequences of the public-private partnership for environmental data practices and information infrastructures? And, what can biodiversity management look like in the era of surveillance capitalism? To unpack these questions, I present four key themes from interviews with the GEO BON community.

5   Findings

5.1   Support for the on the Ground Data Collection is More Important than AI, But is Not as Sexy

Despite the promise of the Planetary Computer, GEO BON members exhibit healthy skepticism to its—often notably exaggerated—claims. For example, one interviewee compared the potential of biodiversity modeling to climate modeling and explained that there is a serious potential for a unified platform for biodiversity monitoring resembling the platforms for climate modelling. But his view is that any centralized modelling platform would be only as good as the data it hosts:

> "I'm skeptical to what extent it only begets like a garbage in garbage out situation. [The Planetary Computer] will only be as good as the data that's going into it. I'm not convinced that machine learning can completely replace the need for on the ground data collection still."

The above quote exemplifies the attitude of "data care" [5] in arguing that quality on the ground data collection is more important than infrastructure development. Continuing the reflection about the potential of the Planetary Computer, this GEO BON member states that data collection is not as "sexy" as an image of a Planetary Computer. In their own words:

> "Part of the problem with the biodiversity conservation issue is that everybody wants to fund the latest, sexy technology platform. They want to fund conservation projects that lead to specific actions, and that's all totally needed, but nobody wants to fund data production. Nobody wants to fund a bunch of people out on the ground collecting data."

This interviewee came back to the problem of on the ground data collection and the fact that funding such efforts is less PR-worthy than a "flashy" Planetary Computer:

> "[Data collection] doesn't get promoted, but it will likely have a much bigger impact for conservation than anything that Microsoft does with the Planetary Computer. It's the really boring non flashy stuff that's actually making a difference on the ground. They just don't make kick-ass videos about it."

This section illustrates that in the views of the GEO BON community, Microsoft is more interested in promoting its charismatic technology, rather than considering funding programs which reflect the actual needs of given scientific communities and the quality of data. This situation might indeed change as the company grows more sensitive to the needs of the biodiversity informatics community.

5.2   Transnational Legitimacy and Expertise Inequalities

Many of my interlocutors mentioned the worry about whether Microsoft takes the needs and political-economic reality of the potential users seriously. One of the key themes in the interviews was the question of political legitimacy. As one person made clear, for a Planetary Computer to work, it needs to gain certain international legitimacy and trust. For them "the planetary computer could come to ground if [Microsoft] focused on partnership with a couple of countries." To illustrate this problem, they asked:

"Is the government of Indonesia going to actually use a Microsoft planetary computer to change how they manage things on the ground in terms of conservation? I'm not so sure, because [the government of Indonesia] is not involved in it. There's no ownership, there's no trust."

In other words, for the Planetary Computer to work, there needs to be trust between the state-specific decision makers and the company. As other scholars presented this problem in the context of geoscience cyberinfrastructure, the designers of new infrastructures always risk that the intended community will not engage with the new initiative [13]. This interviewee offered the following example on how Microsoft could engage with decision-makers:

"Why not work with Costa Rica in partnership around applying the planetary computer around really clearly articulated on the ground problems in that country that the planetary computer can solve? And if you do that, then you suddenly get credibility because then Panama, Columbia, Ghana, and Uganda will go: 'Oh, wait, it's not Lucas Joppa at Microsoft telling me how wonderful [Planetary Computer] is, because I'm totally skeptical when he talks.'"

Even when international legitimacy could be achieved, free and open data has a capacity to exacerbate global inequalities if the expertise required to process and analyze this data is not equally distributed. Therefore, trust and legitimacy are linked to the problem of expertise inequalities and the analysis of geopolitics in media and information studies should not take the second place [1]. This fact is in the forefront of the members of the biodiversity informatics community. For example, after delivering his Keynote at the 2020 ESA's annual meeting, Lucas Joppa was asked:

"One question that comes into my mind is how AI for Earth can make accessibility and inclusivity a priority. My concern is that there is an overrepresentation of white men in tech and CS in general. Where are indigenous peoples in this picture? (…) I fear that the tools you describe will further the gap between those using land and those deciding how land should be used unless those land users are part of the process."

Sociotechnical systems like the Planetary Computer bring forth novel conditions of inclusion and exclusion. More work needs to be done to understand how big data and machine learning create and re-create systems of inequality in environmental sciences. For example, machine learning experts in contemporary ecology might be reinforcing a new system of inequality, in this case, expertise inequality. In this light, designers of transnational environmental information infrastructure need to take into consideration the accessibility of such technologies to local communities and infrastructural conditions around the globe. It is likewise imperative for the private sector to create scientific and political ties with international governing bodies and local governments to build trust in the new tools.

5.3 Informating of Environmentalism

Data aggregation and modeling activities of the GEO BON require novel approaches to computational infrastructure. Hence, although Microsoft competes for the market niche of environmental data cloud infrastructure, from the perspective of the GEO BON community, there is a discernible enthusiasm that Azure infrastructure is exactly what they need for their flagship data product, the EBVs. While one interlocutor told me that "[Microsoft] came to GEO BON and said: what kind of tools would you like to see on the planetary computer?" It was hard for me to unpack the details of how this exchange took place. As a conjecture, I assume that the EBVs on the Cloud funding project were one consequence of Microsoft's initiative to customize the Planetary Computer towards the GEO BON. However, mentioned above ambivalence on the part of the GEO BON community about what the Planetary Computer really is signals a disconnect between the company and the GEO BON.

At least in principle, Microsoft promotes a user-driven approach to technology design. For example, the Chief Environmental Officer at the company Lucas Joppa sees the Planetary Computer as a perfect boundary infrastructure (citation) for a collaboration between computer science and ecology. In one of the interviews describing the vision for the Planetary Computer, Lucas Joppa explained that this platform is an attempt for bringing two worlds—that of tech developers and environmental scientists—together. In Joppa's words,

> "I think one of the biggest risks is a disconnect between the users and the developers and kind of the two types of knowledge bases that we need to bring together. (…) most of those developers don't come to this space with a significant background or understanding in environmental systems and environmental science and the way that their skills can be put to use in helping to improve the state of the world. And most actors in the environmental sustainability space, the potential users, they're not as educated as we would like them to be about what solutions already exist or could be built to help them."

Despite Joppa's intentions, the interviews with the GEO BON secretariat revealed the separation between designers and users of environmental information systems—a separation anthropologist Kim Fortun claims is a defining feature of what she calls the "informating of environmentalism" [23]. While my research thus far can only gesture at the aggregation of problems associated with the "informating of environmentalism," interviews are in themselves insufficient to capture the nuance of a separation between designers and users. Hence, my future work will need to incorporate more ethnographic methods. As with the problem of global expertise inequalities, the above statement by Joppa points towards a need for a dialogue and mutual education between technology developers and, in this context, conservation biologists and ecologists. One promising mode of proceeding forward is to draw on the literature on participatory design [10, 36].

5.4 Funding and the Culture of Innovation: Corporate vs. State

Despite the above-mentioned problematic aspects of the projects like a Planetary Computer, AI and other computational techniques developed in the private sector have a very practical application for biodiversity data processing. And the GEO BON community is enthusiastic about those applications. In the words of one of the former members of the GEO BON leadership:

> "AI for earth has been a great way to create some simple solutions to problems like processing speed, using machine learning algorithms to speed up and automate data workflow pipelines"

Continuing with the positive attitudes, one of the current GEO BON leaders expressed his views about the advantages of working with the private sector over national governments. This person spoke specifically about the willingness on the part of the private sector to provide funding which state agencies were unable to provide:

> There is a temptation to work with the private sector because they operate on a different timescale. They are offering six-figure sums 'like that,' that none of the governments that I've worked with are willing to mobilize for [biodiversity monitoring and modeling].

This interviewee underscored "healthy skepticism" while at the same time expressed the attitude that in light of the general lack of funding from governments, GEO BON needs to use any kind of resources it can gather. He also brought up the fact that GEO BON is a voluntary network with no permanent funding model.

Corporate support of biodiversity monitoring has been described to me as an essential element of the larger mobilization of the public and state conservation efforts. For example, one of the early proponents of GEO BON and an expert in biodiversity modelling told me that there is a need for "all hands on deck" philosophy where private and state actors work together to solve problems like biodiversity loss. The corporate sector is just one part of the solution. In his views, "all hands on deck" is the only form of proceeding forward in fighting the biodiversity decline, which he called an "existential issue for our people, our planet." He further explained:

> "Ideally, for [conservation] to work, we're going to need networks that include academia and government, both at the federal and regional or state level, and also the corporate sector and the nonprofit sector. [This includes] the conservation NGOs, as well as the commercial, corporate sector, Microsoft, Google, Amazon, et cetera."

The same person also emphasized the technical requirements of biodiversity monitoring, modeling, decision making, and the role of AI in this effort:

"you can't do this work without networks, and you can't do it without a lot of machine learning and artificial intelligence techniques. And many of [these techniques] have been developed on the private side, the corporate side. I think that's a natural partnership for [GEO BON and Microsoft] to come together."

Given the nuanced debate in the biodiversity informatics community around the role of ML, it is important to note the subjective element of the above perspective. Yet what the quote is intended to highlight is the culture of innovation of the private sector the GEO BON members find appealing. Responding to the question about the culture of innovation, another interviewee said: "I think Microsoft has the history and the culture where they actually do seriously want to make a difference." The same person explained that the innovation pipeline in the private sector allows for a much faster time to implementation and a more effective design process—as a contrast to longer timeline of innovations supported by federal funding. Nonetheless, in both state and private supported infrastructures it is imperative to consider the long-term effects of design on communities of practice [38].

6   Conclusions

In this paper I draw attention of information studies scholars and the industry partners to the need to consider not only the environmental footprint and sustainability of infrastructures [28], but that design for the Anthropocene [48] is likewise about listening to the needs of the communities who try to ameliorate the environmental crises. I likewise emphasize that the design of information infrastructure sits on the confluence of economic, political, and scientific visions. With the possible rise of the importance of private support for environmental information infrastructures—especially in the context of state-operated environmental knowledge infrastructures being "under siege" [17]—it is crucial to understand who the real and potential stakeholders in those systems are, and what are the consequences of sharing open environmental data. As Nicholas A. John writes,

> As a keyword for the digital age, *sharing* bears the promise for a better society, while requiring us always to keep in mind the political economy of the structures— digital and otherwise—through which we carry out our various practices of sharing [34, see also 35].

While a general mode of critique in social studies of data could suggest that involvement of a Big Tech company in environmental data is be a manifestation of virtue signaling, public relations campaign, a case of over-determination of environmental monitoring by market forces, or an encroachment of a particular regime of calculation, this paper shows that the narrative becomes more nuanced if one considers the reception of technologies and funding such as those provided by the Microsoft on the part of the biodiversity informatics community. My account avoids a one-sided recourse to a critique of datafication, data imperialism, imposition of regimes of calculation, or ill-informed corporate environmentalism driven solely by PR interests [e.g., 29][2].

---

2 On Microsoft's attempts to make their data centers green see [47].

"Environmental information systems," argues Kim Fortun, "need to be recognized as significant and contested sites of political action, because they are sites where conventional ways of thinking about the environment are being reconfigured" [24]. Elsewhere, Fortun and colleagues [25] advocates for a "critical data design," where various stakeholders—among them social scientists—make effort to enhance the production of data which makes social and political action possible. In another register, information studies in the Anthropocene are about forging alliances with those who design technoscientific sites of political action, and hence the communication of the critical perspective on environmental information systems must be carefully considered as not to antagonize potential readers in non-information studies circles. For example, we should find ways to adhere to the principles of participatory research design. Kim Fortun's notion of a "critical data practice" is but one example of an analytic which offers a more generous reading of the work of corporate actors. Through this statement, I wish to underscore the need to reckon with the responsibility of ethnographers towards their interlocutors in both public and private sectors.

The question information infrastructure designers need to face is to define "Making at the End of Nature" [51], but also how to design to save nature and its biodiversity. These are indeed monumental and age-defining questions. The theoretical background of my argument is formed by two parallel matters of concern: one, about the political economy of environmental information infrastructures, the second by the question of what makes data analytics industry's foyer into environmental "data care" appealing to biodiversity researchers. Yet understanding of AI is often obscured by this technology's quasi-mythological cultural status. Therefore, it becomes important to ask how AI and cloud infrastructure are reflections of a collective fantasy of society [40]. For example: how to contextualize claims such as "We need artificial intelligence to save us from ourselves," made by Joppa? I find it instructive to follow cultural scholars of technology, such as Tung-Hui Hu, whose historical account of cloud computing conveys that the cloud mirrors an "architecture of our own desire" [32]. Azure, it might be argued, as any other infrastructure, "operate[s] on the level of fantasy and desire" [40]. To reiterate, AI for Earth and the Planetary Computer are embedded in the data capitalist logic, and its collective technoscientific desires. This theoretical framing is not meant to diminish the actual potential of the funding program and the science it supports.

References

1. Aouragh, M., Chakravartty, P.: Infrastructures of empire: towards a critical geopolitics of media and information studies. Media Cult. Soc. **38**, 559–575 (2016)
2. Aronova, E., Baker, K.S., Oreskes, N.: Big science and big data in biology: from the international geophysical year through the international biological program to the long term ecological research (LTER) network, 1957—present. Hist. Stud. Nat. Sci. **40**, 183–224 (2010)
3. Baker, K., Millerand, F.: Infrastructuring ecology: challenges in achieving data sharing. In: Parker, J.N., Vermeulen, N., Penders, B. (eds.) Collaboration in the New Life Sciences: Via Information and Infrastructure to Knowledge Production and Policy (2010)
4. Baker, K.S., Jackson, S.J., Wanetick, J.R.: Strategies supporting heterogeneous data and interdisciplinary collaboration: towards an ocean informatics environment. Presented at the Proceedings of the 38th Annual Hawaii International Conference on System Sciences (2005)

5. Baker, K.S., Karasti, H.: Data care and its politics: designing for local collective data management as a neglected thing. Presented at the Proceedings of the 15th Participatory Design Conference: Full Papers-Volume 1 (2018)
6. Baker, K.S., Mayernik, M.S.: Disentangling knowledge production and data production. Ecosphere **11**, e03191 (2020)
7. Baker, K.S., et al..: What does infrastructuring look like in STS? when? Workshop report. In: EASST Conference: Meetings–Making Science, Technology and Society together, p. 8. European Association for the Study of Science and Technology (2018)
8. Benson, E.: Wired Wilderness: Technologies of Tracking and the Making of Modern Wildlife. JHU Press, Baltimore (2010)
9. Benson, E.: One infrastructure, many global visions: the commercialization and diversification of Argos, a satellite-based environmental surveillance system. Soc. Stud. Sci. **42**, 843–868 (2012)
10. Botero, A., Hyysalo, S., Kohtala, C., Whalen, J.: Getting participatory design done: from methods and choices to translation work across constituent domains. Int. J. Des. **14**, 17 (2020)
11. Chrun, E., Dolšak, N., Prakash, A.: Corporate environmentalism: motivations and mechanisms. Annu. Rev. Environ. Resour. **41**, 341–362 (2016). https://doi.org/10.1146/annurev-environ-110615-090105
12. Crawford, K.: The Atlas of AI. Yale University Press, New Haven (2021)
13. Cutcher-Gershenfeld, J., et al.: Build it, but will they come? A geoscience cyberinfrastructure baseline analsys. Data Sci. J. **15**, 1 (2016)
14. Doel, R.E.: Constituting the postwar earth sciences: the military's influence on the environmental sciences in the USA after 1945. Soc. Stud. Sci. **33**, 635–666 (2003)
15. Dourish, P.: HCI and environmental sustainability: the politics of design and the design of politics. Presented at the Proceedings of the 8th ACM Conference on Designing Interactive Systems (2010)
16. Edwards, P.N.: Knowledge infrastructures for the Anthropocene. Anthropocene Rev. **4**, 34–43 (2017)
17. Edwards, P.N.: Knowledge Infrastructures under Siege. Data Polit. **21** (2019)
18. Edwards, P.N.: The Closed World: Computers and the Politics of Discourse in Cold War America. MIT Press, Cambridge (1996)
19. Ensmenger, N., Slayton, R.: Computing and the environment: introducing a special issue of information & culture. Inf. Cult. **52**, 295–303 (2017)
20. Espinoza, M.I., Aronczyk, M.: Big data for climate action or climate action for big data? Big Data Soc. **8**, 2053951720982032 (2021)
21. Finn, M., Rosner, D.K.: Troubled worlds: new directions in information research, practice and pedagogy, vol. 8 (2019)
22. Finn, M., et al.: Troubled worlds: a course syllabus about information work and the anthropocene. J. Crit. Libr. Inf. Stud. **3** (2020). https://doi.org/10.24242/jclis.v3i1.137
23. Fortun, K.: From Bhopal to the informating of environmentalism: risk communication in historical perspective. Osiris **19**, 283–296 (2004)
24. Fortun, K.: 10. Biopolitics and the informating of environmentalism. In: Lively Capital, pp. 306–326. Duke University Press, Durham (2012)
25. Fortun, K., Poirier, L., Morgan, A., Costelloe-Kuehn, B., Fortun, M.: Pushback: critical data designers and pollution politics. Big Data Soc. **3**, 2053951716668903 (2016)
26. Gabrys, J.: Practicing, materialising and contesting environmental data. Big Data Soc. **3**, 2053951716673391 (2016)
27. Gabrys, J.: Smart forests and data practices: from the internet of trees to planetary governance. Big Data Soc. **7**, 2053951720904871 (2020)
28. Hogan, M.: Data flows and water woes: the Utah data center. Big Data Soc. **2**, 2053951715592429 (2015)

29. Hogan, M.: Big data ecologies. Ephemera **18**, 631 (2018)
30. Hogan, M., Shepherd, T.: Information ownership and materiality in an age of big data surveillance. J. Inf. Policy **5**, 6–31 (2015)
31. Hong, S.: Technologies of Speculation. New York University Press, New York (2020)
32. Hu, T.-H.: A Prehistory of the Cloud. MIT Press, Cambridge (2015)
33. Jetz, W., et al.: Essential biodiversity variables for mapping and monitoring species populations. Nat. Ecol. Evol. **3**, 539–551 (2019)
34. John, N.A.: 24. Sharing. In: Digital Keywords, pp. 269–277. Princeton University Press, Princeton (2016)
35. John, N.A.: The Age of Sharing. Wiley, Hoboken (2017)
36. Karasti, H.: Infrastructuring in participatory design. Presented at the Proceedings of the 13th Participatory Design Conference: Research Papers-Volume 1 (2014)
37. Karasti, H., Baker, K.S.: Infrastructuring for the long-term: ecological information management. Presented at Proceedings of the 37th Annual Hawaii International Conference on System Sciences (2004)
38. Karasti, H., Baker, K.S., Millerand, F.: Infrastructure time: long-term matters in collaborative development. Comput. Support. Coop. Work (CSCW) **19**, 377–415 (2010)
39. Kolbert, E.: The Sixth Extinction: An Unnatural History. A&C Black, London (2014)
40. Larkin, B.: The politics and poetics of infrastructure. Annu. Rev. Anthropol. **42**, 327–343 (2013)
41. Light, A., Powell, A., Shklovski, I.: Design for existential crisis in the anthropocene age. Presented at the Proceedings of the 8th International Conference on Communities and Technologies (2017)
42. Lindgreen, A., Swaen, V.: Corporate social responsibility (2010)
43. Millerand, F., Baker, K.S.: Data infrastructures in ecology: an infrastructure studies perspective (2020)
44. Neff, G., Tanweer, A., Fiore-Gartland, B., Osburn, L.: Critique and contribute: a practice-based framework for improving critical data studies and data science. Big Data **5**, 85–97 (2017)
45. Group on Earth Observations Biodiversity Observation Network Report (2010)
46. Oui, J.: Commodifying a "good" weather data: commercial meteorology, low-cost stations, and the global scientific infrastructure. Sci. Technol. Hum. Values (2021). https://doi.org/10.1177/0162243921995889
47. Pasek, A.: Managing carbon and data flows: fungible forms of mediation in the cloud. Cult. Mach. **16** (2019)
48. Peters, J.D.: The Marvelous Clouds. University of Chicago Press, Chicago (2015)
49. Randalls, S.: Weather profits: weather derivatives and the commercialization of meteorology. Soc. Stud. Sci. **40**, 705–730 (2010)
50. Randalls, S.: Commercializing environmental data: seeing like a market (2017)
51. Ratto, M.: Making at the end of nature. Interactions **23**, 26–35 (2016)
52. Sunder Rajan, K.: Lively capital: biotechnologies, ethics, and governance in global markets (2012)
53. Taylor, A.: The data center as technological wilderness. Cult. Mach. **18** (2019)
54. West, S.M.: Data capitalism: redefining the logics of surveillance and privacy. Bus. Soc. **58**, 20–41 (2019)
55. Zuboff, S.: Big other: surveillance capitalism and the prospects of an information civilization. J. Inf. Technol. **30**, 75–89 (2015)
56. Zuboff, S.: The Age of Surveillance Capitalism: The Fight for a Human Future at the New Frontier of Power: Barack Obama's Books of 2019. Profile Books (2019)
57. Microsoft and GEO BON Announce the Winners of the Essential Biodiversity Variables on the Cloud Grant Programme. https://www.earthobservations.org/geo_blog_obs.php?id=470. Accessed 09 Dec 2021

Planning and Running a Low-Contact UX Design Workshop During the Pandemic: Challenges and Design Implications

Hong-Chun Chen[1] and Wei Jeng[2(✉)]

[1] Trend Micro Inc., Taipei, Taiwan
[2] National Taiwan University, Taipei, Taiwan
`wjeng@ntu.edu.tw`

Abstract. COVID-19's disruption to global economic activities has affected how UX designers work, with much collaborative work having to take place virtually. This study reports on the preparations for holding a remote UX design workshop, its running, issues that were encountered, and how they were overcome. Based on this experience, the authors recommend that preparations for holding remote UX workshops include ample offline pre-workshop preparation; a playbook for team members who are not physically present; utilization of online collaborative tools; and, where no other suitable options are available, asynchronous working.

Keywords: Pandemic · Online UX design workshop

1 Introduction

As the COVID-19 pandemic ravaged the world, governments and non-governmental organizations have been actively coordinating measures to control its spread. A number of global events for this purpose, including BuildforCOVID19 and Cohack, are being held online to facilitate the rapid collaborative development of solutions. These endeavors highlight an interesting new challenge: How can UX designers and design-project members effectively collaborate without being in the same room when it was used to be held in face-to-face co-design process?

This paper documents and reports on a design project as a case study of how remote team members can effectively generate actionable decisions through a series of virtual UX-related workshops during the early project stages. In general, a design workshop aims to solve problems and generate actionable decisions by gathering diverse stakeholders together for discussion within a limited timeframe [1]. Although such workshops often seem time-consuming and sometimes slow down the development process, they also tend to contribute to convergence in a team's opinions, reach a consensus, and help team members tackle problems from multiple perspectives collectively.

One well-known approach to guiding a design workshop's workflow, which has been found to help designers and non-designers process information and create solutions to complex problems, is the Double Diamond principle [2]. It involves four design processes: Discover, Define, Develop, and Deliver. The Double Diamond model pairs Discover and Define into a Research stage, and Develop and Deliver into a Design stage, as shown in Fig. 1.

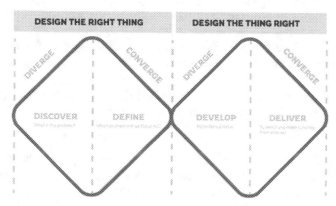

Fig. 1. The double diamond diagram.

Each of the four processes in the model has a different goal, but all are meant to work together in the systematic creation of a solution. The first, Discover, aims to identify actual problems and contextualize them in ways that make it possible to find entry points. Once enough information has been gathered to support such contextualization, not merely about the use scenario but also about all team members' opinions, the team can move to the second stage, Define. In Define, team members are encouraged to elaborate on their ideas and build shared understandings.

Next, following a level of information exchange that is sufficient to the task at hand, the team moves on to the Develop stage, in which potential solutions rooted in different perspectives and various domains of knowledge are all given due consideration. In the final stage, Delivery, these solutions converge and are tested. Many prior studies have adopted the Double Diamond model [3]. However, most have focused on face-to-face workshops, and have rarely discussed virtual or online contexts. As Mueller [4] and Fessenden [5] have pointed out, there are fundamental differences between face-to-face and remote workshops, including (1) the lack of common space, which reduces physical interaction and makes creating immersive experiences difficult; (2) inevitable interference from the participants' various environments; (3) and unfamiliar online tools, which at best take extra time to learn, and at worst can inhibit team members' participation. However, remote workshops also have unique advantages: notably, that online platforms enable people located in different places to co-create.

The outbreak of COVID19 has forced many information product designers, researchers, and engineers to rethink the co-design model, moving away from face-to-face to low-contact design. However, few studies have investigated how the transition. Among the few, Davis et al. proposed an ideal high-level architecture for low-contact design, but they did not evaluate this architecture when it is put in use practice [6]. On the other hand, Kennedy et al. reported the high-level development cycle (including data collection and workshop), but they did not consider the in-depth procedure within an online workshop [7]. The design paper of Gultom et al. [8] documented the design and development process of an epidemic prevention app during the epidemic, yet it did not specify whether low-contact co-design was used.

These differences suggest that approaches familiar from face-to-face workshops may not be fully applicable to online ones. This led us to ask these important questions:

1. How has the Double Diamond approach, which was mostly carried out in face-to-face design workshops before the pandemic, been adapted and adjusted to remote design-workshop use?
2. How does a remote design workshop distribute its participation mode across offline and online sessions? How is this distribution associated with the Double Diamond approach's four stages?

As well as adopting these questions as its research questions, the current study will report on testing workflow and preparation, and discuss key differences between face-to-face and remote design workshops.

2   Case Study Description

2.1   Project Description

The aim of the focal design project was to develop a mobile application with which members of the public could actively self-report, store, and manage their health status (e.g., body temperature, COVID-19 symptoms monitoring from home) during the pandemic without compromising their privacy. The design-project team comprised members of a non-profit organization called MyData Taiwan, which was formally established in January 2020 with official admission of MyData Global, a large international non-profit organization established in 2018 and with more than 600 individual members with the mission to build a fair, sustainable and prosperous digital society by improving the autonomy of personal data. Having the diverse backgrounds typical of members of such organizations, the team members in the Taiwan's Branch began the project with divergent expectations about what app functionalities were desirable; and thus, to reach a consensus about design solutions, a UX design workshop was convened.

2.2   Participants

The attendees of the UX design workshop (n = 15) included UX researchers, designers, software developers, iSchool faculty member and students, and UX interns. These team members had a variety of educational backgrounds, played different roles in the project, and brought different expectations to the table. Table 1 provides an overview of the team members' relevant characteristics.

Table 1. Workshop team members' demographics.

#	Gender	Affiliations	Specialization	Main roles in the project	Goals
P01	Female	Blockchain Company N	Product management	Technological development, project management and marketing. Contributed all company resources to this project for two full months	To use existing technology to build an app that will help the public to contribute to epidemic prevention while maintaining their privacy; promoting the concept of "own your data"
P02	Female	Blockchain Company N	Product management		
P03	Male	Blockchain Company N	Product management		
P04	Male	Blockchain Company N	Software engineering		
P05	Male	Blockchain Company N	Software engineering		
P06	Male	Blockchain Company N	Software engineering		
P07	Male	Blockchain Company N	User interface animation		
P08	Female	Blockchain Company N	Marketing strategy		
P09	Female	University faculty	Pharmacy	Defining key information from the perspective of medical diagnosis	To set medically appropriate epidemic-prevention tasks
P10	Female	iSchool faculty	Information science	1. Rationalizing data collection from the perspective of data ethics 2. Identifying users' needs	To ensure that data collection by the app is ethical and appropriate to users' needs
P11	Female	iSchool students	Information science		
P12	Female	iSchool students	Information science		
P13	Male	Legal Counsel	Law	Examining the legality of data collection	To ensure that data collection by the app is legal
P14	Female	iSchool students	User interface design	Designing a user interface that meets users' needs	To leverage design to understand the concept of "own your data" and to aid epidemic prevention

2.3 Goals of the UX Design Workshop

The UX design workshop aimed to leverage its members' expertise to develop an alpha-testing version of MyData Taiwan's Minimum Viable Product (hereafter: MVP) app concept, based on their respective expert opinions and users' known needs. Before the workshop, the team had set itself a rough goal and held two consensus meetings. The design workshop's outcome would ultimately be as a prototype, developed, and iterated, as shown in Fig. 2.

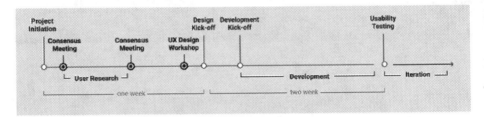

Fig. 2. Milestones of the design process.

3 Designing an Online UX Design Workshop

The overall duration of the online UX design workshop was limited by the team members' tight schedules, which limited their availability to 1–2 h at a time.1 To maximize efficiency, given these time constraints, the researchers split the Double Diamond model into two sections and conducted them separately.

The first, Research half of the model (Discover and Define) was completed by the university faculty and students. Its key output was a set of three user profiles, which clarified the target users' personas, jobs to be done, challenges, and motivations based on user-profiling results. Then, based on the profiles, the full online UX design workshop handled the second, Design half of the diamond (Develop and Deliver), which was further subdivided into three stages.

In the first of these stages, the host recapitulated the project goal and presented the user profiles that had been developed in Research half of the diamond, to ensure that all team members were on the same page. In the second, the team members brainstormed and shared ideas based on the user needs mentioned in the user profiles. And in the last stage, the members discussed everyone's ideas and voted for their three favorites. Those top-three ideas were then used to guide the software engineering of the MVP app.

Notably, because some members were not available to attend the workshop, all were given a playbook with step-by-step details of how to finish the first and second stages offline, thus ensuring that their ideas would also be addressed and thoroughly discussed at a later point. The workshop was planned to be held for 90 min via Zoom, with two online collaborative platforms – Mural and Google Slides – appended. These collaborative platforms were selected because of their easy learning curve: all team members were already registered and familiar with them. Table 2 summarizes the process of the Design half of the online UX workshop.

Table 2. Schedule of the design half of the online UX workshop.

Duration	Stage	Description	Tools
5 min	Warm-up	The workshop host explains the process to the workshop team members	Mural, Zoom
20 min	First stage: restate the consensus	The host recapitulates the consensus and target user profiles that were previously defined	Mural, Zoom
25 min	Second stage: brainstorm and share	Based on the user profiles, the team members begin to propose ideas for suggested features. NB: At this stage, no one can comment on each other's thoughts	Mural, Zoom
15 min		Each team member introduces their ideas in turn	Mural, Zoom
15 min	Third stage: give feedback Decision-making stage	Each team member gives feedback on each other's ideas	Google Slides, Zoom
10 min		Each team member votes for up to three MVP features	Google Slides, Zoom

Pre-workshop preparation comprised finishing the first diamond (Discover and Define), creating the playbook, and preparation of materials. Four days before the workshop, the research team made these preparations and completed the tasks listed below.

3.1 Reaching a Consensus on Project Goals

As noted above, the people involved the project did not all come from the same work sector or similar educational backgrounds. As such, even with a common goal, they held different expectations about what could be achieved and how it could be achieved. To facilitate discussion among team members in the workshop based on the shared goal, the research team pre-collected everyone's expectations about the product and displayed them throughout the workshop.

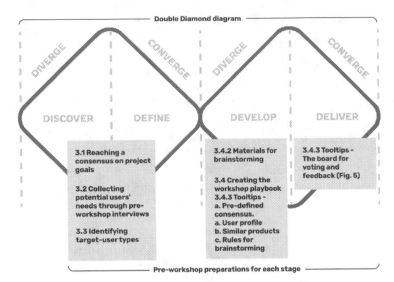

Fig. 3. Pre-workshop preparations for each stage.

3.2   Collecting Potential Users' Needs Through Pre-workshop Interviews

Because the project's aim was to develop a personal health record-keeping app, the pre-workshop team narrowed down its potential users to three types, and recruited between four and six individuals whom they felt exemplified each type. This resulted in a pool of 15 participants who were given semi-structured interviews and questionnaires aimed at understanding their needs.

3.3   Identifying Target-User Types

Based on the insights gained in the user interviews and questionnaires, the pre-workshop team created three user profiles, intended to guide the full design team's activities.

3.4   Creating the Workshop Playbook

The aim of the playbook, created by the research team using Mural, was to facilitate team members' brainstorming based on the project goal and users' needs, not only within the workshop, but also offline if they could not attend one or more of its stages. Specifically, the playbook contained the following information.

3.4.1   Pre-defined Consensus

This was the consensus agreed by all members, incorporating the project goal and the profiles of the target users, as a means of evoking design ideas and inspiring the team's discussion.

3.4.2 Materials for Brainstorming

(1) Each of the user profiles presented a particular set of "motivations", "challenges", and "behaviors", and also included respondents' quotes, to allow the design team to imagine the relevant type of user more clearly. (2) A list of similar products, including their value proposition and design features, was provided to inspire the team members while brainstorming.

3.4.3 Tooltips

The playbook also included rules created to facilitate open-minded and egalitarian discussion. First, it was deemed essential to ensure that the team members' suggested features were (1) well-aligned with user needs, and (2) intelligible by all team members. Each workshop member was required to abide by the dictum that "The proposed idea should always solve users' challenges or fit users' motivations," which could be elaborated as: "If we provide users with [concept], we might help them achieve [motivation]/ solve [challenge]". In this way, the workshop members were allowed to add more information to help others flesh out their ideas, including through illustrations or descriptions. This approach was also intended to support asynchronous participation by some team members.

The playbook also included the step-by-step workshop guidelines illustrated in Fig. 3, in which the information needed for effective participation in each stage of the second diamond is divided into blocks, linked by arrows (Figs. 4 and 5).

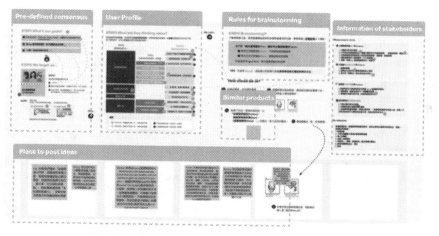

Fig. 4. Playbook on Mural for the "Develop" stage.

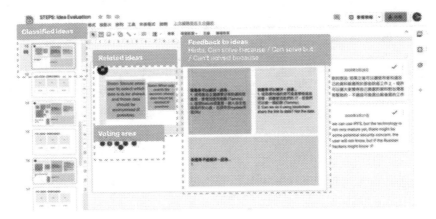

Fig. 5. Playbook on Google Slides for the "Deliver" stage.

4   Workshop Outcome

The workshop ultimately produced many ideas, and settled on a concept for the alpha-test version of the MVP app via voting and discussion. As expected, completing the first diamond beforehand allowed the team members to gain a sufficient understanding of user needs in a time-efficient way. Clear tooltips also efficiently prevented team members from becoming lost in the process, and ensured that they could express their own ideas and thoughts even if they were unable to attend.

After voting in the final stage, however, some team members still had doubts about the results. Therefore, the workshop was extended by about 1 h to resolve these dis-agreements; and some of the workshop members actually dropped out at this point. A key reason for this appears to have been insufficient discussion of potential design flaws in the early stage.

More specifically, throughout the workshop, a great deal of time was provided for team members to brainstorm individually, which as well as being time-consuming appeared to increase their fatigue. This highlighted a clear difference between online and face-to-face workshops: that maintaining focus during the former is particularly chal-lenging. Secondly, in the early stage, team members were not used to speaking up via Zoom, and it took a while for the discussion to warm up. And lastly, insufficient Internet connections meant that the system could not always support multiple people talking at once, and this could have further discouraged some team members from speaking up. Based on these factors, we recommend that online workshops' warm-up times be longer than the norm for face-to-face ones, i.e., 10–15 min or perhaps even longer.

We can conclude that the Double Diamond model is valid and readily adapted to a remote-workshop modality. Nevertheless, we recommend that it be separated into several offline and online sessions, to maintain team members' energy and attention throughout. We also recommend that the teams conducting such workshops settle on some ground rules and tooltips in advance, especially – though not exclusively – to accommodate those members who can only work asynchronously at certain points in the process.

5   Managerial Implications and Concluding Remarks

Although new challenges are associated with hosting workshops online, our experience suggests that many or most of them are soluble. Additionally, online design workshops have the potential for achievements that would be difficult or impossible in face-to-face settings. For example, a participant who cannot attend the workshop can nevertheless follow the same steps offline and complete his/her work asynchronously. Documentation of an online workshop is also easier, insofar as everything is already digitized. Further reflections are provided below.

5.1   Creating the Workshop Playbook

5.1.1   Separate the Double Diamond Model

As mentioned earlier, participating in the two diamonds of the Double Diamond model separately may help mitigate team members' fatigue during workshops. Where there are severe time constraints, we recommend only the core team members (e.g., workshop host, chief designer) complete the first diamond, and convey the results to the remaining members.

5.1.2   Allow Offline Participation with a Clear Playbook

Per the Double Diamond model, Convergence is the most critical stage, in that it requires everyone's participation. However, in our case, the convergence process took longer than expected, and thus contributed to team members' fatigue. We therefore recommend that online design workshops' hosts build playbooks for all their members, regardless of whether their participation in the workshop is expected to be synchronous or asynchronous.

5.1.3   Ensure that the Digital Workspace is Easy to Follow

Given the impossibility of physical interaction, we also recommend that hosts clearly point out relevant materials in their playbooks. Moreover, selecting appropriate online collaborative tools – i.e., ones that establish a digital shared space – is essential to remote design workshops' success.

5.2   Ensuring Members Completely Express Their Ideas to One Another

Do not skimp on ice-breaking. As team members are unlikely to be highly familiar with online-workshop protocol, we recommend that any design team working remotely dedicate a full session to ice-breaking. This will allow team members to better understand one another, adopt a suitable new communication style, and prevent voices from going unheard.

We expect the outcomes of this to stimulate further discussion on building UX workshop protocols during the pandemic, and to shed some light on new forms of communication within design teams.

Acknowledgements. This work was financially supported by the Ministry of Science and Technology (MOST) in Taiwan, under MOST 111-2636-H-002-004- and MOST 110-2634-F-002-045, and the Center for Research in Econometric Theory and Applications (Grant no. 110L900204) from The Featured Areas Research Center Program within the framework of the Higher Education Sprout Project by the Ministry of Education (MOE) in Taiwan.

References

1. UX Workshops and When to Use Them: A Cheat Sheet. https://www.nngroup.com/articles/5-ux-workshops/. Accessed 28 Apr 2021
2. A Study of the Design Process. https://www.designcouncil.org.uk/sites/default/files/asset/document/ElevenLessons_Design_Council%20(2).pdf. Accessed 28 Apr 2021
3. Design Thinking 101. https://www.nngroup.com/articles/design-thinking/. Accessed 28 Apr 2021
4. How to Run Great Remote Workshops. https://uxdesign.cc/how-to-run-great-remote-workshops-da4720777bbe. Accessed 28 Apr 2021
5. Tools for Remote UX Workshops. https://www.nngroup.com/articles/tools-remote-ux-workshops/. Accessed 28 Apr 2021
6. Davis, A., Wallace, N., Langley, J., Gwilt, I.: Low-contact co-design: considering more flexible spatiotemporal models for the co-design workshop. Strateg. Des. Res. J. **14**(1), 124–137 (2021)
7. Kennedy, A., Cosgrave, C., Macdonald, J., Gunn, K., Dietrich, T., Brumby, S.: Translating co-design from face-to-face to online: an Australian primary producer project conducted during COVID-19. Int. J. Environ. Res. Publ. Health **18**(8), 4147 (2021)
8. Gultom, R., Hirzirahim, A., Nugraha, Y., Nursyufa, Z., Hamdi, Suherman, A.L.: Developing a framework for self-isolation app: a case study of Jakarta's COVID-19 mitigation. IOP Conf. Ser. Mater. Sci. Eng. **1077**(1), 012020 (2021)

Testing the Generalization of Neural Language Models for COVID-19 Misinformation Detection

Jan Philip Wahle[1]([✉])(iD), Nischal Ashok[2](iD), Terry Ruas[1](iD),
Norman Meuschke[1](iD), Tirthankar Ghosal[3](iD), and Bela Gipp[1](iD)

[1] University of Wuppertal, Rainer -Gruenter -Straße, 42119 Wuppertal, Germany
{Wahle,Ruas,Meuschke,Gipp}@uniwuppertal.de
[2] Indian Institute of Technology Patna, Bihar 801106, India
1801cs33@iitp.ac.in
[3] Charles University, Malostranské Náměstí 25, 118 00 Praha, Czech Republic
ghosal@ufal.mff.cuni.cz

Abstract. A drastic rise in potentially life-threatening misinformation has been a by-product of the COVID-19 pandemic. Computational support to identify false information within the massive body of data on the topic is crucial to prevent harm. Researchers proposed many methods for flagging online misinformation related to COVID-19. However, these methods predominantly target specific content types (e.g., news) or platforms (e.g., Twitter). The methods' capabilities to generalize were largely unclear so far. We evaluate fifteen Transformer-based models on five COVID-19 misinformation datasets that include social media posts, news articles, and scientific papers to fill this gap. We show tokenizers and models tailored to COVID-19 data do not provide a significant advantage over general-purpose ones. Our study provides a realistic assessment of models for detecting COVID-19 misinformation. We expect that evaluating a broad spectrum of datasets and models will benefit future research in developing misinformation detection systems.

Keywords: COVID-19 · Transformers · Health · Social media.

1 Introduction

The COVID-19 pandemic has claimed more than four million lives by the time of writing this paper, and the number of infections remains high[1]. The behavior of individuals strongly affects the risk of infection. In turn, the quality of information individuals receive strongly influences their actions [10,23]. The novelty and rapid global spread of the SARS-CoV-2 virus has also led to countless life-threatening incidences of misinformation spread on the topic. Controlling

---

[1] https://coronavirus.jhu.edu/map.html.

J. P. Wahle and N. Ashok—Equal contribution.

M. Smits (Ed.): iConference 2022, LNCS 13192, pp. 381–392, 2022.
https://doi.org/10.1007/978-3-030-96957-8_33

COVID-19 and combating possible future pandemics early, requires reducing misinformation and increasing the distribution of facts on the subject [5,35].

Researchers worldwide collaborate on automating the detection of false information on COVID-19.[2] The initiatives build collections of scientific papers, social media posts, and news articles to analyze their content, spread, source, and propagators [7,19,33].

Natural Language Processing (NLP) research has extensively studied options to automate the identification of fake news [27], primarily by applying recent language models. Researchers proposed adaptions of well-known Transformer models, such as COVID-Twitter-BERT [20], to identify false information on COVID-19 from specific sources. However, most prior studies analyze specific content types (e.g., news) or platforms (e.g., Twitter). These limitations prevent reliable conclusions regarding the generalization of the proposed language models.

To fill this gap, we apply 15 Transformer models to five COVID-19 misinformation tasks. We compare Transformer models optimized on COVID-19 datasets to state-of-the-art neural language models. We exhaustively apply models to different tasks to test their generalization on unknown sources. The code to reproduce our experiments,[3] and the datasets used are publicly available.

2   Related Work

The same way word2vec [18] inspired many models in NLP [4,25,26], the excellent performance of BERT [8], a Transformer-based model [28], caused its numerous adaption for language tasks [6,29,30,34]. Domain-specific models build on top of Transformers typically outperform their baselines for related tasks [12]. For example, SciBERT [2] was pre-trained on scientific documents and typically outperforms BERT for scientific NLP tasks, such as determining document similarity [22].

Many models for COVID-19 misinformation detection employ domain-specific pre-training to improve their representation. COVID-Twitter-BERT [20] was pre-trained on 160M tweets and evaluated for sentiment analysis of tweets, e.g., about COVID vaccines. BioClinicalBERT [1] was trained into clinical narratives to incorporate linguistic characteristics from the biomedical and clinical domains.

Cui et al. [7] investigated the misinformation detection task by comparing traditional machine learning and deep learning techniques. Similarly, Zhou et al. [36] explored statistical learners, such as SVM, and neural networks to classify news as credible or not. The results of both studies show deep learning architectures as the most prominent alternatives for the respective datasets.

---

[2] We collectively refer to fake news, disinformation, and misinformation as false information.

[3] https://github.com/ag-gipp/iConference22_COVID_misinformation.

As papers on COVID-19 are recent, some contributions are only available as pre-trained models. COVID-BERT[4] and COVID-SciBERT[5] are pre-trained on the CORD-19 dataset and only available via the Huggingface API. Others, such as COVID-CQ [19] and CMU-MisCov19 [17] are used to either investigate intrinsic details (e.g., how dense misinformed communities are) or to explore the applicability of statistical techniques.

Although related works provide promising approaches to counter misinformation related to COVID-19, none of them explore multiple datasets. Research in many NLP areas already uses diverse benchmarks to compare models [31,32]. To the best of our knowledge, our study is the first to systematically test Transformer-based methods on different data sources related to COVID-19.

3   Methodology

Models. Our study includes 15 Transformer-based models, which are detailed in Appendix A.2. We categorize the models into the following three groups:

General-Purpose Baselines. The first group consists of general-purpose Transformer models without domain-specific training, i.e., BERT [8], RoBERTa [16], BART [15], DeBERTa [11]. These baselines show how vanilla Transformer-based models perform on the COVID-19 misinformation detection task.

Intermediate Pre-Training. The second group contains models trained on specific content types and domains, i.e., SciBERT [2], BERTweet [21], and Bio-ClinicalBERT [1]. For example, SciBERT adapts BERT for scientific articles. These models show the effect of intermediate pre-training on specific sources compared to general-purpose training (e.g., whether BERTweet is superior to BERT for misinformation on Twitter). Moreover, we compare the models in this group to language models optimized using intermediate pre-training on COVID-19 data (third group).

COVID-19 Intermediate Pre-Training. The third group comprises models employing an intermediate pre-training stage on COVID-19 data. Due to task-specific pre-training, we expect these models to achieve better results than the models in groups one and two. We include a model that optimizes the pre-training objective on a large Twitter corpus, i.e., CT-BERT [20], two models trained on the CORD-19 dataset (COVID-BERT[6] and COVID-SciBERT[7]), and two popular models from the huggingface API for which the intermediate pre-training sources are not released yet (ClinicalCOVID-BERT[8] and BioCOVID-BERT[9]). We pre-train RoBERTa, BART, and DeBERTa on the CORD-19 dataset to compare them to the models we used as general-purpose baselines.

---

[4] https://tinyurl.com/86cpx6u2.
[5] https://tinyurl.com/9w24pc93.
[6] https://tinyurl.com/86cpx6u2.
[7] https://tinyurl.com/9w24pc93.
[8] https://tinyurl.com/kebysw.
[9] https://tinyurl.com/4xx9vdkm.

Data. We compile an evaluation set from six popular datasets for detecting COVID-19 misinformation in social media, news articles, and scientific publications, i.e., CORD-19 [33], CoAID [7], COVID-CQ [19], ReCOVery [36], CMU-MisCov19 [17], and COVID19FN.[10] Table 1 gives an overview of the datasets and Appendix A.1 presents more details. For CORD-19, we only use abstracts in the dataset, as they provide an adequate trade-off between size and information density. Additionally, less than 50% of the articles in CORD-19 are available as full texts. For CoAID and ReCOVery, we only extract news articles to reduce a bias towards Twitter posts in our evaluation. All remaining datasets are used in their original composition.

We use CORD-19 to extend the pre-training of general-purpose models and all other datasets to evaluate the models for a downstream task. CORD-19 consists of scientific articles, while the other datasets primarily contain news articles and Twitter content. We chose different domains for training and evaluation to test the models' generalization capabilities and avoid overlaps between the datasets.

Table 1. An overview of the COVID-related datasets. CORD-19 has no specific *Task* or *Label* as it provides a general collection of documents. [†]Details on the labels are given in Memon et al. [17].

Corpus	|Corpus|	Task	Domain	Source(s)	Label(s)
CORD-19 [33]	497 906	–	Scientific articles	CZI, PMC, BioRxiv, MedRxiv	–
CoAID [7]	302 926	Misinformation detection	Healthcare misinformation	Twitter, news, social media	{*true, false*}
ReCOVery [36]	142 849	Credibility classification	Low information credibility	Twitter, news	{*reliable, unreliable*}
COVID-CQ [19]	14 374	Efficacy of treatments	Drug treatment	Twitter	{*neutral, against, for*}
CMU-MisCov19 [17]	4 573	Communities detection	Misinformed communities	Twitter	{*17 labels*[†]}
COVID19FN (2020)	2 800	Misinformation detection	Misinformation in news	Poynter	{*true, false*}

4   Experiments

Overview. Our study includes three experiments. The first experiment tests how static word embeddings and frozen contextual embeddings perform compared to fine-tuned language models. The second experiment studies whether tokenizers specifically tailored to a COVID-19 vocabulary are superior to general-purpose ones.[11] The third experiment evaluates and compares all 15 Transformer models on the five evaluation datasets.

---

[10] https://tinyurl.com/4ne9vtzu.
[11] General-purpose refers to the tokenizers released with the pre-trained models.

Training and Evaluation. To compare general-purpose baselines and COVID-19 intermediate pre-trained models, we perform *pre-training* on the CORD-19 dataset for three models (RoBERTa, BART, and DeBERTa) and use pre-trained configurations for the remaining models (BERT, SciBERT, BioCOVID-BERT, ClinicalCOVID-BERT). We then *fine-tune* all models for each of the five test tasks (COVID-CQ, CoAID, ReCOVery, CMU-MisCov19, and COVID19FN). We use a split of 80% and 20% of the documents in a dataset for training and testing, respectively. This split is the most common configuration for the tested datasets [19,36] and is comparable to other studies [7]. We use 10% of the train dataset as a hold-out validation set.

5 Results and Discussion

Static and Frozen Embeddings. Table 2 compares the classification results of a baseline composed of BiLSTM and GlobalVectors (GloVe) [4] to the frozen embeddings of three Transformer models for the COVID-CQ dataset. The results show no significant difference between GloVe and the frozen models. However, fine-tuning the same three models end-to-end generally increases their performance. Therefore, we choose to fine-tune neural language models for the classification of COVID-19 misinformation.

Tokenizer Ablation. Table 3 shows the results on COVID-CQ for the best configuration of the models using a standard[12] tokenizer for pre-training and fine-tuning. We expected adjusting the tokenizer to the CORD-19 dataset would improve the results, as it adds valuable tokens to the vocabulary, which are often not present in standard tokenizers. However, using specialized tokenizers decreased the performance. The content in CORD-19 originates from the scientific domain. We hypothesize tweets lack similar token relations, which causes the performance drop on the COVID-CQ dataset. Therefore, we use the standard tokenizer for our full evaluation experiments.

Full Evaluation. Table 4 reports the results of our full evaluation. All results are statistically significant using bootstrap and permutation tests ($p < .05$) [9]. General-purpose baselines achieved the best result for two of the five datasets (BART on CoAID and BART on COVID19FN). For two datasets (ReCOVery and COVID-CQ), a model we pre-trained on CORD-19 data (COVID-RoBERTa) performed best. CT-BERT achieved the best result on CMU-MisCov19, an expected outcome as the datasets consist only of Twitter content. BERTweet, which was also trained on Twitter data, does not achieve better results than general-purpose baselines. We expected a minor drop in performance for BERTweet compared to CT-BERT as the former was not trained on COVID-19 vocabulary, but better a performance than general-purpose models as BERTweet was trained mainly on Twitter data.

---

[12] Pre-Trained tokenizer provided by HuggingFace.

Table 2. F1-Macro scores of neural language models and a baseline (BiLSTM+GloVe) for the COVID-CQ dataset. The *static* and *frozen* models use a stacked BiLSTM; *fine-tuned* models were pre-trained on the CORD-19 dataset and fine-tuned for the task.

Type	Models	F1-Macro
static	GloVe	.71
frozen	BERT	.72
frozen	RoBERTa	.70
frozen	SciBERT	.68
fine-tuned	BERT	**.75**
fine-tuned	RoBERTa	**.80**
fine-tuned	SciBERT	**.76**

Table 3. F1-Macro scores of BART and RoBERTa on the COVID-CQ dataset using different **Pre-Training** and **Fine-Tuning** Tokenizers. All models were pre-trained on the CORD-19 dataset.

Models	PT Tok.	FT Tok.	F1-Macro
RoBERTa	Standard	Standard	**.78**
RoBERTa	COVID	Standard	.73
RoBERTa	COVID	COVID	.72
BART	Standard	Standard	**.77**
BART	COVID	Standard	.73
BART	COVID	COVID	.70

All models achieved low scores for CMU-MisCov19, making it the most challenging dataset in our evaluation. The best results were obtained for CoAID. Overall, general-purpose baselines achieved comparable results to COVID-19 intermediate pre-trained models for all datasets. For example, the best mean

Table 4. Average F1-Macro scores and standard deviation over three randomly sampled runs of neural language models for COVID datasets. The table is divided into three parts: general-purpose baselines, intermediate pre-trained, and COVID-19 intermediate pre-trained models. **COVID A**ware means the model was pre-trained on CORD-19 (✓), pre-trained on a different dataset (✗), or the dataset was not reported (?). **Intermediate Training** means the model was pre-trained in a specific domain. **Boldface** indicates the highest value for each dataset. [†]Models trained on CORD-19. [*]Large version of the model.

IT	CA	Model	CMU-MisCov19	CoAID	ReCOVery	COVID19FN	COVID-CQ
—	—	BERT	.54 ± .03	.93 ± .01	.78 ± .02	.65 ± .01	.76 ± .01
—	—	RoBERTa	.53 ± .03	.95 ± .01	.81 ± .01	.73 ± .02	.64 ± .01
—	—	BART	.49 ± .03	**.96 ± .01**	.90 ± .01	**.83 ± .01**	.75 ± .01
—	—	DeBERTa	.52 ± .04	.95 ± .01	.75 ± .01	.67 ± .03	.63 ± .02
✓	—	SciBERT	.46 ± .02	.95 ± .01	.77 ± .01	.76 ± .01	.61 ± .02
✓	—	BioClinicalBERT	.48 ± .02	.89 ± .01	.82 ± .01	.81 ± .02	.63 ± .02
✓	—	BERTweet	.51 ± .03	.88 ± .02	.84 ± .03	.65 ± .01	.75 ± .01
✓	✗	CT-BERT [*]	**.58 ± .04**	.94 ± .01	.80 ± .02	.40 ± .01	.63 ± .02
✓	?	ClinicalCOVID-BERT	.50 ± .03	.93 ± .01	.82 ± .01	.78 ± .02	.74 ± .02
✓	?	BioCOVID-BERT [*]	.45 ± .01	.91 ± .02	.81 ± .01	.68 ± .03	.63 ± .02
✓	✓	COVID-BERT [†]	.46 ± .02	.94 ± .01	.85 ± .03	.73 ± .02	.72 ± .01
✓	✓	COVID-SciBERT [†]	.34 ± .02	.92 ± .03	.78 ± .03	.67 ± .02	.76 ± .03
✓	✓	COVID-RoBERTa	.40 ± .04	.92 ± .04	**.91 ± .03**	.67 ± .03	**.78 ± .03**
✓	✓	COVID-BART	.33 ± .01	.91 ± .06	.89 ± .03	.66 ± .05	.77 ± .07
✓	✓	COVID-DeBERTa	.30 ± .01	.92 ± .05	.89 ± .02	.81 ± .03	.73 ± .01

result for the dataset ReCOVery was achieved by COVID-RoBERTa (F1 = .91, std = .03) while the general-purpose model BART (F1 = .90, std = .01) was only .01 score points worse. We observe similar results for COVID-CQ, where the best model COVID-RoBERTa (F1 = .78, std = .03) has a score difference of .02 to the second-best model BERT (F1 = .76, std = .01). We conclude that pre-training language models on COVID data before fine-tuning on a misinformation task did not generally provide an advantage for the tested datasets in this paper.

6   Conclusion and Future Work

This study empirically evaluated 15 Transformer models for five COVID-19 misinformation tasks. Our analysis shows domain-specific models and tokenizers do not generally perform better in the classification of misinformation. We conclude that the vocabulary related to COVID-19 and possibly text-patterns about COVID-19 do not have a significant effect on the models' ability to classify misinformation.

The main limitation of our study is the non-standardized pre-training of models due to the models' diversity. To reliably detect misinformation across content types and platforms, researchers need access to diverse data. We see this study as an initial step to compile a benchmark for COVID-19 data similar to widely adopted natural language understanding benchmarks (e.g., GLUE, SuperGLUE) which enable an evaluation across diverse sets of misinformation domains, sources, and tasks.

Controlling the current and future pandemics requires reliable detection of false information propagated through many streams and having different unique features. This study is a first step for researchers and policymakers to devise and deploy systems that reliably flag misinformation related to COVID-19 from a broad spectrum of sources.

The usefulness of NLP models increases significantly if they are applicable to multiple tasks [31]. We anticipate future NLP technologies for detecting misinformation need to adopt the trend of evaluating on several benchmark datasets. This work provides a first milestone in evaluating general model capabilities and questioning the advantage of domain-specific model pre-training.

Although COVID-19 accelerated the propagation of misinformation and disinformation, these problems are not unique to the current pandemic. The effects of COVID-19 misinformation and disinformation on elections, ethical biases, and the portrayal of ethical groups [3] can have similar or even more severe consequences on society than misinformation related to COVID-19. Therefore, identifying false information streams across domains will remain a challenging problem, and identifying which models can generalize for many sources is crucial.

A   Appendix

A.1   Dataset Details

COVID-19 Open Research Dataset (CORD-19) [33] is the largest open source dataset about COVID-19 and coronavirus-related research (e.g. SARS, MERS). CORD-19 is composed of more than 280K scholarly articles from PubMed,[13] bioRxiv,[14] medRxiv,[15] and other resources maintained by the WHO.[16] We use this dataset to extend the general pre-training from selected neural language models (cf. Sect. 3) into the COVID-specific vocabulary and features.

Covid-19 heAlthcare mIsinformation Dataset (CoAID) [7] focuses on healthcare misinformation, including fake news on websites, user engagement, and social media. CoAID is composed of 5 216 news articles, 296 752 related user engagements, and 958 posts about COVID-19, which are broadly categorized under the labels *true* and *false*.

Twitter Stance Dataset (COVID-CQ) [19] is a dataset of user-generated Twitter content in the context of COVID-19. More than 14K tweets were processed and annotated regarding the use of *Chloroquine* and *Hydroxychloroquine* as a valid treatment or prevention against the coronavirus. COVID-CQ is composed of 14 374 tweets from 11 552 unique users labeled as *neutral*, *against*, or *favor*.

ReCOVery [36] explores the low credibility of information on COVID-19 (e.g., bleach can prevent COVID-19) by allowing a multimodal investigation of news and their spread on social media. The dataset is composed of 2 029 news articles on the coronavirus and 140 820 related tweets labeled as *reliable* or *unreliable*.

CMU-MisCov19 [17] is a Twitter dataset created by collecting posts from unknowingly misinformed users, users who actively spread misinformation, and users who disseminate facts or call out misinformation. CMU-MisCov19 is composed of 4 573 annotated tweets divided into 17 classes (e.g., *conspiracy*, *fake cure*, *news*, *sarcasm*). The high number of classes and their imbalanced distribution make CMU-MisCov19 a challenging dataset.

COVID19FN[17] is composed of approximately 2 800 news articles extracted mainly from Poynter[18] categorized as either *real* or *fake*.

A.2   Model Details

General-Purpose Baselines. BERT [8] mainly captures general language characteristics using a bidirectional *Masked Language Model* (MLM) and *Next*

---

[13] https://pubmed.ncbi.nlm.nih.gov/.
[14] https://www.biorxiv.org/.
[15] https://www.medrxiv.org/.
[16] https://www.who.int/.
[17] https://tinyurl.com/4mryzj5k.
[18] https://www.poynter.org/ifcn/.

Sentence Prediction (NSP) tasks. RoBERTa [16] improves BERT with additional data, compute budgets, and hyperparameter optimizations. RoBERTa also drops the NSP as it contributes little to the model representation. BART [15] optimizes an auto-regressive forward-product and auto-encoding MLM objective simultaneously. DeBERTa [11] improves the attention mechanism using a disentanglement of content and position.

Intermediate Pre-Trained. SciBERT [2] optimizes the MLM for 1.14M randomly selected papers from Semantic Scholar[19]. BioClinicalBERT [1] specializes on 2M notes in the MIMIC-III database [13], a collection of disidentified clinical data. BERTweet [21] optimizes BERT on 850M tweets each containing between 10 and 64 tokens.

COVID-19 Intermediate Pre-Trained. COVID-Twitter-BERT [20] (CT-BERT) uses a corpus of 160M tweets for domain-specific pre-training and evaluates the resulting model's capabilities in sentiment analysis, such as for tweets about vaccines. BioClinicalBERT [1] fine-tunes BioBERT [14] into clinical narratives in the hope to incorporate linguistic characteristics from both the clinical and biomedical domains.

Cui et al. [7] propose CoAID and investigate the misinformation detection task by comparing traditional machine learning (e.g., logistic regression, random forest) and deep learning techniques (e.g., GRU). In a similar layout, Zhou et al. [36] compare traditional statistical learners, such as SVM and neural networks (e.g., CNN), to classify news as credible or not. In both studies, the results show deep learning architectures as the most prominent options.

A.3   Evaluation Details

Pre-Training. We use the data from the abstracts of the CORD-19 dataset for pre-training. For pre-processing the CORD-19 abstract data, we consider only alphanumerical characters. We use a sequence length of 128 tokens, which reduces training time while being competitive to longer sequence lengths when fine-tuning [24]. We mask words randomly with a probability of .15, a common configuration for Transformers [8,11], and perform the MLM with the following remaining parameters: a batch size of 16 for all the base models, and eight for the large models, the Adam Optimizer ($\alpha = 2e - 5$, $\beta_1 = .9$, $\beta_2 = .999$, $\epsilon = 1e - 8$), and a maximum of five epochs. All experiments were performed on a single NVIDIA GeForce GTX 1080 Ti GPU with 11 GB of memory.

Fine-Tuning. The classification model applies a randomly initialized fully-connected layer to the aggregate representation of the underlying Transformer (e.g., [CLS] for BERT) with dropout ($p = .1$) to learn the annotated target classes with cross-entropy loss for five epochs and with a sequence length of 200 tokens. We use the same configuration of the optimizer as in pre-training.

---

[19] https://www.semanticscholar.org/.

References

1. Alsentzer, E., et al.: Publicly Available Clinical BERT Embeddings. arXiv:1904.03323 [cs], June 2019. http://arxiv.org/abs/1904.03323
2. Beltagy, I., Lo, K., Cohan, A.: SciBERT: a pretrained language model for scientific text. In: Proceedings of the 2019 Conference on Empirical Methods in Natural Language Processing and the 9th International Joint Conference on Natural Language Processing (EMNLP-IJCNLP), pp. 3613–3618. Association for Computational Linguistics, Hong Kong, China (2019). 10/ggcgtm
3. Benkler, Y., Farris, R., Roberts, H.: Network Propaganda, vol. 1. Oxford University Press, October 2018. https://doi.org/10.1093/oso/9780190923624.001.0001
4. Bojanowski, P., Grave, E., Joulin, A., Mikolov, T.: Enriching word vectors with subword information. Trans. Assoc. Comput. Linguist. **5**, 135–146 (2017). 10/gfw9cs
5. Cinelli, M., et al.: The COVID-19 social media infodemic. Sci. Rep. **10**(1), 16598 (2020). https://doi.org/10.1038/s41598-020-73510-5
6. Clark, K., Luong, M.T., Le, Q.V., Manning, C.D.: ELECTRA: Pre-training Text Encoders as Discriminators Rather Than Generators. arXiv:2003.10555 [cs], March 2020. http://arxiv.org/abs/2003.10555
7. Cui, L., Lee, D.: CoAID: COVID-19 Healthcare Misinformation Dataset. arXiv:2006.00885 [cs], August 2020. http://arxiv.org/abs/2006.00885
8. Devlin, J., Chang, M.W., Lee, K., Toutanova, K.: BERT: Pre-training of Deep Bidirectional Transformers for Language Understanding. arXiv:1810.04805, May 2019. http://arxiv.org/abs/1810.04805
9. Dror, R., Baumer, G., Shlomov, S., Reichart, R.: The hitchhiker's guide to testing statistical significance in natural language processing. In: Proceedings of the 56th Annual Meeting of the Association for Computational Linguistics (Volume 1: Long Papers), pp. 1383–1392. Association for Computational Linguistics, Melbourne, Australia, July 2018. https://doi.org/10.18653/v1/P18-1128
10. Hele, T., et al.: A global panel database of pandemic policies (oxford COVID-19 government response tracker). Nat. Hum. Behav. **5**(4), 529–538 (2021). https://doi.org/10.1038/s41562-021-01079-8
11. He, P., Liu, X., Gao, J., Chen, W.: DeBERTa: Decoding-enhanced BERT with Disentangled Attention. arXiv:2006.03654 [cs], January 2021. http://arxiv.org/abs/2006.03654
12. Howard, J., Ruder, S.: Universal language model fine-tuning for text classification. In: Proceedings of the 56th Annual Meeting of the Association for Computational Linguistics (Volume 1: Long Papers), pp. 328–339. Association for Computational Linguistics, Melbourne, Australia, July 2018. https://doi.org/10.18653/v1/P18-1031
13. Johnson, A.E., et al.: MIMIC-III, a freely accessible critical care database. Sci. Data **3**, 160035 (2016). https://doi.org/10.1038/sdata.2016.35 Moody, B., Szolovits, P., Celi, L.A., Mark, R.G.: MIMIC-III, a freely accessible critical care database. Scientific Data **3**, 160035 (May 2016). https://doi.org/10.1038/sdata.2016.35
14. Lee, J., et al.: BioBERT: a pre-trained biomedical language representation model for biomedical text mining. Bioinformatics, pp. 1–7 (2019). https://doi.org/10.1093/bioinformatics/btz682

15. Lewis, M., et al.: BART: denoising sequence-to-sequence pre-training for natural language generation, translation, and comprehension. In: Proceedings of the 58th Annual Meeting of the Association for Computational Linguistics, pp. 7871–7880. Association for Computational Linguistics, Online, July 2020. https://doi.org/10.18653/v1/2020.acl-main.703

16. Liu, Y., et al.: RoBERTa: A Robustly Optimized BERT Pretraining Approach. arXiv:1907.11692 [cs], July 2019. http://arxiv.org/abs/1907.11692

17. Memon, S.A., Carley, K.M.: Characterizing COVID-19 Misinformation Communities Using a Novel Twitter Dataset. arXiv:2008.00791 [cs], September 2020. http://arxiv.org/abs/2008.00791

18. Mikolov, T., Sutskever, I., Chen, K., Corrado, G., Dean, J.: Distributed Representations of Words and Phrases and their Compositionality. arXiv:1310.4546 [cs, stat], October 2013. http://arxiv.org/abs/1310.45464

19. Mutlu, E.C., et al.: A stance data set on polarized conversations on Twitter about the efficacy of hydroxychloroquine as a treatment for COVID-19. Data in Brief **33**, 106401 (2020). https://doi.org/10.1016/j.dib.2020.106401

20. Müller, M., Salathé, M., Kummervold, P.E.: COVID-twitter-bert: a natural language processing model to analyse COVID-19 content on twitter. arXiv:2005.07503 [cs], May 2020. http://arxiv.org/abs/2005.07503

21. Nguyen, D.Q., Vu, T., Tuan Nguyen, A.: BERTweet: a pre-trained language model for English tweets. In: Proceedings of the 2020 Conference on Empirical Methods in Natural Language Processing: System Demonstrations, pp. 9–14. Association for Computational Linguistics, Online (2020). https://doi.org/10.18653/v1/2020.emnlp-demos.2

22. Ostendorff, M., Ruas, T., Blume, T., Gipp, B., Rehm, G.: Aspect-based document similarity for research papers. In: Proceedings of the 28th International Conference on Computational Linguistics, pp. 6194–6206. International Committee on Computational Linguistics, Barcelona, Spain (Online) (2020). https://doi.org/10.18653/v1/2020.coling-main.545

23. Pennycook, G., McPhetres, J., Zhang, Y., Lu, J.G., Rand, D.G.: Fighting COVID-19 misinformation on social media: experimental evidence for a scalable accuracy-nudge intervention. Psychol. Sci. **31**(7), 770–780 (2020). https://doi.org/10.1177/0956797620939054

24. Press, O., Smith, N.A., Lewis, M.: Shortformer: better language modeling using shorter inputs. arXiv:2012.15832 [cs], December 2020. http://arxiv.org/abs/2012.15832

25. Ruas, T., Ferreira, C.H.P., Grosky, W., de França, F.O., de Medeiros, D.M.R.: Enhanced word embeddings using multi-semantic representation through lexical chains. Inf. Sci. **532**, 16–32 (2020). https://doi.org/10.1016/j.ins.2020.04.048

26. Ruas, T., Grosky, W., Aizawa, A.: Multi-sense embeddings through a word sense disambiguation process. Expert Syst. Appl. **136**, 288–303 (2019). https://doi.org/10.1016/j.eswa.2019.06.026

27. Shu, K., Sliva, A., Wang, S., Tang, J., Liu, H.: Fake news detection on social media: a data mining perspective. ACM SIGKDD Explor. Newslett. **19**(1), 22–36 (2017). https://doi.org/10.1145/3137597.3137600

28. Vaswani, A., et al.: Attention is all you need. In: Proceedings of the 31st International Conference on Neural Information Processing Systems, pp. 6000–6010. NIPS 2017, Curran Associates Inc., Red Hook, NY, USA (2017). https://arxiv.org/abs/1706.03762

29. Wahle, J.P., Ruas, T., Foltynek, T., Meuschke, N., Gipp, B.: Identifying machine-paraphrased plagiarism. In: Proceedings of the iConference, February 2022

30. Wahle, J.P., Ruas, T., Meuschke, N., Gipp, B.: Are neural language models good plagiarists? a benchmark for neural paraphrase detection. In: Proceedings of the ACM/IEEE Joint Conference on Digital Libraries (JCDL). IEEE, Washington, USA, September 2021

31. Wang, A., et al.: SuperGLUE: a stickier benchmark for general-purpose language understanding systems. In: Wallach, H., Larochelle, H., Beygelzimer, A., d' Alché-Buc, F., Fox, E., Garnett, R. (eds.) Advances in Neural Information Processing Systems 32, pp. 3266–3280. Curran Associates, Inc. (2019). https://arxiv.org/abs/1905.00537

32. Wang, A., Singh, A., Michael, J., Hill, F., Levy, O., Bowman, S.R.: GLUE: A Multi-Task Benchmark and Analysis Platform for Natural Language Understanding. arXiv:1804.07461 [cs], February 2019. https://arxiv.org/abs/1804.0746

33. Wang, L.L., et al.: CORD-19: The COVID-19 Open Research Dataset. arXiv:2004.10706 [cs], July 2020. http://arxiv.org/abs/2004.10706

34. Yang, Z., Dai, Z., Yang, Y., Carbonell, J., Salakhutdinov, R., Le, Q.V.: XLNet: generalized autoregressive pretraining for language understanding. arXiv:1906.08237 [cs], June 2019. https://arxiv.org/abs/1804.0746

35. Zarocostas, J.: How to fight an infodemic. Lancet **395**(10225), 676 (2020). https://doi.org/10.1016/S0140-6736(20)30461-X

36. Zhou, X., Mulay, A., Ferrara, E., Zafarani, R.: ReCOVery: A multimodal repository for COVID-19 news credibility research, pp. 3205–3212. Association for Computing Machinery, New York, NY, USA (2020). https://doi.org/10.1145/3340531.3412880

Identifying Machine-Paraphrased Plagiarism

Jan Philip Wahle[1]([✉]) [ID], Terry Ruas[1] [ID], Tomáš Foltýnek[2] [ID],
Norman Meuschke[1] [ID], and Bela Gipp[1] [ID]

[1] University of Wuppertal, Rainer-Gruenter-Straße, 42119 Wuppertal, Germany
{wahle,ruas,meuschke,gipp}@uni-wuppertal.de
[2] Mendel University in Brno, 61300 Brno, Czechia
tomas.foltynek@mendelu.cz

Abstract. Employing paraphrasing tools to conceal plagiarized text is
a severe threat to academic integrity. To enable the detection of machine-
paraphrased text, we evaluate the effectiveness of five pre-trained word
embedding models combined with machine learning classifiers and state-
of-the-art neural language models. We analyze preprints of research
papers, graduation theses, and Wikipedia articles, which we paraphrased
using different configurations of the tools SpinBot and SpinnerChief. The
best performing technique, Longformer, achieved an average F1 score
of 80.99% (F1 = 99.68% for SpinBot and F1 = 71.64% for SpinnerChief
cases), while human evaluators achieved F1 = 78.4% for SpinBot and
F1 = 65.6% for SpinnerChief cases. We show that the automated classification alleviates shortcomings of widely-used text-matching systems,
such as Turnitin and PlagScan.

Keywords: Paraphrase detection · Plagiarism · Document
classification · Transformers · BERT · Wikipedia

1 Introduction

Plagiarism is a pressing problem for educational and research institutions, publishers, and funding agencies [12]. To counteract plagiarism, many institutions
employ *text-matching software*. These tools reliably identify duplicated text yet
are significantly less effective for paraphrases, translations, and other concealed
forms of plagiarism [11,12].

Studies show that an alarming proportion of students employ *online paraphrasing tools* to disguise text taken from other sources [36,38]. These tools
employ artificial intelligence approaches to change text, e.g., by replacing words
with their synonyms [53]. Paraphrasing tools serve to alter the content so that
search engines do not recognize the fraudulent websites as duplicates.

In academia, paraphrasing tools help to mask plagiarism, facilitate collusion,
and help ghostwriters with producing work that appears original. These tools
severely threaten the effectiveness of text-matching software, which is a crucial
support tool for ensuring academic integrity. The academic integrity community

© The Author(s), under exclusive license to Springer Nature Switzerland AG 2022
M. Smits (Ed.): iConference 2022, LNCS 13192, pp. 393–413, 2022.
https://doi.org/10.1007/978-3-030-96957-8_34

calls for technical solutions to identify the machine-paraphrased text as one measure to counteract paraphrasing tools [38].

The International Journal for Educational Integrity recently devoted a special issue[1] to this topic.

We address this challenge by devising an automated approach that reliably distinguishes human-written from machine-paraphrased text and providing the solution as a free and open-source web application.

In this paper, we extend Foltýnek et al.[13] work by proposing two new collections created from research papers on arXiv[2] and graduation theses of "English language learners" (ELL), and explore a second paraphrasing tool for generating obfuscated samples. We also include eight neural language models based on the Transformer architecture for identifying machine-paraphrases.

To facilitate future research, all data[3], code[4], and two web applications[5,6] showcasing our contributions are openly available.

2   Related Work

The research on plagiarism detection technology has yielded many approaches that employ lexical, syntactical, semantic, or cross-lingual text analysis [12]. These approaches reliably find copied and moderately altered text; some can also identify paraphrased and machine-translated text. Methods to complement text analysis focus on non-textual features [25], such as academic citations [27], images [26], and mathematical content [28], to improve the detection of concealed plagiarism.

Most research on paraphrase identification quantifies to which degree the meaning of two sentences is identical. Approaches for this task employ lexical, syntactic, and semantic analysis (e.g., word embedding) as well as machine learning and deep learning techniques [12,47].

The research on distinguishing machine-paraphrased text passages from original content is still in an early stage. Zhang et al. [53] provided a tool that determines if two articles are derived from each other. However, they did not investigate the task of distinguishing original and machine-fabricated text. Dey et al. [9] applied a Support Vector Machine (SVM) classifier to identify semantically similar tweets and other short texts. A very recent work studied word embedding models for paraphrase sentence pairs with word reordering and synonym substitution [1]. In this work, we focus on detecting paraphrases without access to pairs as it represents a realistic scenario without pair information.

Techniques to accomplish the task of paraphrase detection, dense vector representations of words in documents have attracted much research in recent

---

[1] https://edintegrity.biomedcentral.com/mbp.

[2] https://arxiv.org.

[3] https://doi.org/10.5281/zenodo.3608000

[4] https://github.com/jpelhaW/ParaphraseDetection

[5] http://purl.org/spindetector

[6] https://huggingface.co/jpelhaw/longformer-base-plagiarism-detection

years. Word embedding techniques, such as word2vec [29], have alleviated common problems in bag-of-words (BOW) approaches, e.g., scalability issues and the curse of dimensionality. Representing entire documents in a single fixed-length dense vector (doc2vec) is another successful approach [22]. Word2vec and doc2vec can both capture latent semantic meaning from textual data using efficient neural network language models. Prediction-based word embedding models, such as word2vec and doc2vec, have proven themselves superior to count-based models, such as BOW, for several problems in Natural Language Processing (NLP), such as quantifying word similarity [40], classifying documents [39], and analyzing sentiment [34]. Gharavi et al. employed word embeddings to perform text alignment for sentences [14]. Hunt et al. integrated features from word2vec into machine learning models (e.g., logistic regression, SVM) to identify duplicate questions in the Quora dataset [16]. We, on the other hand, consider text documents generated with the help of automated tools at the paragraph level.

Recently, the NLP community adapted and extended the neural language model BERT [8] for a variety of tasks [2,5,31,32,42,46,51], similar to the way that word2vec [29] has influenced many later models in NLP [4,39,40]. Based on the Transformer architecture [45], BERT employs two pre-training tasks, i.e., *Masked Language Model* (MLM) and *Next Sentence Prediction* (NSP), to capture general aspects of language. MLM uses a deep bidirectional architecture to build a language model by masking random tokens in the input. The NSP task identifies if two sentences are semantically connected. The ALBERT [20], DistilBERT [41], and RoBERTa [24] models are all based on BERT and either improve their predecessor's performance through hyperparameter adjustments or make BERT less computationally expensive. Different from ELMo [35] and GPT [37], BERT considers left-to-right and right-to-left context simultaneously, allowing a more realistic representation of the language. Although ELMo does use two LSTM networks, their weights are not shared during training. On top of MLM and NSP, BERT requires fine-tuning to specific tasks to adjust its weights accordingly.

Other recent models proposed architectural and training modifications for BERT. ELECTRA changes BERT's MLM task to a generator-discriminator setup [5]. Tokens are substituted with artificially generated ones from a small masked language model and discriminated in a noise contrastive learning process [15]. BART pre-trains a bidirectional auto-encoding and an auto-regressive Transformer in a joint structure [23]. The two-stage denoising auto-encoder first corrupts the input with an arbitrary function (bidirectional) and uses a sequence-to-sequence approach to reconstruct the original input (auto-regressive) [23]. In XLNet, a permutation language modeling predicts one word given its preceding context at random [51]. Longformer proposed the most innovative contribution by exploring a new scheme for calculating attention [3]. Longformer's attention mechanism combines windowed local with global self-attention while also scaling linearly with the sequence length compared to earlier models (e.g., RoBERTa).

Foltýnek et al. [13] tested the effectiveness of six word embedding models and five traditional machine learning classifiers for identifying machine-paraphrased.

We paraphrased Wikipedia articles using the SpinBot[7] API, which is the technical backbone of several widely-used services, such as Paraphrasing Tool[8] and Free Article Spinner[9] [38]. The limitations of [13] are the exclusive use of one data source, the lack of recent neural language models, and the reliance on a single paraphrasing tool. In this paper, we address all three shortcomings by considering arXiv and graduation theses as new data sources (Sect. 3.2), eight neural language models (Sect. 3.5), and SpinnerSchief[10] as an additional paraphrasing tool (Sect. 3.1).

Lan et al. [19] compared five neural models (e.g., LSTM and CNN) using eight NLP datasets, of which three focus on sentence paraphrase detection (i.e., Quora [17], Twitter-URL [18], and PIT-2015 [50]). Subramanian et al. presented a model that combines language modeling, machine translation, constituency parsing, and natural language inference in a multi-task learning framework for sentence representation [43]. Their model produces state-of-the-art results for the MRPC [10] dataset. Our experiments consider a multi-source paragraph-level dataset and more recent neural models to reflect a real-world detection scenario and investigate recent NLP techniques that have not been investigated for this use case before.

Wahle et al. [47] is the only work, to date, that applies neural language models to generate machine paraphrased text. They use BERT and other popular neural language models to paraphrase an extensive collection of original content. We plan to investigate additional models and combine them with the work on generating paraphrased data [47], which could be used for training.

3   Methodology

Our primary research objective is to provide a free service that distinguishes human-written from machine-paraphrased text while being insensitive to the topic and type of documents and the paraphrasing tool used. We analyze paragraphs instead of sentences or entire documents since it represents a more realistic detection task [38,49]. Sentences provide little context and can lead to more false positives when sentence structures are similar. Fulltext documents are computationally expensive to process, and in many cases the extended context does not provide a significant advantage over paragraphs. We extend Foltýnek et al.'s [13] study by analyzing two new datasets (arXiv and theses), including an extra machine-paraphrasing tool (SpinnerChief), and evaluating eight state-of-the-art neural language models based on Transformers [45]. We first performed preliminary experiments with classic machine learning approaches to identify the best-performing baseline methods for paraphrasing tools and datasets we investigate. Next, we compared the best-performing machine learning techniques to neural language models based on the Transformer architecture, representing the latest advancements in NLP.

---

[7] https://spinbot.com/.

[8] https://paraphrasing-tool.com/.

[9] https://free-article-spinner.com/.

[10] http://www.spinnerchief.com/.

3.1   Paraphrasing Tools

We employed two commercial paraphrasing services, i.e., *SpinBot* (see Footnote
3) and *SpinnerChief* (see Footnote 6), to obfuscate samples in our training and
test sets. We used SpinBot to generate the training and test sets and Spinner-
Chief only for the test sets.

SpinnerChief allows specifying the ratio of words it tries to change. We experimented with two configurations: the *default frequency (SpinnerChief-DF)*, which
attempts to change every fourth word, and an *increased frequency (SpinnerChief-
IF)*, which attempts to change every second word.

3.2   Datasets for Training and Testing

Most paraphrasing tools are paid services, which prevents experimenting with
many of them. The financial costs and effort required for obtaining and incorporating tool-specific training data would be immense. Therefore, we employed
transfer learning, i.e., used pre-trained word embedding models, trained the classifiers in our study on samples paraphrased using SpinBot, and tested whether
the classification approach can also identify SpinnerChief's paraphrased text.

Training Set: We reused the paragraph training set of Foltýnek et al. [13] and
paraphrased all 4,012 *featured articles* from English Wikipedia using SpinBot
(see Footnote 3). We chose featured Wikipedia articles because they objectively
cover a wide range of topics in great breadth and depth[11]. Approx. 0.1% of all
Wikipedia articles carry the label *featured article*.

Thus, they are written in high-quality English by many authors and unlikely
to be biased towards individual writing styles.

The training set comprises of 200,767 paragraphs (98,282 original, 102,485
paraphrased) extracted from 8,024 Wikipedia articles. We split each Wikipedia
article into paragraphs and discarded those with fewer than three sentences, as
Foltýnek et al. [13] showed such paragraphs often represent titles or irrelevant
information.

Test Sets: Our study uses three test sets that we created from preprints of
research papers on arXiv, graduation theses, and Wikipedia articles. Table 1
summarizes the test sets. For generating the **arXiv** test set, we randomly
selected 944 documents from the *no problems* category of the arXMLiv project[12].
The **Wikipedia** test set is identical to [13]. The paragraphs in the test set were
generated analogously to the training set. The **theses** test set comprises paragraphs in 50 randomly selected graduation theses of ELL at the Mendel University in Brno, Czech Republic. The theses are from a wide range of disciplines, e.g.,
economics, computer science, and cover all academic levels. Unlike the arXiv and
Wikipedia documents, the theses were only available as PDF files, thus required

---

[11] https://en.wikipedia.org/wiki/Wikipedia:Content_assessment.
[12] https://kwarc.info/projects/arXMLiv/.

conversion to plain text. We removed all content before the introduction section of each thesis, the bibliography, and all appendices to avoid noisy data (e.g., table of contents).

Table 1. Overview of the test sets.

No. of paragraphs	arXiv		Theses		Wikipedia	
	Original	Para-phrased	Original	Para-phrased	Original	Para- phrased
SpinBot	20,966	20,867	5,226	3,463	39,261	40,729
SpinnerChief-DF	20,966	21,719	2,379	2,941	39,261	39,697
SpinnerChief-IF	20,966	21,671	2,379	2,941	39,261	39,618

3.3   Word Embedding Models

Table 2 summarizes the word embedding models analyzed in our experiments: GloVe[13] [33], word2vec[14] (w2v) [29], fastText[15] (FT-rw and FT-sw) [4], and doc-2vec (d2v) [22] that we trained from scratch. The d2v model uses a distributed bag-of-words training objective, a window size of 15 words, a minimum count of five words, trained word-vectors in skip-gram fashion, averaged word vectors, and 30 epochs. All word embedding models have 300 dimensions. Parameters we do not explicitly mention correspond to the default values in the *gensim* API[16].

Our rationale for choosing the pre-trained word embedding models was to explore the most prominent techniques regarding their suitability for the plagiarism detection task. GloVe [33] builds a co-occurrence matrix of the words in a corpus and explores the word probabilities ratio in a text to derive its semantic vectors as a count-based model. The training of w2v tries to predict a word given its context (cbow) or the context given a word (skip-gram) [29].

Even though numerous NLP tasks routinely apply GloVe and w2v [6,39,40], they do not consider two important linguistic characteristics: word ordering and sub-wording. To explore these characteristics, we also included fastText [4] and the paragraph vector model [22]. FastText builds its word representation by extending the skip-gram model with the sum of the n-grams of its constituent sub-word vectors. As the paraphrasing algorithms used by plagiarists are unknown, we hypothesize rare words can be better recognized by fastText through sub-wording. Two training options exist for the d2v model—Distributed Memory Model of Paragraph Vectors (pv-dm) and Distributed Bag of Words version of Paragraph Vector (pv-dbow). The former is akin to w2v cbow, while the latter is related to w2v skip-gram. Both options introduce a new paragraph-id vector that updates each context window on every timestamp. The paragraph-id vector seeks to capture the semantics of the embedded object. We chose a pv-dbow over a pv-dm model because of its superior results in semantic similarity tasks [21].

---

[13] https://nlp.stanford.edu/projects/glove/.
[14] https://code.google.com/archive/p/word2vec/.
[15] https://fasttext.cc/docs/en/english-vectors.html.
[16] https://radimrehurek.com/gensim/models/doc2vec.html.

Table 2. Word embedding models in our experiments.

Algorithm	Main characteristics	Training corpus
GloVe	Word-word co-occurrence matrix	Wikipedia Dump 2014 + Gigaword 5
word2vec	Continuous Bag-of-Words	Google News
pv-dbow	Distributed Bag-of-Words	Wikipedia Dump 2010
fastText-rw	Skip-gram without sub-words	Wikipedia Dump 2017 + UMBC
fastText-sw	Skip-gram with sub-words	Wikipedia Dump 2017 + UMBC

In our experiments, we represented each text as the average of its constituent word vectors by applying the word embedding models in Table 2 [39,40]. All models, except for d2v, yield a vector representation for each word. D2v produces one vector representation per document. Inferring the vector representations for unseen texts requires an additional training step with specific parameter tuning. We performed this extra training step with hyperparameters according to [39] for the *gensim* API: $\alpha = 10^{-4}$, $\alpha_{min} = 10^{-6}$, and 300 epochs [21]. The resulting pv-dbow embedding model requires at least 7 GB of RAM, compared to 1–3 GB required for other models. The higher memory consumption of pv-dbow can make it unsuitable for some use cases.

3.4   Machine Learning Classifiers

After applying the pre-trained models to our training and test sets, we passed on the results to three machine learning classifiers: Logistic Regression (LR), Support Vector Machine (SVM), and Naïve Bayes (NB).

We employed a grid-search approach implemented using the scikit-learn package[17] in Python for finding the optimal parameter values for each classifier (Table 3)

3.5   Neural Language Models

We investigate the following neural language models based on the Transformer architecture: BERT [7], RoBERTa [24], ALBERT [20], DistilBERT [41], ELECTRA [5], BART [23], XLNet [51], and Longformer [3]. Our rationale for testing Transformer-based models is their ability to generally outperform traditional word embedding and machine learning models in similar NLP tasks (e.g., document similarity). We chose the aforementioned models specifically because of two reasons. First, we explore models closely related or based on BERT that improve BERT through additional training time and data (RoBERTa) or compress BERT's architecture with minimal performance loss (DistilBERT, AlBERT). Second, we use contrasting models to BERT that, although relying on the Transformer architecture, significantly change the training objective (XLNet), the underlying attention mechanism (Longformer), or employ a discriminative learning approach (ELECTRA, BART).

---

[17] https://scikit-learn.org.

Table 3. Grid-search parameters for ML classifiers.

Classifier	Parameter	Range
Logistic Regression	Solver	Newton-cg, lbfgs, sag, saga
	Maximum iteration	500, 1000, 1500
	Multi-class	Ovr, multinomial
	Tolerance	0.01, 0.001, 0.0001, 0.00001
Support Vector Machine	Kernel	Linear, radial bases function, polynomial
	Gamma	0.01, 0.001, 0.0001, 0.0001
	Polynomial degree	1, 2, 3, 4, 5, 6, 7, 8, 9
	C	1, 10, 100

To classify whether a paragraph is paraphrased, we attach a randomly initialized linear layer on top of the model's embedding of the aggregate token (e.g., [CLS] for BERT) to transform the embedding into binary space. The final layer predicts whether a paragraph has been paraphrased using cross-entropy loss. For all models, we use the base version, the official pre-trained weights, and the following configurations: a sequence length of 512 tokens, an accumulated batch size of 32, the Adam optimizer with $\alpha = 2e - 5$, $\beta_1 = 0.9$, $\beta_2 = 0.999$, $\epsilon = 1e - 8$, and PyTorch's native automated mixed-precision format. Using a common sequence length of 512 tokens allows for a fair comparison of the models without losing important context information[18]. Section 4.1 provides more details about the models' characteristics.

4   Evaluation

To quantify the effectiveness of classification approaches in identifying machine-paraphrased text, we performed three experiments. Section 4.1 presents the results of applying the pre-trained word embedding models in combination with machine learning classifiers and neural language models to the three test sets. Section 4.2 and 4.3 indicate how well human experts and a text-matching software identify machine-paraphrased text to put the results of automated classification approaches into context.

4.1   Automated Classification

This section presents the micro-averaged F1 scores (F1-Micro) for identifying paragraphs we paraphrased using either SpinBot or SpinnerChief and classified using combinations of pre-trained word embedding models and machine learning classifiers or Transformer-based language models.

---

[18] 99.35% of the datasets' text can be represented with less than 512 tokens.

Results of ML Techniques for SpinBot: Section 4.1 shows the results for classifying SpinBot test sets derived from arXiv, theses, and Wikipedia using combinations of pre-trained word embedding models and machine learning classifiers. GloVe, in combination with SVM, achieved the best classification performance for all test sets. The combination of w2v and SVM performed nearly as well as GloVe+SVM for all test sets. For the theses and Wikipedia test sets, the performance difference between GloVe+SVM and w2v+SVM is less than 2%, and for the arXiv test set 6.66%. All pre-trained word embedding models achieved their best results for the Wikipedia test set (Table 4).

Table 4. Classification results (F1-Micro) of ML techniques for SpinBot.

	GloVe	w2v	d2v	FT-rw	FT-sw
arXiv	**86.46**	79.80	72.40	78.40	74.14
LR	76.53	74.82	69.42	75.08	65.92
SVM	86.46	79.80	72.40	76.31	74.15
NB	79.17	74.23	57.99	78.40	64.96
Theses	**83.51**	81.94	61.92	72.75	64.78
LR	68.55	72.89	59.97	69.17	64.03
SVM	83.51	81.94	61.92	72.75	64.78
NB	75.22	74.18	42.30	72.11	61.99
Wikipedia	**89.55**	87.27	83.04	86.15	82.57
LR	80.89	84.50	81.08	85.13	78.97
SVM	89.55	87.27	83.04	86.15	82.57
NB	69.68	69.84	58.88	70.05	64.47

➤ **Boldface** indicates the best score for each test set, i.e., arXiv, theses, and Wikipedia. The score of the best-performing combination of embedding model and classifier is repeated in the row of the test set.

All classification approaches, except for w2v+SVM, performed worst for the theses test set. However, the drop in performance for theses test cases is smaller than we expected. The F1-Micro score of the best approach for the theses test set (GloVe+SVM) is 6.04% lower than for the Wikipedia test set and 3.09% lower than for the arXiv test set. This finding suggests that the quality of writing in student theses mildly affects the detection of machine-paraphrased text.

Although d2v seeks to mitigate shortcomings of its predecessor w2v, such as ignoring word order and producing a variable-length encoding, w2v surpassed d2v for all test sets. A possible reason is the short length of the paragraphs we consider. Lau et al. found that d2v's performance decreases for short documents [21]. The results for paragraphs in Sect. 4.1 and for documents in our preliminary study [13], where d2v was the best-performing approach, support this conclusion.

For fastText (FT-rw and FT-sw in Sect. 4.1), we observe the same behavior as for w2v and d2v. The sub-word embeddings of FT-sw should provide a benefit over FT-rw, which encodes whole words, by capturing sub-word structures [4]. Therefore, we expected a better performance of FT-sw compared to FT-rw. However, FT-rw and simpler models, i.e., GloVe and w2v, performed better than FT-sw for all test sets.

Results of ML Techniques for SpinnerChief: Table 5 shows the results of applying the pre-trained word embedding models and machine learning classifiers to the arXix, theses, and Wikipedia test sets containing cases paraphrased by the SpinnerChief tool. We either used the tool's default setting, i.e., attempting to replace every fourth word (SpinnerChief-DF), or increased the frequency of attempted word replacements to every other word (SpinnerChief-IF).

Table 5. Classification results (F1-Micro) of ML techniques for SpinnerChief.

	SpinnerChief-DF					SpinnerChief-IF				
	GloVe	w2v	d2v	FT-rw	FT-sw	GloVe	w2v	d2v	FT-rw	FT-sw
arXiv	58.48	**59.78**	56.46	57.42	59.72	64.34	**65.89**	59.27	63.70	63.66
LR	52.14	55.43	56.46	57.42	58.64	54.92	59.61	59.07	61.74	61.57
SVM	58.42	57.65	56.43	56.43	59.72	64.12	62.77	59.27	62.97	63.66
NB	58.48	59.78	51.58	51.58	55.21	64.34	65.89	52.21	63.70	59.33
Theses	52.63	53.60	**59.09**	53.08	57.25	58.57	58.24	**63.15**	59.13	61.27
LR	48.42	53.60	59.09	52.51	55.63	52.08	57.94	62.88	59.13	60.65
SVM	52.63	51.54	59.00	53.08	57.25	58.57	57.78	63.15	58.12	61.27
NB	50.90	53.32	54.94	52.78	46.99	55.62	58.24	55.09	57.19	50.13
Wikipedia	57.86	**60.30**	55.99	59.19	59.62	64.16	**66.83**	60.94	65.35	66.41
LR	52.97	55.90	55.64	56.40	59.62	55.68	61.32	60.16	62.51	66.41
SVM	57.09	57.48	55.99	57.15	58.72	64.16	64.56	60.94	63.61	64.81
NB	57.86	60.30	51.64	59.19	57.29	63.46	66.83	52.64	65.35	62.06

➤ *-DF* default frequency, *-IF* increased frequency (attempt changing every fourth or every second word).
➤ **Boldface** indicates the best score for each test set. The score of the best-performing combination of embedding model and classifier is repeated in the row of the test set.

We observe a drop in the SpinnerChief's classification performance compared to the results for SpinBot. The average decrease in the F1-Micro scores was approx. 17% when using SpinnerChief-DF and approx. 13% for -IF. The comparison between the results of SpinBot and SpinnerChief-IF is more informative than comparing SpinBot to SpinnerChief-DF since the IF setting yields a similar ratio of replaced words to SpinBot.

As in SpinBot, all approaches performed best for the Wikipedia and worst for the theses. However, the performance differences were smaller for SpinnerChief than for SpinBot. For all SpinnerChief (DF and IF), the lowest F1-Micro scores were at most 6.5% below the highest scores, and the runner-ups were generally within an interval of 2% of the best scores.

The characteristics of ELL texts, e.g., sub-optimal word choice and grammatical errors, decreased the classification performance less than we had expected. The highest scores for the SpinBot theses are approx. 6% lower than the highest scores for any other dataset for SpinBot. For SpinnerChief, this difference is approx. 2%.

Notably, SpinnerChief's settings for a stronger text obfuscation (SpinnerChief-IF) increased the rate with which the classification approaches identified the paraphrases. On average, SpinnerChief-DF replaced 12.58% and SpinnerChief-IF 19.37% of the words in the text (Sect. 3.1). The 6.79% increase in the number of replaced words for SpinnerChief-IF compared to SpinnerChief-DF increased the average F1-Micro score of the classification approaches by 5.56%. This correlation suggests that the classification approaches can recognize most of the characteristic word replacements that paraphrasing tools perform.

Text-matching software, such as Turnitin and PlagScan, are currently the de-facto standard technical support tools for identifying plagiarism. However, since these tools search for identical text matches, their detection effectiveness decreases when the number of replaced words increases (Table 7). Including additional checks, such as the proposed classification approaches, as part of the text-matching software detection process could alleviate the weaknesses of current systems.

We attribute the drop in the classification performance and the overall leveling of the F1-Micro scores for SpinnerChief test sets compared to SpinBot test sets to our transfer learning approach. As explained in Sect. 3, we seek to provide a system that generalizes well for different document collections and paraphrasing tools. Therefore, we used the machine-paraphrased text samples of SpinBot and applied the pre-trained word embedding models from Table 2 to extract the vector representations. We then used these vectors as the features for the machine learning classifiers for both Spinbot and SpinnerChief test sets.

We selected the combinations of word embedding models and machine learning classifiers that performed best for SpinBot (Sect. 4.1) and SpinnerChief (Table 5) as the baseline to which we compare the Transformer-based language models in the following section.

Results for Transformer-Based Language Models: Table 6 shows the classification results of neural language models applied to all SpinBot and SpinnerChief test sets. The machine learning technique that performed best for each test set (Sect. 4.1 and Table 5) is shown as *Baseline*.

Table 6. Classification results (F1-Micro) of best ML techniques and neural language models for SpinBot and SpinnerChief.

Techniques	SpinBot			SpinnerChief-DF			SpinnerChief-IF		
	arXiv	Theses	Wiki	arXiv	Theses	Wiki	arXiv	Theses	Wiki
Baseline	86.46[a]	83.51[a]	89.55[a]	59.78[b]	59.09[c]	60.30[b]	65.89[b]	63.15[d]	66.83[b]
BERT	99.44	94.72	99.85	50.74	50.42	43.00	64.59	63.59	57.45
ALBERT	98.91	96.77	99.54	66.88	47.92	50.43	75.57	56.75	59.61
DistilBERT	99.32	96.61	99.42	38.37	45.07	37.05	47.25	51.44	46.81
RoBERTa	99.05	97.34	99.85	57.10	47.40	48.03	66.00	58.24	58.94
ELECTRA	99.20	96.85	99.41	43.83	44.95	56.30	60.77	63.11	**75.92**
BART	99.58	99.66	99.86	69.38	53.39	48.62	76.07	63.57	58.34
XLNet	**99.65**	98.33	99.48	69.90	53.06	50.51	**80.56**	71.75	61.83
Longformer	99.38	**99.81**	**99.87**	**76.44**	**70.15**	**63.03**	78.34	**74.82**	67.11

➤ [a]GloVe+SVM   [b]w2v+NB   [c]d2v+LR   [d]d2v+SVM
➤ The first horizontal block shows the best results of machine learning techniques, the second of models that optimize BERT, and the third of models that use new architectural or training approaches.
➤ **Boldface** indicates the best score for each test set.

For the SpinBot, all Transformer-based models outperformed their machine learning counterparts on average by 16.10% for theses, 13.27% for arXiv, and 10.11% for Wikipedia. Several models consistently achieved F1-Micro scores above 99% for all SpinBot cases. These findings show that the models could capture the intrinsic characteristics of SpinBot's paraphrasing method very well. We stopped the training for each model after one epoch to avoid overfitting.

All techniques performed worse for SpinnerChief than for SpinBot, which we expected given the transfer learning approach. The drop in the classification performance was consistently lower for SpinnerChief-IF, which exhibits a similar ratio of replaced words as SpinBot, than for SpinnerChief-DF, which contain fewer replaced words than SpinBot. The most significant improvements in the scores for SpinnerChief-IF over SpinnerChief-DF are 16.94% for arXiv (ELECTRA), 18.69% for the theses (XLNet), and 19.62% for Wikipedia (BART).

These results show that the ratio of replaced words is a significant indicator of a models' performance. However, since the paraphrasing methods of SpinBot and SpinnerChief (DF and IF) are unknown and could be different for each setting, one can interpret this finding in two ways. First, the models may capture the frequency of replaced words intrinsically and increase their attention to more words, which would mean the models can better detect more strongly altered paragraphs, such as those produced by SpinnerChief-IF. Second, SpinnerChief-IF cases might be better detectable because the paraphrasing method associated with the SpinnerChief-IF setting might be more akin to the one of SpinBot than the method associated with the SpinnerChief-DF setting.

For all SpinnerChief-DF cases, Longformer consistently achieved the best results, surpassing the F1-Micro scores of the machine learning baselines by 10.15% on average and 16.66% for arXiv. For SpinnerChief-IF, XLNet,

Longformer, and ELECTRA achieved the best results with an improvement in the F1-Micro scores of 14.67%, 11.67%, and 9.09% over the baseline scores for the arXiv, theses, and Wikipedia, respectively. As ELECTRA was pre-trained using a Wikipedia dump and the Books Corpus [54], we assume it also captured semantic aspects of Wikipedia articles.

The larger diversity in the training data of Longformer and XLNet (i.e., Gigaword 5 [30], CC Stories [44], and Realnews [52]) seems to enable the models to capture unseen semantic structures in the arXiv and theses better than other models.

BERT and its derived models performed comparably to the baselines for most SpinnerChief cases. DistilBERT, which uses knowledge distillation to reduce the number of parameters by 40% compared to BERT, performed significantly worse than its base model. For the SpinnerChief, the F1-micro scores for DistilBERT were on average 10.63% lower than for BERT, often falling into a score range achievable by random guessing. Although we expected a slight decline in the accuracy of DistilBERT compared to BERT due to the parameter reduction, the results fell well below our predictions. In comparison, for the General Language Understanding (GLUE) dataset [48], DistilBERT performed only 2.5% worse than BERT. ALBERT's parameter reduction techniques, e.g., factorized embedding parametrization and parameter sharing, seem to be more robust. ALBERT outperformed BERT on average by 4.56% on the SpinnerChief test sets. With an average improvement of 0.99%, RoBERTa performed slightly better than BERT. However, as RoBERTa uses more parameters than most other BERT-related models and has exceptionally high computational requirements for pre-training, we rate this performance benefit as negligible.

In summary, improvements of BERT's attention mechanism or training objective outperformed other BERT-based models for the machine-paraphrase detection task. We hypothesize the windowed local and global self-attention scheme used in Longformer allowed the model to generalize better between different paraphrasing tools. In eight out of nine scenarios, Longformer was either the best or second-best model overall. Also, for almost all cases, the neural language models surpassed the machine learning approaches' results, thus providing a better solution to the problem of identifying machine-paraphrases. We see the SpinnerChief-DF test results set as a lower bound regarding the detection effectiveness for unseen spinning methods, even if the frequency of word replacements is significantly different from the frequency in our training set.

4.2   Human Baseline

To complement the earlier study of Foltýnek [13], we conducted a user survey with excerpts from ten randomly selected Wikipedia articles. We paraphrased three of the ten excerpts using SpinerChief-DF, three others using SpinnerChief-IF, and kept four excerpts unaltered. Using QuizMaker[19], we prepared a web-based quiz that showed the ten excerpts one at a time and asked the participants

---

[19] https://www.quiz-maker.com/.

to vote whether the text had been machine-paraphrased. We shared the quiz via e-mail and a Facebook group with researchers from the academic integrity community and 32 participants joined our study.

The participants' accuracy ranged between 20% and 100%, with an average of 65.59%. Thus, the F1-Micro score of the 'average' human examiner matched the average of the best scores of automated classification approaches for the SpinnerChie-IF test sets (65.29%). Some participants pointed out that oddness in the text of some excerpts, e.g., lowercase letters in acronyms, helped them identify the excerpts as paraphrased. For SpinBot, 73 participants answered the survey with an accuracy ranging from 40% to 100% (avg. 78.40%) according to [13].

Our experiments show that experienced educators who read carefully and expect to encounter machine-paraphrased text could achieve an accuracy between 80% and 100%. However, even in this setting, the average accuracy was below 80% for SpinBot and below 70% for SpinnerChief. We expect that the efficiency will be lower in a realistic scenario, in which readers do not pay special attention to spotting machine paraphrases.

4.3   Text-Matching Software Baseline

To quantify the benefit of our automated classification over text-matching software, we tested how accurately current text-matching tools identify paraphrased text. We tested two systems—Turnitin, which has the largest market share, and PlagScan, which was one of the best-performing systems in a comprehensive test conducted by the European Network for Academic Integrity (ENAI) [11]. Our main objective was to test the tools' effectiveness in identifying patchwriting, i.e., inappropriately paraphrasing copied text by performing minor changes and substitutions. Patchwriting is a frequent form of plagiarism, particularly among students.

For this test, we created four sets of 40 documents each (160 documents total). We composed each document by randomly choosing 20 paragraphs from Wikipedia articles (2 × 40 documents), arXiv preprints (40 documents), and theses (40 documents). For each set of 40 documents, we followed the same scheme regarding the length and obfuscation of the chosen paragraphs. First, we created ten documents by varying the paragraphs' length taken from the source from one to ten sentences. In addition to using the ten documents unaltered, we also paraphrased all ten documents using SpinBot, SpinnerChief-DF, and SpinnerChief-IF.

To ensure this test is objective and comparable across the data sets, we exclusively report the overall percentages of matching text reported by a system (Table 7). In most cases, the systems identified the correct source. However, the systems often reported false positives caused by random matches, which means the systems' actual retrieval effectiveness is slightly lower than reported.

Table 7. Percentage of text overlap reported by the text-matching systems Turnitin and PlagScan

Detection	Corpus	arXiv	Theses	Wikipedia
Turnitin	Original	84.0	5.4	98.7
	SpinBot	7.0	1.1	30.2
	SpinnerChief-DF	58.5	4.0	74.5
	SpinnerChief-IF	38.8	1.2	50.1
PlagScan	Original	44.6	22.3	65.0
	SpinBot	0.0	0.1	0.5
	SpinnerChief-DF	9.2	12.0	19.1
	SpinnerChief-IF	1.8	0.5	3.1

The results show that PlagScan struggled to identify patchwriting. Even though the system indexes Wikipedia and could identify entirely plagiarized documents in the ENAI test [11], the average percentage of matching text reported for our patch-written documents was 63%. Paraphrasing documents using SpinBot and SpinnerChief-IF consistently prevented PlagScan from identifying the plagiarism. The average reported percentage of matching text was only 1% for SpinBot and 3% for SpinnerChief-IF test cases. For SpinnerChief-DF test cases, PlagScan could identify 19% of plagiarism present in documents, likely due to the lower ratio of altered words. Nevertheless, we can conclude obfuscating patch-written documents using a machine-paraphrasing tool likely prevents PlagScan from identifying plagiarism.

As shown in Table 7, Turnitin performed better for patch-written documents than PlagScan. For Wikipedia test cases, Turnitin reported 100% matching text for almost all cases. The average percentage of matching text Turnitin reported for machine-paraphrased documents was much higher than for PlagScan—31% for SpinBot, 74% for SpinnerChief-DF, and 50% for SpinnerChief-IF. However, machine-paraphrasing still prevents Turnitin from identifying a significant portion of the plagiarized content. Notably, Turnitin appears to index fewer theses than PlagScan, thus failing to report suspiciously high percentages of matching text for any theses test set, including ones containing unaltered paragraphs copied from theses.

For both systems, we observed the longer a plagiarized passage is, the more likely text-matching tools identified it. This result corresponds to the results of our classification approaches, which also yielded higher accuracy for longer passages.

From our experiments with text-matching software, we conclude that if plagiarists copy a few paragraphs and employ a paraphrasing tool to obfuscate their misconduct, the similarity is often below the text-matching tool's reporting threshold, thus causing the plagiarism to remain undetected. Our classification approaches for machine-paraphrased text can be a valuable complement

Table 8. An illustrative sample of three examples for each paraphrasing tool, data source, and classification method.

Original Parapgraphs:

- A mathematically rigorous approach to quantum field theory based on operator algebras is called an algebraic quantum field theory...
- "Nuts" contains 5 instrumental compositions written and produced by Streisand, with the exception of "The Bar", including additional writing from Richard Baskin. All of the songs were recorded throughout 1987...
- Most of activities are carried out internally using internal resources. The cost and financial demandingness of the project are presented in the table below...

SpinBot Paraphrased	Source	Turnitin[†]	PlagScan[†]	ML[*]	NLM[*]
A numerically thorough way to deal with quantum field hypothesis dependent on administrator algebras is called an arithmetical quantum field hypothesis...	arXiv	25.30	0.00	73.11	99.99

SpinnerChief-IF Paraphrased					
"Nuts" consists of five instrumental compositions written and created by Streisand, with the exception of "The Bar", which includes extra writing from Rich Baskin. All of the music were recorded in 1987...	Wiki	35.80	23.90	98.87	72.46

SpinnerChief-DF Paraphrased					
The majority of activities are carried out internally making use of internal resources. The cost and economic demandingness of the project are illustrated in the table below...	Thesis	0.00	0.00	49.81	63.81

➤ [†] text-match in %.
➤ [*] prediction score in % for the best performing models Longformer and w2v+NB (see Sect. 4).
➤ Red background highlights changed tokens of the original version.
➤ Ellipsis ("...") indicates the remainder of the paragraph.

to text-matching software. The additional analysis step could alert users when indicators of machine-obfuscated text have been identified.

We provide an illustrative example for text from arXiv, Wikipedia, and theses, their modified versions using SpinBot and SpinnerChief, and classification scores using text-matching software (Turnitin, PlagScan), the best performing neural language model (Longformer), and the best combination of machine learning classifier and word embeddings (w2v+NB) in Table 8.

5   Conclusion

In this paper, we analyze two new collections (arXiv and theses), an additional paraphrasing tool (SpinnerChief), eight neural language models based on the Transformer architecture (Table 6), and two popular text-matching systems (Turnitin and PlagScan). We selected training and test sets that reflect documents particularly relevant for the plagiarism detection use case. The arXiv collection represents scientific papers written by expert researchers. Graduation theses of non-native English speakers provide writing samples of authors whose style varies considerably. Wikipedia articles represent collaboratively authored documents for many topics and one of the sources from which students plagiarize most frequently.

We investigated the use of traditional, pre-trained word embedding models in combination with machine learning classifiers and recent neural language models. For eight of our nine test sets, Transformer-based techniques proposing changes in the training architecture achieved the highest scores. In particular, Longformer achieved the best classification performance overall.

Transferring the classifiers trained on the SpinBot training set to Spinner-Chief test sets caused a drop in the approaches' average classification performance. For SpinnerChief-IF, a test set exhibiting a similar ratio of altered words as the training set, the average F1-Micro scores of the best-performing classifiers dropped by approx. 21%, that of human evaluators by approx. 13%. However, the best-performing models were still capable of classifying machine-paraphrased paragraphs with F1-Micro scores ranging between 74.8% to 80.5%. We partially attribute the loss in performance in recognizing SpinnerChief test cases to the obfuscation's strength and not exclusively to deficiencies in the transferred classifiers.

We showed that our approaches can complement text-matching software, such as PlagScan and Turnitin, which often fail to identify machine-paraphrased plagiarism. The main advantage of machine learning models over text matching software is the models' ability to identify machine-paraphrased text even if the source document is not accessible to the detection system. The classification approaches we investigated could be integrated as an additional step within the detection process of text-matching software to alert users of likely machine-paraphrased text. The presence of such obfuscated text is a strong indicator of deliberate misconduct.

The classification approaches we devised are robust to identifying machine-paraphrased text, which educators face regularly. To support practitioners and facilitate an extension of the research on this important task, the data[20] and code[21] of our study, as well as a web-based demonstration system for the best-performing machine learning classifier[22] (NB+w2v) and neural language model[23] (Longformer) are openly available.

6   Future Work

Our experiments indicate that obtaining additional training data is a promising approach for improving artificial intelligence-backed approaches for identifying machine-paraphrased text. Additional training data should cover more paraphrasing tools, topics, and languages. We see a community-driven open data effort as a promising option for generating a comprehensive training set. We encourage researchers investigating machine-paraphrase detection to share their data and contribute to the consolidation and extension of datasets, such as the one we publish with this paper.

Obtaining effective training data is challenging due to many paraphrasing tools, nontransparent paraphrasing approaches, frequent interconnections of paraphrasing tools, and the questionable business model of the tool providers. If paying paraphrasing services to obtain data proves prohibitive, a crowdsourcing effort could overcome the problem. Another interesting direction would be

---

[20] https://doi.org/10.5281/zenodo.3608000.

[21] https://github.com/jpelhaW/ParaphraseDetection.

[22] http://purl.org/spindetector.

[23] https://huggingface.co/jpelhaw/longformer-base-plagiarism-detection.

to use auto-encoding language models to paraphrase text or generate new text with auto-regressive models. This setup will be more realistic in the future as language models are publicly available and generate text that is difficult to distinguish from human writing.

References

1. Alvi, F., Stevenson, M., Clough, P.: Paraphrase type identification for plagiarism detection using contexts and word embeddings. Int. J. Educ. Technol. High. Educ. **18**(1), 42 (2021)
2. Beltagy, I., Lo, K., Cohan, A.: SciBERT: a pretrained language model for scientific text. In: Proceedings of the 2019 Conference on Empirical Methods in Natural Language Processing and the 9th International Joint Conference on Natural Language Processing (EMNLP-IJCNLP), Hong Kong, China, pp. 3613–3618. Association for Computational Linguistics (2019). 10/ggcgtm
3. Beltagy, I., Peters, M.E., Cohan, A.: Longformer: the long-document transformer. arXiv:2004.05150 [cs], April 2020
4. Bojanowski, P., Grave, E., Joulin, A., Mikolov, T.: Enriching word vectors with subword information. Trans. Assoc. Comput. Linguist. **5**, 135–146 (2017). 10/gfw9cs
5. Clark, K., Luong, M.T., Le, Q.V., Manning, C.D.: ELECTRA: pre-training text encoders as discriminators rather than generators. arXiv:2003.10555 [cs], March 2020
6. Conneau, A., Kiela, D., Schwenk, H., Barrault, L., Bordes, A.: Supervised learning of universal sentence representations from natural language inference data. In: Proceedings Conference on Empirical Methods in Natural Language Processing (2017). https://doi.org/10.18653/v1/d17-1070
7. Devlin, J., Chang, M.W., Lee, K., Toutanova, K.: Bert: pre-training of deep bidirectional transformers for language understanding. arXiv:1810.04805 (2018)
8. Devlin, J., Chang, M.W., Lee, K., Toutanova, K.: BERT: pre-training of deep bidirectional transformers for language understanding. arXiv:1810.04805 [cs], May 2019
9. Dey, K., Shrivastava, R., Kaushik, S.: A paraphrase and semantic similarity detection system for user generated short-text content on microblogs. In: Proceedings International Conference on Computational Linguistics (COLING), pp. 2880–2890 (2016)
10. Dolan, W.B., Brockett, C.: Automatically constructing a corpus of sentential paraphrases. In: Proceedings of the Third International Workshop on Paraphrasing (IWP 2005) (2005)
11. Foltýnek, T., et al.: Testing of support tools for plagiarism detection. Int. J. Educ. Technol. High. Educ. **17**(1), 1–31 (2020). https://doi.org/10.1186/s41239-020-00192-4
12. Foltýnek, T., Meuschke, N., Gipp, B.: Academic plagiarism detection: a systematic literature review. ACM Comput. Surv. **52**(6), 112:1-112:42 (2019). https://doi.org/10.1145/3345317
13. Foltýnek, T., et al.: Detecting machine-obfuscated plagiarism. In: Sundqvist, A., Berget, G., Nolin, J., Skjerdingstad, K.I. (eds.) iConference 2020. LNCS, vol. 12051, pp. 816–827. Springer, Cham (2020). https://doi.org/10.1007/978-3-030-43687-2_68

14. Gharavi, E., Veisi, H., Rosso, P.: Scalable and language-independent embedding-based approach for plagiarism detection considering obfuscation type: no training phase. Neural Comput. Appl. **32**(14), 10593–10607 (2019). https://doi.org/10.1007/s00521-019-04594-y
15. Gutmann, M., Hyvärinen, A.: Noise-contrastive estimation: a new estimation principle for unnormalized statistical models. In: Proceedings of the International Conference on Artificial Intelligence and Statistics (AISTATS). JMLR W&CP, vol. 9, pp. 297–304 (2010)
16. Hunt, E., et al.: Machine learning models for paraphrase identification and its applications on plagiarism detection. In: Proceedings 10th IEEE International Conference on Big Knowledge, pp. 97–104 (2019). https://doi.org/10.1109/ICBK.2019.00021
17. Iyer, S., Dandekar, N., Csernai, K.: First quora dataset release: Question pairs (2017). https://data.quora.com/First-Quora-Dataset-Release-Question-Pairs
18. Lan, W., Qiu, S., He, H., Xu, W.: A continuously growing dataset of sentential paraphrases. In: Proceedings of the 2017 Conference on Empirical Methods in Natural Language Processing, Copenhagen, Denmark, pp. 1224–1234. Association for Computational Linguistics (2017). https://doi.org/10.18653/v1/D17-1126
19. Lan, W., Xu, W.: Neural network models for paraphrase identification, semantic textual similarity, natural language inference, and question answering. arXiv:1806.04330 [cs], August 2018
20. Lan, Z., Chen, M., Goodman, S., Gimpel, K., Sharma, P., Soricut, R.: ALBERT: a lite BERT for self-supervised learning of language representations. arXiv:1909.11942 [cs], September 2019
21. Lau, J.H., Baldwin, T.: An empirical evaluation of doc2vec with practical insights into document embedding generation. In: Proceedings Workshop on Representation Learning for NLP (2016). https://doi.org/10.18653/v1/w16-1609
22. Le, Q., Mikolov, T.: Distributed representations of sentences and documents. In: Proceedings 31st International Conference on Machine Learning, vol. 32, pp. 1188–1196 (2014)
23. Lewis, M., et al.: BART: denoising sequence-to-sequence pre-training for natural language generation, translation, and comprehension. arXiv:1910.13461 [cs], October 2019
24. Liu, Y., et al.: RoBERTa: a robustly optimized BERT pretraining approach. arXiv:1907.11692 [cs], July 2019
25. Meuschke, N.: Analyzing non-textual content elements to detect academic plagiarism. Doctoral thesis, University of Konstanz, Department of Computer and Information Science, Konstanz, Germany (2021). https://doi.org/10.5281/zenodo.4913345
26. Meuschke, N., Gondek, C., Seebacher, D., Breitinger, C., Keim, D., Gipp, B.: An adaptive image-based plagiarism detection approach. In: Proceedings 18th ACM/IEEE Joint Conference on Digital Libraries, pp. 131–140 (2018). https://doi.org/10.1145/3197026.3197042
27. Meuschke, N., Stange, V., Schubotz, M., Gipp, B.: HyPlag: a hybrid approach to academic plagiarism detection. In: Proceedings 41st International ACM SIGIR Conference on Research & Development in Information Retrieval, pp. 1321–1324 (2018). https://doi.org/10.1145/3209978.3210177
28. Meuschke, N., Stange, V., Schubotz, M., Kramer, M., Gipp, B.: Improving academic plagiarism detection for STEM documents by analyzing mathematical content and citations. In: Proceedings ACM/IEEE Joint Conference on Digital Libraries, pp. 120–129 (2019). https://doi.org/10.1109/JCDL.2019.00026

29. Mikolov, T., Sutskever, I., Chen, K., Corrado, G., Dean, J.: Distributed representations of words and phrases and their compositionality. arXiv:1310.4546 [cs, stat], October 2013
30. Napoles, C., Gormley, M., Van Durme, B.: Annotated gigaword. In: Proceedings of the Joint Workshop on Automatic Knowledge Base Construction and Web-scale Knowledge Extraction (AKBC-WEKEX), Montréal, Canada, pp. 95–100. Association for Computational Linguistics, June 2012
31. Ostendorff, M., Ash, E., Ruas, T., Gipp, B., Moreno-Schneider, J., Rehm, G.: Evaluating document representations for content-based legal literature recommendations. In: Proceedings of the Eighteenth International Conference on Artificial Intelligence and Law, São Paulo Brazil, pp. 109–118. ACM, June 2021. https://doi.org/10.1145/3462757.3466073. https://arxiv.org/pdf/2104.13841.pdf
32. Ostendorff, M., Ruas, T., Blume, T., Gipp, B., Rehm, G.: Aspect-based document similarity for research papers. In: Proceedings of the 28th International Conference on Computational Linguistics, Barcelona, Spain (Online), pp. 6194–6206. International Committee on Computational Linguistics (2020). https://doi.org/10.18653/v1/2020.coling-main.545. https://aclanthology.org/2020.coling-main.545.pdf
33. Pennington, J., Socher, R., Manning, C.D.: GloVe: global vectors for word representation. In: Proceedings Conference on Empirical Methods in Natural Language Processing, vol. 14, pp. 1532–1543 (2014). 10/gfshwq
34. Perone, C.S., Silveira, R., Paula, T.S.: Evaluation of sentence embeddings in downstream and linguistic probing tasks. arXiv:1806.06259 (2018)
35. Peters, M., et al.: Deep contextualized word representations. In: Proceedings of the 2018 Conference of the North American Chapter of the Association for Computational Linguistics: Human Language Technologies, Volume 1 (Long Papers), New Orleans, Louisiana, pp. 2227–2237. Association for Computational Linguistics (2018). https://doi.org/10.18653/v1/n18-1202
36. Prentice, F.M., Kinden, C.E.: Paraphrasing tools, language translation tools and plagiarism: an exploratory study. Int. J. Educ. Integr. 14(1), 1–16 (2018). https://doi.org/10.1007/s40979-018-0036-7
37. Radford, A., Wu, J., Child, R., Luan, D., Amodei, D., Sutskever, I.: Language models are unsupervised multitask learners (2019)
38. Rogerson, A.M., McCarthy, G.: Using Internet based paraphrasing tools: original work, patchwriting or facilitated plagiarism? Int. J. Educ. Integr. 13(1), 1–15 (2017). https://doi.org/10.1007/s40979-016-0013-y
39. Ruas, T., Ferreira, C.H.P., Grosky, W., de França, F.O., de Medeiros, D.M.R.: Enhanced word embeddings using multi-semantic representation through lexical chains. Inf. Sci. 532, 16–32 (2020). https://doi.org/10.1016/j.ins.2020.04.048
40. Ruas, T., Grosky, W., Aizawa, A.: Multi-sense embeddings through a word sense disambiguation process. Expert Syst. Appl. 136, 288–303 (2019). https://doi.org/10.1016/j.eswa.2019.06.026
41. Sanh, V., Debut, L., Chaumond, J., Wolf, T.: DistilBERT, a distilled version of BERT: smaller, faster, cheaper and lighter. arXiv:1910.01108 [cs], October 2019
42. Spinde, T., Plank, M., Krieger, J.D., Ruas, T., Gipp, B., Aizawa, A.: Neural media bias detection using distant supervision with BABE - bias annotations by experts. In: Findings of the Association for Computational Linguistics: EMNLP 2021. Dominican Republic, November 2021. tex.pubstate: published tex.tppubtype: inproceedings
43. Subramanian, S., Trischler, A., Bengio, Y., Pal, C.J.: Learning general purpose distributed sentence representations via large scale multi-task learning. arXiv:1804.00079 [cs], March 2018

44. Trinh, T.H., Le, Q.V.: A simple method for commonsense reasoning. arXiv:1806.02847 [cs] (2019)
45. Vaswani, A., et al.: Attention is all you need. In: Guyon, I., et al. (eds.) Advances in Neural Information Processing Systems 30, pp. 5998–6008. Curran Associates, Inc. (2017). https://arxiv.org/abs/1706.03762
46. Wahle, J.P., Ashok, N., Ruas, T., Meuschke, N., Ghosal, T., Gipp, B.: Testing the generalization of neural language models for COVID-19 misinformation detection. In: Proceedings of the iConference, February 2022
47. Wahle, J.P., Ruas, T., Meuschke, N., Gipp, B.: Are neural language models good plagiarists? A benchmark for neural paraphrase detection. In: Proceedings of the ACM/IEEE Joint Conference on Digital Libraries (JCDL), Washington, USA. IEEE, September 2021
48. Wang, A., Singh, A., Michael, J., Hill, F., Levy, O., Bowman, S.R.: GLUE: a multi-task benchmark and analysis platform for natural language understanding. arXiv:1804.07461 [cs], February 2019
49. Weber-Wulff, D.: Plagiarism detectors are a crutch, and a problem. Nature (2019). https://doi.org/10.1038/d41586-019-00893-5
50. Xu, W.: Data-drive approaches for paraphrasing across language variations. Ph.D. thesis, Department of Computer Science, New York University (2014). http://www.cis.upenn.edu/~xwe/files/thesis-wei.pdf
51. Yang, Z., Dai, Z., Yang, Y., Carbonell, J., Salakhutdinov, R., Le, Q.V.: XLNet: generalized autoregressive pretraining for language understanding. arXiv:1906.08237 [cs], June 2019
52. Zellers, R., et al.: Defending against neural fake news. arXiv:1905.12616 [cs] (2019)
53. Zhang, Q., Wang, D.Y., Voelker, G.M.: DSpin: detecting automatically spun content on the web. In: Proceedings Network and Distributed System Security (NDSS) Symposium, pp. 23–26 (2014). https://doi.org/10.14722/ndss.2014.23004
54. Zhu, Y., et al.: Aligning books and movies: towards story-like visual explanations by watching movies and reading books. In: The IEEE International Conference on Computer Vision (ICCV), December 2015

An Ensemble Framework for Dynamic Character Relationship Sentiment in Fiction

Nikolaus Nova Parulian[✉], Glen Worthey, and J. Stephen Downie

HathiTrust Research Center, School of Information Sciences,
University of Illinois at Urbana-Champaign, Champaign, USA
{nnp2,gworthey,jdownie}@illinois.edu

Abstract. Fictional characters in a narrative text can experience various events in the narrative timeline as the progress of character development. Relationships between characters can also dynamically change over time. Summarizing the relationship dynamics in fiction through manual annotation can be very tedious even at a small scale, but highly impractical or even impossible in a large corpus. With the recent development of machine learning models in Natural Language Processing, many tasks have been introduced to help humans extract information from text automatically. Motivated by this development, we propose a conceptual model and an information extraction framework that combines two state-of-the-art machine learning algorithms to extract character relationships directly from an event sentence in a fictional narrative. For our use case, as we consider sequence in a story line, we also infer the dynamic sentiment relationships among characters over time. Since this approach is by nature unsupervised, we also preserve the provenance of each relation extracted in order to prepare a dataset to use in training a supervised model. We hope this approach can be a step toward more robust automatic character relation and event extraction from fictional texts.

Keywords: Digital library · Information extraction · Machine learning · Network analysis

1 Introduction

Fictional characters in a narrative can experience various events in the narrative timeline as milestones in the progress of their own character development. Relationships between characters can also dynamically change over time. For example, a protagonist such as Romeo is portrayed in interactions with his friends, through which he slowly develops as a lover of Juliet, and becomes an enemy to Tybalt. These relationships can be interesting to explore, especially for Digital Humanities researchers who want to analyze the presentation of society and social networks are embodied in the text. However, this information is often not expressed explicitly in the story itself, so that a person needs to read and examine each interaction in order to annotate the development of a relationship over time.

M. Smits (Ed.): iConference 2022, LNCS 13192, pp. 414–424, 2022.
https://doi.org/10.1007/978-3-030-96957-8_35

Thus summarizing relationship dynamics in fiction through manual annotation can be very tedious (or nearly impossible for long texts or large corpora). To some extent, a group of people can perform this manual effort collaboratively, or have it down with crowdsourcing, such as what we can find on Wikipedia or DBpedia. However, the contributions and completeness of this approach often depend on a community that values these stories for reasons other than as data preparation for research. Besides, the written summaries in Wikipedia and DBpedia do not focus on addressing relationships among the entities in the story, but rather on simply providing more descriptive summaries.

With the recent development of machine learning models in Natural Language Processing, many tasks have been successfully adapted in ways that can help humans extract and summarize information from text automatically. For example, Named Entity Recognition algorithms, which extract from a text all mentions of the sorts of objects that can be identified with proper nouns, have achieved surprisingly high accuracy. Even though most of these models are trained on public domain data such as news or Wikipedia knowledge bases, there is potential to use this model as a first stage of extracting character relations from the fictional text. Furthermore, this stage can be considered a step in preparing a domain-specific dataset for more general relation extraction from fictional narratives.

Motivated by these developments, we hope to answer the following questions in our research:

- How we can provide a conceptual model that can represent relations among characters in a story based on mentions of these character and of events that involve them?
- How can we combine existing machine learning models to flesh out the information in the model?
- How can we analyze the relationship dynamics among characters as they occur in a story's timeline?

2   Related Works

There has been some prior research into automatic character relation extraction from a fictional text. Shahsavari et al. [13] proposed an automated extraction approach for stories that made use of "Good Reads" book reviews. Although this approach can reduce the noise inherent in algorithmically inferred relations, it does not preserve the actual story timeline because it extracts its information from readers' summaries. In contrast to this approach, our extraction framework is applied to the story itself, extracting character relations based on the event depictions in the story. Skorinkin et al. [14] and Li et al. [10] try to extract and analyze relationship dynamics based largely on co-occurrence between pairs of characters at both the sentence and the scene levels. However, relationship *types* are not preserved with this approach; furthermore, we find that the plot dynamics extracted mainly focus on the text's depicted social network growth, and on simple clustering among the characters. We, on the other hand, preserve events as proxies for relationships: analyzing the sentiment associated with a relationship between two characters, we can infer information about their dynamic relationship. Furthermore, we combine two existing state-of-the-art machine learning methods to infer these relationship dynamics so as to make this approach mainly unsupervised.

To further extract character relations directly from a sentence while preserving the story line, we propose a conceptual model and system that can automatically extract the characters mentioned in a narrative, then use sentiment to infer the nature of the relationship between these characters, in order to represent relationship dynamics within the story line. We have combined two pre-existing machine learning models, a Named Entity Recognition (NER) model to extract the entities (people) mentioned, and an OpenIE model to find and characterize the event or relation that exists between these entities or people. We use a transfer learning model of knowledge-based extraction for character relationships using these two pre-trained models as an ensemble to find and characterize the connections among entities. We also propose a conceptual model that expresses the relationship dynamic as a knowledge graph. Inspired by the FOAF ("friend of a friend") ontology [1], we provide a domain specific character relation by adding event mentions as a feature that can help infer the type of relationship; a temporal feature in the form of sentence sequence; and the provenance of each bit of extracted knowledge in order to keep track of the sentences and the rationale behind the extracted relations. In this way we provide some methodological transparency for the resulting knowledge graph; furthermore, since each stage of the extraction process is mainly unsupervised, we preserve provenance information in the interests of data curation and documentation, and as a means for confirmation of the correctness of the extracted information.

3   Methodology

3.1   Dataset

Since we focus on extracting character relations from a fictional narrative, we use plain text from a scanned book as our dataset. For our experiment, in order to avoid copyright issues while providing complete provenance information for our eventual extracted graph, we use open-access fiction titles as classified by Project Gutenberg [5]. The plain-text, produced from scanned pages provided by HathiTrust (HT) [2], is the primary source of our experiment. The reason for using HT volumes rather than those in Project Gutenberg is to leave open later possibilities for expanding this experimental knowledge graph extraction framework into studies of much larger corpora. Additionally, we make us of a non-consumptive computing environment [6] provided by the HathiTrust Research Center (HTRC) that allows users to perform unrestricted analyses of copyrighted texts that otherwise have restricted access. This allows us, as part of the contribution of our research, to provide a script or analytic notebook for non-consumptive knowledge graph extraction that can be used by the community directly in the HTRC environment.

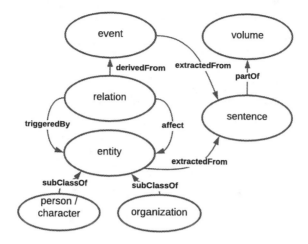

Fig. 1. ChaRelEx conceptual model: The model consists of the entities required to capture and characterize relations between characters in a fictional narrative. Events and entities are extracted from a sentence. Intersections between the event and the two characters further become a proxy of the relationship between them.

3.2   Information Extraction Framework

We have developed a conceptual model to represent characters' relationships based on entities and events extracted from a sentence. Figure 1 shows the relationship between the steps associated with this task. First, a **volume** object, representing a physical or digital volume of a fictional work, is defined. Second, we recognize that this **volume** consists of **sentences** that may or may not contain interactions among character **entities**. When a **sentence** contains an interaction between or among characters, we preserve information about the interaction, the **event**, and the **entity**. Furthermore, we infer a **relation** by combining the **event** and **entity** models, where a subject is **triggered by**, and an object is **affected by** the event.

Next, we propose an Information Extraction (IE) Framework to construct the information as described in the conceptual model presented in Fig. 2. There are three main components for the IE framework:

1. the **entity** extraction, which identifies the subject (i.e., a character, usually a person) in a sentence;
2. the **event** extraction, which identifies the verb as a part of speech, and summarizes the sentence as a triple $< s, v, o >$;
3. the **relation** aligner, which combines the two outputs above, inferring a relation between entities by looking at the co-occurrence of the entity and event expressed by the triples.

Thus, starting with a single **sentence** from a **volume**, the framework will extract the graph for that **sentence**, and if we combine all of the **sentence** graphs from

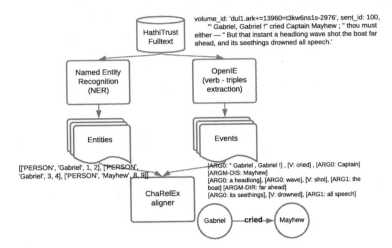

Fig. 2. ChaRelEx IE framework: The framework incorporates a state-of-the-art Named Entity Recognition model for detecting **entities**, and an OpenIE model to detect **events**. Because the OpenIE model does not associate an entity with a type, we need to align the two outputs to further construct a relationship network based on the event trigger between two characters.

a **volume** together, we will have constructed a complete graph of the narrative, using **sentence** sequence as a temporal feature.

Entity Extraction. Automated extraction of entity mentions has gained more attention recently, especially with the development of deep neural networks for natural language processing. Moreover, several pre-trained models for entity extraction have been developed in the general/news domain, which are specifically designed to extract specific entity types such as people, locations, organizations, etc. With the addition of transformer models such as BERT [3], entity extraction is proven to have fairly high accuracy on Named Entity Recognition (NER) tasks within the news/web content domain [8].

We use spaCy's transformer NER model for entity extraction [7]. The entity extraction aims to identify entity mentions in a text, and to classify them into pre-defined entity types. The spaCy NER model is trained on the OntoNotes dataset, which includes 18 entity types. Still, for our proposed Character Relation Extraction (ChaRelEx) framework, we only used the two types most encountered in fiction: PERSON, obviously representing a person named in a sentence, and ORG, which represents an organization.

Event Extraction. After we identify the entities in a sentence, the second part of the framework is relation inference. This is the task of identifying and assigning a relation *type* to a pair of entity mentions. We identify a relationship between two entities in a sentence by filtering an event triggered by a subject and affecting other characters as the object. The event extraction entails identifying event triggers (the words or phrases that most clearly express event occurrences) and their arguments (the words or phrases for participants in those events) in unstructured texts, and classifying these phrases, respectively, into their types and roles. English language structures allow us to understand these event triggers as being analogous to a verb/predicate pair.

We used OpenIE (Open Information Extraction) for event extraction, a model that transforms a sentence into fragments (subject, predicate, and object) that can be expressed as triples $< s, v, o >$ [4]. OpenIE attempts to compress information from a sentence's complex structure into smaller triple chunks that summarize the ideas of a sentence. For this purpose, we used a pre-trained OpenIE model [15] to extract all the triples from a single sentence.

Algorithm 1. Character relation extraction aligner

Require: $volume \in s_1, s_2, s_3, ..., s_n$ ▷ **volume** is a set of **sentences**
   $fullGraph \leftarrow Graph()$
   while $sentence \leftarrow getSentence(volume)$ **do**   ▷ for each **sentence** in a **volume**
      $entities \leftarrow entityExtract(sentence)$ ▷ extract **entities**
      $events \leftarrow openIExtract(sentence)$ ▷ extract **events**
      $sentenceGraph \leftarrow Graph()$ ▷ initiate sentence graph
      while $event \leftarrow fetch(events)$ **do**   ▷ for each **event**
         while $entity \leftarrow fetch(entities)$ **do**   ▷ for each **entity**
            if $entity \cap event$ **then**   ▷ if entity part of the **event**
              if $entity \in subject$ **then**   ▷ if the **entity** is the subject
                $sentenceGraph.addEdge(entity, event)$
              else if $entity \in object$ **then**   ▷ if the **entity** is the object
                $sentenceGraph.addEdge(event, entity)$ ▷ add object graph
              end if
            end if
         end while
      end while
      $relationGraph \leftarrow findTriad(sentenceGraph)$ ▷ find $< s, v, o >$
      $fullGraph.addGraph(relationGraph)$ ▷ add the sentence graph to the
   fullGraph
   end while

Sentence Graph for Character and Relation Extraction. The next task is figuring out the relations between extracted character entities based on the event proxy. We can infer a person (i.e., a character) from the entity extraction model, and an event from the OpenIE model. However, as these two models work independently, as a default their outputs are not connected in any essential way. To ascertain the connections between characters based on entities and events mentioned in a sentence, we developed an alignment procedure, as depicted in Algorithm 1. This "aligner" algorithm aims to find the intersection between outputs from the entity and event extractions, and to combine the two character

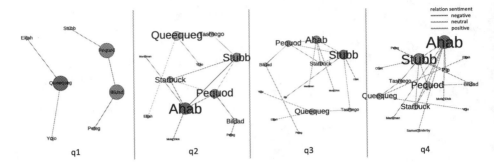

Fig. 3. Moby Dick's character relationship storyline: The Character Relation Network consists of nodes that represent characters, and edges that represent their relations. The relationship sentiment is represented by the color of the edges. Each of the networks shown represents about a quarter (q1-q4) of the storyline's length. As we can see, the network grows over time: in the first quarter of the story, we see two clusters between Queequeg and the Pequod, and as the story progresses, more character relationships are introduced. The sentiment also changes over time, perhaps most interestingly in the relationship between Starbuck and Ahab, which is positive at the beginning of the story but shifts toward the negative at the end of the story. (It is notable that the NER algorithm identified "Pequod" as a name, which it indeed is, but a non-human one: it is of course the name of the whaling ship. While it may be an error from a human reader's point of view to identify a "relationship" between a person and an inanimate object, one could argue that there may actually be interpretive value in such an analysis.) (Color figure online)

entities with the event, using its name as the name of the relation. Thus, a sentence will produce a small graph that will generate a full graph when all the sentence graphs from a volume are combined. The extraction system and examples on open access dataset are shared on our github repository [12].

4   Analysis and Result

The character-relation knowledge graph resulting from our ChaRelEx framework enables a researcher to perform further network analysis and machine learning using fictional mentions as inputs. We provide two analyses in this paper. First, we provide a visualization of the network's growth over the storyline. In addition to this growth, we also visualize a sentiment for each particular stage of the story. Second, we perform a sentiment-based temporal network visualization of the relation mentions among characters in order to understand how characters' relationships progress over time. Understanding this character sentiment is important in producing a general idea of the relationship dynamic of the story.

Our choice of story was informed by the volumes listed as fiction in Project Gutenberg, a collection of open-access literature, in order to preserve the provenance, at the sentence level, of the ChaRelEx framework. We apply our framework to the *Moby Dick* [11] volume as a proof of concept for analyzing the network dynamically.

4.1   Network Dynamic Visualization

In this analysis, we first preserved all the relations, extracted in sequence order, as our temporal identifier. A relation can of course have multiple mentions in the sequenced events (because character relations are not one-time occurrences, but generally extend through some period of narrative time). For simplicity, even though the extracted network is a directed graph based on the event trigger, we assume that the sentiment relation is mutual between two characters, making direction irrelevant in this analysis. Secondly, we compute the sentiment based on the event keyword as a proxy for understanding whether the relation is positive, negative, or neutral. Finally, we use the Vader sentiment analysis model [9] to express the sentiment as a numeric score. We compute the moving average of this score within a temporal window's size in order to aggregate the sentiment value over time. This aggregation is relevant for avoiding sudden turnovers (from positive to negative, and vice versa) within character relationships that can change over time. As a popular saying goes, "Yesterday's friend is today's enemy." In this spirit, it is appropriate both that sudden back-and-forth changes be smoothed (using a researcher-defined parameter), and that older sentiments should expire after some certain period. We choose here a window size of 3, which aggregates sentiment score within the three latest mentions of each character relation.

The Fig. 3 shows the evolution of relationships among the characters from the novel *Moby Dick* in four time frames (representing about a quarter of the text each). The nodes represent characters, and the edges represent the relationships, colored according to sentiment, between two characters. As we can see from the network visualization, new characters are introduced, leading to relationship development among these different characters as the story progresses. The size of the nodes highlights the characters with higher centrality than other characters in the story. We use degree centrality metrics to represent how many interactions a character has compared to the others. A bigger node represents a character with a higher degree, having multiple connections and interactions with different characters.

4.2   Relation Sentiment Dynamic

To further visualize the sentiment dynamic, The Fig. 4 shows the relationship dynamic for the two characters in the network with the highest degree of centrality, "Ahab" and "Stub," and with all of their companion pairs in the network. The relationship sentiment between "Moby Dick" and "Ahab" seems stable over time, characterized by a negative sentiment, as would be expected for an antagonist-protagonist relationship that barely evolves as it progresses over time. The dropping sentiment within the "Starbuck" and "Ahab" relationship further is confirmed knowing how their relation breaks down toward the end from positive to negative. In comparison, the "Stub" and "Ahab" relationship, which was not very good initially, starts moving positively in the middle of the story. Table 1 shows top five pairs of characters in terms of whose relationship

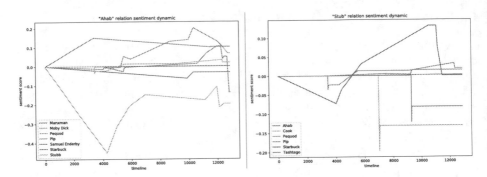

Fig. 4. "Ahab" and "Stub" relation sentiment comparisons: The plot shows the relationship dynamic between two characters within their network pair. As we can see, and interesting dynamic has occurred between the two characters over the course of the story. For example, the relationship between "Moby Dick" and "Ahab" is stable, and characterized by a negative sentiment, which represents the expected contrast between the protagonist and the antagonist of the story. Another interesting development is seen in the evolution of the relationship between "Starbuck" and "Ahab," which begins positively, but by the end has a completely turned toward negative sentiment.

Table 1. Top five characters with greatest sentiment development

Char #1	Char #2	n	Relations (samples)	Average sentiment	Progress
Ahab	Moby Dick	15	Run, shouted, cried, personified	-0.211 ± 0.073	4.035
Ahab	Starbuck	14	Cried, motioned, hailed, grasped	0.023 ± 0.069	2.351
Ahab	Pequod	12	Evincing, glided, stood	0.083 ± 0.071	1.889
Cook	Stubb	3	Cried, said	-0.164 ± 0.046	1.182
Bildad	Peleg	8	Said, cried, laid	-0.064 ± 0.053	0.895

shows the most progress in sentiment through the storyline, with progress being the total delta sentiment for each time frame.

5   Conclusions

This research proposes a conceptual model and an information extraction framework for character relationships in a fictional narrative. Character relations in a narrative, and especially their evolution over the course of that narrative, are a fitting topic for digital humanities researchers, and the quantification and visualization enabled by our framework offer a new way to approach that topic. Manually annotating each relationship in a narrative, especially a long narrative, can be very tedious. But with our character relation model and automated information extraction framework, we can infer the relationships among characters based on their interactions and triggering events as expressed in the narrative text. The benefit of extracting the relations directly from the story is that we can trace the relationship's progress based on the story timeline. Assuming each sentence or page in a story represents a timeline with a linear storyline, we can preserve and combine these time-specific relationships into a dynamic network.

In addition to the extraction of relationships, we also preserve each entity and event mention from the original sentence in order to further assess the relation's sentiment. As we consider the timeline in a network, we can also infer a relationship sentiment's dynamism over time. For example, we showed that the character networks from the novel *Moby Dick* have particular and meaningful sentiment dynamics between certain pairs characters, where yesterday's friend can become today's enemy.

There are several things we want to do to improve and continue our work. First, we want to apply this framework to a larger dataset to make it easier for researchers to explore the character relationship in any particular volume. Next, we want to train a domain-specific supervised classifier for extracting relationships in fiction, hoping to improve upon a generic classifier, allowing us to include "humans in the loop" for the evaluation and curation of a supervised training set deeply rooted in human experience. Finally, we would note that this work is not a panacea for extracting and evaluating all the complexities of fictional interpersonal relationships, but rather a step toward a more robust model and analytical framework for this still unsolved challenge.

References

1. Brickley, D., Miller, L.: FOAF vocabulary Specification (2014). http://xmlns.com/foaf/spec/
2. Christenson, H.: HathiTrust. Libr. Resour. Tech. Serv. **55**(2), 93–102 (2011)
3. Devlin, J., Chang, M.W., Lee, K., Toutanova, K.: BERT: pre-training of deep bidirectional transformers for language understanding. arXiv preprint arXiv:1810.04805 (2018)
4. Etzioni, O., Banko, M., Soderland, S., Weld, D.S.: Open information extraction from the web. Commun. ACM **51**(12), 68–74 (2008)
5. Gutenberg, P.: Project Gutenberg (2021). https://www.gutenberg.org/
6. HathiTrust: Operationalizing "Non-Consumptive" Fair Use to Revolutionize Humanities Research. HathiTrust Digital Library (2020). https://www.hathitrust.org/blogs/perspectives-from-hathitrust/operationalizing-non-consumptive-fair-use-to-revolutionize
7. Honnibal, M., Montani, I.: spaCy 2: Natural language understanding with Bloom embeddings, convolutional neural networks and incremental parsing (2017, to appear)
8. Hovy, E., Marcus, M., Palmer, M., Ramshaw, L., Weischedel, R.: OntoNotes: the 90% solution. In: Proceedings of the Human Language Technology Conference of the NAACL, Companion Volume: Short Papers, pp. 57–60 (2006)
9. Hutto, C., Gilbert, E.: VADER: a parsimonious rule-based model for sentiment analysis of social media text. In: Proceedings of the International AAAI Conference on Web and Social Media, vol. 8 (2014)
10. Li, J., Zhang, C., Tan, H., Li, C.: Complex networks of characters in fictional novels. In: 2019 IEEE/ACIS 18th International Conference on Computer and Information Science (ICIS), pp. 417–420. IEEE (2019)

11. Melville: Moby-Dick, Or, the Whale/by Herman Melville. Harper & Brothers, New York (1851). https://babel.hathitrust.org/cgi/pt?id=dul1.ark%3A%2F13960%2Ft3kw6ns1s&view=1up&seq=11
12. Parulian, N.: ChaRelEx (2021). https://github.com/htrc/ChaRelEx
13. Shahsavari, S., et al.: An automated pipeline for character and relationship extraction from readers literary book reviews on Goodreads.com. In: 12th ACM Conference on Web Science, pp. 277–286 (2020)
14. Skorinkin, D.: Extracting character networks to explore literary plot dynamics. In: Komp'juternaja Lingvistika i Intellektual'nye Tehnologii, pp. 257–270 (2017)
15. Stanovsky, G., Michael, J., Zettlemoyer, L., Dagan, I.: Supervised open information extraction. In: NAACL-HLT (2018)

The Origin and Value of Disagreement Among Data Labelers: A Case Study of Individual Differences in Hate Speech Annotation

Yisi Sang$^{(\boxtimes)}$ and Jeffrey Stanton

Syracuse University, Syracuse, NY 13244, USA
{yisang,jmstanto}@syr.edu

Abstract. Human annotated data is the cornerstone of today's artificial intelligence efforts, yet data labeling processes can be complicated and expensive, especially when human labelers disagree with each other. The current work practice is to use majority-voted labels to overrule the disagreement. However, in the subjective data labeling tasks such as hate speech annotation, disagreement among individual labelers can be difficult to resolve. In this paper, we explored why such disagreements occur using a mixed-method approach – including interviews with experts, concept mapping exercises, and self-reporting items – to develop a multidimensional scale for distilling the process of how annotators label a hate speech corpus. We tested this scale with 170 annotators in a hate speech annotation task. Results showed that our scale can reveal facets of individual differences among annotators (e.g., age, personality, etc.), and these facets' relationships to an annotator's final label decision of an instance. We suggest that this work contributes to the understanding of how humans annotate data. The proposed scale can potentially improve the value of the currently discarded minority-vote labels.

Keywords: Data labeler · Label · Disagreement · Hate speech · Multidimensional scale · Content moderation

1 Introduction

With currently predominant machine learning techniques, humans support the training of machine learning algorithms by providing annotation data [36], often in the form of binary categorizations. Such data work well for training perceptual-level classifiers – for example, those used for labeling a photograph as a cat or dog. In contrast, consider a more complex "social computing" application, where we want to develop a system that can characterize the toxicity of a social media post. Taking into account the messiness of social reality, people's perceptions of toxicity vary substantially. Their labels of toxic content are based on their own perceptions. We refer to the first type of data labeling tasks as "objective data labeling", and the second type of tasks as "subjective data labeling", and in this paper, we are interested in the labelers' disagreements for subjective data labeling tasks.

© The Author(s), under exclusive license to Springer Nature Switzerland AG 2022
M. Smits (Ed.): iConference 2022, LNCS 13192, pp. 425–444, 2022.
https://doi.org/10.1007/978-3-030-96957-8_36

Subjectiveness usually arises from what some researchers refer to as "latent content". The idea of latent content refers to the presence in text of meaning that must be inferred because it is not manifest in the dictionary meanings of individual words. In an influential paper about the validity of content analysis, Potter and Levine-Donnerstein [42] distinguished latent content into pattern and projective subtypes. "Pattern" latent content can be inferred by recognizing a meaningful pattern across recurrent cues present in the text. The detection of pattern latent content depends on a judge's recognition of key configurations of elements in the material. As an example, imagine a statement that on its face seems to indicate one thing, but the subsequent appearance of a sarcasm indicator reverses that meaning. In contrast, "projective" latent content may require a more complex approach. Key elements in projective latent content are symbols that "require viewers to access their pre-existing mental schema in order to judge the meaning in the content" [42]. This point highlights the fact that different annotators may bring different mental schemas to the stimulus evaluation process and thereby may also produce differing judgments about the same content.

The present study is concerned with the annotation of latent content in hate speech, where the mental schemas that human annotators bring to the annotation process may result in systematic variation in judgments about content. Psychometrically sound measurement instruments are generally construed to reflect the underlying dimensional structure of the unobservable concepts they measure. A psychometrically sound instrument that captures the dimensionality of judgments about a set of stimuli (i.e., examples of hate speech) may thus reveal some aspects of how annotators conceptualize content and may also offer analytical insights about variability in their judgments about the content. Therefore, in this study we first developed a multidimensional scale to capture hate speech judgments using standard psychometric scale development methods. Then we conducted multigroup confirmatory factor analysis on n = 170 annotators' evaluations of hate speech. Our analysis focused on addressing these research questions:

Research Question 1: What are some basic judgment dimensions for human annotations of hate speech?
Research Question 2: How does the age of a human judge relate to the annotation of hate speech?
Research Question 3: How do personality factors relate to the annotation of hate speech?

2   Related Work

2.1   Definitions and Elements of Hate Speech

Legal frameworks, social science research, and social media companies have all generated definitions of hate speech, with their particular goals driving the definitional approach they take [50]. Legal frameworks for hate speech are influenced by the social values of speech regulation in particular national contexts [41]. For example, Article 20 of the International Covenant on Civil and Political Rights (ICCPR) states that "[a]ny advocacy of national, racial or religious hatred that constitutes incitement to discrimination, hostility or violence shall be prohibited by law." In 2016, to counter online hate speech, the commission of EU developed a "code of conduct" agreement with

Facebook, Microsoft, Twitter and YouTube. The government of China has established similar mechanisms to counter online hate speech as a part of its Internet censorship policy [53].

Social media platforms have developed their own definitions of hate speech. These definitions guide their content moderation strategies. For instance, Facebook defines hate speech as "a direct attack on people based on what we call protected characteristics – race, ethnicity, national origin, religious affiliation, sexual orientation, caste, sex, gender, gender identity, and serious disease or disability" [60]. Twitter has a hateful conduct policy using the definition of promoting violence, "against or directly attacking, or threatening other people on the basis of race, ethnicity, national origin, caste, sexual orientation, gender, gender identity, religious affiliation, age, disability, or serious disease" [61].

One early academic effort to define hate speech was Richard Delgado's article "Words that Wound" [17]. Based on Delgado's work, Matsuda argued that a narrow class of racial hate speech that causes serious harm should be considered as a crime [30, 31]. Moran and Ward emphasized the intention of hate speech. Moran defined hate speech as "speech that is intended to promote hatred against traditionally disadvantaged groups" [35]. Marwick and Miller [29] proposed three distinct elements that were used in defining hate speech: 1) a content-based element; 2) an intent-based element; and 3) a harms-based element [29]. Benesch [6] defined five aspects of dangerous hate speech: the speaker, the audience, the speech act itself, the social and historical context, and the means of dissemination. Parekh emphasized the target of hate speech [40]. Sellars [50] proposed a framework to conceptualize hate speech including considering the target, content, harm, speaker, result, and context of verbal hate speech.

In summary, our literature review suggests that hate speech judgments re multidimensional in nature. Previous work has considered the status of the source, the status of the target – including whether the target is a (member of a) protected class, the intent of the speech, and the impacts of the speech in the world. While this is probably not an exhaustive list of the aspects or dimensions of hate speech, these perspectives clearly indicate that a binary approach to detecting, flagging, or moderating hate speech oversimplifies the underlying judgments that people make about toxic content.

2.2 Annotation of Hate Speech

Hate speech could be construed as an umbrella term that includes many kinds of problematic user-generated content [49]: abusive language [38, 54], cyberbullying [1, 52], offensive language [11, 58], misogynist language [18, 22], toxic language [23, 34], threatening language [39], aggression [26], and hate speech [24, 55]. In various research communities, these terms are sometimes considered distinctive and sometimes considered as overlapping. Many previous annotation efforts have used simple binary classification decisions to annotate content in any one of these categories or to designate a choice among a small number of mutually exclusive categories. For example, in Chen et al. [11], YouTube comments were labeled based on whether they are offensive or not. Some researchers have constructed datasets that distinguish facets in various expressions of online hate speech. For example, in Founta [19], annotators were required to label tweets as offensive, abusive, hateful speech, aggressive, cyberbullying, spam, and normal. Some researchers have devised hierarchical annotation schemas that require annotators to code texts on nested levels. For example, in Basile et al. [4], tweets were first coded as hateful or non-hateful. Hateful tweets were further coded based on 1) whether the target was a generic group of people or a specific individual; 2) whether the tweet was aggressive or not. In applying annotation schemes to hate speech, much research has assumed that every instance can be placed into two or more of these mutually exclusive categories. As an alternative, Sanguinetti et al. [48] designed an annotation method that considered factors contributing to the definition of hate speech. Assimakopoulos et al. [2] considered the polarity of hate speech and annotated hate speech based on discursive strategies including who was the attitude target and how the attitude was expressed.

Among the annotation approaches described above, two popular methods for assessing quality are inter-rater agreement and gold standard corpus test, which assume that there is a single correct truth with respect to assignment of speech examples to particular annotation classes. However, given the complex dimensionality of hate speech, it may be erroneous to assume that there is only one universally acceptable annotation choice for a given stimulus. People's perceptions of hate speech are influenced by many factors. Previous research has found that gender [32], ethnicity [14], racial attitudes [47, 56], value placed on freedom of speech [15], context [14], target [27], empathy [13], ways of knowing [13, 57], implicitness of the hate speech [7], and relationality [13] may all influence people's perception of hate speech. For example, Roussos and Dovidio found that for Black-targeted hate speech, people higher in anti-Black prejudice tended to invoke freedom of speech rights and perceived it less as a hate crime. When the hate target was Black versus White, people with low-prejudice rated the act as less protected by freedom of speech rights and more strongly as a hate crime [47]. Cowan and Hodge found that in the public setting, when an argumentative response occurred, speech was perceived as more offensive than when no response occurred. In a private setting, no response by the target led to higher offensiveness rating than when the target responded [14]. Cowan and Cowan illustrated that the perceived harm of hate speech was positively related to empathy [13].

Both the proliferation of alternative conceptualizations and the widespread use of simplistic annotation methods are arguably hindering the progress of research on online hate speech. For example, Ross et al. [45] found that showing Twitter's definition of hateful conduct to annotators caused them to partially align their own opinions with the definition. This realignment resulted in very low interrater reliability of the annotations (Krippendorff's $\alpha = 0.29$). Davidson et al. [16] found racial bias in hate speech and abusive language detection datasets. Classifiers trained on these datasets tend to predict tweets written in African-American English vernacular as abusive at substantially higher rates than expected. Awal et al. [3] found that there was annotation inconsistency in popular datasets that are widely used in online hate speech detection. Even expert content moderators often disagree with each other: A Fleiss' kappa for comments annotated by two moderators was only 0.46 [28].

In summary, many alternative annotation methods exist for hate speech. Most of these take the approach of assuming that all speech examples can be assigned to mutually exclusive categories. Gold standard databases take this assumption to its logical conclusion by converging opinions of experts on a set of class assignments assumed to be immutable. While some research considered the possibility that characteristics of hate speech may exist on a set of continua [25], little work has explored the possibility that characteristic differences among human evaluators may influence annotation decisions – whether those decisions include class assignment, ordered ratings, or both. In this light, developing a deeper understanding of how differences among hate speech evaluators cause variation in class assignments or ratings could be valuable in creating and deploying hate speech detection and mitigation systems.

3 Method

3.1 Development of a Multidimensional Scale for Evaluating Hate Speech

We planned to use confirmatory factor analysis on a set of newly created scale items in an effort to establish some basic evaluative dimensions of hate speech. In the initial work towards this goal, we followed Netemeyer et al.'s 4-step scale creation process [37].

Construct Definition and Content Domain: In this step, we identified the facets and domains of the constructs to be assessed. We began by conducting a literature review on the definitions of hate speech and collated 98 definitions from academic papers, law, and online platforms. From the collected material, we compiled a raw list of distinctive elements of online hate speech. To understand people's understanding of online hate speech, we conducted seven semi-structured interviews in October 2020 with researchers who experienced online hate speech or whose research is related to hate speech. We started with questions such as "What do you consider to be hate speech?" Then we examined how participants evaluate hate speech including what factors make them feel that a certain speech instance is hateful. We also asked participants their reactions to hate speech they encountered. Each interview lasted approximately 30 min. An inductive coding method [8] was conducted to document the themes of people's evaluations of hate speech. We matched these coded themes to elements from the literature. If the theme of the interview did not appear in the literature, it was treated as a new element. Then we presented each theme to ten hate speech researchers on index cards using an online research platform Optimal Workshop [62]. The experts sorted these cards into categories of their own individual devising. By collapsing across the many similarities among these expert-generated categories, we developed an eight-facet taxonomy of hate speech: Characteristics of the Speaker, Characteristics of the Target, Content of the Speech, Context of the Speech, Impact of the Speech, Intentions of the Speech, Language Style, and Miscellaneous Identification Cues. Table 1 depicts the eight categories.

Table 1. Interview results: eight-facets of hate speech

Factor	Description
Characteristics of the speaker	Hate speech initiator's attributes
Characteristics of the target	Hate speech recipient/victim's attributes
Content	Whether the speech instance expressed violence tendencies, insults to human dignity, slander, moral violation, radicalization, showing fear, and/or groundless accusation
Context	The circumstances where the speech is conducted including cultural, social, political contexts and the condition of the circumstance i.e., private, or public
Impact of the speech	The outcomes of the speech instance on the targeted individual or on individuals in general
Intention of the speech	The idea or plan of posting the speech instance
Language style	The language style of the speech instance including vocabulary/word choice, sentence structure, figure of speech, whether it is dialogue, monologue, or reported speech etc
Miscellaneous identification cues	Catch-all category for other elements of the speech instance

Generating and Judging Candidate Items: In the present study, we focused on Content of the Speech, Characteristics of the Target, and Impact of the Speech in item generation. We used the subcategories of Content of the Speech (i.e., violence tendencies, insult to human dignity, slander, moral violation, radicalization, showing fear, and groundless accusation). We generated and had experts evaluate an initial pool of items to reflect the constructs and ensured that the items were understandable by prospective respondents. The 10 experts who familiar with the elements were tapped again to create items based on the definitions of constructs. Then the experts evaluated these items based on the construct definition and content domain, i.e., whether the item was representative of the construct and the wording of item is understandable. This step resulted in 39 proposed items.

Developing and Refining the Scale: In this step, we fielded a survey with one hate speech example and one neutral (non-hateful speech) example each harvested from a popular social media platform. We collected two rounds of data ($n = 50$ and $n = 120$) with slight wording adjustments to the survey between the two rounds. Most respondents were recruited from the research platform Prolific.co [63], where we ensured a minimum pay rate of $9.60 USD per hour. Each survey was completed in less than 10 min. Table 2 shows the constructs and items. The median age group of participants was 18–33. 96 participants were male, 69 participants were female, three participants identified themselves as non-binary, and two participants preferred not to report their gender.

Analyzing the Scale: In this step, we used Exploratory Factor Analysis (EFA) to identify possible underlying factor structures and refined the item set to its most efficient form, while maintaining acceptable reliability. Then we used Confirmatory Factor Analysis (CFA) to assess the previously identified underlying factor structure.

Table 2. Constructs and items

Constructs	Description	List of items
Violence tendency	Violence tendency refers to the verbal attack, the commitment, threat, or incitement of violence [6]	1. This post encourages violence
		2. This post threatens violence toward a specific group
		3. This post attacks someone
		4. This post could cause a public safety problem
		5. This post is a threat of an attack
Impact	Impact of the speech describes the influence and outcomes of the speech such as distorting a perception of a fact, stirring up social panic, delivering conspiracy, and causing social secession. The impact can be on the individual or on the society	6. This post probably distorts the facts
		7. This post uses exaggeration to stir up trouble
		8. This post refers to rumors that are untrue
		9. This post tries to divide people into a good group and an evil group
		10. This post injures the status of the target group
		11. This post results in mental distress to the target
Insult to human dignity	Insult to human dignity describes the insult of an individual's humanity such as degrading/judging/discriminating/denigrating people based on their identity, vulnerability, or stereotypes	12. The post degrades people based on who they are

(continued)

Table 2. (*continued*)

Constructs	Description	List of items
		13. The post judges people based on stereotypes
		14. This post discriminates against vulnerable people
		15. This post describes other people as inferior
		16. This post criticizes people unfairly
Slander	Slanderous remark refers to the false spoken statement damaging to a person's reputation	17. This post insults other people
		18. This post tries to damage someone's reputation
		19. This post criticizes others falsely
		20. This post paints others with a broad brush
Moral violation	Moral violation refers the violation of moral standards such as fairness, respect, care, and sanctity	21. This post shows bigotry
		22. This post shows intolerance
		23. This post shows a lack of respect for others
Radicalization	Radicalization refers to the extreme political, social, or religious ideals and aspirations shown in the speech	24. This writer dislikes minorities
		25. This writer takes an uncivilized viewpoint
		26. This writer probably believes that one group is superior and another group is inferior

(*continued*)

Table 2. (*continued*)

Constructs	Description	List of items
Showing fear	Showing fear refers to expressing fear towards a specific population such as misogyny, homophobia, and xenophobia	27. This writer probably dislikes transgender people
		28. This writer probably fears foreigners
		29. This writer probably dislikes gay men
		30. This writer probably fears women
		31. The writer of this post probably feels powerless
Target	The characteristics of the targets focuses on the personality and features of the receivers and victims of the speech [59]	32. This post targets a large number of people
		33. This post targets a specific person
		34. This post targets people based on who they are
		35. This post targets people based on their ethnic background
Groundless accusation	Groundless accusation refers to a claim or allegation of wrongdoing that is untrue and/or otherwise unsupported by facts	36. The target of this post has done nothing to provoke this attack
		37. The target of this post cannot address the writer's problem
		38. The writer of this post believes that the target cannot change
		39. The target of this post is powerless to address the writer's concern

3.2 Multiple Group Confirmatory Factor Analysis

Multiple group analysis is a common method to assess group differences, which amounts to doing separate latent variable models of some kind across the groups of interest. We used multiple group analysis to uncover the influence of age and personality on the evaluation of hate speech.

When collecting participants' evaluations of hate speech using the multidimensional scale, we also asked them to complete the big five personality inventory (BFI-10) [44]. The Big Five Inventory (BFI) is a widely used self-reported personality measurement that has five dimensions: Extraversion is characterized by sociability, talkativeness, excitability, and lots of emotional expression [43]; Agreeableness includes traits like sympathetic, kind, and affectionate; Conscientiousness is featured by high levels of thoughtfulness, good impulse control, and goal-directed behaviors [43]; Neuroticism include tense, moody, and anxious; Openness is characterized by having wide interests and being imaginative and insightful. We used the BFI-10 to reduce the length of the questionnaire. Completion time for self-report surveys is negatively correlated with initial willingness to participate [20] and low response rates can adversely affect reliability and validity [44].

To understand the differences of evaluations of hate speech, we analyzed measurement invariance in latent variables. We grouped respondents by personality profile and estimated separate models using a typical sequence for assessing measurement invariance: configural, weak, strong, and strict invariance [5]. Configural invariance is the most basic level, and just indicates that the latent variable model has the same structure in all the groups. Weak invariance constrains loadings to be equal between groups for a given indicator. Latent (co)variances are allowed to vary among groups. In the measurement of strong invariance, all intercepts are constrained to be equal among groups but can vary within a group. Latent means may change among groups. The measurement of strict invariance constrains the error variances to be the same across groups.

4 Result

4.1 Exploratory Factor Analysis

The scale building process concludes with weeding out poorly functioning items to establish a subset of items that addresses each subscale dimension with an acceptable level of reliability. As a diagnostic, we first conducted exploratory factor analysis (EFA) for each construct. The Cronbach's alpha based upon the covariances of all subscales were above 0.80 except for Target, which had an alpha of 0.66. Item statistics showed that after deleting item 2 the Cronbach alpha of Target increased to 0.73. Cronbach alpha above 0.7 is considered acceptable [12] in scales under development. A parallel analysis of eigenvalues suggested that either a four-factor or a five-factor solution was the best fit for the data. The results of the five-factor solution appear in Table 3.

Table 3. Five-factor EFA results

Items	Factor					Dimension
	1	2	3	4	5	
1	**0.796**					Violence tendency
2	**0.911**					
3	**0.676**				0.240	
4	**0.922**					
5	**0.918**					
6			**0.538**	0.202		Impact
7	0.225	−0.105	**0.585**		0.141	
8	0.191		**0.620**		−0.161	
12	**0.412**	0.113	0.315		0.197	Insult to human dignity
13			**0.618**	0.104	0.177	
14	0.324	0.227	**0.405**			
15	0.286	0.258	0.199	0.117	0.296	
16	0.112	0.217	**0.642**		−0.135	
17	0.298	0.162	0.268		0.328	Slander
18			**0.713**			
19	0.111	0.221	**0.464**		0.135	
20		0.208	0.388	0.115	0.272	
22	0.145	0.180	0.266	0.116	**0.461**	Moral violation
23	0.223	0.118	0.236	0.121	**0.486**	
24	0.343	0.326			0.260	Radicalization
25	**0.428**	0.261	0.109		0.303	
26	0.304	0.275	0.135	0.101	0.355	
27	0.161	**0.657**			0.153	Showing fear
28	0.194	**0.523**		0.160	0.213	
29		**0.921**				
30		**0.740**		0.109		
31		**0.551**		0.253		
32	0.211	0.111			0.169	Target
34	0.236	0.165	0.172		0.387	
35		**0.617**	0.284		−0.134	
36	0.255	0.157	−0.130	**0.634**	−0.261	Groundless accusation
37				**0.836**		
39			0.109	**0.777**		

The EFA suggested a sufficient set of items for these five factors: (a) Violence tendency - This factor has an eigenvalue of 4.889 and accounts for 14.8% of the variance; (b) Showing fear - This factor has an eigenvalue of 3.474 and accounts for 10.5% of the variance; (c) The third factor is measured by items from Impact, Insult to human dignity, and Slander. This factor has an eigenvalue of 3.403 and accounts for 10.3% of the variance. (d) Groundless accusation - This factor has an eigenvalue of 2.007 and accounts for 6.1% of the variance; (e) Moral violation - This factor has an eigenvalue of 1.596 and accounted for 4.8% of the variance. Items 15, 17, 20, 24, 26, 32, and 34 were dropped from subsequent analysis based on a poor pattern of loadings.

4.2 Confirmatory Factor Analysis of the Five-Factor Model

We fit a five-factor confirmatory model using lavaan [46] in R. We standardized the latent factors, allowing free estimation of all factor loadings and used maximum likelihood to estimate the model.

We started the model fitting with the Violence Tendency latent variable. Modification indices suggested that item 5, item 12, and item 25 had excess correlations to other items. After dropping these, CFI increased from 0.94 to 0.99 and RSMEA dropped from 0.194 to 0.037. Then we added the Showing fear latent variable. Modification indices indicated that the model fit would improve by removing item 29, item 31, and item 35. We removed these items and added the Moral violation latent variable. The results indicated that item 38 should be removed. After removing item 38, RMSEA decreased from 0.067 to 0.04 and CFI increased from 0.978 to 0.994. Next, we added Groundless Accusation. The results showed that item 38 should be dropped. After dropping item 38 the RMSEA decreased from 0.067 to 0.040 and the CFI increased from 0.978 to 0.994. Finally, items 22 and 23 were retained as indicators of Impact. This modification improved CFI from 0.945 to 0.991 and decreased RMSEA from 0.082 to 0.042. For the final model, fit statistics were as follows: CFI = .991, RMSEA = .042, SRMR = .032, BIC = 6054.32. These are generally considered acceptable levels for CFA models, except for BIC, which is not a standardized measure. Figure 1 visualizes the model.

Results from the exploratory factor analysis and confirmatory analysis thus provided initial evidence about the dimensionality of hate speech. Five distinctive factors were modeled adequately using 13 items. Three of the correlations between latent variables were in excess of r = .75 which would typically be a concern for discriminant validity. In this case, however, because only two stimuli have been used to generate variance in item responses, it is too early in the research process to combine or eliminate constructs on the basis of high inter-construct correlations. We plan to expand the amount of rated content in a future study, and with the addition of more examples of hate speech, a clearer picture of the inter-construct correlations will emerge.

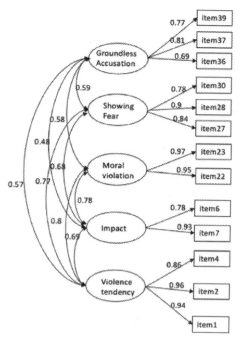

Fig. 1. Five-factor model

4.3 Measurement Invariance Based on Age Differences

hen collecting data, participants report their age based on five age groups, but n = 143 participants were in the age group 18–33, so we run the multigroup analysis with two groups: older than 33 and younger than 33. We fitted the five-factor latent variable models and the subscales with different constraints. Our results showed that when constraining the error variance between age groups, the chi-squared differences were significant, which means that the two age groups do not exhibit measurement invariance. Table 4 shows this result. Tables 5 and 6 are follow-up analyses showing that Violence Tendency and Groundless Accusation were the sources of the invariance.

Table 4. Chi-squared difference test of different age groups on the five-factor model

	DF	AIC	BIC	Chisq	Chisq diff	DF diff	Pr(>Chisq)
Configural	110	5987.5	6294.8	155.52			
Weak	118	5980.3	6262.5	164.32	8.806	8	0.3589
Strong	126	5968.7	6225.9	168.73	4.410	8	0.8184
Strict	139	5986.7	6203.1	212.73	43.993	13	3.078e−05***

Signif. codes: 0 '***' 0.001 '**' 0.01 '*' 0.05 '.' 0.1 ' ' 1

Table 5. Chi-squared difference test of different age groups on Violence Tendency

	DF	AIC	BIC	Chisq	Chisq diff	DF diff	Pr(>Chisq)
Configural	0	1458.8	1515.3	0.0000			
Weak	2	1459.7	1509.8	4.8633	4.8633	2	0.0878904
Strong	4	1456.1	1500.0	5.2587	0.3954	2	0.8206158
Strict	7	1469.9	1504.4	25.0856	19.8269	3	0.0001844***

Signif. codes: 0 '***' 0.001 '**' 0.01 '*' 0.05 '.' 0.1 ' ' 1

Table 6. Chi-squared difference test of different age groups on the Groundless Accusation scale

	DF	AIC	BIC	Chisq	Chisq diff	DF diff	Pr(>Chisq)
Configural	0	1480.5	1537.0	0.0000			
Weak	2	1476.7	1526.9	0.1513	0.1513	2	0.92716
Strong	4	1475.1	1519.0	2.6015	2.4503	2	0.29371
Strict	7	1479.7	1514.2	13.1349	10.5333	3	0.01454*

Signif. codes: 0 '***' 0.001 '**' 0.01 '*' 0.05 '.' 0.1 ' ' 1

4.4 Measurement Invariance Based on Personality Profiles

We used median splits to group personality profiles using the same logic as described above for age groups. The scores of each dimension are divided into high and low groups according to the comparison with the median. Our results showed that constraining the error variance between low and high groups, the chi-squared differences are significant on the five-factor multidimensional model. Besides performing significant differently on the five-factor model, high and low Extraversion significantly changed the evaluation of hate speech on Showing Fear ($p = .01811$) and Groundless Accusation ($p = .017$). High and low Agreeableness also influenced participants' evaluations on Groundless Accusation ($p = .042$) and Showing Fear ($p = .018$). High and low Conscientiousness significantly influenced the evaluation of hate speech on Showing Fear ($p < .01$) and Violence Tendency ($p < .01$). High and low Neuroticism significantly influenced the evaluation of Violence Tendency ($p < .01$) and Showing Fear ($p < .01$). High and low Openness to Experience significantly influenced the evaluation of hate speech on Violence tendency ($p < .01$). The significant p-value implies that the free and constrained models are significantly different. Some paths vary for different age groups and personality groups. In the other words, when evaluating hate speech, the aforementioned factors do not exhibit measurement invariance for different age groups and personality groups. For example, when constraining loadings and intercepts, different levels of Conscientiousness have significant influence on people's evaluation of hate speech related to violence. Table 7 shows the Chi-Squared different test of low and high Conscientiousness on the subscale Violence tendency.

Table 7. Chi-squared difference test of low and high Conscientiousness on Violence tendency

	DF	AIC	BIC	Chisq	Chisq diff	DF diff	Pr(>Chisq)
Configural	0	1414.2	1470.6	0.0000			
Weak	2	1410.9	1461.1	0.7420	0.7420	2	0.690056
Strong	4	1413.0	1456.9	6.8724	6.1304	2	0.046645*
Strict	7	1420.7	1455.2	20.5401	13.6677	3	0.003394**

Signif. codes: 0 '***' 0.001 '**' 0.01 '*' 0.05 '.' 0.1 ' ' 1

5   Discussion

5.1   Annotator's Subjectiveness in Hate Speech Annotation

Our results showed that age and personality differences were connected with the dimensional evaluation of hate speech. We used multi-group confirmatory factor analysis to assess measurement invariance across older and younger respondents, as well as across respondents who had high or low standing on each of the big five personality characteristics. Measurement invariance on self-report items examines differences in the ways that individuals respond to particular stimuli. In our study, respondents rated a particular content stimulus with a variety of items. Our significant results on strict invariance indicated that people had different patterns of responding to the items based on age and personality factors. Although these patterns do not directly tell us how their beliefs about hate speech may differ, we can strongly conclude that annotators' individual differences have a systematic relationship with variance in item responses to items designed to assess dimensional aspects of hate speech.

These results suggest that subjectivity plays a critical role in hate speech annotation. Older adult respondents, by dint of previous experience or knowledge that they possess relative to younger respondents, express different beliefs about content that advocates violence or that makes groundless accusations. Likewise, personality factors such as extraversion and agreeableness impact the patterns of item responses for content with respect to ratings of groundless accusations and fear towards a specific target population (such as a religious minority).

5.2   Design Implications

A key implication from these findings is that, while training annotators may provide improvements to inter-annotator agreement values, these improvements come at the expense of meaningful differences in how different people interpret different examples of speech. As Potter and Levine-Donnerstein [42] suggested, essential elements in projective latent content such as hate speech are symbols whose evaluation depends upon accessing pre-existing mental schemata. Those schemata vary across the lifespan and are based on naturally occurring individual differences, also implying that inter-annotator agreement of hate speech will only be strong to the extent that the annotators themselves are highly homogeneous.

These results also provide design insights for content moderation tools: Some evaluative dimensions that exhibit lesser degrees of inter-annotator variability could be construed as being more universal, and thus easier for an automated system to evaluate. On the other hand, evaluative dimensions with greater inter-rater variability would require a system or method that was adaptable to differing content moderation situations. If we assume that these latter dimensions cannot be consistently annotated (at least without an annotator training process that forces annotators all into the same "box"), then we will need to develop a more sophisticated understanding of the sources of variation in order to be able to develop a satisfactory annotation system.

Additionally, in manual content moderation, a community's moderators can decide the destiny of both posts and users in their community by promoting or hiding posts, as well as honoring, shaming, or banning the users. Moderators' decisions influence the content delivered to community members and audiences [21] and by extension also influence the community's experience of the discussion. Assuming that a human moderator is a community member who has demographic homogeneity with other community members, it seems possible that the mental schema they use to evaluate content will match those of other community members.

In contrast, both hybrid and fully-automated content moderation systems depend on trained machine learning models – the data for training these models comes from annotation processes [21]. These systems play an increasingly important role in content regulation [33]. For example, for identifying hate speech [10], pornography [51], and eating disorder-related content [9]. Given the apparent subjectivity of evaluations of certain dimensions of hate speech, hybrid and fully automated content moderation systems will need to either learn or be pre-programmed with an understanding of how speech evaluations may differ across demographic groups or communities. Further research will be needed to increase understanding of which evaluative dimensions generate the greatest variance in annotation results and how demographic differences are connected to specific patterns of evaluations. Conceivably, a machine learning system that is trained on not just on mean evaluations of speech examples, but also on degrees of variation, and demographic characteristics of annotators that are sources of variance, could then serve as the core of a content moderation system that was adaptable to different audiences or community contexts.

6   Limitations and Future Work

The present research was limited by the use of newly developed evaluative scales and by the use of the minimum number of speech instances needed to obtain variation in dimensional evaluations. Further validation work should be conducted to retest the items developed for this study. Additionally, the items should be tested on a wider variety of speech content, preferably using a method that includes multiple evaluations of each speech instance in order to partition evaluator variance from other sources of variance. In this study we use hate speech as an example. Our multi-dimensional scale approach is also applicable in other subjective data labeling tasks. For example, labeling misinformation and arthritics. We will explore these labeling tasks in the future.

7 Conclusion

In this paper we developed a multidimensional evaluative scale for hate speech and conducted several multigroup analysis to uncover the origin and value of disagreement among hate speech labelers. Our findings shown that personality and age had a substantial influence on the dimensional labeling of hate speech. These findings suggest that efforts to obtain annotation consistency among labelers with different backgrounds and personalities for hate speech may never fully succeed. Implications for the use of labeled data in automated or hybrid content moderation systems were discussed. Future research should be conducted to obtain additional validation evidence on these scales and to generalize to a wider variety of speech instances.

References

1. Aggarwal, A., Maurya, K., Chaudhary, A.: Comparative study for predicting the severity of cyberbullying across multiple social media platforms. In: 2020 4th International Conference on Intelligent Computing and Control Systems (ICICCS), pp. 871–877 (2020)
2. Assimakopoulos, S., Muskat, R.V., van der Plas, L., Gatt, A.: Annotating for hate speech: the MaNeCo corpus and some input from critical discourse analysis. In: Proceedings of the 12th Language Resources and Evaluation Conference, pp. 5088–5097 (2020). https://www.aclweb.org/anthology/2020.lrec-1.626. Accessed 23 Sept 2020
3. Awal, Md.R., Cao, R., Lee, R.K.-W., Mitrović, S.: On analyzing annotation consistency in online abusive behavior datasets. arXiv:2006.13507 [cs] (2020). http://arxiv.org/abs/2006.13507. Accessed 10 Aug 2020
4. Basile, V., et al.: Semeval-2019 task 5: multilingual detection of hate speech against immigrants and women in twitter. In: Proceedings of the 13th International Workshop on Semantic Evaluation, pp. 54–63 (2019)
5. Beaujean, A.A.: Latent Variable Modeling Using R: A Step-by-Step Guide. Routledge, London (2014)
6. Benesch, S.: Dangerous speech: a proposal to prevent group violence. In: Voices That Poison: Dangerous Speech Project (2012)
7. Benikova, D., Wojatzki, M., Zesch, T.: What does this imply? Examining the impact of implicitness on the perception of hate speech. In: Rehm, G., Declerck, T. (eds.) GSCL 2017. LNCS (LNAI), vol. 10713, pp. 171–179. Springer, Cham (2018). https://doi.org/10.1007/978-3-319-73706-5_14
8. Boyatzis, R.E.: Transforming Qualitative Information: Thematic Analysis and Code Development. Sage, Thousand Oaks (1998)
9. Chancellor, S., Kalantidis, Y., Pater, J.A., De Choudhury, M., Shamma, D.A.: Multimodal classification of moderated online pro-eating disorder content. In: Proceedings of the 2017 CHI Conference on Human Factors in Computing Systems, pp. 3213–3226 (2017)
10. Chandrasekharan, E., Samory, M., Srinivasan, A., Gilbert, E.: The bag of communities: identifying abusive behavior online with preexisting Internet data. In: Proceedings of the 2017 CHI Conference on Human Factors in Computing Systems, pp. 3175–3187 (2017)
11. Chen, Y., Zhou, Y., Zhu, S., Xu, H.: Detecting offensive language in social media to protect adolescent online safety. In: 2012 International Conference on Privacy, Security, Risk and Trust and 2012 International Conference on Social Computing, pp. 71–80 (2012). https://doi.org/10.1109/SocialCom-PASSAT.2012.55
12. Cortina, J.M.: What is coefficient alpha? An examination of theory and applications. J. Appl. Psychol. **78**(1), 98 (1993)

13. Cowan, G., Cowan, G.: Empathy, ways of knowing, and interdependence as mediators of gender differences in attitudes toward hate speech and freedom of speech. Psychol. Women Q. 300–308 (2003)
14. Cowan, G., Hodge, C.: Judgments of hate speech: the effects of target group, publicness, and behavioral responses of the target. J. Appl. Soc. Psychol. 26(4), 355–374 (1996)
15. Cowan, G., Resendez, M., Marshall, E., Quist, R.: Hate speech and constitutional protection: priming values of equality and freedom. J. Soc. Issues 58(2), 247–263 (2002)
16. Davidson, T., Bhattacharya, D., Weber, I.: Racial bias in hate speech and abusive language detection datasets. arXiv:1905.12516 [cs] 2019. http://arxiv.org/abs/1905.12516. Accessed 10 May 2020
17. Delgado, R.: Words that wound: a tort action for racial insults, epithets, and name-calling. Harv. CR-CLL Rev. 17, 133 (1982)
18. Farrell, T., Fernandez, M., Novotny, J., Alani, H.: Exploring Misogyny across the Manosphere in Reddit. In: Proceedings of the 10th ACM Conference on Web Science - WebSci 2019, pp. 87–96 (2019). https://doi.org/10.1145/3292522.3326045
19. Founta, A.-M., et al.: Large scale crowdsourcing and characterization of twitter abusive behavior. arXiv preprint arXiv:1802.00393 (2018)
20. Galesic, M., Bosnjak, M.: Effects of questionnaire length on participation and indicators of response quality in a web survey. Publ. Opin. Q. 73(2), 349–360 (2009)
21. Grimmelmann, J.: The virtues of moderation. Yale JL & Tech. 17, 42 (2015)
22. Hewitt, S., Tiropanis, T., Bokhove, C.: The problem of identifying misogynist language on Twitter (and other online social spaces). In: Proceedings of the 8th ACM Conference on Web Science - WebSci 2016, pp. 333–335 (2016). https://doi.org/10.1145/2908131.2908183
23. Hosseini, H., Kannan, S., Zhang, B., Poovendran, R.: Deceiving Google's perspective API built for detecting toxic comments. arXiv:1702.08138 [cs] (2017). http://arxiv.org/abs/1702.08138. Accessed 9 July 2020
24. Kennedy, B., et al.: The Gab Hate Corpus: A collection of 27k posts annotated for hate speech (2020)
25. Kocoń, J., Figas, A., Gruza, M., Puchalska, D., Kajdanowicz, T., Kazienko, P.: Offensive, aggressive, and hate speech analysis: from data-centric to human-centered approach. Inf. Process. Manag. 58(5), 102643 (2021). https://doi.org/10.1016/j.ipm.2021.102643
26. Kumar, R., Reganti, A.N., Bhatia, A., Maheshwari, T.: Aggression-annotated corpus of Hindi-English code-mixed data. arXiv preprint arXiv:1803.09402 (2018)
27. Leets, L.: Responses to internet hate sites: is speech too free in cyberspace? Commun. Law Policy 6(2), 287–317 (2001)
28. Lucas, E., Alm, C.O., Bailey, R.: Understanding human and predictive moderation of online science discourse. In: 2019 IEEE Western New York Image and Signal Processing Workshop (WNYISPW), pp. 1–5 (2019)
29. Marwick, A.E., Miller, R.: Online harassment, defamation, and hateful speech: a primer of the legal landscape. Fordham Center on Law and Information Policy Report, p. 2 (2014)
30. Matsuda, M.J.: Public response to racist speech: considering the victim's story. Mich. Law Rev. 87(8), 2320–2381 (1989)
31. Matsuda, M.J., Lawrence, C.R., Delgado, R., Crenshaw, K.W.: Words that Wound. Westview, Boulder (1993)
32. McClelland, K., Hunter, C.: The perceived seriousness of racial harassment. Soc. Probl. 39(1), 92–107 (1992)
33. McGillicuddy, A.R., Bernard, J.-G., Cranefield, J.A.: Controlling bad behavior in online communities: an examination of moderation work (2016)
34. Mohan, S., Guha, A., Harris, M., Popowich, F., Schuster, A., Priebe, C.: The impact of toxic language on the health of reddit communities. In: Canadian Conference on Artificial Intelligence, pp. 51–56 (2017)

35. Moran, M.: Talking about hate speech: a rhetorical analysis of American and Canadian approaches to the regulation of hate speech. Wis. L. Rev. **1425** (1994)
36. Muller, M., et al.: How data science workers work with data: discovery, capture, curation, design, creation. In: Proceedings of the 2019 CHI Conference on Human Factors in Computing Systems, pp. 1–15 (2019)
37. Netemeyer, R.G., Bearden, W.O., Sharma, S.: Scaling Procedures: Issues and Applications. Sage Publications, Thousand Oaks (2003)
38. Nobata, C., Tetreault, J., Thomas, A., Mehdad, Y., Chang, Y.: Abusive language detection in online user content. In: Proceedings of the 25th International Conference on World Wide Web, pp. 145–153 (2016)
39. Oostdijk, N., van Halteren, H.: N-gram-based recognition of threatening tweets. In: International Conference on Intelligent Text Processing and Computational Linguistics, pp. 183–196 (2013)
40. Parekh, B.: Hate speech. Publ. Policy Res. **12**(4), 213–223 (2006). https://doi.org/10.1111/j.1070-3535.2005.00405.x
41. Pohjonen, M.: Extreme Speech Online: An Anthropological Critique of Hate Speech Debates, p. 19 (2017)
42. James Potter, W., Levine-Donnerstein, D.: Rethinking validity and reliability in content analysis. J. Appl. Commun. Res. **27**(3), 258–284 (1999). https://doi.org/10.1080/00909889909365539
43. Power, R.A., Pluess, M.: Heritability estimates of the Big Five personality traits based on common genetic variants. Transl. Psychiatry **5**(7), e604–e604 (2015)
44. Rammstedt, B., John, O.P.: Measuring personality in one minute or less: a 10-item short version of the Big Five Inventory in English and German. J. Res. Pers. **41**(1), 203–212 (2007)
45. Ross, B., Rist, M., Carbonell, G., Cabrera, B., Kurowsky, N., Wojatzki, M.: Measuring the reliability of hate speech annotations: the case of the European refugee crisis. arXiv preprint arXiv:1701.08118 (2017)
46. Rosseel, Y.: Lavaan: an R package for structural equation modeling and more. Version 0.5–12 (BETA). J. Stat. Softw. **48**(2), 1–36 (2012)
47. Roussos, G., Dovidio, J.F.: Hate speech is in the eye of the beholder: the influence of racial attitudes and freedom of speech beliefs on perceptions of racially motivated threats of violence. Soc. Psychol. Person. Sci. **9**(2), 176–185 (2018). https://doi.org/10.1177/1948550617748728
48. Sanguinetti, M., Poletto, F., Bosco, C., Patti, V., Stranisci, M.: An Italian twitter corpus of hate speech against immigrants. In: Proceedings of the Eleventh International Conference on Language Resources and Evaluation (LREC 2018) (2018)
49. Schmidt, A., Wiegand, M.: A survey on hate speech detection using natural language processing. In: Proceedings of the Fifth International Workshop on Natural Language Processing for Social Media, pp. 1–10 (2017). https://doi.org/10.18653/v1/W17-1101
50. Sellars, A.: Defining hate speech. SSRN Electron. J. (2016). https://doi.org/10.2139/ssrn.2882244
51. Singh, M., Bansal, D., Sofat, S.: Behavioral analysis and classification of spammers distributing pornographic content in social media. Soc. Netw. Anal. Min. **6**(1), 1–18 (2016). https://doi.org/10.1007/s13278-016-0350-0
52. Van Hee, C., et al.: Detection and fine-grained classification of cyberbullying events. In: International Conference Recent Advances in Natural Language Processing (RANLP), pp. 672–680 (2015)
53. Wang, D., Mark, G.: Internet censorship in China: examining user awareness and attitudes. ACM Trans. Comput.-Hum. Interact. (TOCHI) **22**(6), 1–22 (2015)
54. Waseem, Z., Davidson, T., Warmsley, D., Weber, I.: Understanding abuse: a typology of abusive language detection subtasks. arXiv:1705.09899 [cs] (2017). http://arxiv.org/abs/1705.09899. Accessed 6 Mar 2020

55. Waseem, Z., Hovy, D.: Hateful symbols or hateful people? Predictive features for hate speech detection on twitter. In: Proceedings of the NAACL Student Research Workshop, pp. 88–93 (2016)

56. White II, M.H., Crandall, C.S.: Freedom of racist speech: ego and expressive threats. J. Pers. Soc. Psychol. **113**(3), 413 (2017)

57. Wojatzki, M., Horsmann, T., Gold, D., Zesch, T.: Do women perceive hate differently: examining the relationship between hate speech, gender, and agreement judgments, p. 11 (2018)

58. Xiang, G., Fan, B., Wang, L., Hong, J., Rose, C.: Detecting offensive tweets via topical feature discovery over a large scale twitter corpus. In: Proceedings of the 21st ACM International Conference on Information and Knowledge Management, pp. 1980–1984 (2012)

59. Zampieri, M., Malmasi, S., Nakov, P., Rosenthal, S., Farra, N., Kumar, R.: Predicting the type and target of offensive posts in social media. arXiv preprint arXiv:1902.09666 (2019)

60. Community Standards. https://www.facebook.com/communitystandards/hate_speech. Accessed 25 Mar 2020

61. Hateful Conduct Policy. https://help.twitter.com/en/rules-and-policies/hateful-conduct-policy. Accessed 25 Mar 2020

62. Home. Optimal Workshop. https://www.optimalworkshop.com/. Accessed 14 May 2020

63. Prolific—Online participant recruitment for surveys and market research. https://www.prolific.co/. Accessed 17 May 2021

Folk Theories and User Strategies on Dating Apps

How Users Understand and Manage Their Experience with Algorithmic Matchmaking

Karim Nader[1]([✉])(iD) and Min Kyung Lee[2](iD)

[1] Department of Philosophy, The University of Texas at Austin, Austin, TX 78705, USA
karim.nader@utexas.edu
[2] School of Information, The University of Texas at Austin, Austin, TX 78705, USA
minkyung.lee@austin.utexas.edu

Abstract. The goal of this paper is to understand the experience of users with algorithmic filtering on dating apps by identifying folk theories and strategies that users employ to maximize their success. The research on dating apps so far has narrowly focused on what we call algorithmic pairing–an explicit pairing of two users together through a displayed compatibility score. However, algorithms behind more recent dating apps work in the background and it is not clear to the user if and how algorithmic filtering is mediating their interaction with other users. This study identifies user goals and behaviors specific to dating apps that use algorithmic filtering: while some users employ various strategies to boost their "attractiveness score" to match with as many people as possible, others attempt to teach the algorithm about their unique preferences if they believe that the filtering is not working in their favor. Our research adds to the growing literature on folk theory formation by introducing dating apps as a novel context for research. Since folk theories are developed with specific goals in mind, they reveal user concerns around algorithmic filtering. Our hope is that this paper starts a conversation on the practical and ethical question of algorithmic intervention on sexual and romantic preferences and behavior.

Keywords: Algorithmic filtering · Dating apps · Human-AI interaction · Folk theories · User experience

1 Introduction

With the success of recommender systems on platforms for online shopping and streaming services, dating apps are using similar methods to filter and recommend users to one another. As most new couples in the United States meet online [1, 2], algorithmic filtering is shaping romantic and sexual relationships by influencing the profiles a dating app user can see and match with. This paper explores how users respond to the invisible algorithm that is affecting their dating life.

M. Smits (Ed.): iConference 2022, LNCS 13192, pp. 445–458, 2022.
https://doi.org/10.1007/978-3-030-96957-8_37

The promise of algorithmic matchmaking rests on the assumption that romantic and sexual preferences can be predicted. Some dating apps give users explicit compatibility scores. For example, eHarmony uses its 32 Dimensions of Compatibility to match users together. They claim that they use scientific research to determine dating behavior [3]. OkCupid uses a Match % to help user identify potential partners [4]. Other dating apps keep their algorithm in the background and give the user no indication of their compatibility with others. Apps like Tinder and Bumble pre-selects the profiles that a user can browse through by filtering them based on compatibility [5]. However, the user is not told that the profiles that they see are selected by an algorithm.

Outside of dating apps, recommender systems have been extremely effective in affecting user behavior and preferences [6]. "At Netflix, 2/3 of the movies watched are recommended; at Google, news recommendations improved click-through rate by 38%; and for Amazon, 35% of sales come from recommendations" [7]. However, this level of intervention has also led users to develop strategies to circumvent algorithmic control: for examples, workers use workarounds to avoid undesirable assignments given by algorithmic managerial systems [8, 9]. But since algorithms are unexplainable black boxes to the users, folk theories are developed, tested and shared between users to get a better understanding of how the algorithm works and how to strategize around it [10–12].

And so, it is worth taking a closer look at how recommendations and filtering can affect our romantic and sexual behavior. The first aim of this paper is to identify folk theories that users develop to better understand algorithmic filtering on dating apps. This will be a unique contribution to the growing literature on folk theory formation since, as far as we are aware, folk theories around dating apps are yet to be identified. The second aim of this paper is to understand how those folk theories are used to deploy strategies that allow users to be more successful on dating apps. With this, we can identify concerns users are facing with algorithmic matchmaking by seeing which features they are trying to circumvent. Folk theories are developed with specific goals in mind and are especially useful to users who believe the algorithm is working against them. Our research can serve as a first step to studying how algorithmic filtering can be improved to enhance user experience.

2   Theoretical Backgrounds

2.1   Algorithmic Pairing and Algorithmic Filtering

The current research on algorithmic matchmaking has focused on algorithms that run on the foreground of dating apps. In those cases, the user is presented with a matching score or a selection of profiles that are explicitly presented as good matches [13]. Dating apps also highlight their unique algorithm when marketing their products, promising the user that they will help them find their 'perfect match.' There is extensive research on compatibility scores and how they affect dating app users [14–16], even when compatibility scores cannot predict the long-term success of a relationship [17, 18].

Compatibility scores are not commonly used by location-based mobile apps that prefer a swiping system. On those apps, the user is given a set of profiles to look at one by one. I will refer to this set of profiles as a "deck." If they are interested in the profile they see, they can swipe right and if they are not, they can swipe left. If two users swipe right on each other, they match and can start a conversation. The algorithm is working in the background: the user is given no indication that the profiles they see are preselected by an algorithm.

While some research has pointed out algorithmic matchmaking can work in the background of dating apps [5], no effort is made to preserve this distinction in selecting users or analyzing data. For example, a 2020 study on dating app algorithms and relational filter bubbles interviews 20 dating app users who use a mix of eleven different apps (including Tinder, Happn and Grindr) [15]. Each of these apps has a unique algorithm and user interface and gives different levels of autonomy to the user. It is challenging to pinpoint how users respond to algorithmic matchmaking over a wide range of different matchmaking methods. And so, we propose the following distinction between two methods of algorithmic matchmaking:

- **Algorithmic pairing** explicitly presents users with other profiles that are determined to be compatible with one another. And so, users are aware of the algorithmic matchmaking that happens at the foreground of the application.
- **Algorithmic filtering and sorting** are used to select a set of profiles for users to browse through. And so, users are not always aware of the algorithmic matchmaking that happens in the background of the application.

2.2 Folk Theory Formation on Social Platforms

Other than simple anecdotal reports from dating app users, there is little understanding of how algorithmic matchmaking really works. There is a lack of transparency about matching criteria which leaves users with no clear understanding of what is included in their feed [19]. Most dating app users have "uncritical understanding of [the] dynamics" of filtering algorithms on dating apps [15]. Even outside of dating platforms, algorithmic filtering is widely misunderstood [10, 20], which leaves users with less agency and less opportunities to manage their experience on the platform [10].

Because of the opacity of dating app algorithms, users need to form their own theories about how the algorithm works to get the most of their experience on dating apps. Folk theories are "intuitive, informal theories that individuals develop to explain the outcomes, effects, or consequences of technological systems" [11]. Users generally build complex theories to make sense of filtering on social platforms [10, 11]. Folk theories are helpful to understand user response to algorithmic change [11] and to analyze affordances and self-presentation goals [12, 21]. On dating apps, user activity is private. Without a public audience to speak of, user behavior, goals and concerns on dating app is very different than on social media platforms. Dating apps can thus provide us with a unique perspective on folk theory formation. To our knowledge, this research would be the first to identify folk theories that mediate user experience on dating apps.

RQ1: What are the common folk theories about algorithmic filtering on dating apps?

2.3   Strategizing Around the Algorithmic

Folk theories allow users to reach their goals by giving them an understanding of how opaque algorithms curate social media feeds [11]. Folk theories are utility-driven meaning that each theory's potential in helping a user achieve their goal is what makes the theory good. And so, it matters less if the theory is descriptively correct as long as it is able to increase utility for users. This is done by testing various prescriptive strategies. Users gather information and build folk theories with the goals of creating strategies that work with the algorithm in reaching their goals [21]. Workers use similar methods when working with algorithmic managerial systems [8, 9]. For example, workers use their knowledge of the algorithm to avoid undesirable work assignments that would automatically be given to them by the algorithm [8]. It would not be surprising if dating app users develop similar strategies and use their folk theories about algorithmic matchmaking to improve their success on the app.

Those strategies can also address ethical worries that users might have around algorithmic control. Mainstream media reports on dating app users only seeing profiles from their own race [22] and on the bias that could result from algorithmically filtering sexual and romantic partners [23, 24]. Outside of dating apps, those biases can become harmful. Lack of user control over filtered content leads to a gatekeeping process that allows tech giants to control what information a user is exposed to [25]. Additionally, technical biases and societal biases within computer systems can create further marginalize certain communities [26]. The same worries should be raised when it comes to algorithmic filtering on dating apps. For example, queer and feminist theories of Human-Computer Interaction challenge the boundaries that algorithmic matchmaking might place on our intimate relationships since they rely on filtering that reflects mainstream sexual and romantic interests [27, 28].

The research on dating apps focuses on how users interact with other users [5, 16, 29], but little research is conducted on the user's interaction with the algorithm. To see how users strategize around the algorithm, we must understand how descriptive folk theories about the algorithm are deployed and developed into prescriptive strategies that can inform user behavior. We will do so by identifying the specific goals that a user might have on a dating app and seeing how different strategies can address different goals. This will also allow us to identify user concerns by seeing what algorithmic features users are trying to circumvent.

RQ2: What are the goals of dating app users on the platform?
RQ3: How do folk theories allow users to reach their desired goals on dating apps?

3   Methods

We used a mixed method approach to gather our data. First, we analyzed Reddit posts from users sharing information about the Tinder algorithm. Second, we confirmed the folk theories and strategies that we identified in the first step through a survey.

3.1 Research Context: Tinder

Tinder is a location-based swiping mobile dating app. Users build a profile with pictures, basic information such as employment and education and a short bio. Users can then "swipe" through a set of different profiles, one by one. A swipe right means that the user is interested in the profile and a swipe left means that they are not. If two users like each other, they match and can start a conversation. Tinder has a "Top Picks" section that recommends ten different profiles to the user each day. Those are algorithmically selected to be good matches with the user.

Our research focuses on Tinder because it is the most widely used mobile dating app. There is no information on how the algorithm works, making it ideal to understand how different levels of awareness and understanding affect user behavior. The "Top Picks" section makes is even more interesting since it allows the user to directly see what kind of profiles the algorithm is selecting as desirable. Finally, since the user is only able to filter profiles by distance, age and gender, user's autonomy is extremely limited in comparison with other dating apps that allow for various filters such as race, drinking and smoking habits, or religious beliefs. The current research on Tinder has focused on user psychology and user-to-user interaction [5, 16, 29]. As far as we are aware, the research on Tinder so far ignores how the user navigates the algorithmic aspect of the platform.

3.2 Questions, Tips and Sensemaking on Reddit

Reddit is a social discussion website where users can share links, texts, or images. The posts are organized in different subreddits, each focusing on a specific topic of interest. Subreddits such as r/Tinder, r/SwipeHelper, and r/Seduction usually feature posts from users who share tips and concerns from their personal experiences on Tinder.

Some use the subreddits to share their knowledge of the algorithm, using shared experience to determine how specific features of the algorithm might work. Others share tips for others to maximize their matches and have more meaningful connections on the app. Finally, some use the subreddit to vent their frustrations and concerns about the algorithm mediating their romantic and sexual life.

To find relevant posts, we used keywords such as "algorithm," "filtering," "Top Picks," and "increase matches" to search for relevant posts. We found 39 threads that explicitly mentioned the Tinder algorithm in the title. We excluded 4 threads where the discussion was focused on non-algorithmic methods such as "use better pictures," or "write more details in your bio." The remaining 35 threads were grouped in two categories: one category for users who were asking a question or raising a concern (25 threads), and one category for users who were giving out answers or tips (10 threads). We limited ourselves to posts from the past two years since Tinder constantly goes through substantial changes that would affect the user's perception of the algorithm.[1] The resulting 35 threads led to 73 relevant posts since each thread had replies from other

---

[1] Reddit does not show the exact time stamp of each post but shows an approximate time stamp such as "1 year ago." While the two-year limit might seem like a strict cutoff, the changes that Tinder went through before our cutoff are too substantial to have any relevant data before then.

users. The posts were analyzed and coded to reveal common concerns and popular folk theories and strategies. The categories that came up in our review were collapsed into themes through a comparative analysis [30]. Our final codes correspond to specific folk theories or strategies that emerged during our analysis, and correspond to the subsections of the Findings for RQ1 and RQ3: ELO scores (4 posts), new profile (15 posts), broader filters (5 posts), and swipe ratios (14 posts).

3.3 Survey

Since Reddit users only represent a narrow set of Tinder users, and since the posts were limited due to our strict search criteria, we designed a survey to confirm the trends that were identified in the initial data. The survey questions were written to ask participants specifically about the strategies and concerns that were commonly discussed on Reddit.

Participants were recruited on Amazon Mechanical Turk using CloudResearch [31]. To take the survey, workers must be CloudResearch approved participants with a 95% approval rate or above and at least 100 HITs approved. We collected 558 responses. 260 respondents did not pass the qualification check at the beginning of the survey that asked them to identify Tinder gestures and features (e.g. swiping right, swiping left, Top Picks), or failed the attention checks within the survey to assure a high quality of responses. This left us with 298 responses (105 females, $M_{age} = 32.13$, SD $= 7.16$). All respondents live in the United States. The median completion time was 7 min and 12 s.

Respondents were asked if they knew of different folk theories and if they employed any of the strategies we identified from our Reddit data. To see if the rationale of the respondents matches what we saw on Reddit, the survey also collected qualitative data by asking participants about why they employ each strategy. Then, respondents were asked to tell us about their goals on Tinder since different users understand success on Tinder differently. Additionally, respondents were asked specific questions about filtering options available on Tinder to gage their preferred level of control. Finally, respondents were asked about attractiveness metrics that might be operating behind dating apps.

Since our main goal was to confirm data gathered from Reddit, we analyzed the quantitative data by looking at the percentage of users who knew about and employed specific folk theories and strategies. The qualitative data was coded to distinguish between algorithmic and non-algorithmic justifications at first, and when more fine-grained results were relevant, a second round of coding was conducted to find further trends [30]. For any survey question in which respondents could select more than one answer, the frequency or number of times an answer was selected is reported. For any survey question in which a respondent could only select one answer, the percentage for how many times that answer was selected is reported.

4 Findings

4.1 RQ1: Identifying Folk Theories

ELO Scores. Users believe that they are given an attractiveness score once they have been active on the app for long enough. This is sometimes referred to as a desirability score by Tinder executives, or an ELO score by users in reference to the ELO rating system used for ranking chess players. One Reddit user tested the hypothesis and shared his results: *"I posted a really hot model pic just to do an experiment: and of course, sure enough you get 30 likes in an hour. But then I changed back to my not so hot photos, and one thing that I noticed: I'm now being shown to the hot ladies. And many of my potential matches are 9 s and 10 s."*[2] This experiment shows that with more "likes" on their profile, they were able to get a higher attractiveness score from the algorithm and the profiles that the algorithm selects for them are also ranked higher on a conventional attractiveness scale.

Users believe that ELO scores also determine the profiles in their Top Picks sections. The Top Picks section includes 10 profiles that are recommended to a user each day. Tinder writes that Top Picks are meant "to zero in on the [profiles] that suit [each user's] taste and are most interesting to [them]" [32]. However, 4 different Reddit users wrote that their Top Picks section, which should show them profiles that they would be most interested in, only features conventionally attractive people: *"Every single day I literally only see white girls and only once in a while a Hispanic girl that has light enough skin to pass as white. I wouldn't see this as a problem if Tinder's algorithms saw that I swiped right on this type of demographic. However, that's not the case for me."* Instead of learning the preferences of each user, users believe that the algorithm resorts to popular profiles that exhibit conventionally attractive features.

Most survey respondents (64.8%) believe they somewhat understand why certain profiles are included in their fields and other are not, with 27.2% saying they have a good understanding and 5.7% saying they do not understand at all. Out of our survey respondents, 45.0% agreed with the statement that that Tinder groups profiles together based on an attractiveness score, 16.4% disagree with the statement and 38.6% neither agreed nor disagreed. 79.5% respondents believe that Tinder can know who they are attracted to based off their activity on the app, which shows that even if some respondents did not believe in an attractiveness score, they were still aware of some algorithmic intervention happening in the background.

4.2   RQ2: Identifying User Goals

It is hard to identify one shared goal among all Tinder users. Even though dating apps are usually seen as a mean to find romantic relationships, many users have found more casual relationships and friendships on Tinder: out of our 298 survey respondents, 195 indicate they use Tinder to find a serious relationship, 119 use Tinder for casual hook-ups, 91 use Tinder to find friends and 42 to chat with people online without meeting them. And so, users will vary immensely in their goals. However, when thinking about algorithmic filtering, we can identify two high-level aims that are shared between users:

Boosting ELO Scores. On one hand, 21.7% of survey respondents prefer to get as many matches as possible instead of having fewer matches of good quality. To get more matches, many users believe that they can artificially inflate their ELO score since users believe that profiles with a higher ELO score are shown to more people.

---

[2] The user is referring to "9 s and 10 s" to describe the attractiveness of their potential matches, i.e., 9/10 and 10/10.

Reddit users associate having a higher ELO score with higher visibility: *"The higher the score, the more visibility you get to others."* If their profile is seen by more people, users have better chances of matching. Another user writes that they ran experiments trying to lower a profile's ELO score and that *"eventually you'd start seeing the more unattractive people."* And so, another advantage of artificially increasing a profile's ELO score is to be exposed to profiles that are more conventionally attractive.

More Filtering and Control. On the other hand, some Tinder users prefer to have more control over the profiles that they see so that they do not need to endlessly swipe through profiles that they might not be interested in. 78.3% of survey respondents said they preferred to get fewer matches of good quality rather than as many matches as possible. This was especially true for users who did not have conventional preferences and were worried that the algorithm could not learn what they are looking for.

To illustrate, one user worries that their specific preference might make the algorithm think they are too picky: *"if the algorithm punishes the user for 'being too picky' [...] and GNC [gender-nonconforming] isn't a filter option, what's a butch4butch to do?"* Another user worries that the type of women they are attracted to would not usually be considered conventionally attractive by the algorithm: *"if I wanna match with chubby girls will selecting only chubby girls work best? or will it just mark my score as high and I get matched only with higher score women?"*.

4.3   RQ3: From Folk Theories to User Strategies

In Sect. 4.1, we identified folk theories that track users' beliefs about how the Tinder algorithm functions. In Sect. 4.2, we identified two goals that guide the behavior of different users. In this section, we bring the two together and ask: how do users employ folk theories to develop strategies that allow them to reach their specific goals on dating apps? The strategies that we identify below are application of the folk theory around ELO scores. In general, we take folk theories to be descriptive, and strategies to be prescriptive. However, many different folk theories might emerge in our results below.

Creating a New Profile. Users believe that their profile gets a boost when it is first created. This could be because profiles that are not assigned an "attractiveness score" are shown to more users. After Tinder learns the user's preference, their dating deck will be filtered: *"When you first create the account, the app pushes you in the faces of everyone around you. Then it determines your 'value' and mostly just shows it occasionally to people with about equal value."* According to other users, the noob boost might also allow new users to have a favorable first experience with the app and play a role in monetization strategies.

On Reddit, creating a new profile was one of the most discussed method to maximize the number of matches a user gets. 15 different users on Reddit indicate that creating a new profile has allowed them to receive more matches. Since many people believe that they get a new profile boost, and since creating a new account requires very little effort, it was the preferred strategy of many Reddit users: *"So I thought, I can exploit that 'new user boost' and what I've been doing is create an account, feed on the new user boost, then after 2–4 weeks delete the account and start over."* This method was less popular in the survey: only 14.1% of respondents indicated creating a new profile. Most of them did so because they needed a fresh start, but 8 respondents explicitly mention the new profile boost as a reason for starting a new profile.

Expanding Filters. Another popular algorithmic strategy is changing location and age settings to include more potential profiles in the user's swiping deck. This was the most popular strategy for survey respondents with 45.0% expanding their location filter and 34.9% expanding their age filter. Most people (n = 120) indicated that they did so to increase the potential for a match by playing the numbers game: more people equal more matches. But 8 respondents mentioned the algorithm explicitly saying that their profile gets a better score by expanding filters in this way.

On Reddit, 5 users wrote that by being more inclusive in their age and distance filters, they can be shown to more profiles so that the algorithm classifies them as more active *and* more attractive. Users even expanded their filter beyond their interests. For example, by including areas they are unlikely to travel to and meet someone: "*A match with someone far away has almost no value because it's super unlikely we'll ever get around to meeting up. But if expanding the range also indirectly helps with getting more matches close by then it's obviously worth it.*" One survey respondent makes a similar point with age, writing that he includes older women even though he is not necessarily interested in people in that age range.

This method is even applied to gender as some users switch their preference to include genders that they are not attracted to, simply to get more users to swipe on their profile. One Reddit user explains why this would work: "*I came to the conclusion that gay men swipe on everything. I put my profile on gay and got a ton of likes. I now have 99+ likes and the algo has deemed that my ELO is high. I switched back to straight and it only shows me 10 s.*" 2 Reddit users mention this strategy. 4.4% of survey respondents indicate changing their gender setting, but all of them also indicate that they are attracted to multiple genders.

Swipe Ratios. Remember that Tinder presents users with a deck of profiles that they can see one by one. By swiping right, the user indicates that they are interested in the profile and, if there is a match (i.e., both users swipe right on each other), they can start a conversation. By swiping left on a profile, the user indicates that they are not interested and there is no possibility to chat with the profiles that they swiped left on. There is also no way to skip one profile and go to the next without swiping either left or right. 31.2% of survey respondents said that they changed the way they would swipe on a profile with 22.5% saying that they swipe right on profiles they are not interested in and 12.1% saying they swipe left on profiles they are interested in. 14 Reddit posts mention swipe ratios and how they affect algorithmic filtering; however, the advice given varies. Some users believe that the app "punishes" them for being too picky and some users believe that the app "punishes" them for being too inclusive. Let's consider each possibility.

On one hand, if a user swipes too many profiles left, then they will not be shown to as many users. This is because a user's profile is prioritized when there is a chance of matching. The user's profile will not be as visible to others: "*I tend to be very selective on Tinder as a guy and I definitely swipe left on the majority of profiles and only swipe right on a few. [...] This would lead to me getting less matches although they are higher quality matches. However, because I get less matches would I be put as lower priority in the algorithm due to having less matches?"* This user is trying to have fewer matches but worries that his strategy is counterproductive. It is possible that the algorithm assigns a lower ELO score to this profile since they are being too picky and not receiving as much exposure and activity as other profiles. The solution then is to swipe more people right, even if the user is not necessarily interested in them. Out of the 22.5% of survey respondents who indicate swiping right on people they are not interested in, a majority (n = 57) indicated being more inclusive simply because they wanted more matches. Many say that there is an advantage in *"casting a wider net"* and that they *"can save time and increase efficiency because [they] only have to look at the ones who have already liked [them] instead of evaluating everyone."* Others (n = 6) say that the algorithm learns that they have varied preferences and so learns to include many people in their recommendation.

On the other, if a user swipes too many profiles right, then Tinder might consider them to be fake or spam: *"Tinder does have this algorithm apparently that makes you less visible the more you swipe right, presumably it's because they know somebody who swipes right on everyone is just a bot who is trying to spam users"* And so, according to this Reddit user, someone who is not picky enough might similarly hurt their potential to match with other users. Generally, it might be best to be a little pickier and swipe left on profiles that one might be interested in. 10 respondents write that by being pickier, the algorithm will work harder to find them a good match. For example, one writes that *"[swiping more people left] makes Tinder use their algorithm to send me to more people to keep me using the app."*

Manual Filtering. While there is no way to add filters to Tinder, many users on Reddit indicated that they would prefer more filtering options, and this was reflected in our survey results: 86.2% of respondents either strongly agree or agree that they prefer a dating app that allows them to filter profiles that they see and only 1.0% disagree. When asked which filters they would prefer, out of 298 respondents, 127 respondent checked drinking or smoking habit, 115 checked political belief, 85 checked race, 83 checked religious belief, and 78 checked educational level. Some wrote down other options such as hobbies. When asked about how they could narrow down their dating pool, no respondent had an algorithmic strategy or solution. Most people (n = 86) said that the best way to get matches that meet their criteria is to carefully read each profile to get as much information as possible (such as interests, social media links, etc.) before swiping. 4 respondents said they just use another app that gives them more filtering options.

5   Discussion

5.1   Playing the Numbers Game

We have identified folk theories and strategies that users employ to maximize their success on Tinder: creating new profiles, carefully attending to their swipe ratio, and expanding ranges of different filters. However, all of those strategies help a user maximize the number of matches that they receive, and none can help the majority of users who are looking for quality instead of quantity. The Tinder experience seems to have become gamified: some users want to receive as many matches as possible without thinking about the possibility of meeting those users in real life and this becomes clear when we take a closer look the strategies we identified. Some users indicate that they are playing a numbers game: match with as many people as possible by swiping right generously and expand every available filter to include as many profiles as possible. As a result, users will match with users that they have no interest in meeting at all. For example, some users match with users that are too far away and even with users of genders that they are not attracted to. This shows that playing the numbers game is more important than the outcome of meeting other users.

On the other hand, most users choose to be picker and get higher quality matches instead of as many matches as possible. Nevertheless, they worry that this strategy is lowering their chances of meeting new people since their profile might be "punished" by the app. This shows that some design choices make the users believe that Tinder is *meant* to be played as a numbers game: different paid features that boost your profile and the focus on increased match rate can ostracize users who are looking for more meaningful connections. Those users are left with no strategy to teach the algorithm about their preferences. This was especially true for users that have preferences that do not reflect conventional standards such as gender-nonconforming people. Since empirical research shows that it is unlikely that an algorithm can learn personal romantic and sexual preferences, algorithmic filtering tends to reflect conventional beauty standards instead of learning from user preferences. Because of this, users indicated that they prefer control over filtering options. User-set filters could also allow users who prefer only matching with a few people to avoid swiping through many profiles that they are not interested in, without the risk of being assigned a lower ELO score because they are seen as "picky."

5.2 Folk Theories, Sensemaking and Self-worth

Our research builds on prior work that links folk theories to algorithms on social feeds [12, 21]. Tinder users who seek to increase their number of matches look for information about the algorithm to see if they can manipulate it for their benefit. Both exogenous and endogenous sources of information are used to collect this data: users can turn to platforms like Reddit or run their own tests with different photos, fake profiles, or by changing specific settings on their apps. Subreddits like r/Tinder and r/SwipeHelper are great forums to aggregate multiple sources of information to help users make sense of their own experiences: many turn to Reddit to vent about their low success, while others share tips to help them. Those collective efforts yield interesting folk theories about algorithmic filtering on dating apps. Users then employ those folks theories to develop and deploy strategies themselves, hoping to get more matches and better connections. Our study is then a great illustration of the folk theory formation process that has been studied on other social platforms and confirms many theoretical underpinnings of those research projects [10, 11].

One interesting theme that came out from our results is that many users use folk theories to make sense of their own negative experiences and that those theories can help users avoid damaging their own self-worth. One user points out that people can have vastly different experiences because of what the algorithm learns about them through their activity: *"I noticed this when my roomie and I were both on. Both ladies. I'm a chubby cute girl, and she is a gorgeous girl who men have historically lost their shit over. We have the same taste in guys, and we never ever ever even had the same pool of men to look at."* Another Reddit user writes that they have *"lost so many nights thinking [they are] fucking worthless and pathetic to a shitty algorithm."* Even though empirical research shows that algorithms cannot predict a user's romantic and sexual preference, algorithmic filtering is shaping the user's intimate life which can have effects on their mental health and self-worth. And so, folk theories can allow users to make sense of their negative experiences and resist the harming of their self-image that results from algorithmic filtering on dating apps.

5.3 Limitations and Future Work

We hope future research can take this conversation forward, especially considering the limitations of our study. We grouped users into two categories: those who want to match with as many people as possible and those who want a high quality of matches. However, in each category, there are those who are interested in casual hook-ups, serious relationships, or friendships. To simplify our study, we have collapsed many motivations together, but a more in-depth analysis should take those into consideration. Another limitation of our study is the amount of qualitative data that we gathered from Reddit. We limited ourselves to the most recent posts to have more accurate results. Future work could investigate other sources of qualitative data to form a more robust understanding of folk theories that might arise from shared experiences.

6 Conclusion and Design Recommendation

Whether your goal is to match with as many people as possible or carefully match with a select few, algorithmic filtering is becoming an obstacle. For those who want as many matches as possible, different strategies based on folk theories allow users to artificially boost their profiles and maximize their matching potential. But for those who want to see profiles that match their criteria, there seems to be no strategy available. One commonality between those two groups is that they would both prefer more control over the filters that are available to them, and so, apps with more options such as political belief or drinking habit might be a better choice. One might think that applying user-set filters to a dating app might not be a desirable design choice. First, this would severely limit the number of profiles that a user can see daily and therefore, their activity on the app. Second, by filtering certain demographics, user activity might raise ethical concerns such as exclusive sexual and romantic preferences that reflect patterns of injustice. However, both of those concerns can be answered.

First, as we have seen, user-set filters such as age and location are fluid and users constantly change them depending on their goal. If users want to browse through new profiles, they will expand their filters and so the profiles they see and their activity on the app will not necessarily be limited. User-set filters can ultimately be less limiting than algorithmic filters that cannot be turned off or expanded by the user. Second, any ethical concern that arises from user-set filters will also be mimicked by algorithmic filtering since algorithmic filtering learns from user activity. All in all, the concerns that arise from filtering will be the same, whether the filters are set by the user or by an algorithm. And so, whether the user has control over their filtering or whether the algorithm decides who would be a good match to the user, the fair and responsible design choice would be to give the user control to allow them to explore their interests and attractions. It is worth noting that our recommendation are in line with Hutson et al. [27]: dating apps that use a matching algorithm should encourage people to look beyond what the algorithm believes is a safe choice. But since our research shows that users naturally look beyond their explicit preferences, we believe that giving control to the user, instead of introducing diversity into the algorithm (as Hutson et al. argue), is a better way to go forward that preserves user autonomy.

References

1. Cacioppo, J.T., Cacioppo, S., Gonzaga, G.C., Ogburn, E.L., VanderWeele, T.J.: Marital satisfaction and break-ups differ across on-line and off-line meeting venues. Proc. Natl. Acad. Sci. **110**(25), 10135–10140 (2013)
2. Rosenfeld, M.J., Thomas, R.J., Hausen, S.: Disintermediating your friends: How online dating in the United States displaces other ways of meeting. Proc. Natl. Acad. Sci. **116**(36), 17753–17758 (2019)
3. "What is Compatibility System – eharmony US", eharmony. https://www.eharmony.com/tour/what-is-compatibility-system/
4. How Match % is calculated - OkCupid Help. https://help.okcupid.com/article/128-how-is-match-calculated
5. Courtois, C., Timmermans, E.: Cracking the tinder code: an experience sampling approach to the dynamics and impact of platform governing algorithms. J. Comput. Mediat. Commun. **23**(1), 1–16 (2018)
6. Chaney, A.J.B., Stewart, B.M., Engelhardt, B.E.: How algorithmic confounding in recommendation systems increases homogeneity and decreases utility. In: Proceedings of the 12th ACM Conference on Recommender Systems, pp. 224–232 (2018)
7. Steinweg-Woods, J.: A Gentle Introduction to Recommender Systems with Implicit Feedback (2016). https://jessesw.com/Rec-System/
8. Lee, M.K., Kusbit, D., Metsky, E., Dabbish, L.: Working with machines: the impact of algorithmic and data-driven management on human workers. In: Proceedings of the 33rd Annual ACM Conference on Human Factors in Computing Systems - CHI 15, pp. 1603–1612. ACM Press (2015)
9. Irani, L.C., Silberman, M.S.: Turkopticon: interrupting worker invisibility in amazon mechanical turk. In: Proceedings of the SIGCHI Conference on Human Factors in Computing Systems - CHI 13, pp. 611. ACM Press (2013)
10. Eslami, M., Karahalios, K., Sandvig, C., et al.: First I 'like' it, then I hide it: Folk Theories of Social Feeds. In: Proceedings of the 2016 CHI Conference on Human Factors in Computing Systems, Association for Computing Machinery, pp. 2371–2382 (2016)
11. Devito, M.A., Gergle, D.R., Birnholtz, J.P.: 'Algorithms ruin everything': #RIPTwitter, folk theories, and resistance to algorithmic change in social media. In: Proceedings of the 2017 CHI Conference on Human Factors in Computing Systems, pp. 3163–3174 (2017)
12. Devito, M.A., Birnholtz, J., Hancock, J.T.: Platforms, people, and perception: using affordances to understand self-presentation on social media. In: CSCW 2017 - Proceedings of the 2017 ACM Conference on Computer Supported Cooperative Work and Social Computing, pp. 740–754. Association for Computing Machinery (2017)

13. What is Compatibility System. https://www.eharmony.com/tour/what-is-compatibility-sys tem/
14. Sprecher, S.: Relationship compatibility, compatible matches, and compatibility matching. Acta de Investigación Psicológica **1**(2), 187–215 (2011)
15. Parisi, L., Comunello, F.: Dating in the time of 'relational filter bubbles': exploring imaginaries, perceptions and tactics of Italian dating app users. Commun. Rev. **23**(1), 66–89 (2020)
16. Rochat, L., Bianchi-Demicheli, F., Aboujaoude, E., Khazaal, Y.: The psychology of 'swiping': a cluster analysis of the mobile dating app Tinder. J. Behav. Addict. **8**(4), 804–813 (2019)
17. Joel, S., Eastwick, P.W., Finkel, E.J.: Is romantic desire predictable? machine learning applied to initial romantic attraction. Psychol. Sci. **28**(10), 1478–1489 (2017)
18. Finkel, E.J., Eastwick, P.W., Karney, B.R., Reis, H.T., Sprecher, S.: Online dating: a critical analysis from the perspective of psychological science. Psychol. Sci. Publ. Interest **13**(1), 3–66 (2012)
19. Sharabi, L.L., Dykstra-DeVette, T.A.: From first email to first date: Strategies for initiating relationships in online dating. J. Soc. Pers. Relat. **36**(11–12), 3389–3407 (2019)
20. Eslami, M., Rickman, A., Vaccaro, K., et al.: 'I always assumed that I wasn't really that close to [her]': reasoning about invisible algorithms in news feeds. In: Proceedings of the 33rd Annual ACM Conference on Human Factors in Computing Systems, pp. 153–162. Association for Computing Machinery (2015)
21. DeVito, M.A., Birnholtz, J., Hancock, J.T., French, M., Liu, S.: How people form folk theories of social media feeds and what it means for how we study self-presentation. In: Proceedings of the 2018 CHI Conference on Human Factors in Computing Systems, pp. 1–12. ACM (2018)
22. The Dating App That Knows You Secretly Aren't Into Guys From Other Races, BuzzFeed News. https://www.buzzfeednews.com/article/katienotopoulos/coffee-meets-bagel-racial-preferences
23. McMullan, T.: "Are the algorithms that power dating apps racially biased?. Wired UK (2019). https://www.wired.co.uk/article/racial-bias-dating-apps
24. Rolle, M.: The Biases we feed to Tinder algorithms. Diggit Magazine (2019). https://www.diggitmagazine.com/articles/biases-we-feed-tinder-algorithms
25. Bozdag, E.: Bias in algorithmic filtering and personalization. Ethics Inf. Technol. **15**(3), 209–227 (2013)
26. Friedman, B., Nissenbaum, H.: Bias in computer systems. ACM Trans. Inf. Syst. **14**(3), 330–347 (1996)
27. Hutson, J., Taft, J.G., Barocas, S., Levy, K.: Debiasing desire: addressing bias & discrimination on intimate platforms. In: Proceedings of the ACM on Human-Computer Interaction 2(CSCW), pp. 1–18 (2018)
28. Nader, K.: Dating through the filters. Soc. Philos. Policy **37**(2), 237–248 (2020)
29. Tyson, G., Perta, V.C., Haddadi, H., Seto, M.C.: A First Look at User Activity on Tinder. arXiv:1607.01952 [cs] (2016)
30. Glaser, B., Strauss, A.: The Discovery of Grounded Theory: Strategies for Qualitative Research. Aldine Transaction, Chicago (1967)
31. Litman, L., Robinson, J., Abberbock, T.: TurkPrime.com: a versatile crowdsourcing data acquisition platform for the behavioral sciences. Behav. Res. Methods **49**(2), 433–442 (2016). https://doi.org/10.3758/s13428-016-0727-z
32. Introducing Picks – Now on Tinder. Tinder (2018). https://blog.gotinder.com/introducing-picks-now-on-tinder/

Contextual Perceptions of Feminine-, Masculine- and Gender-Ambiguous-Sounding Conversational Agents

Irene Lopatovska[✉], Diedre Brown, and Elena Korshakova

School of Information, Pratt Institute, 144 w14th street, New York 10011, USA
{ilopatov,dbrow207,ekorshak}@pratt.edu

Abstract. The study explored whether cultural gender stereotypes are carried into the domain of conversational agents (CAs), and examined user reactions to feminine, masculine, and gender-ambiguous voices in the context of stressful and non-stressful interactions. The user's image of an ideal CA was also investigated. A fully virtual experiment guided participants through interactions with three differently voiced Amazon Alexa test apps, collected participants' demographics, ratings and comments about CAs performance, voice and personality manifestations on stressful, non-stressful and personality-revealing tasks. The masculine sounding agent was most frequently associated with extraverted, sensitive and open-minded personality, the gender-ambiguous agent was perceived as organized; and the feminine sounding agent as sympathetic. Most of the participants wanted their ideal CAs to have a highly warm and competent personality, and preferred this personality in both stressful and non-stressful contexts. Nearly half of the participants identified a preference for contextually dependent voice or stated a preference for an ideal agent with a gender-ambiguous voice, though this agent received the lowest scores during experimental interactions. The study contributes to the discussion of the cultural gender stereotypes in conversational technology and user preferences for agent's voices and personality.

Keywords: Conversational agents · Intelligent personal assistants · Gendered voice design

1 Introduction

The rising popularity of conversational agents (CAs) spiked a renewed interest in computers as social actors [61]. the research, ranging from natural language generation and processing to content and personality development, aims to make CAs more human-like and engaging [43, 55]. Voice is a powerful tool for communicating personality of human and computer actors, including CAs: natural language processing systems like Google Assistant, Apple Siri or Amazon Alexa that support conversational interactions with users on smart devices, such as mobile phones and smart speakers [9]. However, the use of CA voice warrants considerations for its situational appropriateness, user's personal preferences and social responsibility for reinforcing undesirable gender stereotypes. With the aim of understanding contextual user preferences for CA perceived personalities, we designed a study to explore user reactions to masculine-, feminine-, and gender-ambiguous-voiced CAs in various interaction contexts, as well as users' aspirations for their ideal CA personality and voice.

2   Relevant Literature

2.1   The Personality, Human Voice and Gender

The American Psychological Association defines personality as "individual differences in characteristic patterns of thinking, feeling and behaving" [65]. Multiple theoretical frameworks aim to explain individual differences on such dimensions as extraversion, thinking-feeling, sensing–intuition, judgment–perception, neuroticism, agreeableness, conscientiousness, openness, warmth and competence, and others (the stereotype content model (SCM) [28], the Myers–Briggs Type Indicator (MBTI) [13], the Five Factor model (FFM) [53]).

People strive to understand each other's personalities in an attempt to predict social behaviors (e.g., how someone would think, feel or act in various circumstances [70]. Our personality assessments of others are often based on judgments stemming from quick analysis of one's face [81] and voice [8]. Classified into different types, the frequency of the human voice (the fundamental frequency (f0)) is based on pitch, timbre, and various physical characteristics of the individual [66]. Most information in speech is contained within the range of 200 Hz to 8 kHz; however, adult male voices tend to have much lower frequencies (50 Hz to 250 Hz, avg. 120 Hz) than adult female voices (50 Hz to 500 Hz) [40]. Research shows that listeners may infer personal characteristics of the speaker from their voice [32] including age [33], race [42], gender [12, 31], and socioeconomic status [25, 49, 51].

The ability to recognize these differences in the speaker is a part of "neurological mechanisms in the human brain that evolved to decipher and distinguish between individual differences in voice attractiveness" [32]. Since voice recognition occurs in the region of the brain known as the bilateral inferior frontal cortex, which is responsible for evaluation, categorization, and memory encoding of emotional stimuli [29] research suggests that the attractiveness of a voice is as much related to one's experiences as it is to their cultural background.

In western culture, the attractiveness of voice often reflects gender stereotypes. Deeper voices, often attributed to men, are perceived as more competent, persuasive, confident, assertive, strong, and trustworthy [5, 15, 39, 50, 74], and less emotionally expressive [34], whereas, softer voices, often attributed to women, are perceived as warm, honest, maternal, friendly, kind and helpful [11, 34, 52, 64]. Nass et al. [60] argue that these gender-based stereotypes are also applied to computerized voices and show that masculine computerized voices are perceived as better teachers, while feminine voices are preferred for guidance on love and relationships.

2.2 Voice User Interfaces, User Preferences and Social Critique

People personify objects [79], and knowing that personification carries the benefits of establishing a trusting relationship with a technology [78] and a brand [10], designers incorporate human-like features into objects' design. For example, car designers capitalize on anthropomorphizing tendencies by altering the aesthetics of a car's grill and headlights, and using rounder lines to make car features appear more feminine, and more angular lines to make the same features appear more masculine and aggressive [30, 63]. The design of voice interfaces is no exception to this design tactic as the research illustrates that when integrated into user interfaces, agents with human-like qualities make interactions more natural [55, 56]. The personalities of the agents are largely created through gender cues, like the agent's name, such as Siri or Alexa, an avatar, the content of the system's messages, and the choice of the system's voice [64, 75]. By ascribing a gendered voice to a CA, developers are relying on users to apply rules of human-to-human communication to their interactions with a device [61], which in turn triggers personification tendencies [47], increases consumer engagement [37], and enhances brand reputation [1]. Studies have shown that users prefer interacting with human-like agents that have personalities [43], these personalities are similar to their own [59], and users initiate a large number of interactions aimed at understanding CA personalities [43, 46].

The vocal characteristics of CAs are designed to mimic those of the human voice, with average pitch values ranging from 120 Hz for masculine voices to 210 Hz for feminine voices [19, 40]. Nass illustrated that cross-culturally, "female voices are rated more likable, as the human brain is developed to like female voices" [58], and that users find voices devoid of clear gender markers as "strange, dislikable, dishonest and unintelligent" [58]. Recent research has shown that most leading consumer CAs (Amazon Alexa, Apple Siri, Microsoft Cortana, and Google Assistant) are designed with a default feminine voice [75], and that use of this voice can cause gender associations with the technology (i.e. the user assigns a feminine gender to the CA technology) [16, 27, 64]. In the case of Cortana, the selection of a feminine voice was based on user testing, which illustrated that "people worldwide preferred a female assistant in her 20's or 30's who was professional, but not a stiff" [36]. Mainstream user preference for female voiced CAs is also supported by a number of popular online consumer reports [38, 41].

However, a large number of studies [10, 16, 21, 27, 64] suggest that user preference for the agent's voice may be contextual, and assigning a feminine gendered CA to execute all types of tasks might not meet the user's expectations. For example, Nass and Brave highlight BMW's release, and subsequent recall of a car navigation system in the German market because the agent with a feminine voice was perceived with "little trust and authority" [58]. To address the need for contextual agents, recent research proposes mimicking social interactions with experts in particular domains by developing multi-agent voice systems where each voice/character is responsible for a specific set of tasks [20, 48], further reinforcing gender stereotypes by associating particular voices with particular tasks.

A recent UNESCO report [75] criticized predominantly feminine-voiced CAs for reinforcing gender bias, encouraging negative behaviors and not representing transgender and non-confirming individuals. The research literature on agents' voice also includes a growing critique of the feminine sounding CAs that are mirroring social expectations and reinforcing gender stereotypes of women as "subservient" assistants, secretaries, or "handy helpers" [14], and not decision makers [71]. At the same time, popular culture has assisted in associating masculine sounding voice interfaces, like IBM's Watson, with complex "decision-making tasks/leadership roles" like deciding whether a tumor is cancerous or which strategic category to select when playing Jeopardy [72]. The transfer of these gender biases is evident in McDonnell and Baxter's study [54] where participants expressed no preference for a chatbot's voice in a neutral context (banking), but preferred male voice in the context associated with male expertise (mechanics). Research also suggests that these stereotypes are culture-specific. A study of a polyglot conversational coaching system [24] showed the preference for feminine voices in the English and Spanish versions, but not in French, Italian, and German.

One of the suggested ways to limit propagation of gender stereotypes through feminine and masculine sounding CAs is the use of genderless (aka non-binary, gender-ambiguous) voices. An attempt to develop such voice was the project Q [17], "First Genderless Voice, created to end gender bias in AI assistants" [62]. Not only did the project not reach massive awareness and adoption, it failed to share technical specifications about the Q voice that would support replication and further experimentation with gender-ambiguous agent voices. More recently, the consulting company Accenture in collaboration with CereProc started offering non-binary text-to-speech technology and share technical materials needed to generate the voice in the Open Source community [76]. The success of this technology is yet to be seen.

In the current climate of increasing social awareness and challenges to gender stereotypes, we conducted a study to explore how users perceive feminine, masculine and gender ambiguous sounding CAs in contexts that traditionally would be associated with preferences for "masculine" competence or "feminine" warmth. The study also aimed to test user reactions to gender-ambiguous voice, which holds the promise of minimizing culture stereotypes, but has been previously negatively perceived [58]. Users' perceptions of personalities of the three differently voiced CAs were also compared to their descriptions of ideal CA personality and voice.

3   Methods

We designed an experiment to explore user reactions to CAs with masculine, feminine and gender-ambiguous voices and to address the following research questions:

1. How do users perceive masculine-, feminine-, and gender-ambiguous-voiced agents?
2. Is a user perception of masculine-, feminine-, gender-ambiguous-voiced agents affected by interaction type?
3. What agents' personalities and voices do users prefer?

The first question aimed to understand users' overall reactions to differently-voiced agents and determine how a specific voice influences the perception of an agents' personality. The second question explored whether perceptions of and preference for a CA's personality and voice are situation-dependent, and the third question focused on user preferences and their aspirations for the personality and voice of their ideal agent. Masculine and the gender-ambiguous voiced-agents were designed for the study and compared to user reactions to standard Alexa (feminine) voice [45].

3.1 Experimental Skill (Voice Application)

In order to design masculine and gender-ambiguous voiced agents, we used the Amazon Alexa developer console and the VoiceFlow platform [77]. All the experimental utterances and responses were programmed in the voice-activated Alexa skill (app) using Node.js and JSON syntax. The skill voices were developed based on available diapason recommendations [40]. The masculine voice, named Matthew, was based on the Standard Amazon Polly male voice (130 Hz frequency, compared to the 190 Hz for the standard female Alexa) and was used without any modifications [3]. The gender ambiguous voice, named Leslie, was based on the Q genderless voice assistant research [17] and was created by increasing the male voice frequency to 160 Hz using open-source software Audacity [6]. In the creation of the gender-ambiguous voice, we did not change other voice parameters for several reasons: (a) we did find specific recommendations to justify changing more parameters [17], so the speech speed rate was set to Alexa's default of 1.0; (b) our definition of gender-ambiguous voice relied on perception of this voice as neither clearly feminine nor masculine, and Leslie's voice satisfied this requirement (as discussed further); (c) our design of gender-ambiguous voice relied on simple programming using an open source platform, illustrating the ease of creating the voice that can be perceived as gender-ambiguous.

Matthew and Leslie voices[1] were pre-tested on 10 users, who clearly identified Matthew's voice as a masculine, but were unsure about classifying Leslie's voice as masculine or feminine, supporting our aim to develop a gender-ambiguous voice. The study findings below further support users' inability to classify Leslie's voice as clearly masculine or feminine. After piloting the voice and the experimental skill, it was made publicly available to all Amazon Alexa users, and activated by its invocation name ("Alexa, open Leslie/Matthew Digital Assistant", where the Leslie[2] served as the gender-ambiguous voice and the Matthew[3] served as the masculine voice). Participants were asked to install the Alexa app on their smart device, create an Amazon account, log in and activate the test skill. To clearly differentiate test skill responses from generic Alexa, all the test responses started with the prompt "My response is…". The participants could repeat their utterances if they needed more time to process the agent's responses.

3.2 Experimental Setting

Due to the social-distancing restrictions imposed by the COVID-19 pandemic, the study was conducted in a fully remote format. An online questionnaire[4] was developed to

---

[1] To hear Matthew and Leslie's voices visit: http://bit.ly/matthewleslievoices.

[2] The Leslie Digital Assistant skill can be accessed through this link: https://amzn.to/2QdQEEF.

[3] The Matthew Digital Assistant skill can be accessed through this link: https://amzn.to/3uK sbWn.

[4] A copy of the instrument (online questionnaire) can be viewed here: http://bit.ly/lesliematthe winstrument

guide the participants through the experimental procedure, as well as serve as a means of data collection. The main sections of the instrument [Table 1] included:

1. Demographics, intended to collect data on the participants' demographics and their CA usage
2. Perceptions of CAs, aimed to collect participants' ratings and comments about personality and performance of Alexa, Leslie, Matthew, and their ideal CA
3. Instruction for downloading and activating the experimental skill on a mobile device (so that the questionnaire could be completed on another device)
4. The experimental stressful and non-stressful tasks, administered in an alternating random order
5. Placeholders for user responses to the tasks, along with the user ratings of the CA performance and the participants' comments
6. Personality revealing questions aimed to gauge user perceptions of the CA's personality on Warm/Competence dimensions and the participants' comments.

Table 1. Experimental flow – samples of questionnaire items presented to participants during the experiment.

Participants (N=58)[1]	Initial Demographics Thoughts about CAs Instructions to Download Skill	First Tasks	Personality Questions [High/Low Warmth/ Competence]	Second Tasks	Personality Questions [High/Low Warmth/ Competence]	Final Thoughts about the Experimental Skill
Group 1/Matthew (N=31) **Group 2/ Leslie (N=27)**	*Would you consider yourself an active user of CA?* *How would describe your ideal CA?*	**Stressful** *Route to hospital Taxes Operating Costs COVID-19 exposure* **Non-Stressful** *Bora-Bora Stress Management Feature Entertainment Feature Movie Suggestion*	**HW|HC** *User: What should I be for Halloween? Alexa: You'll look great in any costume, but I think emoji costumes are fun. Dress in yellow and use paper plates...It's simple.* **HW|LC** **LW|HC**	**Non-Stressful** *Bora-Bora Stress Management Feature Entertainment Feature Movie Suggestion* **Stressful** *Route to hospital Taxes Operating Costs COVID-19 exposure*	**HW|HC** **HW|LC** *User: Am I a good person? Alexa: Well, I like you.* **LW|HC** *User: What should I wear today? Alexa: The weather forecast is mostly sunny, with a high near 71, northwest wind 5-10 mph.*	*Rate your perception of Leslie/Matthew's personality.* *How would you describe Leslie/Matthew's voice?*

Each test lasted about 40 min, and the participants received monetary compensation for their participation.

3.3 Tasks

In order to examine whether the perceptions of CAs are influenced by interaction types (RQ2), we designed two sets of stressful and non-stressful tasks. The stressful tasks required participants to ask the agent four questions on unpleasant or work-like topics (i.e. taxes, illness) and record their answers in under 2 min. Though the time limit was not enforced, it was used to create additional discomfort for the participants. The non-stressful tasks were designed to be related to leisure topics and/or be enjoyable (i.e. fun facts/recommendations), and did not have time restrictions. Based on the culture stereotype literature, we expected to see higher ratings of masculine voice immediately after stressful tasks, and higher ratings of feminine voice after leisurely tasks. A longer list of tasks was initially developed and piloted. The tasks that scored the highest on the stressful/non-stressful dimensions were selected for the study, and this choice was further confirmed by the study participants' evaluation of the experimental tasks as stressful/non-stressful. The four "stressful" and four "non-stressful" scenarios are listed in Table 2. Additional information about the tasks' development can be found in Lopatovska et al. [45]. The participants rated the CA's responses to each stressful or non-stressful utterance using a 7-point Likert scale (1 = poor and 7 = excellent) and provided an explanation for their rating in a required comment field.

Table 2. Stressful and non-stressful tasks.

Stressful tasks	Non-stressful tasks
• The route to the closest hospital for a neighbor who has a heart attack • Tax bracket and tax rate information • What to do after coming into contact with someone with COVID-19 virus • Business-related fact for a work email	• Request interesting information about Bora-Bora for vacationing friend • Test of a short meditation instruction • Request for a joke • Ask an agent for a new movie recommendation

3.4 Personality Revealing Interactions and Measures

In addition to giving participants stressful and non-stressful tasks, we designed interactions that would help them assess the CA's "personality" manifested in responses and vocal characteristics. The study relied on personality frameworks to measure the users' perceptions of the personalities of the different-voiced experimental agents. A short version of the Big-Five Inventory (BFI-10) was used to measure the participants' overall impression of the five personality dimensions of the experimental agents, and their ideal CA (i.e., "I want my ideal Alexa to be…"). The five assessed personality dimensions included openness, conscientiousness, extroversion, agreeableness and neuroticism [53, 57, 67–69]. In addition to using the BFI-10 for assessing perceptions of the overall CA's "personality", the SCM was used right after stressful and non-stressful tasks to assess the participants' perceptions of the agent's competence and warmth. The warmth dimension aims to capture manifestations of trustworthiness, friendliness, and tolerance, while competence includes intelligence, confidence, skillfulness [28]. SCM is extensively used in marketing and branding, where the products are recommended to evoke perceptions of high warmth and high competence [2, 37], and we wanted to see if after stressful tasks participants would be more inclined to value competence over warmth (see discussion above about perceptions of competent masculine sounding IBM Watson and feminine sounding "friendly" Cortana).

We selected a set of the utterances that were previously shown to solicit high-warmth/high-competence (HW/HC), high warmth/low-competence (HW/LC), and low-warmth/high-competence (LW/HC) responses (Table 3) [44]. The utterances that were shown to solicit LW/LC responses were not included as they were considered the least desirable by users in any situation. The participants were given different sets of three personality-revealing questions after the stressful and non-stressful tasks and asked to provide general ratings of the agent's responses on a 7-point Likert scale (poor-excellent), rate its responses on the warmth and competence 7-point scale, and provide brief comments to explain their ratings (Table 1 illustrates how personality revealing interactions were injected between tasks to assess users' preferences for agent's warmth and/or competence right after stressful or non-stressful interactions).

Table 3. Examples of utterances and responses on warmth/competence dimension.

Personality Type	Definition	Examples
High Warmth/High Competence (HW/HC)	Someone who is capable, well-liked and respected. A response is informative and supportive	User: What am I thinking right now? CA: You are thinking about a big cake, drizzled in chocolate, with a cherry on top. And if you weren't before, now you are
High Warmth/Low Competence (HW/LC)	Someone who is friendly and pleasant but does not address the question directly	User: Am I a good person? CA: Well, I like you!
Low Warmth/High Competence (LW/HC)	Someone who is knowledgeable, but not likable. A response lacks pleasantries	User: Can I kiss you? CA: I can't kiss you, I lack corporeal form

3.5 Study Participants

The study of masculine and gender-ambiguous voices was conducted separately from the baseline study of the female sounding default Alexa, so that the participant group sizes/characteristics varied. However, all three test groups included the majority of participants who identified as female, ages 25–34, CA users and English speakers [Table 4].

Table 4. Participants' demographics.

Demographic Group (total N/% for 3 groups)	Number/Percent of Participants in Each Group		
	Alexa[a]	**Matthew**	**Leslie**
Gender (1 participant didn't respond)			
Female (71 | 66%)	32 | 64%	19 | 61%	20 | 74%
Male (34 | 31%)	16 | 32%	11 | 35%	7 | 26%
Non-binary (2/2%)	1 | 2%	1 | 3%	0 | 0%
Age (1 didn't respond, 0 participants in 55-64 bracket)			
18-24 (18/17%)	11 | 22%	4 | 13%	3 | 11%
25-34 (61/56%)	32 | 64%	18 | 58%	11 | 41%
35-44 (19/18%)	4 | 8%	5 | 16%	10 | 37%
45-54 (8/7%)	2 | 4%	3 | 10%	3 | 11%
65+ (1/1%)	0 | 0%	1 | 3%	0 | 0%
Primary language			
English (79/72%)	37 | 74%	22 | 72%	20 | 74%
Chinese (18/17%)	7 | 14%	5/16%	6/22%
Others (Korean, Japanese, Polish, Ukrainian, Russian, Afrikaans, German) (11/11%)	6 | 12%	4 | 12%	0 | 0%
Total	50 | 46%	31 | 29%	27 | 25%

[a] Demographics for the baseline study of Alexa

4 Results

4.1 User Perceptions of Masculine-, Feminine- Gender-Ambiguous-Voiced Agents

The personality inventory of the experimental agents revealed that more participants perceived all three agents as extraverted, but Matthew (masculine) and Leslie (gender-ambiguous) were rated as extraverted more frequently compared to the default feminine-voiced Alexa [Table 5].

Table 5. Perceptions of the differently-voiced agents on the Big Five Inventory dimensions.

Dimensions	Description	Matthew (male) (N/%)	Leslie (ambiguous) (N/%)	Alexa (female) (N/%)	Ideal CA (N/%)
Extraversion	Extrovert	29 | **93.5%**	22 | 81.5%	27 | 54%	47 | **81%**
	Introvert	2 | 6.5%	5 | 18.5%	23 | 46%	11 | 19%
Agreeableness	Sympathetic	21 | 67.7%	22 | 81.5%	48 | **96%**	49 | **84.5%**
	Antagonistic	10 | 32.3%	5 | 18.5%	2 | 4%	9 | 15.5%
Conscientiousness	Organized	29 | 93.5%	27 | **100.0%**	43 | 86%	55 | **94.8%**
	Disorganized	2 | 6.5%	0 | 0.0%	7 | 14%	3 | 5.2%
Neuroticism	Sensitive	23 | **74.2%**	16 | 59.3%	18 | 36%	47 | **81%**
	Resilient	8 | 25.8%	11 | 40.7%	32 | 64%	11 | 19%
Openness	Open-Minded	28 | **90.3%**	24 | 88.9%	37 | 74%	41 | **70.7%**
	Conservative	3 | 9.7%	3 | 11.1%	13 | 26%	17 | 29.3%

All three agents frequently scored high on the agreeableness dimension, but Alexa was most frequently identified as agreeable/sympathetic. Leslie was perceived as a highly conscientious/organized agent by all of the participants who rated it, with the frequencies on the conscientiousness dimension for Matthew and Alexa nearing that of Leslie. All three systems were scored more frequently as open-minded/non-conservative (with Matthew scoring the highest in the openness dimension). The only dimension where the perceived personalities of masculine, feminine and gender-ambiguous voices differed was neuroticism: more participants found Matthew to be sensitive, Alexa - resilient, and Leslie as somewhere in between.

The participants' comments describing Leslie and Matthew's *personalities* were analyzed using the coding schema for warmth and competence dimensions developed in an earlier study [45]. Alexa received the highest number of positive comments related to its competence and warmth manifestations. Matthew came close to Alexa in the number of positive comments about competence, but not warmth. Leslie's competence was also praised more frequently than its perceived warmth [Table 6]. Overall, Leslie and Matthew were perceived as competent (though by fewer participants than the female-voiced Alexa). However, on the perception of warmth, gender-ambiguous Leslie and masculine-voiced Matthew received more negative adjectives than Alexa, indicating that the users perceived the feminine-voiced agent to be warmer, friendlier, and more empathetic.

The participants' comments describing Leslie and Matthew's *voices* were content analyzed by three researchers using an emergent coding technique [73]. Following Weber's recommendations for identifying categories in the qualitative data [80], three main categories of themes in the participants' comments emerged: (a) the agent's personality manifested through its voice, (b) the technical characteristics of the voice (including timbre, speed, and tone), and (c) the gender characteristics of the agent's voice.

Table 6. Comments analysis results for tested and ideal CA.

CA Voice	Comments about experimental CA				Comments about Ideal CA (N | %)	Difference (%)
	Positive (N | %)	Negative (N | %)	Neutral (N | %)	Total (N | %)		
Competence						
Leslie	12 | 60% -- Knowledgeable, Reliable	7 | 35% -- Inaccurate, Slow	1 | 5% -- Neutral	20| 44%	22 | 52% -- Smart, Reliable	+8%
Matthew	18 | 69% -- Informative, Useful	7 | 27% -- Inconsistent, Desultory	1 | 4% -- Generic	26| 52%	28 | 57% -- Accurate, Effective	+5%
Alexa	31 | 78% -- Accurate, Efficient	6 | 15% -- Non-functional, Limited	3 | 7% -- Generic Neutral	40| 51%	78 | 54% -- Competent, Quick	+3%
Warmth						
Leslie	11 | 44% -- Kind, Attentive	14 | 56% -- Intimidating, Creepy	0 | 0% --	25| 56%	20 | 48% -- Calm, Easygoing	-8%
Matthew	8 | 33% -- Amusing, Easygoing	15 | 63% -- Boring, Dry	1 | 4% -- Average	24| 48%	21 | 43% -- Humorous, Kind	+5%
Alexa	29 | 74% -- Friendly, Funny	8 | 21% -- Stiff, Insincere	2 | 5% -- Adequate, Serious	39| 49%	67 | 46% -- Cheerful, Funny	-3%

Personality.

Based on the participants' comments about Matthew's voice, the following personality characteristics of this agent emerged:

- Middle-aged ("It's just like the voice of an ordinary man in his 30s", "Male, 30 ~ 45 years old");
- Unemotional, boring and cold ("Matthew's voice is not very interesting", "… very very cold", "This voice is very neutral and boring", "makes a happy question feel like he doesn't care");
- Professional, competent and trustworthy ("…Delivery is at a cadence that is purposeful and that makes the voice sound… reliable, even if the information may seem questionable.").

The "personality" behind the gender-ambiguous voice of the Leslie's agent emerged as:

- Calm ("Calm and soothing", "Pretty calm and relaxed"),
- Unhappy ("The guy have couple divorced marriages", "Unhappy"), and
- Creepy ("It sounds sketchy like a hacker behind a screen", "sounds like a scary movie villain on the phone").

The prior baseline study of Alexa did not include direct questions about agent's voice (and relied on other personality manifestations), so comparable comments about Alexa's feminine voice were not collected.

Voice Characteristics.
Matthew's voice was described by participants as deep ("His deep voice…") and monotone ("he's pretty monotonous "). Leslie's voice was described as deep ("Deep, a little surprising"), low ("Low"), monotone ("Her voice is very monotone"), and slow ("…Leslie also speaks slow and while I appreciate the slower manner in which he/she talked…I would describe it as a weird voice.") Leslie's voice also did not sound clear to many participants ("[it] likes to mumble"). One of the participants mentioned the good timbre of Leslie's voice ("…Good timbre").

Gender.
Matthew's voice was clearly identified as portraying masculine features ("Distinctly male, but pretty robotic"; "Masculine"). However, the participants struggled to identify Leslie's gender, confirming the success of our design of gender-ambiguous voice. Five participants identified Leslie's voice as non-binary/androgynous voice ("A bit androgynous and mechanical, like a filter someone would put on to mask a person's real voice"); five participants stated that Leslie is masculine ("It sounds like male's voice", "Like a younger male"); one described the voice as feminine ("she sounds like she smokes and wants to cough."); two more participants could not clearly identify the gender association of a voice ("The voice is a little weird…not sure if it's a man or a women or man trying to sound like a women or vice versa…"). Both Matthew and Leslie's voices were also described as robotic ("sounds like robot", "computer modulated", "boring and it sounds robotic").

4.2 Effects of Interaction Type on a user's Perception of Masculine-, Feminine-, Gender-Ambiguous-Voiced Agent

We examined the user ratings of agents' responses to personality revealing utterances right after stressful and non-stressful tasks to see if stressful tasks carried over higher appreciation of agent's competence, or a need for more "warmth" in agent's responses after stressful tasks. The statistical comparison of the mean ratings of agents' responses (Table 7) did not show significant differences on the Mann-Whitney U test (appropriate for not normally distributed study data, [26]). In all three voice conditions and after both stressful and non-stressful tasks, participants tended to appreciate CA personality responses that manifested high warmth-high competence (HW/HC, followed by high warmth-low competence (HW/LC), and low warmth-high competence dimensions (LW/HC, Table 8). The largest number of low ratings for CA personality responses were associated with low warmth-high competence responses.

Table 7. Average ratings of differently-voiced responses to stressful, non-stressful tasks and personality questions.

CA Voice	Tasks Scores		Scores on Personality Questions		
	Non-stressful M | SD Median	Stressful M | SD Median	Warmth M | SD Median	Compe- tence M | SD Median	Overall M | SD Median
Alexa	4.97 | 1.59 5.00	4.91 | 1.89 5.00	5.35 | 1.60 6.00	**4.89 | 1.82** **5.00**	**4.73 | 1.80** **5.00**
Matthew	5.06 | 1.80 5.50	5.07 | 1.79 6.00	4.53 | 1.87 6.00	4.52 | 1.85 4.50	4.55 | 1.94 5.00
Leslie	4.93 | 1.81 5.00	4.69 | 1.86 5.00	5.10 | 1.78 6.00	4.71 | 1.80 5.00	4.63 | 1.72 5.00

Participants' comments about their ratings of CA personality responses reflected the design of responses as HW/HC, HW/LC, and LW/HC, for example:

- HW/HC responses were described as "Alexa gives me a real suggestion and not what seems like a search result. It is nice that she complimented me",
- HW/LC as "she [Alexa] avoided the question, but that is probably best coming from an AI that's spent very little time with me", and
- LW-HC as "Technically correct, but Matthew could express more interest, or figurative interpretations."

Table 8. Ratings of CA responses on personality revealing utterances after stressful and non-stressful tasks.

Test Stage	High/low rated CA Responses*: Total N	High Warmth/High Competence Responses (N | %)	High Warmth/Low Competence Responses (N | %)	Low Warmth/High Competence Responses (N | %)
Post-Stressful Tasks	Alexa			
	High Ratings: 89	32 | 64%	30 | 60%	27 | 54%
	Low Ratings: 36	10 | 20%	12 | 24%	14 | 28%
	Matthew			
	High Ratings: 48	22 | 71%	13 | 42%	13 | 42%
	Low Ratings: 27	5 | 16%	9 | 29%	13 | 42%
	Leslie			
	High Ratings: 49	21 | 78%	14 | 52%	14 | 52%
	Low Ratings: 22	2 | 7%	8 | 30%	12 | 44%
Post Non-Stressful Tasks	Alexa			
	High Ratings: 92	37 | 74%	26 | 52%	29 | 58%
	Low Ratings: 41	10 | 20%	14 | 28%	17 | 34%
	Matthew			
	High Ratings: 51	24 | 77%	12 | 39%	15 | 48%
	Low Ratings: 22	3 | 10%	10 | 32%	9 | 29%
	Leslie			
	High Ratings: 54	28 | 67%	14 | 52%	12 | 44%
	Low Ratings: 27	5 | 19%	10 | 37%	12 | 44%

Analysis of comments associated with highly rated personality responses showed participants' appreciation for highly competent/informative responses (for ex., "[response] informative and instructive"), responses that are warm/friendly (for ex., "I like that Leslie is my friend"), or responses that are both competent and warm ("Matthew gave a funny detailed response").

Analysis of comments associated with low rated personality responses did not uncover strong patterns except for post-stress task assessments of Matthew and Alexa responses. A significant portion of comment associated with low scores focused on the LW dimension of Matthew's personality responses (10/37%). A few representative comments include:

- "Informative, but very cold"
- "Matthew says of course and claims to be glad, but doesn't want to engage with me more than that…"
- "Did not sound genuine, in fact, sounded somewhat impatient."

In case of low scores for Alexa personality responses, 67% (N = 24) comments focused on LC dimension in CA's personality responses, for example:

- "I would expect an answer about ethics and morals and maybe a prompt that would allow me to explore these topics more"
- "[Response] Too brief, and not convincing at all."
- "[Alexa] Gave a non-answer."

In summary, while participants' ratings of personality responses were statistically similar for all three agents after stressful and non-stressful tasks, their explanations for low ratings seem to emphasize lack of competence in Alexa and lack of warmth in Matthew after stressful tasks.

4.3   User Preferences for CA Personalities and Voices

Analysis of the personality inventory of ideal agents [Table 5] indicated a preference for extraversion, high agreeableness, conscientiousness, neuroticism and openness. None of the test agents mapped into these requirements perfectly. Matthew came close to the ideal agent on extraversion, neuroticism, and openness dimensions, while Leslie received higher scores on organization/conscientiousness. Alexa was perceived as agreeable by the majority of the participants.

The analysis of the adjectives about an ideal assistant revealed an almost even split between requirements for a warm and competent agent, regardless of its voice character- istics. Out of the total 108 descriptors of the ideal CA, 52% (N = 56) included adjectives describing competence dimension, while 48% (N = 52) referred to warmth.

At the beginning of the study, the participants identified their preference for the voice gender of their ideal CA: masculine, feminine, gender-ambiguous, context-dependent. Out of 65 responses (participants could pick more than one option), 26 preferred the voice gender choice being dependent on interaction context, 26 specified preferences for a gender-ambiguous voice, followed by feminine (15) and masculine (3) voices. However, in sharing their likes and dislikes of Matthew and Leslie's voices, Leslie received more dislikes (17/63%) than Matthew (15/48%). We noted that after the stressful tasks at the end of the study, the dislikes for Matthew grew to 62%.

5   Discussion and Conclusion

Comparison of the users' reactions to masculine-, feminine- and gender-ambiguous voiced CAs confirmed prior findings that voice contributes to personality perception [55, 56]. In our study, the masculine agent was most frequently identified as extraverted, sensitive and open-minded, the gender-ambiguous agent as organized; and the feminine agent as sympathetic. The participants' comments made this difference even more nuanced, as Matthew was described as having a particular age (middle aged), professional demeanor, and an unemotional and boring personality; while Leslie was described as calm, but also creepy (in line with prior research on gender-ambiguous systems [58]. Most of our participants wanted their ideal CAs to have a highly warm and competent personality, that is also extraverted, empathetic, organized, sensitive and open-minded. This user preference is probably known to the designers, considering that Amazon is aiming to develop its Alexa with the Extraverted/Sensing/Feeling/Judging personality [35].

We did not confirm some of the prior theories related to the contextual "appreciation" for different voices, e.g., masculine in stressful and feminine in non-stressful tasks [16, 22, 23, 58]. Right after stressful and non-stressful tasks, responses that projected both high warmth and high competence from all three agents received more positive ratings than responses that were perceived as low on warmth or competence. Despite similarities in ratings, participants' explanations for the low scores after stressful tasks hinted on unfulfilled expectations of Alexa's competence, and Matthew's warmth. This observation further reinforces the finding that participants value both competence and warmth in all types of interactions, and expect agents to deliver informative and friendly responses in stressfully and non-stressful contexts.

One of the more original findings of the study is a dissonance between the users' reactions to masculine, feminine and gender-ambiguous voiced CAs and their ideal agent. Almost half of the participants expressed interest in having a context-specific voice, though this preference was not confirmed by significant differences in ratings of masculine, feminine and gender-ambiguous sounding agents in stressful and non-stressful interactions in the study. The same number of participants expressed a desire for a non-binary sounding CA, yet, the study's gender-ambiguous sounding agent consistently received the lowest ratings. While user preference for binary sounding systems is known [58], our participants expressed a general preference for non-binary/gender-ambiguous voiced agents, but did not appreciate the personality projected by the gender-ambiguous voice in the study. This finding could inform several lines of inquiry in the future:

1. It is possible that that low appreciation of the gender ambiguous voice in our study was caused by our particular implementation of this voice. Further work is needed to design and test various gender-ambiguous voices that users would find acceptable. The will to interact with a gender-ambiguous CA seems to be present at least in a subset of the user population, and the performance scores given to Leslie's responses were comparable to those of Alexa and Matthew.

2. Prior research suggests that a gender ambiguous voice might cause discomfort [58], so it is also possible that users' dislike of Leslie's voice in our study was grounded in their general preferences and not particular voice characteristics. If gender-ambiguous voices do indeed score lower than masculine and feminine sounding voices, CA designs face an interesting dilemma: should CAs continue using voices (and project CA personalities) that users are familiar with and desire, but the ones that also reinforce social gender stereotypes of "competent" masculine and "warm" feminine voices and corresponding personalities? Or should designer try,

at least for the interested users, to change cultural stereotypes by using non-binary voices, or challenge the users to accept feminine and masculine sounding responses in unexpected professional, leisure and other types of interactions?

The study had a number of limitations. Due to resource constraints, the study of CA voice perceptions was designed for masculine and gender-ambiguous sounding experimental agents. The prior, almost identical baseline study of perceptions of feminine-sounding Alexa personality did not include explicit questions about user perceptions of voice, limiting our ability to draw some direct comparisons between the three voices. Due to small and uneven group sizes of participants who tested different systems, some of the statistical tests did not show statistically significant results. Given that the sample included a large number of graduate students with a high understanding of information systems as they relate to social justice issues, it is possible that desire for a gender-ambiguous voiced agent is reflecting aspirations of a largely liberal and socially-conscientious student body. The sample of participants included more self-identified women than men or non-binary participants, possibly affecting the ratings of CA voices and perceived personalities. However, prior research mentions how both men and women prefer lower pitched voices in "authoritative" situations, suggesting that the gender difference among the sample of participants may not be a significant variable affecting agent's voice perceptions/preferences [4, 7, 39]. Further work is also needed to understand the effects of primary language and cultural background of a user on their perceptions of CA voice and personality. The study was designed as a self-guided experiment, where user reactions were artificially stimulated by experimental tasks. A naturalistic study might have revealed more accurate data on user contextual perceptions of different CA voices and their corresponding personalities.

We hope that our research contributes to the ongoing discussion of ways to balance user preferences and socially responsible design of CAs [18, 22]. Should we continue keeping our users happy by transferring our often-dated cultural norms into digital environments? Can we design an acceptable gender-neutral voice, or at least give users an option to challenge themselves by accepting unexpected voices/personas for their various interactions with conversational agents? More work is needed to tackle these questions.

Acknowledgment. We are grateful to our participants and the Pratt Institute for supporting the study.

References

1. Aaker, J., Vohs, K.D., Mogilner, C.: Nonprofits are seen as warm and for-profits as competent: firm stereotypes matter. J. Consum. Res. **37**(2), 224–237 (2010). https://doi.org/10.1086/651566
2. Aaker, J.L., Garbinsky, E.N., Vohs, K.D.: Cultivating admiration in brands: warmth, competence, and landing in the 'golden quadrant.' J. Consum. Psychol. **22**(2), 191–194 (2012). https://doi.org/10.1016/j.jcps.2011.11.012
3. "Amazon Web Services (AWS) Cloud Computing Services", Amazon Web Services, Inc. https://aws.amazon.com/. Accessed 06 Jan 2021

4. Anderson, R.C., Klofstad, C.A.: Preference for leaders with masculine voices holds in the case of feminine leadership roles. PLOS ONE 7(12), e51216 (2012). https://doi.org/10.1371/journal.pone.0051216
5. Apple, W., Streeter, L.A., Krauss, R.M.: Effects of pitch and speech rate on personal attributions. J. Pers. Soc. Psychol. 37(5), 715–727 (1979)
6. Audacity, 2020, *Audacity* ® (2.4.1). https://www.audacityteam.org. Accessed 01 June 2020
7. Banai, I.P., Banai, B., Bovan, K.: Vocal characteristics of presidential candidates can predict the outcome of actual elections. Evol. Hum. Behav. 38(3), 309–314 (2017)
8. Belin, P., Bestelmeyer, P.E.G., Latinus, M., Watson, R.: Understanding voice perception. Br. J. Psychol. 102(4), 711–725 (2011). https://doi.org/10.1111/j.2044-8295.2011.02041
9. Bentley, F., Luvogt, C., Silverman, M., Wirasinghe, R., White, B., Lottrjdge, D.: Understanding the long-term use of smart speaker assistants. Proc. ACM Interact. Mobile Wearable Ubiquit. Technol. 2(3), 1–24 (2018). https://doi.org/10.1145/3264901
10. Benyon, D., Mival, O.: Landscaping personification technologies: from interactions to relationships. In: Cerwinski, M., Lund, A., Tan, D., (eds.) CHI EA 08 Extended Abstracts on Human Factors in Computing Systems, pp. 3657–3662. Association for Computing Machinery, New York, NY, USA (2008). https://doi.org/10.1145/1358628.1358908
11. Berry, D.S.: Vocal attractiveness and vocal babyishness: effects on stranger, self, and friend impressions. J. Nonverbal Behav. 14(3), 141–153 (1990). https://doi.org/10.1007/BF00996223
12. Bishop, J., Keating, P.: Perception of pitch location within a speaker's range: fundamental frequency, voice quality and speaker sex. J. Acoust. Soc. Am. 132(2), 1100–1112 (2012). https://doi.org/10.1121/1.4714351
13. Briggs Myers, I.: Introduction to Type: A Guide to Understanding Your Results on the MBTI Instrument, 6th edn. CPP Inc, Mountain View, California (1998)
14. Budiu, R.: Mental Models for Intelligent Assistants. Nielsen Norman Group. https://www.nngroup.com/articles/mental-model-ai-assistants/. Accessed 29 Dec 2020
15. Burgoon, J.K., Bullar, D.B., Woodall, W.G.: Nonverbal Communication: The Unspoken Dialogue. McGraw-Hill Inc., New York (1996)
16. Cambre, J., Kulkarni, C.: One Voice Fits All?: social implications and research challenges of designing voices for smart devices. Proc. ACM Hum. Comput. Inter. 3(CSCW), 1–19 (2019). https://doi.org/10.1145/3359325
17. Carpenter, J.: Why project Q is more than the world's first nonbinary voice for technology. Interactions 26(6), 56–59 (2019). https://doi.org/10.1145/3358912
18. Cercas Curry, A., Robertson, J., Rieser, V.: Conversational Assistants and Gender Stereotypes: public perceptions and desiderata for voice personas. In: The Second Workshop on Gender Bias in Natural Language Processing COLING-GeBNLP Conference, Barcelona, Spain [online], Association for Computational Linguistics, pp. 72–78 (2020). https://www.aclweb.org/anthology/2020.gebnlp-1.7
19. Chang, R.C.-S., Lu, H.-P., Yang, P.: Stereotypes or golden rules? Exploring likable voice traits of social robots as active aging companions for tech-savvy baby boomers in Taiwan. Comput. Hum. Behav. 84, 194–210 (2018). https://doi.org/10.1016/j.chb.2018.02.025
20. Chaves, A.P., Gerosa, M.A.: Single or multiple conversational agents? an interactional coherence comparison. In: Proceedings of the 2018 CHI Conference on Human Factors in Computing Systems, Association for Computing Machinery, New York, NY, USA, pp. 1–13 (2018). https://doi.org/10.1145/3173574.3173765
21. Cowan, B.R., et al.: "What can I help you with?": infrequent users' experiences of intelligent personal assistants". In: Proceedings of the 19th International Conference on Human-Computer Interaction with Mobile Devices and Services (Mobile HCI 17), ACM Press, Vienna, Austria, pp. 4–7 (2017). https://doi.org/10.1145/3098279.3098539

22. Danielescu, A.: Eschewing gender stereotypes in voice assistants to promote inclusion. In: Proceedings of the 2nd Conference on Conversational User Interfaces, CUI 20. Association for Computing Machinery, New York, NY, USA, pp. 1–3 (2020). https://doi.org/10.1145/340 5755.3406151

23. Danielescu, A., Christian, G.: A Bot is Not a Polyglot: designing personalities for multi-lingual conversational agents. In: CHI EA 18 Extended Abstracts of the 2018 CHI Conference on Human Factors in Computing Systems, Association for Computing Machinery, New York, NY, USA, pp. 1–9 (2018). https://doi.org/10.1145/3170427.3174366

24. Danielescu, A., Lovis-McMahon, D., Christian, G.: Designing for Radar Pace: a conversational system for coaching. In: ACM Computer Human Interaction (CHI 18), 22 April, Montreal QC Canada (2018). https://voiceux.wordpress.com/position-papers/

25. Ellis, D.S.: Speech and social status in America. Soc. Forces **45**(3), 431–437 (1967)

26. Emerson, R.W.: Parametric tests, their nonparametric alternatives, and degrees of freedom. J. Vis. Impairment Blindness **110**(5), 377–380 (2016). https://doi.org/10.1177/0145482X1611 000511

27. Feine, J., Gnewuch, U., Morana, S., Maedche, A.: Gender Bias in Chatbot design. In: Følstad, A., et al. (eds.) CONVERSATIONS 2019. LNCS, vol. 11970, pp. 79–93. Springer, Cham (2020). https://doi.org/10.1007/978-3-030-39540-7_6

28. Fiske, S.T., Cuddy, A.J.C., Glick, P.: Universal dimensions of social cognition: warmth and competence. Trends Cogn. Sci. **11**(2), 77–83 (2007). https://doi.org/10.1016/j.tics.2006. 11.005

29. Frühholz, S., Grandjean, D.: Processing of emotional vocalizations in bilateral inferior frontal cortex. Neurosci. Biobehav. Rev. **37**(10), 2847–2855 (2013). https://doi.org/10.1016/j.neubio rev.2013.10.007

30. Glass, R.L.: Frivolous research. Inf. Syst. Manage. **26**(2), 209–210 (2009). https://doi.org/10. 1080/10580530902797631

31. Honorof, D.N., Whalen, D.H.: Identification of speaker sex from one vowel across a range of fundamental frequencies. J. Acoust. Soc. Am. **128**(5), 3095–3104 (2010). https://doi.org/10. 1121/1.3488347

32. Hughes, S.M., Gallup, G.G.: Why are we attracted to certain voices? Voice as an evolved medium for the transmission of psychological and biological information. In: Izdebski, K. (ed.) Emotions in the Human Voice, vol. 2, pp. 8 (2008)

33. Hughes, S.M., Rhodes, B.C.: Making age assessments based on voice: the impact of the reproductive viability of the speaker. J. Soc. Evol. Cult. Psychol. **4**(4), 290–304 (2010). https://doi.org/10.1037/h0099282

34. Ivy, D.K.: Gender Speak: Personal Effectiveness in Gender Communication, 5th edn. McGraw-Hill Inc, New York (2012)

35. Johnson, K.: Amazon says Alexa is an ESFJ (Updated). VentureBeat (2018). https://ventur ebeat.com/2018/10/25/amazon-says-alexa-is-an-estj/. Accessed Oct 2019

36. Kedemey, D.: Here's What Really Makes Microsoft's Cortana So Amazing. Time (2015). https://time.com/3960670/windows-10-cortana/. Accessed 23 Dec 2020

37. Kervyn, N., Fiske, S.T., Malone, C.: Brands as intentional agents framework: how perceived intentions and ability can map brand perception. J. Consum. Psychol. **22**(2), 166–176 (2012). https://doi.org/10.1016/j.jcps.2011.09.006

38. Kinsella, B., Mutchler, A.: Voice Assistant Consumer Adoption in Healthcare. Voice-bot.AI (2019). https://voicebot.ai/2018/04/03/over-half-of-smartphone-owners-use-voice-ass istants-siri-leads-the-pack/. Accessed 11 Mar 2020

39. Klofstad, C.A., Anderson, R.C., Peters, S.: Sounds like a winner: voice pitch influences perception of leadership capacity in both men and women. Proc. Royal Soc. B Biol. Sci. **279**(1738), 2698–2704 (2012). https://doi.org/10.1098/rspb.2012.0311

40. Kumar, P., Jakhanwal, N., Bhowmick, A., Chandra, M.: Gender classification using pitch and formants. In: ICCCS 11 Proceedings of the 2011 International Conference on Communication, Computing & Security, 12–14 February 2011, ACM Press, Rourkela, Odisha, India, p. 319 (2011). https://doi.org/10.1145/1947940.1948007

41. Kunst, A.: Preferences for male or female voices for digital voice assistant among residents of the United States, as of April 2017. Statista (2019). https://www.statista.com/statistics/702911/united-states-digital-voice-assistants-survey-gender-preferences/. Accessed 14 Dec 2020

42. Lass, N.J., Hughes, K.R., Bowyer, M.D., Waters, L.T., Bourne, V.R.: Speaker sex identification from voiced, whispered, and filtered isolated vowels. J. Acoust. Soc. Am. **59**(675), 675–678 (1976). https://doi.org/10.1121/1.380917

43. Lopatovska, I.: Personality dimensions of intelligent personal assistants. In: CHIIR 20: Proceedings of the 2020 Conference on Human Information Interaction and Retrieval, 14–18 March 2020, Association for Computing Machinery, Vancouver BC Canada, pp. 333–337 (2020). https://doi.org/10.1145/3343413.3377993

44. Lopatovska, I.: Classification of humorous interactions with intelligent personal assistants. J. Libr. Inf. Sci. **52**(3), 931–942 (2020). https://doi.org/10.1177/0961000619891771

45. Lopatovska, I., Korshakova, E., Brown, D., Li, Y., Min, J., Pasiak, A., Zheng, K.: User perceptions of an intelligent personal assistant's personality: the role of interaction context. In: CHIIR 21: Proceedings of the 2021 Conference on Human Information Interaction and Retrieval, pp. 15–25 (2021). https://doi.org/10.1145/3406522.3446018

46. Lopatovska, I., Oropeza, H.: User interactions with 'Alexa' in Public Academic Space. In: Proceedings of the Association for Information Science and Technology, 10–14 November 2018, Vancouver, Canada, pp. 309–318 (2018). https://doi.org/10.1002/pra2.2018.14505501034

47. Lopatovska, I., Williams, H.: Personification of the Amazon Alexa: BFF or a mindless companion. In: CHIIR 18 Proceedings of the 2018 Conference on Human Information Interaction & Retrieval, 11–15 March, Association for Computing Machinery, New York, NY, USA, pp. 265–268 (2018). https://doi.org/10.1145/3176349.3176868

48. Luria, M., Reig, S., Tan, X.Z., Steinfeld, A., Forlizzi, J., Zimmerman, J.: Re-embodiment and co-embodiment: exploration of social presence for robots and conversational agents. In: DIS 19 Proceedings of the 2019 on Designing Interactive Systems Conference, 23–28 June, Association for Computing Machinery, New York, NY, USA, pp. 633–644 (2019). https://doi.org/10.1145/3322276.3322340

49. Manstead, A.S.R.: The psychology of social class: how socioeconomic status impacts thought, feelings, and behaviour. Br. J. Soc. Psychol. **57**(2), 267–291 (2018). https://doi.org/10.1111/bjso.12251

50. Mayew, W.J., Parsons, C.A., Venkatachalam, M.: Voice pitch and the labor market success of male chief executive officers. Evol. Hum. Behav. **34**(34), 243–248 (2013). https://doi.org/10.1016/j.evolhumbehav.2013.03.001

51. Mays, D.V.: Cross cultural social status perception in speech. Stud. Second. Lang. Acquis. **5**(1), 52–64 (1982). https://doi.org/10.1017/S0272263100004599

52. McAleer, P., Todorov, A., Belin, P.: How Do You Say 'Hello'? Personality impressions from brief novel voices. PLoS ONE **9**(3), e90779 (2014). https://doi.org/10.1371/journal.pone.0090779

53. McCrae, R.R., Costa, P.T.: Personality in Adulthood: A Five-Factor Theory Perspective, 2nd edn. Guilford Press, New York, NY (2003)

54. McDonnell, M., Baxter, D.: Chatbots and gender stereotyping. Interact. Comput. **31**(2), 116–121 (2019). https://doi.org/10.1093/iwc/iwz007

55. Moussawi, S., Benbunan-Fich, R.: The effect of voice and humour on users' perceptions of personal intelligent agents. Behav. Inf. Technol. **40**(3), 1–24 (2020). https://doi.org/10.1080/0144929X.2020.1772368

56. Mulder, M.P., Nijholt, A.: Humor research: state of art. In: CTIT Technical Report Series, vol. 2, no. 02–34, Center for Telematics and Information Technology (CTIT) (2002). http://www.ub.utwente.nl/webdocs/ctit/1/0000009e.pdf

57. Müller, S.L., Richert, A.: The big-five personality dimensions and attitudes to-wards robots: a cross sectional study. In: PETRA 18 Proceedings of the 11th PErvasive Technologies Related to Assistive Environments Conference, 26–29 June, Association for Computing Machinery, New York, NY, USA, pp. 405–408 (2018). https://doi.org/10.1145/3197768.3203178

58. Nass, C., Brave, S.: Wired for Speech: How Voice Activates and Advances the Human-Computer Relationship. The MIT Press, Cambridge (2005)

59. Nass, C., Moon, Y.: Machines and mindlessness: social responses to computers. J. Soc. Issues **56**(1), 81–103 (2000). https://doi.org/10.1111/0022-4537.00153

60. Nass, C., Moon, Y., Green, N.: Are machines gender neutral? Gender-stereotypic responses to computers with voices. J. Appl. Soc. Psychol. **27**(10), 864–876 (1997)

61. Nass, C., Steuer, J., Tauber, E.R.: Computers are social actors. In: CHI 94 Proceedings of the SIGCHI Conference on Human Factors in Computing Systems Celebrating Interdependence, 24–28 April, ACM Press, Boston, Massachusetts, United States, pp. 72–78 (1994). https://doi.org/10.1145/191666.191703

62. Norgaard, N., Equal, A.I.: Meet Q The First Genderless Voice (2019). https://www.genderlessvoice.com. Accessed 01 July 2021

63. Norman, D.A.: How might people interact with agents. Commun. ACM **37**(7), 68–71 (1994). https://doi.org/10.1145/176789.176796

64. Obinali, C.: The perception of gender in voice assistants. In: SAIS 2019 Proceedings of the Southern Association for Information Systems Conference, 22–23 March, St. Simon's Island, GA, USA, vol. 39, No.7, pp. 1–6 (2019). https://aisel.aisnet.org/sais2019/39/

65. Personality, n.d.: American Psychological Association. https://www.apa.org/topics/personality. Accessed 26 Mar 2021

66. Pittam, J.: Voice in Social Interaction: An Interdisciplinary Approach. Sage Publications, Inc., Thousand Oaks (1994)

67. Porter, C.M., Rigby, J.R.: Relationship context and personality shape people's preferences for network relationship partners. Pers. Relat. **26**(2), 310–330 (2019). https://doi.org/10.1111/pere.12275

68. Rammstedt, B.: The 10-item big five inventory. Eur. J. Psychol. Assess. **23**(3), 193–201 (2007). https://doi.org/10.1027/1015-5759.23.3.193

69. Rammstedt, B., John, O.P.: Measuring personality in one minute or less: a 10-item short version of the big five inventory in english and german. J. Res. Pers. **41**(1), 203–212 (2007). https://doi.org/10.1016/j.jrp.2006.02.001

70. Snyder, M., Cantor, N.: Understanding personality and social behavior: a functionalist strategy. In: Gilbert, D.T., Fiske, S.T., Lindzey, G. (eds.) The Handbook of Social Psychology, pp. 635–679. McGraw-Hill, Inc., New York (1998)

71. Søndergaard, M.L.J., Hansen, L.K.: Intimate futures: staying with the trouble of digital personal assistants through design fiction. In: DIS 18 Proceedings of the 2018 Designing Interactive Systems Conference, 9–13 June, Association of Computing Machinery, Hong Kong China, pp. 869–880 (2018). https://doi.org/10.1145/3196709.3196766

72. Steele, C.: The Real Reason Voice Assistants Are Female (and Why it Matters). PCMAG (2018). https://www.pcmag.com/opinions/the-real-reason-voice-assistants-are-female-and-why-it-matters. Accessed 29 Dec 2020

73. Stemler, S.: An overview of content analysis. Pract. Assess. Res. Eval. **7**(17), 1–6 (2019). https://doi.org/10.7275/z6fm-2e34

74. Tigue, C.C., Borak, D.J., O'Connor, J.J.M., Schandl, C., Feinberg, D.R.: Voice pitch influences voting behavior. Evol. Hum. Behav. **33**(3), 210–216 (2012). https://doi.org/10.1016/j.evolhumbehav.2011.09.004

75. UNESCO: I'd blush if I could: closing gender divides in digital skills through education. UNESCO Digital Library (2019). https://unesdoc.unesco.org/ark:/48223/pf0000367416.page=1. Accessed 23 July 2019

76. Unkefer, H., Sophie, R.: Accenture and CereProc Introduce and Open Source the World's First Comprehensive Non-Binary Voice Solution. Accenture Newsroom (2020). https://newsroom.accenture.com/news/accenture-and-cereproc-introduce-and-open-source-the-worlds-first-comprehensive-non-binary-voice-solution.htm. Accessed 01 July 2021

77. Voiceflow: Design, prototype, and build voice apps. Voiceflow (0.1.0). https://www.voiceflow.com/. Accessed 06 Jan 2021

78. Waytz, A., Heafner, J., Epley, N.: The mind in the machine: anthropomorphism increases trust in an autonomous vehicle. J. Exp. Soc. Psychol. **52**, 113–117 (2014). https://doi.org/10.1016/j.jesp.2014.01.005

79. Waytz, A., Morewedge, C.K., Epley, N., Monteleone, G., Gao, J.-H., Cacioppo, J.T.: Making sense by making sentient: effectance motivation increases anthropomorphism. J. Pers. Soc. Psychol. **99**(3), 410–435 (2010). https://doi.org/10.1037/a0020240

80. Weber, R.: Basic Content Analysis, 2nd edn. Thousand Oaks, California (2021). https://doi.org/10.4135/9781412983488

81. Willis, J., Todorov, A.: First impressions: making up your mind after a 100-Ms exposure to a face. Psychol. Sci. **17**(7), 592–598 (2006). https://doi.org/10.1111/j.1467-9280.2006.01750.x

Author Index

Printed in the United States
by Baker & Taylor Publisher Services